2995

W9-CJR-385

ASIC 808.82 B56   86-05219
(1984-85)
The Best plays of 1984- 85 and
 the Year book of the drama in
 America

DISCARDED
STARK COUNTY DISTRICT LIBRARY

STARK COUNTY
DISTRICT LIBRARY
CANTON, OHIO 44702

14
DAY

MAR 1 0 1986   OEMCO

THE BEST PLAYS OF 1984–1985

THE
BURNS MANTLE
YEARBOOK

THE
BEST PLAYS
OF 1984–1985

EDITED BY OTIS L. GUERNSEY JR.

*Illustrated with photographs and
with drawings by* HIRSCHFELD

ASIC 86–05219

DODD, MEAD & COMPANY
NEW YORK

Copyright © 1985 by Dodd, Mead & Company, Inc.

ISBN: 0-396-086128

Library of Congress Catalog Card Number 20-21432

Printed in the United States of America

"Scheherazade": by Marisha Chamberlain. Copyright © 1985 by Marisha Chamberlain. Reprinted by permission of Helen Merrill, Ltd. See CAUTION notice below. All inquiries concerning stock and amateur production rights should be addressed to: Dramatists Play Service, Inc., 440 Park Avenue South, New York, NY 10016. All other inquiries should be addressed to: Helen Merrill, Helen Merrill, Ltd., 361 West 17th Street, New York, NY 10011.

"The Shaper": by John Steppling. © Copyright 1985 by John Steppling. All rights reserved. Reprinted by permission of William Morris Agency, Inc. See CAUTION notice below. All inquiries should be addressed to: William Morris Agency, Inc., 1350 Avenue of the Americas, New York, NY 10019, Attention: George Lane.

"A Shayna Maidel": by Barbara Lebow. Copyright © 1984 by Barbara Lebow. Reprinted by permission of the author. See CAUTION notice below. All inquiries should be addressed to: Mary Harden, Brett Adams Limited, 448 West 44th Street, New York, NY 10036.

"Split Second": by Dennis McIntyre. Copyright © 1980 by Dennis McIntyre (under the title "The Saddest Summer of Val"). Copyright © 1984, 1985 by Dennis McIntyre. Reprinted by permission of Rosenstone/Wender on behalf of the author. See CAUTION notice below. All inquiries concerning stock and amateur production rights should be addressed to: Samuel French, Inc., 45 West 25th Street, New York, NY 10010. All other inquiries should be addressed to: Rosenstone/Wender, 3 East 48th Street, New York, NY 10017.

"Hurlyburly": by David Rabe. Copyright © 1985 by Ralako Corp. Reprinted by permission of Grove Press, Inc. See CAUTION notice below. All inquiries should be addressed to: Grove Press, Inc., 196 West Houston Street, New York, NY 10014.

"Ma Rainey's Black Bottom": by August Wilson. Copyright © 1981, 1985 by August Wilson. Reprinted by arrangement with New American Library. See CAUTION notice below. All inquiries should be addressed to: New American Library, 1633 Broadway, New York, NY 10019.

"The Foreigner": by Larry Shue. © Copyright 1983 by Larry Shue as an unpublished dramatic composition. © Copyright 1985 by Larry Shue. All rights reserved. Reprinted by permission of William Morris Agency, Inc. on behalf of the author. See CAUTION notice below. All inquiries concerning stock and amateur production rights should be addressed to: Dramatists Play Service, Inc., 440 Park Avenue South, New York, NY 10016. All other inquiries should be addressed to: William Morris Agency, Inc., 1350 Avenue of the Americas, New York, NY 10019, Attention: Jeffrey R. Alpern.

"Tracers": by, and copyright © 1983, 1985, John DiFusco, Vincent Caristi, Richard Chaves, Eric E. Emerson, Rick Gallavan, Merlin Marston, Harry Stephens with Sheldon Lettich. Reprinted by permission of Hill and Wang, a division of Farrar, Straus and Giroux, Inc. See CAUTION notice below. All inquiries concerning performance rights should be addressed to: Frank J. Gruber, 9601 Wilshire Boulevard, Suite 700, Beverly Hills, CA 90210. All other inquiries should be addressed to: Hill and Wang, a division of Farrar, Straus and Giroux, Inc., 19 Union Square West, New York, NY 10003.

"Pack of Lies": by Hugh Whitemore. Copyright © 1983, 1985 by Hugh Whitemore Ltd. Reprinted by permission of Rosenstone/Wender on behalf of the author. See CAUTION notice below. All inquiries concerning stock and amateur production rights should be addressed to: Samuel French, Inc., 45 West 25th Street, New York, NY 10010. All other inquiries should be addressed to: Rosenstone/Wender, 3 East 48th Street, New York, NY 10017.

"As Is": by William M. Hoffman. Copyright © 1985 by William M. Hoffman. Reprinted by permission of International Creative Management. See CAUTION notice below. All inquiries concerning stock and amateur productions should be addressed to: Dramatists Play Service, Inc., 440 Park Avenue South, New York, NY 10016. All other inquiries should be addressed to: Luis Sanjurjo, International Creative Management, 40 West 57th Street, New York, NY 10019.

"Biloxi Blues": by Neil Simon. Copyright © 1985 by Neil Simon. Reprinted by permission of Random House, Inc. See CAUTION notice below. All inquiries should be addressed to: Random House, Inc., 201 East 50th Street, New York, NY 10022.

"Doubles": by David Wiltse. Copyright © 1985 by David Wiltse. Reprinted by permission of William Morris Agency, Inc. See CAUTION notice below. All inquiries concerning stock and amateur rights should be addressed to: Samuel French, Inc., 45 West 25th Street, New York, NY 10011. All other inquiries should be addressed to: William Morris Agency, Inc., 1350 Avenue of the Americas, New York, NY 10019, Attention: Esther Sherman.

"The Marriage of Bette and Boo": by Christopher Durang. Copyright © 1985 by Christopher Durang. Reprinted by permission of Helen Merrill, Ltd. See CAUTION notice below. All inquiries should be addressed to: Helen Merrill, Helen Merrill, Ltd., 361 West 17th Street, New York, NY 10011.

CAUTION: Professionals and amateurs are hereby warned that the above-mentioned plays, being fully protected under the Copyright Law of the United States of America, the British Commonwealth, including the Dominion of Canada, and all other countries of the Copyright Union, the Berne Convention, the Pan-American Copyright Convention and the Universal Copyright Convention, are subject to license and royalty. All rights including, but not limited to, reproduction in whole or in part by any process or method, professional use, amateur use, film, recitation, lecturing, public reading, recording, taping, radio and television broadcasting, and the rights of translation into foreign languages, are strictly reserved. Particular emphasis is laid on the matter of readings, permission for which must be obtained in writing from the author's representative or publisher, as the case may be with the instructions set forth above.

Al Hirschfeld is represented exclusively by The Margo Feiden Galleries, New York.

EDITOR'S NOTE

OUR American Theater's center of creative gravity seems to be shifting downward in the scale of New York production and outward in a broadening base of new-play production in cross-country theater. To keep up with developments as always, this *Best Plays* series of theater yearbooks allots an ever-larger proportion of its New York coverage to the tributary area known as "off Broadway" (six of the ten Best Plays selections this year) and "off off Broadway," the latter documented annually and thoroughly in Camille Croce's listing and reviewed in a summary of the OOB season by Mel Gussow, distinguished New York *Times* drama critic.

In its coverage of cross-country theater, too, *The Best Plays of 1984–85* is changing its shape to fit the circumstances, in the best tradition of this 66-volume series in continuous annual publication by Dodd, Mead & Company beginning with the season of 1919–20. In the recent past, a committee of the nationally-organized American Theater Critics Association has chosen a single outstanding new play in cross-country production to be synopsized like a Best Play in our volume. Broadening this project, the ATCA committee this year has chosen three outstanding new scripts, with excerpts designated for publication in these pages to illustrate quality and style. Our factual Directory of cross-country theater concentrates on the credits of *new* plays, as it did in last year's volume, so that we can include a comprehensive record of new work. The compilation for this volume was prepared by Sheridan Sweet, taking over from the estimable Ella A. Malin, who originated the concept of such a widely inclusive record of regional theater productions while she was at ANTA and assembled it for *The Best Plays of 1964–65*, the first of Ms. Malin's 20 Directories of painstakingly compiled information. With the 1984–85 *Best Plays* volume, and with our profound thanks, Ms. Malin has passed the baton of this worthy task to Mrs. Sweet for its 21st year in this 1984–85 volume.

It's obvious to Best Plays readers how much each succeeding volume owes to its decorative aspects—the unique drawings of Al Hirschfeld heightening the highlights of the New York season; the reproductions of outstanding scenery and costume designs by Heidi Landesman, Patricia McGourty and David Mitchell, recording some of the "look" of each theater season together with the expressive photographs by Martha Swope and Bert Andrews, John Brown, Marc Bryan-Brown, Bernard Cohen, Susan Cook, Peter Cunningham, Chris Davies, Zoe Dominic, Kenn Duncan, Gerry Goodstein, Henry Grossman, Martha Holmes, Diana Kassir, Ken Kauffman, K.C. Kratt, James J. Kriegsmann, Adam Newman, Carol Rosegg, Jay Thompson and Van Williams.

Not so obvious, but indispensable to the accuracy and clarity of the huge amount of material contained in these pages, are the annual contributions of Jonathan Dodd of Dodd, Mead & Company, and of the editor's willingly and assiduously collaborative wife. Our heartfelt editorial and readership thanks are also due to literally scores of contributors including Rue Canvin (necrology and publications), Stanley Green (cast replacements), playwrights Jeffrey Sweet and Sally Dixon Wiener (Best Plays synopses), William Schelble and Richard Hummler (Tony and Critics Awards data), Henry Hewes and Dan Sullivan of ATCA, Ralph Newman of the Drama Book Shop, Robert Nahas of the Theater Arts Book Shop, Thomas T. Foose (historical data on revivals), and side by side with these, the many helpers in the theater's public relations departments whose generous assistance is a major bulwark of every *Best Plays* volume's every section. As editor, reader and theatergoer, we offer our sincere and tripled gratitude to all these and others including the many dramatists who founded this feast of art and entertainment, who persevered through the 1984–85 theater season and succeeded in celebrating their ideals of drama, comedy and music in a less than ideal environment.

OTIS L. GUERNSEY Jr.

July 1, 1985

CONTENTS

Drawings by HIRSCHFELD

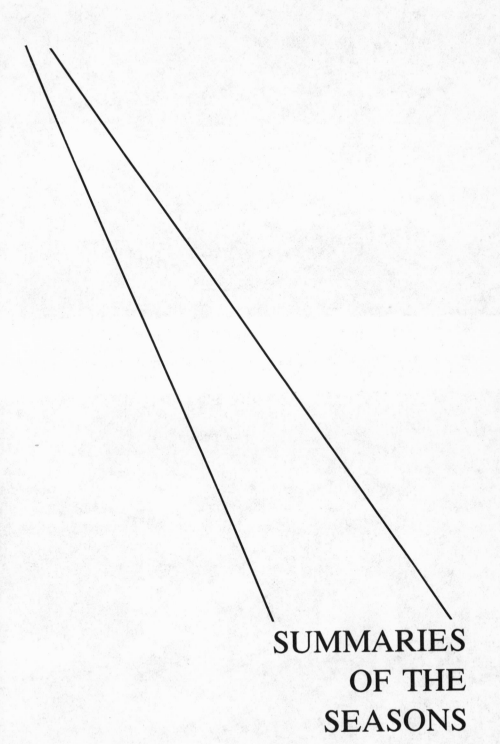

SUMMARIES
OF THE
SEASONS

BILOXI BLUES—David Mitchell's businesslike 1943 Mississippi army base scene design *(above)* is contrasted *(below)* with a moment of barracks camaraderie with Matthew Broderick, Brian Tarantina, Matt Mulhern, Alan Ruck and Barry Miller in Neil Simon's Tony Award-winning comedy

THE SEASON IN NEW YORK

By Otis L. Guernsey Jr.

THAT conspicuous ingredient in all reflections on the 1984–85 theater season on and off Broadway—disappointment—wasn't universally deserved. The glaring multi-million-dollar failure of large-scale Broadway musicals accounted for most of that sinking feeling, in the absence of a blockbusting new musical hit. Production costs were another downer (even off Broadway they were edging ever-closer to the $500,000 line), influencing dramatists to think and write small (two characters, one set preferred) if they wanted to be produced, thus aggravating the shortage of scripts with potentially broad audience appeal. And Broadway's shortcomings were further exposed in the Tony ceremonies summing up a season which offered so little in three of the musical categories (leading actor, leading actress, choreography) that they were dropped from consideration.

On the other hand, the Tony TV show sparkled with past musical glories of Jule Styne, Andrew Lloyd Webber and Cy Coleman, with enticing samples of new ones to come from all three, and it achieved a couple of important firsts: the first best-play Tony to Neil Simon and the first best-scenery award to a woman, Heidi Landesman, for *Big River*. And 1984–85 *did* find the New York theater's creative and interpretive artists in their usual dynamic mode, generating enough excitement to make the rounds of every special taste. And if shows of broad appeal were few, they weren't entirely lacking. No season which treated its audiences to a new Neil Simon comedy like *Biloxi Blues*, with the author remembering his World War II basic training in full comedic power, can be entirely discounted; nor did Hugh Whitemore's spy drama *Pack of Lies*, a visitor from the London stage, deserve anything but cheers. And in a living theater whose wonders never cease, the past rallied to support the present with the triumphant return engagement of Yul Brynner in his memorable character of the King of Siam in *The King and I* (it showed what might have been in store for a new musical hit by grossing $605,546 in its final week, a new record for a single Broadway week, topping its own previous record of $553,245, according to *Variety*). And a series of stunning straight-play revivals—*Much Ado About Nothing, Cyrano de Bergerac, Strange Interlude* and *Aren't We All?* from London and *Joe Egg* from the Roundabout off Broadway—were the arenas for some of the year's outstanding individual achievements.

And yes, there were many more than ten good plays around the town in 1984–85 and certainly ten Best Plays including David Rabe's *Hurlyburly*, a comedy-drama of modern societal decadence directed by Mike Nichols and emerging from off Broadway to be received by Broadway audiences as the year's

3

major new American drama by an "established" playwright. August Wilson's Critics Award-winning *Ma Rainey's Black Bottom*, depicting a recording session by a 1927 blues singer and her accompanists under the direction of Lloyd Richards, was the outstanding Broadway playwriting debut. The only one of the Best Plays produced originally and directly for Broadway—and "middle Broadway" at that—was David Wiltse's *Doubles*, a comedy of male friendship. Off Broadway chimed in with Larry Shue's *The Foreigner*, which ran where the brave dare not go into the perilous realms of situation farce and was nothing but funny; with Dennis McIntyre's *Split Second*, the guilt-haunted dilemma of a black policeman who shoots a taunting white suspect in a fit of justifiable anger; with William M. Hoffman's *As Is*, a tribute to a lover's loyalty to an AIDS sufferer, transferred from Circle Repertory to Broadway; with a collective reminiscence of Vietnam agonies, *Tracers*, created by John DiFusco and other members of its Vietnam Veterans Ensemble Theater Company original cast (Vincent Caristi, Richard Chaves, Eric E. Emerson, Rick Gallavan, Merlin Marston, Harry Stephens and a writer, Sheldon Lettich), now "frozen" as a scripted show imported to New York by New York Shakespeare Festival and exported by them to London in their exchange arrangement with the Royal Court; and with Christopher Durang's acerbic commentary on the stresses of family life and ties, *The Marriage of Bette and Boo*. With the aforementioned *Biloxi Blues* and *Pack of Lies*, the 1984–85 Best Plays list is made up of three Broadway productions (*Ma Rainey*, *Biloxi*, *Pack of Lies*), one middle Broadway (*Doubles*) and six off Broadway (*Hurlyburly*, *As Is*, *The Foreigner*, *Split Second*, *Tracers*, *Bette and Boo*), two of the latter (*Hurlyburly*, *As Is*) moving to Broadway. As a matter of fact, most of them had already moved to New York from somewhere else. *Six* of this year's ten Best Plays had first been produced in cross-country theater, as follows: *Ma Rainey* (Yale Repertory Theater), *Tracers* (Odyssey Theater Ensemble), *Biloxi* (Ahmanson Theater, Los Angeles, and Curran Theater, San Francisco), *Foreigner* (Milwaukee Repertory), *Hurlyburly* (Goodman Theater, Chicago), *Bette and Boo* (as a work-in-progress at Yale and elsewhere). *Pack of Lies* began as a London hit, so only *Doubles*, *As Is* and *Split Second* were original New York productions.

And finally, any difficulty in Best Play selection for 1984–85 was one of elimination, not of accumulation. Only the tyranny of the number ten prevented us from including such distinctly worthy plays as *Alone Together* by Lawrence Roman, *Blue Window* by Craig Lucas, *Kennedy at Colonus* by Laurence Carr, and two *more* New York Shakespeare Festival offerings, *The Normal Heart* by Larry Kramer and *Rat in the Skull* by Ron Hutchinson.

The precipitous 1983–84 drop in Broadway production reported in last year's *Best Plays* volume leveled off in 1984–85. A year ago there were 34 Broadway productions (including 8 new American plays, 4 new foreign plays, 10 new musicals), while this year there were 35 Broadway productions (including 10 new American plays of which two were transfers, two new foreign plays, 6 new musicals). Two large-scale cabaret revues and three specialties padded the list. So did the 12 revivals (there were 11 the season before), including three massive musical revivals which in a sense stood in for the missing "new" musical productions. Broadway production in 1984–85 was indeed down from the historical and even the recent past, which recorded 58 shows in 1979–80, 51 in 1980–81, 45 in 1981–82 and 49 in 1982–83. 1984–85 certainly held to 1983–84's slower pace.

The extent to which the 35 Broadway shows of 1984–85 were audience-pleasers is another matter, possibly reflected in *Variety's* statistical summary, which estimated that the season's total gross for the 52 weeks was $208,006,181 (down from 1983–84's $226 million gross for a "53-week" year owing to a calendar anomaly, but still well ahead of the $203 million the year before). The 1984–85 road gross of touring Broadway shows was almost $226 million, way ahead of the previous year's $206 million, bringing the combined take to almost $444 million, the highest in Broadway history. The *average* Broadway admission price was $29.75 in June 1984, but it had *fallen* to a *Variety*-estimated $27.33 as of June 1985 (owing in part to the proliferation of twofers), so that the sustained high grosses cannot be entirely credited to inflation. The 1984–85 decline in the overall Broadway gross was matched by a decline in playing weeks from 1,097 in 1983–84 to 1,062 (if ten shows play ten weeks, that's 100 playing weeks) and in total paid attendance from 7.9 million to 7.1 million. All of this amounts to a warning signal, perhaps, that the year's shows didn't run as long and didn't pull audiences as they should, and that the theater must resolve to redouble its creative efforts in the coming year; but it is so far from a chronicle of disaster that those who are looking for sensational bad news to report should look elsewhere than at the state of our legitimate theater.

The year's big losers were the failed Broadway musicals including *Grind* which lost its entire capitalization of $4,750,000 and the Goodspeed Opera House production of *Take Me Along*, which folded after its opening night. The big winner was *The King and I*; or perhaps it was *La Cage aux Folles*, which had recouped its $5 million cost and was grossing more than $1.5 million weekly from the combination of its New York, West Coast and national companies; or perhaps it was the Broadway long-run champ *A Chorus Line*, whose eight-figure profit was augmented this year by a $2 million advance for its stock and amateur rights. *Cats* was still selling out and had accumulated a *Variety*-estimated $8 million on its $5 million cost, while another British holdover, *Noises Off*, recouped its $850,000 cost and was netting $30,000 weekly before it left town. The only 1984–85 shows to have paid off by the end of this season, according to *Variety*, were *The King and I*, the Whoopi Goldberg specialty and *Hurlyburly*, which was showing a $550,000 profit on the original $400,000 investment for its off-Broadway production.

This $400,000 cost level wasn't uncommon off Broadway in 1984–85, though of course many shows came in for much less and a few like the musical *3 Guys Naked From the Waist Down* for more (estimated at $500,000 but would have been twice that uptown). The Broadway revival of *Strange Interlude* came in from London at $900,000 but could take in $150,000 for its weekly 6 performances at a $50 top. A guesstimate for the production cost of a frugally-mounted straight play on Broadway would be somewhere around $600,000, with musicals in seven figures as high as they would dare to go (but one of the losers, *Home Front*, was estimated by *Variety* to have gotten onto the Broadway stage this season for an astonishingly small $313,000). One of 1984–85's

BIG RIVER—This Roger Miller-William Hauptman musical based on Mark Twain's *The Adventures of Huckleberry Finn* was a standout in scene design by Heidi Landesman (whose model for the set is pictured here, *above*) and costume design by Patricia McGourty (three of whose sketches are pictured here, *below*), as well as in performances by Ron

Richardson as Jim and Daniel H. Jenkins as Huck *(right)* and Bob Gunton as the King and Rene Auberjonois as the Duke (with Huck, *below*)

mightier economic struggles was waged by *The Tap Dance Kid*, which opened last year for $2.8 million, upped to $4 million when the show changed theaters in mid-run, and had returned about $1.9 to its backers on the eve of its national tour.

Among producers, Joseph Papp was far and away the standout as well as the most active of the season, putting on a spate of 15 new and revival productions, including two Best Plays, on his various indoor and outdoor stages. Apart from Mr. Papp's and some other off-Broadway institutions, the most active producers in 1984–85 were, understandably, those with some interest in keeping theaters occupied: James M. Nederlander with participation in at least six shows (*Much Ado About Nothing, Cyrano de Bergerac, Doug Henning and His World of Magic, Strange Interlude, Grind, Aren't We All?*); The Shubert Organization with a more adventurous five (*Whoopi Goldberg, Harrigan n' Hart, Joe Egg, Pacific Overtures, As Is*), and Roger L. Stevens/Kennedy Center with four (*Quilters, Take Me Along, When Hell Freezes Over I'll Skate, Master Class*), the latter two of which closed before reaching New York. Ivan Bloch distinguished himself by participating in four, including two Best Plays, *Hurlyburly* and *Ma Rainey*, plus *Requiem for a Heavyweight* and the out-of-town closer *Peccadillo*. Emanuel Azenberg came up with three hits including a Best Play (*Whoopi Goldberg, Joe Egg, Biloxi Blues*), Elizabeth I. McCann and Nelle Nugent helped put on three (*Much Ado, Cyrano, Pacific Overtures*), while Roger Berlind's three were *Joe Egg, After the Fall* and *In Trousers*. Frederick M. Zollo concerned himself with only two but batted a thousand with them (*Hurlyburly, Ma Rainey*), as did Douglas Urbanski (*Strange Interlude, Aren't We All?*) and the Richard Horner-Lynne Stuart-Hinks Shimberg team (*Kennedy at Colonus, Doubles*). As can be deduced from the above, New York play production in 1984–85 was more often than not a matter of teamwork rather than individual daring. As far as we can determine, *Grind* had the largest number of production groupies billed above the title—seven and two associates.

It took almost 100 directors to put on this season's New York shows, usually at the rate of one per director. But Jerry Zaks did three including *two* Best Plays: *The Foreigner, Bette and Boo* and *Crossing the Bar*. Double success was achieved by Mike Nichols (*Hurlyburly, Whoopi Goldberg*) and Clifford Williams (*Pack of Lies, Aren't We All?*). Others who essayed two shows with outstanding results were Arvin Brown (*Joe Egg, Requiem for a Heavyweight*), Samuel P. Barton (*Split Second, Henrietta*) and Douglas Turner Ward (*Ceremonies in Dark Old Men, District Line*). Over on the distressed musical side, Joe Layton struggled with *The Three Musketeers* and *Harrigan n' Hart*, while Harold Prince threw himself into *Grind* and *Diamonds*; but the most satisfactory results were obtained by Ran Avni (*Kuni-Leml*), Andrew Cadiff (*3 Guys Naked From the Waist Down*) and Des McAnuff (*Big River*).

And the year's directors should take extra bows for finely tuned ensembles in a goodly number of this year's shows: some of those mentioned above plus Lloyd Richards (*Ma Rainey*), Terry Hands (Royal Shakespeare), Norman Rene (*Blue Window*) and John DiFusco (*Tracers*). Among other 1984–85 directorial standouts were Marshall W. Mason's *As Is*, Keith Hack's *Strange Interlude*, Gene

Saks's *Biloxi Blues*, Stephen Zuckerman's *Kennedy at Colonus*, Lindsay Anderson's *In Celebration*, Morton Da Costa's *Doubles* and Max Stafford-Clark's *Rat in the Skull*. George C. Scott (*Design for Living*) and Gary Sinise (*Orphans*) achieved notable success as actors who were directing in 1984–85, shared to some degree by such colleagues as Sinise's Steppenwolf confrere John Malkovich (*Arms and the Man*), Alvin Epstein (*Endgame*), Geraldine Fitzgerald (*The Return of Herbert Bracewell*) and Daniel Gerroll (*She Stoops to Conquer*).

More than 50 scene designers and 50 costume designers, and a dozen others who did both, provided the imaginative environment for shows of all sizes. Most active among the scenic artists in 1984–85 were Loren Sherman with six shows, John Lee Beatty and Thomas Lynch with four and Marjorie Bradley Kellogg, Tony Walton, Ralph Koltai, Santo Loquasto and Charles Henry McClennahan with three apiece. Among the musical designers, Heidi Landesman with *Big River* and Clarke Dunham with *Grind* were standouts, while among straight plays the sets of Karl Eigsti (*Alone Together*), Douglas W. Schmidt (*Dancing in the End Zone*), David Mitchell (*Biloxi Blues*), Karen Schulz (*The Foreigner*) and Robert Fletcher (*Doubles*) seemed particularly well suited to their material.

Among costume designers, the most active were Ann Roth, Bill Walker and Rita Ryack with four and Jane Greenwood and David Woolard with three apiece. Standouts in the eye of this beholder were the designs of Alexander Reid for Royal Shakespeare, Patricia McGourty (*Big River*), David Navarro Velasquez (*Tracers*), Rita Ryack (*The Foreigner*), Karen Hummel (*Kuni-Leml*) and Florence Klotz (*Grind*).

Disappointment was certainly the lot of Jonathan Pryce, Patti LuPone and Bill Irwin of *Accidental Death of an Anarchist*, Carroll O'Connor and Frances Sternhagen of *Home Front*, Laurence Luckinbill and Pat Carroll of *Dancing in the End Zone*, Anne Pitoniak, Nancy Marchand, Peggy Cass et al of *The Octette Bridge Club* and John Lithgow (except that he was nominated for a Tony) and George Segal of *Requiem for a Heavyweight*, all of whom appeared in vehicles too fragile to bear the weight of their outstanding performances. Among the year's unforgettable images of drama, comedy and song enhanced by performance was Yul Brynner's farewell engagement as The King in *The King and I* after 34 years and 4,625 performances in that role. And then there were Matthew Broderick playing Neil Simon as an army recruit, Bill Sadler as sergeant and Barry Miller as misfit in *Biloxi Blues* . . . Brian Cox playing Edmund in *Strange Interlude* and then turning savage as the interrogator in *Rat in the Skull* . . . Patrick McGoohan with Rosemary Harris, Dana Ivey and George N. Martin in the intricate games of *Pack of Lies* . . . And the presence of Glenda Jackson, Derek Jacobi, Edward Petherbridge, Rex Harrison, Claudette Colbert and George Rose in the visiting British revivals . . . Stubby Kaye with Leilani Jones and untiring Ben Vereen in *Grind* . . . Kevin Kline and Raul Julia in classic and neoclassic roles all over town . . . Douglas Turner Ward re-doing his wonderful *Ceremonies in Dark Old Men* and Hal Holbrook playing up to *The Country Girl* . . . Whoopi Goldberg, Avner Eisenberg, Alec McCowen and Ekkehard Schall filling the stage in solo shows . . . Jim Dale and Stockard Channing coping in *Joe Egg* . . . The Jonathans, Hogan and Hadary, in *As Is* on and off Broadway . . . Kevin McCarthy and Janis Paige parentally comic in *Alone Together* . . . Linda Ronstadt's Mimi in *La Boheme*, Kate Nelligan's Virginia Woolf, Edward Herrmann's T.S. Eliot and Jessica Tandy in *Salonika*, all jewels in the Public Theater's 1984–85 crown . . . The sometimes inimitable, sometimes abrasive *Doubles* players, John Cullum, Tony Roberts, Ron Leibman and Austin Pendleton . . . Ron Richardson and on occasion his understudy, Elmore James, rolling out the songs of Huck's friend Jim in *Big River* . . . John Danelle and Norman Matlock, two generations of police in *Split Second* . . . The ensembles gifted with the extra value of acting nuggets like Anthony Heald's dead-pan poses in *The Foreigner*, the outbursts of Theresa Merritt and Charles S. Dutton in *Ma Rainey's Black Bottom*, J. Kenneth Campbell as a sergeant exercising tyranny in order to toughen his Vietnam trainees in *Tracers*, William Hurt's gropings for eternal meanings in *Hurlyburly*, Christopher Durang as a narrator trying to explain Joan Allen's aberrant maternal instincts in *The Marriage of Bette and Boo*. These and others were visible evidence of the broad-based support of our theater by a throng of talented, devoted performers who give it their best shot on every occasion, whether the occasion deserves it or not.

The ultimate insignia of New York professional achievement (we insist) are the Best Plays citations in these volumes, 16 years older than the Critics Award and only three years younger than the Pulitzer Prizes. Each Best Play selection is now made with the script itself as the first consideration, for the reason (as we've stated in previous volumes) that the script is the spirit of the theater's physical manifestation. It is not only the quintessence of the present, it is most of what endures into the future. So the Best Plays are the best scripts, with as little weight as humanly possible given to comparative production values. The choice is made without any regard whatever to a play's type—musical, comedy or drama—or origin on or off Broadway, or popularity at the box office, or lack of same.

We don't take the scripts of bygone eras into consideration for Best Play citation in this one, whatever their technical status as American or New York "premieres" which didn't happen to have a previous production of record. We draw the line between adaptations and revivals, the former eligible for Best Play selection but the latter not, on a case-by-case basis. We likewise consider the eligibility of borderline examples of limited-engagement and showcase production case by case, ascertaining whether they're probably "frozen" in final script version and no longer works-in-progress before considering them for Best Play citation (and in the case of a late-season arrival the determination may not be possible until the following year).

If a script influences the very character of a season, or by some function of consensus wins the Critics, Pulitzer or Tony Awards, we take into account its future historical as well as present esthetic importance. This is the only special consideration we give, and we don't always tilt in its direction, as the record shows.

The Best Plays of 1984–85 are listed below for visual convenience in the order in which they opened in New York (a plus sign + with the performance numbers signifies that the play was still running after June 2, 1985.)

Split Second
(Off B'way, 147 perfs.)

Hurlyburly
(Off B'way, 45 perfs; B'way, 343 perfs.)

Ma Rainey's Black Bottom
(B'way, 265+ perfs.)

The Foreigner
(Off B'way, 242+ perfs.)

Tracers
(Off B'way, 169+ perfs.)

Pack of Lies
(B'way, 120 perfs.)

As Is
(Off B'way, 49 perfs.; B'way, 35+ perfs.)

Biloxi Blues
(B'way, 74+ perfs.)

Doubles
(B'way, 27+ perfs.)

The Marriage of Bette and Boo
(Off B'way, 18+ perfs.)

Broadway

Comedy was king this season, where once musical comedy reigned. The laughter was crowned on Broadway by Neil Simon's new *Biloxi Blues* and richly caparisoned by David Wiltse's *Doubles*, Lawrence Roman's *Alone Together* and the reappearance of masterworks by Noel Coward (*Design for Living*), William Shakespeare (*Much Ado About Nothing*), Frederick Lonsdale (*Aren't We All?*) and George Bernard Shaw (*Arms and the Man*).

The Neil Simon of his 12th Best Play, *Biloxi Blues*, is the Neil Simon of *Brighton Beach Memoirs*, with an added dynamic that pulls the play up through its sitcom levels into Simon's tickling (and sometimes stabbing) insights into human nature and the way we look at life now. Eugene Morris Jerome, the semi-autobiographical Simon figure, painfully adolescent in *Brighton Beach Memoirs*, has grown old enough to be drafted into the World War II army in *Biloxi Blues*. Now he has become a green twig of middle-class innocence being vigorously bent in the basic training program. Played once again by Matthew Broderick with youthful diffidence and the mannerisms of a magician distracting the audience's attention from the mechanics of a trick, Eugene sets out on his odyssey from Brooklyn to Biloxi, determined to 1) lose his virginity, 2) stay alive and 3) become a successful writer. We know the outcome of 2 and 3, and here we watch him pursue 1, in a scene with Randall Edwards as a busy prostitute, directed by Gene Saks on a fine line between prurience and farce. But it is Eugene's preparation to achieve his second goal that provides most of the fun in this play. Yes, the sergeant-vs.-recruit confrontation of ruthless discipline in order to turn civilians into soldiers is an oft-told tale in both comedy and drama (c.f. this season's Best Play *Tracers*). But this time they put the young Neil Simon through it, and he noticed that it was agonizing to obey but very difficult to outwit the sergeant (crisp and indomitable in the performance of Bill Sadler)—difficult but not impossible for a misfit individualist (Barry Miller in his Tony-winning performance) willing to pay any price to retain his identity and dignity. He noticed that the training has little effect on the essential character of the slobs and goof-offs among his barracks mates (Brian Tarantina, Matt

COMEDY—Whoopi Goldberg as a surfer chick *(left)* in her one-woman show and *(right)* Kevin McCarthy and Janis Paige in Lawrence Roman's *Alone Together*

Mulhern, Alan Ruck and Geoffrey Sharp). Simon shares his findings with us in a flow of gags and situations, many of them hilarious, toward the ironic conclusion that with all this effort nothing much has been improved or lost, except virginity.

Likewise David Wiltse, whose only other major New York production was *Suggs* at Lincoln Center in 1972, came on strong with *Doubles*, a verbal and sight gag-loaded locker room farce about the ways of friendship among men, the paradox of commitment even when they may actually not like each other all that much. Their occasion in this Best Play is a weekly tennis foursome of a grocer (Ron Leibman, a bull in a china shop), a tennis reporter (John Cullum), a lawyer (Austin Pendleton) and a stockbroker (Tony Roberts) in the well-scrubbed, stylish locker room setting designed by Robert Fletcher. However these four may perform on the court (we never see that), under Morton Da Costa's direction their affectionate/abrasive relationships hilariously expose the conceits and finally the fears of the male animal in the 1980s jungle. This *Doubles* was a canny script well

The 1984–85 Season on Broadway

PLAYS (10)

HURLYBURLY
(transfer)
MA RAINEY'S BLACK BOTTOM
Alone Together
Home Front
Dancing in the End Zone
The Octette Bridge Club
Requiem for a Heavyweight
BILOXI BLUES
AS IS
(transfer)
DOUBLES

MUSICALS (6)

Gotta Getaway!
Quilters
Harrigan 'n Hart
Leader of the Pack
Grind
Big River

FOREIGN PLAYS IN ENGLISH (2)

Accidental Death of an Anarchist
PACK OF LIES

REVUES (2)

Haarlem Nocturne
Streetheat

REVIVALS (12)

Circle in the Square:
Design for Living
The Loves of Anatol
Arms and the Man
Oedipus Rex
Royal Shakespeare:
Much Ado About Nothing
Cyrano de Bergerac
The Three Musketeers
The King and I
Strange Interlude
Joe Egg
(transfer)
Take Me Along
Aren't We All?

SPECIALTIES (3)

Kipling
Whoopi Goldberg
Doug Henning and His World of Magic

HOLDOVER WHICH BECAME A HIT IN 1984–85

La Cage aux Folles

Categorized above are all the new productions listed in the Plays Produced on Broadway section of this volume.
Plays listed in CAPITAL LETTERS have been designated Best Plays of 1984–85.
Plays listed in *italics* were still running after June 2, 1985.
Plays listed in **bold face type** were classified as successes in *Variety's* annual estimate published June 5, 1985.

served in design and direction and superbly in its four-star acting, one of the very pleasant surprises of the Broadway year.

Lawrence Roman's *Alone Together* was another comedy of contemporary manners, with Kevin McCarthy and Janis Paige as a Los Angeles couple breathing a deep sight of relief when the last son goes off to college, only to soon find all three sons drifting back home. The nest mom and dad hoped could now be exclusively devoted to champagne for two and other delights of a well-earned rest is bulging instead with full-grown fledglings, refugees from the real world. This timely theme was sympathetically and amusingly spun out, in an ideal Broadway comedy which deserved a wider audience than it managed to attract this time around.

The human comedy was also a strong element in two bittersweet Best Plays, August Wilson's *Ma Rainey's Black Bottom* and David Rabe's *Hurlyburly*. The former, whose title refers to a popular dance of the 1920s, the decade in which it was set, depicted a Chicago recording session of a blues pioneer, Ma Rainey (who could give Bessie Smith lessons), with her black accompanists and hangers-on and the white managers of the record company in attendance. Ma Rainey's proudly tyrannous attitude, the musicians' shop talk and the fawning of the satellite characters were strongly comedic elements under the direction of Lloyd Richards, who staged this play at Yale first and then on Broadway. The heart—or rather, the black bottom—of this matter, however, was the downhearted echo of racial injustice in the all-too-vivid memories of the jazz musicians portrayed by Joe Seneca, Robert Judd, Leonard Jackson and Charles S. Dutton, and in the chip-on-the-shoulder strut of Theresa Merritt as Ma. The play ends in a tragedy not quite as believable as the humor plastered over the scars, or as the very adroit synchronization of action with a recorded sound track which created a perfect illusion that the actors playing the musicians were also really playing their instruments in the sequences of music.

Hurlyburly was the season's dominant American play, appearing off Broadway in June, then transferring to Broadway in August for a run that carried it right to the end of the theater year. As directed by Mike Nichols in both venues, Rabe's newest Best Play was an account of the "me" generation in fading flower in the Hollywood hills, living on the borders of show business and from moment to cocaine-enhanced, sex-troubled moment. William Hurt and Judith Ivey received Tony nominations for their portrayals of two of the seven characters blended into an ensemble of self-destruction so wanton that it was hard to develop strong allegiance to any of them. But even to that segment of the audience which remained emotionally distant from it, *Hurlyburly* offered rewards of writing and stagecraft.

Another American Best Play transferred triumphantly from off Broadway was William M. Hoffman's *As Is*, one of two scripts coming to grips with the subject of the deadly Acquired Immune Deficiency Syndrome (AIDS) this season (the other was Larry Kramer's hard-hitting *The Normal Heart*, of which more in the off-Broadway chapter of this report). With a marvellous economy of means and imaginative direction by Marshall W. Mason in production at his Circle Repertory, this fine play viewed the subject from the perspective of a discarded but still faithful lover (Jonathan Hadary) who stands by his former lover (Tony-

GRIND—Timothy Nolen, Leilani Jones and Ben Vereen (arms linked) and dancers in the burlesque musical directed by Harold Prince

nominated Jonathan Hogan), though the latter has jilted him, caught AIDS and then drifted back to the only person who will instantly accept him "as is" (his family, his partner and others shy away when they learn of the illness). *As Is* dwelt upon loyalty and commitment rather than the horrors or sociological implications of the disease itself, relieving the compression of its relentless, intermissionless sequence of events with a sort of gallows humor. The broader consequences of AIDS are sketched in around the intense personal drama of failing health and unfailing affection, one of the season's major achievements of writing, acting and direction.

Another major social strain—the distress of an American family trying to reassimilate a son home from the Vietnam war but unable to relieve his trauma —was the concern of James Duff's *Home Front*, with Carroll O'Connor in an exceptionally strong performance as the father. O'Connor buried Archie Bunker, his TV series character, invisibly deep inside his portrayal of a parent who is less than perfect but doing his determined best to understand and help. The father finally reaches the point of no more putting up with a son who goes out of his way to upset and hurt and finally exhausts the audience's profound sympathy along with the father's.

Also a more effective stage instrument than its short run would indicate was *Dancing in the End Zone* by Bill C. Davis, about a football coach (Laurence

ACCIDENTAL DEATH OF AN ANARCHIST—Jonathan Pryce, Gerry Bamman and Bill Irwin in a scene from the Broadway production of Dario Fo's Italian farce, adapted by Richard Nelson

Luckinbill) who takes a fatherly interest in his star quarterback but pushes him to risk permanent injury in order to win games. Douglas W. Schmidt's flexible setting suggesting anything from a classroom to a football stadium was one of the play's considerable assets. Two other American plays which made the Broadway scene this year were P.J. Barry's *The Octette Bridge Club*, with a star-studded cast playing eight sisters in family reunions ten years apart, and the Arvin Brown-directed stage version of the late Rod Serling's 1956 television play about a has-been boxer, *Requiem for a Heavyweight*, with John Lithgow in a Tony-nominated performance of the title role that is now memorable to all too few members of the Broadway audience.

Among foreign plays in English (or rather, between them, because there were only two this season), Dario Fo's *Accidental Death of an Anarchist* travelled no better than a very fragile regional wine in transit from the Italian stage to Richard Nelson's Broadway adaptation, even with Jonathan Pryce giving another of his shrewd comic performances as The Fool, the butt of the authorities. Hugh Whitemore's spy drama *Pack of Lies* travelled admirably, however, from the London stage to Broadway and Best Play status. Like much of its author's work, it was based on real events and persons, in this case a suburban family's reactions to having a counterespionage team borrow their house as an observation post to keep watch on suspected neighbors—and not merely neighbors, but the householders' (Rosemary Harris, George N. Martin and Tracy Pollan as their daughter) best friends (Dana Ivey and Colin Fox). With Patrick McGoohan as an unflappable and coldly efficient government agent nearly freezing the warm blood of this gentle family, the play gave out its secrets liberally and soon (this caper was part of Gordon Lonsdale's 1960–61 spying activities in Britain) while dramatizing the effects of all this duplicity on the nonprofessionals caught up in it. Rosemary Harris as the mother was most deeply affected and effective under the direction of Clifford Williams, in the obligatory annual major attraction borrowed from the London stage.

The bad news about Broadway's bad 1984–85 musical season was widely broadcast and has to do with the absence of any sign of a successful new show for most of the year, in the midst of failing large-scale efforts. The good news was that *Big River: The Adventures of Huckleberry Finn* finally showed up at the end of April and turned some of the lights back on with an entertaining and sometimes touching book adapted by William Hauptman from Mark Twain's novel. It also enjoyed a strong visual personality in the designs of Heidi Landesman (scenery, with Huck and Jim's raft moving freely downstage while the Mississippi winds back into the distance) and Patricia McGourty (costumes of the homespun era). The inner strength of character of the runaway slave Jim was stressed and forcefully projected in action and song by Ron Richardson, and on occasions by his capable understudy Elmore James, under Des McAnuff's conscientiously stylized direction. Rene Auberjonois sank his teeth and everything else into the role of the Duke, clown as well as villain. Roger Miller's score with simplistic, repetitive, rock-style lyrics had the grace to keep its decibels at a painless level so that its melodious moments came over the footlights handsomely, helping to establish *Big River* as a positive and welcome asset in the Broadway balance.

There is no questioning the effort and expertise that was poured into *Grind*, the Harold Prince-directed, Lester Wilson-choreographed, Clarke Dunham and Florence Klotz-designed, Ben Vereen, Stubby Kaye and Leilani Jones-acted period musical trying to depict a slice of burlesque life in 1933 Chicago. What they were driving at was sometimes unclear, as in its tale of a remorseful IRA killer converted into a burlesque performer; but that they were indeed driving was obvious in every energetic moment. Certainly the Vereen song-and-dance solos and the backstage spectacle of comedians, strippers, etc., were diverting in a vaudeville kind of way, while missing the collective payoff of a Broadway musical. Another musical backward glance, *Harrigan 'n Hart*, celebrated the careers of the renowned pair of 19th century musical stage stars, but not even with a Michael Stewart book under Joe Layton's direction could it find the handle to musicalize its subject effectively.

Radio City Music Hall's summer musical was *Gotta Getaway!*, with Liliane Montevecchi and Tony Azito front and center and with the perpetually amazing Rockettes, taking audiences around the world on a luxury cruise as directed and choreographed by Larry Fuller. *Quilters*, extrapolating the lives of pioneer women from the patterns in their quilts, was a charming concept born and raised in regional theater, with score and direction by Barbara Damashek and book co-authored by her, and with Lenka Peterson as prototype and narrator. The more boisterous rock musical *Leader of the Pack* was more comfortable on Broadway, with Ellie Greenwich recapitulating the life and songs of Ellie Greenwich, herself as herself in the 1980s and Dinah Manoff as her younger self, directed and choreographed by Michael Peters. The musical season was further embellished by a pair of cabaret-style revues: *Haarlem Nocturne*, conceived by and with Andre De Shields, and *Streetheat*, devised by Michele Asaf and Rick Atwell around New York's "now" culture. It was the revival sector, however, which provided New York's musical year with its only solid hit, *The King and I*, its most dramatic misstep, the closing of *Take Me Along* after only one performance, and perhaps its greatest disappointment, the faltering of *The Three Musketeers* despite a new book.

In the specialty category, Mike Nichols supervised the meteoric rise to Broadway stardom and acclaim of Whoopi Goldberg in her solo presentation of character sketches, all sharply pointed and generally loaded with humor. Doug Henning also stopped off in New York for one of his mystifying sessions of magic, and Roy Dotrice recreated the personality and explored some of the works of Rudyard Kipling in a one-man reminiscence.

Here's where we list the Best Plays choices for the outstanding individual achievements of the season in New York, on and off Broadway. In the acting categories, clear distinction among "starring," "featured" or "supporting" players can't be made on the basis of official billing, which is as much a matter of contracts as of esthetics. Here in these volumes we divide acting into "primary" and "secondary" roles, a primary role being one which might some day cause a star to inspire a revival in order to appear in that character. All others, be they vivid as Mercutio, are classed as secondary. Furthermore, our list of individual standouts makes room for more than a single choice when appropriate. We believe that no useful purpose is served by forcing ourselves into an arbitrary selection of a single best when we come upon multiple examples of equal distinction.

Here, then, are the *Best Plays* bests of 1984–85:

PLAYS

BEST PLAY: *Biloxi Blues* by Neil Simon; *Ma Rainey's Black Bottom* by August Wilson

BEST FOREIGN PLAY: *Pack of Lies* by Hugh Whitemore

BEST REVIVAL: *Joe Egg* by Peter Nichols, directed by Arvin Brown

BEST ACTOR IN A PRIMARY ROLE: Matthew Broderick as Eugene Morris Jerome in *Biloxi Blues*; Jim Dale as Bri in *Joe Egg*

BEST ACTRESS IN A PRIMARY ROLE: Joan Allen as Bette Brennan in *The Marriage of Bette and Boo*; Stockard Channing as Sheila in *Joe Egg*; Glenda Jackson as Nina Leeds in *Strange Interlude*

SPECIAL CITATION: Avner Eisenberg and Whoopi Goldberg in solo performances

BEST ACTOR IN A SECONDARY ROLE: Charles S. Dutton as Levee in *Ma Rainey's Black Bottom*; Barry Miller as Arnold Epstein and Bill Sadler as Sgt. Merwin J. Toomey in *Biloxi Blues*

BEST ACTRESS IN A SECONDARY ROLE: Dana Ivey as Helen Kroger in *Pack of Lies*; Theresa Merritt as Ma Rainey in *Ma Rainey's Black Bottom*

BEST DIRECTOR: John DiFusco for *Tracers*; Jerry Zaks for *The Foreigner* and *The Marriage of Bette and Boo*

BEST SCENERY: David Mitchell for *Biloxi Blues*

BEST COSTUMES: Alexander Reid for *Cyrano de Bergerac* and *Much Ado About Nothing*

MUSICALS

BEST MUSICAL: *Big River*; *Kuni-Leml*

BEST BOOK: William Hauptman for *Big River*

BEST MUSIC: Roger Miller for *Big River*

BEST LYRICS: Richard Engquist for *Kuni-Leml*

BEST REVIVAL: *The King and I* by Richard Rodgers and Oscar Hammerstein II, directed by Mitch Leigh

BEST ACTOR IN A PRIMARY ROLE: Yul Brynner as The King in *The King and I*; John Kassir as Kenny Brewster in *3 Guys Naked From the Waist Down*; Ben Vereen as Leroy in *Grind*

BEST ACTRESS IN A PRIMARY ROLE: Lenka Peterson as Sarah in *Quilters*

BEST ACTOR IN A SECONDARY ROLE: Ron Richardson as Jim in *Big River*

BEST ACTRESS IN A SECONDARY ROLE: Leilani Jones as Satin in *Grind*

BEST DIRECTOR: Ran Avni for *Kuni-Leml*

BEST CHOREOGRAPHY: Lester Wilson for *Grind*

BEST SCENERY: Heidi Landesman for *Big River*

BEST COSTUMES: Florence Klotz for *Grind*; Patricia McGourty for *Big River*

3 GUYS NAKED FROM THE WAIST DOWN—Jerry Colker, John Kassir and Scott Bakula in the Michael Rupert-Jerry Colker musical

Off Broadway

In the season of 1984–85, off Broadway was looking more and more like the major creative stimulus in the New York theater, holding a virtual monopoly on innovation and generating a vigor essential to the survival of the fiercely commercial theater uptown. This was a year in which off Broadway supplied Broadway with three of its major attractions in transfer: *Hurlyburly*, *As Is* and the memorable revival of *Joe Egg*. Its institutions and independents produced on their own or brought up from OOB six Best Plays and an outstanding musical, *Kuni-Leml*. Of course, overcommercialization is an insidious penalty of success like this. With its over-$20 ticket and six-figure production costs, off Broadway is certainly sailing on the edge of the troubled waters in which storm-tossed Broadway is barely managing to keep afloat. As of this season, though, the applause was much louder than the warnings.

Production volume of musicals was off sharply to only 4 as compared with 13 a year ago, but the production of new American plays was up, and there were works of remarkably high quality in all categories. Off Broadway produced 52

The 1984–85 Season Off Broadway

PLAYS (39)

Danny and the Deep Blue Sea
SPLIT SECOND
Playwrights Horizons:
Elm Circle
Romance Language
Life and Limb
Young Playwrights Festival
Kennedy at Colonus
Public Theater:
Found a Peanut
Ice Bridge
The Ballad of Soapy Smith
TRACERS
Coming of Age in Soho
The Normal Heart
THE MARRIAGE OF BETTE AND BOO
HURLYBURLY
Blue Window
Circle Rep:
Bing and Walker
Dysan
AS IS
Medea and the Doll
The Miss Firecracker Contest (return engagement)

Manhattan Theater Club:
Husbandry
Messiah
Digby
California Dog Fight
The Pretender
THE FOREIGNER
Losing It
Negro Ensemble:
District Line
Henrietta
Two Can Play
Cliffhanger
The Mugger
Crossing the Bar
Orphans
Eden Court
Rommel's Garden
Man Enough
The Return of Herbert Bracewell

MUSICALS (4)

Kuni-Leml
3 Guys Naked From the Waist Down
In Trousers
Mayor

FOREIGN PLAYS IN ENGLISH (9)

Public Theater:
The Nest of the Wood Grouse
Tom and Viv
Virginia
Salonika
Rat in the Skull
All Strange Away
In Celebration
Before the Dawn
Childhood & For No Good Reason

SPECIALTIES (10)

An Evening With Ekkehard Schall
The Chinese Magic Revue
Elvis Mania
Viva Vittorio!
Avner the Eccentric
Zelda
Between Rails
Hannah Senesh
The Singular Dorothy Parker
Penn & Teller

REVUES (7)

Shades of Harlem
Rap Master Ronnie
I Hear Music
Hang on to the Good Times
Diamonds
Ann Reinking . . . Music Moves Me
Lies & Legends

REVIVALS (40)

Delacorte:
Henry V
The Golem
Harold Clurman:
Endgame
A Kurt Weill Cabaret
Roundabout:
Come Back, Little Sheba
She Stoops to Conquer
Joe Egg
The Playboy of the Western World
An Enemy of the People
The Voice of the Turtle
After the Fall

LOOM:
The New Moon (12 operettas in running repertory)
Love's Labor's Lost
The Country Girl
Pacific Overtures
La Boheme
CSC:
Agamemnon
Elektra/Orestes
George Dandin
The Underpants
Total Eclipse
Mirror Rep:
The Madwoman of Chaillot
Clarence
Vivat! Vivat! Regina!
Ceremonies in Dark Old Men
Acting Company:
A New Way to Pay Old Debts
As You Like It
The Skin of Our Teeth

Categorized above are all the productions listed in the Plays Produced Off Broadway section of this volume.
Plays listed in CAPITAL LETTERS have been designated Best Plays of 1984-85.
Plays listed in *italics* were still running off Broadway after June 2, 1985.

new plays and musicals (including one return engagement) compared to 57 a year ago and 59 in 1982–83. This season's new-play contingent comprised 39 American straight-play programs, the 4 abovementioned musicals and 9 foreign plays, as compared with last year's 32-13-12 and the 39-7-13, 45-9-7, 33-14-8 and 39-7-12 of the previous four seasons. In addition to this year's 52 new-scripted productions, there were 7 revues, 10 specialties and 40 revivals (see the one-page summary of the season accompanying this report), making a grand total of 109 programs—only one fewer than last year's total—presented off Broadway during the past 12 months.

We must take pains to explain what we mean by "off Broadway," because it is a non-place, or never-never land, whose border lines are blurring at both the Broadway and off-off-Broadway boundaries. Most other publications apply the term loosely, sometimes to plays that are clearly OOB (weekend or Wednesday-to-Saturday performances only, reduced ticket prices, Equity concessions, limited runs). We can't draw indelible lines, but we try to distinguished between professional and experimental theater; between what is probably a work-in-progress which may evolve as it rises to a higher level of commitment, and what is probably a "frozen" script facing the world for better or for worse as a finished work in production or publication. Only the latter is regularly considered for Best Play designation on the same terms as those classified under the Broadway heading, whereas works-in-progress are not.

By the lights of these *Best Plays* volumes, then, an off-Broadway production is one a) with an Equity cast b) giving 8 performances a week c) in an off-Broadway theater d) after inviting public comment by reviewers. And to the best of our information, an "off-Broadway theater" is a house eligible to operate under the off-Broadway contract because it is of a specific size in a specific area, i.e.: seating 499 or fewer and situated in Manhattan *outside* the area bounded by Fifth and Ninth Avenues between 34th and 56th Streets, and by Fifth Avenue and the Hudson River between 56th and 72d Streets.

Obviously, we make exceptions to each of these rules; no dimension of "off" or "off off" can be applied exactly. In each *Best Plays* volume we stretch somewhat in the direction of inclusion—never of exclusion. The point is, "off Broadway" isn't an exact location either geographically or esthetically, it's a state of the art, a level of expertise and economic commitment. In these volumes we'll continue to categorize it as accurately as we can, as long as it seems useful for the record, while reminding those who read these lines that distinctions are no longer as clear as they once were—and elsewhere in this volume we offer the most comprehensive list of 1984–85 off-off-Broadway productions anywhere, compiled by Camille Croce, plus a review of the OOB year by Mel Gussow.

The New York theater season was only a week old in June when off Broadway's first 1984–85 Best Play, Dennis McIntyre's *Split Second*, appeared in independent production. Here a black policeman (John Danelle) is goaded by the racial taunting of a white car-thief to such fury that he draws his gun and shoots his handcuffed prisoner dead. This wasn't a melodrama, however, but an inner conflict: does the policeman tell the truth like a good officer and take the consequences, or does he arrange the details of his unwitnessed act to look like self-defense?—the latter not only in self-interest but to avoid a charge of racist

FACES OF *BLUE WINDOW*—Lawrence Joshua with Maureen Silliman *(left)* and Brad O'Hare with Randy Danson in the play by Craig Lucas

violence which might rub off onto all the other black officers. His best friend and his wife (Peter Jay Fernandez and Michele Shay) pull him toward coverup; his father (Norman Matlock), a retired policeman of some renown, pushes him toward full confession, a conflict which was dramatically stated and fully explored under Samuel P. Barton's direction, building toward the play's final lesser-of-two-evils choice.

And the season was less than a month old when *Hurlyburly*, discussed in the previous chapter, made its appearance with Mike Nichols and company using off Broadway as a tryout town in transit to Broadway. And the autumn leaves had hardly turned when a third Best Play appeared in independent off-Broadway production: *The Foreigner*, a situation farce in which a painfully shy Englishman (Anthony Heald), in order to avoid conversation, arranges to have the inhabitants of a Georgia fishing lodge believe he is an exotic who speaks no English. The author, Larry Shue, played a take-charge character who sets up the situation, goes away and then comes back to mop up after it boils over with really boisterous skullduggery flavored with a dash of romance. Under the direction of Jerry Zaks, the deception and its hilarious consequences came off splendidly.

The early part of the season provided yet another highlight of independent production which slipped into a commercial run from its off-off-Broadway origin: Craig Lucas's *Blue Window*, an imaginatively conceived and constructed examination of one evening in the lives of a group of Manhattanites preparing for a dinner party. Under Norman Rene's direction, it broke up space and time to serve its special purpose of exposing the emotions and ambitions of the characters one by one and two by two. This comedy-drama, which won the newly-established George and Elisabeth Marton Award to encourage a new American playwright, first appeared in June as an offering of Rene's off-off-Broadway Production Company and was raised to full off-Broadway status without moving from its original theater, a process that is being repeated these days, as it holds down some of the original production cost until it's clear that a new work is going to succeed.

Another standout in independent off-Broadway production was Laurence Carr's exceptionally theatrical *Kennedy at Colonus*, directed by Stephen Zuckerman. It was an ensemble rendering of major events in the life and career of Robert F. Kennedy, with Christopher Curry playing the late Senator, beginning on, flashing back from and finally ending on the day of his assassination in California in 1968. In the course of the season, the independents also came up with a return engagement of Beth Henley's 1983–84 Best Play *The Miss Firecracker Contest* and a modern Russian play about the 1941 friendship of two Kiev families, one Christian and one Jewish, entitled *Before the Dawn* and adapted by Joseph Stein from an English translation. Other American scripts in independent off-Broadway production concerned themselves with a straight young man pretending to be gay in order to approach closer to a desirable young woman (*The Pretender*); rustics philosophizing over their beers (*Losing It*); a college professor, played by Henderson Forsythe, weaving a tangled web of murder around a particularly irritating female colleague (*Cliffhanger*); street crime as an occupation for the unemployed (*The Mugger*); the life and times of tavern owners (*Crossing the Bar*); marital problems among the mobile-home set (*Eden Court*); a lovable turn-of-the-century character actor and his actress-wife (Milo O'Shea and Frances Sternhagen in *The Return of Herbert Bracewell*) and a well-made study of a family reassessing its values under the influence of a handicapped member (Patty Gideon Sloan's *Man Enough*).

On the institutional side of 1984–85 off-Broadway production, it seemed that Joseph Papp's New York Shakespeare Festival was coming up with a challenging new theater piece every week. In fact, he lit up the Manhattan sky more often than once a month with two Central Park revivals, five foreign imports (including two in an exchange program with London's Royal Court Theater), one musical revival (*La Boheme* with a new English libretto, new English lyrics by David Spencer and with Patti Cohenour, Linda Ronstadt and Caroline Peyton alternating as Mimi under Wilford Leach's direction) seven new American plays (including two Best Plays), making an imposing total of 15 productions by the Lafayette Street group. One of the Best Plays was a Los Angeles visitor to the Public Theater, *Tracers*, a tattoo of incidents of training and combat in the Vietnam war, with a pre-recorded rock score giving it sometimes the extra dimension of a musical. It was conceived, directed and co-developed by John DiFusco and six other members of its original Vietnam Veterans Ensemble Theater Company cast, plus one writer—all of them having lived through real experiences of Vietnam training and combat. It had a smell of blood and powder in its battle scenes and a whiff of resentment in its reflections from a present-day perspective. Three of the original cast (DiFusco, Vincent Caristi and Richard Chaves) appeared in the New York production, a controlled explosion of ensemble performance.

The large number of Papp's 1984–85 programs included some like *Tracers* which were not materially developed at the Public Theater. Others like Christopher Durang's provocative *The Marriage of Bette and Boo*, a black comedy about an ill-starred marriage and its emotional consequences, were what might be termed Public Theater originals (*Marriage* had been performed elsewhere, but in a much shorter version). In fact, originality was a long suit of this Best Play—not structure or appeal but originality in the conception, expression and staging of its ironies of husband-wife hostility, interfamily scorn, flippant attitudes toward death and emotional disaster, etc., glittering like a polished knife blade and often cutting to the bone. Joan Allen played a forbiddingly unsympathetic wife and mother obsessed with bearing babies doomed to die from RH factor and overburdening her only living child with fulsome sentimentality and guilt. The latter, the only really heartstruck and heartstriking character in the play, served as a narrator to link the many episodes not always in time sequence. He was played by the author in a touching portrayal of the real victim of these ironic fantasies. Only a highly skilled ensemble under strong direction by Jerry Zaks in Loren Sherman's wonderfully adaptable setting of sliding screens could have maintained the style and concentration of this work, which was a sort of random conversation suddenly become all too revealing.

Albert Innaurato also swelled the Public Theater's 1984–85 agenda with *Coming of Age in Soho*, with John Procaccino as a bisexual ex-husband and father whose solitude is continually disturbed by a flow of children, women and even gangsters through his spacious loft—a diffuse but substantial play directed by its author. Larry Kramer's *The Normal Heart* was another of the Public's important contributions to the season, a polemical but dramatic protest against government and other organizational indifference to the growing threat of AIDS. It exposed societal foot-dragging with relentless determination and in rather more depth than the year's other AIDS drama, but without achieving its personal intensity. Michael Weller's *The Ballad of Soapy Smith* was a wide-angle saga of a con man's adventures during the Alaska gold rush, intriguing enough to attract a best-play vote in the Critics' balloting. Donald Margulies examined some of the conflicts of childhood with adults playing characters age 5 to 12 in *Found a Peanut*, while the abovementioned Vietnam Veterans Ensemble Theater Company made an early-season appearance, seven months prior to their *Tracers*, as troops guarding an Arctic nuclear installation in *Ice Bridge*.

Papp himself helped to focus his organization's attention on scripts from abroad early in the season by directing a translation of Victor Rozov's *The Nest of the Wood Grouse*, a Russian family comedy so contemporary that it was playing at the Satire Theater in Moscow while the New York version was being offered at the Public. Later in the year, stars shone downtown in foreign scripts as an exchange program with the Royal Court Theater brought over their production of *Tom and Viv* by Michael Hastings, a closeup of T.S. Eliot's home life with Edward Herrmann playing the poet. Jessica Tandy brightened Louise Page's *Salonika* (a script also previously produced at the Royal Court) as an octogenarian widow visiting the seaside grave of her soldier-husband killed decades before in World War I, still finding pleasure and identity in life while her resentful daughter (Elizabeth Wilson) cannot. This was a play made like a patchwork quilt of small conflicts between flesh and spirit, with the flesh graphically symbolized

KUNI-LEML—Susan Friedman and Stuart Zagnit in the musical by Nahma Sandrow, Raphael Crystal and Richard Engquist

onstage by a sunbathing youth whose stark nakedness is taken in stride by the other characters. Another British import, *Virginia*, provided Kate Nelligan with the opportunity of appearing as Virginia Woolf in a character study based on the Woolfs' writings.

Papp's 1984–85 New York Shakespeare Festival season at the Public Theater closed with another exchange production from the Royal Court, a sledghammer political tract by Ron Hutchinson entitled *Rat in the Skull* (a metaphor for the gnawing intrusion of doubt into a fanatic's thoughts), with a would-be bombthrowing IRA terrorist (Colum Convey) arrested by British police officers in London (Philip Jackson and Gerard Horan) and interrogated by an Ulster policeman (Brian Cox), a protestant, with shattering insistence that their north-south Irish brotherhood is stronger than their religious and political enmity, however deeply rooted in bloody history. This was powerful punctuation for the Public Theater season, directed by Max Stafford-Clark and acted with total conviction by an astonishingly practised and perfected Royal Court cast.

Viewed in 12-month perspective, Papp's season was as exceptionally distinguished as it was active—and profitable, if that word can be applied to a not-for-profit, semi-subsidized theater group. The box office, which normally provides 10 to 12 per cent of the New York Shakespeare Festival's annual income, brought in almost 25 per cent with the successes of 1984–85. It might not be unreasonable to wish that this wonderfully versatile Lafayette Street facility, with its many theaters built into the former Astor Library, could have been filled more often for developmental and less often for hospitable purposes of housing work prefabricated elsewhere. But it would be unreasonable to lean too heavily on this point, especially in a year when Papp gave Herrmann, Nelligan and Tandy vehicles for major performance, brought in the timely and vivid reminder *Tracers* and offered Durang, Innaurato, Weller and Margulies—four of America's leading younger playwrights—the opportunity to develop and display their latest work.

Marshall W. Mason's Circle Repertory Company also reached the Best Play peak with one of their new American plays, *As Is*, which moved uptown and was discussed in the previous chapter of this report. The Circle season included two more new American scripts—James Paul Farrell's *Bing and Walker*, with a self-sacrificing spinster trembling on the brink of happiness, and Patrick Meyers's *Dysan*, a chronicle of enduring love—plus a revival of *Love's Labor's Lost*. Lynne Meadow's and Barry Grove's Manhattan Theater Club expanded this season into the City Center Theater space, while maintaining some operations on 73d Street. The standout on their schedule was David Storey's 1969 play *In Celebration* in its first major New York production, directed by Lindsay Anderson—a British drama of family strife, as three sons come home to Yorkshire to celebrate their parents' wedding anniversary and settle a few old scores. The new American plays at MTC on both sides of town were a Martin Sherman script, *Messiah*, in which a 17th century village of Polish Jews fantasizes a hero to relieve them from oppression; plus three others taking up the plight of the American farmer (*Husbandry*), platonic romance (*Digby*) and the pitting of bull terriers (*California Dog Fight*). MTC also offered a Richard Maltby Jr.-directed revue of Gretchen Cryer-Nancy Ford songs, *Hang on to the Good Times*.

A visiting organization, Chicago's Steppenwolf Theater Company, brought in *Orphans*, a Lyle Kessler dark comedy explosively dramatizing the changing relationships among two brothers—one a criminal and one a shut-in—and their kidnap victim, similar in tone to the group's previous version of Sam Shepard's *True West* and as flamboyantly acted (by Kevin Anderson and Terry Kinney as the brothers and John Mahoney as the victim who turns the tables on them). *Orphans* was directed in Steppenwolf's acrobatic, irresistably theatrical style by Gary Sinise, who won an Obie for *True West*. Steppenwolf was recognized as one of America's major theatrical forces by a special Tony Award this year, voted by the members of the American Theater Critics Association, and it was further importantly represented in this New York season by its member Joan Allen's performance in *The Marriage of Bette and Boo* and its member John Malkovich's direction of the Circle in the Square revival of *Arms and the Man*.

Speaking of Chicago visitors, Jeffrey Sweet reminds us that "Another Chicago institution which has made immeasurably large contributions to world theater, The Second City, didn't happen to send a show to New York this season (its most recent visit was with *Orwell That Ends Well* last year), but it made news when, on Dec. 16, it celebrated its 25th anniversary. Born during the Eisenhower years, this cabaret theater has reflected the subsequent turmoil of American values and politics in a series of cheerfully satiric revues. From the start in 1959, when it was under the artistic direction of Paul Sills, its material has been created and developed improvisationally, frequently on the spot in response to audience suggestions. The result has been described as urban folk theater; almost as soon as an issue appears in the public consciousness it finds comedic representation onstage. Though primarily identified with Chicago (the name "The Second City" was drawn from a *New Yorker* article portraying the Windy City as a cultural wasteland), the company has played Broadway, off Broadway, Los Angeles and London, while maintaining long-running Canadian companies in Toronto and Edmonton.

"The troupe is perhaps most famous for the people who have started their careers there. The company's enthusiasts believe that the discipline of facing a house with nothing but your wits develops talent, and it's hard to argue with an alumni list which includes Alan Arkin, Barbara Harris, Mike Nichols, Alan Alda, Bill Murray, Paul Mazursky, John and Jim Belushi, Robert Klein, Severn Darden, Gilda Radner, John Candy, David Steinberg, Joan Rivers, Martin Short, Dan Aykroyd, Paul Sand, Melinda Dillon, Zohra Lampert, Harold Ramis, Andrea Martin, Paul Dooley, Peter Boyle, Dave Thomas, Catherine O'Hara, Shelley Long, Bob Dishy, Valerie Harper, John Monteith and Suzanne Rand. A surprising number of these flew to Chicago for a private birthday performance at which they revived scene after scene till the wee hours of the morning. Even as the past was celebrated, the future was being charted. Shortly after the celebration, Bernard Sahlins, who has been producer since the beginning, sold his interest to Andrew Alexander, the Canadian sponsor of the long-running Toronto branch of Second City. In addition to maintaining troupes in Chicago and Canada, Alexander is planning on opening a resident company in Los Angeles and is looking into the feasibility of a continued presence in New York."

The Andre Bishop-Paul Daniels group Playwrights Horizons put on an ambitious fantasy-panorama of events of the American past, *Romance Language* by Peter Parnell, and an expose of the American lifestyle in the return to his family of a Korean War veteran, *Life and Limb* by Keith Reddin, directed by Thomas Babe. They also allied themselves with Dramatists Guild projects this season, presenting Mick Casale's *Elm Circle* as part of the Foundation of the Dramatists Guild/CBS New Plays Program and, later in the season, the Young Playwrights Festival of new plays by authors up to 18 years of age, selected in the Guild's annual contest designed to encourage young people to write plays.

The Negro Ensemble Company began its season later than any of the other major groups and also paid homage to its distinguished past with a revival of Lonne Elder III's *Ceremonies in Dark Old Men* with Douglas Turner Ward, the group's artistic director, re-creating under his own direction his original performance as an ex-vaudevillian living with his daughter in the Harlem of the 1950s. The new plays offered at NEC this year concerned themselves with cab drivers on the Washington-Maryland border (*District Line* by Joseph A. Walker), a

ORPHANS—John Mahoney, Kevin Anderson (holding football) and Terry Kinney in the Steppenwolf production of Lyle Kessler's play

Harlem bag lady graphically portrayed by Frances Foster (*Henrietta*) and a two-character anti-male-chauvinism farce (*Two Can Play*). In other off-Broadway group activity, the Barbara Barondess Theater Lab brought in a drama of a psychiatrist dealing with an instance of child abuse, *Medea and the Doll*. Both the Circles—the Square and the Rep—joined in an early-season co-production of John Patrick Shanley's *Danny and the Deep Blue Sea*, a drama of violence-prone lovers previously produced at Actors Theater of Louisville and presented at Circle in the Square's downtown facility. In a season it devoted mostly to revivals and showcases for foreign artists (including *Childhood*, a Simone Benmussa adaptation of a childhood memoir by Nathalie Sarraute), Jack Garfein's Harold Clurman Theater offered a one-character stage version of a 1976 Samuel Beckett prose piece, *All Strange Away*, and a two-character World War II cliff-hanger under Garfein's direction, *Rommel's Garden*. And the American Place Theater was given over this season to guest productions and OOB activities including its ongoing Women's Project.

On the musical side, off Broadway provided two of the year's three best new musicals, plus an important revival of *Pacific Overtures*, plus a collection of high-quality revues. *Kuni-Leml*, the operetta-like romance of an heiress and her two suitors, one an ill-favored rabbi-to-be and one a handsome but impecunious student, began as an OOB project of the Jewish Repertory Theater and was brought uptown for a season-long commercial run. It was based on a popular 19th century Yiddish Theater farce and was played with the earnest and charming suspension of disbelief of a fairy tale under Ran Avni's direction. The Raphael Crystal music and Richard Engquist lyrics, the Nahma Sandrow book and the high spirits of an appealing ensemble fitted together smoothly and brought off the season's most uniformly beguiling musical.

On the other hand, another durable off-Broadway musical, *3 Guys Naked From the Waist Down*, sputtered with brilliant comedy within a smothering score. The title is backstage argot for a stand-up comic, not a porno reference, and the show concerned three such performers aspiring to the Johnny Carson-sized big time. The humor was at its most penetrating in the dark-edged clowning and miming of John Kassir, reminiscent of Jonathan Pryce in *Comedians*, but with the sound of its rock numbers turned up to assault the eardrums and smash the lyrics to smithereens.

Warren Leight (book) and Charles Strouse (music and lyrics) took up the subject of New York Mayor Edward I. Koch and his administration as reported in his autobiography *Mayor*. The cabaret musical of that title was produced by a consortium at the Top of the Gate and was well received as what might be called a tart and tuneful topical revue, except that its songs and sketches concentrated on a single topic, the colorful Mayor of New York and satellite personalities: Carol Bellamy, the Helmsleys, Donald Trump, Harrison Goldin and ex-Mayors Lindsay and Beame. And another 1984–85 off-Broadway musical, *In Trousers*, was written by William Finn of *March of the Falsettos* but could not find much of an audience for its examination of confused sexuality in a husband and father who finds himself increasingly attracted to members of his own sex.

Revues too were an important part of the off-Broadway scene. In addition to MTC's abovemmentioned Cryer-Ford session, the 1984–85 program consisted of a revisit by *A Kurt Weill Cabaret* at the Harold Clurman Theater, with Martha Schlamme and Alvin Epstein in this 15-year-old touring pot pourri of Weill numbers; *Shades of Harlem*, a Cotton Club cabaret with music of the 1920s mingled with new songs; the politically satirical *Rap Master Ronnie* with music by Elizabeth Swados, lyrics by Garry Trudeau and with Reathel Bean as the President (it closed shortly after Election Day, when the Reagan run was extended); Jo Sullivan in a recapitulation of her career (*I Hear Music . . . of Frank Loesser and Friends*) with songs of major Broadway composers; the Harold Prince-directed, multi-authored collection of baseball songs and episodes, *Diamonds*; the song-and-dance session *Ann Reinking . . . Music Moves Me*, made to order for its star; and the "story songs" of the late Harry Chapin in a revue at the Village Gate.

Among the specialty attractions, while Broadway was enjoying its Whoopi Goldberg, off Broadway was relishing the carryings-on of Avner Eisenberg in *Avner the Eccentric*, a one-man extravaganza of clowning, juggling and other engaging accomplishments. The off-Broadway program also included one-performer studies of Elvis Presley (*Elvis Mania*) performed by Johnny Seaton, Zelda Fitzgerald (William Luce's *Zelda*) by Olga Ballin, a renowned Hungarian Jewish heroine (*Hannah Senesh*) by Lori Wilner, Dorothy Parker (*The Singular Dorothy Parker*) by Jane Connell, as well as an anonymous black housekeeper reviewing the events of her life (*Between Rails*) by Thelma Louise Carter. The distinguished Berliner Ensemble actor Ekkehard Schall visited New York with a one-man program of excerpts from the works of his distinguished father-in-law, Bertolt Brecht, performed in the original German. The distinguished Italian actor Vittorio Gassman brought to town his internationally-performed showcase of sketches. And a stopover by *The Chinese Magic Revue* represented still another culture and continent among the year's off-Broadway speciality programs, while native talent was conspicuously and ably represented by the two title stars of the magic-and-comedy show *Penn & Teller*.

With its spate of revivals as reported in the next chapter, off Broadway provided three times the action of Broadway on its stages during the season of 1984–85; stages that were smaller than Broadway's but big enough to hold more than half the Best Plays and other major excitements of the theater year. It shares to some extent Broadway's increasingly prominent characteristics as a showcase for material developed in less demanding economic circumstances, i.e. OOB or regional theater, areas in which *Blue Window*, *Tracers*, *Hurlyburly*, *Kuni-Leml*, *The Foreigner* and other outstanding off-Broadway programs were first produced. But as of this season off Broadway continued also to function as a proving ground, for better or for worse, for relative newcomers like the authors of *As Is* and *3 Guys Naked From the Waist Down*, as well as for such treasured talents as David Storey, Michael Weller, Joseph A. Walker, William Finn, Patrick Meyers, Martin Sherman, Christopher Durang and Albert Innaurato, not to mention fresh looks at the work of an Arthur Miller, a Stephen Sondheim. No such proving-ground function was really viable in 1984–85 on Broadway, with its ballooning costs; but for another year, at least, in the face of the growing menace of similar commercialization, it still stood on a broad base in the narrower byways of New York professional theater.

JOE EGG—Jim Dale and Stockard Channing in the Arvin Brown-directed revival of the Peter Nichols play, presented at the Roundabout and then brought to Broadway

Revivals on and off Broadway

The history of the theater is measured in millenia, and nothing so convincingly demonstrates its immortality as a season like this one, in which the past came forward to bolster the present in revivals all over town. Our corresponding historian, Thomas T. Foose, observes that "1984–85 will be remembered for three classics staged on Broadway, and not off as is usually the case, which three were among the principal artistic successes of the season." He was speaking of *Cyrano de Bergerac* in an Anthony Burgess translation (the 13th New York stage production of the Rostand work, by Mr. Foose's calculations), *Much Ado About Nothing* ("highly popular in New York during the entire 19th century, but for the first four decades of the present century there was little interest in this work") and *Strange Interlude* (Lynn Fontanne opened in the original 1927–28 New York production of "this taxing play" and was later replaced by Judith Anderson). And Broadway produced 9 other revivals this season, making a total of 12 to off Broadway's 40, or a grand New York revival total of 52. If dramatists enjoyed temporary reincarnation along with their works, in 1984–85 we could have seen Shakespeare catching up on the news of O'Neill and Ibsen, Molière smiling at the pleasantries of Goldsmith, Coward or Shaw, Aeschylus marveling at the lyric imagination of Puccini, Victor Herbert, Franz Lehar and of course the Messrs. Gilbert and Sullivan.

It was the late great team of Rodgers and Hammerstein who scored the season's biggest Broadway hit with the revival of *The King and I*, billed as Yul Brynner's farewell appearance in the role of the King of Siam (June 30 was the date of his final performance) which he created so vividly opposite Gertrude Lawrence in the original 1951 production. Its enormous success, including setting a new all-time record for a week's Broadway gross ($605,546) was achieved in the absence of new musical hits, but not merely so, *faute de mieux*. It was a combination of glorious, untarnished script and score and performance that would have succeeded in any competition.

Likewise, the Jim Dale-Stockard Channing performance of Peter Nichols's *Joe Egg* under Arvin Brown's direction did credit to both major areas of New York theater production, originating off Broadway on the Roundabout schedule. This American production of the British play soon moved up to Broadway to share its spotlight with an English production of an American play, Eugene O'Neill's abovementioned *Strange Interlude* starring Glenda Jackson under Keith Hack's direction. The British stage didn't send over as many potent new scripts as in some seasons past, but important revivals like those Royal Shakespeare Company versions of *Cyrano* and *Much Ado*, directed by Terry Hands, with Derek Jacobi as Benedick and Cyrano, took their place. Finally from the London stage Broadway welcomed Frederick Lonsdale's 1923 comedy *Aren't We All?* staged by Clifford Williams with Rex Harrison and Claudette Colbert charming audiences in a glittering cast which included Lynn Redgrave, George Rose and Jeremy Brett. Also visiting from Europe this season was the Greek National Theater's Epidaurus production of Sophocles's *Oedipus Rex*, presented at the Vivian Beaumont in the modern Greek language in a translation from the ancient tongue by Minos Volanakis, who also staged the classic.

It was a directors' year at Circle in the Square. There George C. Scott proved that Noel Coward's *Design for Living* is indeed a lively design, as he staged an energetic version with Raul Julia, Frank Langella and Jill Clayburgh in the three-cornered romance. Ellis Rabb followed, directing his own co-adaptation of Arthur Schnitzler's *The Loves of Anatol*. Finally, John Malkovich of last year's *Death of a Salesman* (acting) and *Balm in Gilead* (directing) fame grappled with the ironies of Shaw's *Arms and the Man* performed by a cast headed by Kevin Kline, Raul Julia and Glenne Headly.

A revival-producing equivalent of Broadway's Circle in the Square (as always, under the direction of Theodore Mann and Paul Libin) is off Broadway's Roundabout Theater Company (continuously under the direction of Gene Feist), ingeniously bringing to the New York stage a flowing series of top-drawer productions of scripts which seem almost invariably well-timed for a fresh viewing. This season, the Roundabout acquired and refurbished new quarters at 100 E. 17th Street, signaling its determination not to permit real estate problems to slow the pace of its contribution to our theater. Its 1984–85 program included the electrifying *Joe Egg* which went on to Broadway, the classic Oliver Goldsmith comedy *She Stoops to Conquer*, directed by Daniel Gerroll, with Kaye Ballard and E.G. Marshall, Synge's *The Playboy of the Western World*, Ibsen's *An Enemy of the*

STRANGE INTERLUDE—James Hazeldine, Glenda Jackson, Edward Petherbridge and Brian Cox in a scene from the visiting London revival of the Eugene O'Neill play

People in a new English version, with Roy Dotrice pursuing his American career in the role of Dr. Stockmann, and, just before the season ended, a new look at John van Druten's comedy *The Voice of the Turtle*.

Death deprived the Light Opera Company of Manhattan of its dedicated and inspiring founder-producer-director William Mount-Burke in July. He had started his first LOOM in Miami in the 1950s after graduating from the university there. He didn't even have to change the last initial letter when he brought it to Manhattan in August 1968 with a performance of *The Pirates of Penzance* in the Mount-Burke living room. LOOM went on to weekend performances at St. Michael's Episcopal Church on East 74th Street, then across that street to its present quarters in the Eastside Playhouse. A statement by Jean Dalrymple, president of LOOM, read in part as follows: "Saddened as we all are by his untimely death, we can also be proud and happy for him, for he leaves behind him a legacy of which few can boast: a living and flourishing memorial. We at LOOM are dedicated to keeping his dream alive, to continue his work of bringing joy and music into the world." Raymond Allen and Jerry Gotham were named co-directors to succeed Mr. Mount-Burke, and LOOM maintained a steady 1984–85 pace of 12 Gilbert and Sullivan, Sigmund Romberg, Victor Herbert and Franz Lehar operettas in running repertory, plus a new production of *The New Moon*.

In other parts of the city, the organizations principally devoted to the gems of the theatrical past were doing their thing in stately defiance of current economic difficulties. New York Shakespeare Festival annually justifies its name these days with summer action at the Delacorte in Central Park, this year offering a *Henry V* with Kevin Kline in the title role, and an English translation of the Yiddish melodrama *The Golem* by H. Leivick (our Mr. Foose notes that he is listed as "Halper Levick" in *The Oxford Companion to the Theater*), with Richard Foreman directing a cast headed by F. Murray Abraham, who later in the year won the best-acting Academy Award for his performance of Salieri in the movie version of *Amadeus*. He also figured in the season of Mirror Repertory in a guest appearance for two weeks in their production of *The Madwoman of Chaillot* (that company also offered revivals of Booth Tarkington's *Clarence* and Robert Bolt's *Vivat! Vivat Regina!* this season under the artistic direction of Sabra Jones).

Ancient Greek tragedy was a preoccupation of Christopher Martin's City (formerly Classic) Stage Company, presenting Aeschylus's Oresteia divided into two programs with inserted excerpts from Sophocles and Euripides. CSC also found time for a Molière (*George Dandin*, as adapted by Alex Szogyi), and an Eric Bentley translation of a German comedy *The Underpants*. They also worked on a version of *Frankenstein* intended for the CSC schedule in the fall of 1985. And the John Houseman-Michael Kahn Acting Company, touring under the auspices of Kennedy Center, made a brief but eclectic appearance in New York with a one-week repertory of *A New Way to Pay Old Debts* by Philip Massinger, Shakespeare's *As You Like It* and Thornton Wilder's *The Skin of Our Teeth*.

Much was hoped for in the re-mounting of Rudolf Friml's *The Three Musketeers*, a seven-figure Broadway production with a new book by Mark Bramble. The old melodies marched bravely through the score, but the show remained a weak echo of its former self, like a musketeer in middle age. Another full-blown Broadway musical in its Goodspeed Opera House production, *Take Me Along*, closed after its opening night, so that these two large-scale musical revivals played a combined total of only ten performances. The theater's musical repertory was more effectively represented this season by the aforementioned revamped *La Boheme* at the Public Theater, and most notably by an exceptionally distinguished revival of the Stephen Sondheim-John Weidman-Hugh Wheeler musical *Pacific Overtures* directed by Fran Soeder in independent production off Broadway by The Shubert Organization and McCann & Nugent. The Sondheim score is one of the most haunting in the modern theater, so sophisticated that its flavor seems to improve by repetition. It is eminently revivable, and its presence here this season was both a pleasure and a powerful reminder that we lack an organized facility for sampling such masterworks *every* season, doing for the later part of the 20th century what LOOM has been doing for the earlier part.

The voice of Samuel Beckett was heard at the Harold Clurman, with Alvin Epstein directing and performing in an *Endgame*. Arthur Miller's semi-autobiographical reminiscence of his life and times with Marilyn Monroe, *After the Fall*, with Frank Langella and Dianne Wiest, was staged by John Tillinger, who later put on a revival of Christopher Hampton's *Total Eclipse*, a 1974 play about the attachment between the French poets Verlaine and Rimbaud. Clifford Odets was well represented by his *The Country Girl* as played by Hal Holbrook and Christine Lahti, as was Lonne Elder III in The Negro Ensemble Company's revival of *Ceremonies in Dark Old Men* with Douglas Turner Ward starring and directing. The multiplicity of such noble projects at the New York theater's commercial levels should not obscure the fact that our revival season annually spreads far afield from Broadway and off Broadway into many of the experimental and special-project channels. For example, Mr. Foose notes, "Two rarities seen in New York City in 1984–85 were Molière's *Les Précieuses Ridicules* and the Nahum Tate version of *King Lear*. The former was given for 3 performances at the Marymount Manhattan by a company from Nantes, France, the Théâtre du Nombre d'Or. The point of special interest is the play's rarity in New York. So far as I know, it has never been done here in English. The five productions in French were in 1888, 1894, 1917, 1938 and 1965.

"Nahum Tate's *The History of King Lear* was revived by the Riverside Shakespeare on March 8, 1985 for the first time in many decades. The Tate version was first staged in London in 1681. Both in London and New York it held the stage, to the total exclusion of Shakespeare's original, all through the 18th century and well into the 19th. In London, Shakespeare's text was partly restored by Edmund Kean in the 1820s and fully restored in 1838 by Charles Macready, who brought this restored version to New York in 1844–45. For the remainder of the 19th century, the Tate version was by no means driven off the New York stage."

Sondheim and Romberg, Beckett and Ibsen, Shakespeare (and Tate) and Molière, Miller and Inge and Odets, and of course, Aeschylus, Sophocles and Euripides—the work of these dramatists speaks to us in revival year after year and certainly spoke with special eloquence in this one, when so many new voices were muted, so many new songs unsung.

Offstage

The playhouses themselves were in the forefront of concern during 1984–85, partly because of a leftover feeling of uneasiness over the destruction of the Morosco, Helen Hayes and Bijou Theaters to make way for a hotel complex looming ever-higher over the Broadway area as the season progressed. A major defensive development at the very beginning in June was an 84-page report by the Theater Advisory Council to the City Planning Commission containing what the New York *Times* called "provisions that would make it difficult for a theater to be demolished unless it was actually deemed unsafe." The Council, consisting of 14 theater professionals including representatives of the Shubert, Nederlander and Jujamcyn holdings, had been appointed in 1982 by New York City Mayor Edward I. Koch to suggest ways to safeguard theaters from further demolition. The report recommended continuing requirement (already in force) of a special permit from the Planning Commission before a theater can be torn down. It also suggested the formation of a theater trust fund to purchase any playhouse threatened with demolition and recommended the banning of further large-scale development from the theater district. Matters of landmark status and air-rights of builders were taken up but not resolved in the report. Orville H. Schell, chairman of the Council, was quoted by the *Times*, "The message to the City of New York is: the theater is worth preserving."

Also on the positive side was the Morton Gottlieb experiment with *Dancing in the End Zone* at Broadway's Ritz Theater, shutting off the balcony and roping off 49 of the 548 orchestra seats to convert the Ritz from a full to a "middle" Broadway house (300 to 499 seats), therefore eligible for materially reduced production and operating costs at lower levels of contractual obligations. For example, under Actors' Equity regulations this procedure reduced the actors' minimum from $650 (Broadway) to $430 (middle Broadway) weekly, with corresponding concessions from other theater unions across the board. The price of a ticket in this arrangement was required to be lowered under $30, whereas $37.50 for straight plays and $45 for musicals was the going Broadway top this season.

Mr. Gottlieb believes that this tradeoff of fewer-seats-at-lower-prices in exchange for materially reduced costs (*Dancing in the End Zone* was estimated by *Variety* to have come in for $450,000) is an economically efficient means of encouraging the Broadway production of straight plays and the utilization of its smaller theaters. Then too, if one of these middle-Broadway offerings proved to be a hit, down could come the artificial barriers and up could go the play's status to full Broadway, raising prices and running expenses together with capacity. This is already done on a smaller scale with successful tributary-theater productions like *Blue Window*, frugally mounted at the off-off-Broadway level and then moved up to full off-Broadway status by a few strokes of the pen, without breaking performance stride or even changing theaters (it's also possible to move *down* a notch from off-Broadway to OOB, as *Man Enough* did this year). *Dancing in the End Zone* wasn't able to attract enough of an audience to provide a full test of this Gottlieb plan at the Ritz, but a later arrival, the Best Play *Doubles*, tried the same arrangement at the same theater. *Variety* estimated that it cost about $400,000 to bring in and could break even at $62,000 weekly under middle-Broadway circumstances, about two-thirds of what its operating cost would be as a full Broadway production in the same theater. *Doubles* was still running at season's end and could eventually prove the advantages of this plan all the way out.

One of the most glaring New York theater vacancies in recent seasons has been that of the Vivian Beaumont at Lincoln Center, a theater designed for repertory but now used all too infrequently for one-at-a-time visiting attractions like the Peter Brook *Carmen* or the Greek National Theater's *Oedipus Rex* or *And a Nightingale Sang . . .* in the little Mitzi E. Newhouse space downstairs. Vivian Beaumont management controversies seem to have been finally smoothed away by the appointment in September of ex-Mayor John V. Lindsay (admittedly no theater person, but an organizational live wire) as chairman of the theater's board. The board's search for an artistic director for the Lincoln Center Theater Company to replace Richmond Crinkley, who resigned, settled on Gregory Mosher, former artistic director of Chicago's Goodman Theater, a 1983–84 Tony nominee for his staging of *Glengarry Glen Ross* and winner this year of the prestigious Margo Jones Award. And Bernard Gersten, a former associate of

DANCING IN THE END ZONE—Dorothy Lyman, Laurence Luck-inbill and Matt Salinger in the Bill C. Davis play produced by Morton Gottlieb at the Ritz Theater in a middle Broadway experiment

Joseph Papp, was named executive producer by the Lincoln Center board to handle the business side of the enterprise.

In other positive developments, the Roundabout Theater Company found and renovated a new home base in the Park Avenue South area at 100 E. 17th St., converting the former I.L.G.W.U. and Tammany Hall 1,100-seat auditorium into a 499-seat theater with seating on the radius, plus executive offices. The Roundabout also retained its 150-seat Susan Bloch Theater at 307 W. 26th St. Off Broadway added the Chelsea Playhouse, a 199-seater at 519 W. 23d St., which opened its doors with the revival of *The Country Girl*. And the established performing groups on the Upper East Side of Manhattan formed themselves into an Eastside Theaters consortium to hold festivals and otherwise call attention to their activities.

On Broadway, the Joseph Nederlander ownership in the Nederlander Organization-owned Mark Hellinger, Neil Simon, Lunt-Fontanne, 46th Street, Nederlander and New Amsterdam Theaters was purchased by Jerry Weintraub, a film and music executive. And speaking of the New Amsterdam, the multi-million-dollar plan to convert 42d Street's Lyric and Selwyn Theaters for modern legitimate stage use received opposition from the Brandt Organization, which owns them as well as the already-converted Apollo Theater.

One of the conflicts which have arisen in recent years between branches of the theater profession—exacerbated by the constantly changing nature of the economic environment—was resolved with a new Approved Production Contract between the Dramatists Guild (the playwrights, lyricists, composers and librettists) and the League of New York Theaters and Producers (Broadway producers and theater owners). The statement announcing the settlement of outstanding legal disagreements, as well as the contract, stated in part as follows: "The terms of the new agreements involve meaningful alterations of the royalty structure which will assist the producers and backers of plays and musicals to recoup their production costs more quickly. In return, authors will receive substantial improvements in option and advance payments, and in the sharing of subsidiary uses, thereby offering them the opportunity to spend more time writing exclusively for the theater as well as to enjoy a greater portion of long-range income that dramatists have come to consider their retirement benefits.

"In addition, the Guild and the League have provided for the creation of a Theatrical Conciliation Council, a body comprised of equal numbers of authors and producers, to be convened whenever problems arise with an individual contract and which is empowered to adjudicate such problems."

Since the first contract negotiated between dramatists and producers in the early 1920s, stage authors (who lease their scripts to producers but retain ownership of them, unlike authors in other dramatic media, who usually sell their work outright) have received very little cash "up front" but have been recompensed by a royalty percentage off the top as soon as and as long as ticket sales occur. What *Variety* called a "sweeping overhaul of the decades-old standard contract" now provides for a substantial cash payment to the Broadway author "up front" in exchange for greatly reduced royalties until a show has recouped its production cost. It seemed likely that this new principle, established and defined for Broadway, would be extended to other levels of production in future agreements.

Relations between dramatists and actors continued strained, however, over the Actors' Equity Association's showcase code provisions requiring job offers or reimbursement for showcase performers in the event that the script they helped to showcase (and which showcased their acting) goes on to commercial production. In the view of authors and their agents, such a lien on a playscript inhibits future productions of it, since it can add to the production cost. Offered the choice between an encumbered and an unencumbered script of equal appeal, producers would tend to select the latter. In several instances during the season, authors were denying production rights to avoid such a lien, or losing production opportunities because of it.

Members of the Society of Stage Directors and Choreographers too were causing concern to dramatists by requesting in some instances a guarantee of first refusal of directing or choreographing assignments for future commercial production of a script they had directed or choreographed at the showcase stage. The Dramatists Guild issued a statement to its members over the signature of its vice president, Terrence McNally, warning against giving such guarantees, as "a play encumbered in writing with the services of a director may have difficulty in finding another director or producer." And the Dramatists Guild also was troubled by its own house in the instance of the musical *Grind*, suspending from Guild membership and placing in bad standing the show's authors (Fay Kanin book, Larry Grossman music, Ellen Fitzhugh lyrics, Harold Prince co-author) for agreeing to an arrangement which fell short of minimum standards of the Dramatists Guild-League contract at that time. Harold Prince also found himself at odds with the League and resigned his membership in it, as did Alexander H. Cohen following his Tony Awards ceremonies. No specific reason for the resignation was given in either case, but a Harold Prince statement did indicate the presence of intra-League controversy: "I have not felt for some time that the League represented my interests or realistically the Broadway theater's best interests. I do not subscribe to the well-publicized theory, held by some of the most powerful members of the League, that the price of the ticket is not an issue. And I don't think there was sufficient control of escalating labor costs. The truth is, for some absurd reason, no one is willing to admit that the interests of the producers and the theater owners are not the same." Harvey Sabinson, the League's executive director, defended League policies and expressed his regret that Mr. Prince had "never participated in any League programs, activities or decisions, or helped to sustain that sense of community," in the past decade.

In other developments, the League is changing its name from New York Theaters and Producers to American Theaters and Producers, wanting to add to its membership its colleagues in the key road cities. The League also came to an agreement with the musicians' Local 802 on a new three-year contract with annual 5 per cent raises which will bring the weekly Broadway minimum from $620 to $720 in the third year (and from $77.50 to $90 extra for playing a second instrument). The SSDC and the League rolled over the directors' and choreographers' contract for another 18 months; meanwhile the SSDC won substantial increases from the League of Regional Theaters and brought artistic directors into their fold.

Equity reached an impasse over how many non-Equity actors would be permitted in LORT shows but agreed to roll over the existing contract, plus a 4.5 per cent cost-of-living increase, for 14 months of further negotiations (the actors' contract for dinner theaters was also renewed, with allowance for future cost-of-living raises). And Equity and the League of Off-Broadway Theaters and Producers came to terms on a new sliding-scale reimbursement for actors in each of the five off-Broadway categories, with new weekly minimums as follows: Category A (100–199 seats) $225, B (200–250 seats) $275, C (251–299 seats) $320, D (300–350 seats) $385 and E (351–499 seats) $435, with the percentage of increase weighted toward the lower end of the scale. And Colleen Dewhurst was elected president of Actors' Equity to succeed Ellen Burstyn, who did not run for reelection.

The New York Drama Critics Circle named Howard Kissel of *Women's Wear Daily* president for a two-year term, succeeding Edwin Wilson of the *Wall Street Journal.* Allan Wallach of *Newsday* moved up from secretary to vice president, Richard Hummler of *Variety* was elected secretary (it is to him we are indebted for details of the Critics Award balloting in the Facts and Figures section of this volume) and Marilyn Stasio of the New York *Post* continued as treasurer. Two new members, Michael Kuchwara of the Associated Press and Sylviane Gold of the *Wall Street Journal* were elected to the organization. Benedict

Nightingale resigned the post of Sunday drama critic of the New York *Times* previously held by Walter Kerr. Theater commentary in that paper's Sunday arts section was taken over, not by a single replacement, but by occasional contributions from members of the *Times* cultural staff—including Mr. Kerr speaking out from time to time from his retirement.

Badmouthing a New York theater season has always been a popular sport, especially in seasons like the one just past. Certainly the first traits visible on the horizon of an overall view of 1984–85 are its shortcomings: attenuation of audience, continued low-volume Broadway production, absence of a new blockbuster musical, hyping of revivals, a general scarcity of glitter and glamor in the personality of the season as a whole. Look a little closer, though, and you will see excellence in the foreground: humor (*Biloxi Blues, The Foreigner, Doubles*), imagination in writing and staging (*The Marriage of Bette and Boo, As Is, Blue Window*) and in design (*Big River*), tragedy (*Tracers*), suspense (*Pack of Lies*) and an abundance of social concerns (*Split Second, Ma Rainey's Black Bottom, Hurlyburly, The Normal Heart, Rat in the Skull*).

It can be said of 1984–85 that it offered nothing for everyone but something for each, with many offerings limited, not in skill or intensity, but in the scope of their appeal. Too much of our theater today seems directed only to this or that segment of the potential audience. Its economics are so heavily biased in favor of the two-character, one-set idea that we probably shouldn't look for much encouragement or inspiration for the whole-audience kind of show. 1984–85's Best Play authors are a distinguished group of dramatists, but among them only Neil Simon and Hugh Whitemore appeared to be trying to address the broadest possible theater audience. That whole audience won't respond to every good play or musical, nor should all dramatists attempt to write for it all the time. But it is always there, it always will be there, and the best hope for the future is that the theater's creators will continue to keep it in mind.

OFF OFF BROADWAY

By Mel Gussow

The eclectic arena of off off Broadway expressed its growing heritage with an exhibition of memorabilia from the legendary Caffe Cino (at the Lincoln Center Library) and with mini-retrospectives of the work of Samuel Beckett, Sam Shepard and Ping Chong. Beckett, whose plays have become increasingly distilled over the years, was represented by a triple bill at LaMama two previously unproduced short pieces entitled *Theater One* and *Theater Two*, and a revival of the one-character *That Time*. The first two are throwbacks to an earlier, more openly comic Beckett; the three featured a trio of prominent off-off-Broadway actors: George Bartenieff, Frederick Neumann and Julian Beck. On other stages, there were dramatizations of the Beckett short prose pieces, *All Strange Away* and *Fizzles*.

George Ferencz, who has had notable past success reviving Shepard, directed a trilogy of his plays at LaMama, grouped together as jazz plays, with music by Max Roach. Under the umbrella "Shepardsets," Ferencz offered *Angel City*, *Suicide in B Flat* and *Back Bog Beast Bait*. It was the third, a metaphorical comedy about toxic waste, that proved to be a rediscovery. Ping Chong's banner season began with the American premiere of *The Games*, his latest collaboration with Meredith Monk, an intergalactic Olympiad and a look at a faceless futuristic society. *The Games* was a highlight of the Brooklyn Academy of Music's exploratory Next Wave Festival. At the crest of the Next Wave was a revival of the Robert Wilson-Philip Glass imagistic opera, *Einstein on the Beach*. Later in the year, again at the busy LaMama, there was a Ping Chong festival—a revival of his haunting *Nuit Blanche* and *Nosferatu*, his chilling contemporary version of the Dracula story.

Another off-off-Broadway favorite, Spalding Gray, is his own traveling festival. He packs up his card table and goes from city to city. America's foremost public anecdotalist and confessor, this performance artist has given us—in a cycle of expository monologues—a grand tour of his life as man and actor. Gray's musings climaxed this year with *Swimming to Cambodia*, a two-part tale in which he vividly detailed his experiences acting in the movie *The Killing Fields*. The one-man show was simultaneously an on-location report from the movie front, a travel adventure and a commentary on the war in Cambodia. Perhaps in emulation, perhaps in envy, other monologuists tried going it alone this season (Beth Lapides, David Cale, Beatrice Roth, among others). It is not as easy as it looks. At the end of the season, however, Ron Litman dashed into town with a devastating political satire called *On a Clear Day You Can See Armageddon*. In the neatest double-take of the year, Litman transformed himself, in full view of the audience, from Henry Kissinger to Jeane Kirkpatrick.

Charles Ludlam, founder and major domo of the Ridiculous Theatrical Company, presented one of his most Ridiculous and one of his funniest shows

PUERTO RICAN TRAVELING THEATER—Miriam Colon, Freddy Valle and Laura Elena in a scene from *Simpson Street* by Edward Gallardo

in *The Mystery of Irma Vep*, a multi-character, two-actor send-up of Gothic yarns from *Wuthering Heights* to potboiler depths. Rushing on and off stage, Ludlam and Everett Quinton played all the roles—sneering villains and cringing heroines—with mercurial wit. Doubling their artistry, the two of them were also responsible for the show's imaginative sets and costumes. Bill Irwin, the first performance artist to win a prestigious MacArthur Award, returned with *The Courtroom*, a clown romp that he conceived, wrote, directed and starred in. Playing two roles, as an accidental witness and an overbearing judge, he led his comedy troupe through a rapturous hour of new vaudeville comedy. *The Courtroom* was one of the year's events for the Music Theater Group/Lenox Arts Center, which also brought back, in finished form, Martha Clarke's extraordinary theater-dance piece, *The Garden of Earthly Delights*.

The jury in *The Courtroom* was played by puppets, the creation of Julie Taymor; puppets also made news on other stages. Theodora Skipitares, who designs puppet landscapes, engineered the complete three-part version of her epic *Age of Invention*, a glance at Yankee tinkerers, featuring animated replicas of Benjamin Franklin and Thomas Edison. The Bread and Puppet Theater, which specializes in theater-politics, offered *The Nativity, Crucifixion and Resurrection of Archbishop Oscar Romero of El Salvador*, a self-explanatory title.

Good new plays were as scarce here as they were in other theatrical arenas, but there were a few of quality or of promise. *The Cruelties of Mrs. Schnayd*, a black comedy about urban renewal and survival, introduced a talented new playwright, David Suehsdorf. Ronald Tavel returned to the ridiculous metier he does so well with *My Foetus Lived on Amboy Street*. In *The Fool*, Michael Dorn Moody offered the epic adventures of Francis Drake on a tiny tabletop stage. In the WPA season were *The Incredibly Famous Willy Rivers*, a step ahead for Stephen Metcalfe, and *The Hitch-Hikers*, an evocative adaptation by Larry Ketron of a Eudora Welty story. Jeff Weiss furnished another shaggy chapter in *And That's How the Rent Gets Paid*, with *Part IV, or the Confessions of Conrad Gehrhardt*. Terrence McNally's *The Lisbon Traviata* was a Callas-worshipping, grand operatic treatment of the homosexual experience.

As usual, one-act plays were in fashion, especially at the Ensemble Studio Theater. The outstanding plays in this year's one-act Marathon were Horton Foote's *The Road to the Graveyard*, poignant period Americana about a self-sacrificial daughter, and Edward Allan Baker's *North of Providence*, an explosive 30 minutes about a shattered blue-collar family. Other one-acts of note were Shel Silverstein's kleptomaniacal romp, *One Tennis Shoe* (Silverstein's *The Crate* was also on view at the Ensemble Studio); Jane Willis's *Men Without Dates* and Richard Greenberg's *Life Under Water* (an advancement over his full-length, *The Bloodletters*, presented earlier in the season at the Ensemble Studio). The Pan Asian Repertory Theater had another prolific year with such cross-cultural plays as Donald G. McNeil Jr.'s *Chipshot*, Linda Kalayaan Faigao's *State Without Grace*, Edward Sakamoto's *Manoa Valley* and, most enticingly, Ernest Abuba's adaptation of the Louis Chu novel, *Eat a Bowl of Tea*. There was equal activity in New York's other ethnic companies, including Repertorio Espanol, INTAR, the Puerto Rican Traveling Theater, Henry Street Settlement's New Federal Theater, the Jewish Repertory Theater and the Irish Arts Center.

Reflecting Broadway, it was a pallid year for musicals. Among the few contributions were *Once on a Summer's Day*, a musical about Lewis Carroll and Alice Liddell; *Almos' a Man*, adapted from a Richard Wright story, and *Sit Down and Eat Before Our Love Gets Cold*, Barbara Schottenfeld's ode to single women in the city. New York's smaller institutional theaters generally had an off year, as exemplified by the disappointing work at the Hudson Guild—with lesser new plays from England and America's regions.

As usual, experimental companies expressed idiosyncratic sensibilities. Paul Zimet's Talking Band offered *Holding Patterns*, three small performance pieces, and *Big Mouth*, an adaptation of *Crowds and Power*. Richard Foreman united his Ontological-Hysteric Theater and the Wooster Group for *Miss Universal Happiness*, an inchoate attempt at theatricalizing Third World politics. The Wooster Group itself waded into controversial seas with its production of *L.S.D. (. . . Just the High Points . . .)*, which took off loosely from Arthur Miller's *The Crucible*, relocating the witchhunt at a hearing of the House Un-American Activities Committee—a time-machine reve.sal. The author objected, and the Wooster Group dropped *The Crucible* from *L.S.D.* Heiner Muller's *Hamlet-machine*, an inversion of *Hamlet*, received a dismal New York premiere. Simultaneously, Ethyl Eichelberger, a transvestite actor-director presented his version of the play entitled *Hamlette*, starring Black-Eyed Susan, the endearing leading lady of the Ridiculous Theatrical Company, as the title Dane.

It was not an auspicious year for classics. The CSC was at less than its best with a double-decker *Elektra/Orestes* and a pairing in repertory of Molière's *George Dandin* and Carl Sternheim's *The Underpants*. The Classic Theater presented the New York premiere of Brecht's *The Roundheads and the Pointheads*, and the Riverside Shakespeare Company offered a real curio, *The History of King Lear*, the notorious Nahum Tate adaptation—*Lear* with a happy ending: Cordelia lives and marries Edgar. With a ridiculous lady Hamlette and a lively Cordelia, this was, in fact, open season on Shakespeare.

O
O
O

THE SEASON
AROUND THE UNITED STATES

with

A DIRECTORY OF NEW-PLAY
PRODUCTIONS

and

OUTSTANDING NEW PLAYS
CITED BY
AMERICAN THEATER CRITICS
ASSOCIATION
O
O
O

THE American Theater Critics Association (ATCA) is the organization of 250 leading drama critics in all media in all sections of the United States. One of this group's stated purposes is "To increase public awareness of the theater as a *national* resource" (italics ours). To this end, ATCA has cited three outstanding new plays produced this season around the country, to be represented in our coverage of The Season Around the United States by excerpts from each of their scripts demonstrating literary style and quality.

The process for the selection of these outstanding plays is as follows: any ATCA member critic may nominate a play if it has been given a production in a professional house. It must be a finished play given a full production (not a reading or an airing as a play-in-progress). Nominated scripts were studied and discussed by an ATCA play-reading committee chaired by Dan Sullivan of the Los Angeles *Times* and comprising Ann Holmes of the Houston *Chronicle,* Bernard Weiner of the San Francisco *Chronicle,* Julius Novick of the *Village Voice,* Damien Jaques of the Milwaukee *Journal* and John Habich of the Tallahassee *Democrat.* The committee members made their choices on the basis of script rather than production, thus placing very much the same emphasis as the editor of this volume in making his New York Best Play selections. There were no eligibility requirements except that a nominee be the first full professional production of a new work outside New York City within this volume's time frame of June 1, 1984 to May 31, 1985. If the timing of nominations and openings prevented some works from being considered this year, they will be eligible for consideration next year if they haven't since moved on to New York production. We offer our sincerest thanks and admiration to the ATCA members and their committee for the valuable insight into the 1984–85 theater season around the United States which their selections provide for this *Best Plays* record.

Cited by American Theater Critics
as Outstanding New Plays
of 1984–85

SCHEHERAZADE

A Full-Length Play in One Act

BY **MARISHA CHAMBERLAIN**

SCHEHERAZADE: Returning home late at night, Ann is forced inside her apartment by a young man wearing a ski mask. He proceeds to rape her. During the act she tears off his mask. "Now I have to kill you," he says. Ann diverts her captor with talk, games, flirtation—whatever she can come up with—as Scheherazade did in *Arabian Nights,* and she is free by sunrise. But this is not a fairy tale. Ann is still in thrall to her ordeal, and her rescuer almost pays the price of her assault.

In this early scene, Ann seems to have aroused the sympathy of her assailant, Joe, by telling him about her recent breakup with her boy friend, after an abortion. "He says he should have been there with me—that I didn't trust him enough —that I don't love him. And there's absolutely nothing I can say. I do love him."

> *She cries. He reaches out tentatively, pats her arm.*
> JOE: I'm sure it'll work out.
> *He goes to the refrigerator, gets out an apple, takes a bite of it, puts it back, closes the refrigerator door. She gets to her feet, gets down a lipstick, faces herself in the mirror, applies the lipstick. He goes to the bathroom door, opens it. Ann's hand slips, smearing the lipstick down her face. She collects herself, turns to him.*
> ANN: I want to ask you something straight out. Straight from the shoulder. Why don't you let me go?
> JOE: Nah. Why should I?

"Scheherazade": by Marisha Chamberlain. Copyright © 1985 by Marisha Chamberlain. Reprinted by permission of Helen Merrill, Ltd. See CAUTION notice on copyright page. All inquiries concerning stock and amateur production rights should be addressed to: Dramatists Play Service, Inc., 440 Park Avenue South, New York, NY 10016. All other inquiries should be addressed to: Helen Merrill, Helen Merrill, Ltd., 361 West 17th Street, New York, NY 10011.

ANN: *(takes a step toward him):* Because I want you to.

JOE: You're a nice girl.

> *He puts his arm around her, faces them toward the mirror, takes a tissue and cleans the lipstick off her cheek, then takes the knife and cuts her cheek where the lipstick had been.*

Doesn't that look nice? Nah, that looks awful.

> *Opens the medicine cabinet, puts a butterfly bandage over her cut.*

Hold still. There . . . That'll do for the moment . . . We've had enough, haven't we?

ANN: I want to say a prayer.

JOE: This is no place to pray.

> *He leads her to the livingroom.*

Are you Catholic?

> *He turns off the radio.*

ANN: No, I'm going to make it up. *(Kneels.)*

JOE: Pray out loud.

ANN: Dear God . . . if there is anyone watching over me . . .

JOE: No? *(Beat.)* No.

ANN: I'm going to pray to my friends. Margaret— *(Aside, to Joe.)* I work with her— *(Prays.)* Margaret, please think of me now. See me, here, Margaret. Jim — *(Aside.)* He's the one with the red motorcycle. *(Prays.)* Please, be with me now. Please come to me, Jimmy. Put your arms around me. Peter, please—

JOE *(gets up, stands over her):* Where are my friends? Do you see any of my friends here? You don't have friends.

ANN: They don't know this is going on.

JOE: Shouldn't they? I keep better track of you than they do. Shit!

> *Shoves her head down to the floor.*

Pray to your turtle.

ANN: I want to say goodbye to him.

> *He lets her up. She crosses to the terrarium, picks up the tortoise.*

I want to read you my love letters.

> *Clutching the tortoise to her, she takes down a carved wooden box, opens it. He advances on her. She dumps the box, steps up with the tortoise to meet his advance.*

I want to kill him.

> *They kneel on the floor, amidst the scattered letters. He puts the knife on the tortoise's neck.*

Wait. Let me do it.

> *Puts her hand on Joe's.*

It's going to be okay, Jeez.

> *They cut. She cries.*

It's okay. It's okay.

JOE: All right.

ANN: I'm putting him back. It's okay, Jeez.

> *Takes the tortoise to the terrarium, turns to Joe.*

Now, me.

JOE: I don't have any choice.

ANN: That's all right.

JOE: You want to do it yourself?

> *He offers her the knife. She takes it, puts the point against her stomach, presses. Presses harder. Decides she's going to make him do it. Flings the knife away.*

I'm sorry for you.

> *He picks up the knife.*

ANN: Would you put your arm around me?

JOE: Okay.

ANN: They say—you know, the ones who've died and come back—they say someone comes to meet you—the one of all the dead people that you loved the most . . .

JOE: I know it.

ANN: It would be my mother—

JOE: I'd be in the mountains, fishing.

ANN:—so I might meet my mother tonight.

JOE: I'd hike back in, far from the road, with Shep, deep in the pine trees. And my brother Dick would be with me, and Marjorie—there in the mountains.

ANN: Who's Marjorie?

JOE: My wife.

ANN: That's all right. Listen, I know I'm not Marjorie.

> *Touches his chest.*

Are you worried about being unfaithful to her?

> *He doesn't answer. She kisses him.*

JOE: That's nice . . . She's not to know about this. She'd never understand.

ANN: Okay . . .

> *He begins to unbutton her shirt. He takes over, unbuttons her shirt, throws off her shoes.*

Say, you take your clothes off, too. . . .

Scheherazade *was produced by the Cricket Theater in Minneapolis on April 18, 1984.*

THE SHAPER

A Play in Two Acts

BY JOHN STEPPLING

THE SHAPER: Bud, 36, and Del, slightly younger, are in an alley. Bud makes surf boards in his shop; his buddy Del recently got out of jail for selling coke. They're lost.

To stir up some action, and get some money, they've just pulled off a robbery of a late-night grocery store, aided by information provided by Del's flirtatious half-sister Reesa.

> *Lights up. Alley, front edge of playing area, night. Del and Bud, both a little out of breath, Bud more so as he enters. Both dressed in jackets and knit caps.*

DEL: What happened?

BUD: Nothing. What do you mean?

DEL: What'd she do? *(Short pause.)* Jesus. *(Walks a few steps, comes back.)* What was it? She wouldn't do what you said?

BUD: I got it. Christ.

DEL: You got it? You did it—it was O.K.? She did it all?

> *Bud walks across stage to extreme left. Del follows, stopping a moment to look behind—in direction Bud entered from.*

So, what is it?

BUD *(irritated):* What?

DEL *(angrier):* Well, something fuckin' came down. It took forever, so what the fuck was it?

BUD: Shit. *(Pause.)* Aw shit, God Del . . . Damnit, damnit, damnit. Damnit!

> *Bud looks at Del. Pause.*

DEL: So? *(Pause.)* Fuck. *(Pause.)* Forever. It felt like forever out here. *(Pause.)* What's she say?

"The Shaper": by John Steppling. © Copyright 1985 by John Steppling. All rights reserved. Reprinted by permission of William Morris Agency, Inc. See CAUTION notice on copyright page. All inquiries should be addressed to: William Morris Agency, Inc., 1350 Avenue of the Americas, New York, NY 10019, Attention: George Lane.

L.A. THEATER WORKS, LOS ANGELES—Noreen Hennessy, Laura Owens, Scott Paulin, Lee Kissman and Jack Slater in *The Shaper* by John Steppling

BUD: She said O.K. I told her to open the safe. She said O.K. and then we opened it.

    Bud takes out money bags. Pause.

DEL: Count it.

BUD: I don't want to count it.

DEL: You wanna' know what we got?

BUD: Yeah.

    Pause.

DEL: You want me to count it?

BUD: I don't care.

DEL: I'll count it, O.K.? *(Pause.)* All right?

    Bud walks a few feet off. Del begins counting the bills. Lights fade out.

    Lights up. Shop, night.

DEL: You were very cool. This slow walk, casual, not the kind of guy who hurries— *(Pause.)* I didn't think you'd done it.

BUD: I didn't point it—I gave her a glimpse in my bag, opened the flap, let her look in.

DEL: She knew when she peeped it. *(Short pause.)* Bet your ass—got her attention in a hurry—army issue .45 automatic. *(Pause.)* You load the gun?

BUD: Did I load it?

DEL: Yeah—was the gun loaded?

BUD: What do you mean?

DEL: When you went in—did you have a loaded gun? Did it have bullets in it?

BUD *(short pause):* No, I didn't put in any bullets.

DEL *(pause):* I don't get that. *(Pause.)* Like trying to fuck with a limp dick.

    Long pause.

BUD: You're right. Going in that way.

DEL: You got to do something like this all the way.

BUD: I know that. *(Pause.)* I didn't think I'd use them.

DEL: It's protection—it's insurance, for you. For both of us.

BUD: I pray we never use them. I pray to Christ.

DEL *(pause):* In a situation—the unexpected—I'm not laying some heavy thing on you here.

> *Del sits down next to Bud, their shoulders touching. Silence.*

You don't want this any more—say so and it's over—no bad feelings. We end the partnership right here and now.

> *Silence. Del leans over, shoulder against Bud. Their faces almost touching.*

(Quiet.) That's one thing—all right, I can see what space you could get yourself into—but inside information is a whole other ride at the fair.

BUD: This is Reesa?

DEL: That's right. *(Pause.)* I jumped at it, when she told me—shit, it's a gift, I mean it's fuckin' gift wrapped.

BUD: You want me to ask you about this?

DEL: I would like you to think about it.

BUD: She's only been there a week.

DEL: She saw an opportunity—she fell into something—she saw there was an opportunity, that's all. *(Pause.)* Dumb luck, call it what you like.

> *Long silence. Del reaches over and picks something out of Bud's ear.*

You got all this foam shit in your ear.

> *Del gently holds Bud's shoulder with one hand while he picks out fiberglass shavings from his ear with the other.*

There . . . let's see the other one.

> *Bud turns his head—Del examines other ear.*

Winter swell's coming in—blowin' out today but was a good six feet, six and a half.

> *Del finishes.*

BUD: I went down this morning and watched. *(Pause.)* There were eight-foot sets early, six-thirty. A couple guys were out but it was all junk—choppy—

> *Pause.*

DEL *(quietly):* We have no idea what we're doing. *(Pause.)* We've no idea of what could come down behind this— *(Vague smile, silent laugh.)*

> *Pause. Bud looks at Del who has head down. He starts massaging Del's neck, slowly.*

But I don't feel it—I can't seem to get a good hold on it at all . . . I mean . . . I know, I know about being in over your head.

> *Bud pushes hair off Del's forehead and then runs his hand through his hair once. Bud then stops, stands up, looking around.*

What?

BUD *(softly):* I think we're on fire— *(Short pause.)* The shop has caught on fire.

DEL *(looks around, concerned, then confused):* Hey Bud, what is this?

BUD *(sits back down):* Let it go—it's nothing, nothing.

> *Lights fade out.*

The Shaper *was produced by L.A. Theater Works at the Night House November 2, 1984.*

A SHAYNA MAIDEL

A Play in Two Acts

BY BARBARA LEBOW

A SHAYNA MAIDEL: This is an unusually moving drama about a family forever divided by a difficult, enigmatic father and the cruel turn of world events. Set in a Manhattan apartment in 1946, the principal characters are Mordechai Weiss, the aging Jewish father; Rose, or Rayzel, his adult daughter whom he brought to America as a young child before World War II; Lusia, Rose's older sister, who was left behind in Poland with her mother; and Mama, Mordechai's wife and the girls' mother, who was killed by the Nazis.

Mama is present in both memory flashbacks and fantasy moments. In the following scene, Lusia has recently arrived in America, having survived a concentration camp. Her infant is among the victims of the Holocaust, and her husband has been missing for years. A Countess, who is not Jewish and was a friend of the family in Poland, delivered to Mordechai a package given to her by Mama shortly before the Countess fled Poland and the Nazis. Mordechai is opening the package. Memories and fantasies mix with the realistic action.

MORDECHAI: It was many years since I heard anything from mine wife. The first thing I found, in here, like this, was a letter for me. It was from over three years before. Since then I never knew was she alive or not or what was happening. So this letter was from three years and came before I heard the news of what happened. The Countess carried it around the world until she came to America. Even if not Jewish, they ran from Hitler. They couldn't run fast enough. But they got plenty money, believe me, and once out of Poland was safe since they wasn't Jewish. Anyway, this from your mother she carries like a holy package, I couldn't believe it. The next is some pictures you never seen of your sister here when she graduated school and this is a wedding . . .

"A Shayna Maidel": by Barbara Lebow. Copyright © 1984 by Barbara Lebow. Reprinted by permission of the author. See CAUTION notice on copyright page. All inquiries should be addressed to: Mary Harden, Brett Adams Limited, 448 West 44th Street, New York, N.Y. 10036.

ACADEMY THEATER, ATLANTA—Andrea Alexander, Mary Jo
Ammon, Ellyn Eaves, Gus W. Mann, Shawna McKellar and Michael
Maschinot in *A Shayna Maidel* by Barbara Lebow

> *Mordechai is passing the pictures to Rose, intending her to hand them
> on to Lusia. Rose is very aware of her sister's fragile state.*

ROSE: Papa, can't we look at these later? I think it's hard for her. It's much
too painful.

> *Lusia is on her way to the bedroom. Voices fade.*

MORDECHAI: All these pictures she's got here, inside, already. This paper don't
make the pain, believe me.

> *Rose starts to follow Lusia. Mordechai holds her back. They continue
> to look quietly at photos while the scene in the bedroom continues.*

LUSIA: Mama, you've got to go with her!

MAMA: Don't argue.

LUSIA: But she wants to protect you, to take a chance herself because she thinks
so much of you.

MAMA: She's a wonderful woman.

LUSIA: Then go!

MAMA: All right. She said they have room for one more. You. But not the baby.
Not Sprinze. You want to come too?

LUSIA: How dare you! Don't be crazy, Mama!

MAMA: You stay with your child, I stay with my child.

LUSIA: But this is different. I'm not helpless like the baby. You have another
daughter, too. You could be with Rayzel again. Finally, Mama. And Papa.

MAMA: When you have a grandchild, you have two children. Here, where I am, I have two. There, where I may never arrive, is one I lost long ago. I won't take the chance of losing more.

LUSIA: But, Mama, then you had no choice. This time, you do.

MAMA: It only looks like a choice. If God wanted us to be in America, you never would have caught scarlet fever. Your father would not have had such business troubles—

LUSIA: I'll never agree with you, never! About God.

MAMA: God doesn't care if you agree with Him or not. He does what He does. God doesn't argue and God doesn't change His mind. Besides, maybe where they're sending us this time will be an improvement. In the country somewhere. At least not a ghetto. Trees, maybe, some flowers—

LUSIA (overlapping): Mama, listen. Please! Anything the Nazis do will only be worse, never better. You go with the Countess. I'm young. I'll do all right. I have the medicine for Sprinze. It puts her to sleep for two days so she won't cry. I'll carry her in my knapsack. Others have done it. They won't even know I have a baby.

Mama closes the suitcase with finality, folds her arms.

MAMA: Ich blayb mit mayn kind.

ROSE: Lusia, look!

Rose is on her way to the bedroom, as Lusia comes out. Rose is holding a small silver spoon and a sealed letter.

Papa says this is my baby spoon! I used to eat with it.

LUSIA (takes the spoon): Sometimes I feed you with this.

ROSE: And a letter for me, from Mama!

Rose is holding the letter out to Lusia. Lusia takes it and hands it back, with the spoon. She goes directly, angrily to Mordechai.

LUSIA: How long ago this Countess visits?

MORDECHAI: November, December, maybe.

LUSIA: Mama sends these things for Rayzel. Why don't you give them before?

MORDECHAI: Until I know—

Mama is in the bedroom doorway; she will soon enter the living room again and watch Lusia.

LUSIA: And now you already know for a long time!

MORDECHAI: I was hoping we should all be a family again—

LUSIA (overlapping): Is no more hoping! Mama's dead! We was supposed to come here! Was your promise. I want Rayzel should know this. (To Rose.) Mama was all ready we should come here when he sends in a letter about the bad money times, we should wait. So we wait. Then comes a letter from your Tanta Perla. She's asking us why Papa won't take no money. Some group in Brooklyn is giving him the money so we could come and he should pay it back later. But Papa says no. He won't take from no one.

MORDECHAI: This you should understand. Not to owe nothing.

ROSE: But, Papa!

MORDECHAI: Every penny what I made since went to bring them over myself.

Rose is looking hard at Mordechai.

LUSIA: Then it don't matter no more. Is too late. (To Mordechai.) And now you don't want even to read to her what Mama is saying. Now you don't want even to touch something of Mama's. From shame. From shame!

MORDECHAI (*calmly, quietly*): Rayzel, who do you want should read you Mama's letter, me or your sister? Say only the truth.

Rose holds out the letter to Lusia.

It should better be a woman. Tanta Perla, maybe.

Rose holds the letter out again. Lusia takes it, holding it away from herself. Mordechai gets up, goes to the closet to get his hat. Lusia's anger is soothed by Mama.

Lusia, read the letter for your sister. I'll wait for you downstairs. When you're finished, you come. I got some new places we should leave word about your husband.

Mordechai is almost out the door, remembers something. He comes back and removes a billfold from his vest pocket, takes out a photograph, shows it to Lusia and Rose. Lusia does not respond to the photo, but watches Mama's reactions.

ROSE: A pretty girl.

MORDECHAI: Age sixteen only.

ROSE: Who is it, Papa? (*Whispers.*) Mama?

MORDECHAI (*nods*): A shayna maidele.

Mama kisses Mordechai on the cheek. Lusia looks away. Mordechai puts the photo back into his pocket and leaves. Lusia gives the letter to Rose.

LUSIA: You open, please. Is your letter.

ROSE (*opens the envelope carefully*): It's very fresh. Like it was just written.

LUSIA: Mama saves the paper, I think, for long time before she sends this letter. Was all ready for time someone comes like Countess. I never seen her write nothing.

Rose is holding the open letter to her face, eyes closed. Then she hands it to Lusia, who hesitates, then also smells the scent of the letter. Lusia can hardly speak. Mama is watching them both from a short distance away.

Is Mama. Before . . . (*She clutches the letter to herself and runs to the bedroom.*) Ich ken nit . . . (*She is holding the letter pressed to her chest, shaking her head.*) Ken nit!

Mama follows Lusia to the bedroom, holds her arms open toward her.

MAMA: Come, Lushke, I'll help you.

Mama leads Lusia to the living-room couch, sits with her arms around her during the reading of the letter. Rose sits in one of the chairs. As Lusia reads, Mama begins to hum and sing softly the Yiddish lullaby heard previously (at the end of Act I, Scene 2).

LUSIA: "My dearest daughter, Rayzel: I'm not a learned woman. I wish I could be so I could say everything to you the right way. For a long time I have written and I know it could happen you don't get the letters. This one is meant by God's will to reach you. Maybe it is the last one for a time so I want to tell you everything how I feel.

"If I could really be with you and put around you my arms, it would be much better, but that is impossible. It cannot be. If I cannot hold you in my arms, I hold you anyway in my heart and this is true for every day in your life since you was born, if you was in Chortkov, Poland, or Brooklyn, New York, America.

"I want you should have your baby spoon. Your favorite, just your size and you could first feed yourself with it. Every day since you and Papa went away, I keep it in a pocket with me, to touch what you touch. I knew I would give it back to you before you were five years old and now look what happened! Well, who are we to question the plan from God? Now when you have this baby spoon, you must get a feeling from your mother. Sometime you will have a child to use it, too, and she will feel from her grandmother. Or, who knows, maybe the family will be together by then.

"You would think I would have more to tell you besides this baby spoon; advice and so forth, but I can't think of anything more important right now. You can't put life on a piece paper. Or love. I am not a smart person with writing down words, but I wish you understand how I am feeling for you, my pretty little girl.

"Your only mother, Liba Eisenman Weiss, Chortkov, Poland, June four, nineteen hundred and forty-two."

> *Lusia and Rose sit silently for awhile, then Lusia puts the letter back in the envelope and gives it to Rose. Lusia is peaceful in Mama's embrace.*

ROSE: Thank you, Lusia.

> *Silence again for a time, then Lusia stands up, encouraged by Mama, who stays close to her.*

LUSIA: Papa's waiting.

> *Rose nods. Lusia and Mama walk toward the front door, Mama picking up her suitcase on the way. Rose sees the scarf in which everything was wrapped, lying on the table. She picks it up, hurries to Lusia and gives it to her. Lusia smiles and puts it on, tying it under her chin. She leans over and gives Rose a maternal kiss. Lusia and Mama exit. Rose opens the letter again, tries to drink in the scent. The Voices are tugging at her gently. Rose clasps the letter and the spoon, which she is still holding, to herself, The Voices continue intermittently.*

ROSE: Mama.

> *All at once, her body is seized by great, dry, wracking sobs. She wants to scream, to cry out, but cannot. She begins to run in and out of each room. The sound that comes from her is a controlled chant, an intoning that is trying to make something happen. Each repetition is more intense.*

Mamamamamamamamamama ma. Mamamamamamamamamama ma. Mamamama-mamamamama ma!

> *Rose is in the bedroom, standing still. Suddenly she moves to the mirror, looks hard at herself. She puts down the letter and spoon and goes into the bathroom, beginning to undo her clothes on the way. She returns wearing Lusia's plain bathrobe, carrying cold cream and tissues. In front of the mirror, face set, she brushes her hair back tightly and ties it. She cleans her face with the cold cream and looks at herself, plain and drawn. She takes eyebrow pencil and rubs it in to make deep*

hollows under her eyes. The Voices are growing louder and are almost continuous. She stares at herself, then goes to the night table and finds a pen. She rolls up her left sleeve and draws a number on her forearm. Arms extended, she looks at herself in the mirror again. The Voices' crying-wailing increases. She sits on the bed and begins to rock. The sound is a comfort to her. She curls up in a fetal position, still rocking. As the Voices grow to their fullest, surrounding her, she slowly stands on the bed, arms outstretched, welcoming them. Her face is a mixture of anguish and joy. She falls to her knees, arms around herself, gratefully embracing the grief and pain. The lights fade. The Voices continue at full volume in the darkness, then stop.

A Shayna Maidel *was produced by the Academy Theater in Atlanta April 18, 1985.*

A DIRECTORY OF NEW-PLAY PRODUCTIONS

Compiled by Sheridan Sweet

Professional 1984–85 productions of new plays by leading companies around the United States which supplied information on casts and credits of first productions at Sheridan Sweet's request, plus a few reported by other reliable sources, are listed below in alphabetical order of the locations of the producing organizations. Figures in parentheses following titles give number of performances, and date given is opening date, both included whenever a record of these facts was obtainable from the producing managements. All League of Regional Theaters (LORT) and other Equity groups were queried for this comprehensive Directory. Those not listed here either did not produce new or newly-revised scripts in 1984–85 or had not responded by press time.

Albany, N.Y.: Empire State Institute for the Performing Arts

(Producing director, Patricia B. Snyder)

RAGGEDY ANN AND ANDY (musical) book by William Gibson; music and lyrics by Joe Raposo. December 7, 1984. Directed by Patricia Burch.
ON THE HOME FRONT by Gail Kriegel. Jan-

uary 15, 1985. Directed by W.A. Franconis.
THE PRINCE AND THE PAUPER (musical) adapted by John Vreeke; music by Diane Leslie; lyrics by Ronald Alexander. March 15, 1985. Directed by W.A. Franconis.

Allentown, Pa.: Pennsylvania Stage Company

(Producing director, Gregory S. Hurst)

JUST SO (musical) book, Mark St. Germain; music, Doug Katsaros; lyrics, David Zippel. September 19, 1984. Director, Julianne Boyd; musical director, Paul Sullivan; orchestrator, vocal arranger, Doug Katsaros; scenery, Atkin Pace; lighting, Craig Miller; costumes, Ann Hould-Ward.
Eldest Magician............ Larry Marshall
Leopard .... Bebe Neuwirth
Rhino .... Clent Bowers
Elephant Child .... Tina Johnson
Giraffe .... Michael Connolly
Camel..................... Pamela Tyson
Man .... David Cady
  Time and Place: The world's first day.

A WALK OUT OF WATER. By Donald Driver. January 9, 1985. Director, Gregory S. Hurst; scenery, Atkin Pace; lighting, Curtis

Dretsch; costumes, Martha Kelly.
Gramma Rinn............ Katherine Squire
Lettie .... Jacqueline Knapp
Little Lyle .... Danny Gerard
Jennie Mae.................. Dorrie Joiner
Earl....................... John Spencer
  Place: The front porch of an Oregon farmhouse in June. Act I: Before noon. Act II, Scene 1: After supper. Scene 2: Late that night.

Staged Readings

MISS MARY. By Muriel Resnick. November 11, 1984.
SMALL TOWN SYNDROME. By Gary Scott Thompson. January 14, 1985.
CARP LAKE. By Bill Sonnega. January 21, 1985.
ETHYL ZUPP'S AMAZING CHEESE-CAKE. By Adriana Trigiani. January 28, 1985.

Atlanta—Academy Theater

(Artistic director, Frank Wittow)

THE WISHING PLACE by Beverly Trader. February 7, 1985. Directed by Ken Leon.

A SHAYNA MAIDEL. By Barbara Lebow. April 18, 1985. Director, Barbara Lebow; scenery, Michael Halpern; lighting, Stoney Johnson, Gregg Wallace; costumes, Judy Winograd; music and sound, Phillip DePoy.

Rose Weiss.............. Mary Jo Ammon
Mordechai Weiss............ Gus W. Mann
Lusia Weiss Pechenik..... Shawna McKellar

Duvid Pechenik......... Michael Maschinot
Hanna.................. Andrea Alexander
Mama....................... Ellyn Eaves
Time: March 1946. Place: Rose Weiss's apartment, New York City, West Side. One intermission. See the introduction to this section.

CANTERBURY TALES: PART II. Adapted by Frank Wittow. May 14, 1985. Directed by Frank Wittow.

Atlanta: Alliance Theater Company

(Acting artistic director, Kent Stephens)

HIGH STANDARDS by Tom Huey. February 12, 1985. Directed by Skip Foster.
SO LONG ON LONELY STREET by Sandra

Deer. May 8, 1985. Directed by Kent Stephens.

Baltimore: Center Stage

(Artistic director, Stan Wojewodski Jr.)

ON THE VERGE OR THE GEOGRAPHY OF YEARNING. By Eric Overmyer. January 4, 1985. Director, Jackson Phippin; scenery, Tony Straiges; lighting, James F. Ingalls; costumes, Del W. Risberg; composer, Paul Sullivan; sound, Paul Sullivan, Janet Kalas.

Fanny..................... Brenda Wehle
Mary...................... Mary Layne
Alexandra................. Marek Johnson
Alphonse; Grover; The Gorge Troll;
  The Yeti; Gus; Madame Nhu; Mr. Coffee;
  Nicky Paradise......... James McDonnell
Time: 1888. Place: Terra Incognita. One intermission.

HOW THEY ARE AND HOW IT IS WITH THEM. By Grace McKeaney. April 4, 1985. Director, Jackson Phippin; scenery, Hugh Landwehr; lighting, James F. Ingalls; costumes, Jess Goldstein; sound, Janet Kalas.

Biz .... James Handy
Finny .... William Foeller
Man-with-a-Tie; Bum; Curtis; Purse;
  Cop; Mack Cianci; Virgil;
  William .... Anderson Matthews
Elizabeth; Whore; Girl From Biz's Past;
  Biz's Mother; Finny's Wife; Campfire Girl;
  Nancy Ann Cianci.......... Brenda Wehle
Place: In the park, memory, the shadows, a graveyard, a diner, various exteriors and a hospital ward, in continuous shifts. One intermission.

Buffalo, N.Y.: Studio Arena Theater

(Artistic director, David Frank)

THE DOOM OF FRANKENSTEIN. By Geoffrey Sherman and Paul Wonsek. November 30, 1984. Director, Geoffrey Sherman; scenery and lighting, Paul Wonsek; costumes, Bill Walker; music, Bob Volkman; sound, Rick Menke.

Johann .... Timothy Meyers
Gregor; Inspector Clerval.. David Hyde-Lamb

Victor Frankenstein.......... Robert Spencer
Elizabeth Abelman .... Melissa Smith
Lucian .... John Curless
The Monster .... Michael Quill
Kurt ..... Paul A. Connolly, Jonathan Lamb
Gerda .... Sarah Lamb, Robin Weiss
Time: 1882. Place: Middle Europe. Act I,

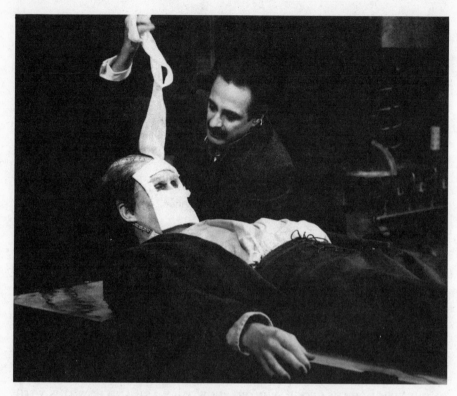

STUDIO ARENA THEATER, BUFFALO—Michael Quill as
the Monster and Robert Spencer as Frankenstein in *The Doom
of Frankenstein* by Geoffrey Sherman and Paul Wonsek

Scene 1: Courtyard. Scene 2: The anatomy laboratory. Scene 3: The salon. Scene 4: The anatomy laboratory. Scene 4: The tower. Act II,
Scene 1: An antechamber. Scene 2: The tower.

Scene 3: A church graveyard. Scene 4: The
tower. Scene 5: Elizabeth's bedroom. Scene 5:
The tower.

Cambridge, Mass.: American Repertory Theater

(Artistic director, Robert Brustein)

In Repertory March 27–April 28, 1985
GILLETTE. By William Hauptman. Director,
David Wheller; scenery, Karen Schulz; lighting,
Thom Palm; costumes, Lynn Jeffery; sound,
Randolph C. Head.
Mickey Hollister . . . . John Bottoms
Brenda . . . . Diane D'Aquila
Jack Cisco . . . . Rodney Hudson
Jody . . . . Cherry Jones
Dar . . . . Harry S. Murphy
Bobby Nobis . . . . Jack Stehlin
Cathy . . . . Gayle Keller
CLAP DEATHTRAP. By Ken Friedman. Di-
rector, Robert Drivas; scenery, Karen Schulz;

lighting, Thom Palm; costumes, Karen Eister;
sound, Randolph C. Head.
Sam . . . . Harry S. Murphy
Sara . . . . Cherry Jones
Mom . . . . Rose Arrick
Harvey . . . . Treat Williams
Sybil . . . . Ursula Drabik
One intermission.

JACQUES AND HIS MASTER. By Milan
Kundera. January 16, 1985. Director, Susan
Sontag; scenery, Douglas Stein; lighting, Jennifer
Tipton; costumes, Jane Greenwood; original
music, Elizabeth Swados.

Jacques................... Thomas Derrah
Jacques' Master.............. Robert Drivas
Innkeeper................... Priscilla Smith
Chevalier de Saint-Ouen....... Jeremy Geidt
Young Bigre.............. Richard Grusin
Old Bigre; Police Officer.... Harry S. Murphy
Justine .... Diane D'Aquila
Marquis .... Dennis Bacigalupi
Mother; Agatha's Mother.... Frances Shrand
Daughter; Agatha .... Lynn Chausow

THE CIVIL WARS: A TREE IS BEST MEA-
SURED WHEN IT IS DOWN. Act III, Scene
E by Robert Wilson; Act IV, Scene A and Epi-
logue by Robert Wilson and Heiner Muller. Feb-
ruary 27, 1985. Director, Robert Wilson; sce-
nery, Robert Wilson, Tom Kamm; lighting,
Jennifer Tipton, Robert Wilson; costumes,
Yoshio Yabara; compositions and sound, Hans
Peter Kuhn.
    Cast: Child—Seth Goldstein; Father, Man Be-
hind Counter, Doctor—Ben Halley Jr.; Freder-
ick the Great, Snow Owl—Priscilla Smith;
Young Woman; Abraham Lincoln—Diane
D'Aquila; Aunt, Abandoned Woman, Woman
with Cigar, Sophi Dorothea, Earth Mother—
Frances Shrand; Young Man, Dog, Smiler—
Thomas Derrah; Mother, White Scribe, Woman
with Bubble Gum, Katte—Shirley Wilber; Old
Man, Grandfather, King Lear—Jeremy Geidt;
Soldiers, Scribes, Submariners, Men with Poles,
Furniture Movers, White Guard, Brown Bear,
Polar Bear—Ensemble.

Staged Readings:
SERVICE WITH A SMILE. By Rodney
Hudson.
TALKING THINGS OVER WITH CHEK-
HOV. By John Ford Noonan.
BULLPEN. By Steve Kluger.
POLLYANNA (musical) book and lyrics,
Geoffrey Bush; music, Loudon Wainwright
III.

Chicago: Goodman Theater

(Artistic director, Gregory Mosher)

THE CHERRY ORCHARD. By Anton
Chekhov; adapted by David Mamet. March,
1985. Director, Gregory Mosher; scenery, Mi-
chael Merritt; lighting, Kevin Rigdon; costumes,
Nan Cibula.
Lyubov Ranevskaya .... Lindsay Crouse
Anya....................... Nessa Rabin
Varya .... Lisa Zane
Leonid Gaev .... Colin Stinton
Yermolay Lopakhin .... Peter Riegert
Petya Trofimov .... W.H. Macy
Semyonov-Pishchik .... Mike Nussbaum
Charlotta .... Linda Kimbrough
Yepikhodov .... Lionel Mark Smith
Dunyasha............... Kathleen Dennehy
Firs....................... Les Podewell
Yasha .... Jose Santana
A Stranger; Station Master .... Robert Scogin
    Time: 1904. Place: Ranevskaya's estate.

THE SPANISH PRISONER and THE
SHAWL By David Mamet. April 19, 1985. Di-
rector, Gregory Mosher; scenery, Michael
Merritt; lighting, Kevin Rigdon; costumes, Nan
Cibula.
The Spanish Prisoner
    Cast: Peter Riegert, Sheila Welch
The Shawl
John .... Mike Nussbaum
Miss A .... Lindsay Crouse
Charles....................... Gary Cole
    Place: John's office.

THE FLYING KARAMAZOV BROTHERS
IN THE 3 MOSCOWTEERS. Commissar of
dialogue, Dmitri Karamazov. June 1, 1985. Di-
rector, Robert Woodrugg; composer and music
director, Douglas Wieselman; scenery, Kate
Edmunds; lighting, James F. Ingalls; costumes,
Susan Hilferty; sound, Micheal Schweppe.
Musicians...... Steven Bernstein, Bud Chase,
            Danny Frankel, Douglas Wieselman
Stalin; Gruchenka............ Laurel Cronin
Lenin; Paderewsky .... Robert Dorfman
Cheka......... Chas Elstner, Jan Kirschner,
    Daniel Mankin, Jeff Raz, Mark Sackett,
                        Missy Whitchurch
Rochfortsky......... Timothy Daniel Furst
Inessa Armand .... Gina Leishman
d'Artagnan.................... Paul Magid
Athos .... Randy Nelson
Aramis .... Howard Jay Patterson
Trotsky; Bonacieuxski......... Eric Peterson
Milady; Konstantina........ Sophie Schwab
Porthos..................... Sam Williams
    Time: Three years after the Russian Revolu-
tion. Place: Most of the time, Moscow.

Chicago: The Organic Theater

(Producing director, Stuart Gordon; artistic director, Thomas Riccio)

3 CARD MONTE, OR THE FURTHER AD-VENTURES OF ROBIN HOOD. By Wayne Juhlin; story by Stuart Gordon and Wayne Juhlin. September 6, 1984. Director, Stuart Gordon; scenery, James Dardenne; lighting, Geoffrey Bushor; costumes, Marta Baumiller; original music and arrangements, Joe Nathan.

Prime Minister of Wamba; Marine;
Teller .... Victor Cole
Ed's Wife; Bystander; Teller ... Julie Crisman
Washington .... Bob Curry
Mike; Guard;
   Russian Ambassador .... Frank Farrell
Curtis .... Aaron Freeman
Mrs. Reagan; Polish Lady;
   Harriet Rojack ..... Carolyn Purdy-Gordon
Yolanda .... Synthia L. Hardy
Reagan; Nate; Remco....... Richard Henzel
Ed; Man #1; Bank President;
   Russian Ambassador ..... Dick Sollenberger
Johnny .... Robert Stewart
Fred; Cop; Jim ..... Brian Van Den Broucke

Marian .... Val Ward
Assorted Roles............. Tony Alcantar
One intermission.

Lab Series

DOPE. By Louis Dilenge and Shawn Wong in collaboration with Stuart Gordon and Norm Langill; based on the novel by Sax Rohmer. April 26, 1985. Directed by Stuart Gordon; scenery, Jerry Fortier; lighting, Larry Schoenemann; costumes, Louise Dilenge; music, Keith Uchima; choreography, Julie Crisman.

Rita Dresden .... Julie Crisman
Jean Adams; Lola Sin;
   Kazmah........... Carolyn Purdy-Gordon
Sir Lucien Pyne; Red Kerry ...... Alex Kerr
Minstrel; Sin Sin Wa....... Russell Kuzuhara
Quentin Gray.................. Andrew May
Stage Manager; Frederick; Coombes;
   Bartender.................... Gene Shuldt
Minstrel; Greville Seton .... Tom Towles
Lord Monte Irvin .... Peter Van Wagner

Chicago: The Steppenwolf Theater Company

(Artistic directors, Terry Kinney, Gary Sinise)

STAGE STRUCK by Simon Gray. September 26, 1984. Directed by Tom Irwin.
COYOTE UGLY by Lynn Siefert. January 30, 1985. Directed by John Malkovich. With Gary

Sinise, Glenne Headly, Moira Harris.
ORPHANS by Lyle Kessler. February 3, 1985. Directed by Gary Sinise.

Chicago: Victory Gardens Theater

(Artistic director, Dennis Zacek)

THE FIFTH SUN. By Nicholas Patricca. September 26, 1984.

THE GOD OF ISAAC. By James Sherman. May 29, 1985.

Cincinnati: Playhouse in the Park

(Producing director, Michael Murray)

THE BIG HOLIDAY BROADCAST (company developed). Directed by Arne Zaslove; a Bathouse Theater production.
AMATEURS (musical) book and lyrics by Winnie Holzman; music by David Evans. January 20, 1985.

PARADISE (musical) book and lyrics by George Wolfe, music by Robert Forest. February 20, 1985. Directed by Worth Gardner.
HAVE by Julius Hay. March 17, 1985. Directed by Robert Kalfin.

Cleveland: The Cleveland Play House

(Director, Richard Oberlin; managing director, Al Milano)

THE ARCHBISHOP'S CEILING. By Arthur Miller. October 12, 1984. Director, Jonathan Bolt; scenery, Gary C. Eckhart; lighting, Richard Gould; costumes, Frances Blau.

Adrian .... Morgan Lund
Maya.................... Lizbeth MacKay
Marcus.................... John Buck Jr.
Irina .... Sharon Bicknell
Sigmund .... Thomas S. Oleniacz
   Time: Some time ago. Place: The sitting room in the former residence of the archbishop; a capital in Europe. One intermission.

THE WAITING ROOM. By Catherine Muschamp. October 19, 1984. Director, William Rhys; scenery and lighting, James Irwin; costumes, Kirk A. Dow; sound, Matthew Wiener.

Kapitan von Planetz .... David O. Frazier
Leutenant von Buhring..... Wayne S. Turney
Field Security Policeman ..... Frank J. Lucus
   Place: Potsdam Station, Berlin. Act I: Evening of April 11, 1917. Act II, Scene 1: About four hours later. Scene 2: Evening of the following day.

DRAMATIC LICENSE. By Kenneth Ludwig. January 18, 1985. Director, Dennis Zacek; scenery and lighting, Richard Gould; costumes, Frances Blau.

Maude Redding............... Carol Bates
William Gillette.......... Thomas S. Oleniacz
Bobby Carlyle .... Wayne S. Turney
May Dison................ Catherine Long
Marion Barrett .... Cassandra Wolfe
Leo Barrett .... John Buck Jr.
Lilly Warner .... Providence Hollander
Louise Parradine........... Sharon Bicknell
   Place: The living room of "Gillette Castle," home of William Gillette in Hadlyme, Conn. Act I, Scene 1: A Sunday morning in April 1921, 3 a.m. Scene 2: One year later, a Saturday night, about 11:30. Scene 3: An hour later. Scene 4: A half hour later. Act II, Scene 1: The following evening about 6:15. Scene 2: That night, about 10 o'clock.

Costa Mesa, Calif.: South Coast Repertory

(Producing artistic director, David Emmes; artistic director, Martin Benson)

THE GIGLI CONCERT. By Thomas Murphy. October 23, 1984. Director, Martin Benson; scenery, Susan Tuohy; lighting, Cameron Harvey; costumes, Barbara Cox.

J.P.W. King............. Kenneth Danziger
Irish Man.................... Dana Elcar
Mona .... Pamela Dunlap
   Place: J.P.W. King's office and living quarters, Dublin. Two intermissions.

SHADES. By David Epstein. November 9, 1984. Director, John Frank Levey; scenery, Mark Donnelly; lighting, Paulie Jenkins; costumes, Deborah Slate.

Lou-Ann Butcher .... Kerry Noonan
Barney "Moonlight" Meade. . Michael MacRae
Bobby Fugazy .... Randy Rocca
Andy Lowell .... Sean Coleman
Natalie Konigsberg .... Terri Hanauer
Dee Ryder .... Eileen Seeley
   Place: A basement apartment in New York City, near Central Park. Act I, Scene 1: A June night. Scene 2: The next day. Act II: As before.

SALT-WATER MOON. By David French. March 15, 1985. Director, Martin Benson; scenery, Michael Devine; lighting, Peter Maradudin; costumes, Sylvia Moss.

Mary Snow .... Juliana Donald
Jacob Mercer............... Marc Epstein
   Time: An August night in 1926. Place: The front porch and yard of the Dawe's summer house in Coley's Point, Newfoundland.

THE DEBUTANTE BALL. By Beth Henley. April 9, 1985. Director, Stephen Tobolowsky; scenery, Mark Donnelly; lighting, Tom Ruzika; costumes, Robert Blackman.

Violet Moone............... Penny Johnson
Teddy Parker.................. Ann Hearn
Willhite Turner .... Jeffrey Combs
Hank Turner .... Kurtwood Smith
Bliss White................ Diane Salinger
Bundy Dugan .... Laurence O'Dwyer
Jen Dugan Parker Turner ..... Joanna Miles
Frances Walker .... Phyllis Frelich
   Place: The upstairs parlor and connecting bathroom in the Turner mansion, located in Hattiesburg, Miss. Act I, Scene 1: An autumn morning. Scene 2: That afternoon. Scene 3: That evening, before the ball. Act II, Scene 1: Late the same evening after the ball. Scene 2: The following morning.

SOUTH COAST REPERTORY, COSTA MESA—Phyllis Frelich,
Laurence O'Dwyer, Diane Salinger, Kurtwood Smith *(foreground)*
and Penny Johnson and Jeffrey Combs *(background)* in *The Debutante
Ball* by Beth Henley

Dallas: Theater Three

(Artistic director, Norma Young)

OUTSIDE WACO. By Patricia Griffith. October
19, 1984. Director, June Rovenger; scenery,
Charles Howard; lighting, Peter Metz; costumes,
Cheryl Denson.

Sarah Matthews Phillips..... Georgia Clinton
Georgia Lee Matthews .... Joan Welles
Juanita Matthews Buchanan .... Susan Oakey
Lashondra Phillips .... Susan Norman
George Harold Matthews....... Hugh Feagin
    Time: The present. Place: The Matthews
Home, Bright Light, Tex. Act I, Scene 1: Pro-
logue, the present. Scene 2: The Matthews
House, 6 hours later. Scene 3: Two days later.
Act II, Scene 1: Two days later. Scene 2: One
week later. Scene 3: One week later.

Staged Readings:

A DAY IN THE LIFE OF . . . By Paulara
Hawkins.
O DAMMIT! AN EVENING WITH THE
"ICONOCLAST." By Jerry Flemmons.
3 ONE-ACTS. By Sharon Ratcliffe.
WARHORSE. By Bill Hare.
THE ELEVENTH ROUND. By Barry Cham-
bers.
DISTILLING SPIRITS. By Dean-Michael
Dolan.
TALK RADIO & PIANO. By David Hall.
OBLOMOV. By F.J. Morlock.
ASSAULT & ASSUAGEMENT. By Charlene
Redick.
THE DEER AND THE ANTELOPE PLAY.
By Jack Bonham.

Denver: Denver Center Theater Company

(Artistic director, Donovan Marley; executive director, Sarah Lawless)

RINGERS. By Frank X. Hogan. October 30, 1984. Director, Donovan Marley; scenery, Richard L. Hay; lighting, Marty Contente; costumes, Andrew V. Yelusich.

Rank...................... Jamie Horton
Gerry .... Mike Regan
Griffin.................... Julian Gamble
Vickie.................... Leticia Jaramillo
  Time: The fall of 1984. Place: Denver, Colo. One intermission.

LAHR & MERCEDES. By James McLure. December 11, 1984. Director, Peter Hackett; scenery, lighting and costumes, Pavel M. Dobrusky.

Lahr .... Bill Buell
Mercedes .... Penelope Miller
The Boy .... Ken Sonkin
  Time: 1956. Place: A rehearsal hall in Miami. One intermission.

THE IMMIGRANT. By Mark Harelik; conceived by Mark Harelik and Randal Myler. February 12, 1985. Director, Randal Myler; scenery, Catherine Poppe; lighting, Marty Contente; costumes, Anne Thaxter Watson.

Haskell Harelik .... Mark Harelik
Ima Perry.................. Ann Guilbert
Milton Perry .... Guy Raymond
Leah Harelik .... Adrienne Thompson
  Time: 1909 through today. Place: Begins in a tiny Jewish village of Russia and ends (where our play begins) in Hamilton County, Tex. One intermission.

THE FEMALE ENTERTAINER. By Elizabeth Levin. April 9, 1985. Director, Edward Pay-

son Call; scenery and lighting, Eric Fielding; costumes, Andrew V. Yelusich; music, Larry Delinger.

Molly .... Maryedith Burrell
Harry .... Michael X. Martin
Old Man................ Archie Smith
Old Woman.................. Ann Guibert
Jimmy-the-Bartender......... Henry Bolzon
Lacy Blossom .... Carol Halstead
Pearl Thompson .... Lori Preisendorf
Daisy; Scene Shifter .... Karen Foster
Fanny; Scene Shifter......... Rebecca Prince
  Time and Place: A Saturday during deer hunting season. One intermission.

Staged Readings May 20–24:
WHEN THE SUN SLIDES. By Stephen D. Parks. Director, Donovan Marley.
NOVEMBER. By J. Ranelli. Director, Archie Smith.
PLEASURING GROUND. By Frank X. Hogan. Director, Peter Hackett.
A WOMAN WITHOUT A NAME. By Romulus Linney. Director, Donovan Marley.
PUBLIC LIVES. By Julia Cameron. Director, Sylvie Drake.
noRmal Doesn't Mean peRfect. By Don Gordon. Director, Peter Hackett.
DEAL WITH A DEAD MAN. By Tom DeMers. Director, Sylvie Drake.
EMILY & KATE. By Ruth Phillips. Director, Randal Myler.
HOPE OF THE FUTURE. By Shannon Keith Kelley. Director, Randal Myler.
TELLING TIME. By Laura Shamas. Director, Laird Williamson.

Evanston, Ill.: Northlight Repertory Theater

(Artistic director, Michael Maggio)

CITY ON THE MAKE adapted from Nelson Algren stories by Denise McClue, Jeff Berkson and John Karraker. Sept. 19, 1984. Directed by Michael Maggio.

HEART OF A DOG adapted from the Mikhail Bulgakov novel by Frank Galati. March 27, 1985. Directed by Michael Maggio; with Frank Galati.

Hartford, Conn.: Hartford Stage

(Artistic director, Mark Lamos)

AMERICA'S SWEETHEART (musical) book, John Weidman and Alfred Uhry, based on the book *Capone* by John Kobler; music, Robert

Waldman; lyrics, Alfred Uhry. March 5, 1985. Director, Gerald Freedman; musical director, Liza Redfield; choreographer, Graciela Daniele; scenery, Kevin Rupnik; lighting, Pat Collins; costumes, Jeanne Button.

Al Capone . . . . Stephen Vinovich
Mae Capone. . . . . K.T. Sullivan
Sonny Capone . . . . Trevor Keeth
Jake Bensick . . . . Nicholas Gunn
Frankie Rivaldo. . . . . Michael McCormick
Tony Rivaldo. . . . . Tom Robbins
Officer Zwick; Jerry Allen; Badger;
    Grown Sonny . . . . Wayne Bryan
Edna Beal. . . . . Carolyn Casanave
Lulu Blombeck . . . . Lucinda Hitchcock Cone
Barney; Schemer Drucci; Senator Krauss;
    President . . . . Gary-Michael Davis

Bernice Madden;
    Muriel Wilson. . . . . Donna English
Bugs Moran; Attorney General;
    Judge Fox . . . . Jeff Etjen
Harry Wilzak; Dion O'Bannion;
    Stone . . . . Tom Henning
Nate Beal; Dr. Bailey . . . . Richard Levine
Radio Lady; Gladys . . . . K.K. Preece
Max Chase; Hymie Weiss;
    Frank Wilson . . . . Steve Routman
Vicki Chase; Fay; Stern . . . . Deanna Wells
    Time: Days of Al Capone. Place: In and around Chicago. One intermission.

Houston: Alley Theater

(Artistic director, Pat Brown; managing director, Tom Spray)

STARRY NIGHT. By Monte Merrick. December 17, 1984. Director, George Anderson; scenery, Mo Holden; lighting, Richard W. Jeter; costumes, Ainslie G. Bruneau; sound, Jan Cole.

Bo . . . . Jeff Bennett
Len . . . . Brandon Smith
Katie. . . . . Johanna Leister

Place: The backyard of a small house and inside a planetarium. Act I, Scene 1: Morning, early September. Scene 2: Noon, two weeks later. Act II, Scene 1: Mid-afternoon of the same day. Scene 2: Two hours later. Scene 3: 6 P.M. Scene 4: Early evening, an hour later.

Los Angeles: East West Players

(Artistic director, Mako)

AN AMERICAN STORY by Ernest K. Abuba. January 2, 1985.
MONKEY MUSIC by Margaret Lamb. March 13, 1985.

THE MUSIC LESSONS by Wakako Yamauchi. April 30, 1985. Directed by Mako.

Los Angeles: L.A. Theater Works

(Producing director, Susan Albert Loewenberg)

THE SHAPER. By John Steppling. November 2, 1984. Director, John Steppling; scenery, Debbie Krikun, Lance Crush; lighting, Karen Musser; costumes, Iona Crush.

Bud. . . . . Lee Kissman
Jill. . . . . Laura Owens
Sherri . . . . Noreen Hennessy
Reesa . . . . Elizabeth Ruscio

Felix . . . . Jack Slater
Del . . . . Scott Paulin
    One intermission. See the introduction to this section.

PROJECT 1984 A.D. By Ljubisa Ristic. March 5, 1985. Directed by Ljubisa Ristic.

Los Angeles: Los Angeles Actors' Theater

(Artistic/producing director, Bill Bushnell)

SECRET HONOR. By Donald Freed and Arnold M. Stone. Director, Robert Harders; scenery and lighting, Russell Pyle.

Mr. Nixon . . . . Philip Baker Hall
    Place: The study of Richard M. Nixon. Time: 1980s.

THE WHITE CROW. By Donald Freed. Director, Charles Marowitz; scenery and lighting, Timian.
Dr. Lillian Baum............. Salome Jens
Adolf Eichmann .... Gerald Hiken
The Guard.................. Dick De Coit
  Place: Jerusalem. Time: 1960.

SHERLOCK'S LAST CASE. By Charles Marowitz. June 29, 1984. Director, Charles Marowitz; scenery, Timian; lighting, Russell Pyle.
Dr. Watson .... Dakin Matthews
Sherlock Holmes .... David Fox-Brenton

Mrs. Hudson .... Toni Lamond
Liza...................... Judith Hanson
Inspector Lestrade......... Peter Bromilow
Sherlock Holmes
  Look-Alike .... Edgar Landudno
Damion.................... Leif Sarraday
  Place: Victorian England. Time: September, 1897. One intermission.

A TASTE FOR THE FORBIDDEN. By Tim Kelly. Director, R.S. Bailey; scenery, A. Clark Duncan; lighting, Jose Lopez; costumes, Armand Coutu.

Los Angeles: Los Angeles Public Theater

(Artistic director, Peg Yorkin)

MELODY SISTERS. By Anne Commire. September 28, 1984. Director, Anne Commire; scenery John Kavelin; lighting, Barbara Ling; costumes, Garland Riddle; musical direction, Larry Kenton.
Dia .... Marcia Rodd
Shay .... Janie Sell

Joyce..................... Yvonne Wilder
Freda .... Betty McGuire
Rowe .... Peg Shirley
Marce..................... Diana Verlain
Seated Lady............... Beverly Dixon
  Time: 1968. Place: Bass River, Mich. One intermission.

Los Angeles: Mark Taper Forum

(Artistic director, Gordon Davidson)

THE HANDS OF ITS ENEMY by Mark Medoff. September 29, 1984. Directed by Gordon Davidson; with Phyllis Frelich, Richard Dreyfuss.

TRAVELER IN THE DARK (revised version). By Marsha Norman. January 24, 1985. Director, Gordon Davidson; scenery, Ming Cho Lee; lighting, Marilyn Rennagel; costumes, Susan Denison.
Sam......................... Len Cariou
Glory .... Deborah May
Stephan.................... Scott Grimes
Everett .... Claude Akins
  One intermission.

Louisville, Ky.: Actors Theater of Louisville

(Producing director, Jon Jory; literary manager, Julie Crutcher)

1984 Shorts, 5 bills October 31-November 18
Bill #1 (2 performances):
SUMMER. By Jane Martin. Director, Jon Jory.
Jennifer Landis .... Gretchen Kehde
Esposito .... Michael Kevin
Lilian Landis .... Dorothy Holland
Driver.................... Lanny Flaherty
Dilly McGregor............. Gretchen West
Marta McGregor......... Kathleen Chalfant
Cairn McGregor .... Bob Burrus
Doc....................... Rob Knepper
  Time: May to August, 1949. Place: A garden

in Philadelphia, at the McGregor ranch outside Billings, Mont., on a Cunard Liner and in various locations in France.
THE AMERICAN CENTURY. By Murphy Guyer. Director, Jon Jory.
Woman..................... Debra Monk
Man .... Christian Kauffmann
Stranger .... Dana Mills
  Time: Spring of 1945.

Bill #2 (3 performances):
THE BLACK BRANCH. By Gary Leon Hill and Jo Hill. Director, Jackson Phippin.

Eli Crooner .... Delroy Lindo
The Black Branch .... Adale O'Brien
Donna Car .... Janna Gjesdal
Aide .... Dana Mills
Wilmer Allen Norris.... Christian Kauffmann
Aunt Hyadle .... Sylvia Short
   Time: July. Place: Morning at Ash Manor, a
state-run mental hospital.
THAT DOG ISN'T FIFTEEN. By Roy Blount
Jr. Director, Alan Duke.
Irene .... Sylvia Short
Virginia .... Adale O'Brien
Little Girl .... Raye Lankford
   Time: The present. Place: An American living
room.
MY EARLY YEARS. By Charles Leipart. Di-
rector, Robert Spera.
Karl Widdoes .... Richard M. Davidson
Amelia Campion .... Susan Bruyn
   Place: A sunny afternoon in a corner of a city
park.

Bill #3 (2 Performances):

THE PERSON I ONCE WAS. By Cindy Lou
Johnson. Director, Robert Spera.
Blaise de Francaux .... Rob Knepper
Mattie Silver .... Janna Gjesdal
Catherine Silver .... Gretchen Kehde
   Time: Winter, but spring is just around the
corner. Place: A town in Georgia.
I'M USING MY BODY FOR A ROAD-
MAP. By Patrick Tovatt. Director, Jackson
Phippin.
Ellis .... Steve Rankin
Jill .... Kathleen Chalfant
Roxie .... Debra Monk
Otis .... Andy Backer
   Place: The Fortune of War Hotel in Sydney.

Bill #4 (2 performances):

THE LOVE SUICIDE AT SCHOFIELD
BARRACKS. By Romulus Linney. Director,
Frazier W. Marsh.
Captain Martin .... Alan Duke
Staff Sgt. Bates .... Christian Kauffmann
Lorna Ann Bates .... Dorothy Holland
Col. Moore .... Dana Mills
Lucy Lake .... Sylvia Short
Katherine Nomura .... Jodi Long
Sgt. Maj. Ruggles .... Andy Backer
Commanding Officer .... Vaughn McBride
Edward Roundhouse .... Lanny Flaherty
   Time: Just after Halloween, 1970. Place: Scho-
field Barracks in Oahu, Hawaii.
THE ROOTS OF CHAOS. By Douglas
Soderberg. Director, Larry Deckel.
Wilma Cernikowski .... Adale O'Brien

Skeeter .... Steve Rankin
Doublemint .... Gretchen West
Joe Cernikowski .... Andy Backer
Officer of Surface Mining .... Bob Burrus
   Time: Dinnertime. Place: The kitchen and din-
ing area of a house in Centralia, Pa.

Bill #5 (3 performances):

PRIVATE TERRITORY. By Christopher
Davis. Director, Frazier W. Marsh.
Tom Brody .... Joe Morton
Vittorio Vincenza .... John Anania
Lottie Clanese .... Marita Geraghty
   Time: 1950. Place: A room in a once wealthy
house in a Roman suburb.
THE COOL OF THE DAY. By Wendell
Berry. Director, Robert Spera.
Edgar .... Bob Burrus
Ellie .... Susan Bruyn
Billy .... Will Oldham
Doc .... Michael Kevin
Pascal .... Vaughn McBride
Bertha .... Kathleen Chalfant
   Time: Evening in early June, 1910. Place: A
farm along the Kentucky River near Port Wil-
liam.
ADVICE TO THE PLAYERS. By Bruce
Bonafede. Director, Larry Deckel.
John Tyler .... Michael Kevin
Oliver Manzi .... Joe Morton
Robert Obosa .... Delroy Lindo
Tony Jones .... Steve Rankin
Randall Moore .... Lanny Flaherty
Emily Ngome .... Cheryl Lynn Bruce
   Time: Recent past. Place: A theater stage in
the United States.

*Humana Festival of New American Plays, Febru-
ary 19–March 30, 1985*

WAR OF THE ROSES. By Lee Blessing. Direc-
tor, Bill Partian; scenery, Paul Owen; lighting,
Jeff Hill; costumes, Marcia Dixcy; sound, James
M. Bay.
David Rose .... Paul Collins
Carolyn Rose .... Cara Duff-MacCormick
   Time: Night in early September. Place: St.
James Hotel in Red Wing, Minn.

THE VERY LAST LOVER OF THE RIVER
CANE. By James McClure. Directors, Ray
Fry, Steve Rankin; scenery, Paul Owen; lighting,
Jeff Hill; costumes, Marcia Dixcy; sound, James
M. Ray.
River Cane .... Debra Monk
Toinette .... Donna Harrison
R.L. .... Bob Burns
Mange .... Dana Mills

Intercourse................. Steve Rankin
Carlyle .... Rob Knepper
Jeeter .... Levi Lee
Bonney McMasters......... Leo Burmester
Will Pike .... Christian Kauffmann
Place: Tranquility Lounge, on Highway 70
near Muleshoe, Tex.

DAYS AND NIGHTS WITHIN. By Ellen
McLaughlin. Director, Jon Jory; scenery, Paul
Owen; lighting, Jeff Hill; costumes, Marcia
Dixcy; sound, James M. Bay.
Elsa Weber.................... Beth Dixon
The Interrogator .... Ken Jenkins
Man .... Frederic Major
Stewardess .... Kathy Bates
Time: February 1950–March 1952. Place: A
prison in East Berlin.

RIDE THE DARK HORSE. By J.F. O'Keefe.
Director, Robert Spera; scenery, Paul Owen;
lighting, Jeff Hill; costumes, Marcia Dixcy;
sound, James M. Bay.
Dierdra.................... Melody Combs
Joel.................... Steven McCloskey
Lennie....................... Zoe Jackson
Elise .... Marilyn Rockafellow
Matt .... Walter Atamaniuk

Jacob.................... Frederic Major
Carl........................ Steve Decker
Dr. Bannerman .... Andy Backer
Time: Between early September and late February. Place: The dining room of a middle-class
home in the Chicago suburbs. One intermission.

AVAILABLE LIGHT. By Heather McDonald. Director, Julian Webber; scenery, Paul
Owen; lighting, Jeff Hill; costumes, Marcia
Dixcy; sound, James M. Bay.
Pierre Riviere, age 15........ Rob Knepper
Victoire Riviere............. Wanda Bimson
Daniel Riviere................. Bob Burrus
Clothilde Riviere, age 14 ..... Melody Combs
Adrien Postel........... Walter Atamaniuk
Dr. Gabriel Fortin .... Michael Kevin
Marguerite............ Marilyn Rockafellow
Robert .... Dana Mills
Father Suiriray .... Ray Fry
Jules, age 17.......... Christian Kauffmann
Jacques, age 13 .... Larry Larson
Eric, age 15 .... Robert Foster
Anne, age 12 .... Patrick Frontain
Beatrice, age 10........... Annemarie Potter
Charles, age 16 .... Joe McCullough
Time: 1832. Place: Normandy, France. One
intermission.

Malvern, Pa.: The People's Light and Theater Company

(Producing director, Danny S. Fruchter)

*New Play Festival, June 8–August 19, 1984
Program B:*
VALENTINES AND KILLER CHILI. By
Kent R. Brown. Director, Israel Hicks; scenery,
Joe Ragey; lighting, Arden Fingerhut; costumes,
Megan Fruchter.
Jackie .... Alda Cortese
Jason........................ Lee Devin
Time: The present. Place: Outside of Amarillo,
Tex.

CITY LIGHTS—AN URBAN SPRAWL. By
J. Rufus Caleb. Director, Murphy Guyer; scenery, Joe Ragey; lighting, Arden Fingerhut; costumes, Megan Fruchter.
Panhandler; Professor.......... Ray Aranha
Landlady .... Carol Dellavecchia
Hero .... Daryl Edwards
Princess; Christian Woman .... Joyce Lee
Sule.................... Rozwill Young
Dice Player .... Daryl S. Smith
Keyboard .... Bernard Samuels
Saxophone .... Marion Salaam
Drums .... Spike Coleman

Place: An apartment and the streets of an
American city.

Program C:
THE AMERICAN CENTURY. By Murphy
Guyer. Director, Steven D. Albrezzi; scenery,
Norman B. Dodge Jr., lighting, Arden Fingerhut; costumes, Megan Fruchter.
Man .... Bill Smitrovich
Woman.................... Jessie K. Jones
Stranger .... Murphy Guyer
Time: 1945. Place: An American kitchen.

Program D:
MALEK'S DEPENDENTS. By Gary Slezak.
Director, Steven D. Albrezzi; scenery, Norman
B. Dodge Jr.; lighting, Arden Fingerhut; costumes, Megan Fruchter.
Bud Malek................ Greg Alexander
Meg Malek................. Shaw Purnell
Jack Malek................ Gerald Richards
Father McKenna........... Bill Smitrovich
Place: A neighborhood liquor store on the
Southwest side of Chicago. One intermission.

Milwaukee: Milwaukee Repertory Theater

(Artistic director, John Dillon)

A WOMAN WITHOUT MEANS. By William Stancil, based on *Dowerless* by Alexander Ostrovsky. April 5, 1985. Director, Kenneth Albers; scenery, Bil Mikulewicz; lighting, Dan J. Kotlowitz; costumes, Sam Fleming.

Jabez Turner .... Peter Callender
Edgar Deloach .... Peter Silbert
William Arthur
  Tisch .... Charles Michael Wright
Jasper Hamish Crow .... Daniel Mooney

Eugenia Sutphen .... Joan Hotchkis
Larissa Claire Sutphen ..... Pamela Woodruff
Eulogius Tarquin Boggs ..... James Pickering
Luther Wesley Barnes .... John Austin
John Hesquith Laprade ...... Dan Desmond
Myrtiss Ratcliff .... Brendan Burke
Eudoxia Athene Boggs .... Rose Pickering
  Time: July 4, 1879. Place: Araby, Mo., a prosperous town on the Mississippi, south of St. Louis. One intermission.

New Haven, Conn.: Long Wharf Theater

(Artistic director, Arvin Brown)

RAINSNAKES by Per Olov Engquist, translated by Harry C. Carlson. November 2, 1984. Directed by Jose Quintero; with Colleen Dewhurst.
THE COMMON PURSUIT by Simon Gray. January 11, 1985. Directed by Kenneth Frankel.

ALBERT HERRING (opera) by Benjamin Britten and Eric Crozier. April 19, 1985. Directed by Arvin Brown; musical direction, Murry Sidlin.
BULLIE'S HOUSE by Thomas Keneally. April 26, 1985. Directed by Kenneth Frankel.

New Haven, Conn.: Yale Repertory Theater

(Artistic Director, Lloyd Richards)

A PLAY OF GIANTS. By Wole Soyinka. November 27, 1984. Directed by Wole Soyinka; scenery, James D. Sandefur; lighting, Mary Louise Geiger; costumes, Claudia Marlow Brown.

Field Marshal Kamini ...... Roger Robinson
Benefacio Gunema .... Leon Morenzie
Emperor Kasco .... Michael Rogers
Gudrum .... Avril Gentles
Sculptor .... Christopher Noth
Chairman,
  Bugara Central Bank .... Tyrone Wilson
Task Force Special .... Gregory Wallace
Ambassador .... L. Scott Caldwell
Gen. Barra Tuboum .... Herb Downer
Beadle; Guard .... Dwight Bacquie
Mayor of Hyacombe .... Lloyd Hollar
Prof. Batey .... Ray Aranha
Secretary General .... Manuel Sebastian
Guard .... Kimberly Scott
1st Russian Delegate .... Neal Lerner
2d Russian Delegate .... Ed Setrakian
1st U.S. Delegate ...... Mary-Alan Hokanson
2d U.S. Delegate .... Don Harvey
Task Force Special .... Steven R. Blye
  Time: A few years before the present. Place:

The Bugara Embassy to the United Nations, New York. One intermission.

FENCES. By August Wilson. April 30, 1985. Director, Lloyd Richards; scenery, James D. Sandefur; lighting, Danianne Mizzy; costumes; Candice Donnelly.

Troy Maxson .... James Earl Jones
Jim Bono .... Ray Aranha
Rose .... Mary Alice
Lyons .... Charles Brown
Gabriel .... Russell Costen
Cory .... Courtney B. Vance
Raynell .. Cristal Coleman, LaJara Henderson
  Place: The front yard of the Maxson house, in an urban neighborhood of a northern American industrial city. Act I: Fall, 1957. Act II, Scene 1: Fall, 1957. Scenes 2–4: Spring, 1958. Scene 5: Summer 1965.

Winterfest (in repertory) January 14–February 9, 1985

BETWEEN EAST AND WEST. By Richard Nelson. Director, John Madden; scenery Basha Zmyslowski; lighting, David Alan Stach; costumes, Rusty Smith.

Gregor Hasek .... Thomas Hill
Erna Hasek .... Jo Henderson
Place: A one-room apartment sparsely furnished on the Upper East Side, New York City.
RUM AND COKE. By Keith Reddin. Director, William Partlan; scenery, Clare Scarpulla; lighting, Donald Holder; costumes, David Peterson.
Jake Seward.................. Michael Ayr
Rodger Potter; Fidel Castro...... Jon Korkes
Tod Cartmell; Raul Castro...... Dylan Baker
Bar Patron; Ramon;
Castro's Driver.......... Christopher Noth
Waiter; Child #1;
Soldier #2 .... Steven R. Blye
Linda Seward............ Deborah Hedwall
George; Ernesto Herrera; Child #2;
Soldier #1 .... Courtney B. Vance
Miguel Santimos .... Ted Sod
Thomas Tanner; President of Guatemala;
Cmdr. Tyler .... Dan Ziskie
Bob Stanton; Felix Duque .. Thomas Costello
Richard Nixon; Larry Peters... Reathel Bean
Patricia Nixon............... Cheryl Mintz
Time: 1960–1961. Place: Various locations in Miami, Washington, D.C., New York, Guatemala, Caracus, Havana, and the Bay of Pigs. One intermission.

FAULKNER'S BICYCLE. By Heather McDonald. Director, Julian Webber; scenery, Pamela Peterson; lighting, Mary Louise Geider; costumes, Scott Bradley.
Mama...................... Kim Hunter
Claire .... Cara Duff-MacCormick
Jett .... Tessie Hogan
Faulkner.................. Addison Powell
Time: 1962. Place: Oxford, Miss.
VAMPIRES IN KODACHROME. By Dick Beebe. Director, Evan Yionoulis; scenery, Charles E. McCarry; lighting, Donald Holder; costumes, Arnall Downs.
Mrs. Renfield............. Susan Blommaert
Mr. Renfield.......... William Duff-Griffin
Seward .... Victor Raider-Wexler
Harker .... Don Harvey
Artie..................... Jordan Schwartz
Van Helsing................. Jean DeBaer
Lucy.................... Amanda Atkinson
Solescu .... Warren Manzi
Time: A prologue describes events taking place in 1939. All subsequent action occurs in 1945. Place: Bathory Island, just off the southeastern coast of Maine, in and around the solarium of a small, private clinic for the alcohol dependent. One intermission.

Norfolk, Va.: Virginia Stage Company

(Artistic director, Charles Towers; managing director, Dan J. Martin)

MOROCCO. By Allan Havis. February 1, 1985. Director, Christopher Hanna; scenery, Michael Miller; lighting, Steve Pollack; costumes, Candice Cain.

Park Forest, Ill.: Illinois Theater Center

(Artistic director, Steve S. Billig)

PACK UP YOUR TROUBLES! (musical). Book, music and lyrics, Steve S. Billig. April 19, 1985. Director, Steve S. Billig; musical director, Jonathan Roark; musical staging, Mark Donaway; scenery, Nancy Eads; lighting, James Lindquist.

1st Man .... Mark Donaway
2d Man...................... Shole Milos
3d Woman; Narrator .... Etel Billig
1st Woman............... Karen J. Wheeler
2d Woman .... Jane Petrongelli
Time: All about 1914–1918.

Philadelphia: Philadelphia Drama Guild

(Producing director, Gregory Poggi)

LOVE GIFTS. By Charles R. Traeger. January 11, 1985. Director, Steven Schachter; scenery, Kevin Rupnik; lighting, Craig Miller; costumes, Cynthia O'Neal.
Jennifer Kane........... Jeannine Costigan
Mrs. McGitzen .... Anna Nestyrev
Lathan Kane .... Peter Syvertsen

Sara Kane .... Susan Gordon-Clark
James Braddock............. Peter Brouwer
Agnes Schulnitz.............. Anne Gartlan
Time: The present, mid-October. Place: The Kane home in the country in the Midwest. One intermission.

PHILADELPHIA DRAMA GUILD—Peter Syvertsen, Susan Gordon-Clark and life-sized doll in a scene from *Love Gifts* by Charles R. Traeger

THE POWER AND THE GLORY. By Graham Greene; adapted by Denis Cannan. November 23, 1984. Director, William Woodman; scenery, George Tyspin; lighting, Frances Aronson; costumes, Kurt Wilhelm; sound, Charles Cohen.

Cast: Victor Arnold, Don Auspitz, Vasili Bogazianos, Bryn Lauren Dubow, James Harper, Barrett Heins, Arlene Lencioni, C.J. Meoli, Taro Meyer, John Milligan, Hector Osorio, Tony Rizzoli, Jose Santana, Norman Snow, Fiddle Viracola.

Time: Early 1930s. Place: Southern Mexico, during the anti-clerical period. One intermission.

Playwright's project: Staged Readings.

FRANKLIN'S CHILDREN. By Philip Bosakowski. May 20, 1985. Director, Kay Matschullat.

SHOULDERS. By Jeffrey Kinghorn. May 21, 1985. Director, Maureen Shea.

SISTER CARRIE. Adaptation by Karolyn Nelke of Theodore Dreiser's novel. May 23, 1985. Director, Steven Schachter.

Princeton, N.J.: McCarter Theater

(Artistic director, Nagle Jackson)

FAUSTUS IN HELL. Adapted by Nagle Jackson from the works of Marlowe, Goethe, Molière, et al., with *The Show of the Seven Deadly Sins* by Edward Albee, Christopher Durang, Amlin Gray, John Guare, Romulus Linney, Joyce Carol Oates, and Jean-Claude van

Itallie. January 23, 1985. Directed by Nagle Jackson; scenery, Elizabeth K. Fischer; lighting, Richard Moore; costumes, Kathleen Blake.

John Faustus . . . . Harry Hamlin
Mephistophilis . . . . Barry Boys
Lucifer . . . . Jay Doyle

Gretchen...................... Stacy Ray
Wagner................... Bruce Somerville
Don Juan................ Mario Arrambide
The Devils: Keith Curran, Dan Diggles, Danielia Fulmer, Jason P. Jones, Henson Keys, Randy Lilly, Mary Martello, Janine Santana, Greg Thornton, Kerry Waters.
GREED. By Amlin Gray.
Emperor.................... Henson Keys
Steward.................... Greg Thornton
Centurion.................. Jason P. Jones
GLUTTONY. By John Guare.
The Messiah................. Keith Curran
Gabriel..................... Randy Lilly
WRATH. By Romulus Linney.
Savonarola................. Greg Thornton
PRIDE. By Jean-Claude van Itallie.
Jogger...................... Dan Diggles
Woman.................... Mary Martello
Doctor .... Henson Keys

ENVY. By Edward Albee.
Envy....................... Keith Curran
SLOTH. By Christopher Durang.
Son .... Dan Diggles
Mother.................... Mary Martello
LECHERY. By Joyce Carol Oates.
Stripper.................... Kerry Waters
One intermission.

Staged Readings:
THE MOUNTAINS OF ARARAT. By Geoffry Brown. March 18, 1985.
SECRET THIGHS OF NEW ENGLAND WOMEN. By Jan Paetow. March 25, 1985.
DALTON'S BACK. By Keith Curran. April 15, 1985.
BASEMENT BLUES. By Judith Gilhousen. April 29, 1985.
THE HEROES OF XOCHIQUIPA. By Rick Foster. May 13, 1985.

Richmond, Va.: Virginia Museum Theater

(Artistic director, Tom Markus)

FINAL TOUCHES. By Kenneth O. Johnson. October 4, 1984. Director, Tom Markus; scenery, Charles Caldwell; lighting, Lynne M. Hartman; costumes, Bronwyn J. Caldwell.
Mary Connally .... Frances Helm
Lester Connally................ Gil Rogers
Ruby Meyers.............. Scottie Wilkison
Flora Jenkins................ Anne Sheldon
Bobby Connally.............. Jake Turner
Time: The Present, summer. Place: The Connally house in a small town on the Gulf Coast of Texas. Act I, Scene 1: Mid-morning. Scene 2: Later that day. Act II, Scene 1: Early the next morning. Scene 2: Later that day. Scene 3: Early the following morning.

THE MISTRESS OF THE INN. By Carlo Goldoni; adapted by Freyda Thomas and David Carlyon. November 8, 1984. Director, Tom Markus; scenery, Charles Caldwell; lighting, Lynne M. Hartman; costumes, Julie Keen.
Frank Thoroughgood .... Mark Hattan
Count d'Argent.............. David Pursley
Duke of Bawlingbrook .... Robert Foley
Cap. Adam Stoutheart .... Dan LaRocque
Miranda .... Janet Zarish
John .... Hubert Kelly Jr.
Anna Malaskaya .... Joanna Morrison
Time: April 1775. Place: A fine inn of Colonial Williamsburg. One intermission.

Rochester, N.Y.: GeVa Theater

(Producing director, Howard J. Millman)

PLANET FIRES. By Thomas Babe. March 30, 1985. Director, John Henry Davis; scenery, Ray Recht; lighting, F. Mitchell Dana; costumes,

Pamela Schofield; music, John Franseschina.
Time: Close of the Civil War. Place: Circus setting.

St. Paul: Actors Theater of St. Paul

(Artistic director, Michael Andrew Miner)

BULLY. By Paul D'Andrea. March 29, 1985. Director, Michael Andrew Miner; scenery, Marty Helen Horty, Michael Andrew Miner;

lighting, Chris Johnson; costumes, Nayna Ramey.
Clay Bayliss................ David Lenthall

Sally Faye Redmund.......... Sally Wingert
Orus Woodard................ Paul Boesing
Francine Gates Woodard...... Delores Noah

Hayden Emory .... D. Scott Glasser
Time: Two months in 1981. Place: New Liberty, Mo. One intermission.

San Jose, Calif.: San Jose Repertory Company

(Executive producer, James P. Reber; producing director, David Lemos)

YUP!: A MUSICAL LAMPOON OF MODERN LIFE. Music and words, Roy Zimmerman; conceived by J. Stephen Coyle, Kathryn Garcia, David Lemos, Kathryn Nymoen and Roy Zimmerman. June 22, 1984. Director, David Lemos; scenery, Kevin Short; lighting, Joseph Driggs.
Cast: J. Stephen Coyle, Kathryn Nymoen, Roy Zimmerman.

Seattle: A Contemporary Theater

(Founder/director, Gregory A. Falls; new plays manager, Barry Pritchard)

THE COMMUNICATION CORD by Brian Friel. October 25, 1984. KING LEAR by William Shakespeare; in a new style based on Japan's Kabuki Theater. May 2, 1985. Directed by Arne Zaslove; co-produced with The Bathouse Theater.

Stamford, Conn.: Hartman Theater

(Producing artistic director, Edwin Sherin; executive director, Harris Goldman)

OVER MY DEAD BODY. By Anthony J. Fingleton and Michael Sutton; suggested by the novel The Murder League by Robert L. Fish. November 2, 1984. Director, Edwin Sherin; scenery, Victor Capecce; lighting, Jeff Davis; costumes, Judianna Makovsky.
Trevor Foyle .... Fritz Weaver
Dora Winslow .... Tammy Grimes
Bert Cruikshank .... Thomas Toner
Charters .... William Preston
Desmond Grubb .... Mordecai Lawner
Simon Vale................ Stephen Newman
Chief Inspector Smith........ Richard Clarke
Detective Sergeant Trask .. Walter Atamaniuk
Time: The present. Place: The reading room of The Murder League, London.

BELOVED FRIEND. By Nancy Pahl Gilsenan. December 28, 1984. Director, David Chambers; scenery, Oliver Smith; lighting, Arden Fingerhut; costumes, Marie Anne Chiment; incidental music, Mel Marvin.
Mrs. Halvorson .... Barbara Sohmers
Kristin Halvorson .... Dana Delany
Rachel Kativhu............. Sheila Dabney
Betty Kativhu; Anna .... Kim Staunton
Shopkeeper; 1st Soldier;
Rhodesian Policeman....... Matthew Lewis

Mrs. Mitchell; Mrs. Campbell; Exercise Leader;
Airport Announcer.............. Mary Jay
Pavu Mlambo .... Robert Jason
Gary Davis................ Richard Backus
Pass Officer; 2d Soldier; Prison Guard;
Hospital Orderly........... David Combs
Black Women; Esther........ Cheryl Rogers
Kenneth .... Kim Sullivan
Policeman at Bus; Dr. Mills;
British Bobby .... Max Jacobs
Exercisers: Phran Clulow, Terry Neylan, Barbara Ferrero.
Time: 1967–1982. Place: Scenes alternate between America and Rhodesia (Zimbabwe). One intermission.

THE TEAM. By Terence Feely; based on a story by Brian Clemens and Terence Feely. March 22, 1985. Director, Edwin Sherin; scenery, Guido Tondino; lighting, Jeff Davis; costumes, Mariann Verheyen.
Paul Walton................. Richard Dow
Dan Moore .... Lenny Von Dohlen
Salina Proby.......... Alexandra O'Karma
John Charters .... Richard Clarke
Place: A basement flat in Earl's Court, London. Act I: Spring and Summer. Act II: Autumn and winter, one year later. One intermission.

Syracuse, N.Y.: Syracuse Stage

(Artistic director, Arthur Storch)

HANDY DANDY by William Gibson. December 14, 1984. Directed by Arthur Storch. (Co-produced with Empire State Institute for the Performing Arts.)

Washington, D.C.: Folger Theater Group

(Artistic director, John Neville-Andrews)

CROSSED WORDS, A PANTO by Mike Laflin and Hugh Atkins. November 19, 1984. Directed by Davey Marlin-Jones.

THE MARRIAGE OF FIGARO adapted into English by John Neville-Andrews. January 15, 1985. Directed by John Neville-Andrews.

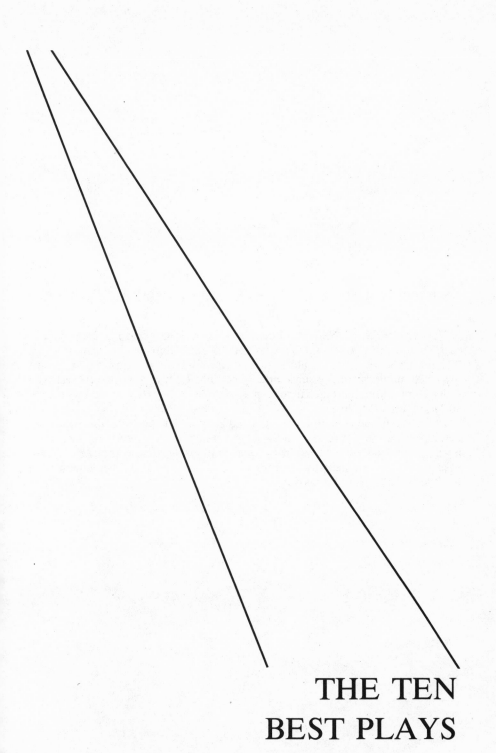

THE TEN
BEST PLAYS

Here are details of 1984–85's Best Plays—synopses, biographical sketches of authors and other material. By permission of the publishing companies which own the exclusive rights to publish these scripts in full in the United States, most of our continuities include substantial quotations from crucial/pivotal scenes in order to provide a permanent reference to style and quality as well as theme, structure and story line.

In the case of such quotations, scenes and lines of dialogue, stage directions and descriptions appear *exactly* as in the stage version or published script unless (in a very few instances, for technical reasons) an abridgement is indicated by five dots (. . . . .). The appearance of three dots (. . .) is the script's own punctuation to denote the timing of a spoken line.

SPLIT SECOND

A Play in Two Acts

BY DENNIS McINTYRE

Cast and credits appear on pages 346–347

DENNIS McINTYRE was born in Detroit in 1942, the son of an advertising executive (his father) and a teacher (his mother). He was educated at the University of Michigan, where he was encouraged to write plays by one of his teachers, Kenneth Rowe, graduating in 1961 and later, in 1968, obtaining his M.F.A. from Carnegie-Mellon University. His first New York production of record was Children in the Rain *off Broadway at the Cherry Lane Oct. 2, 1970—for only one performance. It was not until May 3, 1978 that his next play,* Modigliani, *appeared in an off-off-Broadway production at the Direct Theater and then, skipping a season, opened Nov. 11, 1979 for an acclaimed off-Broadway engagement of 119 performances, cited as a close contender for the Best Plays list in our volume. His* The Saddest Summer of Val *was presented in staged readings in 1980 and 1981 at the New Dramatists, of which he is a member. His* Split Second *appeared as an OOB production by Amstad World Theater in February 1984 and went on to become its author's second major success and first Best Play in its off-Broadway production June 7, 1984 for 147 performances. Another of his scripts,* National Anthem, *has been twice produced in cross-country theater, and he is the author of a novel,* The Divine Child.*

McIntyre, who lives in New York City, is a member of the Circle Repertory Playwriting Lab as well as the New Dramatists and has been the recipient of an Avery and Jule Hopwood Award in Playwriting and Fiction, an MCA Fellowship, two Shubert Fellowships, a Tufts University Commission in Playwriting, a Playbill Award and Rockefeller and National Endowment grants.

"Split Second": by Dennis McIntyre. Copyright © 1980 by Dennis McIntyre (under the title "The Saddest Summer of Val"). Copyright © 1984, 1985 by Dennis McIntyre. Reprinted by permission of Rosenstone/Wender on behalf of the author. See CAUTION notice on copyright page. All inquiries concerning stock and amateur production rights should be addressed to: Samuel French, Inc., 45 West 25th Street, New York, NY 10010. All other inquiries should be addressed to: Rosenstone/Wender, 3 East 48th Street, New York, NY 10017.

Time: The present, July 4

Place: Manhattan

ACT I

Scene 1

SYNOPSIS: The setting for a continuous flow of action is a series of platforms suggesting locales with a minimum of objects. An occasional musical background is *"comparable to the sound of wind chimes . . . . . mysterious, haunting and melancholy."* At first, in darkness, the music fades, and the sound of pursuit is heard, together with the order, "Freeze!" The noise of July 4 firecrackers and other city sounds can be heard as the lights come up on a late-night confrontation at 28th Street and 11th Avenue: Val Johnson, a black New York City policeman in street clothes, is pointing a revolver and holding at bay William H. Willis, a white man in street clothes who has been caught trying to steal an Oldsmobile. Willis, ordered to stand with his back to the officer and hands raised, hopes they can talk this over.

WILLIS: Have a heart, would you? It's the Fourth of July, for Christ's sake!

VAL *(right behind Willis):* Just another night to me, fucker.
　　　Val, his service revolver at his hip, pushes Willis forward and kicks his legs apart.

WILLIS: *(as it happens):* You don't got to do that, do you?

VAL: You want to bet?

WILLIS: Just where in the hell am I going to go? Tell me that.

VAL: That's the point, asshole.
　　　Val begins to frisk Willis.

WILLIS: I'm clean. Really. Hey, be a little more careful, would you? I'm a citizen.
　　　Val takes a large pocket knife out of Willis's right jacket pocket.

VAL *(as he does so):* I'll keep that in mind.

WILLIS: You'd better keep that in mind, man.
　　　Val puts the knife in a jacket pocket. He takes a wallet out of Willis's right back pocket, opens it, quickly checks the identification, and then puts the wallet in a jacket pocket. He removes his handcuffs from his belt and snaps them on Willis, one at a time.

Willis protests that he wasn't doing anything wrong, as Val reads him his rights from a card. Val ignores Willis's continued protests and calls Police Headquarters on his two-way radio to request transportation for his arrest. As he does so, Willis turns around and sees for the first time that the officer arresting him is black. "You got a white voice, you know that?" Willis comments, then his attitude

Peter Jay Fernandez as Charlie and John Danelle as Val Johnson in
Split Second by Dennis McIntyre

changes somewhat. He becomes almost confiding as he deprecates the condition of the car he was going to steal—he'd be doing the city a favor taking it away. He suggests that it was a Spanish-owned car, decorated with religious symbols. He is only a small-time lawbreaker, he pleads, with a long record but only for minor offenses.

WILLIS: . . . . . The spics are breathing down my neck. They're starting to dress better than me. That car, that heap, that was to buy a new suit. So I could go to court. So I could look decent. So I could make a favorable impression. My ex, she's breaking my balls. Alimony. Child support. You might appreciate that. I've been around black chicks. Marlene, my ex, she's just like a lot of black chicks. Gorgeous in bed, real nifty, you know what I mean, right? But one step away from the sheets, all of a sudden, she's putting a bat between your legs, just for fucking practise.

VAL (low): You're not helping your case.

WILLIS: Look, brother—

VAL (low—dangerous): Don't call me fucking "brother."

WILLIS: What else am I supposed to call you? You and me, we're in the same category.

VAL: The fuck we are!

WILLIS: No, listen, we're deprived, that's all I'm saying. Economically deprived. We always have been—always will be. My father was a prick. Yours just happened to be colored, right?

    Val flinches—visibly.

Willis goes on to try to bribe Val to let him go with $1,000 he can get from his brother, who owns two dry-cleaning places. Val refuses, and Willis calls him "nigger," raising his offer to a couple of thousand and taunting Val with ugly references to his wife and his children, ignoring Val's obvious efforts to control his mounting fury.

WILLIS: . . . . . They ought to take all you nigger cops and ship you back to Africa. That's what they ought to do. Let you be jungle cops. Give you some beads and a spear. Let you direct traffic in the jungle. Because that's where you belong, nigger! Don't you know that?! I mean, like don't you miss the smell of elephant shit?!

    Val slowly removes his service revolver. He points the revolver at Willis, his arm trembling. Willis laughs—moves closer—a bravado.
Just try it! Go on! See where it fucking gets you!

    Val continues to point his revolver at Willis, then slowly holsters it.
You don't got the balls, do you? Well, I can understand that. Really. Most niggers, they only come with one ball, that's what I hear. (Moves slightly closer.) Hey, I got a joke for you. You want to hear a joke? What's the difference between a nigger cop and a pile of shit? No difference, man! Get it!

    Val draws his service revolver, points it at Willis and pulls the trigger. An explosion from the revolver. Willis is thrown backward. He sags to the ground, jerks and then lies still. Val replaces his revolver in his *holster, turns away from Willis, takes several steps, and then stops. He turns back, stumbles to Willis, searches in his own pockets for the handcuff key, finds it, unlocks the handcuffs, locks them again, replaces them on his belt, takes out Willis's knife, opens it, wipes it with his jacket, puts the knife in Willis's right hand and then begins to back away. He remembers the wallet. He takes it out, wipes it on his jacket, moves back to Willis and puts it in Willis's back pocket. He backs away again, panting, taking deep breaths. He removes his service revolver and begins moving upstage. Blackout.*

Scene 2

At a New York City Police precinct later that evening, Parker, a black police captain, is going over Val's report while Val sips from a container of coffee. Parker comments on Val's use of only one shot to get Willis through the heart—most officers would have fired again, for good measure.

Parker inquires about Val's background in Pittsburgh; in those days, Val carried two guns in his tough neighborhood. He got permits for them because his father was a policeman.

Val has filled out a full report of the Willis killing and wants to get home, but Parker feels that "there must be something else"—Parker is the investigating officer of this incident, over which there is scheduled to be a departmental hearing Friday morning, which may be just pro forma policy because the victim was white and the officer black.

Parker is accustomed to an officer being upset for a long time after he uses his gun to kill for the first time, and Val seems strangely cool. Parker agrees that Willis "wasn't any prize" but didn't seem the type who would attack a policeman.

PARKER: . . . . . How come you called for a radio car before you cuffed him?

VAL: I didn't cuff him.

PARKER: That's right. I forgot. You didn't get a chance to cuff him. I hate nights. My mind wanders. All the details get lost. I've been thinking about a Virginia ham on whole wheat for the last five minutes. Maybe a couple of pickles. Why didn't you just call in when you spotted him jerking around with the Olds?

VAL: I figured I could handle it. It was one-on-one.

PARKER: Johnson, most cops in this city, me included, you call "transportation" when you've got the cat laced over a hood. Not when he's just waiting around for you to make a move. Christ, don't you ever watch television?

VAL: I had him covered. He looked docile.

PARKER: A lot of sweet-faced kids, give them a chance and they'll take your ears home with them. Didn't your old man ever tell you that?

VAL: I chased him three blocks. He was out of shape. I didn't think he'd try anything.

PARKER: That's the trouble with being on the street too much—you begin to think you own it. "Procedure" doesn't mean shit when it's one-on-one time, right?

That's what I like about being in the office. You can't fuck up that much. Throw away one piece of paper, you've still got five more. Three feet?

VAL *(indicates the report):* That's what it says, doesn't it?

PARKER: Sure it does. That's how I know.

Questioned by Parker about his service in Vietnam, Val explains that he was there for more than a year, often volunteering for dangerous "point" duty because he felt he had a knack for dealing with snipers and could save lives. He was very careful, and for five months nobody in his squad was hit. He is just as careful with his duty here, but in the case of Willis, "He pulled a knife, so I pulled the trigger," and that was that.

Parker tries to draw an analogy with Vietnam: the darkness in the jungle would get on the soldiers' nerves so that they might fire hundreds of rounds at a twig's snap, and it was dark and deserted in the area where Val met the car thief. Val denies it was that dark on 28th Street.

PARKER: Three feet? You really got that close?

VAL: I got that close.

PARKER: I never liked getting "close." That's why I decided to get off the street. That and my mother-in-law. I just couldn't get used to touching guys I didn't know. Some cops—they really enjoy slamming a guy into a wall. That might even be the reason they join up. But not me. You were patting him down, right?

VAL: It never got that far.

PARKER: You had him "spread out," didn't you?

VAL: It never got that far either.

PARKER: He just turned around, three feet, knife out?

VAL: He turned around, one foot, knife coming out. I backed up two.

PARKER: He must have been desperate.

VAL: He must have been.

PARKER: And that's when you warned him?

VAL: I told him to "drop it." That was his second warning. The first warning, I told him to "freeze."

PARKER: Let me get this straight. He had his knife out, he was coming at you, and you had time to warn him.

VAL: "Drop it" doesn't take a whole lot of time.

PARKER: Well, it's a good thing you didn't say, "Drop that fucking knife, you cocksucking bastard, or I'll put a bullet through your miserable heart!"

Parker insists on reenacting the incident with Val to make it clearer for the investigation coming up this Friday. Parker puts a pen in his belt, turns his back three feet away from Val, who is pointing his finger like a gun. When Parker spins around he pulls the pen from his belt with his left hand and has it against Val's throat in two seconds. Val points out that Willis had the knife in his right hand and was in the process of opening it when he was shot.

Parker is still baffled by Val's shooting, right through the heart in a situation like this. Val insists that he did the right thing under the circumstances, and Parker comments, "I hope so, Johnson," as the scene blacks out.

Scene 3

In a bar a short time later, Val and a fellow black policeman, Charlie, are having a beer. Charlie is trying to cheer Val up, insisting he was right to shoot Willis and probably saved some other cop the trouble of doing it: "I don't get it. They walk around just inviting us to put a hole in them. We all know that. And then, when we finally do it, we're fucking depressed. Beats me . . . . . It was up close, that's all. If you'd shot him off a roof, you'd be home in bed asleep."

Charlie recalls some other bad up-close incidents, then advises Val to take a short leave and try to relax. Val is especially haunted by the thought that if Willis had been black, maybe he wouldn't have pulled the trigger—as it is, Val doesn't remember doing it, and he doesn't remember hearing the shot.

Charlie goes to get them a couple of beers, so he doesn't hear Val, head in hands, saying, "I had him cuffed, Charlie." Slow blackout.

Scene 4

In Val's and Alea's apartment, she is sleeping on the couch when he returns home, takes off his holster and gently wakens her. It is a little after 4 A.M.; she fell asleep and neglected to bolt the door, which troubles Val.

Val suggests they take the day off tomorrow, but Alea has a class to teach and doesn't want to miss it. Val tells her he needs to get out of the city and makes up a tale about the evening's incident: he found himself facing a black teen-ager high on drugs and in possession of them, wielding a kitchen knife. Alea sympathizes and agrees to take tomorrow off, and Friday too—but of course Val can't be absent from the departmental hearing Friday morning. Val exclaims, "I'm telling you, the next punk who comes at me with a knife—the next punk who comes at me with anything, I'm going to pull the trigger!" Alea senses that there was something more than Val is telling, but Val doesn't want to talk about it, he just wants to get away and forget it.

Alea feels she has a right to know about Val's work, but Val resists bringing the ugly street stories home. They talk about her work in the classroom, but not his—that's the way Val wants it, and he insists on being in control.

VAL: You lose it, you let it go for a second, you even snap your fingers, somebody else picks it up, and fast!

ALEA: Is that what your father taught you? Is that Rusty's code?

VAL: No, it's mine. I learned it early—starting at six—starting in Pittsburgh. I got dragged off the "Hill." I got tied to a tree. I got my clothes ripped off with a knife. I got poison ivy rubbed all over me. I hung there for five hours. It got dark out. I was still there. That's when I learned it.

ALEA: You were six years old, Val.

VAL: It could have been yesterday.

ALEA: And so nothing else counts?

VAL: Not a fucking thing. It got me through a war, and it gets me through my job!

ALEA: And what's it do to me, Val? *(He turns away from her.)* What's it do to you?

VAL *(without looking):* Let it go.

Alea insists that she is Val's partner and deserves to experience all of him, not just the half that comes home and leaves the other half, the policeman, outside. Goaded by Alea, Val finally shocks her by confessing, "I offed a white dude," telling her of some of the circumstances of Willis's death, as though it were a clear case of a self-defense—which Alea senses it was not. Val faces her and tells her that Willis was cuffed and "I—I accidentally pulled the trigger," then took the cuffs off and placed the open knife in his hand. "Then there's nothing to worry about—is there?" Alea asks. "No," Val replies, as the scene blacks out. *Curtain.*

ACT II

Scene 1

In his apartment the next evening, Rusty Johnson (Val's father, a retired policeman) is at ease in his armchair, holding a can of beer and watching a police program on TV. Val enters, and Rusty turns the set off after commenting that on these programs, "Ever notice how the black dude trots in second? You think they're trying to tell us something?"

Rusty is wearing cowboy boots and is favoring a leg after a fall from his horse, an accident which he attributes to cheap stirrups. He reminisces about the surprising incompetence of some thieves. He remembers one he arrested: "He was carrying a 21-inch Admiral portable. Right down Forbes. Three in the morning. A streetcar almost hit him. We saved his goddamn life. Anyway, we got him in the black-and-white, stashed the portable—you remember that portable. It was in your grandmother's house . . . . . Worked real well, that Admiral. Your grandmother never had any trouble with it."

Finally it occurs to Rusty to wonder what Val is doing here, and Val tells him he shot a man last evening.

RUSTY: Dead?

VAL: Dead.

RUSTY: First time outside the army?

VAL: I didn't kill anybody in Nam.

RUSTY: Funny. You know, I always assumed you did. We never talked about it. I was always waiting for you to mention it, but you never did. A whole year, and you didn't shoot anybody?

VAL: I did "point." It didn't come up.

RUSTY: It's a real shame.

VAL: What?

RUSTY: All that free ammo, tons of it, and you didn't have anything to show for it.

VAL: Disappointed?

RUSTY: You've either got a target or you don't. You know this guy you shot? Ever see him before?

VAL: No.

RUSTY: One of "us?"

VAL: White.

RUSTY: Well, that's one for our side, isn't it? . . . . .

Questioned, Val tells his father various versions of the incident, originally claiming that Willis had a gun, then a knife, then neglecting to handcuff him and accidentally pulling the trigger of his service revolver. Val shouldn't make a mistake like that, Rusty comments. Val reminds his father that in his day the police carried "throwaway" weapons in case of just such a mistake. Rusty protests, "We didn't have accidents. Guns just didn't go off. People didn't die just because we got jumpy, nervous, distracted or whatever you want to call it."

It is Val's responsibility not to make mistakes and, Rusty adds, "I didn't ask you to be a goddamn cop!" Val pleads that he couldn't have been anything else, the way he was brought up.

VAL: . . . . . I started being a cop at five. The first Christmas I can remember, under the tree, a fingerprint kit. A goddamn fingerprint kit. And a black-and-white, made out of tin, with your name painted on the hood, "Rusty," and the number of your squad car, 183. I broke it Christmas day, winding it up, listening to the siren. My God, you had me in uniform when I was ten . . . . . Fake ribbons. Fake medals. All the ribbons and medals I was supposed to earn when I grew up. First in the army, and then on the force. You got me a flasher for my bike. I was eleven years old, and I was arresting every other kid on the block!

RUSTY: It was my profession! What'd you expect?! We were living on the "Hill." I was a black cop. That was something in those days—a black cop. I was proud of it. And sure, I brought it home. What else was I supposed to bring home? What else was I supposed to do? Pretend I was a goddamn surgeon? Put clamps and a scalpel under the tree? Buy you a book on anatomy? No, I'm not going to listen to this! Why in hell am I defending myself?! I'm not about to swallow a bullet just because you grew up in a cop's house! Just because you lost your cool last night! You're on trial, kiddo! Not me! Manslaughter, that's what you gave those bastards!

VAL: I didn't give them shit!

RUSTY (studies Val): I must be losing my edge. I didn't see it coming. You fixed it, didn't you?

VAL: I fixed it.

RUSTY: You planted the knife.

VAL: I planted the knife.

RUSTY: And that makes it a whole different story, doesn't it?

VAL: It makes it self-defense.

RUSTY: He came at you, right?

VAL: Right.

RUSTY: And you warned him.

VAL: I warned him twice.

Michele Shay as Alea Johnson and Norman Matlock as Rusty Johnson
with John Danelle in a scene from *Split Second*

RUSTY: Neat.
VAL: That's right. Neat.
RUSTY: No witnesses.
VAL: Nobody.
RUSTY: And that's it?
VAL: There's a departmental hearing. Tomorrow morning.
RUSTY: And you're going to lie again?
VAL: When are you going to realize—when are you going to learn—it's not our fucking world! When are you going to understand that?!
RUSTY: Then maybe you should have picked cotton for a living!

If you're going to be a cop, there are rules that you must obey, Rusty insists. Val points out that they are "White rules," and that his father wasn't even promoted to sergeant during his 32 years on the force. But Rusty is proud that he was able to support his family during the Depression and now enjoys a comfortable retirement, after the years of keeping to the rules. In those days, the black policemen got the dirtiest assignments and couldn't complain; nowadays there are black captains. Progress may have been slow, but it has taken place, Rusty argues. Explosions of anger, as in Watts and Detroit and Val's action the previous night, will get them nowhere.

Val fought their war for them, he reminds his father, who taunts him with not having killed any of the enemy man-to-man, "You wasted a lot of ammunition." On the contrary, Val tells him, he caused the enemy to waste a lot of ammunition shooting at him while he was on "point," but he has never talked about this because he has none of the medals his father would like to boast about.

Rusty doesn't want to hear any more about the shooting incident from Val and is not prepared to offer him absolution, but as Val moves to depart Rusty stops him with a question.

RUSTY: If it'd been a black dude, this guy, would you have shot him?
VAL: The gun went off accidentally.
RUSTY: It's too bad.
VAL: What?
RUSTY: If we were still in Pittsburgh, I might have been able to help you.
VAL: I had him cuffed.
RUSTY: I thought so. I didn't think you were that dumb.
   Val exits. Music. The lights slowly fade.

Scene 2

In Val's and Alea's apartment, Alea is insisting that the shooting was an accident and that Val must regard and report it as such. They can live with the knowledge that Val altered the setting, tampering with the evidence, a felony in itself. Val can find within himself no good excuse for his behavior, though Alea argues that anyone else, such as Charlie, would also have arranged things to exonerate himself from any wrongdoing and never have worried about it afterward. "I'm too good a cop," Val insists, "it never should have happened."

Alea sees that Val is even considering telling what really happened, and she warns that there's too much at stake for that: "I don't plan on visiting you twice a week for the next ten years." And even if he punishes himself by taking himself off active duty into a desk job, they'll both still have to live with the memory of what happened.

ALEA: . . . . . There is no decision to be made. It's made. It was made the day you were born—when you ended up black instead of white. It was made, Val!
   They stare at each other.
VAL: A guy like Willis, I always figured I'd be able to handle it. You know, skip the lies, tell the truth, fuck the consequences. I didn't know shit, did I?
ALEA: You're just not Rusty, that's all.
VAL: So what's that make me?
ALEA: You're alive, aren't you? Who cares about the truth any more? Who ever did? Unless they got caught. What's the truth mean, anyway? You recited his record. He was a pimp. He was a hustler. He was a thief. He smuggled cigarettes from North Carolina. He went to prison in New York. He went to prison in Michigan. He carried a knife, and, if you'd given him a chance, he probably would have killed you. That's your fucking truth, Val. But he was white. Don't you ever

forget that. White! You tell them what really happened, and they'll crucify you. And not just you. Me. All of us. The next black man who wants to become a cop, you think they're not going to think twice about giving him a gun? The next black kid they blow away in Bed Stuy, you don't think they're going to bring up your name? Because when black people pull the trigger, that's not insanity, that's spontaneity! Give a gorilla a banana, he's going to eat it! And I'll tell you one thing, Val Johnson, you go to prison, and you won't survive it. The guards are going to hate you. You're the ex-cop who couldn't control himself. The whites are going to hate you. You're the ex-black cop who couldn't control himself. "Control," Val! Remember? But the blacks, they're going to hate you most of all. And do you want to know why? Out of contempt, that's why! Contempt! Why'd you have to go and let them know!

VAL: Then where the hell are we?

ALEA: You tell me! But keep that in mind, tomorrow morning, and keep asking yourself the other question—"Where are we going to be?!"

>   *They stare at each other—hard. He turns and exits the apartment. The lights slowly fade on her as she stares after him.*

Scene 3

A short time later Val joins Charlie on a park bench sipping beer from cans in paper bags. Charlie assures Val that he has nothing to worry about at the hearing. He knows how Val feels—he had to kill a man close up in Vietnam. And there was a white corporal in Saigon who was peddling drugs, good stuff to the white soldiers but bad, brain-damaging stuff to the blacks. "We decided to take him out, this Corporal, and I got the low card," Charlie tells Val. They decided to make him suffer, so Charlie strangled him with a wire: " 'Euthanasia,' that's what I like to call it. I lost maybe a night's sleep over it."

Val needs Charlie's reassurance, and slowly he lets the truth come out: he was nine feet away, not three ("Shit, I would have smoked the motherfucker at fifteen feet—I even saw the tip of a blade," Charlie comments). Val finally admits that he had Willis cuffed ("But they don't know that, do they?" is Charlie's immediate reaction). Val unholstered his revolver to impress Willis, and somehow it went off.

VAL: It was an accident.

>   *They stare at each other. Charlie slowly nods.*

CHARLIE: If that's what it was, then fuck them. It's "street." They don't know anything about it. And the less they know, the better.

>   *Charlie rubs Val's shoulder, but the affection is gone.*

(*As he does so.*) But they've got a shovel for people like you. My advice—don't let the mothers use it. I left it in Saigon. No regrets.

VAL: Did you?

CHARLIE: You leave it on 28th. You play good-guy cop, Johnson, you won't have a friend left in the world. Guaranteed. That's just the way it is, brother.

>   *Charlie exits. Val stares straight ahead. The lights slowly fade on Val as he begins to walk away from the bench.*

Scene 4

A short time later in her apartment, Alea is asking Rusty to help his son, but Rusty maintains that telling the truth is the only way to go for a cop who has taken his oath. If Rusty had ever had such an accident, he would have faced up to it without rearranging the evidence—but he never did. He always managed to keep his feelings and impulses in check.

ALEA: And that's why you can be so calm. That's why it's so easy for you to pass judgment, walk out of here, feed your horses, and start jumping fences!

RUSTY: It's not easy!

ALEA: No?! In case you didn't know it, Rusty, it's our life! It's the next ten years! The next twenty!

RUSTY: I know that.

ALEA: No you don't! You're quoting scripture, that's all you're doing! You could be talking to anybody. Take a goddamn look! I'm your son's wife! Val could go to jail, and you could be dead before he got out! That's what you're promoting! He's your son! Where's your compassion?!

RUSTY: You don't want compassion! You want approval!

ALEA: No, I don't want interference! Your interference! I don't care if Val took off the handcuffs! I don't care if he planted the knife! We don't owe them anything! Nothing!

RUSTY: No, we don't, if we don't want to. But I don't see how that's going to improve anything.

ALEA: I'm not interested in improvement! I'm interested in Val!

RUSTY: Val joined the Police Department! He took an oath! He owes them something!

ALEA: What?! His life?! Mine?!

RUSTY: There are consequences!

ALEA: There are white consequences, and there are black consequences!

RUSTY: No, sister, you're mixing it up! There are consequences! Period!

ALEA: In your mind! Not mine!

Alea doesn't believe that the possibility of remorse or any other consequences are as important as just staying alive and staying together. Rusty warns her that she may find herself living with a Val she doesn't know.

Val comes home and, seeing his father, tells him abruptly that he means to stick to his story. Rusty is disappointed, but Val repeats his catechism of excuses: he has a wife to think of, the victim was a loser, the whole thing was an accident not worth the ruin of his whole career. But whatever Val decides to do, whatever story he tells others, Rusty wants to know the whole truth for its own sake.

RUSTY: . . . . . I want to know if a little bit of me rubbed off on you. Not a lot. Just a little bit. That's all I want to know.

ALEA *(turns away):* Goddamn you, Rusty.

RUSTY: You aimed, didn't you?

ALEA *(turns back):* Goddamn you!

RUSTY: Didn't you?!

VAL: That's right. I aimed.

ALEA: Of course he did! Didn't you know that?! He shot him right through the heart! One bullet, nine, ten feet away! A perfect target! He probably even toyed with the idea of putting it between the fourth and fifth buttons! That's how good Val is! He wanted to turn it off, just once, and he had the power to do it. He didn't want to hear it any more. "Nigger." He didn't want the spit in his face. "Nigger!" He wanted to turn it off forever. "NIGGER!" Just like you did, except you never pulled the trigger. You were afraid to do it. So you took it. And took it. And took it! But you tell me—who gave them the right to say it?! And you tell me—why do we have to take it?! It's wrong. He shouldn't have shot him. He should have ignored him. Like you did. But it never would have happened—he never would have even thought about it—if we didn't have to spend most of our lives being tempted to do it! Val had to do it for you! He had to do it for a lot of people like you! Why'd you have to ask?! You couldn't even let him have that, could you? I believed him. The whole story. And I knew it wasn't true. Why'd you have to ask?!

> *Alea turns away from them.*

RUSTY: You can't turn it off, son. I thought you knew that.

VAL: It seemed like a good idea at the time.

RUSTY: I figured it out early. That's why I never pulled the trigger. Everything's temporary. Most people don't stay in your life that long. Not if you're a cop. I thought I taught you that.

VAL: I suppose you did. But I remember you telling me, six years old, the day you found me tied to that tree—"No difference between a white man and a black man can't be erased by a bullet."

RUSTY: I was angry. What they'd done to you. I didn't mean it.

VAL: You never told me you didn't mean it.

Rusty is trying not to judge Val but he admits he believes Val should be punished for breaking the law—the law that Rusty only bent a little, appropriating a stolen TV set for his mother, for example, but which Val has violently broken. Val admits that he lost his cool, he yielded to the urge to shut Willis's mouth, but he doesn't believe his whole life should be ruined "just because some son of a bitch, the lowest of the low, finally screamed 'nigger' " once too often and once too loud. Rusty doesn't agree; he hopes that if the same thing had happened to him, he would have told the truth and faced the music.

Rusty moves to depart, but before he goes he throws out a last line of affection, telling Val that he moved to this city to be closer to his son, and "If I could—if there was any way, Val—if I were still in uniform—If I could convince anyone—I'd take credit for the guy you shot. I'd claim it. I would. I'd make it mine."

After Rusty leaves, Alea tells Val one more time that they can't afford to listen to Rusty, they have a life to live. Val does not respond one way or the other, and the lights fade to black.

Scene 5

The next morning, Val is sitting in the witness chair at the police hearing and describing what took place at 11:15 the evening of July 4 on West 28th Street off Eleventh Avenue. He tells of spotting the suspect in the act of stealing a car, pursuing him, ordering him at gunpoint to halt, and then calling for transportation. He is looking downward, gripping his legs, and Parker's voice is heard asking him to look up and speak up.

VAL *(without looking up):* I approached the suspect—William H. Willis—And I—I—I ordered him to—Suspect—

PARKER'S VOICE: Officer Johnson, please? We can't hear you, and we can't see your face.

Val grips his legs harder. He doesn't look up.

Officer Johnson?

Val slowly relaxes his hands. He looks up slowly and stares straight ahead.

Thank you, Officer Johnson. That's much better. Please continue.

VAL: I called "transportation." I approached the subject with the specific intention of patting him down and placing him in handcuffs. When I was within three feet of him, the suspect turned on me with an open knife in his right hand. I backed up two feet and ordered the suspect to drop the knife. The suspect did not comply with my order, but instead made a menacing movement in my direction, the knife still in his hand. I fired my service revolver once, the bullet striking the suspect in the chest and killing him instantly.

The lights slowly begin to fade on Val. He remains motionless. He stares straight ahead. The life seems to have gone out of him. Music. Blackout. The music plays in the darkness. Music out. Curtain.

HURLYBURLY

A Play in Three Acts

BY DAVID RABE

Cast and credits appear on pages 320 & 348–349

DAVID RABE was born March 10, 1940 in Dubuque, Iowa, the son of a school teacher. He was educated at Loras Academy and Loras College, both in Dubuque, graduating B.A. in 1962 and going east to get his M.A. in theater at Villanova. He was drafted and served in the Army from January 1965 to January 1967 as a Specialist 4th Class, the final 11 months in Vietnam.

Rabe describes his pre-playwriting career as "formerly egg carrier, bellhop, parking lot attendant, teacher," and meanwhile he studied writing with Raymond Roseliep, Dick Duprey and George Herman. In 1967 and 1968 at Villanova (under a program partly supported by the Rockefeller Foundation) he wrote the first drafts of two plays about the Vietnam war: The Basic Training of Pavlo Hummel *and* Sticks and Bones. *He went from Villanova to the New Haven* Register, *where he won an Associated Press award for feature writing; then, in 1971, he went back to Villanova to teach in the graduate theater department.*

Joseph Papp gave Rabe his professional stage debut with the New York Shakespeare Festival production of Pavlo Hummel *May 20, 1971 for 363 performances, winning its author a citation as "most promising playwright" in* Variety's *poll of drama critics and in the Drama Desk voting, plus an Obie Award and the Hull-Warriner Award voted by the Dramatists Guild Council as the season's best play on a controversial subject. While* Pavlo Hummel *was still running, on Nov. 7, 1971, the Public Theater produced Rabe's* Sticks and Bones *(which had been staged at Villanova in 1969) for 121 performances, then moved it to Broadway for another 245 performances, winning the Tony Award for best play, a special Critics Circle citation and our citation as a Best Play of its season.*

"Hurlyburly": by David Rabe. Copyright © 1985 by Ralako Corp. Reprinted by permission of Grove Press, Inc. See CAUTION notice on copyright page. All inquiries should be addressed to: Grove Press, Inc., 196 West Houston Street, New York, NY 10014.

The New York Shakespeare Festival continued in the 1970s to produce Rabe's work. This has included The Orphan *(an adaptation of the Oresteia as an American drama) March 30, 1973 for 53 performances;* Boom Boom Room *at Lincoln Center Nov. 8, 1973 for 37 performances;* Burning *as a work-in-progress April 13, 1974, and* In the Boom Boom Room *(a revision) Nov. 20, 1974 for 31 performances. Rabe's* Streamers *was produced by Papp at Lincoln Center April 21, 1976 for 478 performances, winning the Critics Award as best American play, the Drama Desk Award as best new play and Rabe's second Best Play citation.*

In the 1980s, Rabe's Goose and Tomtom *was produced by New York Shakespeare Festival May 6, 1982 for 14 performances. His third Best Play,* Hurlyburly *(once known as* Spinoff*), was produced at the Goodman Theater, Chicago in March 1984, then was staged off Broadway by Mike Nichols (who had directed* Streamers*) June 21, 1984 for 45 performances under the aegis of a group of producers who transferred it to Broadway, Aug. 7.*

Other Rabe honors have included an American Academy of Arts and Letters Award (1974) and a Rockefeller Foundation grant (1981). He is the author of the screen play I'm Dancing as Fast as I Can *and the film version of his own* Streamers*. He is married to Jill Clayburgh and lives in New York City.*

The following synopsis of Hurlyburly *was prepared by Jeffrey Sweet. A note by Rabe appended to his script reads in part as follows: "In the characters' speeches, phrases such as 'whatchmacallit,' 'thingamajig,' 'blah-blah-blah' and 'rapateta' abound. These are phrases used by the characters to keep themselves talking and should be said unhesitatingly with the authority and conviction with which one would have in fact said the missing word."*

Time: A little while ago

Place: A house in the Hollywood Hills

ACT I

Scene 1

SYNOPSIS: The audience's view is of a cross-section of the house. The ground floor is an open area with a front door, living room area and a kitchen nook. A stairway leads up from the ground floor to an exposed balcony, off of which feed three doors leading to Eddie's bedroom, a bathroom, and Mickey's bedroom. Through the *"greenhouse-like"* windows can be seen the jungle-like vegetation which surrounds the house. The tangle of vegetation outside is echoed by the clutter of scripts, resumes, and empty liquor bottles inside.

At rise, Eddie is asleep and mostly undressed in the wake of a night of drugs and indiscriminate TV immersion. He snaps to attention as Phil, *"a muscular, anxious man,"* rushes into the house without knocking. Phil has news: "It's over." As they make coffee, roll joints—whatever—what's over emerges: Phil's marriage to Susie. A bad fight. A very bad fight. Eddie offers to call Susie on Phil's behalf to get some kind of peace process going. Phil says he doesn't think that will work because, in the middle of giving him a verbal skinning, Susie had some harsh words in reference to Eddie, too. "She hates you," Phil tells Eddie.

Eddie is offended. He can understand why Susie might hate Arnie. Friend though Arnie is to Eddie and Phil, still Arnie is not a surprising candidate for loathing, given an obnoxiousness which has promoted spontaneous threats of personal mayhem from even his closest buddies. But why Susie should hate Eddie, a person she always gave the appearance of liking, is beyond Eddie. "You're just like me, she says," is the closest thing Phil has for an explanation.

PHIL: We're friends. You know. So she thinks we got somethin' in common. It's logical.

EDDIE: But we're friends on the basis of what, Phil? On the basis of opposites, right? We're totally dissimilar is the basis of our friendship, right?

PHIL: Of course.

EDDIE: I mean, I been her friend longer than I been yours. What does she think, that I've been—what? More sympathetic to you than her in these goddamn disputes you two have? If that's what she thought she should have had the guts to tell me, confront me!

PHIL: I don't think that's what she thought.

EDDIE: SO WHAT WAS IT?

PHIL: I don't know. I don't think she thinks.

EDDIE (settling onto the swivel chair opposite Phil): None of them think. I don't know what they do.

PHIL: They don't think.

EDDIE: They calculate. They manipulate. So what's she up to? They express their feelings. I mean, my feelings are hurt, too.

PHIL (growing frenzied): Mine, too.

EDDIE: They're all nuts.

PHIL (and more frenzied): I pity them, I fuckin' pity them. She makes me crazy. I ain't gonna see her any more.

The cause of the fight emerges. Last night, Phil came home bursting with an idea about how to make a major killing in Las Vegas, which in turn was connected to a profound theory on global politics. In retrospect, Phil will grant that, having been under the influence of intoxicants, his rap was not the product of a sound mind, but Susie wouldn't give him the consideration of paying attention or giving any kind of due respect, the upshot being Phil belted her. He remembers her being like a cloud with a face on it saying these lousy things at him to the point where he struck. And sometime in the middle of this she tossed in how she hated Eddie.

Eddie's theory is that Susie hates men. Evidence? She hates Phil, Arnie and Eddie; and what Phil, Arnie and Eddie have as a common characteristic is being male. "It's a goddamn syllogism," Eddie insists. "You go from the general to the particular." Except something's wrong with that. In this case, they aren't starting with a general and going to particulars, they're going from particulars to a general. Which isn't a syllogism but—what?—"Science!" Science

Christopher Walken as Mickey and Jerry Stiller as Artie *(standing)* and William Hurt as Eddie and Harvey Keitel as Phil *(seated)* in the off-Broadway cast of David Rabe's *Hurlyburly,* directed by Mike Nichols

being defined by Eddie as, "You see all the shit like data and go from it to the law." So what they have is scientific verification that Susie hates all men. In which case, Eddie reasons, Susie has no particular reason to hate him, but, rather, hates him in the abstract—so to hell with her. *"It is important to note that there is an element of play in this whole scene between Phil and Eddie: on some level it is a game, a riff and that Eddie tends to adopt Phil's mannerisms when alone with him."*

Eddie and Phil are having a good time cussing out Susie as Mickey staggers out of his room onto the balcony and makes known his annoyance at having been disturbed by these goings-on. Mickey heads down to the kitchen area, Eddie and Phil following him, making outrageous comments as much to irritate Mickey as to continue the riff with each other. (Eddie, for instance, loudly insists that he will never talk to Phil again if Phil goes back to Susie.) Mickey's every attempt to inject a note of sanity into the discussion prompts more intentionally lunatic replies.

As Mickey bewails the lack of food in the kitchen, Eddie gets ready to snort some coke. When Mickey questions the wisdom of this, Eddie replies that he needs it to wake up. Mickey suggests coffee as an alternative. "The caffeine is fucking poison, don't you know that?" says Eddie. To which Mickey replies, "So what is this, Bolivian health food?" Eddie is indifferent to Mickey's belief that perhaps his coke-snorting is getting out of hand.

Mickey suggests that, in view of Eddie's rough night—which included "crashing around and talking to the TV like a goddamn maniac"—Eddie should consider going to bed. This triggers a rant from Eddie about the horrors and absurdities of contemporary life as brought to him by the 11 o'clock news. After being "just devastated" by the news last night, he got a phone call from his ex-wife which just added to the horror.

Having covered Phil's domestic situation, Mickey moves to the question of Phil's professional situation. Phil, an actor, talks with hope about some parts he's up for. One guy in particular, a director named Leighton, seems to be interested in him for a new cop show. Eddie tells him that that particular director is a lowlife from whom Phil should not expect anything except a runaround. Eddie and Mickey, as casting directors, know what's what in this business, and Phil should take what he—Eddie—has to say seriously. Phil resents these discouraging words from a friend.

Eddie sincerely tries to get the facts of life across to Phil: "Look, you have to exploit your marketable human qualities, that's all. You have certain qualities and you have to exploit them. I mean, basically we all know the M.O. out here is they take an interesting story, right? They distort it, right? Cut whatever little truth there might be in it out on the basis of it's unappealing, but leave the surface so it looks familiar—cars, hats, trucks, trees. So, they got their scam, but to push it they have to flesh it out, so this is where you come in, because they need a lot of authentic sounding and looking people—high-quality people such as yourself, who need a buck. So like every other whore in this town, myself included, you have to learn to lend your little dab of whatever truth you can scrounge up in yourself to this total, this systematic sham—so that the fucking viewer will be exonerated from ever having to confront directly the fact that he is spending his life face to face with total shit. So that's all I'm sayin'. 'Check with me,' is all I'm sayin'. Forget about this Leighton thing."

Phil asks if they're handling anything else which might have a part for him. He hasn't been working, and he's more than a little desperate. Eddie points to a script which might offer something in a month or so. Phil scoops it up and heads up to Eddie's room to read it and take a nap.

Mickey and Eddie are alone now. Mickey says that, between the self-destructive previous night, the crap that's been shoved up his nose and the joint he's beginning to smoke, Eddie is in no shape to go to a business meeting they have scheduled. Eddie's response pushes the conversation into the real issue between them: Darlene.

Eddie met Darlene first, thought she was dynamite and began a serious but non-exclusive relationship with her. Eddie introduced Darlene to Mickey—his roommate, business partner and best friend—and something of a chemical nature seemed to happen between Darlene and Mickey. Mickey asked Eddie for permission to get together with Darlene so that they could "determine the nature of these vibes."

MICKEY: . . . . . I mean, couldn't you have said, "No"? Couldn't you have categorically, definitively said no when I asked? But you said—"Everybody's free, Mickey." That's what you said.

EDDIE: Everybody is free.

MICKEY: So what's this then?

EDDIE: This? You mean this? This conversation?

MICKEY: Yeah.

EDDIE: This is JUST ME trying to maintain a, you know, viable relationship with reality. I'm just trying to make certain I haven't drifted off into some, you know, solitary paranoid fantasy system of my own, totally unfounded and idiosyncratic invention. I'm just trying to stay in reality, Mickey, that's all. Don't you want me to be in reality? I personally want us both to be in reality.

So Mickey and Darlene had gone to dinner last night to discuss what they had to discuss and, as Eddie points out, Mickey returned at six in the morning, indicating that things went beyond the discussion stage. Mickey doesn't deny this, but, given the fact that he asked and got permission from Eddie to explore the situation, he doesn't think he owes Eddie any guilt. But, if the thing between him and Darlene bothers Eddie, Mickey won't see her again. "This is not worth our friendship," he tells Eddie. Besides, says Mickey, although Darlene is obviously dynamite, perhaps she is not as dynamite as Eddie thinks.

Eddie is offended that Mickey is badmouthing the lady Mickey more-or-less stole from Eddie. If he was going to put their friendship in jeopardy by moving in on Eddie's lady, the least Mickey could do is not imply that he did so over a lady not worth the risk. Mickey suggests that Eddie perhaps doesn't have the most balanced perspective on the merits of women either as individuals or in general. Somehow we get the feeling that Eddie is not as upset about this as he represents himself to be.

And now the subject of the phone call from Eddie's ex-wife Agnes comes up.

Given the grief Agnes causes Eddie, Mickey doesn't understand why Eddie talks to her at all. "I have to talk to her," says Eddie defensively. "We have a kid." Mickey says that every time Eddie talks to Agnes he goes crazy, further validating her view of him as a mess.

They are interrupted by the arrival of Artie and Donna. *"Artie is about ten years older than Eddie and Mickey."* One might say he is very L.A. Donna is a 15-year-old blonde in shorts wearing headphones connected to a portable tape player. After a perfunctory introduction to the guys, she heads up to the bathroom.

Artie tells them he kept running into Donna in the elevator of his hotel, figured she was living in the elevator for want of anything better to do, and so he took her in. Artie has no use for her, though, so he thought he'd bring her over to them. Eddie asks what they would do with her. "What do you want to do with her?" Artie replies. He suggests that she would be useful to them. "Just to stay in practise. In case you run into a woman."

Eddie remarks that Donna is of no use or interest to Mickey, seeing as how he has got a real and true thing going with a terrific lady named Darlene. "You guys switched, or what?" says Artie, and he congratulates Mickey on having a serious relationship. "Except I ain't serious about anything, Artie, you know that," says Mickey in reply. Donna returns from the bathroom and it's settled —Donna more or less agrees to stay with Eddie and Mickey. (Of course, she'll continue to walk Artie's dog.)

This arranged, Artie is on his way to his appointment at the studio. If he's bubbly today, it's because things are looking very good on a certain project with a certain producer. Eddie asks if any money has changed hands; if it hasn't, then Artie may be riding for a fall. Artie doesn't like Eddie clouding his sunny day. Says Eddie, "But what I'm after here, I mean ultimately, is for your own good, for your clarity. You lose your clarity in this town next thing you know you're waking up in the middle of the night on the beach with dogs pissing on you, you think you're on vacation."

The name of the producer Artie is dealing with comes out—Herb Simon. Eddie practically howls in response. Herb Simon is a notorious shark, one the worst. Artie insists that Simon is changing his ways, he's looking to make a "turnaround into decency." Evidence? After lunch together one day ("He paid," says Artie), Simon turned to him with a sick look on his face. Artie asked him if the food was bad. "No," said Simon. "It's this town and all the lies it makes me tell."

Eddie is not impressed. "This fucking snake tells you he lies a lot, so you figure you can trust him?" Artie's bubbliness of a few moments ago has been replaced by a sinking feeling in the pit of his stomach. Furious at Eddie, he exits. "Do you think I was too hard on him?" Eddie asks Mickey. "No," says Mickey.

Donna returns, and, against a background haze of beer, dope and TV, she tells Mickey and Eddie a little about herself. She had hitched here from the Midwest with a friend. She moved into the elevator after the friend turned ugly. She overheard a lot of interesting things in the elevator. People talking about clothes and furnishings. "There was sometimes desperation, you couldn't get a handle on it," Donna editorializes. Then Artie found her and was nice to her. Mickey is pulling clothing off of her as she tries to make her serious points. Eddie looks at a record she's been carrying with her. It's one of her prize possessions, Willie Nelson singing standards such as "Stardust" and "All of Me." She is rhapsodizing on the record as Phil emerges in search of a valium.

Eddie introduces Donna, saying that Artie brought her by as a kind of "CARE package for people without serious relationships." As he says this, he takes Donna from Mickey. Mickey initially thinks this is some kind of a joke, but Eddie means what he is saying; as long as Eddie is around, he intends to see to it that Donna is not used by Mickey. Mickey is not amused. "I'll get her sometime you're not around," he tells Eddie. Eddie replies, "I can only do so much for you, Mickey. That'll be on your conscience." The three guys are oblivious to the fact that Donna is "a little stoned and scared" during this exchange. While Mickey sputters with frustration downstairs, Eddie and Phil retreat into Eddie's bedroom upstairs.

Scene 2

That night, Eddie opens the door and discovers Darlene in the house; she has taken the liberty of coming inside to wait for Mickey. Eddie and Darlene are awkward with each other. Darlene begins to hint that maybe she made a mistake getting involved with Mickey. Eddie seems to be torn between his desire to repair things with Darlene and to maintain the appearance of a cool ambivalence. This in turn annoys Darlene. She calls him down for "this total way you exaggerate this enchantment you have with uncertainty—the way you just prolong it and expect us all to think we ought to try and live in it, and it's meaningful. It's shit."

Eddie replies that he could pretend at certainty as well as anybody else, but he chooses instead to confess his confusion and ignorance when that is what is happening in his head. If that is too much for her to handle, maybe it's lucky for them that they found out before they got too far into a relationship.

The squabble continues along these lines until Mickey enters, groceries in arm and story in mouth. He has been standing outside listening to them squabble, and under the squabble he sensed real passion. In the face of real passion, and given the fact that he believes the source of what happened between him and Darlene to be his appearance of being "safe" (he's made no secret of the fact that he expects to go back to his wife and kids sooner or later), he thinks the thing for him to do is to get out of the way of something genuine.

We get the impression that most of this has been said for Eddie's benefit, and, this having been settled between the two of them, Darlene's feelings in the matter consist of a loose end to be tied up without too much hassle. Darlene seems to be trying to put her finger on what is wrong here, but Mickey doesn't give her a chance. With elegant glibness he says to her, "In all honesty, Darlene, you told me this is what you wanted in more ways than I cared to pay attention to." With that, he takes off, leaving Eddie and Darlene to figure out where they are. Eddie is awed by Mickey's performance.

EDDIE: . . . . . Where the hell did he come up with the . . . I mean, clarity to do that?

DARLENE: That wasn't clarity.

EDDIE *(turning to Darlene, he perches on the couch arm):* No, no, I mean, it wasn't clarity. But he had to HAVE clarity.

DARLENE: I don't know what it was. Generosity?

EDDIE: Whatever it was, you don't see it very often. I don't expect that from Mickey, I mean that kind of thing.

DARLENE: Who expects that from anybody? We're all so all over the place.

EDDIE: Self-absorbed.

DARLENE: And distracted. I'm distracted by everything. I mean, I'm almost always distracted, aren't you?

EDDIE: Absolutely.

DARLENE: Everything is always distracting me from everything else.

EDDIE: Everything is very distracting, but what I've really noticed is that mainly, the thing I'm most distracted by is myself. I mean, I'm my own major distraction, trying to get it together, to get my head together, my act together.

DARLENE: Our little minds just buzzzzzzzzz! What do they think they're doing?

EDDIE: However Mickey managed to get through it, though, I know one thing —I'm glad he did.

DARLENE: Are you really?

EDDIE: I really missed you. It was amazing. That was probably it—he got his clue from the fact that I never shut up about you. I think I was driving him crazy. How do you feel?

DARLENE: Great. I think I was, you know, into some form of obsession about you, too, some form of mental loop. I feel scared is what I feel. Good, too. I feel good, but mainly scared.

EDDIE: I'm scared.

DARLENE: I mean, a year ago, I was a basket case. If we had met a year ago, I wouldn't have had a prayer.

EDDIE: Me, too. A year ago, I was nuts. And I still have all kinds of things to think through. Stuff coming up, I have to think it through.

DARLENE: Me, too.

EDDIE: And by thinking, I don't mean just some ethereal mental thing either, but being with people is part of it, being with you is part of the thinking, that's how I'm doing the thinking, but I just have to go slow, there's a lot of scar tissue.

DARLENE: There's no rush, Eddie.

EDDIE: I don't want to rush.

DARLENE: I don't want to rush.

EDDIE: I can't rush. I'll panic. If I rush, I'll panic.

DARLENE: We'll just have to keep our hearts open, as best we can.

EDDIE: No pressure.

DARLENE: And no guilt, okay?

EDDIE: No guilt.

DARLENE: We don't want any guilt. I mean, I'm going to be out of town a lot. We both have lives.

EDDIE: We just have to keep our options open.

DARLENE: And our hearts, okay?

EDDIE: I mean, the right attitude . . .

DARLENE: Exactly. If we have the right attitude . . .

EDDIE: Attitude is so important. And by attitude I don't mean just attitude either, but I mean real emotional space.

DARLENE: We both need space.

EDDIE: And time. We have to have time.

DARLENE: Right. So we can just take the time to allow the emotional space for things to grow and work themselves out.

EDDIE: So you wanna go fuck?

> *They kiss and the music starts: Willie Nelson singing "Someone to Watch Over Me." Blackout.*
>
> *Author's note: It might be that as the scene progresses they end up on the couch, undressing each other as they conduct their negotiations; or perhaps it is more strictly a negotiation between them. Or perhaps it is a combination, so that each time there is a sense of the negotiations being completed so that physical contact can begin—an embrace, a kiss —some bit of outstanding business is then remembered, and one or the other moves away.*

Scene 3

The next day, late afternoon, Phil enters the house to find Donna simultaneously reading a magazine, watching TV and listening to her Willie Nelson record. Phil carries provisions for an afternoon of watching football on TV. Assuming Eddie is upstairs, he begins to beef about Donna's being constantly around and underfoot. Donna informs him that he's yelling to nobody, she's the only one there. Phil's reaction is one of contempt and hostility—and something else. There is something decidedly scary about Phil. He seems to be reacting to stimuli unnoticed by anybody else, and the reactions carry the promise of violence.

Donna gets a bit of a reprieve when Eddie shows up. Phil begins to complain about and to Donna. "I come here to see Eddie, you gotta be here. I wanna watch the football game and talk over some very important issues which pertain to my life, you gotta be here. What the fuck makes you tick?"

Eddie tells them that Darlene will be by soon. If she does come by, he would appreciate it if Phil would introduce Donna as his "ditz." Eddie goes up to his room to change. Donna begins to ask about Darlene. Phil tells Donna he doesn't want even to see her. She distracts him. She is demolishing his privacy. He's trying to think seriously about football and about some problems he is facing, and her tight, scanty clothing makes it impossible for him to think about anything but "tits and ass." Doesn't she know how disruptive she's being?

Donna's non-linear reply is that she likes football. She'd like to watch the game with him. This sets something off in Phil. He insists she doesn't know anything about the game, and, to underscore the point, he grabs her head between his hands and *"butts his head into hers."* She begins to howl from the pain.

The sound brings Eddie out of his room to find out what's going on. Donna tells Eddie that Phil hit her. Phil protests that he was just trying to teach her something about football. Furious, Donna grabs her record and runs upstairs to the bathroom, slamming the door behind her.

Eddie makes a further attempt to find out what happened. Phil says it happened so fast he doesn't know. And he has news for Eddie: he's going back to Susie. "I can't stand it," says Phil. "The loneliness. And some form of totally unusual and unpredictable insanity is creeping up on me about to do I don't know WHAT —God forbid I find out." Maybe if he and Susie were actually to have a kid as Susie's been pressuring them to do . . . Phil could almost get behind that, except he's afraid. He has mental pictures of the baby putting a gun to his—Phil's—head and blowing him away.

It sounds to Eddie as though this question is what has been under all of Phil's and Susie's fights lately. What would be best, as he sees it, would be for them to put aside the idea of the kid until they get some clarity on the issues between them in the marriage. Phil agrees that probably would be best, except Susie seems to absolutely need to have a kid. Phil has tried to dissuade her: "Because, you know, I got three kids, two little boys and a girl who are now, you know, I don't know how old, in Toledo, I haven't seen 'em since I went to prison. I don't want any more kids out there, rollin' around their beds at night with this sick fucking hatred of me. I can't stand it."

Eddie says that if he feels that way, he should definitely not have a kid until the marriage is in shape. "I mean," says Eddie, "no kid and a divorce is who-gives-a-fuck, but you have a kid and it's seismic. A big ten on the Richter scale. Carnage, man, that's what I'm sayin', gore on the highway. Add in the kid and it's a major disaster." (He and Phil are now passing a joint back and forth, which further contributes to the groping nature of the conversation, the missed connections.)

Phil can't just go back and trust to luck that Susie won't get pregnant. He's got that covered—he's taking some kind of medication to decimate his sperm count. Eddie is appalled by this news. Phil can't go on poisoning himself like this. He should face Susie, tell her what he's been doing, get things straight between them. Phil agrees that's what he should do.

PHIL: Without a doubt. And I'm going to do it, I just want to know what kind of latitude I have regarding our friendship if my mind gets changed.

EDDIE: Listen to me—are you a deaf man? Am I only under the delusion that I'm speaking? What you're telling me is a horror story—one part of you is begging another part to stop, but you don't hear you. But I do, I hear—you have got to stop, Phil.

PHIL: I know this, Eddie. But what if I can't? Give me some sort of hint regarding your reaction, so I know.

EDDIE: What's she do, hypnotize you? Is this voodoo? You're a grown man. You have asked me to tell you. I'm telling you: "Tell her!"

PHIL: You're not answering my question. I'm talking about our friendship here!

EDDIE: You're switching the goddamn subject is what you're doing.

PHIL: What the hell are you talking about? Why are you avoiding my question?

EDDIE: Our friendship doesn't matter here. Our friendship is totally, categorically, one hundred percent irrelevant here.

PHIL: Eddie, listen to yourself! This is our friendship—this conversation—these very exchanges. We are in our friendship. What could be more important?

EDDIE: I mean, I don't feel . . . What?
PHIL: Scorn, You feel scorn for me.
EDDIE: No.
PHIL: It's in your eyes.

Phil accuses Eddie of harboring dark thoughts. Phil wants Eddie to focus on him, on their friendship, on the deep trouble he's in. The intensity of Phil's desperation combined with the dope is having a disorienting effect on Eddie. "I feel like you're drillin' little fuckin' chunks of cottage cheese into my brain. I'm gettin' confused here, Phil, I tol' you, I don't feel good." But Phil presses on, more intensely and less coherently than before.

PHIL: . . . . . Cynicism has nothing to do with it, Eddie, I've done my best. The fucking thing is without a clue, except the mess it leaves behind it, the guts and gore. What I'm sayin' is, if my conclusion is contrary to your wishes, at least give me the fucking consideration and respect that you know that at least from my point of view it is based on solid thought and rock hard evidence that has led me to I have no other choice, so you got no right to fuck with me about it. I want your respect, Eddie. *(He ends leaning intently toward Eddie on the couch.)*
EDDIE: You got that, Phil.
PHIL: I do?
EDDIE: Don't you know that? I'm just sayin'—all I'm sayin' is, "Don't have the baby thoughtlessly."
PHIL: Eddie, for godsake, don't terrify me that you have paid no attention! If I was thoughtless would I be here? I feel like I have pushed through to the brink where it is just noise and of no more use than a headful of car horns, because the bottom line here that I'm getting at is just this—I got to go back to her. I got to go back to Susie, and if it means havin' a kid, I got to do it. I mean, I have hit a point where I am going round the bend several times a day now, and so far I been on the other side to meet me, but one a these days it might be one time too many, and who knows who might be there waitin'? If not me, who? . . . . . No, I need my marriage. I come here to tell you. I got to stay married. I'm lost without her.

Donna reappears, all of her meager belongings in tow. She's leaving. "You can just walk your own dog, and fuck yourselves. These particular tits and ass are taking a hike." Eddie, looking quite ill, watches her storm out of the house and slam the door behind her.

ACT II

One night a year later, Eddie and Mickey are lounging—Eddie downstairs and Mickey on the balcony—as Phil and Artie tell about Phil's latest exploit (to which Artie was exuberant witness): Phil punching out some jerk. What started it? The jerk in question was talking to a homely woman as though she was gorgeous. "You don't talk to some dog in the manner he's talking. It's disgusting!" says Phil.

So he told the jerk to shut up, the jerk didn't, so Phil hit him with a punch that smashed him against a wall, where he hung for a second, as if magnetized, before crashing to the floor.

Artie reports with amazement that the guy somehow managed to get up again, at which point Phil belted him again. Phil has some regrets about belting him the second time, being of the opinion, in retrospect, that the guy probably did not intend to pose a threat. Probably he did not even know where he was, but, as Artie says, got up and came toward Phil as a matter of reflex. Phil hitting him again could also be seen as a matter of reflex. "So," says Phil, "we are both victims of our reflexes." "So," says Mickey, "this is a tragedy here."

The elation of telling the story is gone for Phil. As he does some coke, he broods about coming to understand things too late ". . . . . so the realizations can serve no useful purpose on earth but to torment me with the thought that I am a merciless, totally out of control prick." Artie tells him he just has "violent karma."

PHIL: Yeh, well, I am running out of patience with being good for nothing but whacking people in the face they do some irrelevant thing that drives me nuts. If this is my karma, to be an asshole and have such a thing as this, fuck it.

MICKEY (rising languidly to his feet): Absolutely, right; fuck destiny, fate and all metaphysical stuff.

PHIL (bolting to the base of the stairway where he glares up at Mickey): You, you cynical bastard, watch the fine line you are walking between my self-awareness and my habitual trend to violence. 'Cause on the one hand I might appear worried, but on the other I could give a fuck, you know, and my urge to annihilate anyone might just fixate on you.

MICKEY (descending the stairs toward a bottle of Scotch by the TV): And the vortex get me—fling me, you might say, wallward, magnetically.

PHIL: Exactly. So you can help us both out by watching your goddamn, you know—right? Am I making myself clear?

MICKEY (slipping by Phil): Step.

Eddie suggests that there is a relation between the birth of Phil's baby, the divorce papers he's just signed and the black, violent mood he's in. He further suggests that the first step to getting it together would be for Phil to acknowledge this connection. Phil replies that he understands this connection and his reasons. "My point is that I am wired beyond my reasons. I know my reasons, but I am wired beyond them."

Mickey makes another sarcastic comment. Phil overcomes his urge to work Mickey over and instead turns to Artie, asking for "hard data on this karma stuff." Is there something in this that could be of use to him?

ARTIE: Hey, you know, past lives, you have past lives and the karmic stuff accrues to it. You have debits and credits and you have to work your way out from under the whole thing, so you—

MICKEY: Artie! This is not your investment counselor we're talking about here.

EDDIE: This is not cosmic Visa, Artie.

Mickey and Eddie are both laughing now—Mickey, wanting fun and to keep Phil from being taken seriously by anyone, and Eddie because he is irritated that Phil seems more interested in Artie's opinions than in the advice Eddie himself has tried to give.

ARTIE: We could be in the process of working out the debits and credits of our past lives with the very way we relate to each other at this very instant. It could be that Phil owes some affection to me, I owe him some guidance, and—

EDDIE *(laughing even more now. Mickey and Eddie both breaking up):* Guidance?

MICKEY: The fact that you're talking, Artie, does not necessarily make it destiny speaking, I hope you know this.

ARTIE: And you two pricks owe some negative shit to everybody.

PHIL: Artie, he's right. You make it sound like the cosmos is in your opinion this loan shark. This is disappointing.

ARTIE: You asked me.

PHIL: Because I thought you might know. . . . . .

MICKEY: You disappointed him, Artie. You built him up, you disappointed him.

ARTIE: It happens.

MICKEY: He's at a critical juncture in his life, here.

ARTIE: Who isn't?

EDDIE: You guys need to get laid.

MICKEY: You, however, don't, huh?

EDDIE: I am, in fact, sustaining a meaningful relationship.

ARTIE *(irritated that Eddie and Mickey have teased him, he thinks he will tease back, snapping out his real feelings):* The only thing sustaining that relationship is the fact that she's out of town two out of every three weeks.

EDDIE *(Glaring at Artie):* Well, she's in town tomorrow.

Attention turns to the task of finding an available female for Phil. As Eddie makes the first of several attempts to reach a likely prospect named Bonnie, Phil explains his usual way of attracting interest from the ladies—something about carrying a vibrator with him and pulling it out to show that he's up for anything; except earlier this evening the vibrator routine didn't work terribly well. He's been trying to pick up a lady and so pulled out the vibrator, but, unbeknownst to him, he'd broken it. Consequently the thing whirred and whined in a demented fashion, not making the impression he intended.

ARTIE: This thing's goin', arrrggghhh, arrrghhh. Phil's sayin, "Want to come home with me?"

PHIL: Arrghhhhh, arghhh, want to come home with me? *(Eddie, on the stool by the phone, stares at Phil.)*

EDDIE: You really did this, Phil?

PHIL: Yeah.

EDDIE: Listen to me. You're a rare human being . . . . . I mean, it's unique; this goddamn imagination. You could channel it.

PHIL: I have thoughts sometimes they could break my head open.

EDDIE: Whata you mean?

PHIL: I mean, these big thoughts. These big goddamn thoughts. I don't know what to do with them.

EDDIE: This is what I'm saying: if you could channel them into your talent. I mean, under all this crazed bullshit you've been forced to develop—

PHIL: I get desperate. I feel like my thoughts are all just going to burst out of my head and leave me; they're going to pick me up and throw me around the room. I fight with them. It's a bloodbath this monster I have with my thoughts. Maybe if I channeled them.

EDDIE: I never took you so seriously before. I mean, quite so seriously.

PHIL: Me neither.

Eddie tells Phil he's going to love Bonnie. She dances artistically in a club, which is to say naked and with a balloon. "And," says Eddie, "the best part about her is that she's up for anything," which gives rise to a story about when Eddie and Mickey arranged for her to go with them to the airport to meet an actor named Robbie Rattigan. Robbie was up for a part in a pilot and was nervous, and Bonnie was assigned to take care of his nerves, which she did in the back seat of the car. As they laugh at the memory of the expression on Robbie's face as Bonnie unzipped his fly, Bonnie answers Eddie's call. Eddie's invitation is swiftly made and accepted.

The phone call finished, another detail from the story comes back to Eddie and Mickey: while Bonnie was relaxing Robbie in the back seat, her six-year old daughter was on the verge of freaking in the front seat with Mickey and Eddie. The two guys had tried to take care of the kid.

EDDIE: . . . . . We ended up, I'm holdin' her, we're tellin' her these goddamn stories, remember? She was there. We were makin' up this story about elves and shit, and this kingdom full of wild rabbits, and the elves were getting stomped to death by gangs of wild rabbits.

MICKEY: Jungle Bunnies, I think, is what we called them.

EDDIE: Fuck. Everywhere I turn I gotta face my own depravity. Jungle Bunnies are stomping elves to death so the elves start to hang them. Is that the story?

MICKEY: Yeah. And we're doin' the voices. (Now they are moaning and pounding their heads on the counter in a mix of mock and real remorse.)

EDDIE: I don't wanna think about it. High-pitched, right?

MICKEY: Yeah, high-pitched . . .

MICKEY and EDDIE: And rural!

EDDIE: The kid was catatonic. I think maybe that was it, Mickey; we turned the corner in this venture.

MICKEY: Right. What venture?

EDDIE: Life. That was the nose dive. I mean, where it began. We veered at that moment into utter irredeemable depravity. (As they collapse upon the counter.)

MICKEY: I feel sick to my stomach about myself. A little. That I could do that. How could I do that?

PHIL (leaping to his feet): Hey! You guys! Don't get crazy! You had a WHIM.

This is what happens to people. THEY HAVE WHIMS. So you're sittin' around, Robbie's comin'. You want him to like you, you want him to think well of you. So you have this whim. Did she have to do it? Did anybody twist her arm? *(Mickey and Eddie have straightened slowly.)*

MICKEY: Phil's right, Eddie. What'd we do? I mean, objectively. Did anybody say, "Bring your kid."

EDDIE: It's the airwaves.

MICKEY: Exactly.

But then, on some level, it wasn't Bonnie's fault either. After all, says Eddie, she watches so much TV that the opportunity to get it on with one of the gods from the tube in their back seat could not be resisted.

Bonnie arrives. Eddie digs out some coke for her, as she tells them what a godsend the invitation was. "Doom and gloom have come to sit in my household like some permanent kind of domestic appliance . . . . . I was in mortal longing for someone to call me. I was totally without hope of ever having worthwhile companionship tonight, a decent fucking conversation."

While she talks, Phil puts his arm around her. She wonders casually whether Phil's attentions portend anything sexual. The general reply from the guys is that the possibility exists, but there isn't any particular agenda.

Bonnie takes in the fact that everybody present is by now ripped on something or other. This leads her to explain the constant busy signal Eddie kept getting when he was phoning her—some guy who kept tying up her line with his un-wanted attentions. Phil says that if she tells him who was annoying her, he could make a persuasive case for him to stop. Bonnie finds the threat of violence on her behalf sort of appealing. Artie warns her that Phil is dangerous "in ways you can't imagine." Bonnie doubts that. Bonnie continues to explain about the guy who was bothering her. He's involved with her girl friend Sarah, they're both into EST, and they have been carrying on a campaign to get her to give up drugs. "They will not shut up about it. So I am trying to make to this guy what is for me an obvious point, which is that unlike those who have lost their minds to EST, I am a normal person: I need my drugs!" Everybody's into drugs, she told them—doctors and lawyers even, all snorting up a storm. But they were unmoved by her logic, so she gave them a razz and hung up the phone, at which point Eddie's call came like a miracle. And so here she is.

And now she is more or less informed that she's here for Phil. Though this wasn't quite what she had in mind when she came over, it's okay by her. Does Phil want to go upstairs? No. Phil's in the mood to go out. So Phil and Bonnie go in her car. They'll be back in a little while.

Artie takes the opportunity of Phil's absence to get something off of his chest. Why is it Eddie gives Phil special treatment? Eddie says that he and Phil have "a kind of intuitive thing," and that Artie shouldn't get too upset. But Artie is very upset because Eddie prefers this pathetic nut case to him. Eddie reacts with a distance informed by mockery, which only makes Artie angrier. Artie heads for the bathroom, expressing his intention to leave this place and possibly the friend-ship shortly after he finishes his business in the john. Artie now gone, Eddie looks to Mickey for clarification.

MICKEY *(unmoving):* I think what he was trying to get at is that he, you know, considers your investment in Phil, which is in his mind sort of disproportionate and maybe even—and mind you, this is Artie's thought, not mine—but maybe even fraudulent and secretly self-serving on your part. So you know, blah-blah-blah, rapateta—that this investment is based on the fact that Phil is very safe because no matter how far you manage to fall, Phil will be lower. You end up crawling along the sidewalk, Phil's gonna be on his belly in the gutter looking up in wide-eyed admiration.

   Bolting upright, Eddie heads for the couch, where he grabs up a bottle.

EDDIE: This is what Artie thinks.

MICKEY *(getting slowly to his feet now, he starts dressing to go out with Artie: putting on a belt, tucking in a shirt putting on his shoes):* Yeah. And it hurts his feelings because, you know, he'd like to think he might be capable of an eyeball-to-eyeball relationship with you based not necessarily on equality, but on, nevertheless, some real affinity—and if not the actuality, at least the possibility of respect. So your, you know, decision, or whatever—compulsion—to shortchange yourself, in his estimation, and hang out with Phil is for him a genuine disappointment, which you just saw the manifestation of.

EDDIE *(has been drinking quite a bit throughout the evening and is now taking in great quantities, throwing his head back to drink from the bottle):* That was his hurt feelings.

MICKEY: Yeah.

EDDIE: What's everybody on my case for all of a sudden?

MICKEY: Nobody's on your case.

EDDIE: What do you think you're doing, then, huh? What is this? What was Artie doing?

MICKEY *(having descended the stairs, he is now sitting down in the armchair, putting on his shoes):* You have maybe some misconceptions is all, first of all about how smart you are. And then maybe even if you are as smart as you think you are, you have some misconception about what that entitles you to regarding your behavior to other human beings. Such facts being pointed out is what's going on here, that's all. Don't take it personally.

EDDIE: What would make you mad, Mickey? . . . . . You're just too laid back for human tolerance sometimes, Mickey. A person wonders if you really care.

MICKEY: I get excited.

EDDIE: You have it figured somehow. What's it according to—some schematic arrangement—grids of sophistication—what's the arrangement by which you assess what's what so you are left utterly off the hook?

MICKEY: It's a totally unconscious process. . . . .

EDDIE: That's the fucking bottom line, though, huh, nobody's going to take substantial losses in order to align and endure with what are totally peripheral —I mean, transient elements in their life. I mean, we all know we don't mean shit in one another's eyes, finally.

Artie emerges from the john, and he and Mickey suggest that Eddie join them for a change of scene that will maybe result in a change of tone in the evening. Eddie begs off. He thinks he'll just spend a quiet evening at home

Judith Ivey (*foreground,* as Bonnie) with Jerry Stiller and Harvey
Keitel (*background*) in a scene from *Hurlyburly*

yelling at his TV. The guys exchange a few final insults, and then Eddie is
alone.

On the heels of their exit, Eddie gets a phone call from Agnes, his ex-wife. This
conversation does not go all that well either. He is in the middle of yelling at her
when Bonnie enters, bruised and scratched and limping. Eddie hangs up the
phone to find out where Phil is.

Bonnie is not too moved by Eddie's concern about Phil, as Phil is the reason
for her condition, having just tossed her out of a moving car. *Her* moving car,
in fact. She takes Eddie to task for setting her up with someone who could do
such a thing. Someone so patently crazy and dangerous. She continues to rail at
him as she removes her skirt and pantyhouse in order to see to her scrapes and
bruises. She questions the wisdom of staying friends with Eddie, given the lack
of even a warning from him about Phil's disposition. Eddie, who is *"reacting
increasingly as a little boy,"* doesn't pick up any of Bonnie's cues to express
concern for her. Rather, he asks what Bonnie did to make Phil throw her out.
Dressing again, she insists that she did nothing, certainly nothing to justify

violence. Mainly she tried to be agreeable and get along with him so that there would be some human element to the sex they were going to have. But he started interpreting perfectly innocent comments as signs of hostility. His paranoia built to the point where he was screaming at her and pushing her out of the car. Eddie explains that Phil has been having his difficulties. Bonnie snaps back, "Eddie, it's a rough century all the way around—you say so yourself, Eddie. Who does anybody know who is doing okay? So this is some sort of justification for us all to start pushing each other out of cars?—things aren't working out personally the way we planned?"

Eddie replies that Phil has been experiencing a "form of desperation you are maybe not familiar with it." Bonnie knows that she doesn't exactly bask in the sunshine of Eddie's respect, but she is "a form of human being like any other," and she's trying to support herself and a kid in a mean town by dancing naked with a balloon in front of crowds of frequently terrifying strangers. Such a position, she figures, puts her on regular acquaintance with desperation, making his exposition of same unnecessary. "I'm gonna level with you, Eddie," she says, "I came here for a ride home and an apology."

But Eddie is not forthcoming with either. He points out that Bonnie doesn't discriminate much about who she has sex with, so where does she get off hitting him with recriminations for having set her up with Phil?

BONNIE: He coulda hurt me, Eddie.

EDDIE (*trying to stand up*): I don't care!

BONNIE: Don't tell me that.

EDDIE (*careens backward against the stairway and bounces forward onto the floor on his hands and knees*): You're just some bitch who thinks it matters that you run around with balloons and your tits out. Nobody's going to take substantial losses over what are totally peripheral, totally transient elements. You know, we're all just background in one another's life. Cardboard cutouts bumping around in this vague, you know, hurlyburly, this spin-off of what was once prime-time life; so don't hassle me about this interpersonal fuck-up on the highway, okay? (*Having struggled to the sink, he is putting water on his face.*)

BONNIE: You oughta have some pity.

EDDIE: I'm savin' it.

BONNIE: For your buddies.

EDDIE: For myself.

Now Phil returns. Bonnie, furious at him, yet still afraid, backs away. Phil tells her he knows he flipped out and he's sorry. She has every right to call the cops if she wants. He tries to explain himself to Eddie, but Eddie has finally lost patience. He went out of his way for Phil, and the result is everybody's mad at him. Phil says he knows he's got to take the energy that fuels his craziness and channel it into his work, his acting. Eddie tells him he has no real work. He's nothing more than a prop to be used to make garbage on TV look legitimate.

PHIL: What about my, you know, talent; you said I ought to . . . you know . . . Remember?

EDDIE *(moving to slump down in the rocking chair):* That was hype . . . . .

PHIL: You mean, all that you said about how I oughta, you know, have some faith in myself, it wasn't true.

EDDIE: Whata you think? Did you ever really believe it?

PHIL: Yeah. Sorta.

EDDIE: Not really. No.

PHIL: Well, you know. No.

EDDIE: So who we been kiddin'?

PHIL: Me. We been kiddin' me. *(Moving nearer to Eddie now.)* But this is the real goods . . . now, right? I mean, we're gettin' to the real goods now.

EDDIE: Yeah.

PHIL: So you musta decided it would be best for me to hear the truth.

EDDIE: Naw.

PHIL: So I could try and straighten myself out.

> *By this eerie, unrelenting positiveness, Phil seems to be almost demanding an escalation from Eddie.*

EDDIE: I'm just sick of you, Phil.

PHIL: Oh. How long you been sick of me? It's probably recent.

EDDIE: No.

PHIL: So it's been a long time . . . So what caused it?

EDDIE: I'm gonna let you off the hook now, Phil. I'm not gonna say any more.

But Phil presses him for causes, reasons. What about him disgusts Eddie? "Everything," says Eddie. "You really had me fooled, Eddie," says Phil. Eddie tells him that was the point. And now, very drunk and very depressed, Eddie launches into a speech about the immoral nature of the neutron bomb, which broadens into a general diatribe about the evils of a society that has allowed the growth of its technology to outpace the development of any ethical sense to handle it.

BONNIE: Yeah, well, Eddie, it's no reason to be mean to your friends.

EDDIE: Says you.

BONNIE: Exactly.

EDDIE: You want me to have reasons? I got to have fucking reasons? *(Suddenly woozy, Eddie is trying to move away, collapsing onto his hands and knees and crawling.)* And you probably want me to say them, don't you. And you probably want them to be the right reasons and I say them. They're whores, don't you know that? Logic is a slut. Be consoled that inasmuch as you are indiscreet you are logical.

Phil leaves to get something from the car as Eddie continues. He will not make the effort to behave better. He chooses instead to be a thing. "I will be a thing and loved; a thing and live."

Bonnie wonders at the way he's transformed himself from being someone she admired to this pitiful heap lying at her feet on the floor. Isn't he supposed to be having this great mutually fulfilling thing with Darlene? Supposedly is right. "My girl friend doesn't love me," says Eddie. She is a photographer, and she takes every out-of-town assignment offered to her, which indicates something to him. But even if he's wrong, even if she *does* love him, he doesn't *feel* loved.

Bonnie decides that it's time to go home, at which point Artie and Mickey return and enquire how her date with Phil went. Bonnie tells them all to go to hell. Over her objection, Eddie tells them that Phil threw her out of the car. Artie asks what she's doing tomorrow—She's taking her kid to Disneyland. Artie would like to join them. Her irritation at him abates, and the date is made. She leaves. "So she likes to be thrown out of cars," says Phil.

Phil enters carrying his baby daughter. He stole her away while his ex-wife was asleep. The guys look at the baby, remarking on her resemblance to Phil. It's a resemblance Phil doesn't see himself. He passes the baby to Mickey, who quickly passes her to Artie.

EDDIE *(Taking the baby):* Ohh, she's real cute. What's happenin', little baby? Makes me miss my kid, huh?

ARTIE: Makes me miss my kid.

MICKEY: I got two of 'em.

EDDIE: This really makes me hate my ex-wife. *(Eddie laughs a little, and looks at Mickey, who laughs.)* I mean, I really hate my ex-wife. *(Now they start to make jokes, trying to break each other up, and top each other, all except, of course, Phil.)*

ARTIE: And this little innocent thing here, this sweet little innocent thing is a broad of the future.

MICKEY: Hard to believe, huh?

EDDIE: Awesome.

ARTIE: Depressing.

EDDIE: Maybe if we kept her and raised her, she could grow up and be a decent human being.

MICKEY: Unless it's just biologically and genetically inevitable that at a certain age they go nasty.

PHIL: Except for the great ones.

MICKEY: The great ones come along once in a lifetime.

ARTIE: Not in my lifetime.

PHIL: Like the terrific athletes of any given generation, there's only a few.

MICKEY: You think it might be wise or unwise to pay attention to the implications of what we're saying here?

As Artie takes the baby again, Phil says maybe he'll ask Susie to take him back for one more try. "I'll take the kid back. I'll beg her. I can beg." As if to deny the harsh things Eddie has said to Phil, Eddie speaks again of what Phil could be if he would just channel his potential. Phil pulls away from Eddie, talks of losing three days last week just driving around. He has to get Susie to take him back.

A startled cry from Artie. He passes the baby back to Phil. "Yeah, well, she's a broad already, Phil," he says. "Just like every other broad I ever met, she hadda dump on me."

ACT III

Scene 1

Several days later, in early evening, Eddie enters to find Mickey and Darlene sharing a joke. Echoes from the awkward situation from the first act make them all uncomfortable for a second. Eddie's received some frantic messages from Phil, and he's worried. He asks Mickey if Phil has called. Not that Mickey's aware of, no. From the ensuing conversation, it is apparent that Phil did indeed go back to Susie, but that it again hasn't been working out. Mickey decides to remove himself and leave Eddie and Darlene alone.

Eddie suggests to Darlene that they stick around a little in case Phil calls. Phil would be in an easier situation if it weren't for the fact of his little girl. He could leave Susie without a hassle, but for the baby. Eddie understands some of what Phil feels. "I mean, my little girl is a factor in every calculation I make—big or small—she's a constant. You can imagine, right?"

Darlene thinks she has some sense of what Eddie's talking about. She was once pregnant. Not knowing which of two guys was the father, she had an abortion. The image of the potential person she robbed the world of haunted her for awhile. In fact, she had what sounds like a nervous breakdown. It took a trip to Puerto Rico to bring her back to a vaguely functional mode.

All this happened seven and a half years ago, but Darlene brought it up to indicate that she has some inkling of the parental feelings Eddie was referring to. Eddie, believing for the moment that they are making a true connection with each other, tells her that everybody carries emotional baggage and that you have to find a way to acknowledge it's there without being overwhelmed by it. He asks about the two guys she was going with when the pregnancy happened, wondering if they knew each other. She says no, why does he ask? Eddie speculates that maybe there's a pattern there—a pattern having to do with two guys. She is upset. She was talking about something else entirely, and here he's picking up on something "totally off the wall, and hostile." Eddie says she shouldn't get offended, he was only making a mental association that might have been worth exploring: "I mean, if we don't talk these things out, we'll just end up with all this, you know, unspoken shit, following us around."

Darlene is hungry. Eddie asks where she'd prefer to go, to a Chinese place called Mr. Chou's or to Ma Maison. She doesn't care which: "Honestly, Eddie, I like them both the same. I like them both exactly the same." He says that's impossible, how can she like them the same? They aren't the same thing. "I mean, what is the world, one big blur to you out there in which everything that bears some resemblance to something else is just automatically put at the same level in your hierarchy, for chrissake, Darlene, the only thing they have in common is that they're both restaurants!" With some heat he tells her she seems to be incapable of making "the most rudimentary sort of distinction." Why is she doing this? What is behind this attitude of hers? Darlene tells him he's paranoid.

EDDIE: I'm supposed to trust your judgment of my mental stability? I'm supposed to trust your evaluation of the nuances of my sanity? You can't even tell the difference between a French and a Chinese restaurant!

DARLENE: I like them both.

EDDIE: But they're different. One is French, and the other is Chinese. They are totally fucking different.

DARLENE: Not in my inner, subjective, emotional experience of them.

EDDIE: The tastes, the decors, the waiters, the accents. The fucking accents. The little phrases the waiters say. And they yell at each other in these whole totally different languages, does none of this make an impression on you?

DARLENE: It impresses me that I like them both.

EDDIE: Your total inner emotional subjective experience must be THIS EPIC FUCKING FOG! I mean, what are you on, some sort of dualistic trip and everything is in twos and you just can't tell which is which so you're just pulled taut between them on this goddamn high wire between people who might like to have some kind of definitive reaction from you in order to know!

DARLENE: Fuck you!

EDDIE: What's wrong with that?

DARLENE: Is that what this is all about? Those two guys. I happened to mention two guys!

EDDIE: I just want to know if this is a pattern. Chinese restaurants and you can't tell the difference between people. *(They stand, staring at each other.)*

And we begin to get the sense that indeed something is going on with Darlene. She starts to make moves toward disengagement, saying she likes him, but . . . Eddie can see where this is going and changes course, trying to deflect her from what he can sense is an imminent kiss-off. He tries to explain that some of his negative behavioral stuff is residue from his bizarre childhood with extremely strict, religious parents. The phone starts to ring as Darlene says she has heard this before. Whatever he went through, as far as she's concerned it doesn't enter into what's going on now with them. "I don't care," she says. He presses her on the subject, she says that it doesn't matter. Eddie yells "Hold on," into the phone and grabs Darlene. "No, no: it matters and you care," he tells her. "What you mean is, it doesn't make any difference." She rails at him for his obsessive semantic games.

But he's no longer focussed on their conversation. Something he's being told on the phone now takes all of his attention. He tells the person on the other end that he'll be right over and hangs up. Darlene can sense something is terribly wrong. Eddie tells her that Phil is dead. He got killed in his car. Darlene tries to tell Eddie how sorry she is, but he *"gives her a look and goes,"* leaving her alone.

Scene 2

One evening several days later, Eddie, Mickey and Artie are returning from Phil's funeral. Mickey notes that Phil's agent didn't even show up. The day has thoroughly bummed out Artie. Trying to banish depression, he focuses on tomorrow, which he claims will bring with it a lot of meetings and a development deal —encouraging stuff. Talking about this, Artie has a touch of his old naive vigor again. With a smile, Eddie tells him to be sure and come by after he's finished. Artie says he will and takes off, leaving Eddie and Mickey alone.

Eddie begins to look through the day's mail. It contains a hell of a surprise: a letter from Phil. It reads: "The guy who dies in an accident understands the nature of destiny. Phil." It was mailed on the day Phil died. This is Phil's testament, says Eddie. This is the message he wanted to leave them with.

Mickey doesn't want to get into whatever the message may or may not (probably not) mean. Phil is dead, and no message he has to convey posthumously can be of any value or interest to him. Mickey has little sympathy for Phil even in death. He believes the guy had enough to live for, and if he chose for his own demented reasons to drive like a maniac in the middle of the night down Mulholland Drive and rack himself up, that's too bad, but it's over, and it should be put into the past.

Eddie won't let it go. He must understand why, and he believes that the key to why is in Phil's note.

MICKEY: What why? There's no why in a disaster like this. You know, the earth moved. He was in the wrong place; this big hole opens up, what's he gonna do?

EDDIE: Your attitude, Mickey—will you please examine your fucking attitude?

MICKEY: This is a dead end is all I'm saying. There's no traffic with this thing. You go in, you don't come out. The guy made a decision beyond communication.

EDDIE *(waving the note at Mickey, who grabs it):* He left a note.

MICKEY: The note is tangential. It's part of his goof, you know, that he was a rational human being, when he wasn't. *(Balling up the note, he throws it on the floor.)* I want no part of this fucking, beyond-the-grave extension of his jerk-off sensibility.

EDDIE *(grabbing the note up protectively, he smooths it out on the kitchen counter in preparation to study it):* The note is what he wanted us to think.

MICKEY: Bullshit.

EDDIE: He left it.

MICKEY: To drive us nuts from long distance. Lemme see that—what is this?
   Mickey grabs the note and paces around while Eddie, sitting on the swivel chair on the living room side of the counter, focuses on the dictionary.

EDDIE: I'm gonna look up the words.

MICKEY: It's a fucking fortune cookie. What's to look up? "A guy who." That's him. "Dies." In case we don't know, he gave us a demonstration. "Accident" is to propel yourself into a brief but unsustainable orbit, and then attempt to land in a tree on the side of a cliff-like incline. "Understand" is what he had no part of. "Nature" is the tree, and "destiny" is, if you're him, you're an asshole.

Eddie considers trying to crack the meaning of the note through anagrams. Mickey insists there is no code, no meaning to crack. Eddie tells him to stop being sarcastic. Mickey isn't being "sarcastic," he's being "flip." There's a difference. "Flip" is much lighter than "sarcastic." "Sarcastic is 'heavy,'" says Mickey. "It's mean. Funny, sure, but mean. I do both, but this was flip."

Eddie has looked up all the words in the note in the dictionary and come up with a rewording: "If you die in a happening that is not expected, foreseeon or intended, you understand the inevitable or necessary succession of events."

Mickey rejects the idea that this has any meaning, either in and of itself or in relation to what happened to Phil. The evidence is that Phil did what he did on purpose, which makes it not an accident which makes the note irrelevant. But what, Eddie asks, brought Phil to the point of having an accident on purpose? Mickey observes, "It's not that big a deal—that's the fucking truth, you know, you make an adjustment, that's all—you shift your point a view a little and what was horrible looks okay. All the necessary information that might deter you gets locked away. Little gremlins divert the good thoughts so you don't hear them. You just hear the bad thoughts, which at this point are convincing you they're a good idea. *(Rising, loosening his tie, taking off his jacket, Mickey moves toward the kitchen.)* You get an idea, that's all. You don't understand the scope of it; you just lose the scope of it. So there you are, foot's on the gas, you're flying. So far so good. No big deal. Road, trees, radio. What's a little flick of the steering wheel? Maybe an inch's rotation. Nothing to it. An inch, what's that? So you do it. *(From the cabinets he grabs a bowl and a box of Cheerios.)* But with that, what? You've gone beyond what you can come back from. You've handed control over now, it's gravity and this big machine, which is a car, who are in charge now. Only it's not a car anymore. It's this hunk of metal rearranging itself according to the laws of physics, force and reaction, stress and resistance; heat, friction, collapse, and then you're gone, who knows where. *(With a shrug, he heads triumphantly for the refrigerator to get some milk.)*"

This does not deter Eddie from trying to rope Mickey into attempting anagrams. Mickey resists. Eddie says he needs support instead of Mickey's so-called common sense. Mickey insists that the only sensible thing one can make of Phil's death is, "It happens." Eddie is outraged. "On a friend's death, you absolutely ransack the archives of your whole thing and come up with 'It happens.'"

And now Eddie starts to try to put the blame on Susie. If she hadn't constantly undermined Phil's self-confidence . . . Maybe he should call up and tell her she killed Phil. Mickey says he can't blame Susie. She behaved the way she behaved for the same reason everybody behaves the way they behave. People want things and they do what they do to get what they want.

Eddie is getting set to do some more cocaine. Mickey warns him that he'll kill himself if he keeps this up. Eddie almost doesn't care. What should he take care of himself for? "For some state-of-the-art bitch to get her hooks into me." Mickey thinks Eddie has passed the border of the sensible. He should go to bed. "Phil would want you to get your rest," says Mickey.

EDDIE: Fuck you about him, Mickey. *(Getting to his feet.)* I mean, where do you get the goddamn cynicism, the goddamn scorn to speak his name, let alone—
MICKEY: Eddie, Eddie, is everything my fault?
EDDIE: What'd you ever do but mock him and put him down?
MICKEY: Relent, I beg you.
EDDIE *(advancing on Mickey):* You ain't saying you ever did one good thing for him, are you, not one helpful thing!?
MICKEY: No, Eddie, what I'm saying is that unlike you, I never lied to him.
EDDIE *(trapping Mickey against the counter):* And you never loved him either.

MICKEY: Right, Eddie. Good taste has no doubt deprived me of a great many things. *(Slipping free now, Mickey glides behind the counter to get a drink.)*

EDDIE: You lie to yourself, Mickey.

MICKEY: Who better?

EDDIE: No guts. No originality; no guts. *(He moves toward the couch, as Mickey, behind the counter is furiously pouring himself some vodka in a water glass.)*

MICKEY: You want this goddamn ultra-modern post-hip, comprehensive, totally fucking cost-efficient explanation of everything by which you uncover the preceding events which determined the following events, but you're not gonna find it. *(And Mickey takes a drink.)*

EDDIE: Says you.

MICKEY: You wanna believe that if you do or don't do certain things now, certain other things will or won't happen down the road, accordingly. You think you're gonna parlay this finely tuned circuitry you have for a brain into some form of major participation in the divine conglomerate, man, but all you're gonna really do is make yourself and everyone around, nuts. *(And Mickey drinks again.)*

EDDIE: Hey, I'm just tryin' to level out here, Mick—the lobes are humming, you know—I got sonar bouncing off the moon; I got—

MICKEY: I mean, to whatever extent THIS FUCKING TORMENT OF YOURS is over whatshername, Darlene, believe me, she isn't worth it.

EDDIE: Ohhh, that move you made when you gave her up for her own good, that was genius. Whatever prayer I might have had was gone. She had you down as some form of totally unique, altruistic phenomenon, instead of the fact that you had a low opinion of her and what you really wanted was to fuck the bubble-brain Artie had brought us.

MICKEY: So what?

EDDIE: You're no better off than me.

MICKEY: Just slightly.

EDDIE: You don't have any feelings at all.

MICKEY: I don't have your feelings, Eddie; that's all. I have my own. They get me by.

EDDIE: So what kind of friendship is this?

MICKEY: Adequate. Goodnight.

Eddie tries to get Mickey to stay with him. One senses that he doesn't want to be alone as he faces his desperation. But Mickey isn't up to joining him. He won't yell at the television with him. He's going to bed. Maybe Phil will come by later and join him. "To keep you company. I'm sure he will," says Mickey. "He always did." And he goes into his room and closes the door.

Eddie turns on the TV set. Johnny Carson is on. Eddie rants furiously as Carson does his monologue. Eddie has suggestions for a much richer monologue. Darker, true, but . . . Now he gets furious. Carson's not listening to him. He starts whacking away at the television, furious at Carson's obliviousness.

Donna has entered during this rant, surprising him. Tentatively, she tells him she's not angry any more, and she begins to describe her travels in the interim.

She shows him patches on her clothes which signify where she's been. Her arrival confuses Eddie even more. He tries to convey the nature of his confusion.

EDDIE: . . . . . I don't know what of everything going on pertains to me and what is of no account at all.

DONNA: Everything pertains to you, Eddie.

EDDIE: Yeah?

DONNA: Sure. *(Finding a plate with leftover bread on it.)* It's all part of the flow of which we are a part, too, and everything pertains to everything one way or another, see what I mean?

EDDIE: But I don't know, see, I don't KNOW.

DONNA: It doesn't matter.

EDDIE: So I'm just in this flow, right, like you in your elevator.

DONNA *(finding an open bottle of water):* It wasn't mine.

EDDIE: So how'm I supposed to feel about it? See that's what I don't know.

DONNA *(moving to the armchair to eat):* You have total, utter complete freedom on that score, Eddie, because it doesn't make a bit of difference.

EDDIE *(following her):* What I feel, it doesn't matter? This flow don't care!

DONNA: I don't think so.

EDDIE: So fuck it then! What good is it?

DONNA: I don't know.

He can get no further clarification from Donna, no matter how hard he presses. Basically, as far as she's concerned, once you accept that it's all a mystery, which by definition you can't figure out, that's the end of any point of tying to figure it out. Why waste energy on the impossible?

Eddie tells her that Phil is dead and the funeral was today. She figures that this is why he's in the state he's in. Eddie tries to describe the funeral and his feelings. *"Somewhere, here it hits him, a grief that, though there are tears, is beyond them: It is in his body, which heaves, and wracks him . . . . . He gasps, tries to breathe."*

Donna confesses that she didn't really go to all the places represented on her patches. She only got as far as Oxnard, where she got into a relationship that didn't work out. So, if it's okay with him, she'd like to sleep here.

EDDIE: I'm gonna be up for a while.

DONNA *(standing up, looking around):* Oh, I don't care. I'm just happy to get off the streets at the moment. The desperation out there is paranormal.

EDDIE: I don't know if I'm going to sleep ever again. I might stay awake forever.

DONNA: That's okay; should I lay down on the floor?

EDDIE: No, there's room here.

> Eddie slides to one end of the couch, while Donna, carrying her coat, settles in against him, covering herself with her coat, then she looks up at him.

DONNA: You wanna fuck me or anything, Eddie, before I go to sleep?

EDDIE: No.

DONNA: Great. Not that I don't want to, I'm just sleepy.

EDDIE: You want a lude, or anything?
DONNA: No. *(Turning back to go to sleep.)*
EDDIE: Valium?
DONNA: No. 'Night.
EDDIE: Goodnight.
DONNA: Pleasant dreams.
>   *He holds her. Blackout. Curtain.*

MA RAINEY'S BLACK BOTTOM

A Play in Two Acts

BY AUGUST WILSON

Cast and credits appear on pages 321–322

AUGUST WILSON was born in 1945 in Pittsburgh, where his father worked as a baker and his mother determinedly introduced her son to the written word and had him reading at 4 years old. Despite his early acquaintance and continuing fascination with words, he did not long pursue formal education, attending Central Catholic High School but leaving it before graduating. He can clearly remember when he began to approach writing as a profession: it was April 1, 1965; he had just earned $20 writing a term paper for his sister, and he bought a typewriter which, he says, "represented my total commitment" because it took every penny he had, so that, lacking bus fare, he carried it home.

Wilson started with poetry, and by 1972 he was writing one-acts. His first production was Jitney, *staged in 1978 by Black Horizons Theater, a group which he himself had founded in 1968.* Jitney *was repeated in 1982 by Allegheny Repertory Theater, and meanwhile Wilson's* Black Bart and the Sacred Hills *was produced in 1981 by Penumbra Theater in St. Paul. After a staged reading at the O'Neill Theater Center in Waterford, Conn. in 1982 and production by Yale Repertory Theater April 3, 1984, Wilson's* Ma Rainey's Black Bottom *was brought to Broadway Oct. 11, 1984 to become its author's first full New York production and Best Play.*

Wilson is a member of New Dramatists (which presented his The Mill Hand's Lunch Bucket *in staged readings last season), and he has been a recipient of Bush, McKnight and Rockefeller fellowships in playwriting. His* Fences *was staged in an O'Neill reading in 1984 and is scheduled for production by Yale Repertory. He is married, with one daughter, and lives in St. Paul.*

The following synopsis of Ma Rainey's Black Bottom *was prepared by Sally Dixon Wiener.*

"Ma Rainey's Black Bottom": by August Wilson. Copyright © 1981, 1985 by August Wilson. Reprinted by arrangement with New American Library. See CAUTION notice on copyright page. All inquiries should be addressed to: New American Library, 1633 Broadway, New York, NY 10019.

Time: Early March 1927

Place: The bandroom and recording studio of a record company in Chicago. The "race" division.

ACT I

SYNOPSIS: The divided set is comprised of the bandroom, a slightly larger area, stage left, and the recording studio, stage right. The bandroom, where the musicians wait and rehearse, is a dingy room with rusty exposed pipes. A clutter of old music stands and other paraphernalia of the trade is junked in a corner adjoining the old lockers near the door, upstage left. There is a piano, two chairs, and two old painted wooden benches in the room, which is lit by two overhead hanging lights. In the recording studio, a radiator is just downstage right of the door that is the entrance to the studio. Upstage, below the windowed control booth on an upper level and the wall clock, is a piano, and at right is a circular metal staircase that leads to the control booth. Downstage in the studio there are some high stools, a chair, and a raised platform. The passageway between this unpretentious studio and its bandroom is backstage.

As the play begins, Irvin, Ma Rainey's manager, 40-ish, dark-haired and wearing a brown suit and gold watch chain, comes into the studio with Sturdyvant, the studio owner, 40-ish, with thinning sandy hair and a brown suit and a bow tie, to prepare for the recording session. Sturdyvant goes up to the control room and Irvin, after feeling the radiator, drags the heavy old-fashioned standing mike to the downstage platform so Sturdyvant can test it. Sturdyvant is warning Irvin as they wait for Ma and her accompanying musicians that Irvin must keep Ma "in line." He doesn't care if she's the Mother of the Blues—he doesn't want any of her "Queen of the Blues bullshit." He just wants to record the songs listed and be done with it, and Irvin assures him he'll handle the situation.

STURDYVANT: Yeah . . . yeah . . . you handled it last time. Remember? She marches in here like she owns the damn place . . . doesn't like the songs we picked out . . . says her throat is sore . . . doesn't want to do more than one take . . .

IRVIN: OK . . . OK . . . I was here! I know all about it.

STURDYVANT: Complains about the building being cold . . . and then . . . trips over the mike wire and threatens to sue me. That's taking care of it?

IRVIN: I've got it all worked out this time. I talked with her last night. Her throat is fine . . . we went over the songs together . . . I got everything straight, Mel.

STURDYVANT: Irv, that horn player . . . the one who gave me those songs . . . Is he going to be here?

IRVIN: Yeah.

STURDYVANT: Good. I want to hear more of that sound. Times are changing. This is a tricky business now. We've got to jazz it up . . . put in something different. You know something wild . . . with a lot of rhythm. *(Pause.)* You know,

Scott Davenport-Richards as Sylvester, Charles S. Dutton as Levee, Leonard Jackson as Slow Drag, Theresa Merritt as Ma Rainey, Robert Judd as Toledo, Joe Seneca as Cutler and, *in booth above,* Lou Criscuolo as Irvin and John Carpenter as Sturdyvant in *Ma Rainey's Black Bottom* by August Wilson

what we put out last time, Irv? We put out garbage last time. It was garbage. I don't even know why I bother with this any more.

IRVIN: You did all right last time, Mel. Not as good as you did before, but you did all right.

STURDYVANT: You know how many records we sold in New York? You wanna see the sheet? And you know what's in New York, Irv? Harlem. Harlem's in New York, Irv.

IRVIN: OK, so they didn't sell in New York. But look at Memphis . . . Birmingham . . . Atlanta . . . Christ . . . you made a bundle.

Sturdyvant claims it isn't the money, it's his nerves. He plans to get out of the business in a couple of years and go into "something respectable"—like the textile business.

A buzzer, off, marks the arrival of three of the four band players: Cutler, the trombonist, perhaps in his late 50s, with a short white beard and a plaid suit; Slow Drag, the bassist, 40-ish, heavy, wearing a dark vest over a white shirt that's open at the collar; and Toledo, the pianist, in his late 50s at least, in a green suit and unpolished, old-fashioned high black uncitified shoes. Everyone was supposed to be there by one o'clock, but Ma is not with them, nor is the fourth band player, Levee, the horn player.

Irvin has tried to reassure Sturdyvant that Ma will be along soon, and he has gone to order sandwiches for the band after showing them down to the bandroom so they can rehearse. Cutler has the list of songs they're to record, but when Toledo reads it aloud, Cutler says they aren't the songs that Ma told him they were to do. "This 'Moonshine Blues' wasn't in it," he frets. "That's one of Bessie's songs."

The others tell him not to worry. Slow Drag reports that Levee is out buying shoes, partially with the four dollars he won gambling with Cutler, so he can impress the girl that was with Ma at a club the previous night.

Slow Drag and Toledo are having a drink of bourbon when Levee arrives, wearing a garishly-striped suit and a black hat and wearing a small mustache. About middle-30s, he has a restless energy that seems to fill the bandroom as he comes in with a shoebox and puts on his new shoes. When he comments that the bandroom used to be upstairs and now it's downstairs, Toledo philosophically goes on about how everything changes all the time.

Slow Drag wants to get on with rehearsing, but Levee says it's only "old jug band music" anyway. Cutler, annoyed with Levee, tells him he's no Buddy Bolden or King Oliver.

LEVEE: What is you? I don't see your name in lights.

CUTLER: I just play the piece. Whatever they want. I don't go talking about art and critizing other people's music.

LEVEE: I ain't like you, Cutler. I got talent! Me and this horn . . . we's tight. If my daddy knowed I was gonna turn out like this he would've named me Gabriel. I'm gonna get me a band and make me some records. I done give Mr. Sturdyvant some of my songs I wrote and he say he's gonna let me record them when I get my band together. *(Takes some papers out of his pocket.)* I just gotta finish the last part of this song. Mr. Sturdyvant want me to write another part to this song. . . . .

CUTLER: Well, until you get your own band where you can play what you want, you just play the piece and stop complaining. I told you when you came on here, this ain't none of them hot bands. This is an accompaniment band. You play Ma's music when you here.

Toledo and Levee have an argument about how music is spelled, Levee insisting that it's spelled m-u-s-i-k. Slow Drag again tries to get them to start rehearsing. Levee insists, however, he must finish the song for Sturdyvant, and Ma isn't there yet. He and Toledo go another round, with Toledo insisting that if Levee knew how to read he'd "understand the basic understanding of everything," until Slow Drag interrupts them again.

SLOW DRAG: Both of you all gonna drive me crazy with that philosophy bullshit. Cutler, give me a reefer.

CUTLER: Ain't you got some reefer? Where's your reefer? Why you all the time asking me?

SLOW DRAG: Cutler, how long I done know you? How long we been together? Twenty-two years. We been doing this together for twenty-two years. All up and down the back roads, the side roads, the front roads . . . we done played in the juke-joints, the whorehouses, the barn dances and city sit downs . . . I done lied for you and lied with you . . . we done laughed together, fought together, slept in the same bed together, done sucked on the same titty . . . and now you don't wanna give me no reefer.

CUTLER: You see this nigger trying to talk me out of my reefer, Toledo? Running all that about how long he done knowed me and how we done sucked on the same titty. Nigger, you *still* ain't getting none of my reefer!

Toledo comments that what Slow Drag has been doing is "an African conceptualization." Slow Drag and Cutler both take umbrage.

TOLEDO: Naming all those things you and Cutler done together is like trying to solicit some reefer based on a bond of kinship. That's African. An ancestral retention. Only you forgot the name of the gods.

SLOW DRAG: I ain't forgot nothing. I was telling the nigger how cheap he is. Don't come talking that African nonsense to me.

TOLEDO: You just like Levee. No eye for taking an abstract and fixing it to a specific. There's so much that goes on around you and you can't even see it.

CUTLER: Wait a minute . . . wait a minute. Toledo, now when this nigger . . . when an African do all them things you say and name all the gods and what not . . . then what happens?

TOLEDO: Depends on if the gods is sympathetic with his cause for which he is calling them with the right names. Then his success comes with the right proportion of his naming. That's the way that go.

CUTLER (taking out a reefer): Here, Slow Drag. Here's a reefer. You done talked yourself up on that one.

They begin to rehearse the number called "Ma Rainey's Black Bottom," but Levee, who's playing it differently, stops and insists that they are to do his version. That's what Mr. Irvin had told him. It's on the list Cutler has. He argues with Cutler that there's no point in rehearsing the wrong version, but Cutler won't back down and insists Levee play what he tells him to play.

They begin rehearsing a different song. When Irvin comes in to ask why Ma is delayed, he confirms they are to play Levee's version of the title song. Irvin leaves, and Cutler points out to Levee that "it's what Ma says that counts." Levee argues that the man making the recording is the one who'll decide, "and you heard what the man told you . . . . . Levee's arrangement." Toledo remarks that "As long as the colored man look to white folks to put the crown on what he say . . . as long as he looks to white folks for approval . . . then he ain't never gonna find out who he is and what he's about." He'll just be what whites want him to be.

Cutler claims Levee is mixed up about who's the boss, Ma's the boss. Levee concedes she is, on the road, but this is a recording session, in Chicago. Cutler gives up, and they get on with rehearsing Levee's version.

TOLEDO: How that first part go again, Levee?

LEVEE: It go like this. *(He plays.)* That's to get the people's attention to the song. That's when you and Slow Drag come in with the rhythm part. Me and Cutler play on the breaks. *(Becoming animated.)* Now we gonna dance it . . . but we ain't gonna countrify it. This ain't no barn dance. This is a city dance. We gonna play it like . . .

CUTLER: The man ask you how the first part go. He don't wanna hear all that. Just tell him how the piece go.

TOLEDO: I got it. I got it. Let's go. I know how to do it.

CUTLER: "Ma Rainey's Black Bottom." One . . . Two . . . You know what to do.

They begin to play, Levee stops.

LEVEE: You all got to keep up now. You playing in the wrong time. Ma come in over the top. She got to find her *own* way in.

CUTLER: Nigger, will you let us play this song. When you get your own band . . . then you tell them that nonsense. We know how to play the piece. I was playing music before you was born. Gonna tell me how to play. All right. Let's try it again.

SLOW DRAG: Wait till I fix this. This string started to unravel. *(Playfully.)* And you know I want to play Levee's music right.

As Slow Drag crosses he nearly steps on Levee's new shoes and Levee berates him as begins to shine the shoes with a rag. Cutler is smoking another reefer. They reflect the tension in another argument, about shoes. Cutler thinks anybody who spends a week's pay on shoes is a fool. Slow Drag points out Toledo's "clod-hoppers." Levee sneers, but Toledo says they suit him.

Toledo grumbles that the trouble with colored folks is that they always want to have a good time, and that "there's more to life than having a good time." Slow Drag claims that Toledo's good time is reading books and studying and that he shouldn't pick on other people about having a good time doing other things. Cutler backs him up by adding that "Niggers been having a good time before you was born, and they gonna keep having a good time after you gone." What else they're going to do is what concerns Toledo. He's interested in making "the lot of the colored man better for him here in America." Good times are what makes life worth it, Slow Drag argues. He says Toledo's forgotten how to have a good time, like the white man. The arguing gets more intense, with Toledo insisting that it's every colored man's responsibility to help solve their problems—all of them together, not just as individuals.

Slow Drag claims he knows a man who sold his soul to the devil, and Levee says he'd like to see the devil coming so he could sell him his.

LEVEE: I sure wish I knew where he went. He wouldn't have to convince me long. Hell, I'd even help him sign people up.

CUTLER: Nigger, God's gonna strike you down with that blasphemy you talking.

LEVEE: Oh, shit! God don't mean nothing to me. Let him strike me! Here I am standing right here. What you talking about he's gonna strike me? Here I am! Let him strike me! I ain't scared of him. Talking that stuff to me.

CUTLER: All right. You gonna be sorry. You gonna fix yourself to have bad luck. Ain't nothing gonna work for you.

LEVEE: Bad luck? What I care about some bad luck? You talking simple. I ain't knowed nothing but bad luck all my life. Couldn't get no worse. What the hell I care about some bad luck? Hell, I eat it every day for breakfast! You dumber than I thought you was . . . talking about bad luck.

In the recording studio Irvin is calling down to the bandroom that the sandwiches have arrived. Toledo goes up to get them. Sturdyvant is getting increasingly upset with Irvin about the delay. He tells Irvin he should have gone to the hotel to make sure Ma would be here on time.

Finally the buzzer sounds again, and Ma Rainey comes on in a flurry, with a policeman, Dussie Mae and Sylvester. Ma is a vast, ageless and ample presence, dressed to the nines in shades of red fancied up with fringe and tassels. She is also wearing a long string of pearls, a gold headband and a fur coat and has a red feather fan.

Dussie Mae, a slithering young sexpot, is wearing a light flowered dress of sheer material, pink stockings and shoes and a velvet coat with a fur collar. The policeman is a young white man in uniform. Sylvester, Ma's stuttering, half-grown nephew, is in a knicker suit with wine-colored socks, old-fashioned shoes and a big cap.

MA RAINEY: Irvin . . . you better tell this man who I am! You better get him straight!

IRVIN: Ma, do you know what time it is? Do you have any idea? We've been waiting . . .

DUSSIE MAE *(to Sylvester):* If you was watching where you was going . . .

SYLVESTER: I was watching . . . what you mean?

IRVIN *(notices policeman):* What's going on here? Officer . . . what's the matter?

MA RAINEY: Tell the man who he's messing with!

POLICEMAN: Do you know this lady?

MA RAINEY: Just tell the man who I am! That's all you gotta do.

POLICEMAN: Lady, will you let me talk huh?

MA RAINEY: Tell the man who I am!

Irwin tells the policeman that Ma is a recording artist and tries to get her to sit down so he can find out from the policeman what the problem is. Dussie Mae is blaming it all on Sylvester. She claims he wrecked Ma's car. The policeman tells Irvin Ma's been charged with assault and battery. Dussie Mae interrupts to say that they'd been trying to get a cab, and Ma interrupts her to say that Sylvester had been driving her car. The policeman doesn't seem to believe it was Ma's car, but Ma says it's registered to her and bought and paid for by her. The policeman tells Irvin the car hit another car whose driver reported that "the kid" had run a stoplight.

SYLVESTER: What do you mean? The man c-c-come around the corner and hit m-m-me!

POLICEMAN: While I was calling a paddy wagon to haul them to the station . . . they try to hop into a parked cab. The cabbie said he was waiting on a fare . . .

MA RAINEY: The man was just sitting there. Wasn't waiting for nobody. I don't know why he wanna tell that lie.

POLICEMAN: Look, lady . . . will you let me tell the story?

MA RAINEY: Go ahead and tell it then. But tell it right!

POLICEMAN: Like I say . . . she tries to get in this cab. The cabbie's waiting on a fare. She starts creating a disturbance. The cabbie gets out to try to explain the situation to her . . . and she knocks him down.

DUSSIE MAE: She ain't hit him! He just fell!

SYLVESTER: He just s-s-slipped!

POLICEMAN: He claims she knocked him down. We got her charged with assault and battery.

MA RAINEY: If that don't beat all to hell. I ain't touched the man! The man was trying to reach around me to keep his car door closed. I opened the door and it hit him and he fell down. I ain't touched the man!

IRVIN: OK. OK . . . I got it straight now, Ma. You didn't touch him. All right? Officer . . . can I see you for a moment?

DUSSIE MAE: Ma was just trying to open the door.

SYLVESTER: He j-j-just got in t-t-the way!

MA RAINEY: Said he wasn't gonna haul no colored folks . . . if you want to know the truth of it.

Sturdyvant comes in and wants to know what's happening. Ma tells him to get away from her. Irvin says he'll handle it, and Sturdyvant goes back to the control booth as Irvin and the policeman confer. The policeman says that in addition to charging Ma with assault and battery, Sylvester is charged with threatening the cabbie.

MA RAINEY: You leave the boy out of it. He ain't done nothing. What's he supposed to have done?

POLICEMAN: He threatened the cabbie, lady! You just can't go around threatening people.

SYLVESTER: I ain't done nothing to him! He's the one talking about he g-g-gonna get a b-b-baseball bat on me! I just told him what I'd do with it. But I ain't done nothing cause he didn't get the b-b-bat!

IRVIN *(pulling the policeman aside):* Officer . . . look here . . .

POLICEMAN: We was on our way down to the precinct . . . but I figured I'd do you a favor and bring her by here. I mean if she's as important as she says she is . . .

IRVIN *(slides a bill from his pocket):* Look, officer . . . I'm Madame Rainey's manager . . . it's good to meet you.

He shakes the policeman's hand and passes him the bill.

As soon as we're finished with the recording session . . . I'll personally stop by the precinct house and straighten up this misunderstanding.

POLICEMAN: Well . . . I guess that's all right. As long as someone is responsible for them.

He pockets the bill and winks at Irvin.

No need to come down . . . I'll take care of it myself. Of course we wouldn't want nothing like this to happen again.

IRVIN: Don't worry, officer . . . I'll take care of everything. Thanks for your help.

The policeman leaves and Ma introduces Sylvester and Dussie Mae to Irvin. She tells Irvin to call and see about her car—she wants it fixed today—and she complains about Sturdyvant's pennypinching—the studio is so cold. Irvin, as usual, says he'll take care of everything.

In the bandroom Levee is talking about New Orleans and about a place there called Lula White's, where he'd like to introduce Slow Drag, who's never been to New Orleans, to one of the girls.

CUTLER: Slow Drag don't need you to find him no pussy. He can takes care of his ownself. Fact is . . . you better watch your gal when Slow Drag's around. They don't call him Slow Drag for nothing. *(He laughs.)* Tell him how you got your name, Slow Drag.

SLOW DRAG: I ain't thinking about Levee.

CUTLER: Slow Drag break a woman's back when he dance. They had this contest one time in this little town called Bolingbroke about a hundred miles outside of Macon. We was playing for this dance and they was giving twenty dollars to the best slow draggers. Slow Drag looked over the competition, got down off the bandstand, grabbed hold of one of them gals and stuck to her like a fly to jelly. Like wood to glue. Man had that gal whooping and hollering so . . . everybody stopped to watch. This fellow came in . . . this gal's fellow . . . and pulled a knife a foot long on Slow Drag. 'Member that, Slow Drag?

SLOW DRAG: Boy that mama was hot! The front of her dress was wet as a dishrag!

LEVEE: So what happened? What the man do?

CUTLER: Slow Drag ain't missed a stroke. The gal, she just look at her man with that sweet dizzy look in her eye. She ain't about to stop! Folks was clearing out, ducking and hiding out under tables, figuring there's gonna be a fight. Slow Drag just looked over the gal's shoulder at the man and said . . . "Mister, if you'd quit hollering and wait a minute . . . you'll see I'm doing you a favor. I'm helping this gal win ten dollars so she can buy you a gold watch." The man just stood there and looked at him, all the while stroking that knife. Told Slow Drag, say, "All right then, nigger. You just better make damn sure you win." That's when folks started calling him Slow Drag. The women got to hanging around him so bad after that, them fellows in that town ran us out of there.

Toledo comes into the bandroom and tells the others that Ma is there. He has brought the sandwiches. There are five, and Levee grabs two. Toledo comments that they won't have to worry about any leftovers with Levee around. Levee tells Toledo, who has Slow Drag's sandwich in addition to his own, to look to himself before he looks at him, talking about leftovers.

TOLEDO: That's what you is. That's what you all is. A leftover from history. You see now, I'll show you.

LEVEE: Aw, shit . . . I done got the nigger started now.

TOLEDO: Now, I'm gonna show you how this goes . . . where you just a leftover from history. Everybody come from different places in Africa, right? Come from different tribes and things. Soonawhile they began to make one big stew. You had the carrots, the peas, and potatoes and whatnot over here. And over there you had the meat, the nuts, the okra, corn . . . and then you mix it up and let it cook right through to get the flavors flowing together . . . then you got one thing. You got a stew. Now you take and eat the stew. You take and make your history with that stew. All right. Now it's over. Your history's over and you done ate the stew. But you look around and you see some carrots over here, some potatoes over there. That stew's still there. You done made your history and it's still there. You can't eat it all. So what you got? You got some leftovers. That's what it is. You got leftovers and you can't do nothing with it. You already making you another history . . . cooking you another meal, and you don't need them leftovers no more. What to do? See, we's the leftovers. The colored man is the leftovers. Now what's the colored man gonna do with himself? That's what we waiting to find out. But first we gotta know we the leftovers. Now who knows that? You find me a nigger that knows that and I'll turn any which-a-way you want me to. I'll bend over for you. You ain't gonna find that. And that's what the problem is. The problem ain't with the white man. The white man knows you just a leftover. Cause he the one who done the eating and he know what he done ate. But we don't know that we been took and made history out of. Done went and filled the white man's belly and now he's full and tired and wants you to get out the way and let him be by himself. Now I know what I'm talking about. And if you wanna find out, you just ask Mr. Irvin what he had for supper yesterday. And if he's an honest white man . . . which is asking for a whole heap of a lot . . . he'll tell you he done ate your black ass and if you please I'm full up with you . . . so go on and get off the plate and let me eat something else.

As they eventually begin to rehearse again, up in the studio Dussie Mae is wandering around. Sylvester is by the piano, and Ma is rubbing her feet as she sings to herself. Dussie Mae is wondering where the band is. Ma is getting impatient for Irvin to come back—he's gone off with Sturdyvant. Ma fusses with Dussie Mae's dress and tells her she's going to get her some more clothes before they go to Memphis. She wants Dussie Mae to look nice for her.

"Dussie Mae seductively pulls up her stocking as Irvin enters." Irvin has called the garage and the car will be ready, he tells Ma. *"The strains of "Ma Rainey's Black Bottom" can be heard as the band begins to rehearse."* Ma gradually realizes that it must be Levee's version she's hearing, and she doesn't like it one bit. She says she's going to do it her way, and she's brought her nephew to do the old voice intro. Irvin tells her that Levee's arrangement is what people want now. It excites them. "Times are changing." People want something they can dance to.

MA RAINEY: I don't care what you say, Irvin. Levee ain't messing up my song. If he got what the people want . . . let him take it somewhere else. I'm singing Ma Rainey's song. I ain't singing Levee's song. Now that's all there is to it. Carry my nephew on down there and introduce him to the band. I promised my sister I'd look out for him and he's gonna do the voice intro on the song my way.

IRVIN: Ma . . . we just figured that . . .

MA RAINEY: Who's this we? What you mean we? You and Sturdyvant? You and Levee? Who's we. I ain't studying Levee nothing. Come talking this we stuff. Who's we?

IRVIN: Me and Sturdyvant. We decided that it would . . .

MA RAINEY: You decided, huh? I'm just a bump on the log. I'm gonna go which ever way the river drift. Is that it? You and Sturdyvant decided.

IRVIN: Ma. It was just that we thought it would be better.

MA RAINEY: I ain't got good sense. I don't know nothing about music. I don't know what's a good song and what ain't. You know more about my fans that I do.

IRVIN: It's not that, Ma. It would just be easier to do. It's more what the people want.

MA RAINEY: I'm gonna tell you something, Irvin . . . and you go on up there and tell Sturdyvant. What you all say don't count with me. You understand? Ma listens to her heart. Ma listens to the voice inside her. That's what counts with Ma. Now you carry my nephew on down there . . . tell Cutler he's gonna do the voice intro on that Black Bottom song . . . and that Levee ain't messing up my song with none of his music shit. Now if that don't set right with you and Sturdyvant . . . then I carry my black bottom on back down South to my tour, cause I don't like it up here noways.

Irvin gives up. Ma says she'll take Sylvester down to the bandroom herself. Dussie Mae wants to go along, but Ma tells her, "You stay your behind up here". Irvin says they will be ready in fifteen minutes. Ma says they will be ready when she says so.

In the bandroom, Ma tells Cutler to teach Sylvester the intro to her version of the song. Levee starts to argue with her, but she cuts him off: "These folks done messed with the wrong person this day." She goes off, leaving Sylvester, and Levee complains about "that old circus bullshit" and "tent show nonsense." Cutler tells Levee his job's to play what Ma says. Levee threatens to quit, but Toledo says he won't—that he needs money for shoe polish.

Cutler starts to rehearse Sylvester, who stutters badly on the intro. Levee, incensed, asks how the boy can handle the intro when he can't even speak.

SYLVESTER: W-W-W-Who's you to tell me what to do, nigger! This ain't your band! Ma tell me to d-d-d-do it and I'm gonna do it. You can go to hell, n-n-n-nigger!

LEVEE: B-B-B-Boy, ain't nobody studying you. You go on and fix that one, Cutler. You fix that one and I'll . . . I'll shine your shoes for you. You go on and fix that one!

TOLEDO: You say you Ma's nephew, huh?

SYLVESTER: Yeah. So w-w-what that mean?

TOLEDO: Oh, I ain't mean nothing . . . I was just asking.

SLOW DRAG: Well, come on and let's rehearse so the boy can get it right.

LEVEE: I ain't rehearsing nothing! You just wait till I get my band. I'm gonna record that song and show you how it supposed to go!

CUTLER: We can do it without Levee. Let him sit on over there. Sylvester, you remember your part?

SYLVESTER: I remember it pretty g-g-good.

CUTLER: Well, come on let's do it then.

When Sturdyvant comes into the bandroom, pleased that the band is rehearsing, Levee jumps up and says "Yessir! . . . . . We know them songs real good." Sturdyvant asks Levee if he's finished the song he was working on for him. Levee has, he wrote it the way Sturdyvant said to write it. Sturdyvant takes the song and tells him he wants to see him about his songs as soon as he has the time, and he goes off.

Toledo tells Levee he is just like the rest of them—"Spooked up with the white man." But Levee says just because he said "Yessir" doesn't mean he's spooked, he intends to handle Sturdyvant in his own way and wants to be let alone. He's been handling white folks for thirty-two years. He was eight years old, Levee tells the others, when he watched a gang of white men come into his father's house and "have to do with my mama anyway they wanted." His father had 50 acres of farmland and had gone to Natchez to get seed and fertilizer, telling Levee to take care of his mother while he was gone. She was trying to fight the men off. He went and got his father's hunting knife and tried to cut the throat of one of them, but the man took the knife and "whacked me across with it".

Levee raises his shirt to show a long ugly scar.

LEVEE: That's what made them stop. They was scared I was gonna bleed to death. My mama wrapped a sheet around me and carried me two miles down to the Furlow place and they drove me up to Doc Albans. He was waiting on a calf to be born, and say he ain't had time to see me. They carried me up to Miss Etta, the midwife, and she fixed me up. My daddy came back and acted like he done accepted the facts of what happened. But he got the names of them men from my mama. He found out who they was and then we announced we was moving out of the county. Said goodbye to everybody . . . all the neighbors. My daddy went and smiled in the face of one of them crackers who had been with my mama. Smiled in his face and sold him our land. We moved over with relations in Caldwell. He got us settled in and then he took off one day. I ain't never seen him since. He sneaked back, hiding up in the woods, laying to get them eight or nine men. He got four of them before they got him. They tracked him down in the woods. Caught up with him and hung him and set him afire. *(Pause.)* My daddy wasn't spooked up by the white man. Nosir! And that taught me how to handle them. I seen my daddy go up and grin in this cracker's face . . . smile in his face and sell him his land. All the while he's planning how he's gonna get him and what he's gonna do to him. That taught me how to handle them. So you all just back up and leave Levee alone about the white man. I can smile and say yessir to whoever I please. I got time coming to me. You all just leave Levee alone about the white man.

There is a long pause. Slow Drag begins playing on the bass and sings.

SLOW DRAG (singing): "If I had my way
        If I had my way
        If I had my way
        I would tear this old building down."

    Curtain.

ACT II

The band members are in the studio with their instruments waiting for the recording session to begin. Cutler speaks privately to Irvin about Sylvester's inability to do the spoken intro. Irvin is disgusted and says they'll have to do Levee's version after all. Levee, meanwhile, is standing near Dussie Mae, who has hiked her dress up and crossed her legs for his benefit. This does not go unnoticed by Ma, who tells Cutler to "school" Levee. "He's got his eyes in the wrong place."

Irvin, over the speaker from the control booth, announces they will do "Moonshine Blues" first, but Ma will have none of it—she's doing "Black Bottom" first and demands a microphone for Sylvester. Irvin tells her they'll have to do Levee's version because the musicians say Sylvester can't speak his part. Ma doesn't care if her nephew does stutter—he doesn't all the time—and she's promised him he could do it. They can take the time, or she'll leave.

Irvin enters with a microphone and hooks it up.

MA RAINEY: Come on, Sylvester. You just stand here and hold your hands like I told you. Just remember the words and say them . . . that's all there is to it.

Don't worry about messing up. If you mess up we'll do it again. Now let me hear you say it. Play for him, Cutler.

> *Irvin exits. Cutler plays and Sylvester curls his fingers and clasps his hands together in front of his chest, pulling in opposite directions as he says his lines.*

SYLVESTER: All right boys, you d-d-done s-s-seen the best . . . now I'm gonna show you the rest . . . Ma R-Rainey's gonna show you her B-B-Black B-B-Bottom.

MA RAINEY: That's all right. That's real good. You take your time, you'll get it right.

Irvin says they're all set, but Ma starts complaining because she doesn't have her Coca Cola (Irvin's forgotten to get it).

STURDYVANT *(enters from the control booth):* Now just a minute here, Ma. You come in an hour late . . . we're way behind schedule as it is . . . the band is set up and ready to go . . . I'm burning my lights . . . I've turned up the heat . . . We're ready to make a record and what? You decide you want a Coca Cola?????

MA RAINEY: Sturdyvant, get out of my face.

> *Irvin enters.*

Irvin . . . I told you keep him away from me.

IRVIN: Mel, I'll handle it.

STURDYVANT: I'm tired of her nonsense, Irv. I'm not gonna put up with this!

> *Irvin crosses and takes Sturdyvant's arm and guides him toward the control booth.*

IRVIN: Let me handle it, Mel. I know how to handle her.

> *Sturdyvant exits. Irvin crosses to Ma Rainey.*

Look, Ma . . . I'll call down to the deli and get you a coke. But let's get started, huh? Sylvester's standing there ready to go . . . the band's set up . . . let's do this one song, huh?

MA RAINEY: If you too cheap to buy me a coke . . . I'll buy my own. Slow Drag! Sylvester, go with Slow Drag and get me a Coca Cola.

As Slow Drag and Sylvester leave to get the cokes and Irvin goes to the control booth, Ma explains to Cutler that she's the one to say who does what, and doing the introduction will help Sylvester with his problem. And she wants Cutler to find a replacement for Levee when they get to Memphis. Cutler defends Levee's musicianship, but Ma is adamant.

Cutler questions Ma about singing "Moonshine Blues," one of the songs Bessie Smith sang, but Ma doesn't care: Bessie's only imitating her, she believes, because she was the *first.* Ma is angry at Irvin, complaining about white folks taking her voice and putting it into "fancy boxes" and then being too cheap to spend a nickel on a coke.

MA RAINEY: They don't care nothing about me. All they want is my voice. Well, I done learned that and they gonna treat me like I want to be treated no matter how much it hurt them. They back there calling me all kinds of names

... calling me everything but a child of god. But they can't do nothing else. They ain't got what they wanted yet. As soon as they get my voice down on them recording machines, then it's just like if I'd be some whore and they roll over and put their pants on. Ain't got no use for me then. I know what I'm talking about. You watch, Irvin right there with the rest of them, he don't care nothing about me either. He's been my manager for six years, always talking about sticking together, and the only time he had me in his house was to sing for some of his friends.

CUTLER: I know how they do.

MA RAINEY: If you colored and can make them some money then you all right with them. Otherwise you just a dog in the alley. . . . .

In the bandroom, Toledo is reading the newspaper and Levee has been singing his new song when Dussie Mae comes in. She tells Levee that she thought he was "jiving" her at the club when he told her he wrote music. Levee turns to Toledo for affirmation of the fact that Sturdyvant has some of his songs, but Toledo doesn't want to get involved in this situation and goes off. Dussie Mae wants to know if Levee's really going to have his own band.

LEVEE: That's what I was trying to tell you last night. A man what's gonna get his own band need to have a woman like you.

DUSSIE MAE: A woman like me wants somebody to bring it and put it in my hand. I don't need nobody wanna get something for nothing and leave me standing in my door.

LEVEE: That ain't Levee's style, sugar. I got more style than that. I knows how to treat a woman. Buy her presents and things . . . treat her like she want to be treated.

DUSSIE MAE: That's what they all say . . . till it come time to be buying the presents.

LEVEE: When we get down to Memphis I'm gonna show you what I'm talking about. I'm gonna take you out and show you a good time. Show you Levee knows how to treat a woman.

DUSSIE MAE: When you getting your own band?

LEVEE (moves closer to slip his arms around her): Soon as Mr. Sturdyvant say. I done got my fellows already picked out. Getting me some good fellows know how to play real sweet music.

DUSSIE MAE (moves away): Go on now, I don't go for all that pawing and stuff. When you get your own band maybe we can see about this stuff you talking.

LEVEE (moving toward her): I just wanna show you I know what the women like. They don't call me Sweet Lemonade for nothing.

DUSSIE MAE: Stop it now. Somebody's gonna come in here.

LEVEE: Naw they ain't. Look here, sugar . . . what I wanna know is . . . can I introduce my red rooster to your brown hen?

DUSSIE MAE: You get your band then we'll see if that rooster know how to crow.

> Levee has her in his arms. He grinds up against her and feels her buttocks.

Aleta Mitchell as Dussie Mae *(left)* watches a recording session in a scene from *Ma Rainey's Black Bottom*

In the studio, while she sits with Cutler and Toledo, Ma comments on how quiet it is and how she can't stand silence. Keeping some music in you makes things feel balanced.

MA RAINEY: White folks don't understand about the blues. They hear it come out but they don't know how it got there. They don't understand that's life's way of talking. You don't sing to feel better. You sing cause that's a way of understanding life.

CUTLER: That's right. You get that understanding and you done got a grip on life to where you can hold your head up and go on to see what else life got to offer.

MA RAINEY: The blues help you get out of bed in the morning. You get up knowing you ain't alone. There's something else in the world. Something's been added by that song. This be an empty world without the blues. I take that emptiness and try to fill it up with something.

TOLEDO: You fill it up with something the people can't be without, Ma. That's why they call you the Mother of the Blues. You fill up that emptiness in a way ain't nobody ever thought of doing before. And now they can't be without it.

MA RAINEY: I ain't started the blues way of singing. The blues always been there.

CUTLER: In the church sometimes you find that way of singing. They got blues in the church.

MA RAINEY: They say I started it . . . but I didn't. I just helped it out. Filled up that empty space a little bit. That's all. But if they wanna call me the Mother of the Blues, that's all right with me. It don't hurt none. . . . .

Slow Drag and Sylvester finally appear with the cokes—the store on the corner was closed and they had to find another. Ma tells Sylvester to find Mr. Irvin and say they're ready.

In the bandroom, Levee is kissing Dussie Mae when Slow Drag comes in for a nip of bourbon. He tells Levee they're ready to start and he leaves. Levee tries to kiss Dussie Mae again, but she's worried he'll get her into trouble and runs out.

In the studio Ma is drinking her coke as Levee comes on from the bandroom. The musicians are in their places and Sylvester is at the other mike. Everything's ready to go, and when the band starts Sylvester comes in on cue but stutters. The same thing happens on the second take, but on the third he manages the intro without a single stutter. After Ma's completed the song and they're setting up for the next one, however, Sturdyvant calls over the speaker that something has happened and they don't have anything recorded. Something was wrong with Sylvester's mike. Irvin thinks Levee kicked the mike wire's plug out but then finds that the cord is faulty. They need another cord.

Ma is outraged and tells Irvin she's going home. She calls to Dussie Mae to come on, and she goes off to get their coats. Sturdyvant threatens Irvin and Irvin pleads with Ma. Sturdyvant threatens Ma, telling her she'll be through if she walks out. Irvin begs Ma for just fifteen minutes, assuring her the records will be hits and that "even Sylvester will be a star."

Ma sits, with her coat on, but warns Irvin that fifteen minutes is all. Irvin promises and tells the band to take a break.

Cutler and Slow Drag go to the bandroom to get a drink, and Toledo and Levee follow. It doesn't make any difference to him if Ma left or not, Slow Drag says, but Cutler feels like Mr. Irvin does—"best to go ahead and get something out of it" after all the time they've spent there. Cutler's wondering if Sylvester will ever get that intro right again, though.

Slow Drag remarks that Levee "got one eye on the gal and the other on his trumpet" and Cutler asks Levee if he doesn't realize Dussie Mae is Ma's girl. Levee says he was only talking to her. Cutler tries to explain that if it was some boy's girl, the boy would be liable to kill him, but because it's Ma's girl, "you ass gonna be out there scraping the concrete looking for a job." Levee keeps insisting he hasn't done anything.

Slow Drag asks Toledo if he's ever been a fool about a woman and Toledo assures him he has. Slow Drag's surprised. He's never seen him "mess with no woman;" he thought books interested him more. Toledo says he's been around, "messed" with a lot of them, "gonna mess with some more." And he's been legally married, to a good woman, but she joined the church and began thinking Toledo was a heathen. The church got more important to her, and she moved out. Toledo says he must have been a fool to not know she wanted something he didn't give her. Yeah, he'd been a fool about a woman.

Cutler tells him he's been a fool also, but he claims that what Toledo calls a fool and what he calls a fool are different things. If you can't help what happens, he wouldn't call you a fool. His idea of a fool is someone who causes something to happen to him. "Like Levee . . . if he keep messing with Ma's gal" and loses his job.

Cutler doesn't think life did the fair thing by Toledo, but Toledo thinks life is fair. Levee says life doesn't have any balls. "Now death . . . death got some style!"

Levee sneeringly remarks about a "nigger" talking about life is fair when he hasn't got "a pot to piss in," and Toledo turns philosophical again and says a "nigger" is always going to be dissatisfied, and will make "his own dissatisfaction." "Niggers got a right to," Levee argues. Would you be satisfied with a bone somebody threw you when they're eating the whole hog? he asks Toledo.

Toledo tells Levee he's lucky to be an entertainer, lucky and doesn't even know it, when the others are hauling wood. Slow Drag says there's nothing wrong with hauling wood, but Levee says that's not what he meant. He means they're satisfied to stay put, when they should be moving down the road and keeping an eye out for the devil who's buying up souls and hoping they'll find him.

CUTLER: I done told you about that blasphemy. Talking about selling your soul to the devil.

TOLEDO: We done the same thing, Cutler. There ain't no difference. We done sold Africa for the price of tomatoes. We done sold ourselves to the white man in order to be like him. Look at the way you dressed . . . that ain't African. That's the white man. We trying to be just like him. We done sold who we are in order to become someone else. We's imitation white men.

CUTLER: What else we gonna be living over here?

LEVEE: I'm Levee. Just me. I ain't no imitation nothing!

SLOW DRAG: You can't change who you are by how you dress. That's what I got to say.

TOLEDO: It ain't all how you dress. It's how you act, how you see the world, It's how you follow life.

LEVEE: It don't matter what you talking about. I ain't no imitation white man. And I don't want to be no white man. As soon as I get my band together and make them records like Mr. Sturdyvant done told me I can make . . . I'm gonna be like Ma and tell the white man just what he can do. Ma tell Mr. Irvin she gonna leave . . . and Mr. Irvin get down on his knees and beg her to stay! That's the way I'm gonna be! Make the white man respect me!

CUTLER: The white man don't care nothing about Ma. The colored folks made Ma a star. White folks don't care nothing about who she is . . . what kind of music she make.

SLOW DRAG: That's the truth about that. You let her go down to one of them white folks hotels and see how big she is.

CUTLER: Well, she ain't got to do that. She can't even get a cab up here in the North. . . . .

As an example of how the white man doesn't care about them, Cutler tells a story about the Reverend Gates, a black minister who was traveling by train from Florida to Atlanta to see his sick sister. The train came through Thomasville, then Moultrie and then stopped at the little town of Sigsbee. The reverend got off the train at Sigsbee to check the schedule and had to go to the bathroom, but there were no colored rest rooms. He had to go to an outhouse quite a way from the station. While he was in the outhouse the train left without him. It was growing dark, and a group of white men gathered nearby just watching him, so he started to walk down the railroad tracks. They began to call, "Hey, nigger!" When he heard a gunshot, he stopped. They asked him his name, and if he could dance. He had to dance. They took his cross from his neck, and they took his bible and tore it up and made him keep dancing until they got tired of it. "That's the only way he got out of there alive . . . was to dance." They made him into a clown. And Ma's "just another nigger who they can use to make some money," Cutler sums it up.

If he was a man of God, where was God? Levee asks. He can't see why God didn't strike those crackers down with lightning. " 'Cause he's a white man's God. That's why! . . . . . God take a nigger's prayers and throw them in the garbage."

Cutler can't take any more of Levee's blaspheming. He knocks him down, jumps on him and pounds him. Toledo and Slow Drag finally get Cutler off Levee. Levee is bleeding and takes out a knife, circling Cutler, who grabs up a chair for protection.

LEVEE *(to Cutler):* I'm calling your God! I'm gonna give him a chance to save you! I'm calling you God! We gonna find out whose God he is!

CUTLER: You gonna burn in hell, nigger!

LEVEE: Cutler's God! Come on and save this nigger! Come on and save him like you did my mama! Save him like you did my mama! I heard her when she called you! I heard her when she said, "Lord have mercy! Jesus help me! Please God have mercy on me, Lord Jesus, help me!" And did you turn your back? Did you turn your back, motherfucker? Did you turn your back?

> *Levee becomes so caught up in his dialogue with God that he forgets about Cutler and begins to stab upwards in the air, jumping, trying to reach God.*

Come on! Come on and turn your back on me! Turn your back on me! Come on! Where is you? Come on and turn your back on me! Turn your back on me, motherfucker! I'll cut your heart out! Come on, turn your back on me! Come on! What's the matter? Where is you? . . . . .

> *Levee folds his knife and stands triumphantly.*

Your God ain't shit, Cutler.

We hear Ma's voice singing the last of the final song to be recorded as the action moves again to the recording studio. Irvin is pleased with the session, and Ma is praising Slow Drag's playing. She isn't pleased with Levee's improvising, however, and at the end of an argument about it, she fires him. He's cocky about it and regards it as if she's done him a favor.

While the band members pack up, Irvin is going to get their money. Cutler urges him to make it cash. Checks are difficult for them. As they go off to the bandroom, Irvin explains to Ma that Sturdyvant will have to pay Sylvester his $25 out of Ma's share. Ma claims he was to have been paid like the rest and sends

Irvin off to talk to Sturdyvant again. If he doesn't pay Sylvester, Sturdyvant won't make another record of hers, she threatens.

In the bandroom, the musicians are waiting to be paid. Slow Drag is doing card tricks, but Cutler and Toledo are mostly concerned about whether or not they'll be paid in cash.

Ma is waiting in the studio as Sturdyvant and Irvin come on.

STURDYVANT: Ma, is there something wrong? Is there a problem?

MA RAINEY: Sturdyvant, I want you to pay that boy his money.

STURDYVANT: Sure, Ma. I got it right here. Two hundred for you and twenty-five for the kid, right?

> *Sturdyvant hands the money to Irvin who hands it to Ma Rainey and Sylvester.*

Irvin misunderstood me. It was all a mistake. Irv made a mistake.

MA RAINEY: A mistake, huh?

IRVIN: Sure, Ma. I made a mistake. He's paid, right? I straightened it out.

MA RAINEY: The only mistake was when you found out I hadn't signed the release forms. That was the mistake.

> *Ma Rainey starts to exit.*

STURDYVANT: Hey Ma . . . come on, sign the forms, huh?

IRVIN: Ma . . . come on now.

MA RAINEY: Get your coat, Sylvester. Irvin, where's my car?

IRVIN: It's right out front, Ma. Here . . . I got the keys right here. Come on, sign the forms, huh?

MA RAINEY: Irvin, give me my car keys!

IRVIN: Sure Ma . . . just sign the forms, huh?

> *Irvin gives her the keys, expecting a trade-off.*

MA RAINEY: Send them to my address and I'll get around to them.

IRVIN: Come on, Ma . . . I took care of everything, right? I straightened everything out.

MA RAINEY (*she signs the forms*): You tell Sturdyvant . . . one more mistake like that and I can make my records some place else. (*She turns to exit.*) Sylvester, straighten up your clothes. Come on, Dussie Mae.

> *Ma Rainey exits, followed by Dussie Mae and Sylvester.*

The band members are still waiting in the bandroom for their pay. Levee and Cutler are verbally sniping at each other when Irvin comes in with Sturdyvant who has $25 in cash for each of them.

Sturdyvant is about to follow Irvin out when Levee speaks up about his songs. It seems they're not what Sturdyvant is looking for. He's thought about it—doesn't think people will buy them. Levee tries to persuade him that people would if they could hear the band he's got picked out play them, that people are "tired of jugband music."

Sturdyvant agrees to give him $5 for each of the songs, but Levee wants to record them. Again, Sturdyvant insists they're not the kind they want. Levee wonders why Sturdyvant asked him to write them, and why does he now not want him to record them: "What's the difference between then and now?" Sturdyvant wants no more to do with it, gives Levee $5 for each of them and says he'll take any more he might write off his hands at the same price. Sturdyvant leaves in a rush.

Levee, his hopes dashed, wads the money up and throws it onto the floor, swearing in frustration. Toledo, who has his back to Levee and is gathering up his things, steps accidentally on Levee's shoe. Toledo apologizes, but Levee becomes completely incensed and claims Toledo's ruined his shoe. Toledo tells him that he's said "Excuse me"—what does Levee want him to do?

> *Levee is in a near rage, breathing hard. He is trying to get a grip on himself as even he senses or perhaps only he senses he is about to lose control. He looks around, uncertain of what to do. Toledo has gone back to packing, as have Cutler and Slow Drag. They purposefully avoid looking at Levee in hopes he'll calm down if he doesn't have an audience. All the weight in the world suddenly falls on Levee and he rushes at Toledo with his knife in his hand.*

LEVEE: Nigger, you stepped on my shoe!!
> *He plunges the knife into Toledo's back up to the hilt. Toledo lets out a sound of surprise and agony. Cutler and Slow Drag freeze. Toledo falls backward with Levee, his hand still on the knife, holding him up. Levee is suddenly faced with the realization of what he has done. He shoves Toledo forward and takes a step back. Toledo slumps to the floor.*

He . . . He stepped on my shoe. He did. Honest. Cutler, he stepped on my shoe. What he do that for? Toledo, what you do that for? Cutler . . . help me. He stepped on my shoe, Cutler.
> *He turns his attention to Toledo.*

Toledo! Toledo, get up.
> *He crosses to Toledo and tries to pick him up.*

It's okay, Toledo. Come on . . . I'll help you. Come on, stand up now. Levee'll help you.
> *Toledo is limp and heavy and awkward. He slumps back to the floor. Levee gets mad at him.*

Don't look at me like that! Toledo! Nigger, don't look at me like that! I'm warning you, nigger! Close you eyes! Don't you look at me like that!
> *Cutler takes Levee by the arm.*

Tell him to close his eyes, Cutler. Tell him don't look at me like that.

CUTLER: Slow Drag . . . get Mr. Irvin down here.
> *The sound of a trumpet is heard, Levee's trumpet, a muted trumpet struggling for the highest of possibilities and blowing pain and warning. Curtain.*

THE FOREIGNER

A Comedy in Two Acts

BY LARRY SHUE

Cast and credits appear on page 368

LARRY SHUE was born July 23, 1946 in New Orleans and spent much of his youth in Kansas and Illinois, where his father was a teacher of English and drama and president of a small college, and later a scholar with Kiwanis International. Shue graduated from high school in Illinois and from Illinois Wesleyan in 1968. While in college, he wrote a satyr play, put on there and thus establishing him— he claims—almost certainly as the world's greatest living satyr playwright. In his senior year he also wrote a children's musical, My Emperor's New Clothes, *which won prizes and is still produced.*

After college, Shue embarked on a career of acting, interrupted by Army service during the Vietnam era. In 1977 he began piling up acting credits at Milwaukee Repertory Theater, and in 1979 Milwaukee Rep staged his one-acter Grandma Duck Is Dead. *He became a playwright-in-residence with that group, and there the full-length Shue plays made their first appearance:* The Nerd *(1981 and now in production in England),* The Foreigner *(1983 and its author's New York debut in off-Broadway production Nov. 1, 1984) and* Wenceslas Square *(1984).*

Besides its designation as a 1984–85 Best Play, The Foreigner *has been voted the season's best production and best new American play by the critics of the Outer Circle. Shue maintained a base in Milwaukee, but his acting assignments—including the role of Froggy in* The Foreigner—*kept him recently resident in New York City. His untimely death in an airplane accident in September 1985 leaves the theater bereft of a major talent.*

"The Foreigner": by Larry Shue. © Copyright 1983 by Larry Shue as an unpublished dramatic composition. © Copyright 1985 by Larry Shue. All rights reserved. Reprinted by permission of William Morris Agency, Inc. on behalf of the author. See CAUTION notice on copyright page. All inquiries concerning stock and amateur production rights should be addressed to: Dramatists Play Service, Inc., 440 Park Avenue South, New York, NY 10016. All other inquiries should be addressed to: William Morris Agency, Inc., 1350 Avenue of the Americas, New York, NY 10019, Attention: Jeffrey R. Alpern.

Time: The recent past

Place: Betty Meeks's fishing lodge resort, Tilghman County, Ga.

ACT I

Scene 1: Evening

SYNOPSIS: The high-ceilinged living room of a log farmhouse features what is obviously a hotel-type counter at left with guest register, candy and tobacco supplies, etc. The area is furnished with sofas, a coffee table with a bowl of apples and a stove and wood bin at left. Up left is the front entrance, up right is the access to the rooms occupied by the guests and the stairs to the floor above.

A thunderstorm is in progress, as two Englishmen come in through the front door carrying suitcases. *"They are about the same age—mid-50s, perhaps—but of distinctly different styles. The first, in a British Army fatigue outfit, seems well-fed, flushed with the spirit of adventure and right at home. The other, standing in his forlorn trenchcoat, seems quietly, somehow permanently, lost."*

The first, Froggy, makes himself at home, ringing the bell on the counter, calling for the proprietress, Betty, and pouring himself a drink of whiskey. Froggy shows his companion, Charlie, on the map that they have come about 100 miles south from Atlanta in their hired jeep.

FROGGY: . . . . . Oh, it's lovely in daylight, the lake is—see it right from the window. Lovely. Just wot you need, Charlie—your own forest retreat. Silent? Peaceful? Eh? Wot d'yer think?

CHARLIE: I shouldn't have come.

FROGGY: Now, *now?*

CHARLIE: No, I—oh, don't think me ungrateful, Froggy. I know the enormous trouble you've taken to bring me here—

FROGGY: No, it was no trouble. Yer know wot I told the Yanks? " 'E's my assistant," I says. "If 'e don't go—*I* don't go." One minute later, bingo. On the plane together. *(A proud chuckle.)*

CHARLIE: Yes—your research assistant—that was a good joke—but—

FROGGY: It all depends on my approach; the right approach? That's it.

CHARLIE: Yes . . . Still—

FROGGY: Wot.

CHARLIE: I should have stayed with Mary, at the hospital. When a man's wife is dying, he belongs with her, not—not in Georgia.

FROGGY: We'll only be 'ere three days.

The doctors have told Charlie that his wife has only three months to live. Froggy doesn't believe this, and besides, Mary encouraged Froggy to take Charlie on this trip (that's because his wife doesn't like him very much, Charlie remarks,

Larry Shue, author of *The Foreigner,* in the role of Froggy LeSueur in his own play, with Kathleen Claypool as Betty Meeks (pouring tea, *above*) and Patricia Kalember as Catherine Simms *(below)*

she finds him boring). Charlie is a proof reader for a science fiction magazine: "I'm boring, all right. I've often wondered—how does one acquire personality? What must it be like, to be able to tell a funny story? To arouse laughter. Anger. Respect. To be thought—wise? How must it be?"

Froggy reassures Charlie that he was a good peacetime army officer, and that his wife is faithful to him. The latter, Charlie confesses, turns out not to be true; in fact, by actual count she has been unfaithful to him with 23 different people. But Charlie still loves Mary, quoting "Love is not love which alters when it alteration finds."

FROGGY: 'Ave you talked to anyone else about this?

CHARLIE: I've tried to. But I—I'm no good at it, you see. Talking. Talk. I— One is expected to talk these things out, but I—I can't seem to— I never finish sentences, I— I have an active fear of—of—of—

FROGGY: Talk?

CHARLIE: Yes. Lately. Even idle conversation—terrifies me. Simply knowing that in a moment, it's going to be my turn, again. My turn, to—to—to—

FROGGY: To talk.

CHARLIE: Yes.

FROGGY: Well, ye won't 'ave ter worry 'ere. Betty'll do all the talking for both of yer.

CHARLIE (alarmed): What?

FROGGY: Oh, she's a regular chatterbox, Betty is. Good weather, bad weather, 'ow's yer mum—?

CHARLIE: Oh, God—

FROGGY: And when she's not goin' on about somethin', the other guests will be. So don't—

CHARLIE: Other guests?

FROGGY: Well—

CHARLIE: You mean—strangers?

FROGGY: Well, they won't be strangers long. Why, as soon as you've 'ad one or two—

CHARLIE: Conversations!

FROGGY: Charlie—

CHARLIE: Take me with you. Please.

FROGGY: I—

CHARLIE: Please. Try to understand. I can't—talk to anyone now. Please.

FROGGY: I can't bring a civilian on post, you know that. I—
    Charlie, in a genuine panic, clutches his chest, gasping for air.

Froggy, seeing Charlie's acute distress, promises to fix it so that Charlie doesn't have to talk to anyone. Froggy will think of something; meanwhile, he takes a room key off the board and sends Charlie off to get settled.

Betty Meeks, the proprietress, enters. When she sees Froggy they hug and greet each other warmly. Froggy has arrived on his annual visit to lecture to American Army recruits on his specialty, demolition, and he has brought along a detonating device of his own invention, which he shows to Betty.

Catching up on Betty's news, Froggy learns that two of the guests, Catherine Simms and the Rev. David Marshall Lee, are engaged to be married (and Catherine's somewhat retarded brother apparently has an unfortunate habit of taking one bite out of a perfectly good apple and then throwing the rest of the fruit into the wood bin). After they're married, Catherine and David might buy this house, which Betty is having a hard time keeping in repair—in fact, Owen Musser, the county property inspector has been saying the foundation is rotten. Betty has bought a pile of bricks for repairs but hasn't yet been able to afford the services of a bricklayer.

Froggy suspects there may be some hidden profit motive in getting this place condemned, so that Betty wouldn't be permitted to sell the house, only the land under it. In any case, Catherine could afford to fix it up, her family is very well off. And besides, Betty has a longing to get away and see some of the world that Froggy has described to her: "I lay awake sometimes, wonderin' what them folks 'd be like. Foreigners. Their different kinds a' lives. How they dress up, 'n' talk, 'n' all." This gives Froggy an idea. He tells Betty that he has brought a friend who'll be staying here for three days, in Froggy's old room.

FROGGY: I want yer to take super care of 'im—best of everything, right?

BETTY: Well, yes.

FROGGY: All right. The other thing is—oh, God, 'ow should I put this? 'E musn't be spoken to.

BETTY: He mustn't—when?

FROGGY: Ever.

BETTY: Mustn't be spoken to?

FROGGY: No.

BETTY: Why not?

FROGGY: Well—

BETTY: Somethin' wrong with him?

FROGGY: No. No. Perfectly nice. Terrific fella. But—the fact is—'e doesn't speak English very well.

BETTY: No?

FROGGY: No. In fact—not a word.

BETTY: Oh?

FROGGY: No, poor bloke. Now, I can't say too much, mind. I've got my orders. But I'll tell yer this—if someone 'ere was wishin' ter see a foreigner—a real one —p'raps they wouldn't 'ave ter look too far.

BETTY: Frog!

FROGGY: That's right.

Froggy isn't allowed to tell all he knows about this foreigner, except that he's "as foreign as the day is long" but is definitely *not* a Communist.

BETTY: But—we cain't none of us talk to him?

FROGGY: No, it shames 'im, yer see. Poor bloke—'e can't reply to wot people say, and then 'e feels 'orrible. If yer so much as says "good mornin' " to 'im, 'e walks about, 'angin' 'is 'ead for days. Yer don't want that.

BETTY: Why, no. Poor man.

FROGGY: 'E'll be no trouble. Regular meals, spot o' tea once in a while.

BETTY: My. A real foreigner.

FROGGY: Don't expect Jojo the Jungle Boy. 'E's just a bloke, yer know.

BETTY: Still—

FROGGY: You'll get on great. I wish I could stay, but I'm off. I, uh— *(Smiling.)* I suppose I ought to 'ave just a word with Cha-Oo-Lee.

BETTY: You know how to speak his kinda talk?

FROGGY: Well, the odd phrase. You know—" 'Ello"—"Where's the gents?"— "My hat is brown," that sort o' thing.

BETTY: Oh—

> *Perhaps she is about to ask for a quick language course, but she is interrupted by a sound from the hall.*

FROGGY: That'll be 'im. . . . .

Betty goes to fetch some tea, as Charlie comes in and sits, listlessly. When Betty comes back with the tea, Charlie, not yet briefed on the deception, says "Thank you" distinctly, amazing her with his grasp of this English phrase. Froggy intervenes with some gibberish and then sends Betty off so that he can explain to Charlie that he has fixed it so Charlie won't have to engage in any conversation. He can pretend he's an exotic foreigner who can't speak English, and Betty especially admires foreigners.

Charlie declares he can't go through with this. Froggy points out how disappointed, then, Betty will be. He prepares to leave and let Charlie do the explaining to Betty, when the Rev. David Marshall Lee comes in out of the storm. He *"is neither the stereotypically pallid, remote young divinity student, nor the hearty, backslapping evangelist. He seems rather to be a regular fella—humorous and open."* Before leaving, Froggy learns that David and his fiancee love this lodge and hope Betty won't have to sell but will buy it at her price if she does.

As Froggy leaves, Catherine Simms, David's betrothed, enters, a *"formidable little figure . . . . . Her crossed arms and the basilisk glare from her pretty face tell us that David has stayed too long at the fair."* They fail to notice Charlie in his chair. Catherine blurts out to David that he isn't sterile after all, as they had thought. She is pregnant and thinking about going to Atlanta to have it attended to, so that she won't have to walk up the aisle obviously "all ballooned up" in front of everybody when they get married in November. David will have none of this; he suggests they get married immediately, but Catherine doesn't want to change the carefully planned date. In any case, David sees this as a cause for celebration. As they embrace, Catherine notices Charlie, who is desperately trying to remain invisible. She calls Charlie to David's attention.

CATHERINE: I mean, would you look at that? Would you take a look at the nerve of that? *(To Charlie.)* You were just sitting there this whole *time?*

DAVID: Now honey, I'm sure—

CATHERINE: I don't be*lieve* it!

BETTY *(entering):* What's going on here?

CATHERINE: I can't get over it! We're in here havin' this *real* personal conversation. Then we turn around, what do we see? This *man* sittin' here. Just sittin' here listenin' to every word we *said*.

BETTY: Miz Catherine—

CATHERINE: I can't get over it! I never heard of anything so *rude!* When I think what we were talkin' about, I—

BETTY: Miz—

CATHERINE: I could just *die!*

BETTY: He didn't hear ye, Miz Catherine.

CATHERINE: He was sittin' right here the whole—

BETTY: *Shh,* now? He don't speak no English.

CATHERINE: What?

BETTY: No. Nary a word. So you can just simmer down.

CATHERINE: He doesn't speak English?

BETTY: No. Well, he can say "Thank you," but he jest learned that tonight.

CATHERINE: Who is he?

BETTY: He's a foreign fella, name's Charlie. *(To Charlie, patting him on the shoulder and shouting in his face.) Don't you worry none, Charlie! Everything's gonna be fine!*

> For Charlie, it is surely the moment of truth. If he is to speak, it had better be now. He opens his mouth.

CATHERINE: I'd die if I thought he'd been listenin' to us. I would just die.

> *Charlie closes his mouth, then opens it to speak again.*

DAVID: Honey, he wasn't. No decent person would've just sat there.

> *Again, Charlie wavers.*

BETTY: 'Course not. An' Frog wouldn't lie to me. He's m' friend.

> *Charlie looks miserably from face to face—Catherine's suspicious, David's trusting and Betty's shining with pride. Finally, resignedly— perhaps even with a trace of foreign dialect—he speaks and seals his fate.*

CHARLIE: Thank you.

BETTY: There, y' see? "Thank you." That's all he knows.

CATHERINE: All right, then.

DAVID: All right.

Betty claims that the "foreigner" likes her to talk to him, but no one else should try. She notices that Ellard has put two more half-eaten apples in the wood bin, but both Catherine and David plead for tolerance of his behavior, though it seems to be getting worse.

Owen Musser enters and adds a *"dank presence"* to the room. He is *"a man with two tattoos . . . . . One he may have gotten on a drunk or a dare. But two means he went back."* Betty resents his bad-mouthing this building, but since Owen is the county property inspector, his gossip is the law. A clap of thunder and flash of lightning cause Owen to admit that "They's things out thar" on nights like this that he's afraid of.

Owen wants to talk to David in private, so the women retire to their rooms, Catherine asking David to bring her a candle when he comes upstairs. David assures Owen that Charlie is a foreigner who understands nothing. Owen tests

Charlie, trying to make him flinch by standing behind him and threatening to pour Coke down his neck, but Charlie remains immovable. Owen's idea of fun, then, is to smile at Charlie, pretending he is being friendly, while saying ugly things to him. Charlie continues to reply "Thank you," even to this.

Finally, Owen and David get down to business, with Charlie overhearing. Owen shows David a paper certifying that this building is condemned by the state authorities in Atlanta.

DAVID: So how much can Betty ask for it now?

OWEN: Tops, around twenty thousand.

DAVID: That is a bargain, truly.

OWEN: You gonna buy it, then?

DAVID: As soon as I'm able.

OWEN: You be careful she don't find herself another buyer.

DAVID: No, Betty will wait till I have the funds.

OWEN: She gonna wait six months?

DAVID: If need be.

OWEN: *(with paper):* 'Cause this ain't necessarily permanent, ye know. That there brickwork out front gets repaired, 'n' you got yourself one expensive little property again.

DAVID: Just the brickwork, huh?

OWEN: Thass all. She fixes that up, an' they ain't nothin' I can do. Legally.

They are interrupted by the entrance of Catherine's brother Ellard, *"a lumpy, overgrown, backward youth."* David asks Ellard to take a carrot to Catherine, and Ellard goes off to oblige. It seems that Ellard's and Catherine's father bequeathed to his children about $100,000, to be divided equally if Catherine feels Ellard is intelligent enough to handle it prudently. Owen leaves, as David assures him the Lord will provide them the means to establish what he calls a "Christian hunt club."

Catherine comes in, puzzled as to why Ellard, trailing after her, should have brought her a carrot. David claims he asked Ellard to bring Catherine a *candle* (which Ellard of course denies), seemingly one more small indication of the lad's incompetence, but deliberately engineered by David. After Catherine and Ellard depart, David takes an apple from the bowl, bites it, then throws it in the wood bin, declaring to supposedly obtuse Charlie, "God helps those who help themselves," as the scene blacks out.

Scene 2: The following morning

Betty enters and stamps on the floor, trying without success to signal Ellard, in the cellar, to open the trap door and pass her up a jar of sauerkraut. A few moments later, Charlie enters the now-empty room, goes to the phone, reaches Froggy at the base and begs him to come and get him. He has overheard a good many things he shouldn't have, and "They don't leave me alone. No! The old woman does nothing but shout at me. The others talk about me as if I were a potted palm."

Ellard wanders in and out (he hasn't been fully informed about Charlie yet), and when Betty comes in, Charlie resorts to gibberish on the phone and then hands it to Betty, who tells Froggy how very much she enjoys having the "foreigner" here. Betty hands Charlie back the phone and exits; and Charlie then allows that maybe he can stand it here for a couple more days. He'd like to tell Froggy something else of importance, but is forced by Betty's re-entrance to break off the conversation and hang up the phone.

Betty finally manages to make contact with Ellard, below, who opens the downward-hinged trap door and tries to pass up a handful of sauerkraut and an empty jar. Betty instructs Ellard to close the trap, fill the jar and return by the back door.

Catherine is somewhat irritated when she finds that David has gone out: "Off with the damn poor people again, is where he is. Helpin' 'em skin hogs, and make soap, and lookin' after their damn souls. I just hope he won't mind havin' a wife he has to go visit in the *insane asylum!*" Catherine refuses Betty's offer of breakfast but insists that Ellard must eat something.

BETTY: What do you want? You can have French toast? Pancakes? What?
ELLARD: Eggs.
BETTY: I thought you didn't *like* eggs.
　　　　Pause.
ELLARD: French toast.
BETTY: You can have eggs if you want 'em. I jest thought you didn't want 'em. You want 'em?
ELLARD: Yeah.
BETTY: All *right.* I tell ye, Ellard—these questions ain't that hard. Anybody'd think you 'uz tryin' to make me mad deliberately.
ELLARD: Yes'm.
BETTY: You are?
ELLARD: No'm.
BETTY: All right. How do ye like yer eggs?
ELLARD *(on the spot):* What?
BETTY: *How* do ye *like* yer *eggs?*
ELLARD *(fearfully):* They're real good. Thank you.
BETTY: Ellard!
ELLARD: What?
BETTY: When I say, "How do ye like yer eggs," that means, "How do ye want me to fix 'em."
ELLARD: Oh.
BETTY: So how do ye like 'em?
ELLARD: Fried?
BETTY: All *right,* then! *(She storms out.)*
CATHERINE: Ohhh, boy. *(To Charlie and Ellard.)* You two be up for a game of Scrabble later? If I'm not busy makin' some excitin' cookies, or sump'm. Or readin' one of these delightful up-to-date magazines. *(Picking up a ragged magazine and reading.)* "Princess Diana has given birth to a baby boy—her first. The child is as yet unnamed." When *will* she find a name for that baby? *(Drops the*

magazine and wanders to a window.) Yeah. Shoot. When is that gal—gonna find a name for that—?

> *She has surprised herself with a sudden rush of emotion, which she quietly allays.*

ELLARD: *(finally—helpfully):* Buddy might be good.

CATHERINE: What?

ELLARD: Buddy?

CATHERINE: For what?

ELLARD: That little boy's name?

CATHERINE *(dripping with sarcasm):* Yeah. Prince Buddy. Prince Buddy of England. Be fine. Well. That's settled. I don't know *what* we're gonna do now. We named the prince. Go back to bed, I guess.

ELLARD: That's my favorite name. If I ever catch me that chipmunk, that's what he's gonna be—Buddy the chipmunk.

Betty comes in with the breakfasts for Ellard and Charlie. Again she asks Catherine if she wants some, but she gives up when Catherine refuses edgily.

"How d'ye like them eggs?" Betty asks Ellard, who, having learned his lesson, replies, "Fried."

Catherine leaves to take a walk by the lake. Betty, having explained something of Charlie's foreign-ness to Ellard, leaves the two men alone. Charlie imitates Ellard's motions with fork, orange juice, etc., as though learning what these objects were all about. Ellard turns this into a game and puts a glass on his head. Charlie does the same. Betty comes back and takes this to mean that in Charlie's country they put a glass on their head at breakfast.

Betty leaves, and Ellard tries to explain to Charlie the functions of knife, fork and spoon. In the process, he gets Charlie to imitate him saying "Fork"— "Faw-work"—and soon Charlie is pretending to learn from Ellard the names of many of the objects in the room. Delighted with Charlie's progress, Ellard goes outside to get some objects for further naming, when Betty comes back.

BETTY: Laws. *(Going to clear the remains of breakfast.) You done with yer breakfast, Charlie?* You must be. Ye took off your little head-glass.

> *Charlie, as if to answer, tears his paper napkin in half.*

That mean yo're done? I reckon it must.

> *Experimentally, Charlie stands and, straight-faced, does a brief, wild little dance.*

Ohhh! *(They look at each other.)* That mean ye enjoyed it? *(Charlie does his little smile.)* It does?

> *Charlie dances around some more, shading his eyes a la hornpipe, flapping his arms like wings and doing a fairly complex series of meaningless gestures.*

And—let's see, I don't know if I got all o' that, er not. Sump'm about—was it sump'm about yo're lookin' forward to more o' my cookin'? *(Charlie smiles, watches her.)* And—and ye hope I'll cook ye some chicken? *(Charlie just smiles.)* Well, don't you worry none, Charlie. 'Cause ye know what we're havin' fer dinner this very *night? Chicken! (Flaps her arms.)*

Betty now believes she can read all of Charlie's gestures, and when he wiggles his fingers she assumes he wants her to play the harmonica for him. She goes to get it.

Catherine comes in, signs for Charlie to sit and amuses herself by haranguing him on the subject of the news in today's paper: "Aww—looky here. Somebody's gone out and torched the Klan headquarters, can you beat that? Up in Atlanta. Yes, sir. Burned the place *down*. That's a switch. Some old boys aren't too pleased right now, you can bet on that. Watch out for them, mister, those Klan boys. They'll get you. You're not a hundred per cent American white Christian, you're liable to find yourself some fine mornin' floppin' around in some Safeway dumpster, minus a few little things . . . . ."

Betty turns from the paper and addresses the brick wall she believes Charlie to be, confessing that she was once "one of these little cutie-patooties" like the debutantes in the paper and fears she may not be cut out for anything better, like being a mother and a preacher's wife.

Ellard comes in with a wheelbarrow with an uprooted bush, bricks, hardware and other objects from outdoors. He puts Charlie through his verbal paces, showing Catherine that he's teaching the "foreigner" English words. His pupil appears to be a very fast learner. Betty comes through on her way upstairs and is amazed by Charlie's progress. Then David comes in, somewhat disheveled from having helped clean up fire damage down the road. David witnesses the English lesson, as Ellard shows Charlie a brick.

ELLARD: . . . . . Now wha-at's this?
CHARLIE: "Breek?"
ELLARD: Yeah. This?
CHARLIE: "Boosh."
ELLARD: Real good.
CHARLIE: Ril good.
CATHERINE: Idn' that sump'm?"
ELLARD: This?
DAVID: Well, yes . . .
    With a grin and a jerk of the head toward the kitchen, Catherine exits.
CHARLIE: "Rock?"
ELLARD: "Rock!" Yeah. Okay, some new things. "Jar?"
    Charlie favors David with a big, innocent smile. David returns it, minus a couple of kilowatts.
Charlie? *(Charlie looks back at him.)* "Ja-ar?"
CHARLIE: "Ja-ar?"
ELLARD: "Nail?"
CHARLIE: "Nail?"
    From another room we hear a sprightly hymn—"Bringing in the Sheaves," perhaps, or "In the Sweet Bye-and-Bye"—being played on the harmonica. David, a little disturbed, turns again to regard Charlie, who has continued with his responses.
ELLARD: "Board?"

CHARLIE: "Board?"
ELLARD: "Leaf?"
CHARLIE: "Leaf?"
ELLARD: Together.
BOTH: "Ja-ar?" "Na-ail?" Bo-oard?" "Le-eaf?"

> *The music continues. David is still watching Charlie. Charlie and Ellard are still reciting, as the lights fade. Curtain.*

ACT II

Scene 1: Afternoon, two days later

David enters followed by Owen carrying a corrugated box. They hint at some plan involving money and this lodge of Betty's and possible acts of violence. Owen is inclined toward an immediate use of force.

OWEN: I still think we oughta jest *take* this place. Jest *take* it!
DAVID *(stopping him)*: Now, Owen, listen. Listen to me. *(Owen looks at him.)* We have got an opportunity, here. The whole Georgia empire, what's left of it, it's all out there in that van. The hardware. The uniforms. All of it. And listen —this time tomorrow, I expect to be a happily-married homeowner.
OWEN: Wha—?
DAVID: True. Quietly, legally. So there's no need to get gun-happy. All right? There's no need to arouse the law, until we are the law.
OWEN: Man, if it wadn't fer that money—!
DAVID: I know. All right. Just think of the money. And calm yourself. *(Referring to the box.)* Let's get this open.
OWEN *(opening the box)*: Papers.
DAVID *(pulling out ledgers, labels, mailing lists)*: Good. Records, addresses. We need these. Praise God.
OWEN *(deeper in the box)*: Boy, howdy. Looky here.
> *He extracts a bundle of sticks of dynamite.*
Oh, I do like dynamite.
DAVID: Wait. We just drove up this mountain with a box of dynamite?
OWEN: Don't ye worry. These babies won't go without a charge. These is good little babies.
DAVID: All right, let's put it back.

As they exit to take the box back to the van, David tells Owen he and Catherine are getting married the next day because they're too much in love to wait until November as planned. Ellard and Charlie come in—Charlie appears to be learning the numbers from 1 to 20. Betty comes in with dinners on a tray, and Catherine joins the group, learning that Ellard and Charlie have been down to watch them building the new courthouse, and today they let Ellard help.

Froggy enters and is introduced by Betty to Catherine and her brother, whom he hadn't met. Betty tells Froggy how wrong he was when he said it might be boring to have the "foreigner" as a boarder. They are all enjoying his company, his picturesque little ways like putting a glass on his head at breakfast time. Froggy, pouring himself a drink, allows as how in his own country Charlie is known as quite a raconteur, and Betty insists on hearing Charlie tell one of his stories. Charlie can't get out of it; "Blasny, blasny," he begins and launches upon an outpouring of gibberish—with gestures that can be interpreted as a moral tale about a pretty young girl being eaten by a great beast in a forest. His listeners all enjoy it, though they did not all deduce the same events from Charlie's mouthings and gestures.

Charlie has reached the point where he can now use some of the phrases Ellard has "taught" him.

FROGGY: . . . . . 'E's picked up a bit of English, I see.

BETTY: Oh, yes. Charlie's been in good hands, all right.

CHARLIE: Last night—I learn--to rid.

FROGGY: Ter "rid?"

CHARLIE: To rid book.

FROGGY: Ah!

CHARLIE (referring to Ellard): He teach me.

FROGGY: Yes. (To Ellard.) And 'ow long did it take yer to teach 'im to, uh—ter "rid?"

ELLARD: 'Bout an hour.

FROGGY: One hour, eh?

CHARLIE: Yes! I show you.
He brings a large volume down from the mantel.

CATHERINE: Well, how did I miss this?

CHARLIE (with the book open): You help.

ELLARD: 'Kay.

CHARLIE (reading): "Shall I compare thee to a summer's day? Thou art more lovely—aa—?"
He points to a word.

ELLARD (helping): "And?"

CHARLIE: "And, more temperate." (To Ellard.) Yes?

ELLARD (after studying the page another moment and trying to conceal his astonishment at himself): Yeah. (He looks at the page again.)

CATHERINE: Well, Ellard. (Ellard looks at her.) All that's from just an hour?

ELLARD: Yeah.

CATHERINE: I can't believe that.

ELLARD: I know. Remember how long it took me to learn to read? 'Bout three years.

FROGGY: Wot d'yer think accounts for the difference?

ELLARD: I don't know. (Not naming any names.) I guess he just had a better teacher.

Catherine suggests that maybe she'd better stop confiding her secrets to Charlie, who may now be able to understand what she's saying. Froggy comments to no one in particular, "Gettin' away wiv bloody murder, is wot it is." After hearing from Charlie that "gok" and "blit" mean "yes" and "no" in his language, the others drift off, leaving Charlie alone with Froggy to tell him how much he's

Anthony Heald as Charlie Baker and Kevin Geer as Ellard
Simms in a scene from *The Foreigner*

enjoying this adventure and his ripening friendship with Catherine. Froggy,
feeling a little bit that he has created a monster, leaves.

Owen enters and boasts to Charlie that he's going to become sheriff, "An' I
got that Invisible Empire t' back me up—man, they ain't gonna be none o' you
left in this county. Foreigners. Yeah. Gonna wipe you all right out—all you
dummy boys, black boys, Jew boys . . . . ."

They're going to have a pile of money soon, too, Owen tells Charlie, believing
he can't understand, and he just hopes that some of his victims will give him
pleasure by trying to resist. Charlie replies with sequences of pidgeon English to
which Owen at first pays no attention.

CHARLIE: I loook tru your bones.
> *Owen looks at him, startled by this. Charlie looks back with ancient
> eyes and the ghost of a smile.*
OWEN *(finally):* You say what?
CHARLIE: Yes. Me see. Moon get beeg. You sleep—sleep out, out. All you skin
—bye-bye. I come. I look tru your bones.
OWEN: What you talkin' about, mister?
CHARLIE *(his eyes close):* Round an' round, and in de town—*(His eyes open
slightly, still looking at Owen.)* Gonna look into your bones, when de *bees* come
down.
> *Owen watches him, open-mouthed, for another moment, then is in-
> stantly at the window.*

OWEN: Hey! *(Looks back at Charlie, then out the window again.)* Hey! Somebody get in here! Get in here!

David and Betty enter and see that Owen has been greatly upset by Charlie's "zombie talk" about bones and "bees come down." Catherine comes in and refers somewhat sarcastically to David's absence for a whole day (it was two days, he corrects her, and she is surprised to realize that he's right, and she hadn't realized). He has brought home a green van loaned to him by the people whose place burned down in Atlanta. It will be much needed in his ministry, he claims.

Charlie demonstrates for David what great progress he has made learning new words under Ellard's tutelage—and Catherine boasts that Ellard has now been taught to lay bricks by the people building the courthouse. Ellard's progress has been such that Catherine has decided to give him his family inheritance. David smiles and suggests that they give it to him together after they're married, Catherine agrees.

David is determined to find out more about Charlie—where his native land is, for example. The only map they have is of Georgia. Owen holds it, and Charlie sends Owen farther and farther off, pretending to demonstrate what the relative position of his homeland would be on a world map. When David inquires about Charlie's native language, Charlie ties him in conversational knots, much to David's irritation.

CATHERINE: . . . . . You have to be patient.

DAVID: Patient! You're telling me how to be *pa*tient?

CATHERINE: David.

DAVID: Who the hell are you to tell—!

CATHERINE: I've never seen you like this.

ELLARD *(the forgiving soul):* Maybe it's just a phase.

DAVID: All right. What do you want? You want me to learn some words from this man?

CATHERINE: Well, yes. Look at him. He really just wants to give us something, can't you see that?

CHARLIE *(earnestly, to David):* Yes. I really want geev eet to you.

DAVID: All right.

CHARLIE: Yes? I teach now?

DAVID *(summoning up his calm again):* Yes. Why don't you teach me something?

OWEN *(moving toward the door):* Well, don't that jest cut it? Do anything she says, I reckon, wouldn't ye? I reckon if she said fer you to—

DAVID: Owen, we can discuss this later.

OWEN: Ain't gonna be nothin' to discuss. Not once I go down inta town 'n' tell some friends of mine who's up here shinin' up to foreigners.

DAVID: Owen—if you'd think about it, maybe you'd realize why I'm doing this.

OWEN: I can see why.

CATHERINE: Who cares, David? Let him go.

DAVID: No, honey. *(Looking at Owen.)* Owen is one of God's children too. I think he might profit from a lesson as much as any of us. *(To Owen.)* I think you should stay. Join me in this.

OWEN: I ain't stayin' here talkin' no damn hoodoo talk!

DAVID *(evenly):* Owen. You must learn to be meek. Otherwise you may never inherit the earth.

> *Pause. Then, to nearly everyone's suprise, Owen pulls up a chair and sits, fuming.*

Charlie teaches the group "gok" and "blit," makes Owen repeat it and then makes fun of him because of his pronunciation. Owen's fury deepens when Ellard, too, appears to be laughing at him. The "language" lesson continues, with Charlie managing to needle Owen at almost every turn, until even David can no longer curb him. Owen pulls out his knife, commands silence and makes his declaration: "I'm doin' the talkin' from now on! Me! I got me some friends down thar—they don't think I'm so dumb. Matter fact, they jes' waitin' t' hear one word from me —jes' one little word, before they come ridin', up this mountain in a blaze a' light! Ridin' out, the way they been doin' fer a hunnerd years! More'n a hunnerd years! Takin' care of foreigners like him. So you get yourselves ready. *(To Catherine and Betty.)* Put on yer pretty dresses, women. You fixin' to meet the Klan."

Owen exits. Catherine is shocked to hear that Owen belongs to the Klan and wants to call the police. David persuades her not to do it, assures her he will handle Owen, and he exits.

Catherine warns the others that a visit from the Klan would have serious consequences with a foreigner like Charlie in the house. Betty names various neighbors they could call on for help, but Charlie dials Froggy and gets an answering machine, into which Catherine pours the message that they need help, particularly against "a mean-lookin' fella drivin' a green van."

The phone goes dead, and when they try the lights they find they've been cut off too, with darkness coming soon. Preparing for their defense, Ellard brandishes a croquet mallet. Betty asks Charlie for his advice.

BETTY: You tell us what to do! You been all over the world! You got all them mysterious ways o' doin' things, an' all!

ELLARD: Oh, yeah, I bet Charlie will come up with sump'm.

CHARLIE: Ohhh . . .

CATHERINE: Any idea you have, Charlie. Even a stupid one, at this point.

CHARLIE *(looking around):* Stupid idea. Stupid idea.

CATHERINE: It dudn' *have* to be stupid. Just—

BETTY: He's got an idea right now. I can always tell.

CHARLIE *(sickly):* Oh . . .

CATHERINE: Charlie, if you do, if you have any kind of idea, please tell us.

CHARLIE *(still in dialect, though perhaps he doesn't realize it):* Listen, I . . . I'm not—

> *He is on the verge of confession, but suddenly his attention is arrested by something in the center of the floor. The others look too. The throw-rug? He looks at the mallet in Ellard's hands and back at the spot on the floor. He picks up the rug and tosses it aside, still watching the spot.*

CATHERINE: Charlie? What—what are you thinking? *(Pause.)* Charlie?

CHARLIE *(looks at the spot for another second, then up at Catherine. Pause):* Sheets?

CATHERINE: What?

> Charlie looks at Betty. Then he looks back at Catherine. He does not speak again. Blackout.

Scene 2: That evening

In the calm before the expected onslaught by the Klan, Catherine is curious about Charlie's background. Charlie tells her he's married and that his wife, whom he loves, is sick.

At Charlie's direction, Betty has removed all the light bulbs upstairs. Catherine doubts they can hold the attackers off with the puny forces at their disposal, but "It'd sure give us a chance to find out how brave we all are."

An orange glow outside tells them the Klan has arrived and is lighting torches. It's time for Catherine and Ellard to get upstairs, according to Charlie's plan. Ellard, who has been listening to Catherine voice her doubts, is now scared, and he freezes.

CHARLIE *(to Ellard, improvising wildly):* Leesten! Thees— Eet— croquet mallet! Een my contry, croquet mallet ees great seembol of—of—of—*frid*dom!

ELLARD: Huh?

CHARLIE: Yes! and we hev king. Great, famous, famous—uh—

> *Outside in the distance, we hear sounds—ear horns, and Indian whoops, and an occasional rifle shot.*

CATHERINE: Charlie—

CHARLIE: Famous, uh—*war*rior! Warrior king! Very brave! Many bettles he ween weeth—croquet mallet!

ELLARD: Huh?

CHARLIE: Yes! Ulways fight weeth croquet mallet! Here! Hold!

> *Racing against time now, he raises the mallet in Ellard's hands to a passably regal position.*

Ah! De same! De same! You loook like heem!

ELLARD *(tentatively):* The king?

CHARLIE: Yes! Yes! De *king!* De *king!*

> *Ellard looks at the mallet, still not convinced.*

(Desperately.) King Buddy!

ELLARD *(scarcely able to believe it):* King *Bud*dy?

CHARLIE: Yes!

The invaders are pounding on the door. Ellard and Catherine go upstairs to take their places—but not before Catherine wonders how Charlie learned about Ellard's love of the name "Buddy."

The door opens. Inside there is darkness and noise, the sound of swishing robes and the pounding of boots, with Betty's and Charlie's faces visible in the beam of flashlights. Owen's voice outdoors on a loudspeaker warns the inhabitants of the house that they are about to receive a visit from "the holy tribunal of the Invisible Empire" calling them to account for harboring a foreigner in their midst. Betty protests loudly that Charlie has done nothing wrong. Owen orders the electricity turned back on, and the gang of Klansmen becomes visible ". . . . . *in white robes, some carrying weapons—shotguns, pistols, army rifles. All are hooded. Owen's high rank is designated by colorful insignia sewn on to his own hood.*"

Owen declares that they are going to take Charlie and orders the others to get out of town on the next bus, or "Charlie here's gonna get to see what his innards look like." Starting tomorrow, this house will be abandoned property taken over as a headquarters for the Klan. A Klansman has found Catherine upstairs and brings her down, while Owen orders Charlie to get up onto the table and dance. Instead of obeying, Charlie stares at Owen.

CHARLIE (*slowly, with growing power, his eyes boring straight at Owen*): You—dare—to—affront—*me?* I, who have lain in wait, lo, these many centuries for such a night as this!

OWEN: What!

CHARLIE (*slowly stepping onto the sofa*): I, child of Hrothgar and of Moloch! I whom the Old Ones have given suck, to rise now from the forest mold and smite thee! Klatu! Barada! Nikto!

OWEN: Now, don't you start that! I warn ye!

CHARLIE: There are a thousand serpents in my bowels, and each one squeals with pleasure!

OWEN: Now, don't you—don't you start that hoodoo talk, mister, er somebody's gonna get *hurt.*

CHARLIE (*in his full glory now, standing majestically atop the* sofa): You dare to sneer at me! *You—puny—earthling!*

OWEN (*troubled by this unexpected word*): "Earthling!" What—?

CHARLIE: *Aroint thee, sniveling spawn!*

> *The Klansman holding Catherine releases her and raises his rifle. Charlie wheels on him, pointing at him with ramrod-straight arm and outstretched fingers.*

From my heart, I strike at thee!

> *With a vengeful cry, Charlie makes a sudden upward slash through the air with his arm, and the Klansman's rifle, as though wrenched from him by an unseen force, flies from his grasp and spins across the floor.*

KLANSMAN: Wha—?

OWEN: What th'—?

> *In a flash, Charlie has returned his arm, so that it points again at the offending Klansman.*

BETTY: Charlie! No! No!

> *But there is no stopping Charlie in his wrath. From somewhere deep within him comes a constant, shrill, unearthly sound. We half expect to see glass objects shattering here and there; but instead—can we believe our eyes?—the Klansman claws the air, giving out a cry born of deep, searing pain—deep at first, then higher, like the voice of a*

dwarf, then like that of an insect, as—he grows smaller! His arms retract, his head sinks into his body, and his body itself, writhing in place and possibly seething smoke, slowly melts into the floor, leaving at last only a pile of white and rumpled cloth.

OWEN *(pause; staring at the spot):* Holy shit.

CHARLIE *(turning with eyes ablaze to Owen, now, and bringing his deadly arm into firing position):* De bees come down! De bees come down! Gonna look into your *bones,* when de *bees*—come—!

Suddenly conscious of his mortality, Owen flees, carrying as he goes the only exit-line really worth of him.

OWEN: *AAAAAAAAAAAAAAAAAAAAAH!*

As the Klansmen flee, with similar cries, the others run to the pile of clothing to see if Ellard—who comes back up out of the floor through the trap door—is all right. He is fine, having scared away all the Klansmen except one they hit over the head with the croquet mallet upstairs. Almost at once, David comes staggering in, holding his bruised forehead—he was that "Klansman," and he is very upset to find that Charlie and his friends have scared the others off. They have ruined David's well-laid plan, he admits in front of them all, to take over the Invisible Empire and "clean" the nation of "Foreigners! Jews! Catholics!" Appalled, Catherine realizes that what this monster she was going to marry really wants of her is her money to finance his ambitions, and she wants no more of him.

David has one last hope: they've left him the van and its contents which will perhaps permit him to start all over again on the path of domination, by himself. But Froggy arrives with his detonator attached to wires; and when he learns for sure that the van is David's, it is only the work of a moment to push down the plunger and blow the van to smithereens. David leaves the house with a cry similar to Owen's.

Froggy reassures his friends that the police are rounding up the Klansmen. Betty explains to Froggy how they scared off the invaders according to Charlie's plan. They knocked the one who came upstairs (David) over the head and took his robe for Ellard to act the part of the Klansman stripped of his rifle and shrinking down to the floor.

Catherine has decided that she and Ellard will stay here and help Betty put the place in order (Ellard can do the brick work now). Betty is delighted—but they're all going to miss Charlie, who gathers with them for a communal hug.

Froggy takes Charlie aside and shows him a telegram that came for him today—Charlie has lost his wife and is free to stay on here if he pleases. It is to Charlie's credit that he is obviously saddened by the telegram, and Catherine persuades him to whisper to her the reason for his sadness.

CATHERINE: Ohhh, Charlie *(Hugging Charlie.)* We've both had our losses today, haven't we? *(Charlie nods.)*

FROGGY: I've told 'im 'e could stay 'ere a bit longer, if 'e'd like. I could fix it on my end.

CATHERINE: How about that, Charlie? You want to stay here with us? *(No answer.)* Charlie?

FROGGY: Charlie? Look—I ought to tell yer—I'm a bit worried about 'im. I ought ter tell yer—'e's not wot 'e seems. I mean—

CATHERINE: Shh, now. I think I know.

FROGGY: Yer do? *(She nods.)*

CATHERINE *(to Charlie):* Come on, baby. We'll take care of you.

CHARLIE: I—stay?

CATHERINE *(leading him to the door):* That's right. You stay. And you know what? I bet, if we work real hard, some day you won't be talkin' with any accent at all, any more.

CHARLIE: That may take long . . .

CATHERINE: Well. We've got all the time in the world.

> *They exit. Ellard follows.*

FROGGY: Bet? I'm havin' a drink.

> *He goes to the bar, pours.*

And I never drink alone. My treat.

> *He hands her a drink.*

'Ere you go.

BETTY: My land. What—what was in that telegram he had?

FROGGY: It was from the 'ospital. It was 'is wife.

BETTY: His wife? Did she—? Did she die?

FROGGY: *No.* No. It was *from* 'is wife. No. She recovered completely. Ran off with a proctologist.

BETTY *(shakes her head):* Well—real life's awful hard, sometimes.

FROGGY: It is, Bet. It is that. *(Toasting.)* Blasny, blasny.

BETTY: Blasny, blasny.

> *They drink as the lights fade out. Curtain.*

TRACERS

A Play in Two Acts

CONCEIVED BY JOHN DiFUSCO, WRITTEN BY

VINCENT CARISTI, RICHARD CHAVES,

JOHN DiFUSCO, ERIC E. EMERSON,

RICK GALLAVAN, MERLIN MARSTON

AND HARRY STEPHENS WITH SHELDON

LETTICH

Cast and credits appear on pages 368–370

JOHN DiFUSCO conceived the original idea of Tracers *and directed it during its authorship in the improvisational process (but now "frozen" in script form) by the seven original members of its cast, all Vietnam War veterans—Vincent Caristi, Richard Chaves, Eric E. Emerson, Rick Gallavan, Merlin Marston, Harry Stephens, and DiFusco himself—plus a contributing writer, Sheldon Lettich, also a veteran.*

DiFusco was born Dec. 31, 1947 in Webster, Mass., the son of a road construction worker. He served with the United States forces in the Central Highlands of

"Tracers": by, and copyright © 1983, 1985, John DiFusco, Vincent Caristi, Richard Chaves, Eric E. Emerson, Rick Gallavan, Merlin Marston, Harry Stephens with Sheldon Lettich. Reprinted by permission of Hill and Wang, a division of Farrar, Straus and Giroux, Inc. See CAUTION notice on copyright page. All inquiries concerning performance rights should be addressed to: Frank J. Gruber, 9601 Wilshire Boulevard, Suite 700, Beverly Hills, CA 90210. All other inquiries should be addressed to: Hill and Wang, a division of Farrar, Straus and Giroux, Inc., 19 Union Square West, New York, N.Y. 10003.

165

Vietnam from Nov. 4, 1967 to Nov. 4, 1968, after which he entered California State University in Long Beach and studied to become an actor. Tracers *was an idea he carried around for a decade or more while working as an actor, director and writer. His experience with improvisational techniques led him to believe that* Tracers *might be developed in that process by a group of actors who also had Vietnam War experience and thus knew their subject. Not being acquainted with any such colleagues, he ran an ad in* Drama-Logue *in March 1980 and assembled his creative team under the auspices of Thomas Bird's Vietnam Veterans Ensemble Theater Company on the West Coast. After six months of work described in a New York program note as "personal improvisation, rap sessions, psycho-drama, physical work, trust and ensemble work," with a musical score selected by DiFusco and recorded to coordinate with the action,* Tracers *opened Oct. 17, 1980 at the Odyssey Theater in Los Angeles and was acclaimed by the* Drama-Logue *critics' award for direction and the Los Angeles Drama Critics award for ensemble performance. Its Jan. 21 appearance this season at the Public Theater marked DiFusco's New York directorial debut.*

Our method of synopsizing Tracers *in these pages differs from that of the other Best Plays. In order to illustrate its distinctive action and "look," the play is represented here partly in photographs, with continuity and short excerpts from the script to portray its textual style and flavor. These photographs of* Tracers *depict scenes as produced Jan. 21, 1985 by Joseph Papp in the Vietnam Veterans Ensemble Theater Company production, Thomas Bird artistic director, at the Susan Stein Shiva Theater of the New York Shakespeare Festival Public Theater; and as directed by John DiFusco, and with scenery by John Falabella and costumes by David Navarro Velasquez.*

Our special thanks are tendered to the producer and his press representatives, Merle Debuskey, Richard Kornberg, Bruce Campbell and Don Summa, for making available these selections of excellent photographs of the show by Susan Cook of Martha Swope Associates.

PROLOGUE

Someone just told me
>you were in Vietnam!

Someone just told me
>you carried a gun.

You killed people?
You were only nineteen?
You volunteered?
You must be bullshitting.
Oh, you're one of the lucky ones
>who made it back.

Oh, I am sorry.
Oh, and I suppose
>you don't want to talk about it?

Oh yeah, well we saw that on TV.
How was the heat?
How was the rain?
How were the chicks?
How was Bob Hope?
How does it feel
>to kill somebody? . . . . .

ACT I

1. *(Foreground)* Professor (R.J. Bonds), Doc (Josh Cruze) and Scooter (Jim Tracy) introduce themselves with their buddies *(background)* Habu, Little John, Dinky Dau and Baby San, accompanied by the first of the songs ("Walking on a Thin Line") prerecorded for each of the play's scenes: "Don't you know me, I'm the boy next door/The one you find so easy to ignore. . . . ./Straight off the front line/Labeled as freaks loose on the streets of the city/Walking on a thin line/Angry all the time/Take a look at my face, see what it's doing to me."

2. One by one, vets recite their "tracers," their individual emotions and hangups after their year's service in Vietnam. Scooter has dreams of combat in which no one dies. Little John has unexplained fits of anger. Baby San, unable to cope with his parents' lack of understanding, leaves home for Manhattan. Habu runs streams of red stoplights in his Camaro, explaining, "When you load the magazines, make the first two or three rounds tracers . . . . . when you see two or three red streaks in a row you know you're running out of ammo . . . time to reload."

The "tracer" of Dinky Dau (Richard Chaves, *below*), now in a wheelchair, goes like this: "I'm rolling down the boardwalk in Venice Beach and this Amazon queen in a one-piece string walks right in front of me. I slam on the brakes. Wow, sorry. Wanna dance? Are you crazy, she says, and runs over to her boy friend, a Charles Atlas look-alike. Fuckin' jack off. Fuck her and my ex-wife. Those kind

of women, they don't understand. Some of them can't even look at me. They all think I'm crazy. But at least I'm trying to straighten myself out. Get off the skag and drugs. Maybe they're right. I am Boo Coo Dinky Dau. I don't want to need a woman, but I do. Vietnamese women were different. Appearance didn't matter to them. They knew the value of a smile . . . . . it was special to them. They made me feel special. They weren't whores. I know what you're thinking, but they weren't. They were women. Very special women!"

Professor has fits of nerves: "I'm sitting in my apartment. I'm trying to meditate. Suddenly, I feel myself go numb. My mind separating from my body. The room—my environment—everything around me is moving up and away from me. . . . . I'm losing control. Maybe I'm going insane. All I know is, I'm scared. No, this couldn't have anything to do with Vietnam. I remember certain places, and certain people's faces . . ."

3. Past and future merge in the ritual performed *(above)* by Dinky Dau, Scooter, Professor, Habu (Anthony Chisholm), Baby San (Vincent Caristi) and Little John (Brian Delate). Alternating words and phrases, they whisper then recite their "Saigon list" which evokes the Vietnam experience:

Saigon	Dink	Sorry 'bout that shit
Da Nang	Victor Charles	Wasted
Phu Cat	November Victor Alpha	K.I.A.
Cam Rahn Bay	Skivvie girls	Head wound
The Nam	I souvenir you, G.I.	Stomach wound
Hootch	La Dai, motherfucker!	Medavac
Bunker	Mos Skosh!	Dustoff
Sandbags	Deedee Mou!	Hueys
Concertina wire	There it is, G.I.	Cobra gunships
Gook	I can't feel my legs	Freedom bird!

The six have returned in memory to their first day as recruits, greeting each other, shaking hands and exchanging names. The order, "Find yourselves a pair of yellow footprints, maggots," brings them to attention. They are about to meet Sgt. Williams.

4. On "day one" of training his group of young civilians to become soldiers, Drill Instructor Sgt. Williams (J. Kenneth Campbell, *above center*) begins at the beginning: "The position of attention means: feet at a forty-five-degree angle, thumbs along the seam of their trousers, stomach in, chest out, shoulders back, chin in, head and eyes locked straight to the front! While maggots are at attention they will not talk, they will not eye-fuck the area, they will listen to me and only me! From this day forth, the first word out of a maggot's mouth is 'Sir,' the last word out of a maggot's mouth is 'Sir.' Do maggots understand me?"

"Sir yes sir," the "maggots" reply, at first feebly but later sharply, as Sgt. Williams introduces them to the ways of tough discipline. Finally he gets them into a close-packed line *(bottom of facing page)* and heads them in the direction of the barber.

When the "maggots" have disappeared, Sgt. Williams turns and confides in the audience: "The Union of Soviet Socialist Republics trains its infantry for eighteen months. We train ours for eighteen weeks. Charlie Cong has been at it for twenty-six years. We issue them the most sophisticated equipment in the world; but we do not teach them how to use it. We commit them to the combat zone in units so large that their support facilities become targets for insurgents. They are now eighteen and nineteen years old. Before they are twenty-one, nearly half of them will be killed or wounded. With a two-year draft, we send out amateurs to play against pros in a game for keeps. Ten per cent should not even be here. Eighty per cent are targets; we have no time to train them to be more. Ten per cent are fighters. One in a hundred may become a warrior. I must seek him out. I must come down heavy on him. Upon him the success or failure of our present conflict lies. . . . ."

Sgt. Williams comes to attention, salutes, turns right face and exits.

5. "I lost my sense of judgement yesterday," Baby San *(left in photo below)* muses to himself, "I killed someone. Who? I don't know, we've never met . . . . . Brooklyn seems like a world away."

The men check their weapons, preparing to go on patrol in a free-fire zone, led by Cpl. Habu *(background in photo below)*. They tape anything that might rattle, top off canteens to avoid the sound of sloshing water, "blouse" their trousers, load tracers to tell them when they're nearly out of ammo and check their "autogetem," two clicks from safety on their M-16s.

6. Dinky Dau *(second from right in photo above)* describes the patrol: "We hadn't seen shit all day. Everyone's fatigues were drenched with sweat. . . . We'd been humpin' all day. I could hardly concentrate on the trail in front of me. My whole body was achin'. The jungle on both sides was startin' to get real dense. The trail started to go downhill. And then all of a sudden out of nowhere, there they were. Twelve or thirteen V.C. Right in front of us. If the point man hadn't spotted them, they'd have walked right into us. I watched the point man raise his weapon. It was like a movie in slow motion. The point man opened up on the first two or three V.C. I watched the first two go down, and then I opened up on full automatic. I creamed one of 'em with an entire clip. I watched my bullets as they ripped across his torso. Everyone was up. Everyone was hyper. Everyone was hittin'. . . . . I was eager. I was angry! . . . . . It was the first time I killed anybody. There were eight or nine dead bodies lying on the ground, and I just kept blastin' away at 'em. . . . . It was our little victory."

7. In the hootch, Dinky Dau is haunted by the memory of his killing frenzy. Baby San brings what he thinks is incense but turns out to be heroin. Dinky Dau sniffs it; then, helped by Little John, who's had medical training, he shoots it up *(photo above)*. It unsettles his stomach but relieves his anxiety "Like I'm flying . . . . . like being in a cartoon . . . . . like sex in slow motion."

Preparing for another patrol, Little John tells the audience, "Hunt 'em, kill 'em and count 'em. If we lose any we count them too. Then we call in the count and we get points," like a team scoring touchdowns for a big scoreboard, with the brass checking the tally every day. *Curtain.*

ACT II

8. Dinky Dau gets a "Dear John" letter from his girl. The men are assigned to a "blanket party," trying to fit together the pieces of mutilated corpses.

Professor visits Doc to be treated with rabies shots for a rat bite. They share a joint *(right)* and find they are kindred spirits, readers of Pirandello and Hesse. A month or so later, Professor hears that Doc has killed himself with a bullet from his .45.

9. For some, the ordeal is approaching its end. At a "short-timer's" sendoff for Habu, who has only nine more days to go, an M-16 serves as a limbo stick for Scooter to squeeze under *(photo below),* and the beer flows freely. To the tune of "O Tannenbaum" they sing "We like it here/We like it here/You're fuckin'-A/We like it here/We'll patrol the paddies/Sweep the hills/And triple reports/Of all our kills. . . . ." Habu reminds Little John, "You're the spirit here now. You bring 'em on home alive."

10. And what if they all *did* come home? Their 1984 "tracers" tell the possible story. Professor is in Bangkok, seeking solace from a Thai woman. Dinky Dau has found a woman who will dance with him in a wheelchair—a Vietnamese refugee. Habu re-enlisted and now has his fifth hash mark. Baby San owns night clubs in Manhattan and Miami and wonders whether he left an American child in Saigon.

Little John *(right)* has this 1984 "tracer": "Now I got my little sheet metal business. I pay my own way. I pay all my hospital bills. I never beg for anything. My doc says my cancer's running faster now than I am. I won't live past 40. My little girls will be here. Mary was born without a stomach and Debbie only has one foot. The war drags on. Fuck the Agent Orange lawsuit! . . . . . Fuck it man! . . . . . Fuck it!"

11. But there is another possible ending to the ordeal of these soldiers, and it begins to unfold when the men come in to get their M-16s.

LITTLE JOHN: . . . . . Habu came in the hootch screamin' for everyone to get their gear together and muster on the LZ. That's all I fuckin' know.

SCOOTER: Yeah, but did he say where we're going?

LITTLE JOHN: I told you—I don't know shit.

SCOOTER: You know what I heard? I heard Delta Company got their asses totally wiped out—like totally massacred—and we're gettin' sent in to replace them.

LITTLE JOHN: Where'd you hear that?

SCOOTER: That's all they're talkin' about down at the Commo bunker.
        Dinky Dau enters.

DINKY DAU: Oh fuck! We're in a world of shit now! You guys hear where they're sending us? . . . The Dee-Em-fuckin'-Zee, motherfuckers.

The war seems to be escalating alarmingly, with the enemy "making airmobile assaults in Russian-built helicopters," and the ARVN needs support. Baby San enters, furious that he is being sent on this mission with only a little more than one month left to serve. Habu enters and herds them into the helicopter, and soon they're looking down at the combat, which seems to be heavy. They psych each other up for action as the helicopter lands.

> *All leap out of the chopper. Crouching low, they begin darting back and forth in a confused, haphazard manner.*

ALL *(shouting excitedly):* Where's the firing comin' from? Anybody know what the fuck's goin' on? Who's doin' the shooting? What direction we supposed to be goin' in? Movement in the tree line!

HABU: Form up! Skirmish line!

> *All except Scooter get blown away, culminating with Baby San killing himself. Dinky Dau is still alive.*

DINKY DAU *(screaming):* My legs! Scooter, what happened to my legs?

SCOOTER: *(gets to his knees, dazed):* What the fuck . . . What the fuck . . .

> *He shakes Little John, who is lying beside him.*

Little John, what the fuck happened? *(No response.)*

Scooter shouts for a medic to attend to Dinky Dau's wound, to no avail. He hears firing and grabs for his rifle, but it doesn't function, and he throws it aside. He notices that he is bleeding copiously and he panics, pressing dirt into his wounds to stop the blood. Finally he calms down.

SCOOTER: Keep it together, keep it together. Don't want to go into shock. Most guys die of shock—that's what they taught us. Gotta keep it together. Gotta make a tourniquet. Still bleedin' like crazy. Gotta find a belt—tie it off. *(Begins crawling around.)* I could still die—lose too much blood. God, I don't wanna die. I don't wanna die here. *(Looks to heaven.)* You hear that?! I don't wanna die! *(Back to himself.)* Keep it together. Keep it together. Talkin' to God now. Keep your fuckin' sanity, G.I. *(Crawls up to Baby San.)* Baby San, Baby San, I gotta tie off my fuckin' leg. Baby San, you fucker. You fuckin' killed yourself. Dinky Dau! Medic! Medic! Medic! Please! Gotta have a medic! *(Heavenwards.)* Please God, don't let 'em die. God, don't let everybody die here! Talkin' to God. I need a medic.

Scooter grabs an M-16 *(photo at top of opposite page)* and aims it skyward, cursing at God. Finally, *"He curls into fetus position and screams 'Mama, Mama' over rising music."*

EPILOGUE

Professor and Doc *(background of photo at bottom of opposite page)* and Dinky Dau, Baby San and Habu *(foreground)* join in the final comment:

You were a pawn	You were there?
You were a hero	You were there? . . . . .
You were stupid, you should	How does it feel to kill
have gone to Canada	somebody? *(Blackout. Curtain.)*

PACK OF LIES

A Play in Two Acts

BY HUGH WHITEMORE

Cast and credits appear on page 333

HUGH WHITEMORE *was born in 1936 in Tunbridge Wells, in Kent, and was educated at Tunbridge's Judd School and the Royal Academy of Dramatic Art in London, starting out to become an actor. His writing career began in British television and has included two Emmy Award-winning series, "Elizabeth R" and "Concealed Enemies," the latter based on the Alger Hiss case. His first play for the theater was a dramatization of the life of the British poet Stevie Smith (White-more has made a specialty of writing about real people and events). Entitled* Stevie, *it was produced in London in 1977 with Glenda Jackson in the leading role (and later made into a movie) and brought to New York in an off-off-Broadway production Feb. 7, 1979 by Manhattan Theater Club.*

Whitemore's Pack of Lies *was originally produced at the Lyric Theater in London Oct. 26, 1983 for 367 performances and arrived in New York Feb. 11, 1985 as its author's Broadway debut and first Best Play, following a Boston tryout. It too is based on real events, which took place in a London suburb in the 1960s. A new Whitemore play,* Breaking the Code, *about Alan Turing, a British math genius, is scheduled for West End production.*

Whitemore is also the author of several screen plays including the recent The Return of the Soldier. *He is married to Sheila Lemon, the play agent, with one child, and lives in London.*

"Pack of Lies": by Hugh Whitemore. Copyright © 1983, 1985 by Hugh Whitemore Ltd. Reprinted by permission of Rosenstone/Wender on behalf of the author. See CAUTION notice on copyright page. All inquiries concerning stock and amateur production rights should be addressed to: Samuel French, Inc., 45 West 25th Street, New York, NY 10010. All other inquiries should be addressed to: Rosenstone/Wender, 3 East 48th Street, New York, NY 10017.

Time: The autumn and winter of 1960–61

Place: The London suburb of Ruislip

ACT I

SYNOPSIS: The sitting room of a modest and well-cared-for semidetached suburban home is at right, the kitchen is at left (with door upstage leading to the
garden). Upstage, the front hall connects with both these rooms, with the front
door at right and with stairs leading to the second-floor hall. The window of the
second-floor bedroom, right, fronts on the street, as does the bay window in the
sitting room below.

   The drama—all of whose main events are true—begins in domesticated innocence as Bob Jackson, in his mid-40s and wearing a gray cardigan, alone in the
sitting room, tells a story about a visit from a traveling Bible salesman, mostly
to remind himself how happy he once was, "for no particular reason."

   In the kitchen, Bob's wife Barbara is preparing breakfast, and he goes to her.
Their daughter Julie—"*a teenager wearing school uniform*"—comes downstairs
and joins them. Their typical family breakfast conversation is interrupted by the
front doorbell. The callers are their neighbors, Helen *("tall, large-boned, in her
40s")* and Peter *("about 50")* Kroger, both wearing casual clothes and helping
each other carry in a large easel draped in a tablecloth. They place it in the sitting
room, a surprise gift for Barbara's birthday—which, it turns out, isn't until the
following week.

> *Barbara stands speechless for a moment, unable to find the words to
> express her delight.*
>
> PETER: It's an easel. For your paintings.
>
> HELEN: She knows it's an easel, you dumdum. *(To Barbara.)* Come on—don't
> keep us in suspense—do you like it or don't you?
>
> BARBARA: I love it. It's wonderful. I don't know what to say.
>
> PETER: Now that you're going to these art classes, we thought you ought to
> have all the regular . . .
>
> *He completes the sentence with a gesture towards the easel.*
>
> BARBARA: You shouldn't have done this, it's much too extravagant.
>
> HELEN *(Overlapping):* Now don't give me any of that English phoney-baloney
> about "Oh you shouldn't have," and all that horse shit. You're my very good and
> dear friend, Barbara, and if I want to buy you a fancy birthday present, no one's
> going to stop me, O.K.? O.K.?
>
> BARBARA *(smiling):* O.K.
>
> HELEN: And if it ain't your birthday, who cares—what the hell—we'll call it
> a thanksgiving present.
>
> JULIE: Thanksgiving for what?
>
> HELEN: Thanksgiving for what . . . ? *(Improvising rapidly.)* O.K., I'll tell you

for what. How many people are there living in London? Six million? Eight? Let's say six, O.K.? So that means it was something like three million to one that we'd find ourselves living across the street from wonderful folk like you—and if that ain't the cause for some kind of thanksgiving, I don't know what is!

Barbara laughs and embraces Helen.

BARBARA: Oh Helen—dear Helen, you're priceless!

The lights fade, the two couples exit and when the lights come up again Stewart enters. *"He is in his 40s, wearing a raincoat and a dark blue suit. He might be mistaken for an averagely successful provincial solicitor."* Stewart addresses the audience, describing the neat rows of houses in this suburban locale, where "This particular story began for me—or rather this particular chapter of this particular story, for the case as a whole had been occupying my attention for several months. It is, by the way, by and large—true."

Stewart exits, as Barbara and Helen come into the sitting room, where Barbara proceeds with a fitting of a dress she is making for Helen for Christmas. Barbara is also worrying about her daughter Julie, who has taken up with a young man, Malcolm Granger, who "races around on that motor-bike of his." At Barbara's request, Helen agrees to speak to Julie about the dangers of riding around on a motor-bike with a reckless young man.

Julie comes in from choir practise and observes that "Aunt Helen's" new dress looks "smashing." Soon they move into the kitchen. When the telephone rings, Julie goes into the hall to answer it, then comes back into the kitchen to tell her mother it's for her, some man, Julie doesn't know who.

While Barbara is answering the phone, Helen, alone with Julie, takes the opportunity to caution her about riding on a motor-bike.

JULIE: When did you see me?

HELEN: The other afternoon, with young Mr. you-know-who.

JULIE: Malcolm.

HELEN: Yes, Malcolm. I thought all that was strictly verboten.

JULIE: He was only bringing me home from school—and he's very careful.

HELEN: Your momma doesn't think so.

JULIE: You know what she's like: she worries about everything.

HELEN: Only because she loves you.

JULIE: She keeps treating me like a little girl. She doesn't realize that I'm grown up.

Helen looks at Julie. She smiles affectionately.

HELEN: No. No, and I don't suppose she ever will. O.K., I won't say a word. It'll be our secret. Don't do anything silly, do you hear me?

JULIE *(smiles):* I won't, thanks.

Barbara returns as Julie pours herself a cup of tea and goes upstairs to her bedroom. Barbara complains about Julie's untidyness, but it is clear that Helen envies Barbara having such a wonderful daughter. When Bob comes in, Helen makes her goodbyes and departs. Barbara immediately tells her husband about the phone call they just received.

BARBARA: Bob, listen—somebody's been ringing up for you—I think it's urgent.

BOB: What is? Who?

BARBARA: His name's Stewart.

BOB: Stewart what?

BARBARA: That's his surname—Mr. Stewart.

BOB: Who is he?

BARBARA: I don't know.

BOB: What does he want?

BARBARA: I don't know.

BOB: Didn't you ask him?

BARBARA: Of course I asked him! He said he wanted to talk to you—I told him you weren't here and could he ring back later, and he said no, he'd like to come and see us.

BOB: What about?

BARBARA: I don't know—he got all cagey and said he couldn't explain on the phone.

BOB: He's probably just a salesman.

BARBARA: No, he's something to do with the police.

BOB: The police . . . ?

BARBARA: He said if we were worried about him coming round here, we could ring Scotland Yard and speak to a Superintendant Smith.

Bob stares at her, but says nothing.

And he said it's confidential; we mustn't tell anyone.

Bob checks by phone with Superintendant Smith and learns that the matter is indeed genuine and important. They await Stewart's arrival in person at 8 P.M. to give them the details.

The lights fade and come up on Peter Kroger telling the audience how he and his wife met the Jacksons when they moved in here, and how they began to get to know and like them.

In the sitting room, Barbara is speculating that maybe the police are interested in Malcolm and his motor-bike, when the doorbell rings. Bob opens the door. Stewart *("wearing a trilby hat, a raincoat and a dark blue suit")* comes in and introduces himself. Bob takes him to the sitting room, introducing him to Barbara. Somewhat to the suprise of Bob and Barbara, Stewart wants Julie to join them—he wants to talk to the Jacksons as a family. Barbara goes upstairs to get her daughter.

STEWART: . . . . . It's a bit melodramatic, I suppose, ringing Scotland Yard and all that, but—well, it's a good quick way of telling people that we're—you know —trustworthy, unlikely to run off with the family silver.

Stewart grins. Bob, too tense for light-hearted pleasantries, merely nods.

I gather you're with AirSpeed Research?

BOB: Yes.

STEWART: That must be jolly interesting. Don't you find it interesting?

BOB: Yes, oh yes, I enjoy it.

Patrick McGoohan as Stewart, George N. Martin as Bob Jackson,
Tracy Pollan as Julie Jackson and Rosemary Harris as Barbara Jackson
in *Pack of Lies* by Hugh Whitemore

STEWART: Travel about a bit, do you?

BOB: Well not much; up and down to Liverpool mostly.

STEWART: Ah. *(Smiles.)* One tends to think of people in the aircraft industry
as flying off all over the world at the drop of a hat.

BOB: Not me, I'm afraid.

Barbara comes in with Julie, and when they are all settled in the sitting room,
Stewart expresses his gratitude for their attention, identifies himself as a civil
servant rather than a policemen and regrets that he is unable to go into much
detail about his assignment: they are trying to gather information about a particular individual who visits this area on weekends and is believed to have friends
living here.

STEWART: . . . . . Now we don't know who they are or where exactly they live;
we don't even know why he comes here so regularly. It might just be friendship,
of course, but somehow I rather doubt it.

JULIE: Why?

BARBARA *(a mild reprimand):* Julie.

STEWART: He's a busy man, Miss Jackson. If he takes the trouble to come out here every weekend, then I'm sure he does so for a very good reason. And that's why we think it's important to find out as much as we can about these weekly jaunts—and about these mysterious friends of his. Now—I've got a photograph of him somewhere . . .

He finds the photograph in his jacket pocket.

. . . I'd like you all to take a look at it, if you will, and tell me if you think you've seen him before and if so, where. *(Murmurs of assent.)*

Stewart passes the photo around. They're all positive they've never seen this man. Julie asks what the man's done, but Stewart can't tell her. He urges them to keep their eyes open but their mouths shut in absolute confidence, no gossiping with the neighbors or school chums.

Stewart inquires about the other families living on this street. Barbara knows a little bit about each of them: the Gallifords from Cardiff, with a daughter Julie's age; the Duncans, retired, in their 70s, reclusive; the Krogers (the Jacksons' best friends), Canadians, moved here five years ago, deal in antiquarian books; the Hendersons, both working, been here a year. Stewart then proceeds to inform the Jacksons how they can help him.

STEWART: . . . . . We have to station observers in various parts of the district and find out where this man goes, where he spends his Saturdays and Sundays. The problem is—how can our people observe without being observed? In Piccadilly at rush-hour, it couldn't be easier—but here, everybody knows everybody else, it's really very difficult. There's no other way. *(A brief hesitation.)* So that's what we need. A room. Somewhere. That's how you can help.

A moment of silence.

BOB: You mean a room *here* . . . ?

STEWART: It would only be for a couple of days: tomorrow and Sunday.

Barbara and Bob exchange glances.

BOB: Well, I don't know about that . . .

BARBARA: You mean—one of your men—here, in the house?

STEWART: It would be a young lady. More natural, we thought. If any questions are asked, you can say she's a member of your Art Club. . . . . .

Barbara is surprised that Stewart knows so much about the family, including her painting, which he judges is "very good indeed." He thinks Julie's small bedroom window upstairs would be the best place for an observation post, but Barbara is rather reluctant to have a watcher in the house. She suggests a parked car (too conspicuous) or perhaps somebody else's house—the Krogers', say. Stewart informs her that it takes a long time "to make sure that the people we go to are people we can trust," and the Jacksons have already been screened— Bob already works on classified material at AirSpeed Research.

BOB: What about . . . I mean—would it be dangerous?

STEWART: Dangerous . . . ?

BOB: Well presumably this man's committed a crime of some sort . . .

STEWART: He's not a thug, if that's what you mean. There's no danger of any physical violence.

BOB: But he is a criminal . . . ?

STEWART: Let's say we have every reason to believe that he's involved in some kind of illegal activity.

> Bob turns to Barbara.

BOB: What do you think?

BARBARA: It's up to you.

> Bob hesitates for a moment; he then turns to Stewart and nods his approval.

Stewart is delighted and names 9 A.M. as the time for his watcher to arrive the next day at the Jacksons', surreptitiously by the back garden and kitchen door.

The lighting indicates a change of scene. Stewart's watcher, Thelma ("in her late 20s, a sturdily-built ex-regular army girl; she wears a sweater and slacks") enters and addresses the audience, describing Julie's bedroom, much more comfortable than the settings for most surveillance jobs. From her vantage point upstairs she could hear the Jacksons "talking quietly because there was a stranger in the house." They spoke to her in politely friendly fashion when she left the house at 5:30 P.M.

Alone in the sitting room with Bob in the evening, Barbara is worrying about the man they are watching for.

BARBARA: We don't know anything about him. Nothing. We don't even know what he's done.

BOB: We don't need to.

BARBARA: Because of us he might be arrested. Just think of that. We ought to know something.

> Bob lowers his newspaper.

BOB: Because of *us* . . . ?

BARBARA: Because we let them watch.

BOB (grins): Trust you to say a thing like that.

BARBARA: Like what?

BOB: Trust you to find a way of blaming yourself. Doesn't matter what it is, does it?—if there's a hole in my sock, if the car breaks down—it's always your fault. Well, this isn't.

> Barbara looks at him but says nothing.

So stop worrying.

> Barbara nods her head, but her expression remains troubled and anxious.

Barbara and Bob speculate about the Krogers' sexual relations, "All these wild nights we hear so much about." Barbara finds Peter rather attractive, but Bob thinks of Helen as "Dizzy Lizzie."

Suddenly Barbara remembers an incident from years ago when they saw a pathetically ragged, sobbing man arrested in a bus station. Bob guesses he may have hit someone over the head, but Barbara can't help feeling that "People don't stop being people just because they've done something wrong. They still have feelings." Stewart's business is none of their business, Bob insists—besides, it won't be long before Thelma (whom they like) will be gone and it'll all be over.

The lighting indicates a change of scene. It is Sunday, and Barbara addresses the audience, telling of Sunday chores which took Bob and Julie out of the house. Barbara was chatting with Thelma, "when Thelma suddenly looked out of the window. I looked out too, I don't know why, I just did. Helen's front door was open and somebody was coming out of the house. It was a man. I'd never seen him before. He didn't look round to say goodbye, he just hurried to the gate and went off along the road. He had disappeared before I realized who it was."

Thelma and Barbara both recognized the man in the photo for whom Stewart was searching. Thelma went to make a phone call, after which she told Barbara that Stewart would come around that afternoon.

The lights indicate a change of scene from the monologue to the sitting room, where Stewart has joined the Jacksons. Stewart guesses his quarry spent the night at the Krogers'. Barbara positively identifies him (Bob and Julie didn't see him —they were washing the car). He drives a white Studebaker, somewhat flashy for a man in his line of business, Stewart comments. But when the Jacksons inquire as to what this line of business may be, Stewart becomes evasive, telling them only that the man is suspected of having entered the country illegally under the assumed name of Gordon Lonsdale and may be working in secret for a foreign government.

BOB: You mean he's a spy . . . ?

STEWART: Well, something of that sort—but I'd rather not jump to conclusions until we know a little more.

BOB (almost laughing): But what would a spy be doing in Peter's house?

STEWART: Well, quite . . .

BOB: There must be some mistake.

BARBARA: Shouldn't we tell them? Shouldn't we warn them?

STEWART: All in good time, Mrs. Jackson.

BOB: Oh, come on, you're not suggesting that they're involved with this man, are you?

Stewart responds with an ambiguous shrug.

BARBARA: Oh no—not Helen and Peter—they wouldn't do a thing like that.

Stewart points out that this Mr. Lonsdale visits the Krogers every single weekend, but the Krogers have never mentioned his name to their best friends, the Jacksons. At any rate, Lonsdale is not a bookselling colleague, Stewart declares, he's the director of a burglar-alarm firm in London, with something of a reputation as a high-living man-about-town—an ill-matched companion for the Krogers.

The Jacksons begin to realize that Stewart knows very much more than he's telling. They begin to wonder whether it's just a coincidence that he asked to set up an observation post directly across the street from the Krogers. Stewart reminds them of the Official Secrets Act and that "sensible, reasonable discretion" will be expected, even required, of them.

Openly, Stewart begins asking questions about the Krogers. The Jacksons know little more than they've told already: the Krogers came here from South London; Helen talks about having lived on a farm in Canada; Peter is "bookish" and once had a shop in the Strand but now conducts his business at home by means of mail order; theirs is "a marriage of opposites," but they seem happy.

Stewart observes that it's in all their interests to get to the the bottom of this matter: "We think Lonsdale may be in a spot of trouble. He's had a few business problems just recently—money problems—and this could make him do something rash, reckless. If he does, we want to know about it. And that means keeping an eye on things." To the Jacksons' chagrin, it means particularly that Stewart will want to continue surveillance with a watcher in the Jackson house not just weekends but every day, "just for a week or so."

The Jacksons are particularly troubled about how this might affect Julie. Will she be able to do her homework? ("No problem there. It gets dark at—what?— four-thirty, five—no point us staying after that.") What about her fondness for the Krogers? ("Say it's just a routine investigation—there's no need to go into details.") Why not just go across the street and clear up the Lonsdale matter with the Krogers? ("Supposing they're involved with him in some way?") Stewart's people cannot ignore the fact that Lonsdale has been spotted coming out of the Kroger house, and they must behave appropriately.

BARBARA: I don't think you understand, Mr. Stewart. Helen and Peter are our best friends. We see them every day.
STEWART: Yes, I know.
BARBARA: Helen especially. She's always popping in.
STEWART: Yes, I know.
BARBARA: Well, you can't expect me to talk to her and have cups of tea with her when I know there's somebody spying on her from Julie's bedroom. I can't do that, I can't. Well I won't, I'm sorry.
STEWART: Perhaps you could try . . . just for a day or two.
BARBARA: But why should I?
> *Always the peacemaker, Bob recognizes a bellicose tone in Barbara's voice; he turns pacifically to Stewart.*
BOB: It's asking a hell of a lot, you know.
STEWART *(quietly):* I'm afraid I must insist.
BOB: *Insist . . . ?*
STEWART: Earnestly implore.
BARBARA: Oh, it's not fair, Mr. Stewart.
STEWART: It's not, I agree—but being fair has a pretty low priority at the moment.
> *Pause.*
I really am very sorry.

Stewart reassures them that the watcher would still be Thelma, with an occasional relief, and they'll put in a separate phone to maintain contact. It's clear that Barbara doesn't think they should go on with this; but Bob nods his consent reluctantly, commenting, "Well, if it's only a week . . ."

Barbara is convinced that they've been such close friends of the Krogers, they would have noticed any wrongdoing. Stewart informs her, "Mrs. Jackson, people like Lonsdale and his colleagues spend their lives deceiving people like you. It's their job, their profession, and they do it with the utmost skill and conviction. If they didn't, they'd be finished."

Julie comes in. She is agreeable to having Thelma continue to use her bedroom as a surveillance post (though she is told nothing about why this continues to be necessary), and she promises to maintain silence. She goes upstairs to her room. Stewart, apologetic but purposeful to the last, makes his departure. Alone with her husband, Barbara lets him see that she is angry.

BOB: Don't blame me.
BARBARA: I don't want those people here. I don't want them in the house!
BOB: Be reasonable. There was nothing I could do.
BARBARA: You could have said no, couldn't you?
BOB: Well, hardly.
BARBARA: You're always the same with people like that.
BOB: Like what?
BARBARA: You know what I mean: like a schoolboy in front of the headmaster.
BOB: Look, there's no point in—
BARBARA: I just don't want to talk about it, Bob. I don't want anything to do with it!

Barbara also feels badly about not letting Julie in on the whole truth. But Bob is at least considering what the consequences may be if Stewart is right and Helen and Peter are somehow involved in espionage (Barbara scoffs at this possibility). Bob reminds Barbara that they never see the Krogers on weekends.

The lights indicate a change of scene. Barbara is alone in the kitchen, when Helen's distinctive ring at the doorbell startles her. Uneasily, she goes to the door and lets in the Krogers. They are on their way into town for early Christmas shopping and wonder whether Barbara would like them to pick up anything for her.

Helen and Peter notice that their gift, the easel, is in place, and Barbara tells them again how much she loves it. The Krogers find that they've forgotten their shopping list, so Peter goes to get it. Alone with Barbara, Helen asks, "Who's the mystery man?" she saw coming from this house the day before.

HELEN: . . . . . And don't pretend you don't know what I'm talking about.
BARBARA: What?
HELEN: Yesterday afternoon—about four o'clock—I saw some guy walking across the street. It looked like he was coming from here.
BARBARA: Well yes, he was.
HELEN: Aha! It's lucky I knew your old man was at home, otherwise I might have gotten very suspicious indeed. Who is he?
BARBARA: Oh—just a friend of Bob's.

HELEN: Yeh, I thought so. Didn't I meet him at your wedding anniversary?

BARBARA: No, that was somebody else.

HELEN: Are you sure?

BARBARA: Quite sure.

HELEN: Gee, that's funny. I could have sworn he was the guy Bob introduced me to. What's his name?

BARBARA: Um . . . Stewart.

HELEN: Stewart?

BARBARA: He's never been here before. You can't have met him.

HELEN: O.K., if you say so.

   Helen rises, collecting scarf, coat and handbag.

Now look, about this Christmas shopping—what do you think Julie would like?

BARBARA: Oh look, you mustn't bother . . .

HELEN: It's no bother. I love bringing her presents, it gives me pleasure, she's always so appreciative. I was wondering about a blouse, do you think she'd like that? A silk blouse.

BARBARA: Well yes, that would be lovely, but you mustn't be too extravagant.

HELEN: Why not, for heaven's sake? There's nothing I enjoy more than real sinful extravagance. *(She winks playfully.)* Born to be bad, that's me. I'd better go, I'll see you later, honey. *(Going to the door.)*

BARBARA *(suddenly, impulsively):* Helen—

   Helen pauses, looking back at Barbara.

We're thinking of having a few friends in for a drink on Saturday evening. Would you and Peter like to come?

HELEN: Oh, we can't this Saturday—what a shame. *(Starts out again.)*

BARBARA: We'll change it, we'll make it next Saturday. Saturday week.

HELEN: Saturday's always difficult for us, I'd better say no. Peter likes to do his accounts at the weekend. You know that. We told you. *(She smiles.)* Thanks for asking. Ciao!

   Helen exits. Barbara remains motionless. Curtain.

ACT II

Thelma enters through the kitchen door. Her relief, Sally *("about 30: pleasant, but rather plain, middle class")* comes downstairs to join her. Both are wearing rain gear—it's wet outside, and Thelma is late because of an accident which clogged the traffic. Both are by now obviously familiar with the Jackson household routine. Thelma believes this will be a long job ("Mr. Stewart went to the American Embassy yesterday—twice"), though Mrs. Jackson keeps hinting that the surveillance should end soon.

Barbara comes in with shopping bags. Thelma pours her some tea (she knows how Barbara likes it), as Sally leaves. Barbara has brought some sausages for lunch—she's gotten into the habit of fixing lunch for Thelma. When the doorbell rings, Thelma gathers up her things and rushes upstairs while Barbara admits Helen, who is returning a cake tin which had been filled with Barbara's delicious cookies.

Rosemary Harris and Dana Ivey (as Helen Kroger) in *Pack of Lies*

Helen notices that Barbara is a bit edgier than usual, and she also notices that there are two empty mugs of tea on the kitchen table.

HELEN: . . . . . Don't tell me you've got a lover, hiding away upstairs.
BARBARA: Oh dear—fancy that, I haven't even washed up yet.
    Quickly plunging the cups into the sink.
. . . Isn't that awful?
HELEN *(stares at Barbara):* Are you sure you're all right, honey? You look kinda pale.
BARBARA: No, it's nothing, just a headache.
HELEN: Take a pill.
BARBARA: I have.
HELEN: Take another pill.
BARBARA: Yes, all right.
HELEN: I'll get you one, shall I?
BARBARA: No, please . . .
HELEN: Pills and potions keep me going. I'll run upstairs and see what you've got.
BARBARA: It's all right, Helen, please don't fuss!
    Helen frowns, startled by Barbara's irritability.

But it's all right to shout at friends, Helen reassures Barbara. After advising Barbara to lie down with a good book and get some rest, Helen departs. A few beats after she's gone, Barbara, overcome with emotion and tension, goes to the kitchen sink and vomits.

The lights indicate a change of scene, with Bob receiving an evening visit from Stewart. Stewart has heard from his watchers how unhappy with the situation Barbara has become and has called to see if there's anything he can do about it, perhaps keep her more fully informed.

Stewart notes that the Krogers and the Jacksons drive the same kind of car— a black Ford Consul—and finds this an extraordinary coincidence (the Jacksons got one first, then the Krogers admired it and got one of their own). Stewart asks Bob about the Krogers' hobbies and learns that Peter likes classical music and has a lot of sound and radio equipment, including headphones. Helen (Bob says) is too much of a "Dizzy Lizzie" to have a hobby. How often do the Jacksons visit the Krogers' house? Very seldom, usually just Christmas and birthdays. Does Helen have friends apart from the Jacksons? Yes, "She's friendly with everyone, she's a very friendly woman," Bob replies, and Stewart immediately wants to know in what way she shows her friendliness.

BOB *(angrily):* I don't often see her, Mr. Stewart, I'm at work when she comes round; Barbara's the one she talks to, not me. I don't know what she does or what she says. Anyway, there's nothing sinister about being friendly, is there?
STEWART: Nothing sinister, no. It just adds to the pattern.
BOB: Pattern?
STEWART: Well if the Krogers are mixed up in this business—and I say if— if they are, then it would be essential for them to know what's going on. Any

change of routine, any change of neighbor . . . it could be dangerous for them.

BOB: You can make anything look suspicious if you try hard enough.

STEWART: True.

BOB: I mean all that stuff about cars: why shouldn't they buy a car like ours if they want to?

STEWART: No reason at all—on the other hand, it could be construed as an extremely clever thing to do.

BOB: Clever, why?

STEWART: Because it would certainly confuse anyone who might be watching them; I mean, if one of my chaps saw a black Ford Consul parked in Cranley Drive he couldn't be sure, at a glance, whether the Krogers were at home or whether you were. Might be useful, that.

Bob stares at Stewart; he says nothing.

It's not terribly important, I agree—it's just one of those little details that tend to arouse interest. And it's only when you start adding all these things together that a significant pattern begins to emerge.

Barbara comes in from her Art Club meeting and joins the others in the sitting room (Julie is at the movies). She takes this opportunity to inform Stewart that she cannot tolerate the situation much longer, particularly as it is unsettling for Julie while she's studying for exams. "I know it's important, what you're doing here," Barbara tells Stewart, "but we have got our own lives to lead, after all. You must have known that it would be more than a couple of days, you should have told us." Barbara is losing sleep over this, and every time she sees Helen it makes her feel sick.

Stewart admits that they can never tell how long such a job may take, and they aren't sure yet how Lonsdale and the Krogers fit together. He decides to put the Jacksons further into the picture: the Russians, with their vast fleet of submarines, are especially interested in NATO's development of underwater detection devices, and Lonsdale, undoubtedly a high-ranking KGB officer, is the spy in charge of their activities in this direction in England. The Admiralty wants Lonsdale arrested immediately, but Stewart's colleagues are waiting to trace his associates until they are able to round up Lonsdale's whole espionage network, including whatever assistants he may have recruited.

Once again, Stewart assures the Jacksons there is no danger—after a lifetime of studying the KGB and its methods, he knows that they do not employ violent "hooligans" in this line of work. Demonstrating his detailed knowledge of the enemy, Stewart describes the Moscow living quarters and habits of his opposite number, a man named Shelepin, who has a parquet-floored office near the Lubyanka Prison and is partial to ice cream. "No," he concludes, "there's no danger . . . . . The merest hint of any strong-arm behavior would cause the most almighty diplomatic rumpus—and that's the one thing the Soviets want to avoid at all costs. So there's nothing to worry about. I guarantee it."

The fact of the matter is, however, that Stewart needs to maintain his watchers here for the time being. This clearly upsets Barbara, who goes into the kitchen and stares out the window. After Stewart has departed, she tells Bob, "I've made up my mind what I'm going to do: I'm not going to think about it. We've got to lead a normal life—for Julie's sake, if not our own. Let them do what they like. I'm not going to think about it.''

The lights indicate a change of scene, as Barbara addresses the audience on the subject of Bob's mother who was so diffident and considerate that she didn't like to tell the landlord that the roof leaked, or to call the doctor after 6 P.M. even when she was gravely ill. "Like a child, she thought if she kept very still and didn't say anything, nobody would take any notice of her. And she was right—they didn't.''

Barbara is folding Helen's Christmas dress, now finished and ready for boxing. Thelma, on her way out, admires Barbara's handiwork in passing. Barbara is finally ready to admit that the Krogers "must be involved. It's obvious. Any fool can see that.'' But Thelma can't give Barbara the further information Barbara would like so very much to have, and Thelma's polite refusal sets Barbara to pouring out her resentment of Stewart. When she first realized that the Krogers were involved in deception, she was hurt and hoped they'd be punished, but she doesn't feel that way any more. All Barbara wants to remember is that Helen has been kind to Julie, and "I don't care what she's done, she's still my friend. I'll tell you what chokes me, Thelma: it's that Mr. Stewart not telling us anything, not telling us about Helen and Peter, treating us like a couple of kids who can't be trusted. How dare he! Can you imagine what it's been like? Can you? *(No response.)* Last Friday, when I went shopping, I looked at the women all round me. And I thought, 'I'm not like them, I'm not like the others—I may look like them, but I'm not.' It hurts telling all these lies. It really hurts. It's like a dead weight on my stomach. It's like grief. You can't forget it. And he won't tell us. Why not? Does he think we can't be trusted? Does he think we're too stupid to understand? Or perhaps he thinks it doesn't matter. *(A shaft of bitterness.)* Well that's it, of course—why should he bother about us? We're the sort of people who stand in queues and don't answer back—why should he bother—we'll just do as we're told and not ask any questions. *(With sudden passion.)* Well I hate him! *I hate him!* I want to smack his smiling face and say, 'How dare you!—how dare you treat us like that! Who the hell do you think you are!' *(Her passion subsides.)* I won't though, will I? Of course I won't . . . . .''

Stewart probably knew that the guilty parties were Helen and Peter from the very beginning, Barbara supposes. Thelma tries to console and reassure her that ugly things just seem to happen from time to time, it's no one's fault and no one can do anything about it. Julie comes in as Thelma is leaving. Thelma exits with a comment about Julie's boy friend's handsome motor-bike, inadvertently letting the cat out of the bag about Julie's forbidden rides. Julie apologizes to her mother for deceiving her, but Barbara, already oversentitized to lies and cheating, over-reacts with "I'll never be able to trust you ever again—never again—never!''

The lights indicate a change of scene, as Peter addresses the audience about his past: in the depth of the Depression he was recruited at a meeting which seemed to support the noble ideas of democracy with quotations from the works of Marx and Lenin, presenting Communism so attractively, "That evening, my whole life changed.''

In the next scene there is a Christmas tree in the hall, and the two families are singing "Hark! The Herald Angels Sing.'' Helen has had a bit too much to drink, but Peter manages to keep her in some kind of control. Helen tells a story about Christmases with her Aunt Sophie, to illustrate how strongly she feels that here and now with the Jacksons and the Krogers, everything is perfect. The perfection is interrupted by a phone call from Stewart, who is only calling to wish the Jacksons a Merry Christmas.

This time when the lights indicate a change of scene it is Helen who addresses the audience, on the subject of an apartment she and Peter had in 1950 on East 71st Street. She loved the place, but "One evening, Peter came home early. 'We've got to leave,' he said, 'the Rosenbergs have been arrested; we've got to leave.' I looked at Peter. His mouth had gone dry. He moistened his lips with his tongue. 'When?' I asked. 'Tonight,' he said, 'we've got to get the hell out of here as fast as we can.' And that's what we did. We left our clothes in the closet, books on the shelves, food in the refrigerator. We took a cab to the airport. The driver was talking about a ball game. It all seemed so normal . . . so normal and yet so unreal. We could've stayed, I suppose, and taken our chances—but we didn't. And from then on, there was no turning back."

Later, Stewart calls on the Jacksons to tell them that the surveillance may probably end today. Lonsdale is to be arrested when he makes contact with other agents in London.

BOB: What about Helen and Peter?

STEWART *(evenly):* Yes, we'll pick them up this afternoon. If everything goes according to plan.

BARBARA: This afternoon . . .

BOB: Yes, but what have they done? Helen and Peter?

STEWART: They're Lonsdale's transmitting station. He brings them information which they dispatch to KGB headquarters, either hidden in the books that Peter Kroger posts to fictitious clients in various parts of Europe, or, presumably, by radio. I'm sorry to tell you so bluntly, but there's no doubt about it: your friends are both Communist agents with many years experience behind them. And their name's not Kroger, by the way, and they're American, not Canadian. I thought it better to hear it from me than to read about it in the newspapers.

Barbara and Bob remain motionless, stunned.

BARBARA: When I think of the hours she's spent in this house . . . in this room . . . *(She lapses into silence for a moment; she looks up at Stewart.)* Was it *all* a lie—I mean everything she's ever told us. *(Almost imploringly.)* Was it?

STEWART: Well not everything, I suppose.

BARBARA: I mean all those stories about her life on the farm—wasn't that the truth?

STEWART: Apparently not. Her parents emigrated from Poland. They lived in a place called Utica in New York State. Her father was fairly well off; he made his money during Prohibition. He was a bootlegger. Peter Kroger was a schoolteacher. He became a Communist in the Thirties, and he fought in the Spanish Civil War.

Pause.

BARBARA: How could she do it? How *could* she? I've never had many friends, not close friends, not what you'd call close . . . never. But I trusted Helen. I thought she was brash and noisy and sometimes a bit silly . . . but I trusted her. I loved her.

STEWART (*sympathetically*): Well I'm quite sure that her affection for you is perfectly genuine. There's no reason to doubt that.

BARBARA (*angrily*): No reason . . . ? What do you mean. No reason? There's every reason to doubt everything she's ever said or done!

STEWART: Yes, well, you're bound to feel like that. And there's nothing anyone can do to soften the blow. I only wish there were.

Barbara wishes fervently that Stewart had never entered this house and started them lying even to their daughter; or if not directly lying, at least withholding the truth from her. "We're all playing the same rotten game," is the way Barbara looks at it. She feels that she is as guilty of betrayal on her side of the friendship as Helen is on hers.

Sally comes downstairs carrying the unplugged telephone and exits—the surveillance is finally over. Again, Stewart apologizes to Barbara for causing her pain, as Barbara realizes that the Krogers are bound for prison and separation, though they love each other. Barbara still wishes Stewart had told the whole truth from the beginning. He couldn't, of course, because for all he knew, Barbara might have decided to tip the Krogers off. "What makes you think I won't now?" she flings at Stewart and adds, "If I was brave enough, I would."

The doorbell rings, and Barbara can see through the window that it's Helen. Stewart goes outside the kitchen door, leaving it ajar so that he can hear the conversation inside, while Bob goes to the door. He tells Helen that Barbara is indisposed, with another headache; but Helen insists on coming in, going to Barbara in the kitchen and playing the Jacksons with questions about Barbara's health—she ought to see the doctor, etc.

HELEN: It's not like you, getting all these headaches. You've had three in a month.

BARBARA: I suppose I'm worried, that's all.

HELEN: What about?

BARBARA: Oh—this and that . . . things, you know.

HELEN: What things?

BARBARA: Well nothing special, nothing in particular, nothing serious.

HELEN: Now come on—don't be shy. You just tell your Auntie Helen all about it.

BARBARA: It's nothing.

HELEN: Bob—let me talk to her alone.

BOB: It's Julie and her exams.

BARBARA (*gratefully following Bob's lead*): Yes, it's Julie and her exams.

Helen reassures Barbara that Julie will do well on her exams and advises her to rest and pamper herself (meanwhile Stewart, now assured that the Jacksons don't intend to give the game away, departs across the garden). Helen tells the Jacksons that she and Peter plan to get away for awhile, visiting friends in Australia. Barbara overreacts, declaring, "It's a marvellous idea, Helen" and urging her to go so emphatically that Helen stares at her, wondering. They are interrupted by the ringing phone, which Barbara answers (it's a message for Julie). *"Bob rightly suspects that Helen is puzzled by Barbara's uncharacteristically emotional behavior; he tries to ease the atmosphere,"* chatting about Julie.

> *Barbara replaces the receiver and returns to the kitchen. She and Helen*
> *stand facing each other. Helen's expression is grave and concerned.*

HELEN: Are you sure there's nothing wrong?

> *Barbara nods.*

BARBARA: Quite sure.

HELEN: Will you just let me know if there's anything I can do, O.K.?

> *Barbara nods.*

Take good care of her, Bob—she's a very special lady. Give my love to Julie. Ciao.

> *Helen goes out.*

The lights indicate a change of scene, in which Stewart has come to the Jacksons' house to tell them that everything went smoothly and according to plan. They arrested Lonsdale and his London contacts and then came here at about 6:30 (the Jacksons weren't looking and didn't see anything—not that there was much to see). "Superintendant Smith told the Krogers that they were going to be arrested on suspicion of offenses against the Official Secrets Act," Stewart relates, "Mrs. Kroger asked if she could go and stoke the boiler before they left the house, but Mr. Smith was naturally suspicious. He had a look in her handbag. He found a six-page letter in Russian, apparently from Lonsdale to his wife—a glass slide containing three microdots—and a typed sheet of numbers, presumably some sort of a code. *(A small smile.)* I'm not surprised she wanted to stoke the boiler . . . . . And I was right about the radio transmitter, it's hidden under the kitchen floor."

The Krogers were taken to Bow Street Police Station—and now, after a few days of inevitable press attention, the Jacksons will be left in peace. They won't have to take part in the courtroom proceedings. In fact, Stewart will see to it their names aren't even mentioned.

Julie comes in with the Sunday papers, surprised to have noticed a stir of activity across the street. Stewart tells Julie what has happened, while Barbara and Bob overlap his statements with protestations that they weren't able to tell Julie the truth previously. Julie, greatly upset, can scarcely believe what she is hearing about her beloved Auntie Helen and Uncle Peter.

JULIE: How could she do it? How could she do it? How could she do it?

BARBARA: Oh Julie don't please don't—please!

JULIE *(her voice rising):* How could she do it how could she do it how could she do it how could she do it how could she do it how could she do it how could she . . .

> *Julie breaks away from Barbara and runs upstairs.*

BARBARA *(with a terrible cry of anguish):* Julie!

> *Lights fade. Bob steps forward to address the audience.*

BOB: Julie went up to her room. She collected together all the things that Helen and Peter had ever given her—the handkerchiefs, the necklace, the silk blouse, she took them out into the garden and burnt them. A few days later, Mr. Stewart called round with a present for Barbara, a thank-you present, he said, for looking after his girls for all those weeks. It was a box of six silver-plated fish knives and forks. The Krogers were sentenced to twenty years imprisonment. Julie's bitterness did not last. Curious to see her Aunt Helen again, she went to visit her in Holloway Prison. Towards the end of their conversation, Helen said, "I'll never forgive your mother—never." After eight years, they were released from prison in exchange for an Englishman who had been jailed by the Russians. They flew to Poland to start a new life. A crowd of journalists watched them go. "Let's all be friends," said Helen. A few weeks after that, Sunday afternoon it was, Barbara went into the kitchen, sat down on a chair and died. A heart attack. She was so young, still in her fifties. I miss her more as time goes by. More not less. Is it always like that?

   Curtain.

AS IS

A Full-length Play in One Act

BY WILLIAM M. HOFFMAN

Cast and credits appear on pages 341–342 & 362–363

WILLIAM M. HOFFMAN was born in New York City April 12, 1939, the son of a caterer who specialized in United Nations and show business clients. He was educated at the Bronx High School of Science and City College, where he majored in Latin. As an employee of Hill & Wang, which publishes a good deal of theater material, he found himself getting acquainted with Lanford Wilson, Marshall W. Mason, Robert Patrick and other theater folk who were putting on plays—so he started writing them too, in the early days of Caffe Cino and Cafe LaMama. His first production of record was the one-actor Thank You, Miss Victoria *(1966) on the off-Broadway program of one-actors "Six From LaMama." There followed off-off-Broadway productions of Hoffman's* Spring Play *and* Tonight, I Love You *(both directed by Mason);* Gilles de Rais; The Cherry Orchard Part II; XXXXX *(a title, not a typographical error); and two musicals,* Gulliver's Travels *and* Etiquette, *for which Hoffman wrote the books and collaborated on the lyrics with John Braden. Mason directed Hoffman's first Best Play,* As Is, *which was produced off Broadway by Circle Repertory March 10 for 49 performances before making Hoffman's Broadway debut in a transfer of the production uptown on May 1.*

*Two Hoffman collaborations—*Cornbury *and* Shoe Palace Murray, *a musical —have been produced in regional theater. Among his other activities, he has branched into directing; he was a founding member of the OOB group New York Theater Strategy in the early 1970s; and he recently wrote an opera libretto,* A Figaro for Antonia, *commissioned by the Metropolitan Opera in honor of its 100th anniversary. He has been the recipient of a Guggenheim Fellowship, two National Endowment grants and a New York Foundation for the Arts Fellowship. Hoffman lives in New York City, in SoHo.*

"As Is": by William M. Hoffman. Copyright © 1985 by William M. Hoffman. Reprinted by permission of International Creative Management. See CAUTION notice on copyright page. All inquiries concerning stock and amateur productions should be addressed to: Dramatists Play Service, Inc., 440 Park Avenue South, New York, NY 10016. All other inquiries should be addressed to: Luis Sanjurjo, International Creative Management, 40 West 57th Street, New York, NY 10019.

Time: The present

Place: New York City

SYNOPSIS: The set is flexible and represents many different locales including, at right, *"Saul's fashionable loft space, suggested by a sofa, Barcelona chair, bench and area rug,"* a bar at center and a bench at left. A hospice worker, *"a dowdy middle-aged woman wearing a bright dress and bright lipstick and nail polish"* comes downstage to address the audience. She is a secretary (and a former novice who has left the convent) who works part time tending the dying, though she has failed to discover the spiritual significance or nobility she expected to find in the process of death.

The lights focus on Rich and Saul, *"two casually dressed men around 30 seated in a fashionable loft space living area."* They are quarreling in a lightly sarcastic vein, two former lovers who are trying to be civilized about it as they divide their possessions.

RICH: . . . . . Sell the rug.

SAUL: I will not sell the manikin heads. I don't care what you say.

RICH: Then take them.

SAUL: And the chromium lamp? I love that lamp.

RICH: Take it.

SAUL: And the Barcelona chair?

RICH: The Barcelona chair is *mine! (Beat.)* Fuck it. Take it. Take everything. I won't be Jewish about it.

> *He rises to go.*

SAUL: Why didn't you warn me we were going to play Christians and Jews today? I would have worn my yellow star.

RICH: I've gotta go.

SAUL: Where're you going?

RICH: I'm not feeling so hot. Let's make it another day.

Saul blocks Rich's exit and insists on continuing to divide up their possessions. Rich can have the Barcelona chair for his new lover, Chet, but Saul is undecided what to do with the Paul Cadmus painting and their assortment of collectibles.

Saul resents the fulsome dedication of Rich's latest book, a collection of short stories, to Chet, but he accepts Rich's compliment on the cover photo which Saul provided for it. Somewhat reluctantly, Saul also accepts Rich's check for some money owed him. Saul can't help telling Rich, "He won't make you happy," which drives Rich toward the door again, and again Saul stops him. This time, instead of talking about their possessions, Saul goes on about friends who have become gravely ill: "I visited Teddy today at St. Vincent's. It's very depressing . . . He's lying there in bed, out of it. He's been out of it since the time we saw him. He's not in any pain, snorting his imaginary cocaine, doing his poppers . . . . ." Their friend Jimmy has died, Harry and Matt have developed symptoms of the dreaded disease, obviously Acquired Immune Deficiency Syndrome, or AIDS. And "Sometimes I'm so scared I go back on my resolutions: I drink too much, and I smoke a joint, and I find myself at the bars and clubs, where I stand around and watch. They remind me of accounts of Europe during the Black Plague: coupling in the dark, dancing till you drop. The New Wave is the corpse look. I'm very frightened, and I miss you. Say something, damn it."

What Rich says is, "I have it," startling Saul and Rich's other close associates, who are now onstage.

CHET *(a handsome, boyish man in his early 20s):* You what?
LILY *(a beautiful woman, 30ish):* You have what?
BROTHER *(to his wife, whom we don't see):* He has AIDS.
SAUL: I don't think that's funny.
PARTNER: The idea is ridiculous.
RICH: That's the bad news.
PARTNER: You ran the goddamned marathon.
LILY: Darling!
RICH: The good news is that I have only the swollen glands.
DOCTOR 1: We call it a "Pre-AIDS   DOCTOR 2: "AIDS-related Complex."
Condition."
RICH: And I've lost some weight.
SAUL: I'm in a state of shock.
LILY: Move in with me. Chet doesn't   RICH: I tire easily. My temperature
know how to take care of you.   goes up and down.
DOCTOR 1: Your suppressor cells outnumber your helper cells.
BROTHER: I don't care what he has, Betty, he's my brother.
CHET: You're my lover.
LILY: You're my buddy.

The partner tries to keep their catering business going, and the brother insists to his wife that Rich is coming to visit them this Christmas as he always does. But gradually all of them (except Saul), even Chet, begin to distance themselves from Rich.

CHET: You know I'd do anything for you.
RICH: You're walking out on me.
BROTHER: We're going to Betty's mother for Christmas.
CHET: I need more space to get my head together.
SAUL: What did you expect?
RICH: Chet, please, I need you!
        Rich tries to put his arms around Chet. Everyone except Saul pulls back
        terrified.
CHET, BROTHER, LILY, PARTNER, DOCTORS: *DON'T TOUCH ME!*
        A beat.
LILY: Please forgive me!
CHET: This thing has me blown away.
BROTHER: If it weren't for the kids.

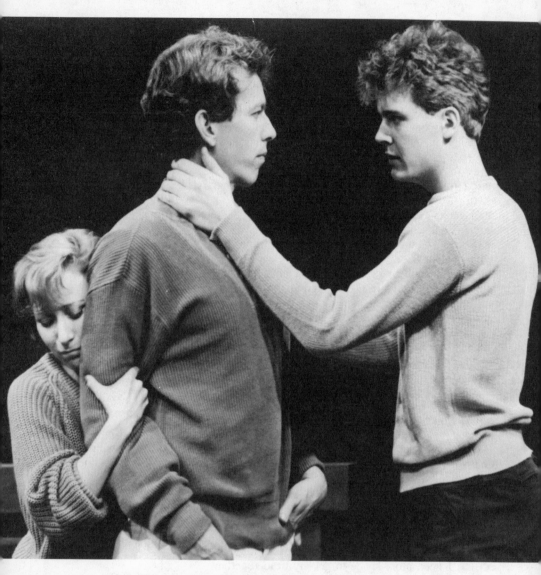

Lily Knight as Lily, Jonathan Hogan as Rich and Steven Gregan as
Chet in *As Is* by William M. Hoffman

PARTNER: I don't know what the hell we're going to do.
SAUL: Bastards!

Doctors tell Rich they don't know enough about AIDS to tell him what his chances might be, while a recorded announcement declares that AIDS victims "may live a normal life span, or they may have only a few weeks. Fortunately, so far this tragic disease has not spread outside its target groups . . . . ."
Back in the loft, Saul's loyalty to Rich remains unshaken.

SAUL: You're my friend. You'll stay with me till you feel better.
RICH: Aren't you afraid I'll infect you?
SAUL: Yes, I'm afraid.
RICH: Paper plates, lysol, face masks—no, I'd prefer to live alone, thank you.
SAUL: You need me.
RICH: Besides, if I live with you, where am I going to bring my tricks?
SAUL: You pick up people?
RICH: I go to bars . . . I pick up guys . . . but I give them a medical report before we leave. . . .

In the bar area, Rich acts out just such an encounter, at which the other man backs off as soon as he learns of Rich's illness. Saul admits he's frightened (and Rich interposes, "How the fuck do you think I feel? My lover leaves me, my family won't let me near them, I lose my business, I can't pay my rent"). Saul insists that he loves Rich and Rich must stay here where Saul can take care of him. But in a kaleidoscope of brief relationships, Rich drifts from bar to bar and from companion to cloned companion, sinking ever deeper into panic, emotional chaos and alcoholic daze.
In one of the bars, Saul prevents Rich from getting into a fight. He has just found Rich after an alarming two weeks' unexplained absence, and he gradually sobers Rich up with bad jokes and exaggeratedly foul-mouthed talk. It's the latter which most amuses Rich: "God, how I love sleaze: the whining self-pity of a rainy Monday night in a leather bar in early spring; five o'clock in the morning in the Mineshaft, with the bathtubs full of men dying to get pissed on and whipped; a subway john full of horny high school students; Morocco—getting raped on a tombstone in Marrakesh. God, how I miss it."
They recall some of the drug-induced and/or sex-induced highlights of their checkered past. In the back room of a porno bookshop, they begin imitating some of the habitues.

SAUL (a black queen): Sistuhs, theyuh's plenty heah fo' ivrybody.
RICH (a tough New York queen): Hey, Mary, the line forms at the rear.
SAUL: And whose rear might that be, sugar?
        Two other men appear in the bookstore.
MARTY: Hey, Vinnie?
VINNIE: Marty?
MARTY: What are you doing here? You said you were gonna buy the papers.
VINNIE: You said you were gonna walk the dogs.

MARTY: You trash!
>*They exit bickering.*
SAUL: I always knew when you were fucking around.
RICH: You did your share.
SAUL: Moi?
RICH: I know why Grand Union wouldn't deliver to our house.
>*They have returned to the loft.*
SAUL: God, I used to love promiscuous sex.
RICH: Not "promiscuous," Saul—nondirective, noncommitted, nonauthoritarian—
SAUL: Free, wild rampant—
RICH: Hot, sweaty, steamy, smelly—
SAUL: Juicy, funky, hunky—
RICH: Sex.
SAUL: Sex. God, I miss it.

Saul tries to kiss Rich, declaring he doesn't care about the disease, but Rich pulls away abruptly. They remember how much fun it was going out together on Saul's photographic excursions. Saul never wanted to break up, partly because he liked the routines of a stable relationship, coming home with his photographs and finding Rich there writing. "We were stagnating," Rich comments, but Saul argues that the daily sameness gave them "a structure to fall back on when life dealt us its wild card or curve balls."

After a long pause, Saul remembers that he was in a hot tub at the St. Marks baths when he first heard about AIDS four years ago. A group enters chatting quietly, with two or more sometimes talking at the same time.

1ST MAN: The first time I heard about AIDS it was a spring day, kind of warm. I was wearing a jacket. I remember I ran into a friend on the corner of 57th and Broadway. He asked me if I'd heard about Joel. It didn't make any sense to me.

3D MAN: I thought AIDS was like Legionnaire's Disease or Toxic Shock Syndrome, or Sickle Cell Anemia, Alzheimer's disease—one of those rare diseases you read about in the papers.

2D MAN: The first time I heard about AIDS was in the Paradise Garage, a disco I used to go to. I won a raffle, the proceeds of which went to help people with this strange new disease. I didn't even know what it was.

1ST WOMAN: It seemed so terribly remote at the time, like an . . .

1ST WOMAN, 2D MAN: . . . epidemic in India . . .

OTHERS: Finland . . . Borneo . . . Java . . .

ALL: Ethiopia.

2D WOMAN: The first time I heard about it . . .
1ST WOMAN, 2D WOMAN: . . . I was standing in my kitchen . . .
1ST WOMAN: I was about to go out shopping . . .
1ST WOMAN, 2D WOMAN: . . . for my youngest's birthday party.

4TH MAN: The phone rang.

2D WOMAN: It was this doctor calling me . . .

2D WOMAN, 3D MAN: . . . about my son Bernard.

1ST WOMAN: He used a lot of big words . . .

1ST WOMAN, 2D WOMAN: . . . and then he said . . .

1ST MAN, 4TH MAN: . . . "Do you understand what I'm saying?"

2D WOMAN: I said . . .

1ST WOMAN, 2D WOMAN: . . . Yes.

1ST WOMAN: Right before he hung up he said . . .

1ST MAN: "So you know he has . . ."

ALL: ". . . AIDS."

1ST WOMAN: That's the first time I heard the word.

2ND WOMAN: I was backstage at Saratoga.

2ND WOMAN, 4TH MAN: I can't remember if it was *The Seagull* . . .

1ST WOMAN: . . . or *Virginia Woolf.*

2ND WOMAN: It was absurd. I had just seen him two weeks before. but there you had it . . .

1ST MAN, 2D MAN, 4TH MAN, 1ST WOMAN, 2D WOMAN: . . . George was dead.

3D MAN: When I first heard that Bill had AIDS and was dying, I thought . . .

2D MAN: I almost died laughing.

3D MAN: . . . my God, we're all going to die.

This group exits as Saul finishes telling Rich that he first heard about AIDS from a friend who called another friend's death from the disease "bizarre." And Rich finally agrees to stay here with Saul "Just until I feel better," as a friend but not as a lover. Medical expenses have wiped out Rich's resources (his health insurance is "pulling a fast one"). He is physically frightened, too, and Saul tries to comfort him. Saul is hugging Rich when the action flashes back to the time when Lily came to the loft, bringing her cousin Chet and introducing him to Rich and Saul, congratulating Rich on the imminent publication of his book and asking Saul to take some publicity photos of her.

LILY *(to Saul):* You're such an artist.

SAUL: Rich is the "artiste" in the family.

LILY: Chet, be an angel and bring Saul his camera. It's by the bar.

    Chet looks for camera.

SAUL *(to Chet):* Don't let your cousin push you around the way she does me.

LILY: Come on, Saul, make click-click.

SAUL: Unless you like that sort of thing.

RICH *(to Saul):* That's all I get?

LILY *(to Rich, about Saul):* Leave the boy alone.

RICH: A hug and a bitchy remark?

SAUL *(to Rich):* That and ninety cents.

RICH *(to Saul):* No "Gee, Rich, I'm so proud of you?"

SAUL *(Smiling falsely):* Gee, Rich, I'm so proud of you.

RICH: I finally have some good news, and he's annoyed.

CHET *(to Lily, holding camera):* What should I do with this?

SAUL: Well, your brother called, while you were out guzzling lunch with your agent, Dr. Mengele. Call him back.

RICH: What'd he have to say?

SAUL: Call him and ask him. I'm not your secretary.

RICH *(imitating him):* I'm not your—

SAUL: He forgot my fucking name again. How long we been together?

RICH: Too long. . . . .

Rich wants to celebrate but continues to be annoyed that Saul won't exclaim over his book. Lily finally prevails on Saul to take her picture. After Rich and Saul lightly apologize to each other, Rich prepares to go out jogging (he's in training for the marathon). Chet goes out of his way to congratulate Rich on the book and comments with enthusiasm on a poem of Rich's he has read. Saul inquires of Lily whether Chet is gay, and Lily promptly shouts the question to Chet, who answers with a loud "Yes." Chet needs a place to stay in New York, and Rich invites him to occupy the loft of a friend who has gone to Los Angeles (and Rich's growing interest in this young man is not lost on Saul).

Lily, Rich and Chet exit after Saul finishes taking the pictures. The hospice worker comes forward to tell the audience how it is to tend the dying: "My job is not to bring enlightenment, only comfort." Here in the Village, about a third of her patients are AIDS victims.

After the hospice worker exits, an AIDS support group is in progress. A young man declares he was never promiscuous and didn't believe his lover was either, but when he got AIDS the lover left him. A pregnant suburban housewife has contracted AIDS from her husband. When Rich's turn comes, he says, "I'm not sure I have it any more. I feel guilty about saying this, like somehow I'm being disloyal to the group. I'm getting better, I know it. I just have these lumps which for some reason won't go away, and a loss of weight, which has made me lighter than I've been for years . . . . . I feel the disease disappearing in me. Only a tiny percentage of those with the swollen glands come down with the rest. I'm going to *not* come here next week. I'm sorry."

Back at the loft, Saul is worried about his own neck glands, but Rich feels them and assures him there is nothing wrong. They start a roughhouse which is about to turn into sex play, when Saul stops and stares at Rich's shoulder.

RICH: What?

    Saul ignores him and looks at the mark carefully.

What? You seduce me, you finally succeed in getting me hot and bothered, and what do you do as I lie here panting? You look at my birthmark.

SAUL: Not the birthmark.

    He looks at Rich's back. He touches some marks.

RICH: What is it?

SAUL: Nothing.

RICH: What is it? Tell me!

SAUL: I'm sure it's nothing.

RICH: What! WHAT! *WHAT!* . . .

The hospice worker draws a curtain around the loft area, while two AIDS hotline volunteers, Barney and Pat, answer a series of incoming calls: "It's not that easy to get it—*if* you take a few precautions," "The disease is spread mainly through the blood and the semen," "American Indians are *not* a risk group," "I would definitely check it out with a physician," etc, answering the phones, answering the questions, offering advice and sometimes reassurance.

BARNEY: I'm sorry you're lonely.
PAT: Just don't exchange any body fluids and you'll be all right.
BARNEY: Madam, we're busy here. I can't stay on the line with you all day.
PAT: You have a nice voice too, but I'm seeing someone.
BARNEY: Hello?
PAT: Thanks.
BARNEY *(to Pat):* Thank God.
PAT: Good luck.
　　　They hang up at the same time.
BARNEY: Spots. I love it.
PAT *(to himself):* I'm not seeing anyone.
BARNEY: What are you talking about?
PAT: I was saying how much I love being celibate.

In the course of their conversation they remind each other that Rich is one of the unruly problem patients: "He throws dishes and curses his roommate and won't cooperate with the doctor and won't see his shrink and isn't interested in support groups." They've had to put Rich in the hospital. The phones start ringing again, and Barney and Pat answer with their opening question, "Are you a gay man?"

The lights fade, and the curtain opens to reveal a hospital bed, chair and table in the former loft and bar area. Rich is in bed, attended by Lily, Saul and a nurse. Rich has just learned from Lily that Chet died of AIDS, and Rich uses this as an excuse to browbeat the nurse until she gives up trying to take his blood pressure.

LILY *(to Saul):* I should have kept my mouth shut.
RICH: Having brought Romeo the news that Juliet is dead, Balthasar makes a tearful exit.
LILY: I don't know what to say.
　　　Lily looks at Rich, then Saul.
RICH: I said: Balthasar makes a tearful exit.
LILY: I know how you're feeling.
RICH: No matter. Get thee gone and hire those horses.
LILY: I loved Chet, too.
RICH: Tush, thou art deceived.
LILY: He told me he was sorry for the way he treated you.
RICH: Do the thing I bid thee.
LILY: He didn't belong in New York. He thought he was so sophisticated, but he was just a kid from Mendocino. I'm sorry I let him go home.

RICH: The messenger must go. The hero wishes to be alone with his confidant. *Rich turns his back on Saul and Lily.*

Lily finally departs, and Rich and Saul toy with the Sunday *Times* crossword puzzle, to which Rich has all the answers, having spent a lot of his childhood time in libraries. Rich wrote his first poem at age 8 or 9: "I was a good kid, but I was lonely and scared all the time. I was so desperate to find people like myself that I looked for them in the indexes of books—under 'H'." Grown up, he moved to the city, became an office worker and writer and met and moved in with Saul. They loved each other, but that wasn't enough: "You weren't my muse, you were . . . *(He searches for the word.)* Saul. *(Saul rises and looks out the window.)* I loved you, but I wanted someone to write poems to. During our marriage I had almost stopped writing and felt stifled, even though our loft had appeared in *New York* magazine. And then I met Chet and left you in the lurch and lived with him at the Chelsea Hotel. He was shallow, callow and selfish, and I loved him, too. We did a lot of coke, and I wrote a lot of poetry, and the catering was booming, and the *New Yorker* published a story of mine, and I ran in the marathon. I was on a roll . . . . . The next morning I woke up with the flu and stayed in bed for a couple of days and felt much better. But my throat stayed a little sore and my glands were a little swollen."

Rich asks Saul to help him collect some Seconal—he's tried to hoard pills here but hasn't been able to get away with it. Saul refuses adamantly, but Rich begs him, "Just have them around. You'll get used to the idea. And when the lesions spread above my neck so that I don't look the same, you'll want me to have them." Saul still refuses, and they are interrupted by the arrival of Rich's brother dressed protectively in surgical mask, gown and gloves and carrying a shopping bag.

RICH *(to brother):* Unless you're planning to come into intimate contact with me or my body fluids, none of that shit you have on is necessary.
BROTHER: The sign says—
RICH: But please restrain your brotherly affection for my sake: who knows what diseases you might have brought in with you?
        Brother removes mask, gown and gloves.
SAUL: You two haven't seen each other for a while, so why don't I just—
RICH: By all means. You need a break, kid. Think about what I said.
SAUL: It stopped raining. I'll take a walk.
RICH: Have a nice walk.
BROTHER: Good seeing ya . . . ? *(He has forgotten Saul's name.)*
SAUL: Saul. Yeah. *(Exits.)*
BROTHER *(after a beat):* I owe you an apology . . .
        Rich won't help him.
I was very frightened . . . I'm afraid I panicked . . . Please forgive me.
RICH: Nothing to forgive.

Rich's brother passes along his wife's love and makes small talk about medical research. When he asks Rich how he's doing, Rich stops him cold with clinical

Jonathan Hogan with Jonathan Hadary as Saul in a scene from *As Is*

detail: "I have Kaposi's sarcoma, a hitherto rare form of skin cancer. It's spreading. I have just begun chemotherapy. It nauseates me. I expect my hair will fall out. I also have a fungal infection of the throat called candidiasis, or thrush. My life expectancy is . . . I have a greater chance of winning the lottery."

After a long silence, Rich's brother tells Rich about his daughter's winning a swimming contest and shows Rich a large fold-out card she has made for him.

RICH: Say, have you heard about the miracle of AIDS?

BROTHER: What?

RICH: It can turn a fruit into a vegetable. What's the worst thing about getting AIDS?

BROTHER *(lets the card fall to the floor):* Stop it!

RICH: Trying to convince your parents that you're Haitian. Get it?

BROTHER: I came here to see if I can help you.

RICH: Skip it. So what do you want?

BROTHER: I don't want anything.

RICH: Everything I own is going to Saul—

BROTHER: I don't want anything.

RICH: Except for the stuff Mom left us. I told Saul that it's to go to you. Except for the Barcelona chair—

BROTHER: I don't care about—

RICH: I'm leaving Saul the copyright to my book—

BROTHER: Why are you doing this to me?

RICH: So you don't want my worldly possessions, such as they are: you want me to relieve your guilt.

BROTHER: Stop it.

RICH (*making the sign of the cross over his brother, chanting*): I hereby exonerate you of the sin of being ashamed of your queer brother and being a coward in the face of—

BROTHER: Stop! Don't!

    Brother grabs Rich's hand.

RICH: No!

BROTHER: Richard, don't! . . .

    Attempts to hug Rich.

I don't care . . . I don't care . . . Rich!

    He grabs Rich and hugs him.

Richie . . . Richie . . .

They hold each other close while Rich confesses he's frightened. An officious hospital worker comes in, draws the wrong conclusion from their embrace and warns them that Saul is on his way back to the room, which sets them to laughing. Rich's brother has to go now but promises to come back the next day with his daughter, who has been wanting to visit her uncle. On the way out, the brother forgets Saul's name again, which Saul continues to resent.

Saul admits to Rich that he decided to get some pills after all—a hundred of them, enough for both of them. "The widow throws herself on her husband's funeral pyre," Rich comments sarcastically, sending Saul into a paroxysm of anger. But later, after he bought them, Saul threw the pills away, he tells Rich, exclaiming "Let me help you live!" Rich climbs out of bed as though in an attempt to get up and go out to find some pills himself, but he collapses with the effort.

Saul gets Rich into a chair and then insists on explaining that he had bought the pills from a pusher and was walking past Sheridan Square in the rain, depressed, thinking about their dual suicides. He stopped in front of a sex shop lit with a red neon sign and found himself asking God for help, "Which is funny coming from an atheist, let me tell you . . . I said it out loud." Saul happened to look down into a puddle at his feet, and there "in this dirty little puddle was a reflection of the red neon sign. It was beautiful. And the whole street was shining with the most incredible colors. They kept changing as the different signs blinked on and off . . . I don't know how long I stood there. A phrase came to my head: 'The Lord taketh and the Lord giveth.' " So Saul threw the $200 worth of pills into the sewer, convinced he has no right to take either of their lives. All he can do is promise Rich, "I'll be here for you no matter what happens."

Rich admits that he needs Saul and gets him to repeat his solemn promise to stick by him no matter what happens. Reflecting on what might happen after death, Rich comments, "I don't feature leaving here and going to a goddamned naphtha swamp in the Z sector of some provincial galaxy to live as some kind of weird insect . . . But if life is a kind of educational process in which each piece of the universe eventually gets to discover its own true divine nature, if it is, then a methane bog on Jupiter might serve just as well as a meadow in the Berkshires."

When Rich gets out of the hospital, he wants Saul to take a picture of him reading his poetry in a certain "scuzzy" coffee house whose customers "look new born but slightly depraved." Saul and Rich express their affection for each other by calling each other vulgar names.

RICH: You're a faggot.
SAUL: You're a fruit.
RICH: You know, if we took precautions . . .
SAUL: What? If what? You always do that.
RICH: I don't know.
SAUL: Would you like to?
RICH: If we're careful. Do you want to?
SAUL: I'd like to. What do you think?
RICH: I think it'd be O.K.
SAUL: What'll we do?
RICH: I don't know.
SAUL: We'll think of something.
RICH: Close the curtain.
SAUL: Do you think we should?
RICH: Well, we can't do it like this.
SAUL: Right.
RICH: Right.
SAUL: What if someone comes in?
RICH: So what?
SAUL: Right.
RICH: So what are you waiting for?
SAUL: I'm scared.
RICH: So am I. Close the curtain.
SAUL: Do you think we should?
RICH: Oh, come on, gimme a break.
SAUL: God, I want to.
RICH: Close the fucking curtain.
          Hospice worker closes the curtain.
Thanks.
SAUL: Thanks.

After the curtain is closed, the hospice worker addresses the audience on the subject of her "new AIDS patient, Richard. He still has a lot of denial about his condition. Which is normal. I think most of us would go crazy if we had to face our own deaths squarely. He's a wonderful man. He writes extraordinarily funny poems about the ward. His lover's there all the time, and he's got a lot of friends visiting and both families. I only hope it keeps up. It's only his second time in the hospital. They get a lot of support at first, but as the illness goes on, the visitors stop coming—and they're left with only me."

Probably this won't happen in Richard's case, the hospice worker continues, because Saul is keeping a close and determined eye on him. "Rich will be out of

the hospital again in a week or so," she continues, "For a while. He's a fighter
. . . The angry phase is just about over, and the bargaining phase is beginning.
If he behaves like a good little boy, God will do what Rich tells Him to do
. . . I certainly hope that God does."

The hospice worker admits that she has fits of denial and anger and is perhaps
suffering from burnout but means to continue this work. She's now caring for a
real "queen" who, though *in extremis*, is sometimes callously treated by other
attendants. But "I've lost some of my idealism, as I said. Last night I painted his
nails for him. *(Showing the audience her vividly painted fingernails.)* Flaming red.
He loved it." *Curtain.*

BILOXI BLUES

A Comedy in Two Acts

BY NEIL SIMON

Cast and credits appear on page 335

NEIL SIMON was born in the Bronx, N.Y. on July 4, 1927. After graduating from DeWitt Clinton High School he managed to find time for writing while serving in the army, not unlike his alter ego Eugene Morris Jerome in Biloxi Blues. *Writing soon became his profession without the formalities of college (except for a few courses at New York University and the University of Denver). His first theater work consisted of sketches for camp shows at Tamiment, Pa., in collaboration with his brother Danny. He became a TV writer, supplying a good deal of material for Sid Caesar* (Caesar's Hour) *and Phil Silvers* (Sergeant Bilko).

On Broadway, Simon contributed sketches to Catch a Star *(1955) and* New Faces of 1956. *His first Broadway play was* Come Blow Your Horn *(1961), followed by the book of the musical* Little Me *(1962). His next play, the comedy* Barefoot in the Park *(1963) was named a Best Play of its season, as was* The Odd Couple *(1965). Neither of these had closed when the musical* Sweet Charity, *for which Simon wrote the book, came along early in 1966; and none of the three had closed when Simon's* The Star-Spangled Girl *opened the following season in December 1966—so that Simon had the phenomonal total of four shows running simultaneously on Broadway during the season of 1966–67. When the last of the four closed the following summer, they had played a total of 3,367 performances over four theater seasons.*

Simon immediately began stacking another pile of blue-chip shows. His Plaza Suite *(1968) was named a Best Play of its year. His book of the musical* Promises, Promises *(1968) was another smash, and his* Last of the Red Hot Lovers *(1969) became his fourth Best Play and third Simon show in grand simultaneous display*

"Biloxi Blues:" by Neil Simon. Copyright © 1985 by Neil Simon. Reprinted by permission of Random House, Inc. See CAUTION notice on copyright page. All inquiries should be addressed to: Random House, Inc., 201 East 50th Street, New York, NY 10022.

on Broadway. Plaza Suite *closed before* The Gingerbread Lady *(1970, also a Best Play) opened, so that Simon's second stack was "only" three plays and 3,084 performances high.*

There followed The Prisoner of Second Avenue *(1971, a Best Play),* The Sunshine Boys *(1972, a Best Play),* The Good Doctor *(1973, a Best Play) and* God's Favorite *(1974). There was no new Neil Simon play on Broadway the following year because he was moving himself and his family from New York to California, partly for personal reasons and partly to base himself closer to his screen activities. Movies or no movies, by April 1976 he had* California Suite *ready for production at Center Theater Group in Los Angeles en route to the Eugene O'Neill Theater—which for a time he owned—in June 1976 as his 15th Broadway show and ninth Best Play.*

To continue: Simon's tenth Best Play was Chapter Two, *also produced at Center Theater Group before coming on to New York in December 1977. He wrote the book for* They're Playing Our Song, *the long-run 1979 musical with a Marvin Hamlisch score and Carole Bayer Sayer lyrics. His 11th Best Play,* I Ought To Be in Pictures, *was seen in Los Angeles prior to its 1980 arrival on Broadway. His shortest-run New York play,* Fools *(1981), survived for only 40 performances, and an attempt to revise and revive* Little Me *in 1982 fell short of expectations, with only 36 performances. But Simon came roaring back with* Brighton Beach Memoirs *in 1983 after pre-Broadway stagings on the West Coast. This was a semi-autobiographical comedy of adolescence, a popular hit which was still running when its sequel, the semi-autobiographical army comedy* Biloxi Blues, *opened this season on March 28, again after West Coast staging, as its author's 22d Broadway production and 12th Best Play.*

Simon's movie writing credits have included the screen plays for his own Barefoot in the Park *(in its time the longest run at the Music Hall),* The Odd Couple *(which broke that record the following year),* Plaza Suite, The Prisoner of Second Avenue, The Sunshine Boys, California Suite, Chapter Two *and* I Ought To Be in Pictures, *plus* The Out-of-Towners, The Heartbreak Kid, Murder by Death, The Goodbye Girl, The Cheap Detective, Seems Like Old Times, Only When I Laugh, Max Dugan Returns *and* The Slugger's Wife.

Simon's many honors and accolades have included Tony Awards every ten years: the 1965 Tony as author of The Odd Couple, *a special 1975 Tony for his over-all contribution to the theater and a 1985 best-play Tony for* Biloxi Blues. *He received the 1982–83 New York Drama Critics Circle best-play award for* Brighton Beach Memoirs, *the Sam S. Shubert Award in 1968, Writers Guild screen awards in 1968, 1970 and 1975 and numerous Tony, Emmy and Academy nominations—and last year Broadway's Alvin Theater was renamed the Neil Simon in his honor. He now divides his time between New York and Los Angeles and has been twice married, with two daughters by his first wife.*

Our method of representing Biloxi Blues *here differs from that of the other Best Plays. The humor of this army comedy is so verbal, on top of character and situation, that too much of the play's wealth would be squandered in the giveaway of a synopsis with excerpts from the script. We therefore represent* Biloxi Blues *with one complete scene, designated by the author himself to appear in these pages as a prime example of the style and quality of his latest Best Play.*

Time: 1943

Place: Biloxi and Gulfport, Miss.

Eugene Morris Jerome, the teenager of *Brighton Beach Memoirs,* is now a young man on his way from his Brooklyn home to basic training in the World War II army. Accompanying him in the facing seats of an old railroad coach on its way to the army base in Biloxi, Miss. are three other 18-to-20-year-old youths: Joseph Wykowski, Roy Selridge and Don Carney. Eugene is writing a description of his companions in a school notebook, shared with the audience in asides: "Roy Selridge from Schenectady, New York smelled like a tuna fish sandwich left out in the rain. . . . . . Joseph Wykowski from Bridgeport, Connecticut had two interesting characteristics. He had the stomach of a goat and could eat anything. His favorite was Hershey bars with the wrappers still on it . . . The other peculiar trait was that he had a permanent erection . . . . . Donald Carney from Montclair, New Jersey was an okay guy until someone made the fatal mistake of telling him he sounded like Perry Como."

A fifth youngster is sleeping in the baggage rack above: "Arnold Epstein of Queens Boulevard, New York was a sensitive, well read, intelligent young man. His major flaw was that he was incapable of digesting food stronger than hard boiled eggs."

Eugene introduces himself to the audience and explains that there are three things he means to do in this war: "Become a writer, not get killed and lose my virginity." Since Eugene is a semi-autobiographical character created by the author, we know that he accomplished the first two, and in the course of *Biloxi Blues* we see him accomplish the third.

In the meantime, he and his four companions settle into their barracks and begin to cope with the army, personified by Sergeant Toomey, a hard-nosed veteran with a plate in his head covering a wound suffered in the North African campaign. Their section of the barracks is furnished with three double bunks for the five and another recruit about their own age, James Hennesey. Eugene's bunk is an upper, and he also has a footlocker where he hides the notebook in which he exercises his writing skills in diary-like fashion. The following scene (Act II, Scene 3) takes place in these quarters.

> *Lights up on section of barracks. It's late Sunday night. Selridge, Carney and Arnold are lying on their bunks. Wykowski, pacing, has Eugene's notebook of memoirs. Carney is on his stomach reading a letter and Arnold is reading a worn paperback of Kafka.*

WYKOWSKI: . . . I can't believe what this creep's been writing about us . . . Listen to this . . . "No matter how lunatic I think Sergeant Toomey is, there is method in his madness. He is winning the game. Each day we drop a little of our own personalities and become more obedient, more robot-like, until what was once an intelligent, thinking human being is now nothing but a khaki idiot.

Yesterday, in front of everybody, he made Epstein unscrew the top of his head and take his brains out."

ARNOLD *(without looking up from his book).* I fooled him. I only took out my mucous membrane.

> *Hennesey comes in from outside.*

HENNESEY: Wow, what a weekend. How'd you guys do?

WYKOWSKI: Hey, Hennesey. You ought to listen to this. You're in this too.

HENNESEY: What is it?

> *He starts loosening his tie.*

WYKOWSKI: "The Secret and Private Memoirs of Eugene J. Jerome."

HENNESEY: He let you read it?

WYKOWSKI: No, but we're going to ask him if it's all right when we get through. *(He and Selridge laugh.)*

HENNESEY: You have no right to read that. That's like opening someone's mail.

WYKOWSKI: Bullshit. It's all about us. Private things about every one of us. That's public domain like in the newspapers.

ARNOLD *(without looking up from his book):* A newspaper is published. Unpublished memoirs are the sole and private property of the writer.

WYKOWSKI: I thought all Jews were doctors. I didn't know they were lawyers too.

ARNOLD: I'm not a Jew any more, Wykowski.

WYKOWSKI: What do you mean?

ARNOLD: I converted to Catholicism yesterday. In six weeks I hope to become a priest and my first act of service to the Holy Father is to have you excommunicated, so get off my ass.

SELRIDGE *(laughs):* That's good. That's funny. God damn Jews are really funny. Hey, Epstein, I'm beginning to like you, I swear to Christ.

WYKOWSKI *(annoyed):* You guys interested in hearing the rest of this or not?

HENNESEY: No, I'm not. *(He starts toward latrine, stops.)* I thought you were Gene's friend, Epstein.

ARNOLD: He didn't lock his locker. Why then would he leave something so private in an open locker? There's no logic to it. I have no interest in illogical things.

HENNESEY *(to Epstein):* You tell Gene I had nothing to do with this. You hear me? *(He exits to latrine.)*

SELRIDGE: Go on. After ". . . still, still of the night."

WYKOWSKI *(reads):* . . ."At night I listen to the others breathing in their sleep and it's then that their fears and self-doubts become even more apparent than during their waking hours . . . One night a sudden scream from Selridge that sounded like he was calling out the name, Louise. Is Louise his girl or possibly his mother?"

SELRIDGE: He's full of crap.

WYKOWSKI: Who's Louise?

SELRIDGE: My mother. But he's full of crap. I never called my mother Louise.

WYKOWSKI: Poor baby, wants his mother.

> *Continues reading.*

CARNEY: I don't want to hear any more of this. I don't like being spied on.

(Front row) Brian Tarantina as Roy Selridge, Alan Ruck as Don Carney, Matt Mulhern as Joseph Wykowski; *(middle row)* Penelope Ann Miller as Daisy Hannigan, Matthew Broderick as Eugene Morris Jerome, Randall Edwards as Rowena; *(back row)* Geoffrey Sharp as James Hennesey, Bill Sadler as Sgt. Merwin J. Toomey and Barry Miller as Arnold Epstein in Neil Simon's *Biloxi Blues*

WYKOWSKI *(looks at book):* Dirty bastard! Wait'll you hear what he writes about me.

> *Suddenly Eugene appears, coming back from town.*

SELRIDGE: It's him. Put it away.

> *Wykowski slips the book under his bunk, pretends to play cards with Selridge. Eugene enters with a big, self-satisfied smile on his face and a very "cocky" walk.*

EUGENE: Hi, guys!

> *They all look up, mutter their hellos and resume their activities. Eugene waits expectantly for someone to ask about his adventure but no one does.*

So, how was your weekend?

CARNEY: Fine.

WYKOWSKI: Great.

SELRIDGE: The best.

EUGENE: Good—good—good—good—good.

CARNEY *(to Eugene):* Well?

EUGENE: Well what?

CARNEY: What was it like? Give us details . . . Was it "Empty Saddles in the Old Corral" or was it "Swing Swing Swing"?

EUGENE: It was sort of—"Moonlight Cocktails" . . . It was chatty.

WYKOWSKI: Chatty? Your first time in the sack with a pro was "chatty"?

EUGENE: She's not a pro. She only does it on weekends.

WYKOWSKI: So what does that make her? A semi-pro?

SELRIDGE *(laughs):* Great! That was great. Perfect remark, Kows . . .

EUGENE: At least we talked to each other. I wasn't in and out of there in two seconds. She was a person to me, not a pro.

ARNOLD: *(still reading book):* Self-righteous, Eugene. Be on guard against self-righteousness.

EUGENE *(unties his tie, starts to unbutton his shirt):* The second time was "Swing, Swing, Swing". *(He smiles.)*

SELRIDGE: The *second* time? You paid twice?

EUGENE: No. It was a "freebie." On the house.

WYKOWSKI: You're full of it.

CARNEY: Why would she give you a free one?

EUGENE: Maybe I was her one millionth customer. *(He chuckles at his joke.)*

WYKOWSKI: Hey, Jerome. Blow it out your barracks bag.

> *Eugene doesn't see what he's looking for. He seems disturbed. He looks through locker, under his bunk and mattress.*

EUGENE: Has anybody seen my notebook?

WYKOWSKI *(very deliberate):* What notebook is that?

EUGENE: The one I'm always writing in . . . Arnold, did you see it?

ARNOLD: Why did you leave your locker unlocked?

EUGENE: Because I lost my key in the shower drain. There was nothing valuable in there except my book. I thought I could trust people around here.

WYKOWSKI: That's really funny, Jerome, 'cause we thought we could trust you too.

EUGENE: What does that mean?

Wykowski reaches under his bunk and takes out the notebook. He opens it up and Eugene makes a move toward it but Wykowski jumps on top of his bunk and extends his foot to ward off Eugene.

WYKOWSKI *(starts to read):* "One night a sudden scream from Selridge that sounded like he was calling out the name, Louise. Is Louise his girl or possibly his mother?"

EUGENE *(furious):* You had no right to read that. Give it to me, Kowski.

CARNEY: Give it to him. Nobody's interested.

WYKOWSKI: No? You interested in what he thinks about you, Donny baby?

EUGENE *(lunges for him):* Give it to me, Goddammit!

Selridge reaches quickly and grabs Eugene's arm and bends it behind his back. Eugene knows one move and it's broken.

SELRIDGE: I'm just gonna hold your arm. If you want it broken, it's up to you.

CARNEY: What does he say about me?

EUGENE: Kowski, please don't read it.

WYKOWSKI: If it gets boring, I'll stop. *(He reads.)* "I can't make Don Carney out yet. Basically I like him and we've had some interesting talks, if you don't mind sticking to popular music and baseball. But there's something about him you can't count on and if I was ever in real trouble, Don Carney's the last one I'd turn to."

Carney and Eugene look at each other. The others are quiet.

CARNEY: Well, let's just hope you never have to count on me.

He is hurt. He gets up, walks to the side and lights up a cigarette.

EUGENE *(to Carney):* It doesn't mean anything. It's just the thoughts in my head when I'm writing it. They change every day.

HENNESEY *(has returned from the latrine):* Let him go, Selridge.

SELRIDGE: You want to take his place? I don't care whose arm I break.

WYKOWSKI: O.K., you ready for the best part? Here's the best part . . . *(He reads.)* "Wykowski is pure animal. His basic instincts are all physical and he eats his meals like a horse eating his oats." Hey, Epstein! Can I sue him for defamation of—what is it?

ARNOLD: Character. Only if his intent is to prove malice and in your case it's not possible.

SELRIDGE: Go on. What else does he say about you?

WYKOWSKI *(reads on):* "He masturbates in bed four or five times a night. He has no shame about it and his capacities are inexhaustible. Sometimes when he has a discharge, he announces it to the room. 'Number five torpedo fired! Loading number six!' " *(To others.)* That's really good reporting. This guy should be on *Time* Magazine or something.

EUGENE *(near tears):* Please stop it. You want to read it, read it to yourself.

WYKOWSKI: What do you mean? You're making me famous. Maybe the movies'll buy this. Great picture for John Wayne.

SELRIDGE: Is there any more?

WYKOWSKI: Yeah. Where was I?

SELRIDGE: You just fired number five.

WYKOWSKI: Oh yeah. Here. *(He reads.)* "Despite Wykowski's lack of culture,

Bill Sadler, Matthew Broderick, Matt Mulhern, Barry Miller, Brian Tarantina, Geoffrey Sharp and Alan Ruck in a barracks scene from *Biloxi Blues*

sensitivity or the pursuit of anything minutely intellectual, his greatest strength
is his consistency of character and his earnest belief that he belongs on the
battlefield. He is clearly the best soldier in the platoon, dependable under pressure, and it would not surprise me if Wykowski came out of this war with the
Medal of Honor." *(Looks at Eugene.)* . . . You really mean that, Jerome?

EUGENE: I told you, I don't mean any of it. I get a thought and I write it down.
Right now I would describe you in three words. "A yellow bastard!"

WYKOWSKI: They don't give the Medal of Honor to yellow bastards . . . Let
him go, Sel.

Selridge lets him go. Eugene rubs his arm in pain.
. . . Why do you want to write this stuff down for? You're just gonna make a lot
of guys unhappy.

EUGENE: What I write is *my* business. Give me my book. *(He reaches for it.)*

ARNOLD: Wait a minute.

As Wykowski extends book, Arnold snatches it from his hand.
I think I deserve to hear *my* life story.

EUGENE: Arnold, I beg you. Don't read it. They're my private thoughts and
if you take them, you steal from me.

ARNOLD: I gather then it's unflattering. Don't you know me by now, Gene?

I can't be unflattered. I'm past it . . . However, if you don't want me to read it, I won't read it. But I don't think we'll be able to be truly honest with each other from this moment on.

EUGENE *(looks at him):* . . . Put it back when you're through.

> *He gets up and walks out of the room. Arnold opens the book and starts to read to himself.*

WYKOWSKI: Don't we get to hear it?

ARNOLD: Sure, Kowski. This is what we're fighting the war about, isn't it? *(He reads.)* "Arnold Epstein is truly the most complex and fascinating man I've ever met and his constant and relentless pursuit of truth, logic and reason fascinates me in the same proportion as his obstinacy and unnecessary heroics drive me to distraction. But I love him for it. In the same manner that I love Joe DiMaggio for making the gesture of catching a long fly ball to center seem like the last miracle performed by God in modern times. But often I hold back showing my love and affection for Arnold because I think he might misinterpret it. It just happens to be my instinctive feeling—that Arnold is homosexual, and it bothers me that it bothers me."

> *He closes the book. He looks at the others who are all staring at him.*

. . . Do you see why I find life so interesting? Here is a man of my own faith and background, potentially intelligent and talented, who in six weeks has come to the brilliant conclusion that a cretin like Wykowski is going to win the Medal of Honor and that I, his most esteemed and dearest friend, is a fairy.

> *He tosses the book on Eugene's bunk.*

This is a problem worthy of a Talmudic scholar. Goodnight, fellas . . . It is my opinion that no one gets a wink of sleep tonight.

> *Blackout.*

DOUBLES

A Comedy in Two Acts

BY DAVID WILTSE

Cast and credits appear on pages 342–343

DAVID WILTSE was born in Lincoln, Neb. June 6, 1940, the son of an attorney. He was educated in Falls City, Neb. and the University of Nebraska. Following a period of service in the U.S. Army, in Germany, he came to New York City in 1966 with the intention of writing plays. His first production of record was an OOB staging Oct. 6, 1971 of his Tall and Rex *in Chelsea Theater Center's experimental series. There soon followed a production of his* Suggs *by the Repertory Theater of Lincoln Center May 4, 1972 for 20 performances, for which he won a Drama Desk citation as most promising playwright—a promise fulfilled by his* Doubles *as of May 8, 1985, his first Best Play.*

In the intervening years, Wiltse wrote more than two dozen films, TV movies and series pilots. In the 1980s he turned to writing novels, and his first one, The Wedding Guest *was selected by the New York* Times *as one of the 100 notable books of 1982. His second and third—*The Serpent *and* The Fifth Angel—*were both book club selections. He has received a grant from the Connecticut State Arts Commission to complete a new play,* A Grand Romance, *scheduled for New York production next season, and he has also been commissioned to write a thriller (his* Revenge of the Stepford Wives *on TV won a Mystery Writers of America Award). He lives in Connecticut with his wife and three daughters.*

"Doubles:" by David Wiltse. Copyright © 1985 by David Wiltse. Reprinted by permission of William Morris Agency, Inc. See CAUTION notice on copyright page. All inquiries concerning stock and amateur rights should be addressed to: Samuel French, Inc., 45 West 25th Street, New York, NY 10011. All other inquiries should be addressed to: William Morris Agency, Inc., 1350 Avenue of the Americas, New York, NY 10019, Attention: Esther Sherman.

Time: The present

Place: The men's locker room of the Norwalk Racquet Club, Norwalk, Conn.

ACT I

Scene 1

SYNOPSIS: The fully equipped tennis club locker room features benches, exercise machine, a cubicle formed by two rows of lockers, doors to the sauna and the showers at right and to the tennis courts at left, and the exit door upstage. The tennis pro, Chuck, pauses to admire himself in the mirror while passing through, but the room is empty when Guy, *"an athletic-looking man in his early 40s . . . He has never been here before and looks just a little bit ill at ease,"* enters, puts down his equipment and starts to undress into an empty locker. Somewhat to his embarrassment, Heather, a very attractive female locker room attendant dressed in tennis clothes, comes in to pick up the used towels, breezily, with a "Don't worry about me, I'm not looking."

Arnie, *"40 but looks and acts older because of a certain prissy primness,"* comes in and greets Heather with shy admiration, complimenting her on her pretty name and on her socks with the pom-poms. Heather exits giggling, while Guy and Arnie get to know each other. Arnie is obviously a regular here, and by chance Guy has put his gear in Arnie's usual place; Arnie doesn't want to trouble Guy, but Guy, eager to fit in, moves it out of Arnie's way.

As Guy goes to get a towel at the front desk, Lennie—*"rough, energetic, very aggressive"* and also a regular—comes in.

LENNIE: Hiya, Arn. I got a new serve tonight. It's gonna kill ya.

ARNIE: Well, I think I've heard that before.

LENNIE: Watch me tonight, Arnold, and do exactly as I do, and you'll finally learn how to play this game. But you will not touch my serve. Want to double the regular stakes, go for fifty? *(No response.)* take it easy on yourself, Arnie, you're having a slow year. Things are tough on you lawyers since they raised the speed limit for ambulances.

ARNIE: Fifty sounds all right to me.

LENNIE: O.K., Arn! Take your choice of partners, Henry or George. I'll play with anybody warm and I'll still kill you.

ARNIE: I'll play with George.

LENNIE: Done. Don't try to weasel out of it later.

> Lennie pushes Guy's bag off the bench onto floor. Sits on bench, putting on his tennis shoes. Guy enters, finds his paraphernalia on floor and Lennie dressing in his place.

GUY: Was I in your way?

LENNIE *(aggressively):* What?

GUY *(very annoyed):* I'll just move my stuff out of your way, All right?

LENNIE: Good idea.

GUY: I didn't know you guys owned this bench. You ought to have little nameplates.

Guy angrily takes his bag and walks upstage to the cubicle.

LENNIE *(loud enough so Guy can hear):* What kind of schmuck? What's he think this is, schul, he bought a seat?

Lennie has had a bad day; he's stuck with 40 cases of canned plums which his customers, the good people of Newark, don't seem to like. Chuck the tennis pro drifts across the locker room with a meaningless "Hi, how'sitgoing, howyadoing, goodtoseeyou!" Lennie envies him because he's probably getting it on with Heather. Lennie speculates that Chuck is "hung like a whale," and at this point Guy manages to get into the conversation—and to stop it cold—by informing the others that "A grey whale has a member twelve feet long and three feet wide."

Even now, Lennie obviously resents Guy's intrusion, and Guy withdraws to his cubicle as George, *"about 40, pleasant, calmer than Lennie and Arnie, with a frequently distracted air,"* comes in and joins what is obviously his regular group. As usual, George is a bit late and reports on his condition: "I'll be going about three-quarters speed tonight," owing to a touch of bursitis. George's lateness upsets Lennie.

LENNIE: It's a few minutes every damn time. And that adds up. And you know what else? Out on the court, you go to pick up the balls, you get one, you don't get the other one that's three feet away. Somebody else has got to come and get it next time. How much time you waste there?

GEORGE: You have trouble with your schwartzes again today?

ARNIE: He bought too many plums.

GEORGE: Trouble with your plums? Too bad, Lennie.

LENNIE: Don't worry about me, worry about that SEC investigation.

ARNIE: The Securities Exchange Commission is investigating George?

GEORGE: No, Arnie.

LENNIE: George has got the Feds sniffing around his firm, haven't you, George?

GEORGE: It's nothing.

LENNIE: Taking advantage of insider information, is what I heard.

GEORGE: It's just routine. It doesn't mean anything.

As George dresses, he pulls on elaborate knee brace with iron rods.

LENNIE: We aren't keeping you from surgery, are we, George? It's like playing with fucking General Hospital.

Lennie produces a huge cigar, plants it in his mouth.

GUY *(to Arnie):* He's not going to smoke that in here, is he?

ARNIE: Better not smoke that, Lennie.

LENNIE: Why not?

GUY: This is a place of health. We come in here to get our lungs opened up from exercise. We don't want to have to breathe somebody else's smoke.

LENNIE: First with the bench, then the whale, now my cigar. What are you hocking me?

GUY: Since you own the locker room, I'll just leave. All right? O.K.? Do you mind if I go? *(Guy exits.)*

Lennie, having offended just about everybody, kicks an open locker door angrily. A phone call for George is announced on the p.a. system, and while George goes to answer it, Arnie tries to calm Lennie down. Lennie admits he feels hostile all the time, probably because so many of the people who come into his grocery store are trying to rip him off in some way. His boss's sons get the prime locations in the chain—like Greenwich—while Lennie, only a son-in-law, is stuck with Newark. His wife Joyce is unsympathetic too, Lennie declares, so angrily that he has to lie down to calm himself.

George comes back with Guy and with the information that their usual tennis doubles fourth can't make it this evening but has sent a substitute—Guy Wallace, whom George introduces to the others. Guy is to be Lennie's partner. George and Arnie go out to practise while Lennie explains to Guy that they have a standing $25 bet on the game which Lennie has doubled tonight to $50 because he has a new hot serve. But Guy makes it clear that he doesn't like to bet on tennis.

LENNIE: If you don't have any money on the side, what do you play for?

GUY: Because I love it, I love the game, I like the exercise. I hope to meet a few nice people . . . I just want a friendly game.

LENNIE: This is a friendly game. Those two guys are my best friends in the world—that doesn't mean I don't like to stick it to them . . . You all right? You look funny.

GUY: Fine.

LENNIE: Let's go. We're going to kill them! . . . Just let me take the overheads . . . What's the matter! You look pale. Hey, relax! Take it easy. It's only a game!
> *He puts a companionable arm around Guy's shoulder as they walk towards the exit.*

GUY: Well, I think tennis is more than just a game. It's life at the most basic. We have to be aggressive and yet we must cooperate with each other, we have to be savage while at the same time respecting a strict code of behavior. We have to do all we can to win, yet remain courteous and gracious . . . it's like medieval combat between knights of honor. It's a struggle to the death, but no one really gets killed . . . At the end of the hour we emerge, victorious or defeated, yet, somehow shriven.

LENNIE: Shriven?

GUY: Anyhow, that's how I see it.

LENNIE: Me too. *(At doorway.)* Arnie! The bet's off!
> *The lights dim out.*

Scene 2

Lennie and Guy come in from the courts, having roundly defeated the others. Arnie and George follow, George now limping more obviously and complaining, "My shoulder was acting up a little." The losers bring out the cash to pay their bets. Guy accepts his and then is left awkwardly holding it when Lennie refuses to take Arnie's money. Arnie insists, but Lennie crumples the bill and throws it on the floor. Guy, not knowing quite what to do, puts his $50 bill on the bench and then goes to his locker to change.

Guy, it seems, is a writer for *Tennis* magazine. The missing foursome member's wife recruited Guy through Guy's wife, whom she met at the Unitarian Church. Lennie wants to talk about religion (Guy is an atheist, he declares), but the others bring the subject back to tennis.

ARNIE: You're a very good player, Guy. It must be hard playing with hackers like us.

GUY: No, I thought you were all pretty good. I just came here hoping to meet a few people. It was fun.

LENNIE: Don't run yourself down, Arnie. We gave him a game, it was a contest. He's not that much better.

ARNIE: He never even took off his warm-up suit.

GEORGE: Did you see anything that might help us improve?

GUY: Well . . . not really.

LENNIE: See?

GEORGE: He's being polite.

LENNIE: Hey, don't ever be polite with me.
          Arnie starts for the shower.

ARNIE: It was great playing with you, Guy.

GUY: Thank you, I enjoyed it.
          Lennie starts toward shower.

LENNIE: Yeah, you played well, Guy.

GUY: Thank you . . . you might try to hit the backhand a little farther in front of your body.

LENNIE: Are you talking to me?

GUY: Just something I noticed.

LENNIE: My backhand's my best shot. *(Exits into shower.)*

Guy tells George how awkward he feels about taking any bet money, or for that matter intruding into this group of three such close friends. "We're just used to each other," George explains, "Don't confuse familiarity with closeness. I do some legal business with Arnie, and Lennie . . . Lennie's a neighbor. The kind you build fences for." In any case, Guy couldn't accept the bet winnings because he believes some of his partner Lennie's calls were "questionable." George admits that Lennie cheats but figures it doesn't really matter, it's only part of Lennie's style. Guy disagrees.

GUY: . . . . . If you cheat during a game where everybody is going on the honor system, what are you going to do in real life with all the ambiguities there? I may be wrong, but it seems to me that tennis is one of the few chances we ever have to really bite the bullet, act honorably even if it hurts, and be proud of ourselves. I may be wrong.

GEORGE: I don't think it's a philosophical judgment with Lennie. He just wants to win.

GUY: What do you do for a living, George?

GEORGE: I'm a stockbroker.

GUY: Let's say you know something about a particular stock, you learn that the company isn't really very sound, but you stand to make a lot of money if you convince your customers to buy it anyway. You wouldn't sell it, would you? Just to make the money?

GEORGE *(pause):* Where are you from, Guy?

GUY: Originally, Duluth.

GEORGE: I've never been to Iowa.

GUY: Minnesota.

GEORGE: It must be very different.

George changes the subject to writing and compliments Guy on a recent article he wrote about tennis shoes. George himself writes song lyrics—just the lyrics, without any music. George confesses that he is pretty good, "a combination between Johnny Mercer and Steve Sondheim." He happens to have a page of his lyrics in his wallet and reads them to Guy: "You tell me that you love me, but I don't know/You swear by stars above me, but I don't know/You fit me like a glove, but I don't know." Meanwhile, Lennie is playing a trick on Arnie (he does this every week), filling an empty tennis can with cold water and throwing it on Arnie in the shower.

George invites Guy to join them again when they need a fourth.

LENNIE: You head of admissions now, George?

GEORGE: You have an objection?

GUY: I don't want to intrude . . .

LENNIE: Maybe we're not good enough for him.

GUY: I'm just here for the social aspects . . . if you really want me, I'd love to.

GEORGE: Of course we want you, that's why I asked. But I want you on my side next time.

LENNIE: Has George shown you his new pin stripe outfit? The Federal government is designing it for him.

GEORGE: Ignore him, if possible.

GUY: I don't get the joke.

GEORGE: Pay no attention.

LENNIE: A guy named Guy. That's terrific. I don't even have to learn your name.

> *Arnie enters from the shower, dripping, but with a towel around him. He carries the tennis-ball can in his hand. He walks angrily, purposefully, toward Lennie.*

ARNIE: That's the last time, Lennie.

LENNIE: Oh, ho-ho.

> *Lennie backs up, mock terrified, hands in the air.*

ARNIE: You think it's funny, but now you're going to find out how funny it is to get a can full of cold water every week.

LENNIE: Wooo-wooo!

Arnie prepares to throw the water. Heather enters, carrying a clean cloth roll for the hand towel dispenser.

HEATHER: I won't look.

Lennie grabs Arnie's towel and yanks it off. Heather, naturally, looks at Arnie. Arnie dies of embarassment and, with a whoop of surprise, dashes to the showers.

HEATHER: Oh, Mr. Lewis!

Lights dim.

Scene 3

A spot comes up on George unburdening himself in monologue to Heather: his wife Danielle is an intelligent, capable woman who does extremely well at enterprises like getting a master's degree in Social Work, or importing wicker baskets —except that, through no fault of her own, she never quite manages to follow such projects through to the end. Their maid, Reba, is "wonderful with children," so Danielle doesn't have to spend all her time with them. Now she's starting an art gallery, "And it's only costing me fifteen thou extra the first year! . . . But, there are always ways to get the extra money . . . Legitimate ways."

Scene 4

Five weeks later, Guy and Lennie come in after a game, Lennie complaining about one of Guy's calls, appealing to Arnie when he joins them. "It could have been either way," Arnie judges, and Guy points out to Lennie that in such cases sportsmanship requires a call in favor of the opponent. Lennie's reaction is, as expected, "Would you stop with the Marquis of Queensbury?"

George comes in and further irritates Lennie by singing to himself calmly— Lennie is upset and wants everyone else to be upset too. When the others exit to the shower, Lennie lets himself go in a series of sobs. The pro, Chuck, passes through the locker room. Not knowing what to make of this sobbing customer, he goes to fetch the others, who come back, size up the situation and try to comfort Lennie. What is really wrong with him, it seems, is a fit of shame because he struck his wife and broke her nose—mixed with embarrassment because everyone is going to notice her injury.

Lennie regains control as Chuck brings him a drink of water and exits. "I feel like a complete bastard," Lennie admits, giving Guy the opening to comment, "I would think so." Lennie doesn't know why he did it, it just happened.

LENNIE: . . . . . I got home from work, nothing unusual, the regular three-hour drive. I walk into the bedroom, she's sitting on the bed, stark naked, cutting her toenails. She's got her foot pulled up like this . . . *(He pulls his foot up onto his knee.)* . . . legs apart, and there it is, staring me in the face. I mean, what if a stranger walks in? I say, "Holy shit, Joyce, cross your legs!"

ARNIE: For heaven's sake!

LENNIE: Don't get me wrong, I like it, but I don't want to have to look at it. Especially if it catches me unawares.

ARNIE *(disgusted sound):* Ooouuu.

LENNIE: I say, "Joyce, where's the mystery?" She says, "You give me romance, I'll give you mystery."

ARNIE: I've told Phyliis, "Don't ever let me see you shaving your armpits. I don't care to know about that."

GEORGE: It's the mustache cream that gets me.

GUY: Your wife has a mustache?

ARNIE: Oouu.

GEORGE: No! It's a cream. She puts in on her lip. You've never seen that?

GUY: For what?

GEORGE: For her mustache.

ARNIE: Oouu.

GEORGE: It's not unusual. All women use it.

ARNIE: Not mine.

LENNIE: Not mine.

GUY: Not mine.

GEORGE: She's a very attractive woman!

LENNIE: Hairy, but nice.

GEORGE: I don't hit her because she flashes it at me, Lennie!

Lennie continues telling his story: he found that his wife had decided not to cook dinner that night, but that isn't what feezed him. He simply went out to get some pizza, which he brought home. Lennie explains, "I'm eating the pizza, and all of a sudden I realize: 'I'm forty-one years old. I *hate* being forty-one years old. What's the best I got to look forward to, the absolute best? Being forty-two' . . . She says, 'Lennie, what's the matter, what are you staring?' I say, 'Joyce, I'm forty-one years old.' She says, 'I know, and I'm thirty-eight.' *Then* I hit her."

Scene 5

Guy is unburdening himself to Heather on the subject of marriage. He has never hit his wife Sooki, "It takes so little to ruin a relationship"—a careless remark, "Then suddenly you can't stand each other . . . . . Marriage is the one friendship you can count on. It's you and her against the world. She's got to take your side. But sometimes, I wish I were ethnic. It might be nice to carry on that way."

Scene 6

It is winter, it's snowing, the club is officially closed but not locked, so that Guy and George have made their way in, hoping for a game. George would overcome any obstacle to get out once in a while, and so would Guy, though they insist their wives are good company. George makes the point that maybe men and women weren't really meant to get married: "When you're a little kid, the last person in the world you want to spend time with is a girl, right? . . . . . But *anything* soft will suffice when you're a teenager. Then you're a young adult, you've spent your whole life with the boys, and suddenly you pick one girl and go off and live *alone* with her. What have you got in common? Years of avoidance."

Their friend Henry has been transferred out of the state, so there is a permanent vacancy in the foursome which Guy would like very much to fill if the others will accept him. Guy has some doubts about Lennie.

Lennie comes in covered with snow, and George relishes telling him "You're late." In retaliation, Lennie stuffs snow in George's tennis pants.

LENNIE: Just want to remind you got something down there, George. *(To Guy.)* His wife keeps his balls in a box. *(Sotto voce.)* The key's under her dress. He never thinks to look there.

GEORGE: I like Joyce's new nose, Lennie. It fits a little better than the other one.

LENNIE: Sing a song, George, while I dress.

GEORGE: She looks good with an Irish nose.

LENNIE: How's the SEC investigation going, George?

GEORGE: Never mind, Len.

LENNIE: Did you get the money transferred to the bank in Costa Rica yet?

GEORGE: Cut it out.

LENNIE: Be sure to send a postcard with your new alias once you get settled.

GEORGE: Goddamn it, Lennie, that's enough! It's not funny! I thought at least here I wouldn't have to talk about it. I figured at least here nobody would nag me about it. *(In a frantic woman's voice.)* "What are you going to do, George? What are you going to do! What will become of us! Everyone at aerobics is talking!" . . . I had *hoped* that with my friends all I had to do was play some tennis.

GUY: George, I hadn't heard. If there's anything I can do.

LENNIE: Can you put in the fix in Washington?

GEORGE: Thanks, Guy. There's nothing you can do, but I appreciate it. This will all blow over. I'd really rather not talk about it. *(Pause.)* You made me wrench my back, Lennie. I was only going about eighty per cent as it was.

George informs Lennie he's asked Guy to join the foursome on a permanent basis. Lennie is still not sure he wants him. Guy leads them onto the subject of primitive ceremonies regarding the penis, but their conversation is interrupted by the entrance of Heather from the sauna with rumpled hair and unbuttoned clothing, pretending that she has been cleaning the sauna and telling the men they must leave, the club is closed today. She makes a hurried exit, but Guy thinks he can see Chuck hiding in the sauna waiting till the coast is clear. At Lennie's suggestion, Guy turns on the sauna to smoke Chuck out.

George invites Guy and his wife to have dinner next week at a Chinese restaurant on the Post Road.

GUY: I'd like that, I really would.

LENNIE: George likes to eat Chinese because he doesn't have to ask his wife to cut his meat for him.

GEORGE: I'd invite you to join us, Lennie, but Danielle is still not speaking to you . . .

*The door to the sauna opens slowly until fully open. The men watch
with expectant amusement.*

LENNIE: Cooked him out.

GUY: Hi, Chuck, how'sitgoing,howyoudoin' . . . Holy shit!

*Out of the sauna, stripped to his shorts by the heat, looking very sheep-
ish, steps Arnie.*

LENNIE, GEORGE, GUY: Arnie!

Curtain.

ACT II

Scene 1

A few months later, Guy and George are getting dressed, while congratulating
themselves on their performance today against Lennie and Arnie. Guy enjoys
manipulating Lennie on the court: "I think Lennie has to be treated like a spoiled
child—firmly but with guidance and affection."

Arnie has a special soap, and of course Lennie comes out of the shower with
it, having swiped it, with Arnie in pursuit. Arnie and Guy try to get it back, to
no avail until Lennie has tired of scrubbing himself with it all over, including his
crotch, and Arnie no longer wants it back. Arnie's unaccustomed fit of anger is
caused partly by Lennie's antics and partly by his emotional upset at his wife
Phyllis's having left him, on the advice of the members of her support group.
Arnie wants her back.

GUY: How did your wife find out about Heather?

ARNIE: She doesn't know about Heather. She found out about some of the
others.

GUY: Others?

ARNIE: I couldn't help it, I'm a very sexy person.

LENNIE: God knows.

ARNIE: You guys have had affairs, haven't you?

Pause. The others look at each other.

LENNIE: You don't have to commute, Arnie.

GUY: While I understand the urge, I don't approve of affairs on principle.

LENNIE *(mocking):* "On principle."

GUY: I do have principles.

LENNIE: Meaning?

GUY: Just a statement.

GEORGE: Who did you have these affairs with, Arnie?

ARNIE: Oh, just about everybody. You know how it is once you get started with
something.

LENNIE: Everybody?

ARNIE: I never did it *against* Phyllis, never to hurt her. I just got married too
young. I never had a chance to sow my wild oats. I was not very attractive to
girls in high school.

John Cullum as Guy, Ron Leibman as Lennie, Austin Pendleton as Arnie and Tony Roberts as George in *Doubles* by David Wiltse

Arnie loves Phyllis, and he made a point of never having an affair with a friend of hers. Lennie is curious about Arnie's technique with married women, and Arnie advises him, "Just be nice to them. Most men don't pay attention to them; they appreciate it when someone does." And Guy advises Arnie not to permit his emotional reaction to his wife's leaving to dominate him: "Don't get your dobber down."

Arnie invites first George and then Guy to have a cup of coffee with him. Neither of them can, but Lennie volunteers his company, even though he has a date with his father-in-law to discuss the possibility of his taking over one of the good stores. When George and Arnie go into the sauna, Guy takes the opportunity to warn Lennie that he should remember Arnie is in a vulnerable, depressed state.

GUY: And you're still treating him in your usual, overbearing manner—this is fine, this is your manner and it's—your manner, but I think he needs sympathy and advice, rather than pubic hair on his soap.

LENNIE: You're telling me how to treat my friends?

GUY: I noticed he asked *me* to have coffee. I didn't have to ask *him*. Don't get mad, it was just an observation.

LENNIE: I'm not mad, do I look mad? Do I sound mad?
    He holds his empty hands in the air.

GUY: Do you know why primitive people hold up an empty hand like that? The Australian aborigine, for instance . . .

LENNIE: How come you never talk about people someone might meet?

GUY: It was just a suggestion, you can take it for what it's worth. I'm not trying to tell you how to behave, believe me.

LENNIE: Good.

GUY *(beat):* But you ought to lay off George. He's under a lot of stress with that SEC business.

LENNIE: Let me tell you something. George and I are like brothers. He loves it when I give him a hard time. Don't tell me how to treat my friends. If there's one thing I know, it's how to treat my friends.

GUY: You treat them like shit.

LENNIE: That's the way I do it! That's how we relate.

GUY: Well, I think you ought to consider how much hostility you're expressing . . .

LENNIE: Here it comes. Whenever they start on me, we always get into Freud.

GUY: I don't believe in Freud.

LENNIE: What do you mean, you don't believe in him? We got pictures of the man.

GUY: I was just trying to tell you as a friend . . . . .

Lennie protests that Guy is not so much a friend as a mere tennis partner who disapproves of almost everything and preaches irritating self-improvement sermons about aborigines and such. Lennie comes here because it's the one place he can be accepted and get the world off his back, and now Guy is ruining even this for him. Lennie states the case simply: he doesn't like Guy. Well, Guy admits, he doesn't like Lennie. As their hostility reaches the boiling point, Chuck comes in, but they pay him no attention. In *"a brief, silly fight of two middle-aged men,"* they fail to land punches but grapple with each other, half wrestling and half kneeing, until their knees hit together and, in pain, they hop apart. "See you next week," Chuck says, exiting.

Lennie now insists that Guy is to remove himself from the doubles foursome, as Lennie is a charter member and doesn't want Guy around any more. Guy decides that probably Lennie is behaving this way because he's "different."

LENNIE: No, pal, you're the one who's different.

GUY: I mean you're Jewish.

LENNIE: Now he tells me!

GUY: And I'm not.

LENNIE: No!

GUY: Do you know what prejudice is, Lennie? It's just fear. Primitive tribesmen felt this way because they were afraid the neighboring tribe might eat them.

LENNIE: You're doing it again!

GUY: Back in Duluth there was a Jewish man who wanted to join our tennis club. He had his faults, but so did the rest of these guys. Only one man had the courage to defend that Jewish person. One man stood alone, like a giant oak in the desert, his outstretched branches providing shade against the cruel sun of intolerance. Do you have that courage now, Lennie? Will you stand like a giant oak and rise above the nasty core in your heart? Not because you want to, but because it's right.

LENNIE: I'm taking notes on you, pal. There are people who would be very interested in this.

GUY: Are you too small?

LENNIE: Don't underestimate yourself. I dislike you for your own sake. You transcend all racial and political barriers.

GUY: Well, then, Lennie, I give up. This group is not one I care to belong to. You'll have to get along without me and George from now on.

LENNIE: George? What's George got to do with it?

GUY: This isn't the only game in town, you know. George asked me to play in a Thursday game. They're stronger players, and they don't throw their racquets.

LENNIE: I know George for years. He wouldn't quit on me.

GUY: Keep telling yourself that. He'll get a better game, and he won't have to put up with you.

LENNIE *(pause):* You're not really going to do that, are you?

GUY: George would rather play with me than you.

LENNIE: Hey, we got a little excited there, I didn't mean it personally.

GUY: They're good players. George would enjoy it.

LENNIE: Guy, don't break up my group. We can work something out.

GUY: I don't come where I'm not wanted. George and I will be able to talk for a change without you running around like a teenager.

LENNIE: Guy, please don't screw around with this.

GUY: What's the matter, Lennie, these the only friends you have?

LENNIE *(unable to face him and beg, turns upstage. Emotionally):* Guy, please don't break up this group! I need it! It may be only an hour and a half a week, but I need it!

GUY *(sadly):* Did it ever occur to you that I might need it too? Damn it, Lennie, do we all have to be just alike? I didn't ask you to be a good tennis player! I didn't even ask you to like me. I just asked to be a friend. That's all! Is that so much to ask?

> *Guy exits. Lennie, alone. He sits for a moment, very depressed. The lights dim out.*

Scene 2

A spot comes up on Lennie unburdening himself to Heather on the subject of a fight he had with his wife Joyce on their wedding anniversary. Lennie swore he wouldn't give Joyce another surprise party—but he broke his promise, and when they got to the party Joyce began to weep, and the other guests were looking at Lennie reprovingly. Lennie figured that everybody realized that Joyce was fed up with him and planning to divorce him—and then in spite of everything Joyce smiled at him. "Oh, when my Joycie smiles at me. It's like a voice from heaven saying, 'I forgive you, Lennie.' I knew I had her then, for another year anyway."

Scene 3

Three weeks later, Guy limps in from the courts supported by George—Guy has just stepped on a tennis ball and sprained his ankle. Guy had joined the foursome again—just this once—as a special favor to George at the last minute. Heather comes in with cold cans of soda for Guy, in lieu of ice for his ankle—the club is out of ice. As Heather leaves, George assures Guy that he'll be able to go 50 per cent after he shows Guy how to tape his ankle.

George is in a euphoric state because he is off the hook on the SEC matter—he had feared he might be facing a jail term. Guy admires the way George seemed cool and collected under the pressure of his troubles. George admits he has learned to conceal his feelings as a member of a family whose other members constantly overreact to everything: "They like to accent the negative so no one should mistake us for happy people . . . . . To my mother, God is punishment. That's how she knows He loves us, when He kicks us."

Out of Guy's sight, George does a little dance of wild jubilation, then suddenly clutches his chest. His breath comes in gasps and his moans get louder, until finally Guy notices something is wrong and becomes alarmed.

GUY: What does it feel like?
GEORGE: Pushing. Squeezing. Can't catch my breath.
GUY: Is it your heart?
GEORGE: Don't say that.
GUY: It's your heart!
GEORGE: He saw me. He saw me dancing.
GUY: Should I call an ambulance?

GEORGE: No, no. I think it's gas.

GUY: Christ, you're sweating so much. George, what are the symptoms of a heart attack?

GEORGE: Pain in the chest. Shortness of breath. Profuse sweating . . . I think it's gas.

GUY: I'm going to call an ambulance.

GEORGE: Call an ambulance.

GUY: Lie down, do you want to lie down?

GEORGE: I don't think so.

GUY: I'll be right back. Don't *do* anything.

GEORGE: What could I do?
          Guy exits.
(To God.) I only cheated a little. It was practically not cheating at all. It was only a few hundred thousand dollars. *(A twinge from his heart.)* All right. *Eight* hundred thousand. Does that deserve this? *(More pain. Sings.)* "You tell me that you love me, but I don't know."

Lennie and Arnie run in, Arnie, to George's disgust, is ready to give him mouth-to-mouth resucitation. Guy joins them—the ambulance is on the way. Knowing it's selfish and hating himself for it, Lennie nevertheless can't bear to take part in this scene and edges away from it.

GEORGE: Arnie!
          Arnie runs to George. Lennie stays in the other cubicle.
Arnie! Did I sign my will?

ARNIE: Everything is just as you want it.

GEORGE: Len . . .
          Lennie is in the other cubicle. He does not come.

GUY: Lennie *(No answer.)* Lennie!

ARNIE: Leave him, Guy.

GEORGE: It's all right.

GUY: No it's not. *(Guy goes angrily to the other cubicle.)* Come on, he wants you.

LENNIE: I can't.

GUY: He's your friend, he wants you.

LENNIE: I *can't!*

GUY: Stop indulging yourself.

LENNIE: You don't tell me how to behave.

GUY: Get in there.

LENNIE: What can I do, George?

GEORGE: Len, I'm sorry.

LENNIE: For what?

GEORGE: I don't remember.

LENNIE: I forgive you.

GEORGE: You don't have to stick around for the rest of this. I understand how you feel. I hate it, too.

LENNIE: I'll stay.

ARNIE: You're a heluva man, George.

GEORGE: My foot's cold. *(To Guy.)* I never showed you how to tape your ankle.

GUY: You can show me tomorrow.

GEORGE: Arnie, you know my mother.

ARNIE: She's a fine woman, George. *(To Guy.)* A fine, fine woman. This will break her heart.

GEORGE: If I die . . .

ARNIE: You're not going to die!

GUY: You're not dying, George.

GEORGE: If I die—don't tell her. I feel about twenty per cent.

> *Lights dim out.*

Scene 4

An hour later, Guy is packing George's clothes from the locker. Lennie wanders in, subdued, admitting that George's illness has shaken him (it could have been *him*). And Lennie doesn't have so many friends that he can afford to lose as close a one as George.

GUY: . . . . . Friendships are hard.

LENNIE: They're not easy.

GUY: That's what I meant. You know, the Masai warriors in Africa have a special initiation ceremony for an entire generation. They all get together and smear each other with mud and cow's urine, then the priest spits something in their face—it's a very moving ceremony, apparently.

LENNIE: Sounds good.

GUY: Then afterwards these warriors are all sworn brothers for life.

LENNIE: It might be worth it.

GUY: Well, it breaks down the barriers, see. That's where the problem is, you've got to break down the barriers, at least for a minute, so you realize you've got something in common. After that it's just work.

LENNIE: The problem is that people judge you by your personality. For instance, people always think I'm hostile. Am I hostile? I'm *playing* with them. I'm being *jocular.* People misunderstand that. Even my wife has never understood this. She says, "Underneath it all, Lennie, you're a very angry man." Well, yes, but underneath *that . . .*

GUY: What's underneath that?

LENNIE: I'm shy.

Underneath it all, Lennie tries to be friendly—he even tried with Guy, in the beginning, but not so that Guy noticed it—and he regrets that people don't seem to like him. Even in high school, his best friend never invited him over to dinner. Guy has the same problem, he tells Lennie—no one likes him because he's too quiet, he makes them nervous. Guy shows Lennie that he could smile a lot and make people like him, if he wanted to, but it would be hypocritical. They see that with their shyness and their habit of offering suggestions and/or criticism to other people, they have a lot in common.

Chuck drifts in and out trying to fill a vacant court, but they don't feel like tennis—they're waiting for news from Arnie about George. On second thought, Lennie feels maybe George would want them to play, a view which Guy labels "wholly inappropriate" with their friend in the hospital. Lennie resents Guy's platitudes about "courage and self-denial," but Guy holds stubbornly to his opinion. "I'm goddamned if I'll put up with a self-satisfied prick like you!" Lennie exclaims, storming out as the scene ends.

Scene 5

Now it's Arnie's turn to take the spotlight and unburden himself to Heather. The impermanence of existence—"One minute you're young and healthy and full of life, and the next you get dizzy tying your shoes"—has made him think of his mother, who doted on him and made him great sandwiches. Arnie's wife Phyllis never quite liked her and influenced Arnie, finally, to put his mother in a nursing home. Now that Phyllis has left him, maybe Arnie will bring his mother back.

Scene 6

Six weeks later, Arnie is decorating the locker room with strands of colored crepe in honor of George's return to the foursome (Arnie's new enthusiasm, Rachel, thinks Arnie is "naturally artistic"). When Guy comes in from the court in tennis clothes, Lennie comments "What's he doing here?" Arnie invited Guy for the celebration but hadn't expected him to take the day off and get here in time for a game of tennis beforehand.

Heather announces George's arrival, and George enters, greeting all hands warmly. After Heather exits, Arnie informs them all, first, that Heather is going back to school to get a degree in clinical psychology, and second, that he's brought champagne to celebrate George's recovery. Lennie announces that he has something to celebrate too: he finally confronted his father-in-law and is being promoted to a purchasing job in the front office. He's brought George a present of some T-bone steaks from Kansas.

George surprises Lennie by wanting to play tennis again, right now, but they don't have a fourth unless they include Guy, who is sitting glumly off by himself. George and Arnie try to persuade Guy to join them, but Guy shakes his head.

The three go off to the court but George, concerned about Guy, returns immediately and wants to know what's the matter. Then Arnie and Lennie come back too, and Guy finally comes out with it.

GUY: I got fired.
GEORGE: Oh Jesus, Guy.
GUY: It's not so bad.
GEORGE: Why not?
GUY: Well . . . *(He can't think of a thing.)*
ARNIE: That's terrible, Guy.
GUY: I don't mind.
LENNIE: Why did he fire you?

GUY: The publisher asked me what I thought of the course the magazine was taking. I made a few suggestions. Just some general advice, a few observations.

LENNIE: It all comes clear.

GUY: They were for his own good.

ARNIE: Oh, you poor guy. Fired in the prime of life.

LENNIE: Hey, it could be worse. You could have had a heart attack and dropped dead, like George.

GEORGE: I'm not dead.

ARNIE: That's true, Guy. You have to keep this in perspective. It's not just George, we could all be dead.

GEORGE: I'm not dead.

ARNIE: Poor George!

GEORGE: Maybe I'm dead!

Guy hasn't been home yet, hasn't told his wife Sooki, who'll be frightened at the news of her husband being out of a job. Guy was already fired from the only other tennis magazine six years before, and he has no savings. Guy is trying to keep his cool, Lennie tries to slough the whole problem off, while George reassures Guy that at least he's got friends. Arnie urges Guy to get his dobber up.

Heather comes in to find out if they want their court, otherwise she can give it to someone else. Lennie assures her they are going to play, and she exits, while George accuses Lennie of heartlessness for wanting to play tennis at a time like this when their friend Guy is in so much trouble. Guy protests that it was Lennie who saved him today, in a way: "There was a moment, after the publisher fired me, when he was willing to take me back if I apologized. I almost did it, but then I thought of Lennie and all the crap he takes from his wife and his wife's family and his customers, just to keep his job. And I figured, no, I didn't do anything wrong, I spoke the truth, I'd rather be right than employed."

The three go out to the court leaving Guy alone, head in hands, but Lennie soon returns to the locker room to remind Guy of what a real jam he's in: no job, too old to find another, wife and child to support: "A middle-aged man cannot possibly find himself in a worse situation than the one you are in now." Guy admits he is "scared shitless" and can barely control himself. And on top of everything else, everybody hates him. Lennie agrees, a lot of people hate Guy, but Lennie doesn't, and he has an idea. George and Arnie come back into the locker room as Lennie makes his suggestion.

LENNIE: I remembered that tall oak thing.

GUY: What are you talking about?

LENNIE: It doesn't matter. The thing is, while you're looking for another job —just a thought—until you get something permanent . . . you might want to work for me.

GUY: Are you serious?

LENNIE: Just an idea. It's up to you.

GUY: Doing what? Stacking shelves?

LENNIE: You're a writer, aren't you? We need a public relations man.

GUY: I don't know anything about public relations.

LENNIE: What's to know? All you need is a pleasant way with people.

GUY: I can do that.

LENNIE: I know. So that's it. It's up to you.

GUY: That's so decent of you.

LENNIE: It's no big deal.

GUY: You don't even like me.

LENNIE: So? What are friends for?

ARNIE: That's a wonderful thing to do, Lennie.

LENNIE: Yeah, I figured what the fuck.

GEORGE: Nice sentiment.

ARNIE: A toast, a toast.

LENNIE: Yeah, let's open this stuff. What are we, old farts?

Lennie opens the champagne.

ARNIE: I just want to say, this is what life is all about. Good friends, champagne, raw meat. To George.

GEORGE: No, no. To Guy.

GUY: No, no. To Lennie.

LENNIE: To *us!* To friendship.

GEORGE: No matter how strange.

ALL: To friendship.

They drink.

LENNIE: The good thing about champagne is we don't have to *drink* this shit.

He shakes up the bottle, proceeds to spray George and Arnie. Guy waits, longing to be included. Lennie pauses, then sprays him with particular relish. Curtain.

THE MARRIAGE OF BETTE AND BOO

A Play in Two Acts and 33 Scenes

BY CHRISTOPHER DURANG

Cast and credits appear on pages 369 & 372

CHRISTOPHER DURANG was born in 1949 in Montclair, N.J., the son of an architect. He was educated at the Delbarton School, a Roman Catholic institution, in Morristown, N.J. He received his B.A. from Harvard in 1971 and his M.F.A. from Yale School of Drama in 1974, having studied playwriting with William Alfred, author of Hogan's Goat, *at the former university and with Richard Gilman, Jules Feiffer and Howard Stein at the latter and having acted in several plays by himself and others, including (as a member of the chorus) the world premiere of the Burt Shevelove-Stephen Sondheim version of Aristophanes's* The Frogs.

Durang's long list of play authorship credits of record begins with The Idiots Karamazov *(which he wrote with Albert Innaurato and in which he played a leading role) and* Death Comes to Us All, Mary Agnes, *both produced by Yale Repertory Theater in the season of 1974–75. His first New York production occurred the following season, as his* Titanic *appeared off off Broadway and then moved up to off Broadway May 10, 1976 for 8 performances. There followed* A History of the American Film *on Broadway March 30, 1978 for 21 performances, for which he received a Tony nomination for best book;* The Nature and Purpose of the Universe *OOB Feb. 21, 1979 for 26 performances;* Das Lusitania Songspiel, *co-authored with Sigourney Weaver, at Chelsea Theater Center Jan. 10, 1980 for 24 performances;* Sister Mary Ignatius Explains It All for You *in an Obie-winning OOB production at Ensemble Studio Theater in the 1979–80 season and then on*

"The Marriage of Bette and Boo": by Christopher Durang. Copyright © 1985 by Christopher Durang. Reprinted by permission of Helen Merrill, Ltd. See CAUTION notice on copyright page. All inquiries should be addressed to: Helen Merrill, Helen Merrill, Ltd., 361 West 17th Street, New York, NY 10011.

a double bill with The Actor's Nightmare *at Playwrights Horizons Oct. 21, 1981 for 947 performances;* Beyond Therapy *at the Phoenix Theater Jan. 1, 1981 for 30 performances and in a revised version on Broadway May 26, 1982 for 11 performances;* Baby With the Bathwater *at Playwrights Horizons Nov. 8, 1983 for 84 performances; and* The Marriage of Bette and Boo, *his first Best Play, which opened May 16 at New York Shakespeare Festival in its present form after having appeared in shorter versions at Yale School of Drama and Williamstown, Mass., and which won Obies for the playwright, the acting ensemble (in which Durang played a major part as the narrator) and Jerry Zaks's direction.*

Some of the regional theaters which have produced Durang's plays over the years are Arena Stage, American Repertory, Mark Taper, American Conservatory and Seattle Repertory, as well as Yale. As an actor, he has appeared in his own plays, Wallace Shawn's The Hotel Play *and others in New York, and he has written three screen plays. He is a member of Ensemble Studio Theater, of the Playwrights Horizons artistic board and of the Dramatists Guild council and has been a recipient of Guggenheim, Rockefeller and CBS fellowships. He lives in New York City.*

ACT I

Scene 1: The wedding

SYNOPSIS: Each of the multiple settings is suggested by the use of symbolic objects (a stained-glass window for a church, a couple of chairs and a table for a living room, etc.), with a bare stage for a hospital corridor or the musings of the character Matt who serves both as narrator and participant. Sliding screens effect the many changes of time and place.

Matt is standing to one side, as all the other characters—the Brennan and Hudlocke families, dressed in wedding attire—gather together to sing a round.

ALL *(sing):*
God bless Bette and Boo and Skippy,
Emily and Boo,
Margaret Matt and Betsy Booey,
Mommy, Tommy too.

Betty Betsy Booey Boozey,
Soot, Karl, Matt and Paul,
Margaret Booey, Joanie Phooey,
God bless us one and all.
        The characters now call out to one another.
BETTE: Booey? Booey? Skippy?
BOO: Pop?
MARGARET: Emily, dear?
BETTE: Booey?
BOO: Bette?

KARL: Is that Bore?

SOOT: Karl? Are you there?

JOAN: Nikkos!

BETTE: Skippy! Skippy!

EMILY: Are you all right, Mom?

BETTE: Booey, I'm calling you!

MARGARET: Paul? Where are you?

JOAN: Nikkos!

BOO: Bette? Betsy?

BETTE: Boo? Boo?

> *Flash of light on the characters, as if their picture is being taken. Lights*
> *off the Brennans and Hudlockes. Light on Matt, late 20s or so.*

MATT: If one looks hard enough, one can usually see the order that lies beneath the surface. Just as dreams must be put in order and perspective in order to understand them, so must the endless details of waking life be ordered and then carefully considered. Once these details have been considered, generalizations about them must be made. These generalizations should be written down legibly, and studied. The Marriage of Bette and Boo.

In the wedding photos which follow, the groom, Boo, is grouped with his parents, Karl and Soot, while the bride, Bette, stands with her mother and father, Margaret and Paul, and her two sisters, Emily and Joan. The latter is pregnant and looks "grouchy" (her husband Nikkos is in the bathroom, feeling unwell). Emily plays the cello (she has brought hers with her) and is suffering from asthma. Bette looks lovely (her mother insists) and can hardly wait to have her first baby. Boo is informed by his father Karl (who calles him "Bore") that at 32 he's "mighty old to be getting married."

Father Donnally comes in to pronounce Bette and Boo man and wife. Paul hurls rice at them. In honor of the occasion, Joan prepares to sing a Schubert lied to Emily's cello and their father Paul's flute accompaniment, but at the last moment Emily can't remember the music, and they have to give it up.

Scene 2: The honeymoon

Matt introduces the scene and Bette enters carrying a pillow and confiding to the audience: "First I was a tomboy. I used to climb trees and beat up my brother Tom. Then I used to try to break my sister Joanie's voice box because she liked to sing. She always scratched me, though, so instead I tried to play Emily's cello. Except I don't have a lot of musical talent, but I'm very popular. And I know more about the cello than people who don't know anything. I don't like the cello, it's too much work and besides, keeping my legs open that way made me feel funny. I asked Emily if it made her feel funny and she didn't know what I meant and then when I told her she cried for two whole hours and then went to confession twice, just in case the priest didn't understand her the first time. Dopey Emily. She means well. *(Calls offstage.)* Booey! I'm pregnant! *(Puts pillow around her waist; to audience.)* Actually, I couldn't be, because I'm a virgin. A married man tried to have an affair with me, but he was married and so it would have

Christopher Durang *(left)*, author of *The Marriage of Bette and Boo,* as Matt, with *(back row)* Mercedes Ruehl as Joan, Joan Allen as Bette, Richard B. Shull as Father Donnally, Graham Beckel as Boo, Patricia Falkenhain as Margaret Brennan, Bill Moor as Karl Hudlocke and *(front row)* Bill McCutcheon as Paul Brennan, Kathryn Grody as Emily and Olympia Dukakis as Soot Hudlocke

been pointless. I didn't know he was married until two months ago. Then I met Booey, sort of on the rebound. He seems fine though."

In regard to her escapades, Bette believes, "As long as your conscience is all right, then so is your soul." She calls for Boo and runs off.

Scene 3: Margaret Gives Emily Advice

Emily wants to apologize in a letter for forgetting the music at the wedding but wonders whether she ought to address the apology to Bette or Boo. Margaret tells her, "Emily, dear, don't go on about it."

Scene 4: The honeymoon, continued

Wrapped in sheets with Boo, Bette declares the experience "better than a cello." Boo is phoning his father about an insurance deal. Bette repeats her wish to have a dozen children, which reminds her how she cried and cried after seeing the movie *Skippy,* and that reminds her of her best friend Bonnie Wilson who ranked at the bottom of the math class with Bette. She tries to tell all this again on the phone to Boo's father, but he hangs up on her. Bette asks for her pocketbook (which is in plain sight) and Boo hands it to her.

Scene 5: Emily practises the cello

Emily still can't remember the music for the lied, though she knows it starts on A. Joanie enters with scissors, commenting, "It may start on A, Emily, but it ends now."

Scene 6: Bette and Boo visit their in-laws

MATT *(to the audience):* At the suggestion of *Redbook,* Bette refashions her wedding gown into a cocktail dress. Then she and Boo visit their in-laws. Bette is pregnant for the first time.

SOOT: How nice that you're going to have a baby.

KARL: Have another drink, Bore.

BETTE *(to Soot):* I think Booey drinks too much. Does Mr. Hudlocke drink too much?

SOOT: I never think about it.

KARL: Soot, get me and Bore another drink.

    Boo and Karl are looking over papers, presumably insurance.

BETTE: Don't have another one, Boo.

SOOT *(smiles, whispers):* I think Karl drinks too much, but when he's sober he's really very nice.

BETTE: I don't think Boo should drink if I'm going to have a baby.

SOOT: If it's a boy, you can name him Boo, and if it's a girl you can call her Soot after me.

BETTE: How did you get the name "Soot?"

SOOT: Oh you know. The old saying, "She fell down the chimney and got covered with soot."

BETTE: What saying?

SOOT: Something about that. Karl might remember. Karl, how did I get the name "Soot?"

KARL: Get the drinks, Soot.

SOOT: All right.

KARL *(to Bette):* Soot is the dumbest white woman alive.

SOOT: Oh, Karl. *(Laughs, exits.)*

Bette annoys Boo by nagging him about his drinking. Karl takes his son's part, warning Bette that if she goes on like this her baby will be "all mouth." Then he tries to lighten the atmosphere with a joke, but Bette leaves, immediately followed by Boo. Soot comes in with the drinks, finds them gone, but still wants to know how she got her name. Karl repeats his comment about Soot being dumb, and again Soot laughs.

Scene 7: Margaret gives Bette advice

With her father Paul and sister Emily present, Bette complains to her mother about Karl's rude manner and Boo's drinking. Margaret responds with a platitude, Bette turns to her father, Paul, who is the victim of a stroke, always taking part in the conversation but seldom intelligible either to the audience or the other characters. Paul utters "On # # # #%t ump oo% # % onoosns # $s. Eggh ing ahm # $" (he is probably trying to say, "Don't jump to conclusions, give things time").

Emily is writing a letter of apology, this one to Father Donnally. She has already written one to Joan, who enters with it in her hand and tries to get it across to Emily: "I *forgive* you. I *forgive* you. I *forgive* you."

Bette asks Joan whether she thinks the arrival of the baby will make Boo stop drinking.

JOAN: I have no idea.

BETTE: Well, but hasn't your having little Mary Frances made things better between you and Nikkos? He isn't still disappearing for days, is he?

JOAN: Are you trying to make me feel bad about my marriage?

EMILY: I'm sorry, Joanie.

JOAN: What?

EMILY: If I made you feel bad about your marriage.

JOAN: Oh shut up. *(Exits.)*

BETTE *(to Margaret):* She's so nasty. Did you punish her enough when she was little?

MARGARET: She's just tired because little Mary Frances cries all the time. She really is a dreadful child.

BETTE: I love babies. Poppa, don't you think my baby will bring Boo and me closer together?

Paul's answer in gibberish might be construed as "That's not a very good reason to have a baby, Bette" as the scene ends.

Scene 8: Twenty years later, Boo has dinner with his son

Out of time sequence, Boo has dinner with Matt, the son he and Bette are about to have, 20 years after the preceding scene. Asked about life at the college he's attending—Dartmouth—Matt replies he's learned that "Tess of the d'Urbervilles was a masochist." Confiding in his son, Boo declares, "A man needs a woman, son. I miss your mother. I'd go back with her in a minute if she wanted. She's not in love with her family any more, and I think she knows that drinking wasn't that much of a problem. I think your old man's going to get teary for a second."

Scene 9: The first child of Bette and Boo

Back in the original time sequence, the Brennan and Hudlocke families are at the hospital waiting with Boo for the baby to arrive. Emily seems to be having sympathetic pains. Karl wants Soot to fetch him and "Bore" a drink, but Soot can't think where she could find one here.

A doctor, played by the same performer who appears as Father Donnally, comes in with a small bundle in his arms and drops it on the floor—the baby, he says, is dead. Paul picks up the bundle and tries to make the others understand that the baby is *not* dead. The doctor grasps his meaning, takes the bundle and comments, "Oh, you're right. It's not dead. Mr. Hudlocke, you have a son."

Bette enters, radiant, takes the baby and announces that she's going to call him Skippy. Emily insists the child must have a saint's name in order receive Roman Catholic baptism. "Why not name it after a household appliance? . . . . . Egg beater. Waffle iron. Bath mat," is Karl's sardonic suggestion. Bette agrees to name the baby Matt, short for Matthew, but she's going to nickname him Skippy after her favorite movie.

Scene 10: Matt's favorite movie essay; arts and crafts with Emily

Matt begins to recite to the audience an essay on "My Favorite Movie," but he soon digresses into an analysis of the novels of Thomas Hardy whose sadness and lack of faith in a benevolent providence is, as Matt sees it, "part of the late Victorian mood. We can see something like it in A.E. Housman, or in Emily's life. Shortly after Skippy's birth, Emily enters a convent, but then leaves the convent due to nerves. Bette becomes pregnant for the second time. Boo continues to drink. If psychiatrists had existed in nineteenth century Wessex, Hardy might suggest Bette and Boo seek counseling. Instead he has no advice to give them, and in 1886 he writes *The Mayor of Casterbridge.*" Skippy studied this novel in college. He also tried his hand at drawing with Emily when he was very little and managed to draw a recognizable dog.

Scene 11: The second child of Bette and Boo

> *Bette enters, carrying a chair. She sits on the chair.*

BETTE *(to audience and/or herself):* I'm going to pretend that I'm sitting in this chair. Then I'm going to pretend that I'm going to have another baby. And then I'm going to have another and another and another. I'm going to pretend to have a big family. There'll be Skippy. And then all the A.A. Milne characters. Boo should join A.A. There'll be Eeyore and Pooh Bear and Christopher Robin and Tigger . . . My family is going to be like an enormous orphanage. I'll be their mother. Kanga and six hundred baby Roos. Baby Roo is Kanga's baby, but she's a mother to them all. Roo and Tigger and Pooh and Christopher Robin and Eeyore and Owl, owl, ow, ow ow, ow, ow, ow, ow, owl! I'm giving birth, Mom. Roo and Tigger and Boo and Pooh and Soot and Eeyore and Karl and Betsy and Owl . . .

> *Enter quickly: Boo, Karl, Soot, Margaret, Paul, Emily, Joan. They stand in their same hospital positions. Enter the doctor with the baby in a blue blanket.*

DOCTOR: The baby's dead.

> *He drops it on the floor.*

MARGARET: Nonsense. That's what he said about the last one, didn't he, Paul?

DOCTOR: This time it's true. It *is* dead.

BETTE: Why?

DOCTOR: The reason the baby is dead is this: Mr. Hudlocke has Rh positive blood.

KARL: Good for you, Bore!

DOCTOR: Mrs. Hudlocke has Rh negative blood.

BETTE: Like Kanga.

DOCTOR: And so the mother's Rh negative blood fights the baby's Rh positive blood and so: THE MOTHER KILLS THE BABY.

EMILY *(rather horrified):* Who did this??? The mother did this???

KARL: You married a winner, Bore.

BOO: The baby came. And it was dead.

SOOT: Poor Booey.

BETTE: But I'll have other babies.

DOCTOR: The danger for your health if you do so and the likelihood of stillbirth are overwhelming considerations.

BOO: The baby came. And it was dead.

BETTE: Mama, tell him to go away.

MARGARET: There, there. Say something to her, Paul.

Paul says nothing. Lights change.

Scene 12: Bette and Margaret visit Emily in a rest home

Trying to keep the conversation on pleasant subjects, Emily asks after Skippy. Bette is lost in her own thoughts, however, and is barely able to understand that Emily is talking about her son, whom she now calls Baby Roo. Emily continues: "Bette, dear, don't feel bad, you have the one wonderful child, and maybe some day God will make a miracle so you can have more children." Bette comes out of her lethargy, electrified by the words "miracle" and "more children" and is seized with hope, shouting "I CAN HAVE MORE CHILDREN!" again and again. Margaret and Bette depart, leaving Emily trying to remember the music she forgot at the wedding.

Scene 13: Father Donnally gives Bette advice

Bette consults Father Donnally on the subject of miracles which, the priest tells her, "Rarely happen." Bette, hearing only what she wants to hear, exclaims, "I do too! Thank you, Father. You've helped me make a decision."

Scene 14: Soot gives Bette advice

Bette, pregnant again, is at the Hudlockes' with Boo.

BETTE: And then Father Donnally said that I should just keep trying and that even if this baby died, there would be at least one more baby that would live, and then I would be a mother as God meant me to be. Do you agree, Soot?

SOOT: I've never met this Father Donnally. Karl, Pauline has a retarded daughter, doesn't she? LaLa is retarded, isn't she? I mean, she isn't just slow, is she?

BETTE: I don't care if the child's retarded. Then that's God's will. I love retarded children. I like children more than I like people. Boo, you're drinking too much, it's not fair to me. If this baby dies, it's going to be your fault.

BOO: I don't think Father Donnally should have encouraged you about this. That's what I think.

BETTE: He's a priest. *(To Soot.)* Did you ever see Jackie Cooper as a child? I thought he was much cuter than Shirley Temple, what do you think, Soot?

KARL: Bore, my wife Soot hasn't said one sensible thing in 30 years of marriage . . .

SOOT: Oh, Karl . . . *(Laughs, flattered.)*

KARL: But your little wife has just said more senseless things in one ten-minute period than Soot here has said in 30 years of bondage.

SOOT: Oh, Karl. I was never one for talking.

BETTE *(to Karl):* Look here, you. I'm not afraid of you. I'm not going to let Boo push me to a breakdown the way you've pushed Soot. I'm stronger than that.

SOOT: Oh, my. *(Laughs.)* Sit down, dear.

KARL: Tell the baby maker to turn it down, Bore.

BOO: Bette, sit down.

BETTE: I want a marriage and a family and a home, and I'm going to have them, and if you won't help me, Boo, I'll have them without you. *(Exits.)*

KARL: Well, Bore, I don't know about you and your wife. Whatever one can say against your mother, and it's most everything, at least she didn't go around dropping dead children at every step of the way like some goddamned giddy farm animal.

SOOT: Karl, you shouldn't tease everyone so.

KARL: I don't like the way you're behaving today, Soot. *(Exits.)*

SOOT *(looks back to where Bette was):* Bette, dear, let me give you some advice. That's right. She left. *(In a moment of disorientation, looks at Boo.)* Boo, Karl's a lovely man most of the time, and I've had a very happy life with him, but I hope you'll be a little kinder than he was. Just a little. Anything is an improvement. I wish I had dead children. I wish I had two hundred dead children. I'd stuff them down Karl's throat. *(Laughs.)* Of course, I'm only kidding. *(Laughs some more.)*
      Lights change.

Scene 15: Matt talks about the Mayor of Casterbridge

Matt points out that Thomas Hardy's mayor sold his wife and child while drunk, and that Boo's alcoholism is not as severe as that. Possibly it is caused by Bette's nagging, or possible the other way around. Anyhow, Bette has gone to the hospital to have another baby.

Scene 16: The third child of Bette and Boo

All but Bette are present when the Doctor enters and drops the dead baby onto the floor without a word.

Scene 17: Bette telephones Bonnie Wilson

Late at night, Bette wakes up her former best friend, Bonnie Wilson, to whom she hasn't spoken since they were 15 years old, with a phone call. Bonnie lives in Florida and is married, with two children. Bette wants to talk about some of their childhood escapades, but Bonnie just wants to get back to sleep. Bette insists on talking about her dead babies, and Boo's drinking (Bonnie's husband Scooter doesn't drink) but finally hangs up after telling her, "Goodbye, Bonnie, it was good to hear your voice."

Scene 18: Bette and Boo celebrate Thanksgiving

Several months later, Bette and Boo and ten-year-old Matt are preparing to have the Brennans and the Hudlockes over for Thanksgiving. Bette and Boo quarrel about Boo's drinking—she thinks he has a bottle stashed in the cellar—while Matt tries to set the table.

Joan arrives with candied sweet potatoes, and Emily brings gravy, but not even their arrival stops the quarrel between Bette and Boo, nor does the arrival of the Brennans (with a cake) and the Hudlockes (with candelabra). In the midst of the quarrel, Boo knocks into Emily, spilling gravy all over the rug. He offers to clean it up and brings in the vacuum cleaner, persistantly running it over the mess. As Bette shouts "You don't vacuum gravy. . . . . Stop it! You're ruining the vacuum!", the Hudlockes make their escape.

BETTE: You don't vacuum gravy. You don't vacuum gravy. You don't vacuum gravy.

BOO *(hysterical):* WHAT DO YOU DO WITH IT THEN? TELL ME! WHAT DO YOU DO WITH IT?

BETTE *(quieter, but very upset):* You get warm water, and a sponge, and you sponge it up.
Bette and Boo stare at one another, spent.

EMILY: Should we put the sweet potatoes in the oven?

JOAN: Come on, Emily. Let's go home.

MARGARET: Betsy, if you and Skippy want to stay at our house tonight, just come over. Goodbye, Boo.

EMILY *(calls):* Goodbye, Skippy.
Margaret, Joan, Emily and Paul exit. Enter Matt with a pan of water and two sponges. He hands them to Bette. Bette and Boo methodically sponge up the gravy. Music to the "Bette and Boo" round in the background.

BOO *(quietly):* Okay, we'll soak it up with the sponge. That's what we're doing. We're soaking it up.
They more or less finish with it.
I'm going to take a nap.
Boo lies down where he is, and falls asleep.

BETTE: Boo? Boo? Booey? Boo?
Enter Soot.

SOOT: Did I leave an earring in here? Oh, dear. He's just asleep, isn't he?
BETTE: Boo? Boo.
SOOT: He must have gotten tired. *(Holds up earring, to Bette.)* If you should see it, it looks just like this one. *(Laughs.)* Booey? *(Laughs.)* I think he's asleep. Goodbye, Booey. *(Exits.)*
BETTE: Boo? Booey?
MATT: Please don't try to wake him up. You'll just argue.
BETTE: All right. I won't try to wake him. *(Pause.)* Boo. Booey.
   She pushes his shoulder slightly.
Boo. *(To Matt.)* I just want to get through to him about the gravy. *(To Boo.)* Boo. You don't vacuum gravy. Are you awake, Boo? Boo? I wonder if he's going to sleep through the night. I can wait. Boo. Booey.
   Bette looks at Matt, then back at Boo. Matt looks at both of them. Lights dim. Curtain.

ACT II

Scene 19: Boo takes a pledge in front of Father Donnally

The families gather to sing "Ninety-nine bottles of beer on the wall," which becomes soft background music as Boo pledges in front of Father Donnally to give up drinking. After the priest comments that all problems can be solved through faith, Bette suggests to Boo that they have another baby.

Scene 20: Bette and Boo go dancing

As they dance, Bette and Boo comment on their families and themselves . . . Joanie's marriage is in trouble . . . Emily is praying daily that the new baby lives . . . Father Donnally is nice . . . Boo's father treats his mother badly. Boo, meanwhile, is worrying that the waiter might think it odd that he ordered only ginger ale. Bette commands him to stop worrying and start having a good time, and he obeys.

Scene 21: Matt's holiday essay; Bette and Boo celebrate Christmas

Holidays were invented to depress almost everybody, Matt observes to the audience. "And so, at this time," he concludes, "the Thanksgiving with the gravy having been such fun, Bette and Boo decide to celebrate the holiday of Christmas by visiting the Hudlockes."

At the Hudlockes', Karl issues his usual instruction to Soot to fetch him and Boo another drink, causing Bette to cry out, "IF BOO HAS ANOTHER DRINK I AM GOING TO SCREAM AND SCREAM UNTIL THE WINDOWS BREAK!" Karl notices that she is pregnant again and supposes that his son must be trying to kill her. Bette goes off to lie down, leaving Matt to watch and report to her if Boo takes another drink, but she soon returns to watch for herself. She continues to criticize Boo's drinking, to his exasperation. Karl pours his drink on Bette's lap, and she has hysterics.

Graham Beckel and Joan Allen in a scene from *The Marriage of Bette and Boo*

Scene 22: Twenty years later, Boo has dinner with his son; twenty years later, Bette has dinner with her son

The conversation 20 years later is much the same as the previous father-and-son conversation, except that Boo is now in Columbia graduate school. Boo still feels that he and Bette might get back together again: "I always found your mother very charming when she wasn't shouting." Again, Boo "is going to get teary for a second."

Matt then joins his mother for dinner. Bette greets him with, "Hello, Skippy dear. I made steak for you, and mashed potatoes and peas and cake. How many days can you stay?" Only one, he says. Bette complains that he never stays long with her, unlike the children of her friends Polly Lydstone and Judith Rankle, who are most attentive to their mothers.

MATT: And some boy from Pingry School came home after class and shot both his parents. So what?

BETTE: There's no need to get nasty.

MATT: I don't want to hear about Polly Lyastone and Judith Rankle.

BETTE: You're the only one of my children that lived. You should see me more often.

MATT: That's not a fair thing to say.

BETTE: You're right. It's not fair of me to bring up the children that died; that's beside the point. I realize Boo and I must take responsibility for our own actions.

Of course, the Church wasn't very helpful at the time, but nonetheless we had brains of our own, so there's no point in assigning blame. I must take responsibility for wanting children so badly that I foolishly kept trying over and over, hoping for miracles. Did you see the article in the paper, by the way, about how they've discovered a serum for people with the Rh problem that would have allowed me to have more babies if it had existed back then?

MATT: Yes I did. I wondered if you had read about that.

BETTE: Yes I did. It made me feel terribly sad for a little while; but then I thought, what's past is past. One has no choice but to accept facts. And I realized that you must live your own life, and I must live mine. My life may not have worked out as I wished, but still I feel a deep and inner serenity, and so you mustn't feel bad about me because I am totally happy and self-sufficient in my pretty sunlit apartment. And now I'm going to close my eyes, and I want you to go out into the world and live your life. Goodbye. God bless you. *(Closes her eyes.)*

MATT: *(to audience):* I'm afraid I've made that conversation up totally.

> *They start the scene over.*

BETTE: Hello, Skippy dear. I made a steak for you, and mashed potatoes and peas and cake. You know, you're the only one of my children that lived. How long can you stay?

MATT: Gee, I don't know. Uh, a couple of days. Three years. Only ten minutes, my car's double-parked. I could stay eight years if I can go away during the summer. Gee. I don't know.

> *Lights change.*

Scene 23: Boo's second pledge in front of Father Donnally

Shortly after the disastrous Christmas celebration, Bette brings Boo back to Father Donnally to pledge again that he will stop drinking. Bette has written out the pledge for him and has added the words "And I promise to tell my father to go to hell." After the priest leaves, Bette declares to Boo that if he will stop drinking, maybe this time God will answer Emily's and her prayers and let them have a live baby. They immediately start quarreling in such a way that it finally provokes them into laughing at their own behavior.

Scene 24: Joan's birthday celebration

Matt and Bette are visiting the Brennans to celebrate Joan's birthday (Boo has stayed home drinking or sulking, they're not sure which). Margaret is delighted to have her children living at home—Emily back from the rest home, Joan because her marriage has broken up—because it gives her someone to talk to besides Paul.

Joan (who is pregnant) and Bette can't keep themselves from bickering over almost any subject that arises, upsetting Emily, who comes in with a birthday cake. Bette warns Skippy not to take a piece of the cake because it hasn't been cooked properly. The dough is wet.

EMILY: It isn't cooked right?

BETTE: It's wet, it's wet. You didn't cook it enough.

JOAN: I don't like cake anyway.

MARGARET: Poor Joanie.

BETTE: Everything's always poor Joanie. But her baby's going to live.

EMILY: Oh, Bette.

JOAN: Well maybe we'll both have a miracle. Maybe yours'll live and mine'll die.

EMILY: Oh, Joanie.

BETTE: Stop saying that, Emily.

MARGARET: Girls, girls. This isn't conversation for the living room. Or for young ears.

PAUL (choking on cake): #%#%#%GHGHR#%#%#*********#@#@#********.

MARGARET: Paul, stop it. Stop it.

Paul falls over dead. Lights change.

Scene 25: *The funeral of Paul Brennan*

Paul is sitting in a chair with a sheet over him as the Brennan family gathers for his funeral. Father Donnally tells a fatuous story which is supposed to teach a moral lesson about bereavement. Joan admits to Paul's dead body that he was right—she has turned against all Greeks after Nikkos.

Scene 26: *The fourth child of Bette and Boo*

At the hospital awaiting the birth of Bette's fourth child, the Hudlockes have gathered but the Brennans are absent. Karl starts to tell an off-color joke. Boo, unable to stand any more, goes off to get a drink. Karl can't remember the punch line and demands that Soot finish the joke for him, but Soot doesn't know it either.

The doctor enters, drops the new baby on the floor without a word, and exits. Boo comes back and learns that the new baby didn't live: "I should probably see Bette, but I don't think I can face her." Karl orders Soot to tell the joke, though Boo doesn't feel like hearing a joke at this time. Karl insists, so Soot starts to retell it and of course gets it wrong.

Scene 27: *Father Donnally gives Bette advice again*

As though she were looking at gravestones, Bette recites the names of her three dead children: Patrick Michael, Christopher Tigger and Pooh Bear Eeyore. She consults Father Donnally about her problem.

BETTE: I know sometimes one can misunderstand the will of God. But sex is for having babies, right? I mean, it's not just for marriage. Well, even if it is somewhat, I feel that I should be a mother; and I think it would be a sin for me not to try again. But I don't think Boo wants me to get pregnant again.

FATHER DONNALLY: Have you tried the rhythm method?

BETTE: But I *want* to get pregnant.

FATHER DONNALLY: What does your doctor say?

BETTE: The problem is that all the babies die. I don't see why I have to go through all this suffering. And Boo never helps me.

FATHER DONNALLY: I give a retreat for young married couples every year in the parish. Why don't you and your husband come to that? I'm sure it will help you if you're having trouble on the marriage couch.

BETTE: All right, I'll bring Booey to the retreat, Thank you, Father.

FATHER DONNALLY: You're welcome, Bette. *(Exits.)*

BETTE *(calls out):* Boo Boo. Booey. Booey. Booey.

BOO: What?

BETTE: Booey, I'm pregnant again. Do you think I'm going to die?
Lights change.

Scene 28: Father Donnally's marriage retreat

Everybody is present at the retreat, including dead Paul with his sheet over him. Father Donnally reminds the group that Jesus blessed a wedding couple at Cana and mentions some typical problems newlyweds might have, such as ill-cooked bacon. This leads Father Donnally to give them his imitation of bacon frying in a pan and coffee percolating. Such things as coffee and bacon, he tells the group, "represent things the wife does to make her husband happy." He admits that unlike other priests who wish they had lived in Jesus's time, he's glad he lives now when they have such creature comforts as showers.

Father Donnally doesn't insist that the wife "obey" her husband, "but if chaos follows, don't blame me." The purpose of marriage, he continues, is "to populate the earth and to glorify God." But it isn't a step to be taken lightly—he reminds the group—because divorce is not permitted and remarriage is a sin.

"So for God's sake," Father Donnally advises, "if you're going to get married, pay attention to what you're doing, have conversations with the person, figure out if you *really* want to live with that person for years and years and years, because you can't change it. . . . . I get so sick of these people coming to me after they're married, and they've just gotten to know one another *after* the ceremony, and they've discovered they have nothing in common and they hate one another. . . . . There is no solution to a problem like that. I can't help them! It puts me in a terrible position. I can't say get a divorce, that's against God's law. I can't say go get some on the side, that's against God's law. I can't say just pretend you're happy and maybe after a while you won't know the difference because, though that's not against God's law, not that many people know how to do that, and if I suggested it to people, they'd write to the Bishop complaining about me and then he'd transfer me to some godforsaken place in Latin America without a shower, and all because these people don't know what they're doing when they get married. *(Shakes his head.)* So I mumble platitudes to these people who come to me with these insoluble problems, and I think to myself, 'Why didn't they *think* before they got married? Why does no one ever *think*? Why did God make people stupid?' *(Pause.)* Are there any questions?"

Bette and Emily raise their hands. Bette wants to know if she should pray for a girl baby, better able to resist infection than a boy. Father Donnally advises her to go ahead, no one can stop her from praying.

Emily wants to know if Father Donnally thinks it might be her fault that Bette's babies died, because she was once in a convent but left it. "Yes, I do," Father Donnally replies, as a joke. Emily has difficulty understanding that it is only a joke. The priest makes a hurried exit after announcing, "Father McNulty will talk to you about sexual problems, which I'm not very good at."

Emily's comment on the session is, "Our Saviour, that's more important than having a shower." Boo's comment is, "He just said that we shouldn't get married, and that if we did, not to bother him with our problems." Soot's comment is that she seems to be going deaf and it's wonderful, "I haven't been able to hear Karl for about three days." They await the arrival of Father McNulty.

Scene 29: The divorce of Bette and Boo

Matt informs the audience, "Twenty years later, or perhaps only fifteen, Bette files for a divorce from Boo. They have been separated for several years, since shortly after the death of the final child; and at the suggestion of a therapist Bette has been seeing, Bette decides to make the separation legal in order to formalize the breakup psychologically, and also to get better, and more regular, support payments. Boo, for some reason, decides to contest the divorce; and so there has to be testimony."

Matt is of course a principal witness in the proceedings, questioned by his mother's lawyer, who reminds him of his grandfather Paul (Paul comes to life to question Matt, still in his almost unintelligible gibberish, but Matt manages to get the drift of most of the questions).

Under Paul's questioning, Matt testifies that his father "drank a fair amount" but he, Matt, isn't qualified to say whether or not Boo is an alcoholic (Bette offers in evidence a 12-year calendar of Boo's drinking). Matt did see Bette and Boo hit each other sometimes; it was "fairly harrowing" when they happened to do it while driving the car. Matt himself does not drink.

PAUL: Ehl ee att, urr oo uhasgee ehn or errens epyrateted? (Tell me, Matt, were you unhappy when your parents separated?)
    Matt is at a loss. Paul must repeat the word "separated" several times, with hand gestures, before Matt understands.
MATT: No, I was glad when they separated. The arguing got on my nerves a lot. *(Pause.)* I'd hear it in my ear even when they weren't talking. When I was a child, anyway.
PAUL: Ehl ee att, oo oo# ink or aher us goooh aher? (Tell me, Matt, do you think your father was a good father?)
MATT: Yes, I am against the war in Vietnam. I'm sorry, is that what you asked?
PAUL: Doo oo# ink ee uz a goooh ahzer? (Do you think he was a good father?)
MATT: Oh. Yes. I guess he's been a good father. *(Looks embarrassed.)*
PAUL: *(pointing at Boo, pushing for some point):* Buh dyoo oo# ink ee ad ohme or uh inking bahblim? (But do you think he had some sort of drinking problem?)
MATT: Yes, I guess he probably does have some sort of drinking problem. I mean it became such an issue it seems suspicious to me that he didn't just stop,

he kept saying there was no . . . well, it was odd he didn't stop. It's really not my place to be saying this. I would prefer I wasn't here.

> Pause. Matt is uncomfortable, has been uncomfortable relating to Boo for the whole scene.

PAUL: Orr ehcoooz, att. (You're excused, Matt)

MATT: What?

BETTE: He said you were excused.

MATT: Oh good.

BETTE: Thank you, Skippy. (Kisses him.)

BOO: Well, son. Have a good time back at school.

MATT: Thank you. I'm behind in this paper I'm doing. (Pause.) I have to get the plane.

BOO: Well, have a good trip. (Looks embarrassed, exits.)

MATT: Thank you.

> Bette and Paul also exit.

Matt addresses the audience on the subject of his paper on Eustacia Vye but soon starts talking about the avoidance of dangers of all kinds, physical and emotional, especially the dangers of associating with crazy people. "It is difficult to totally protect oneself, of course," he concludes, "and there are many precautions that one thinks of only when it's too late. But, as Virginia Woolf pointed out in *To The Lighthouse,* admittedly in a different context, the attempt is all."

Scene 30: Matt has dinner with Karl, Soot, Margaret and Paul

Many years after the divorce, Matt is at the dinner table with his four grandparents (Karl is 80, Margaret is senile and Paul and Soot are dead and so have their heads on the table). Margaret's mind wanders erratically, but Karl still seems to have most of his marbles, and Matt asks him how to avoid the pitfalls of divorce which seem to have caught everyone he knows. "Don't expect too much, that's for starters," Karl replies. "Look at Bette and Bore. She kept trying to change Bore. That's idiotic. Don't try to change anybody."

MATT: You know, I didn't know you and Soot back when you were young, or Margaret and Paul either, for that matter. Maybe your marriages *were* happy. I have no way of knowing.

KARL: I never expected much from life. I wanted to get my way in everything, and that's about all. What did you ask?

MARGARET: Huh-huh-huh. Joan. Emily.

MATT: Why did you marry Soot?

KARL: No reason. She was much prettier when she was younger.

MATT: But surely you didn't marry her because she was pretty.

KARL: Don't tell me what I did.

MATT: And why did everyone call her Soot? How did she get the name Soot?

KARL: I don't remember. Was her name Soot? I thought it was something else.

MATT: I think her name was Soot. Do you think I misheard it all these years?

KARL: I couldn't say.

MATT: Why were you so mean to Soot?

KARL: Why do you want to know?

MATT: Because I see all of you do the same thing over and over, for years and years, and you never change. And my fear is that I can see all of you but not see myself, and maybe I'm doing something similar, but I just can't see it. What I mean to say is: did you all *intend* to live your lives the way you did?

KARL: Go away. I don't like talking to you. You're an irritating young man.
> *Matt leaves the scene. Karl, Margaret, Soot and Paul exit or fade into darkness.*

Scene 31: Matt gives Emily advice

Back in chronology before the divorce, Emily is writing a letter of apology on general principles, though she has no one to send it to just now. Matt advises Emily not to be so hard on herself. Matt is a bit confused about the time sequence but finally figures out that they are at a point when, "some time after Father Donnally's marriage retreat, Bette goes to the hospital for the fifth time."

Scene 32: The last child of Bette and Boo

Matt is waiting at the hospital with his father, when a baby in a pink blanket is thrown in from offstage. Matt, reluctant to talk to his father, goes outside. Bette comes in, and Boo begs her not to have any more babies. Bette's reply is, "I don't love you any more, Boo. . . . . I'm tired of feeling alone talking to you." Boo goes off in search of a drink, and Bette calls for Skippy.

MATT *(enters):* Yes.

BETTE: Would you move this for me?
> *She indicates dead baby on floor. He gingerly places it offstage or behind something.*

Your father's gone away. All the babies are dead. You're the only thing of value left in my life, Skippy.

MATT: Why do you call me Skippy? Why don't you call me Matt?

BETTE: It's my favorite movie.

MATT: My favorite movie is *Citizen Kane.* I don't call you Citizen Kane.

BETTE: Why are you being fresh?

MATT: I don't know.

BETTE: I don't want to put any pressure on you, Skippy dear, but you're the only reason I have left for living now.

MATT: Ah.

BETTE: You're so unresponsive.

MATT: I'm sorry. I don't know what to say.

Bette reiterates that she should have had more babies, then asks Matt to come read her to sleep with A.A. Milne but informs him as she exits, "I don't want to call you Matt."

After this, Matt remembers, he went to high school, then college, then graduate school. He tells the audience, "I'm afraid what happened next will sound rather exaggerated, but after she divorced Boo, Bette felt very lonely and unhappy for several years, and then she married another alcoholic, and then after two years that broke up, and then she got cancer. By this time I'm 30, and I visit her once more in the hospital."

Scene 33: Matt visits Bette; Bette and Boo reminisce

Emily is pushing Bette in a wheelchair when Matt arrives at the hospital. Emily prays to ease Bette's pain and goes to the chapel to continue praying. Bette wonders whether God is punishing her for marrying a second time, but Matt reassures her that He doesn't punish people for specific offenses, "He punishes people in general, for no reason."

Bette asks Matt to pray for healing while he places his hand on her hip, and he does this reluctantly.

BETTE: You're just like your father—unresponsive.

MATT: Let's not argue about this.

BETTE: All right. *(On a pleasanter subject.)* Do you remember when you used to smell your father's breath to see if he'd been drinking? You were such a cute child. I saw your father last week. He came to the hospital to visit.

MATT: Oh, how is he?

BETTE: Well, he's still mad at me about my second marriage, but in some ways he's always been a sweet man. I think the years of drinking have done something to his brain, though. He'll be talking, and then there'll be this long pause like he's gone to sleep or something, and then finally he'll go on again like nothing's happened.

Boo comes in bringing flowers, and Matt fetches him a chair. Boo sits and tells Matt that his mother still looks very pretty.

MATT: Mother said you came to visit last week.

BOO: I came last week.

BETTE: He repeats himself all the time.

BOO: What?

BETTE: I said, you repeat yourself. *(Boo looks annoyed.)* But it's charming. *(To Matt.)* Your father flirted with the second shift nurse.

BOO: Your old man still has an eye for the ladies. I was here last week and there was this . . .
        Long pause; he stares, blank.

BETTE: *(to Matt):* See, he's doing it now. Boo, are you there? Boo?. *(Sings to herself.)* God bless Bette and Boo and Skippy, Emily and Boo.

BOO *(comes back, continues):* . . . nurse, and she liked your old man, I think.

BETTE: She thought he was her grandfather.

BOO: What?

BETTE: You're too old for her.

BOO: What?

MATT: Maybe he's gone deaf.

BOO: No, I can hear. I think it's my brain.

BETTE: Do you remember when you tried to vacuum the gravy?

BOO: No.

BETTE: Well, you did. It was very funny. Not at the time, of course. And how you used to keep bottles hidden in the cellar. And all the dead babies.

BOO: Yes. We had some good times.

Bette remembers that Boo was very helpful when she accidentally killed her pet parakeet—but then he went out and got drunk. Matt takes this opportunity to ask questions of his father ("Why did you drink?"), his mother ("Why did you keep trying to have babies?") and both of them ("Why didn't Soot leave Karl? Why was her name Soot?") but he gets no shred of an answer.

Boo remembers how thrilled he and Bette were when Matt was born. Bette feels a twinge of pain.

> *Bette closes her eyes, and is motionless.*

BOO: Bette? Betsy?

MATT: Is she sleeping?

> *Matt with some hesitation feels her pulse, in her wrist and perhaps in her neck. Enter Emily.*

EMILY: Oh hello, Boo. It's nice to see you. Are you all right, Skippy?

MATT: She died, Emily.

EMILY: Then she's with God. Let's say a prayer over her.

> *Emily and Boo pray by Bette's body. The other characters enter in the background and sing the "God bless Bette and Boo" round softly. Matt speaks to the audience during the prayer and the song.*

MATT: Bette passed into death, and is with God. She is in heaven where she has been reunited with the four dead babies, and where she waits for Boo, and for Bonnie Wilson, and Emily, and Pooh Bear and Eeyore, and Kanga and Roo; and for me.

> *Lights dim. Curtain.*

A GRAPHIC GLANCE

Gordon Connell (*far left*, as Mark Twain), John Short *(with pipe)*, Ron Richardson, Daniel H. Jenkins, Rene Auberjonois and Carol Dennis in *Big River: The Adventures of Huckleberry Finn*

John Mahoney in *Orphans*

Barry Miller in *Biloxi Blues*

Jim Dale *(above)* and Joanna
Gleason *(right)* in the revival of
(A Day in the Death of) Joe Egg

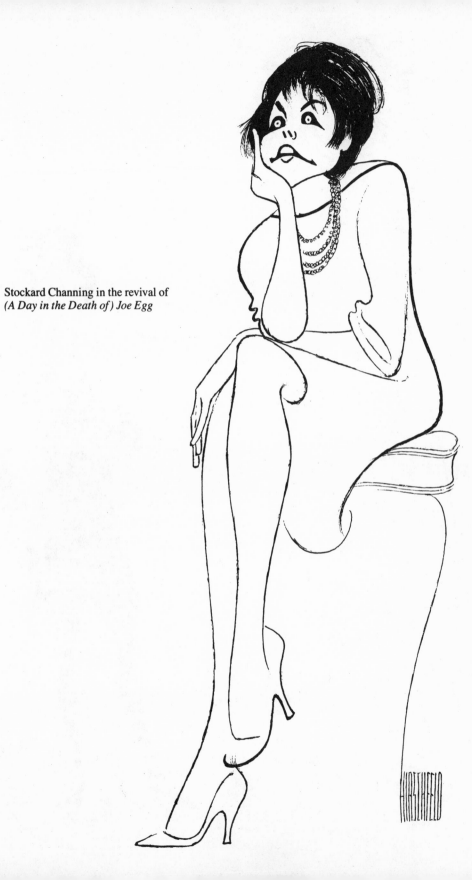

Stockard Channing in the revival of
(A Day in the Death of) Joe Egg

Kate Nelligan as Virginia Woolf in *Virginia*

Robert Joy in *Life and Limb*

Claudette Colbert in *Aren't We All?*

Roy Dotrice in the revival of *An Enemy of the People*

Matthew Broderick, Barry Miller, Brian Tarantina, Matt Mulhern,
Alan Ruck, Geoffrey Sharp and Bill Sadler in *Biloxi Blues*

Jill Clayburgh, Raul Julia and Frank Langella in the revival of Noel Coward's *Design for Living*

The cast of *Hurlyburly (clockwise from lower left)*: Judith Ivey, Harvey Keitel, Christopher Walken, Sigourney Weaver, Jerry Stiller, Cynthia Nixon and William Hurt

Carrie Nye in *The Madwoman of Chaillot*

Janis Paige in *Alone Together*

Tovah Feldshuh in *She Stoops to Conquer*

Everett Quinton in *The Mystery of Irma Vep*

Derek Jacobi and Sinead Cusack in *(left) Cyrano de Bergerac* and *(far right) Much Ado About Nothing* with Christopher Bowen and Clare Byam Shaw *(background)*

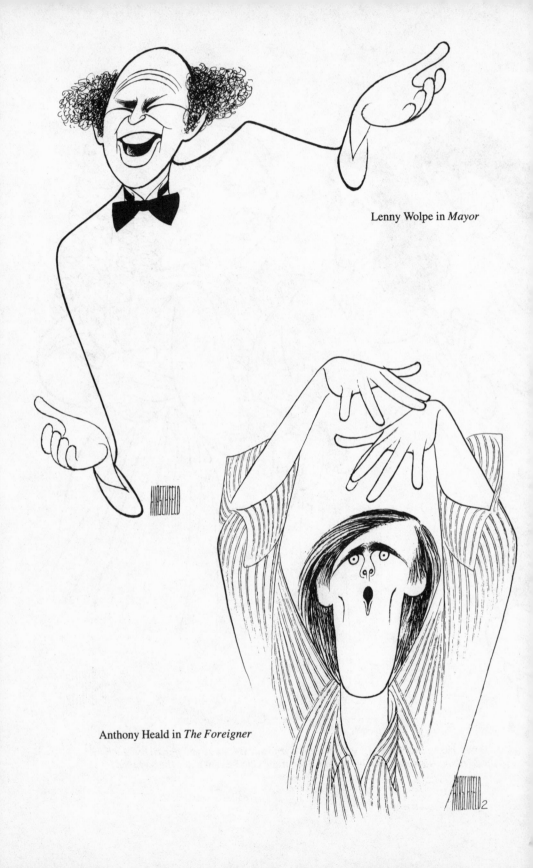

Lenny Wolpe in *Mayor*

Anthony Heald in *The Foreigner*

Elizabeth Wilson in *Salonika*

Mary Beth Hurt in *The Nest of the Wood Grouse*

Leilani Jones in *Grind*

Rene Auberjonois in *Big River: The Adventures of Huckleberry Finn*

(Clockwise from upper right) Jeremy
Brett, Claudette Colbert, Rex Harrison,
Lynn Redgrave and George Rose in the
revival of *Aren't We All?*

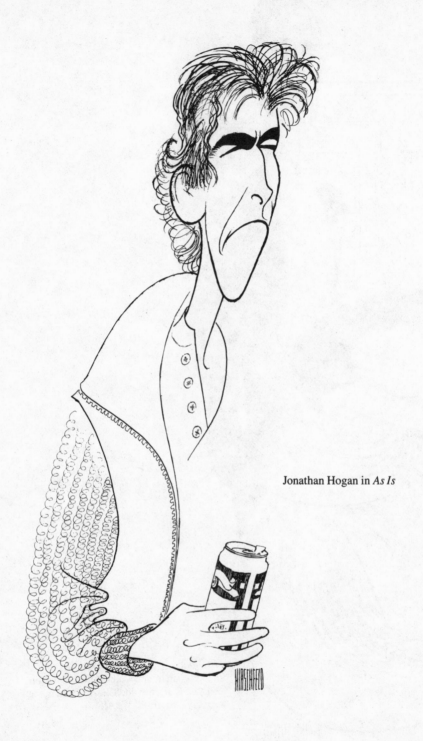

Jonathan Hogan in *As Is*

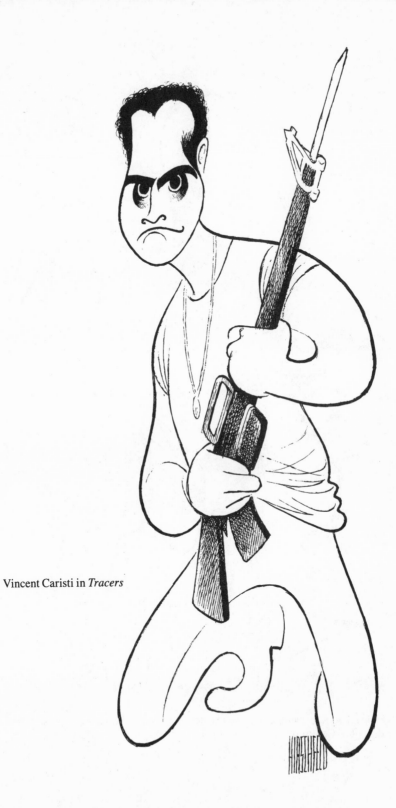

Vincent Caristi in *Tracers*

(Left to right) Kate Nelligan in *Virginia*, John Lithgow in *Requiem for a Heavyweight* and Stephen Collins in *The Loves of Anatol*

John Danelle in *Split Second*

Kevin Kline *(foreground)* with *(left to right)* Vivienne Argent, Mary Elizabeth Mastrantonio, Jack Stehlin and George Guidall in Shakespeare's *Henry V*

Judith Ivey *(above)* and Jerry
Stiller *(right)* in *Hurlyburly*

Candice Bergen in *Hurlyburly*

Rosemary Harris in *Pack of Lies*

Glenda Jackson with *(from left)* Edward Petherbridge, Brian Cox and James Hazeldine
in the revival of *Strange Interlude*

Lenny Wolpe as Mayor Koch with *(counterclockwise from upper left)* Kathryn McAteer, Keith Curran, Ilene Kristen, Douglas Bernstein, Ken Jennings and Nancy Giles in *Mayor*

Theresa Merritt in *Ma Rainey's Black Bottom*

Stephen Joyce in *Maneuvers*

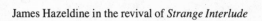

James Hazeldine in the revival of *Strange Interlude*

Chuck Wagner, Ron Taylor, Brent Spiner *(at rear)*, Darlene Anders
and Michael Praed *(far right)* in *The Three Musketeers*

Harry Groener and Mark Hamill in *Harrigan 'n Hart*

Ben Vereen *(center)* with *(clockwise from left)* Stubby Kaye, Leilani Jones,
Carol Woods, Sharon Murray, Timothy Nolen and Joey Faye in *Grind*

Tony Roberts in *Doubles*

Julie Covington in *Tom and Viv*

John Carlisle in *Much Ado About Nothing*

Raul Julia, Glenne Headly and Kevin Kline in the revival of George Bernard Shaw's *Arms and the Man*

Frank Langella in the revival of *After the Fall*

Dianne Wiest in the revival of *After the Fall*

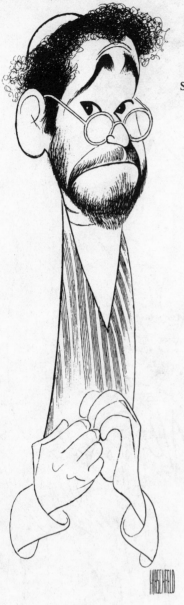

Stuart Zagnit in *Kuni-Leml*

Avner Eisenberg in *Avner the Eccentric*

Gisela Caldwell in *The Octette Bridge Club*

Peter Evans in *Endgame*

The cast of *The Golem (counter-clockwise from upper left)*: Joe Parisi, David Gregory, Carl Don, Christopher McCann, Joseph Wiseman, F. Murray Abraham and *(in background)* Randy Quaid in the title role

Al Carmines in *Romance Language*

Jay O. Sanders in *The Incredibly Famous Willy Rivers*

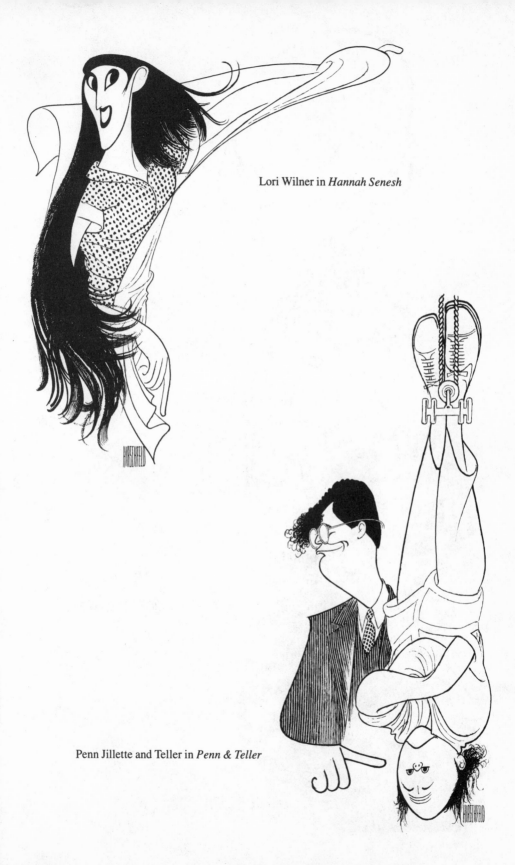

Lori Wilner in *Hannah Senesh*

Penn Jillette and Teller in *Penn & Teller*

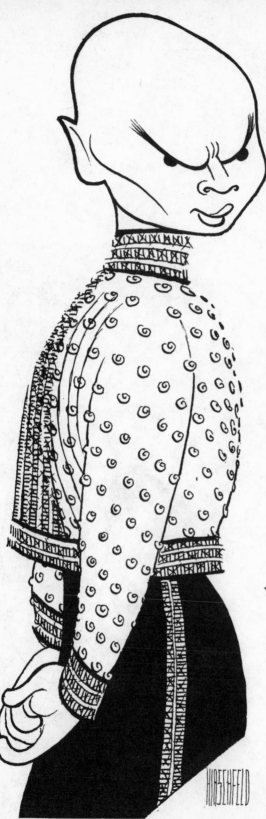

Yul Brynner in *The King and I*

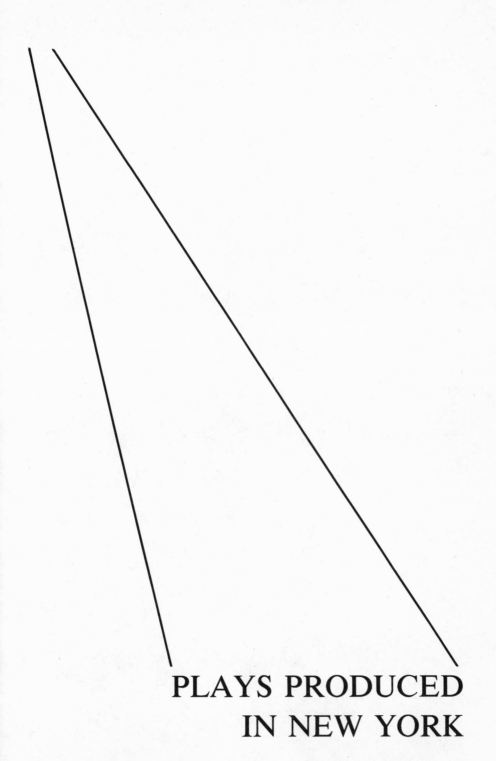

PLAYS PRODUCED
IN NEW YORK

PLAYS PRODUCED ON BROADWAY

Figures in parentheses following a play's title give number of performances. These figures are acquired directly from the production offices and do not include previews or extra non-profit performances. In the case of a transfer, the off-Broadway run is noted but not added to the figure in parentheses.

Plays marked with an asterisk (*) were still running on June 1, 1985. Their number of performances is figured through May 31, 1985.

In a listing of a show's numbers—dances, sketches, musical scenes, etc.—the titles of songs are identified wherever possible by their appearance in quotation marks (").

HOLDOVERS FROM PREVIOUS SEASONS

Plays which were running on June 1, 1984 are listed below. More detailed information about them appears in previous *Best Plays* volumes of appropriate years. Important cast changes since opening night are recorded in the Cast Replacements section of this volume.

*A Chorus Line** (4,086; longest run in Broadway history). Musical conceived by Michael Bennett; book by James Kirkwood and Nicholas Dante; music by Marvin Hamlisch; lyrics by Edward Kleban. Opened April 15, 1975 off Broadway where it played 101 performances through July 13, 1975; transferred to Broadway July 25, 1975.

*Oh! Calcutta!** (3,777). Revival of the musical devised by Kenneth Tynan; with contributions (in this version) by Jules Feiffer, Dan Greenberg, Lenore Kandel, John Lennon, Jacques Levy, Leonard Melfi, David Newman & Robert Benton, Sam Shepard, Clovis Trouille, Kenneth Tynan and Sherman Yellen; music and lyrics (in this version) by Robert Dennis, Peter Schickele and Stanley Walden; additional music by Stanley Walden and Jacques Levy. Opened September 24, 1976 in alternating performances with *Me and Bessie* through December 7, 1976, continuing alone thereafter.

*42nd Street** (1,990). Musical based on the novel by Bradford Ropes; book by Michael Stewart and Mark Bramble; music and lyrics by Harry Warren and Al Dubin; other lyrics by Johnny Mercer and Mort Dixon. Opened August 25, 1980.

*Dreamgirls** (1,439). Musical with book and lyrics by Tom Eyen; music by Henry Krieger. Opened December 20, 1981.

Torch Song Trilogy (1,222). By Harvey Fierstein. Opened January 12, 1982 off Broadway where it played 117 performances through May 30, 1982; transferred to Broadway June 10, 1982. (Closed May 18, 1985)

*Cats** (1,106). Musical based on *Old Possum's Book of Practical Cats* by T.S. Eliot; music by Andrew Lloyd Webber; additional lyrics by Trevor Nunn and Richard Stilgoe. Opened October 7, 1982.

*Brighton Beach Memoirs (904). By Neil Simon. Opened March 27, 1983.

My One and Only (767). Musical with book by Peter Stone and Timothy S. Mayer; music by George Gershwin from *Funny Face* and other shows; lyrics by Ira Gershwin. Opened May 1, 1983. (Closed March 3, 1985)

*La Cage aux Folles (743). Musical based on the play *La Cage aux Folles* by Jean Poiret; book by Harvey Fierstein; music and lyrics by Jerry Herman. Opened August 21, 1983.

Zorba (354). Revival of the musical based on the novel by Nikos Kazantzakis; book by Joseph Stein; music by John Kander; lyrics by Fred Ebb. Opened October 16, 1983. (Closed September 1, 1984)

Baby (241). Musical based on a story developed by Susan Yankowitz; book by Sybille Pearson; music by David Shire; lyrics by Richard Maltby Jr. Opened December 4, 1983. (Closed July 1, 1984)

Noises Off (553). By Michael Frayn. Opened December 11, 1983. (Closed April 6, 1985)

*The Tap Dance Kid (586). Musical based on the novel *Nobody's Family Is Going to Change* by Louise Fitzhugh; book by Charles Blackwell; music by Henry Krieger; lyrics by Robert Lorick. Opened December 21, 1983.

The Real Thing (566). By Tom Stoppard. Opened January 5, 1984. (Closed May 12, 1985)

The Rink (204). Musical with book by Terrence McNally; music by John Kander; lyrics by Fred Ebb. Opened February 9, 1984. (Closed August 4, 1984)

Glengarry Glen Ross (378). By David Mamet. Opened March 25, 1984. (Closed February 17, 1985)

Death of a Salesman (158). Revival of the play by Arthur Miller. Opened March 29, 1984. (Closed July 1, 1984 after 92 performances) Reopened September 14, 1984. (Closed November 18, 1984)

A Moon for the Misbegotten (40). Revival of the play by Eugene O'Neill. Opened May 1, 1984. (Closed June 9, 1984)

*Sunday in the Park With George (450). Musical with book by James Lapine; music and lyrics by Stephen Sondheim. Opened May 2, 1984.

End of the World (33). By Arthur Kopit. Opened May 6, 1984. (Closed June 2, 1984.

The Wiz (13). Revival of the musical based on *The Wonderful Wizard of Oz* by L. Frank Baum; book by William F. Brown; music and lyrics by Charlie Smalls. Opened May 24, 1984. (Closed June 3, 1984)

PLAYS PRODUCED JUNE 1, 1984–MAY 31, 1985

Gotta Getaway! (151). Musical conceived and created by Stephen Nisbet and James Lecesne; written by James Lecesne; title song by Glen Roven; original music by Marc Elliot, Chip Orton, Gene Palumbo, Marc Shaiman and Eric Watson. Produced by Radio City Music Hall Productions, Richard H. Evans president, at Radio City Music Hall. Opened June 16, 1984. (Closed September 3, 1984)

GOTTA GETAWAY!—The Rockettes in their Statue of Liberty
number in the Music Hall's musical

CAST: Liliane Montevecchi, Tony Azito, Loretta Devine, Alyson Reed, Ron & Joy Holiday.

The Rockettes: Pauline Achillas, Carol Beatty, Katherine Beatty, Dottie Belle, Susan Boron, Elizabeth Chanin, Barbara Ann Cittadino, Susan Cleland, Eileen Collins, Brie Daniels, Prudence Gray Demmler, Susanne Doris, Jackie Fancy, Deniene Fenn, Alexis Ficks, Carol Harbich, Jennifer Hammond, Ginny Hounsell, Cindy Hughes, Joan Peer Kelleher, Pam Kelleher, DeeDee Knapp, Judy Little, Sonya Livingston, Leslie Gryszko McCarthy, Mary McNamara, Barbara Moore, Lynn Newton, Kerri Pearsall, Gerri Presky, Terry Spano, Pamela Stacy Pasqalino, Lynn Sullivan, Susan Theobald, Carol Toman, Patricia Tully, Rose Anne Woolsey, Darlene Wendy.

The Cruisettes: Arminae Azarian, Ellia English, Connie Kunkle, Jacqueline Reilly, Freida Williams.

The Stewards: Ciscoe Bruton, John Clonts, Joe DeGunther, Brian Feehan, Darrell Greene, Marc Hunter, David Michael Johnson, Robert Kellett, Lacy Darryl Phillips, Jeff Shade, Paul Solen, Alan Stuart, John M. Wiltberger.

Understudies: Mr. Azito—Robert Kellett; Misses Montevecchi, Reed—Bonnie Schon; Miss Devine —Arminae Azarian.

Directed and choreographed by Larry Fuller; co-choreographer, Marianne Selbert; musical direction, Gene Palumbo; scenery, Eduardo Sicangco; costumes, Michael Casey; lighting, Clarke W. Thornton; music video, Neil Wagman; orchestrations, Michael Gibson, Bill Brohn; conductor, Robert Billig; vocal arrangements, Gene Palumbo, Robert Billig; dance arrangements, Michael Rice; producer and artistic director, Patricia Morinelli; associate producer, Stephen Nisbet; production manager, Steven Rivellino; production stage manager, Raymond Chandler; stage managers, Howard Kolins, Nelson Wilson, Laurie Clark, Susan Green; press, Neil S. Friedman, Ellen M. Schiebelhuth.

Around the world on a luxury cruise liner, revue-style. The play was presented in two parts.

ACT I

Bon Voyage: Gotta Getaway (video sequence directed by Neil Wagman)—Liliane Montevecchi, Alyson Reed, Loretta Devine, Tony Azito; "Gotta Getaway" music and lyrics by Glen

Roven)—Reed, Devine, Azito; "I'm Throwing a Ball Tonight" (music and lyrics by Cole Porter)—Montevecchi, Reed, Devine, Azito, Rockettes, Cruisettes, Stewards; "Use Your Imagination" (music and lyrics by Cole Porter)—Montevecchi.

Shipshape: "Too Marvelous for Words" (music and lyrics by Richard A. Whiting) and "This Heart of Mine" (music by Harry Warren, lyrics by Arthur Freed)—Reed, John Clonts, Robert Kellett, Brian Feehan, Marc Hunter, Stewards.

50,000 Leagues Under the Sea: "Bubble, Bubble" (music by Gene Palumbo, lyrics by Chip Orton)—Devine, Rockettes, Cruisettes (Mermen—Ciscoe Bruton, Darrell Greene, Jeff Shape, Lacy Phillips; Divers—Azito, David Michael Johnson, Alan Stuart; Sea Nymphs—Rose Anne Woolsey, Ginny Hounsell, Susan Cleland, Jennifer Hammond; Seaweed—Mary McNamara, Judy Little, Katherine Beatty; Mermaids—Beth Chanin, Sonya Livingston, Pat Tully, Lynn Sullivan, Terry Spano).

The Poop Deck: La Cumparcita (by G.H. Matos Rodriquez, original choreography by George Reich)—Montevecchi, Joe DeGunther.

Island Hopping: "Here in Minipoora" (music and lyrics by Marc Elliot and Marc Shaiman)—Azito, Devine, Reed, Rockettes, Stewards, Cruisettes; "Hot VooDoo" (music by Sam Coslow, lyrics by Ralph Rainger)—Montevecchi, Company (Dancing Trees—Carol Beatty, Pam Stacy, Lynn Newton).

ACT II

Ohh, La La Paris: "Hello Beautiful" (by Walter Donaldson)—Azito, Folies Showgirls (Brie Daniels, Spano, Cindy Hughes, Barbara Ann Cittadino, Kerri Pearsall, Carol Beatty, Tully, Leslie Gryszko McCarthy, Newton, Woolsey, Cleland, Prudence Gray Demmler; "Le Dernier Pierrot" (music by Pierre Porte, lyrics by Pascal Sevran)—Montevecchi; "Folies Bergeres" (music and lyrics by Maury Yeston)—Montevecchi, Rockettes, Stewards; "Stairway to Paradise" (music by George Gershwin, lyrics by Ira Gershwin)—Montevecchi, Azito, Rockettes, Stewards.

Up in the Air: "Higher and Higher" (by Gary Jackson, Carl Smith and Raynard Miner)—Cruisettes.

A Wild Holiday: The Holidays—Ron and Joy Holiday and cats.

The Forbidden City: "Come to the Super Market in Old Peking" (music and lyrics by Cole Porter)—Devine; "Peking" (original ballet composed by Eric Watson; masks, Willa Shalit)—Reed, Shade, Stewards, Rockettes.

The Stardeck: "Once You've Seen a Rainbow" (music and lyrics by Gene Palumbo and Chip Orton)—Reed, Devine, Montevecchi.

Land Ho: "Manhattan" (music and lyrics by Marc Elliot and Marc Shaiman)—Azito, Stewards; "Take Good Care of That Lady" (music and lyrics by Marc Shaiman and Marc Elliot)—Devine, Reed, Montevecchi, Azito, Company.

Note: Radio City Music Hall also presented a return engagement of *The Magnificent Christmas Spectacular* for 110 performances 11/16/84–1/10/85; conceived, produced and directed by Robert F. Jani; scenery, Charles Lisanby; costumes, Frank Spencer; lighting, Ken Billington; principal staging, Frank Wagner; staging and choreography, Violet Holmes, Linda Lemac, Frank Wagner; orchestrations, Elman Anderson, Robert M. Freedman, Michael Gibson, Arthur Harris; with a cast of John Cunningham (narrator), Thomas Ruisinger, Edward Prostak, Kimberley Moke, Amy Dolan, Sky Ashley Berdahl, Rickie Cramer, Roie Ward, Joan Cooper-Mirabella, David Roman, Phillip Bond, Lou Ann Csaszar, Michael Booker, Ron Chisholm, Darrell Cooper, The Rockettes, The New Yorkers and The Dancers.

*Circle in the Square Theater. Schedule of three revivals. **Design for Living** (245). By Noel Coward. Opened June 20, 1984. (Closed January 20, 1985) **The Loves of Anatol** (46). By Arthur Schnitzler; adapted by Ellis Rabb and Nicholas Martin. Opened March 6, 1985. (Closed April 14, 1985) ***Arms and the Man** (2). By George Bernard Shaw. Opened May 30, 1985. Produced by Circle in the Square Theater, Theodore Mann artistic director, Paul Libin managing director, at Circle in the Square Theater.

DESIGN FOR LIVING

Gilda......................	Jill Clayburgh	Grace Torrence.................	Lisa Kirk
Ernest Friedman...........	Richard Woods	Henry Carver..........	Robertson Carricart
Otto	Frank Langella	Helen Carver.................	Anne Swift
Leo.........................	Raul Julia	Matthew...................	Arthur French
Miss Hodge	Helena Carroll		

Standbys: Messrs. Julia, Langella—Mart Hulswit; Mr. Woods—Donald Buka. Understudy: Miss Clayburgh—Anne Swift.

Directed by George C. Scott; scenery, Thomas Lynch; costumes, Ann Roth; lighting, Marc B. Weiss; wigs, Paul Huntley; production stage manager, Michael F. Ritchie; stage manager, Ted William Sowa; press, Merle Debuskey, David Roggensack.

Time: 1932. Act I: Otto's studio in Paris. Act II, Scene 1: Leo's flat in London, 18 months later. Scene 2: The same, a few days later. Scene 3: The same, the next morning. Act III, Scene 1: Ernest's apartment in New York, two years later. Scene 2: The same, the next morning.

Design for Living was first produced on Broadway 1/24/33 for 135 performances and was named a Best Play of its season. This is its first major New York revival of record.

Frank Converse replaced Frank Langella 7/31/84; Anne Swift replaced Jill Clayburgh 8/14/84; John Glover replaced Raul Julia 11/13/84; Jim Piddock replaced Frank Converse 12/31/84.

THE LOVES OF ANATOL

Max	Philip Bosco	Franz	Reed Jones
Anatol...................	Stephen Collins	Bianca.....................	Pamela Sousa
Cora; Emilie.............	Mary-Joan Negro	Baron Diebl.................	Kurt Johnson
Johann	Louis Turenne	Flieder	Daniel Southern
Annie; Annette	Valerie Mahaffey	Lady in Black (Dancer).......	Pamela Sousa
Gabrielle; Ilona	Michael Learned	Young Gentleman (Dancer)......	Reed Jones

Gentlemen: Louis Turenne, Kurt Johnson, Daniel Southern.

Understudies: Mr. Collins—Kurt Johnson; Mr. Bosco—Louis Turenne; Misses Learned, Negro, Sousa—Wendy Radford; Miss Mahaffey—Cora-Leah Doyle; Messrs. Jones, Southern, Johnson, Turenne—Mark Fotopoulos.

Directed by Ellis Rabb; musical staging, Donald Saddler; scenery, Lawrence Miller; costumes, Robert Morgan; lighting, Richard Winkler; improvisation on solo piano, John Bayless; music design, Catherine MacDonald; production stage manager, Michael F. Ritchie; stage manager, Ted William Sowa; press, Merle Debuskey, William Schelble.

Time: Before and after the turn of the century. Place: Max's study in Vienna, winter, and in Anatol's memory; then, 20 years later, the terrace of an inn some distance from Vienna, fall. The play was presented in two parts.

ARMS AND THE MAN

Catherine Petkoff...........	Dimitra Arliss	Russian Officer	Guy Paul
Raina Petkoff.............	Glenne Headly	Nicola...................	George Morfogen
Capt. Bluntschli..............	Kevin Kline	Maj. Paul Petkoff	Louis Zorich
Louka....................	Caitlin Clarke	Maj. Sergius Saranoff	Raul Julia

Understudies: Messrs. Kline, Julia—Guy Paul; Misses Headly, Clarke—Debra Engle; Miss Arliss —Joanne Dorian; Messrs. Morfogen, Zorich—Tom Brennan.

Directed by John Malkovich; scenery, Thomas Lynch; costumes, Ann Roth; lighting, Richard Nelson; music, Louis Rosen; production stage manager, Michael F. Ritchie; stage manager, Ted William Sowa.

Act I: Night, a lady's bedchamber in Bulgaria, in a small town near the Dragoman Pass, late November 1885. Act II: Maj. Petkoff's garden, March 1886. Act III: The library after lunch.

The last major New York revival of *Arms and the Man* took place off Broadway 6/22/67 for 189 performances.

Oedipus Rex (8). Revival of the play by Sophocles in the Greek language; translated from ancient to modern Greek by Minos Volanakis. Produced by Mel Howard/World Festival Corp. in association with The American Hellenic Alliance in the Greek National Theater's Epidaurus production at the Vivian Beaumont Theater. Opened July 17, 1984. (Closed July 22, 1984)

Oedipus	Nikos Kourkoulos	Men From Corinth	Theodore Mordid,
Priest	Stathis Samartzis		Kostas Tsapekos
Kreon	Nikos Kavvadas	Shepherd of Laios	Andreas Lazaris
Tiresias	G. Danis	Messenger	Spyros Mavadis, Andreas Vaios
Jocasta	Katerina Helmi	Daughters of Oedipus	Paya Veaki, Lambrini Liva

Chorus Leaders: Christos Biros, Christos Demertzis, Yannis Siopis.

Elders of Thebes: Christos Savvas, Antonis Kouselinis, Prokopis Dourvas, Kostas Petroulakis, Pavlos Orkopoulos, Nikos Kavvadas, Andreas Lazaris, Tasos Samartzis, Spyros Mavidid, Andreas Vaios, Constantine Papalexis, Kostas Apostolidid, Vassilis Kouris.

Directed by Minos Volanakis; assistant directors, Vassilis Kyritsis, George Vouros; music, Theodore Antoniou; scenery, Robert Mitchell; costumes, Dionysis Fotopoulos.

Limited engagement of Greek production, prior to a tour of America and Canada. The last major New York revival of the Sophocles drama was by Classic Stage Company off Broadway 10/16/81 for 58 performances.

Hurlyburly (343). Transfer from off Broadway of the play by David Rabe. Produced by Icarus Productions and Frederick M. Zollo with Ivan Bloch and ERB Productions at the Ethel Barrymore Theater. Opened August 7, 1984. (Closed June 2, 1985)

Phil	Harvey Keitel	Donna	Cynthia Nixon
Eddie	William Hurt	Darlene	Sigourney Weaver
Mickey	Ron Silver	Bonnie	Judith Ivey
Artie	Jerry Stiller		

Standbys: Miss Nixon—Alison Bartlett; Messrs Hurt, Silver—John Christopher Jones; Messrs. Stiller, Keitel—Harris Laskawy; Misses Ivey, Weaver—Natalia Nogulich.

Directed by Mike Nichols; scenery, Tony Walton; costumes, Ann Roth; lighting, Jennifer Tipton; sound, Otts Munderloh; associate producer, William P. Suter; production stage manager, Peter Lawrence; stage manager, Jim Woolley; press, Bill Evans and Associates, Sandra Manley, Jim Baldassare.

Time: A little while ago. Place: A house in the Hollywood Hills. The play was presented in three parts.

Assortment of cocaine-era characters on the fringes of show business, self-destructing in a modern Hollywood environment. Previously produced at the Goodman Theater, Chicago and off Broadway 6/21/84 for 45 performances through 7/29/84; see its entry in the Plays Produced Off Broadway section of this volume.

A Best Play; see page 96.

Candice Bergen replaced Sigourney Weaver 10/23/84; John Christopher Jones replaced William Hurt (Sunday matinees only) 11/18/84; Alison Bartlett replaced Cynthia Nixon 12/10/84; Susan Anton replaced Candice Bergen, John Rubinstein replaced William Hurt, Christine Baranski replaced Judith Ivey and Harris Laskawy replaced Harvey Keitel 1/2/85; John Christopher Jones replaced John Rubinstein 2/5/85; Frank Langella replaced John Christopher Jones 3/12/85; Danny Aiello replaced Harris Laskawy 3/20/85.

Quilters (24). Musical based on *The Quilters: Women and Domestic Art* by Patricia Cooper and Norma Bradley Allen; book by Molly Newman and Barbara Damashek; music and lyrics by Barbara Damashek. Produced by The Denver Center for the Performing Arts, The John F. Kennedy Center for the Performing Arts, the American National

Theater and Academy and Brockman Seawell at the Jack Lawrence Theater. Opened September 25, 1984. (Closed October 14, 1984)

Sarah . . . . Lenka Peterson

The Daughters: Evalyn Baron, Marjorie Berman, Alma Cuervo, Lynn Lobban, Rosemary McNamara, Jennifer Parsons.

Musicians Daughters and Sons: Emily Knapp Chatfield, Melanie Sue Harby, John S. Lionarons, Joseph A. Waterkotte, Catherine Way.

Understudies: Miss Peterson—Eda Seasongood; Daughters—Catherine Way, Eda Seasongood, Jennifer Parsons, Rosemary McNamara, Lynn Lobban, Alma Cuervo.

Directed by Barbara Damashek; scenery, Ursula Belden; costumes, Elizabeth Palmer; lighting, Allen Lee Hughes; production stage manager, Bruce A. Hoover; press, Patt Dale Associates, Julianne Waldheim.

The story of American pioneer women as suggested by the patterns in the quilts they made. Previously produced by The Denver Center Theater Company and in Washington and Los Angeles.

MUSICAL NUMBERS, ACT I: "Pieces of Lives" (first four lines from *The Quilt* by Dorothy MacFarlane), "Rocky Road," "Little Babes That Sleep All Night" (lyrics from *Our Homes and Their Adornments* by Almon C. Varney), "Thread the Needle," "Cornelia," "The Windmill Song," "Are You Washed in the Blood of the Lamb" (by E.A. Hoffman), "The Butterfly," "Pieces of Lives" (Reprise), "Green, Green, Green," "The Needle's Eye" (chorus from the lyric of a traditional folk song).

ACT II: "Hoedown" (traditional), "Quiltin' and Dreamin'," "Pieces of Lives" (Reprise), "Every Log in My House" (first line by Eleanor Pruitt Stewart), "Land Where We'll Never Grow Old" (by J.C. Moore), "Who Will Count the Stitches?", "The Lord Don't Rain Down Manna, "Dandelion" (lyrics by Clara J. Denton from the poem *Blooming in the Fall*), "Everything Has a Time," "Hands Around."

Kipling (12). One-performer play by Brian Clark; based on the works of Rudyard Kipling; with Alec McCowen. Produced by Roy A. Somlyo at the Royale Theater. Opened October 10, 1984. (Closed October 21, 1984)

Directed by Patrick Garland; design, Pamela Howard; lighting, Neil Peter Jampolis; production stage manager, Thomas A. Kelly; press, Michael Alpert Public Relations.

Alec McCowen as Rudyard Kipling in a foreign play previously produced in London and including quotations from collected letters and *Something of Myself* as well as from the following material presented in two parts.

PART I: *The Ballad of East and West, If, The White Man's Burden, Gentlemen-Rankers, Gunga Din, The Way Through the Woods, Mandalay, Boots, Recessional, Sussex, The Appeal,* "The Elephant's Child" (from *Just-So Stories*), *I Keep Six Honest Serving Men,* "Ba Ba Black Sheep" (from *Wee Willie Winkie*), *The Way Through the Woods, Kim, If,* "The Flag of Their Country" (from *Stalky and Co.*), *Mesopotamia, The Ladies, That Day, Gentlemen-Rankers, Cells.*

PART II: *Tommy,* "The Friendly Brook" (from *A Diversity of Creatures*), "The Devil and the Deep Sea (from *The Day's Work*), *The Settler, Gunga Din, Chant Pagan, Gethsemane 1914–18, Epitaphs of the War 1914–18, The Children, The Storm Cone 1932, The Waster, The Law of the Jungle, When 'Omer Smote . . . , The Ballad of East and West, When Earth's Last Picture Is Painted, The Children's Song.*

*Ma Rainey's Black Bottom (265). By August Wilson. Produced by Ivan Bloch, Robert Cole and Frederick M. Zollo in the Yale Repertory Theater production at the Cort Theater. Opened October 11, 1984.

Sturdyvant	John Carpenter	Toledo	Robert Judd
Irvin	Lou Criscuolo	Slow Drag	Leonard Jackson
Cutler	Joe Seneca	Levee	Charles S. Dutton

Ma Rainey................ Theresa Merritt   Sylvester......... Scott Davenport-Richards
Dussie Mae .... Aleta Mitchell   Policeman............. Christopher Loomis

Understudies: Messrs. Carpenter, Criscuolo, Loomis—Peter Boyden; Mr. Seneca—Bill Cobbs; Messrs. Jackson, Judd—Arthur French; Misses Merritt, Mitchell—Ebony Jo-Ann; Messrs. Dutton, Davenport-Richards—Brent Jennings.

Directed by Lloyd Richards; scenery, Charles Henry McClennahan; costumes, Daphne Pascucci; lighting, Peter Maradudin; musical direction, Dwight Andrews; sound, Jan Nebozenko; associate producers, Bart Berman, Hart Productions, William P. Suter; production stage manager, Mortimer Halpern; stage manager, K. White; press, Jeffrey Richards Associates, C. George Willard, Robert Ganshaw.

Time: Early March 1927. Place: The bandroom and recording studio of a record company in Chicago, the "race" division. The play was presented in two parts.

Recording session by a black blues singer and accompanists for a white-owned and operated studio gives rise to a drama of racial relations and conflicts as they once existed. Previously produced in a staged reading at the National Playwrights' Conference of the Eugene O'Neill Theater Center, Waterford, Conn. and at the Yale Repertory Theater in New Haven.

A Best Play; see page 124.

Royal Shakespeare Company. Repertory of two revivals. **Much Ado About Nothing** (53). By William Shakespeare. Opened October 14, 1984. **Cyrano de Bergerac** (59). By Edmond Rostand; newly translated and adapted by Anthony Burgess. Opened October 16, 1984. Produced by James M. Nederlander, Elizabeth I. McCann, Nelle Nugent, Cynthia Wood, Dale Duffy and Allan Carr in the Royal Shakespeare Company production, Terry Hands and Trevor Nunn joint artistic directors, at the Gershwin Theater. (Repertory closed January 19, 1985)

PERFORMER	"MUCH ADO ABOUT NOTHING"	"CYRANO DE BERGERAC"
Penelope Beaumont		Precieuse; Lise; Mother Marguerite
Christopher Benjamin	Dogberry	Montfleury
Ken Bones	Don Pedro	Jaloux
John Bowe	Conrade	Le Bret
Christopher Bowen	Count Claudio	Valvert; Gascony Cadet
Raymond Bowers		Jodelet; Renaudot
Alexandra Brook	Margaret	Flower Girl; Sister Claire
John Carlisle	Don John	De Guiche
Amy Chang	(Boy)	(Page)
Robert Clare		D'Artagnan; Gascony Cadet
Simon Clark	4th Watch	Citizen
Richard Clifford	Lord	Cavalryman; Gascony Cadet
Dennis Clinton	Hugh Oatcake	Cuigy
Robert Craig	(Balthasar)	
Sinead Cusack	Beatrice	Roxane
Philip Dennis	(Balthasar)	Flunkey; Gascony Cadet
Jeffery Dench	Antonio	Marquis
Cathy Finlay	Ursula	Food Seller; Sister Marthe
Alex Flagg		Page
Geoffrey Freshwater	Borachio	Musketeer
Jimmy Gardner	Verges	Doorkeeper; Capuchin
David Glover		Marquis
Derek Jacobi	Benedick	Cyrano de Bergerac
Edward Jewesbury	Leonato	Brisaille
Ray Llewellyn	Sexton	Pickpocket
Tom Mannion	3d Watch	Christian

PERFORMER	"MUCH ADO ABOUT NOTHING"	"CYRANO DE BERGERAC"
Samuel Schueffelin Nordberg	(Boy)	(Page)
Niall Padden		Eater; Gascony Cadet
George Parsons	Friar Francis	Ligniere
Brenda Peters		Duenna
Pete Postlethwaite		Ragueneau
Clare Byam Shaw	Hero	Precieuse
David Shaw-Parker	George Seacoal	Bellerose
Jayne Tottman	Josetta	Citizen's Son
John Tramper		Gascony Cadet; Flunkey
Phillip Walsh		Drinker; Gascony Cadet

(Parentheses indicate roles in which the performers alternated)

BOTH PLAYS: Directed by Terry Hands; scenery, Ralph Koltai; costumes, Alexander Reid; music, Nigel Hess; lighting, Terry Hands; American production designed in association with John Kasarda, scenery, and Jeffrey Beecroft, lighting; musical direction, Donald Johnston; sound supervision, T. Richardson Fitzgerald; assistant director, Brigid Larmour; choreography, Doreen Hermitage; company stage manager, Jane Tamlyn; production stage manager, Alan Hall; press, Solters/Roskin/Friedman, Inc., Joshua Ellis, Adrian Bryan-Brown, Keith Sherman, Cindy Valk.

MUCH ADO ABOUT NOTHING: Understudies: Miss Cusack—Alexandra Brook; Misses Shaw, Brook—Cathy Finlay; Miss Finlay—Jayne Tottman; Mr. Jacobi—John Bowe; Messrs. Freshwater, Dennis—Simon Clark; Messrs. Bones, Bowe—Richard Clifford; Messrs. Dench, Parsons—Dennis Clinton; Mr. Llewellyn—Philip Dennis; Mr. Jewesbury—Ray Llewellyn; Mr. Bowen—Tom Mannion; Mr. Carlisle—George Parsons; Messrs. Benjamin, Gardner—David Shaw-Parker.

Musicians: Donald Johnston keyboards; Jacqueline Giat flute, piccolo, recorder; Mathew Goodman clarinet; Bruce Uchitel guitar; Luann Montesi violin; Joan Spergel cello; Brooks Tillotson, Richard Hagen, horn; Dennis Elliot associate conductor, trombone; Gregory Maker double bass; Michael Hinton, Jan Hagiwara percussion.

Fencing consultant, Ian McKay; stage manager, Vikki Heywood.

The play was presented in two parts. The last major New York revival of *Much Ado About Nothing* was by New York Shakespeare Festival in Central Park (with musical numbers by Peter Link added) 8/10/72 for 20 performances and transferred to Broadway 11/11/72 for 136 additional performances.

CYRANO DE BERGERAC: Understudies: Miss Peters—Penelope Beaumont; Miss Beaumont (Duenna)—Alexandra Brook; Miss Cusack—Clare Byam Shaw; Miss Beaumont (Mother Marguerite)—Brenda Peters; Misses Finlay, Brook—Jayne Tottman; Mr. Jacobi—Ken Bones; Mr. Mannion—Christopher Bowen; Mr. Postlethwaite—Raymond Bowers; Messrs. Bowe, Bowen—Robert Clare; Messrs. Bones, Benjamin—Simon Clark; Mr. Carlisle—Richard Clifford; Messrs. Clark, Gardner (Capuchin)—Ray Llewellyn; Mr. Freshwater—Niall Padden; Messrs. Gardner (Doorkeeper) Bowers—David Shaw-Parker; Messrs. Clare, Bowers, Shaw-Parker—John Tramper; Messrs. Parsons, Llewellyn, Clifford—Phillip Walsh.

Musicians: Jacqueline Giat flute, recorder; Harriet Orenstein oboe; Mathew Goodman clarinet; Richard Henly, Robert Zottola trumpet; Brooks Tillotson, Richard Hagen horn; Dennis Elliot associate conductor, trombone; Joan Spergel cello; Gregory Maker double bass; Bruce Uchitel guitar; Michael Hinton, Jan Hagiwara percussion.

Fight arranger, Ian McKay; Cyrano's nose, Christopher Tucker; stage manager, Michael Dembowicz.

Act I: The Hotel de Bourgogne, Paris, an indoor tennis court converted into a theater, an evening in 1640. Act II: Ragueneau's pastry shop, the next morning. Act III: The courtyard outside Roxane's house some weeks later. Act IV: The battlefield at the siege of Arras, some days later. Act V: The garden of a convent, 15 years later. The play was presented in two parts.

The last major New York revival of *Cyrano de Bergerac* was in a Broadway musical version entitled *Cyrano* 5/13/73 for 49 performances.

ROYAL SHAKESPEARE—*Above,* Sinead Cusack as Roxane, Tom Mannion as Christian and Derek Jacobi as Cyrano in *Cyrano de Bergerac* and *on opposite page,* Sinead Cusack as Beatrice and Derek Jacobi as Benedick in *Much Ado About Nothing* in the two-play repertory of the distinguished visiting troupe

Alone Together (97). By Lawrence Roman. Produced by Arnold Mittelman and Lynne Peyser at The Music Box. Opened October 21, 1984. (Closed January 12, 1985)

George Butler	Kevin McCarthy	Michael Butler	Don Howard
Helene Butler	Janis Paige	Elliott Butler	Kevin O'Rourke
Keith Butler	Dennis Drake	Janie Johnson	Alexandra Gersten

Standbys: Miss Paige—Tudi Wiggins; Mr. McCarthy—George Guidall. Understudies: Messrs. Howard, O'Rourke, Drake—William Fichtner; Miss Gersten—Mary Ellen Stuart.

Directed by Arnold Mittelman; scenery, Karl Eigsti; costumes, Jane Greenwood; lighting, Arden Fingerhut; production stage manager, Larry Forde; stage manager, Mark Rubinsky; press, Mark Goldstaub Public Relations, Kevin P. McAnarney, Philip Butler, Daniel Kellachan.

Time: The present. Place: The Butler home in Los Angeles. Act I, Scene 1: A September morning. Scene 2: That evening. Scene 3: A few days later. Act II, Scene 1: A few days later. Scene 2: A few hours later. Scene 3: Four days later.

Domestic comedy, three sons return to the family fold, escaping the hard knocks of the outside world. Previously produced in regional theater, Montclair, N.J.

Whoopi Goldberg (148). One-woman show with Whoopi Goldberg. Produced by Mike Nichols, Emanuel Azenberg and The Shubert Organization at the Lyceum Theater. Opened October 24, 1984. (Closed March 10, 1985)

Production supervised by Mike Nichols; visual consultant, Tony Walton; lighting, Jennifer Tipton; sound, Otts Munderloh; production supervisor, Martin Herzer; stage manager, Lisa M. Hogarty; press, Bill Evans and Associates, Sandra Manley, Jim Baldassare.

Six comic-dramatic character sketches in monologue. The show was presented in two parts.

The Three Musketeers (9). Revival of the musical with book by William Anthony McGuire; music by Rudolf Friml; lyrics by P.G. Wodehouse and Clifford Grey; new version by Mark Bramble. Produced by Irvin Feld, Kenneth Feld, Ina Lee Meibach and Jerome Minskoff at the Broadway Theater. Opened November 11, 1984. (Closed November 18, 1984)

Queen Anne of France . . . . . . Darlene Anders	Cardinal Richelieu . . . . Ed Dixon
Lady Constance Bonacieux . . . . Liz Callaway	Sgt. Jussac . . . . Raymond Patterson

Innkeeper; Selenus;
Major Domo............. J.P. Dougherty
Duke of Buckingham .... Joseph Kolinski
Comte de la Rochefort.... Michael Dantuono
Milady de Winter .... Marianne Tatum
D'Artagnan .... Michael Praed
Athos .... Chuck Wagner
Aramis .... Brent Spiner

Porthos...................... Ron Taylor
Laundress; Tavern Wench ... Susan Goodman
De Beauverais .... Steve Dunnington
Capt. Treville................ Peter Samuel
King Louis XIII .... Roy Brooksmith
Chambermaid................ Elisa Fiorillo
Patrick .... Perry Arthur

The Cardinal's Guards: Bill Badolato, Steve Dunnington, Craig Heath Nim, Steve Marder, Mark McGrath, Sal Viviano, Faruma Williams.

Citizens of Poissy, Paris, Calais; The King's Musketeers, etc.: Janet Aldrich, Perry Arthur, Bill Badolato, Tina Belis, Steven Blanchard, Steve Dunnington, Elisa Fiorillo, Terri Garcia, Susan Goodman, Patty Holley, Jeff Johnson, Steve Marder, Mark McGrath, Craig Heath Nim, Suzan Postel, Wynonna Smith, Sal Viviano, Faruma Williams, Sandra Zigars.

Understudies: Mr. Praed—Jeff Johnson; Mr. Wagner—Mark McGrath; Mr. Taylor—Peter Samuel; Mr. Spiner—Steven Blanchard; Miss Callaway—Elisa Fiorillo, Janet Aldrich; Miss Anders—Suzan Postel; Mr. Dantuono—Craig Heath Nim; Mr. Dixon—Peter Samuel; Mr. Kolinski—Sal Viviano; Mr. Patterson—Faruma Williams; Mr. Brocksmith—J.P. Dougherty; Miss Goodman—Patty Holley; Miss Tatum—Janet Aldrich; Mr. Dougherty—Mark McGrath; Mr. Samuel—Craig Heath Nim; Swings—De Dwight Baxter, Kirsti Carnahan, Craig Frawley, Jacqueline Smith-Lee.

Directed by Joe Layton; choreography, Lester Wilson; scenery, Nancy Winters; costumes, Freddy Wittop; lighting, Ken Billington; sound, Jan Nebozenko; music adapted, arranged and supervised and vocal and fight arrangements, Kirk Nurock; conductor, Gordon Lowry Harrell; orchestrations, Larry Wilcox; dance arrangements, Wally Harper, Mark Hummel; fights, Steve Dunnington; production stage manager, Steven Zweigbaum; stage manager, Arturo E. Porazzi; press, Judy Jacksina, Glenna Freedman, Marcy Granata, Susan Chicoine, Marc P. Thibodeau, Kevin Boyle, Jane Steinberg.

Time: 1626. Place: France and England.

This musical version of the Alexandre Dumas novel was first produced on Broadway 3/13/28 for 318 performances. This version with a new book is its first major New York revival and was previously produced in regional theater in Stamford, Conn.

ACT I

Scene 1: France, April, 1626
    Prologue.................... Three Musketeers, King, Treville, Queen, Constance, Jussac,
                            Innkeeper, Buckingham, Rochefort, Milady, D'Artagnan
Scene 2: Poissy, a market town outside Paris
    "Gascony Bred"..................................... D'Artagnan, Innkeeper, Company
    "All for One"... Three Musketeers
    "Only a Rose" .... D'Artagnan, Constance
    "My Sword and I"... D'Artagnan, Company
Scene 3: Paris the night of All Fools Eve
    Carnival of Fools .... Company
Scene 4: Garden at the Convent of Carmier
    "L'Amour Toujours-L'Amour"................................. Buckingham, Queen
Scene 5: Streets of Paris
    "Come to Us"... Milady, Jussac
Scene 6: The laundry at Number 7 Rue de Colombier
    "March of the Musketeers"................... Three Musketeers, D'Artagnan, Company
Scene 7: The Cardinal's chamber in the Louvre
    "Bless My Soul"..................................... Cardinal, Milady, Rochefort
Scene 8: Garden of the Tuileries
    "Only a Rose" (Reprise) .... Constance, D'Artagnan, Company
Scene 9: Palace corridor into the great hall
Scene 10: On the road to Calais
    Act I Finale................................. D'Artagnan, Three Musketeers, Company

ACT II

Scene 1: The Golden Lily Tavern, Calais
"Vive la France"... King, Company
"The Actor's Life"................................. Three Musketeers, D'Artagnan
"My Belle" .... D'Artagnan, Constance
Scene 2: Streets of Calais and the ship to England
"The Chase".. Company
"My Belle" (Reprise)................................ D'Artagnan, Three Musketeers
Scene 3: The Duke of Buckingham's castle in England
"Dreams" .... Buckingham
Scene 4: Milady's bedroom at the Golden Lily Tavern, Calais
"L'Amour Toujours-L'Amour" (Reprise) .... Milady
Scene 5: The road to Paris
"All for One" (Reprise)............................ Three Musketeers, D'Artagnan
Scene 6: All over Paris
"Gossip" .... Three Musketeers, D'Artagnan, Milady, Jussac, Cardinal,
Constance, Treville, King, Queen, Company
Scene 7: The Hotel de Ville
Finale... Company

Accidental Death of an Anarchist (20). By Dario Fo; adapted by Richard Nelson. Produced by Alexander H. Cohen and Hildy Parks at the Belasco Theater. Opened November 15, 1984. (Closed December 1, 1984)

The Fool	Jonathan Pryce	Capt. Pisani	Joe Grifasi
The Sergeant	Bill Irwin	Chief Bellati	Raymond Serra
Inspector Bertozzo	Gerry Bamman	Reporter	Patti LuPone

Standbys: Mr. Pryce—Seth Allen; Messrs. Irwin, Bamman—Robert Fitch. Understudies: Messrs. Grifasi, Serra—Frank Biancamano; Miss LuPone—Maia Danziger.

Directed by Douglas C. Wager; scenery, Karl Eigsti; costumes, Patricia Zipprodt; lighting, Allen Lee Hughes; co-producer, Bernard Gersten; production stage manager, Robert L. Borod; stage manager, Marc Schlackman; press, Merle Debuskey, William Schelble.

Act I, Scene 1: Rome, Italy—Central Police Headquarters 2d floor office. Scene 2: The same building, 4th floor office. Act II: later that day.

Mysterious death in custody of an accused terrorist is investigated, to the detriment of the authorities. Previously produced in this adaptation by Arena Stage, Washington, D.C. A foreign play previously produced in Italy and London.

Haarlem Nocturne (49). Cabaret revue conceived by Andre De Shields; written by Andre De Shields and Murray Horwitz (see additional authors' credits in list of musical numbers and sketches). Produced by Barry and Fran Weissler at the Latin Quarter. Opened November 18, 1984. (Closed December 30, 1984)

Debra Byrd	Marc Shaiman
Andre De Shields	Freida Williams
Ellia English	

Orchestra: Marc Shaiman piano, Kenyatte Abdur-Rahman percussion, Brian Grice drums, Louis Cortelezzi woodwinds, Jeffrey Ganz bass, Marc Ribot guitar.

Directed by Andre De Shields and Murray Horwitz; musical direction, orchestrations and vocal arrangements, Marc Shaiman; scenery and club interiors, David Chapman; costumes, Jean-Claude Robin; lighting, Marc B. Weiss; sound, Bill Dreisbach; assistant to directors, Gary Sullivan; associate producer, Alecia Parker; production stage manager, Bruce H. Lumpkin; stage manager, Meryl Vladimer; press, Jacqueline Burnham, Edward Callaghan, Merle Frimark.

Collection of songs and sketches presented cabaret-style, previously produced off off Broadway at

LaMama ETC by special arrangement with Black Goat Entertainment. The show was presented without intermission.

MUSICAL NUMBERS AND SKETCHES: "Love in the Morning" (music and lyrics by Steven Lemberg)—Andre De Shields, Ladies; "Wishful Thinking" (music and lyrics by Kenny Moore, Marti McCall and Zedrick Turnbough)—De Shields, Ladies; "New York Is a Party" (music by Marc Shaiman, lyrics by Robert I)—De Shields, Ladies; "Jungle Hip Hop" (music and lyrics by Andre De Shields)—De Shields, Ladies; "Sweet Dreams (Are Made of This" (music by Annie Lennox, lyrics by D.A. Stewart)—Ladies; "What Becomes of the Broken Hearted" (music and lyrics by W. Witherspoon, P. Riser and J. Dean)—De Shields, Ladies; "Love's Sad Glance" (music by Marc Shaiman, lyrics by Ula Hedwig)—Ladies; "Secret Love" (music by Kenny Moore, lyrics by Alex Brown)—Debra Byrd, Ladies; "Say It Again" (music and lyrics by Dennis Andreopoulos)—Freida Williams, Ladies; "Heads or Tails" (music and lyrics by Dennis Andreopoulos)—De Shields, Ladies; "Hit the Road Jack" (music and lyrics by Percy Mayfield) Ellia English, De Shields, Ladies: "Water-faucet Blues"—English.

Also Streetcorner Symphony—De Shields, Ladies; "Release Yourself" (lyrics by Larry Graham), "Bad Boy" (music and lyrics by Lil Armstrong), "Symphony Rap" (music and lyrics by Andre De Shields)—De Shields, Ladies; "Mary Mack"—De Shields, Freida Williams, Ladies; Pastiche (by Alan Bergman, Marvin Hamlisch, Marilyn Keith, Eddie Holland, Brian Holland, Lamont Dozier, Jeff Barry, Ellie Greenwich, Phil Spector, Rudy Clark, Cynthia Weil, Barry Mann, Bob Feldman, Gerald Goldstein, Richard Gottehrer, George Morton, Gene Pitney, Tony Powers, Carole King, Gerald Goffin, Florence Green, Luther Dixon, Burt Bacharach, Hal David, Ronald Mack, George Harrison, Robert Bateman, Freddie Gorman, Burt Russell, Thomas Elliot, Andrew Lloyd Webber, Trevor Nunn)—Ladies; Sermon (by Murray Horwitz and Andre De Shields)—De Shields; "Harlem Nocturne" (music by Earle Hagen, lyrics by Dick Rogers)—Ladies; "B.Y.O.B." (music and lyrics by Andre De Shields)—De Shields, Ladies; "Now Is the Time" (music and lyrics by Andre De Shields)—De Shields, Ladies.

Doug Henning and His World of Magic (56). Magic show conceived by Doug Henning; music by Peter Matz. Produced by James M. Nederlander and Arthur Rubin at the Lunt-Fontanne Theater. Opened December 11, 1984. (Closed January 27, 1985)

CAST: Doug Henning, Debby Henning; Magical Dancers—Victor Heineman, D.J. Mergenthaler, Gina Rose, Kathleen White.

Directed by Doug Henning; staged and choreographed by Charlene Painter; musical direction, Peter Matz; scenery, Bill Bohnert; costumes, Jef Billings; lighting, Michael McGiveney; music designer and coordinator, Jim Steinmeyer; head illusion engineer, William Kennedy; illusion design and construction, John Gaughan; additional illusion construction, William Kennedy; magical consultant, Charles Reynolds; animal training and management, Rick Glassey; illusion engineers, Jon Sipos, Wayne Saks, Frank Carra; sound engineer, Bud Beauchamp; assistant choreographer, Victor Heineman; additional costumes, Bill Hargate; stage manager, Michael McGiveney; press, Michael Alpert Public Relations, Ruth Jaffe.

Series of Doug Henning magic acts with a few production frills, previously produced in a cross-country tour of the U.S. The show was presented in two parts.

Home Front (13). By James Duff. Produced by Richard Barr, Charles Woodward and David Bixler at the Royale Theater. Opened January 2, 1985. (Closed January 12, 1985)

Bob . . . . Carroll O'Connor
Maurine . . . . Frances Sternhagen
Jeremy . . . . Christopher Fields
Karen . . . . Linda Cook

Standbys: Mr. O'Connor—David Leary; Miss Sternhagen—Estelle Kemler. Understudies: Miss Cook—Debbie Silver; Mr. Fields—Steven Weber.

Directed by Michael Attenborough; scenery, Sue Plummer, adapted for Broadway by Frank J. Boros; costumes, John Falabella; lighting, Ken Billington; associate producer, Peter Jedlin; production stage manager, Donald Walters; stage manager, Michael Kasdan; press, Shirley Herz, Sam Rudy, Peter Cromarty.

HOME FRONT—Frances Sternhagen and Carroll O'Connor in the play by James Duff

Time: Thanksgiving Day, 1973. Place: Suburban Dallas-Fort Worth. Act I, Scene 1: Thanksgiving Eve. Scene 2: Early the next morning. Act II, Scene 1: Four hours later. Scene 2: Later that afternoon.

Distressed family cannot assimilate its distressed son, a veteran of the Vietnam war. An American play previously produced in London.

Dancing in the End Zone (28). By Bill C. Davis. Produced by Morton Gottlieb in association with Sally Sears at the Ritz Theater. Opened January 3, 1985. (Closed January 26, 1985)

James Bernard	Matt Salinger	Dick Biehn	Laurence Luckinbill
Madeleine Bernard	Pat Carroll	Jan Morrison	Dorothy Lyman

Understudies: Mr. Luckinbill—Brian Evers; Mr. Salinger—Gavin Troster; Miss Lyman—Jill Larson.

Directed by Melvin Bernhardt; scenery, Douglas W. Schmidt; costumes, Patricia McGourty; lighting, Dennis Parichy; associate producers, Richard Seader, Ben Rosenberg, Milly Schoenbaum; production stage manager, Duane Mazey; stage manager, Warren Crane; press, Milly Schoenbaum, Leo Stern.

Place: A Midwestern university town. The play was presented in two parts.

Parting of the ways between a talented quarterback and the coach who seeks victory at all costs, even permanent injury to his players. Previously produced at the Coconut Grove, Fla., Playhouse.

*The King and I (163). Revival of the musical based on the novel *Anna and the King of Siam* by Margaret Landon; book and lyrics by Oscar Hammerstein II; music by Richard Rodgers. Produced by the Mitch Leigh Company at the Broadway Theater. Opened January 7, 1985.

Louis Leonowens	Jeffrey Bryan Davis	Lady Thiang	Irma-Estel LaGuerre
Capt. Orton	Burt Edwards	Prince Chulalongkorn	Araby Abaya
Anna Leonowens	Mary Beth Peil	Princess Ying	Yvette Laura Martin
Interpreter	Jae Woo Lee	Fan Dancer; Angel	Patricia Weber
Kralahome	Jonathan Farwell	Sir Edward	Edward Crotty
King	Yul Brynner	Uncle Thomas	Hope Sogawa
Lead Royal Dancer;		Little Eva	Evelina Deocares
Eliza	Kathy Lee Brynner	Topsy	Deborah Harada
Lun Tha	Sal Provenza	Simon	Rebecca West
Tuptim	Patricia Welch		

Royal Dancers and Wives: Maria F. Bingham, Young-Hee Cho, Carolyn DeLany, Evelina Deocares, Deborah Harada, Valerie Lau-Kee, Suzen Murakoshi, Hope Sogawa, Sylvia Yamada.

Princes and Princesses: Max Barabas, Michael Bulos, Caroline Ann Cabrera, Lisa Chui, Jamie Chung, Mark Damrongsri, Kate Gwon, Tracie Mon-Ting Lee, Michelle Nigalan, Steven Tom, Luke Trainer.

Nurses and Amazons: Alis-Elaine Anderson, Joyce Campana, Mariann Cook, Janet Jordan.

Priests and Slaves: Cornel Chan, Kaipo Daniels, Gary Bain Domasin, Stanley Earl Harrison, Thomas Heath, Andre Lengyel, Ron Stefan.

Standby: Mr. Brynner—Jonathan Farwell. Understudies: Miss Peil—Mariann Cook; Mr. Edwards—Edward Crotty; Mr. Davis—Luke Trainer; Mr. Lee—Kaipo Daniels; Mr. Farwell—Jae Woo Lee; Miss Welch—Carolyn DeLany; Miss LaGuerre—Joyce Campana; Mr. Abaya—Michael Bulos; Miss Martin—Tracie Mon-Ting Lee; Mr. Provenza—Thomas Heath; Mr. Crotty—Burt Edwards; Miss Weber—Deborah Harada; Miss Brynner (Lead Royal Dancer)—Evelina Deocares; Miss Brynner (Eliza)—Sylvia Yamada; Miss West—Thom Cordeiro Kam; Miss Harada—Sandy Sueoka; Miss Sogawa—Maria F. Bingham; Miss Deocares—Young-Hee Cho; Swings—Sandy Sueoka, Thom Cordeiro Kam.

Directed by Mitch Leigh; original choreography, Jerome Robbins; choreography reproduced by Rebecca West; musical direction, Richard Parrinello; scenery, Peter Wolf; costumes, Stanley Simmons; lighting, Ruth Roberts; sound, Scott Marcellus; original costume designs, Irene Sharaff; production supervision, Conwell Worthington II; producer, Mitch Leigh; executive producer, Milton Herson; associate producer, Manny Kladitis; production stage manager, Kenneth L. Peck; stage managers, John W. Galo, Charles Reif; press, Solters/Roskin/Friedman, Inc., Joshua Ellis, Susan E. Lee.

Time: The 1860s. Place: In and around the King's palace, Bangkok, Siam. The play was presented in two parts.

The King and I was first produced on Broadway 3/29/51 for 1,246 performances. Its most recent major New York revival was on Broadway 5/2/77 for 696 performances with Yul Brynner in the role of the King.

The list of musical numbers in *The King and I* appears on page 361 of *The Best Plays of 1950–51.*

Streetheat (20). Cabaret revue based on an original concept by Michele Assaf and Rick Atwell (see authors' credits in list of musical numbers). Produced by Bert Stratford Productions in association with Gene Cates, Doug Leeds, Christine Mortimer Biddle and Rex Farr at the 54th Street Theater Cabaret. Opened January 27, 1985. (Closed February 24, 1985)

Spinner	Michael DeLorenzo	Character Man	Ron Lee Savin
Leon	James Arthur Johnson	Lucky Louie	Glenn Scarpelli
Victoria	Vicki Lewis	Picasso	Tico Wells

Ensemble: Bryant Baldwin, Nora Cherry, Cecilia Marta, Troy Myers, Rick Negron, Daryl Richardson, Louis Ritarossi, Robin Summerfield, Jorge Vaszuez.

Understudies: Messrs. Wells, Johnson—Rick Negron; Messrs. DeLorenzo, Scarpelli—Louis Ritarossi; Miss Lewis—Aimee Covo; Swings—Aimee Covo, Alan Stuart.

Directed and choreographed by Rick Atwell; music and songs produced by Michael G. Millius, James Gregory; songs developed and supervised by Michael G. Millius; scenery and costumes, Franne Lee; lighting, John McLain; sound, Bob Kerzman; orchestrations, dance arrangements, underscoring, special music, Frank Owens, James Gregory; associate producer, Judee Wales; production stage manager, Mark Baltazar; stage manager, Eric J. Scheps; press, Betty Lee Hunt, Maria Cristina Pucci, James Sapp.

Revue self-described as "a modern-day dream story of New York City's 'now' culture," presented without intermission.

MUSICAL NUMBERS: "We Paint Life" (by Rick Atwell and Perry Arthur Kroeger), "Picasso's Theme" (by Frank Owens), "Uptown Dreamer's Express" (by James Gregory and Rick Atwell), "Hold On" (by Chris Darway), "To Dance Is to Fly" (by Kyra Kaptzan), "Power" (by Vinnie Rich and Dave Moritz), "I'm a Wow" (by Ron Abel and Bob Garrett), "Lucky Louie" (by Frank Owens, Rick Atwell and Perry Arthur Kroeger), "Full Circle" (by Laura Taylor and Charles Mortimer), "Streetheat" (by James Gregory, Charles Mortimer and William Hocher), "I Want A Real Man" (by Geoff Bradford), "Sacrifice Your Body" (by James Gregory, Charles Mortimer and Rick Atwell), "The King Becomes a Clown" (by Laura Taylor), "Nirvana" (by James Gregory and Perry Arthur Kroeger), "Danger Men Working" (by Bob Garrett and Joe Curiale), "Today I Found Me" (by Laura Taylor), "Power" (Reprise), "Full Circle" (Reprise), "The Power Lies Within" (by James Gregory, Joe Hudson and Rick Atwell).

Harrigan 'n Hart (5). Musical based on material compiled by Nedda Harrigan Logan and *The Merry Partners* by E.J. Kahn Jr.; book by Michael Stewart; music by Max Showalter; lyrics by Peter Walker; songs of the period by Edward Harrigan and David Braham. Produced by Elliot Martin, Arnold Bernhard and The Shubert Organization at the Longacre Theater. Opened January 31, 1985. (Closed February 3, 1985)

Stetson; Andrew LeCouvrier;	Martin Hanley............. Oliver Woodall
Judge; Johnny Wild; Captain;	Alfred J. Dugan; Harry Mack;
William Gill .... Mark Fotopoulos	Judge Hilton; Doctor.... Christopher Wells
Edward Harrigan .... Harry Groener	Annie Braham Harrigan........ Tudi Roche
Tony Hart .... Mark Hamill	Chester Fox; Photographer; Newsboy;
Archie White; Sam Nichols;	Newspaperman .... Kenston Ames
Felix Barker; Uncle Albert ... Clent Bowers	Lily Fay; Adelaide Harrigan;
Old Colonel; Billy Gross;	Nurse................ Merilee Magnuson
Nat Goodwin .... Cleve Asbury	Mrs. Annie Yeamons ..... Armelia McQueen
Colonel's Wife; Elsie Fay;	Jennie Yeamons; Newsgirl .. Amelia Marshall
Belle.................... Barbara Moroz	Gerta Granville.......... Christine Ebersole
Eleanor; Ada Lewis........... Roxie Lucas	

Orchestra: Peter Howard conductor; Irving Berger trumpet; Bruce Doctor percussion; Bill Ellison double bass; Jack Gale trombone; Scott Kuney banjo, mandolin; Robert Lawrence violin; Michael Skloff piano, assistant conductor; Robert Stern oboe, flute, clarinet; David Weiss flute, clarinet, alto sax.

Understudies: Messrs. Groener, Hamill—Christopher Wells; Miss Ebersole—Merilee Magnuson; Miss Roche—Barbara Moroz; Miss McQueen—Roxie Lucas; Messrs. Woodall, Bowers—Michael Gorman; Swings—Michael Gorman, Alison Mann.

Directed by Joe Layton; choreography, D.J. Giagni; musical direction, Peter Howard; scenery, David Mitchell; costumes, Ann Hould-Ward; lighting, Richard Nelson; music supervision, orchestrations, arrangements, John McKinney; sound, Otts Munderloh; production stage manager, Mary Porter Hall; stage manager, Marc Schlackman; press, Fred Nathan and Associates, Bert Fink, Anne Abrams, Leslie Anderson, Ted Killmer.

Time: 1871 to 1888.

The life and times of the famous 19th century musical stage duo. Previously produced at Goodspeed Opera House.

ACT I

Scene 1: Stetson's American Music Hall, Galesburg, Ill., 1871
"Put Me in My Little Bed"..Tony Hart
"Wonderful Me"...Harrigan and Hart
Scene 2: New York City
Scene 3: The Theatre Comique
"Mulligan Guard"...Harrigan and Hart
Scene 4: U.S. Courthouse, Worcester, Mass.
"Put Me in My Little Bed" (Reprise) ....Hart
Scene 5: The Theatre Comique
"I Love to Follow a Band"..............................Edward Harrigan, Company
"Such an Education Has My Mary Ann"......................Harrigan, Hart, Company
"Maggie Murphy's Home" .... Annie Braham, Harrigan, Sam Nichols, Company
"McNally's Row of Flats"....................................Mrs. Yeamons, Company
"Something New, Something Different".......................Harrigan, Hart, Company
Scene 6: The Theatre Comique
"That's My Partner" ....Harrigan and Hart
Scene 7: Outside the New Theatre Comique, opening night
Scene 8: Old Nieuw Amsterdam
"She's Our Gretel".................... Harrigan, Hart, Mrs. Yeamons, Company
Scene 9: A restaurant, later that evening
"What You Need Is a Woman".................................... Gerta Granville
Scene 10: The New Theatre Comique
"Knights of the Mystic Star" ....Mrs. Yeamons, Company
"Girl of the Mystic Star" ....Granville, Men
"Mulligan Guard (Reprise)....................................Harrigan and Hart

ACT II

Scene 1: New York City and the Park Theater
"Skidmore Fancy Ball" .... Sam Nichols, Harry Mack, Johnny Wild, Billy Gross
"Sweetest Love" .... Ada Lewis, Elsie Fay
"The Old Barn Floor"..................... Wild, Jennie Yeamons, Chester Fox, Lily Fay
"Silly Boy" .... Granville, Gross, Mack
"Mulligan Guard" (Reprise)..................................Harrigan, Hart, Company
"We'll Be There" ....Harrigan, Hart, Company
Scene 2: Harrigan's Tour, 1880 to 1886
"Ada With the Golden Hair"............................. Annie Harrigan, Wild, Gross
"That Old Featherbed" .... Mack, Fay Sisters
"Sam Johnson's Colored Cakewalk" ....Nichols, Jennie
"Dip Me in the Golden Sea" .... Harrigan, Mrs. Yeamons, Company
"That's My Partner" (Reprise).. Harrigan
Scene 3: Backstage, Wallack's Theater
"I've Come Home to Stay"...Hart
"If I Could Trust Me"..Hart
Scene 4: New York City
"Maggie Murphy's Home" (Reprise) .... Martin Hanley, Lily, Mrs. Yeamons, Lewis
"I've Come Home to Stay" (Reprise)...................................Hart, Girls
Scene 5: New York Hospital
"I Need This One Chance"..Granville
Scene 6: The Park Theater, March 22, 1888
"I Love to Follow a Band" (Reprise)............................... Annie, Company
"Mulligan Guard" (Reprise)........................... Harrigan, Hart, Mrs. Yeamons
"Something New, Something Different" (Reprise) .... Harrigan, Hart, Company

Pack of Lies (120). By Hugh Whitemore. Produced by Arthur Cantor and Bonnie Nelson Schwartz by arrangement with Michael Redington in association with Bernard Sandler and Eddie Kulukundis at the Royale Theater. Opened February 11, 1985. (Closed May 25, 1985)

Bob Jackson	George N. Martin	Peter Kroger	Colin Fox
Barbara Jackson	Rosemary Harris	Stewart	Patrick McGoohan
Julie Jackson	Tracy Pollan	Thelma	Kaiulani Lee
Helen Kroger	Dana Ivey	Sally	June Ballinger

Standbys: Miss Harris—Elizabeth Shepard; Messrs. Martin, McGoohan, Fox—Richard Neilson. Understudies: Misses Ivey, Lee—June Ballinger; Miss Pollan, Ballinger—Juli Cooper.

Directed by Clifford Williams; scenery and costumes, Ralph Koltai; lighting, Natasha Katz; production manager, Mitchell Erickson; associate producer, Harvey Elliott; stage manager, John Handy; press, Arthur Cantor Associates, Tom Siracusa.

Time: The autumn and winter of 1960–61. Place: The London suburb of Ruislip.

Suburban family is drawn reluctantly into a counterespionage caper, with tragic consequences, in a drama whose principal events actually took place. A foreign play previously produced in London. A Best Play; see page 178.

Strange Interlude (63). Revival of the play by Eugene O'Neill. Produced by Robert Michael Gesler, John Roberdeau, Douglas Urbanski and James M. Nederlander in association with Duncan C. Weldon with Paul Gregg, Lionel Becker and Jerome Minskoff at the Nederlander Theater. Opened February 21, 1985. (Closed May 5, 1985)

Mary	Jane Fleiss	Sam Evans	James Hazeldine
Charles Marsden	Edward Petherbridge	Mrs. Amos Evans	Elizabeth Lawrence
Prof. Henry Leeds	Tom Aldredge	Gordon	Patrick Wilcox
Nina Leeds	Glenda Jackson	Madeleine Arnold	Caitlin Clarke
Edmund Darrell	Brian Cox	Young Gordon	Charley Lang

Standbys: Messrs. Petherbridge, Aldredge—Neil Vipond; Mr. Wilcox—Tim Choate; Mr. Cox—Ken Ryan; Miss Clarke—Jane Fleiss; Mr. Lang—Jordan Marder.

Directed by Keith Hack; scenery, Voytek with Michael Levine; costumes, Deirdre Clancy; lighting, Allen Lee Hughes; music, Benedict Mason; sound, Valerie Spradling; production stage manager, Jane E. Neufeld; stage manager, William Hare; press, Marilynn LeVine, Merle Frimark, Meg Gordean.

Act I, Scene 1: Library, the Leeds's home in a small university town in New England, an afternoon in late summer in 1919. Scene 2: The library, a year later, evening. Scene 3: The Evans homestead, late spring of the next year, morning. Scene 4: The same as Scenes 1 and 2, fall of the same year, evening. Act II, Scene 5: Sitting room of a small house Evans has rented in a suburb near New York, the following April, morning. Scene 6: The same, a little over a year later, a summer evening. Act III, Scene 7: A terrace on the Evans's Long Island estate, early fall ten years later. Scene 8: The terrace, ten years later, a summer afternoon. Scene 9: The terrace, fall of the same year, early evening.

Strange Interlude was first produced on Broadway 1/30/28 for 426 performances and was named a Best Play of its season and won the Pulitzer Prize. It was revived on Broadway 3/11/63 for 97 performances.

The Octette Bridge Club (23). By P.J. Barry. Produced by Kenneth Waissman and Lou Kramer in association with MTM Enterprises, Inc. at the Music Box Theater. Opened March 5, 1985. (Closed March 23, 1985)

Martha	Anne Pitoniak	Ann	Elizabeth Huddle
Mary	Bette Henritze	Lil	Peggy Cass
Connie	Nancy Marchand	Betsy	Gisela Caldwell
Nora	Elizabeth Franz	Robert Foster	Nicholas Kaledin
Alice	Lois de Banzie		

Understudies: Misses Marchand, Cass, Pitoniak, Henritze—Jen Jones; Misses Franz, de Banzie, Huddle—Ruth Livingston.

Directed by Tom Moore; scenery, John Lee Beatty; costumes, Carrie Robbins; lighting, Roger Morgan; production stage manager, Steve Beckler; stage manager, Lynne Guerra; press, Betty Lee Hunt, Maria Cristina Pucci, James Sapp.

Place: The living room of Ann (Mrs. John Conroy) in a Rhode Island town. Act I: A Friday night in late October 1934. Act II: The night before Halloween, 1944.

The progressing lives and problems of eight sisters set forth in two family gatherings a decade apart. Previously produced at Actors Theater of Louisville.

Requiem for a Heavyweight (4). By Rod Serling. Produced by Zev Bufman, Ken Butler, Walter Barnett and Ivan Bloch in the Long Wharf Theater production, Arvin Brown artistic director, M. Edgar Rosenblum executive director, at the Martin Beck Theater. Opened March 7, 1985. (Closed March 9, 1985)

Packy; Photographer......	John C. McGinley	Doctor	Daniel F. Keyes
Policeman; The Kid	Kevin Carrigan	Perelli	Cosmo F. Allegretti
Army Hakes	David Proval	Golda	Joyce Ebert
Leo Loomis	Eugene Troobnick	Charlie	John C. Moskoff
Maish Resnick................	George Segal	Morrell......................	Mike Starr
Harlan McClintock..........	John Lithgow	Grace Miller	Maria Tucci
Max Greeny............	Dominic Chianese	Fan	Kit Flanagan

Fighters: Ellis "Skeeter" Williams, Herbert Rubens, John Capodice.

Understudies: Mr. Lithgow—Lanny Flaherty; Mr. Segal—John C. Moskoff; Misses Tucci, Ebert —Kit Flanagan; Mr. Proval—Ellis "Skeeter" Williams; Messrs. Troobnick, Allegretti, Chianese— Herbert Rubens; Messrs. Keyes, McGinley, Fighters—Steven J. Parris; Mr. Moskoff—John Capodice; Messrs. Starr, Carrigan—John C. McGinley.

Directed by Arvin Brown; scenery, Marjorie Bradley Kellogg; costumes, Bill Walker; lighting, Ron Wallace; fight direction, B.H. Barry; produced in association with Jujamcyn Theaters, Richard G. Wolff president; associate producer, Jay M. Coggan; production stage manager, James Harker; stage manager, Tracy B. Cohen; press, Susan L. Schulman, Ted Killmer.

Time: 1956. Place: New York City. Act I, Scene 1: The dressing room and adjacent corridor. Scene 2: The bar. Scene 3: The corridor adjacent to the dressing room. Scene 4: A New York State employment office. Scene 5: Maish's hotel room. Scene 6: The bar. Scene 7: The streets of New York. Act II, Scene 1: Maish's hotel room. Scene 2: The bar. Scene 3: Maish's hotel room. Scene 4: The bar. Scene 5: The dressing room and adjacent corridor of Matthews Arena. Scene 6: Grace's apartment. Scene 7: The dressing room and adjacent corridor of Matthews Arena.

Rod Serling play about a has-been boxer, adapted for television in 1956 and for the screen in 1961. Previously produced in this production at the Long Wharf Theater, New Haven, Conn.

*Joe Egg (76). Transfer from off Broadway of the revival of the play by Peter Nichols. Produced by The Shubert Organization, Emanuel Azenberg, Roger Berlind, Ivan Bloch and MTM Enterprises, Inc. in the Roundabout Theater Company production, Gene Feist artistic director, Todd Haimes managing director, at the Longacre Theater. Opened March 27, 1985.

Bri.............................	Jim Dale	Pam	Joanna Gleason
Sheila	Stockard Channing	Freddie....................	John Tillinger
Joe.........................	Tenney Walsh	Grace	Margaret Hilton

Understudies: Messrs. Dale, Tillinger—Larry Pine; Misses Channing, Gleason—Barbara eda-Young; Miss Walsh—Karyn Lynn Dale; Miss Hilton—Paddy Croft.

Directed by Arvin Brown; scenery, Marjorie Bradley Kellogg; costumes, Bill Walker; lighting, Ronald Wallace; production stage manager, Franklin Keysar; stage manager, Kathy J. Faul; press, Bill Evans and Associates, Sandra Manley, Jim Baldassare, Leslie Anderson.

Time: The late 1960s. Place: The living room of Bri's and Sheila's home. Act I: An evening in winter. Act II: Later the same night.

Revival of 1967–68 Best Play originally entitled *A Day in the Death of Joe Egg*, produced by Roundabout off Broadway 1/6/85–2/3/85 for 34 performances before being transferred to Broadway.

*Biloxi Blues (74). By Neil Simon. Produced by Emanuel Azenberg in association with Center Theater Group/Ahmanson Theater Los Angeles at the Neil Simon Theater. Opened March 28, 1985.

Roy Selridge .... Brian Tarantina	Sgt. Merwin J. Toomey .... Bill Sadler
Joseph Wykowski .... Matt Mulhern	James Hennesey............. Geoffrey Sharp
Don Carney.................. Alan Ruck	Rowena.................. Randall Edwards
Eugene Morris Jerome ... Matthew Broderick	Daisy Hannigan........ Penelope Ann Miller
Arnold Epstein .... Barry Miller	

Standbys: Mr. Broderick—Geoffrey Sharp, Greg Germann; Messrs. Tarantina, Mulhern—Woody Harrelson; Messrs. Ruck, Sharp—Jim Fyfe; Mr. Miller—Greg Germann; Mr. Sadler—Jamey Sheridan; Miss Edwards—Joan Goodfellow; Miss Miller—Joyce O'Brien.

Directed by Gene Saks; scenery, David Mitchell; costumes, Ann Roth; lighting, Tharon Musser; stage managers, Charles Blackwell, Henry Velez; press, Bill Evans and Associates, Sandra Manley, Jim Baldassare, Leslie Anderson.

Time: 1943. Place: Biloxi and Gulfport, Miss. Act I, Scene 1: Coach of an old railroad train, 1943. Scene 2: Section of a barracks, the next morning. Scene 3: Section of a mess hall, that evening. Scene 4: The barracks, later that night. Scene 5: The latrine and barracks, weeks later.

Act II, Scene 1: A hotel room, later that day. Scene 2: Rowena's hotel room, minutes later. Scene 3: The barracks, late Sunday night. Scene 4: Steps outside the barracks, later. Scene 5: The barracks, middle of the night. Scene 6: A church basement, the next week. Scene 7: Sgt. Toomey's room, that night. Scene 8: Gulfport, outside a girls' school, weeks later. Scene 9: Coach of a railroad train, sometime later.

Eugene Jerome, the semi-autobiographical Neil Simon-figure of *Brighton Beach Memoirs*, is now old enough to be drafted into the World War II army and is enduring/enjoying basic training and the masculine rites of passage. Previously produced at the Ahmanson Theater, Los Angeles, and Curran Theater, San Francisco.

A Best Play; see page 211.

*Leader of the Pack (61). Musical with music and lyrics by Ellie Greenwich and others (see additional authors' credits in list of musical numbers); liner notes by Anne Beatts; additional material by Jack Heifner; based on an original concept by Melanie Mintz. Produced by The Pack at the Ambassador Theater. Opened April 8, 1985.

Darlene Love................ Darlene Love	Gus Sharkey .... Dennis Bailey
Annie Golden .... Annie Golden	D.J. Voice .... Peter Neptune
Young Ellie Greenwich	Lounge Singer .... Pattie Darcy
(1960s)................... Dinah Manoff	Dance Couple .... Shirley Black-Brown,
Rosie.................... Zora Rasmussen	Keith McDaniel
Shelley .... Barbara Yeager	Gina .... Gina Taylor
Mickey; Waitress............. Jasmine Guy	Ellie Greenwich (1980s) ..... Ellie Greenwich
Jeff Barry .... Patrick Cassidy	

Girls & Guys: Shirley Black-Brown, Pattie Darcy, Christopher Gregory, Jasmine Guy, Danny Herman, Lon Hoyt, Keith McDaniel, Jodi Moccia, Peter Neptune, Zora Rasmussen, Joey Sheck, Gina Taylor, Barbara Yeager.

Musicians: Jimmy Vivino conductor, guitar; Leo Adamian drums; Ed Alstrom piano; Dennis Espantman bass; Gary Guzio trumpet; Artie Kaplan saxophone; Frank Pagano percussion; Lenny Pickett saxophone; Bob Smith trombone; Jeff Venho trumpet; Jerry Vivino saxophone; William Washer guitar; Daryl Waters associate conductor, synthesizer.

LEADER OF THE PACK—Jasmine Guy, Dinah Manoff and Pattie Darcy in a scene from the rock musical

Understudies: Miss Manoff—Pattie Darcy; Mr. Cassidy—Peter Neptune; Miss Greenwich—Zora Rasmussen; Mr. Bailey—Joey Sheck; Miss Golden—Jasmine Guy; Miss Love—Gina Taylor; Ensemble—Lisa Grant, Kevyn Morrow.

Directed and choreographed by Michael Peters; musical director and adaptor, Jimmy Vivino; scenery, Tony Walton; costumes, Robert de Mora; lighting, Pamela Cooper; vocal arrangements, Marc Shaiman; dance arrangements, Timothy Graphenreed; sound, Abe Jacob; assistant to Mr. Peters, Geneva Burke; production stage manager, William Dodds; stage manager, Kenneth Hanson; press, Solters/Roskin/Friedman, Inc., Joshua Ellis, Cindy Valk, Adrian Bryan-Brown, Keith Sherman.

Time: Here and now . . . and in the days of beehives and 45s. The play was presented without intermission.

The life and songs of Ellie Greenwich, whose compositions for female singing groups were an entertainment fixture of the 1960s.

MUSICAL NUMBERS

(Names of Ellie Greenwich's co-authors appear in parentheses below)
"Be My Baby" . . . . Annie, Girls
    (Jeff Barry, Phil Spector)
"Wait 'Til My Bobby Gets Home" . . . . Darlene, Company
    (Jeff Barry, Phil Spector)
"A . . . My Name Is Ellie" . . . . Young Ellie
"Jivette Boogie Beat" . . . . Young Ellie, Shelley, Mickey
"Why Do Lovers Break Each Others' Hearts" . . . . Darlene, Company
    (Tony Powers, Phil Spector)
"Today I Met the Boy I'm Gonna Marry" . . . . Darlene, Company
    (Tony Powers, Phil Spector)

"I Want to Love Him So Bad" .... Young Ellie, Girls
(Jeff Barry, Phil Spector)
"Do Wah Diddy"... Jeff
(Jeff Barry)
"And Then He Kissed Me" .... Young Ellie, Girls
(Jeff Barry, Phil Spector)
"Hanky Panky" .... Jeff, Guys
(Jeff Barry)
"Not Too Young (To Get Married)"..................................... Darlene, Girls
(Jeff Barry, Phil Spector)
"Chapel of Love"... Company
(Jeff Barry, Phil Spector)
"Baby I Love You" .... Annie, Girls
(Jeff Barry, Phil Spector)
"Leader of the Pack"... Annie, Company
(Jeff Barry, George "Shadow" Morton)
"Look of Love" .... Pattie
(Jeff Barry)
"Christmas—Baby Please Come Home" .... Darlene, Girls
(Jeff Barry, Phil Spector)
"I Can Hear Music" .... Jeff, Annie Pattie, Keith McDaniel
(Jeff Barry, Phil Spector)
"Rock of Rages" .... Young Ellie
(Jeff Kent)
"Keep It Confidential"... Gina Taylor, Company
(Jeff Kent, Ellen Foley)
"Da Doo Ron Ron".. Ellie, Company
(Jeff Barry, Phil Spector)
"What a Guy" .... Ellie, Company
(Jeff Barry, Phil Spector)
"Maybe I Know"... Ellie, Darlene, Annie, Girls
(Jeff Barry)
"River Deep, Mountain High" .... Darlene, Company
(Jeff Barry, Phil Spector)
"We're Gonna Make It (After All)" .... Ellie, Darlene, Annie, Company

Take Me Along (1). Musical revival based on the play *Ah, Wilderness!* by Eugene O'Neill; book by Joseph Stein and Robert Russell; music and lyrics by Bob Merrill. Produced by Kennedy Center in the Goodspeed Opera House production, Michael R. Price executive director, at the Martin Beck Theater. Opened and closed at the evening performance, April 14, 1985.

Nat Miller	Robert Nichols	David Macomber	Richard Korthaze
Essie Miller	Betty Johnson	Sid Davis	Kurt Knudson
Arthur Miller	Stephen McDonough	Belle	Nikki Sahagen
Mildred Miller	Alyson Kirk	Wint	Joel Whittaker
Lily Miller	Beth Fowler	Bartender	David Vosburgh
Muriel Macomber	Taryn Grimes	Salesman	John Witham
Richard Miller	Gary Landon Wright		

Trolley Conductors, Firemen, Townsfolk, Bar Patrons, Ladies of the Evening: Kathy Andrini, Blake Atherton, Michael Kelly Boone, Ed Brazo, Richard Dodd, Andy Hostettler, Richard Korthaze, Patrick S. Murphy, Mercedes Perez, Keith Savage, David Vosburgh, Joel Whittaker, Betty Winsett, John Witham.

Swing Dancers: Kimberly Campbell, Erik Geier.

Directed by Thomas Gruenewald; choreography and musical staging, Dan Siretta; musical direction, Lynn Crigler; scenery, James Leonard Joy; costumes, David Toser; lighting, Craig Miller;

orchestrations, Philip J. Lang; dance arrangements, Allen Cohen; additional orchestrations, Lynn Crigler, Allen Cohen; sound, Jan Nebozenko; associate conductor, Patrick Vacciarello; presented by arrangement with the Shubert Performing Arts Center, New Haven; production stage manager, John Bonanni; stage manager, Bryan Harris; press, David Powers.

Time: 1906. Place: A Connecticut town.

Take Me Along was first produced on Broadway 10/22/59 for 448 performances. This is its first major New York revival.

ACT I

Overture. . . . . Orchestra
Scene 1: The Miller home
  "Marvellous Fire Machine". . . . . Nat, Ensemble
  "Oh, Please". . . . . Essie, Nat
  "Oh, Please" (Reprise). . . . . Essie, Nat, Lily, Arthur, Mildred
Scene 2: The Macomber yard
  "I Would Die". . . . . Richard, Muriel
Scene 3: The Centerville carbarn
  "Sid, Ole Kid" . . . . Sid, Belle, Townspeople
Scene 4: The Miller home
  "Staying Young". . . . . Nat
  "I Get Embarrassed". . . . . Sid, Lily
  "We're Home". . . . . Lily
  "Take Me Along". . . . . Nat, Sid
Scene 5: The picnic grounds
  "Take Me Along" (Reprise) . . . . Company
  "The Only Pair I've Got". . . . . Belle, Ensemble
  "In the Company of Men" . . . . Sid, Nat, Male Ensemble
Scene 6: The Miller home
  "Knights on White Horses" . . . . Lily, Essie
Scene 7: The Miller Home
  "That's How It Starts" . . . . Richard

ACT II

Entr'acte . . . . Orchestra
Scene 1: The Pleasant Beach House
  "If Jesus Don't Love Ya" . . . . Richard, Belle, Ensemble
Scene 2: The Miller home
  "Oh, Please" (Reprise). . . . . Nat, Essie
Scene 3: The Miller Home
  "Promise Me a Rose" . . . . Lily
  "Staying Young" (Reprise) . . . . Nat
Scene 4: Richard's bedroom
  "Green Snake" . . . . Sid
Scene 5: The dock
  "Nine O'Clock" . . . . Richard
  "Nine O'Clock" (Reprise) . . . . Richard, Muriel
Scene 6: The Miller home
  "But Yours" . . . . Sid, Lily
Scene 7: The Miller home
Scene 8: The Centerville carbarn
Finale. . . . . Sid, Lily

*Grind (53). Musical with Book by Fay Kanin; music by Larry Grossman; lyrics by Ellen Fitzhugh. Produced by Kenneth D. Greenblatt, John J. Pomerantz, Mary Lea Johnson, Martin Richards, James M. Nederlander, Harold Prince and Michael Frazier in association with Susan Madden Samson and Jonathan Farkas at the Mark Hellinger Theater. Opened April 16, 1985.

Leroy	Ben Vereen	Mechanical Man	Jackie Jay Patterson
Harry	Lee Wallace	Romaine	Sharon Murray
Gus	Stubby Kaye	Satin	Leilani Jones
Solly	Joey Faye	Louis	Brian McKay
Vernelle	Marion Ramsey	Mike	Oscar Stokes
Ruby	Hope Clarke	Stooge	Leonard John Crofoot
Fleta	Valarie Pettiford	Doyle	Timothy Nolen
Kitty	Candy Brown	Grover	Donald Acree
Linette	Wynonna Smith	Mrs. Faye	Ruth Brisbane
Maybelle	Carol Woods		

Knockabouts, Toughs: Leonard John Crofoot, Ray Roderick, Kelly Walters, Steve Owsley, Malcolm Perry.

Understudies: Mr. Vereen—Jackie Jay Patterson; Miss Jones—Candy Brown; Messrs. Nolen, Stokes—Brian McKay; Messrs. Kaye, Wallace, Faye—Oscar Stokes; Miss Murray—Dana Lorge; Misses Clarke, Brown, Ramsey, Pettiford, Smith—Gayle Samuels; Miss Woods—Ruth Brisbane; Miss Brisbane—Carol Woods; Mr. Acree—Raymond Rickman; Mr. Patterson—Dwight Baxter; Mr. McKay, Swing—David Reitman.

Directed by Harold Prince; choreography, Lester Wilson; musical direction, Paul Gemignani; scenery, Clarke Dunham; costumes, Florence Klotz; lighting, Ken Billington; orchestrations, Bill Byers; dance music arrangements, Tom Fay; additional orchestrations, Jim Tyler, Harold Wheeler; dance music arrangement for "New Man," Gordon Harrell; executive producers, Ruth Mitchell, Sam Crothers; assistant choreographer, Larry Vickers; production stage manager, Beverley Randolph; stage manager, Richard Evans; press, Mary Bryant, Becky Flora.

Time: 1933. Place: In and around Harry Earle's Burlesque Theater, Chicago.

Life, times and talents of an old-time burlesque company during the Chicago Worlds Fair.

ACT I

"This Must Be the Place"	Company
"Cadava"	Solly, Gus, Romaine
"A Sweet Thing Like Me"	Satin, Earle's Pearls
"I Get Myself Out"	Gus
"My Daddy Always Taught Me to Share"	Leroy
"All Things to One Man"	Satin
"The Line"	Leroy, Earle's Pearls
"Katie, My Love"	Doyle
"The Grind"	Gus, Company
"Yes, Ma'am"	Doyle
"Why, Mama, Why"	Satin, Leroy
"This Crazy Place"	Leroy, Company

ACT II

"From the Ankles Down"	Leroy, Earle's Pearls
"Who Is He?"	Satin
"Never Put It in Writing"	Gus
"I Talk, You Talk"	Doyle
"Timing"	Romaine, Solly
"These Eyes of Mine"	Maybelle, Company
"New Man"	Leroy
"Down"	Doyle
"A Century of Progress"	Leroy, Satin, Earle's Pearls
Finale	Company

Big River: The Adventures of Huckleberry Finn (42). Musical based on the novel by Mark Twain; book by William Hauptman; music and lyrics by Roger Miller. Produced by Rocco Landesman, Heidi Landesman, Rick Steiner, M. Anthony Fisher and Dodger Productions at the Eugene O'Neill Theater. Opened April 25, 1985.

ACT I

In St. Petersburg, Mo.; later on the Illinois shore and Jackson's Island:

Mark Twain . . . . Gordon Connell
Huckleberry Finn . . . . Daniel H. Jenkins
Widow Douglas . . . . Susan Browning
Miss Watson;
  Woman in Shanty . . . . Evalyn Baron
Jim . . . . Ron Richardson
Tom Sawyer . . . . John Short
Ben Rogers . . . . William Youmans
Jo Harper . . . . Andi Henig
Simon . . . . Aramis Estevez
Dick . . . . Michael Brian
Pap Finn . . . . John Goodman

Judge Thatcher . . . . Ralph Byers
On the river, south of St. Louis:
  Slaves and Overseers on a Flatboat: Carol Dennis, Elmore James, Jennifer Leigh Warren, Franz Jones, Aramis Estevez, John Goodman, William Youmans, Michael Brian
On the river, near Cairo, Ill.:
  Three Men on a Skiff: Ralph Byers, Reathel Bean, Elmore James.
On the riverbank in Kentucky:
  The King . . . . Bob Gunton
  The Duke . . . . Rene Auberjonois
  Soldiers, Citizens . . . . Company

ACT II

In Bricktown, Ark.:

Hank . . . . William Youmans
Andy . . . . Michael Brian
Lafe . . . . Reathel Bean
Townspeople . . . . Company
In Hillsboro, Ark.:
Young Fool . . . . William Youmans
Mary Jane Wilkes . . . . Patti Cohenour
Susan Wilkes . . . . Peggy Harmon
Joanna Wilkes . . . . Andi Henig
Bill . . . . Franz Jones
Counselor Robinson . . . . Reathel Bean
Alice . . . . Carol Dennis

Alice's Daughter . . . . . Jennifer Leigh Warren
Mourners; Mob . . . . Company
Sheriff Bell . . . . John Goodman
Harvey Wilkes . . . . Ralph Byers
Man in the Crowd . . . . Michael Brian
Harmonia Player . . . . Evalyn Baron
On a farm near Hillsboro:
Sally Phelps . . . . Susan Browning
Silas Phelps . . . . Ralph Byers
Doctor . . . . Gordon Connell
  Hired Hands: Reathel Bean, Michael Brian, John Goodman

Musicians: Don Brooks harmonica; John Guth guitar, banjo; Kenny Kosek fiddle; Bruce Bonvissuto trombone; Vinnie Johnson drums; Jeffrey Ganz bass; Lowell J. Hershey trumpet; Scott Kuney guitar; Robert Steen woodwind; Linda Twine piano.

Understudies: Ensemble—Peggy Harmon, George Merritt; Mr. Richardson—Elmore James; Mr. Jenkins, Ensemble—Andrew Hill Newman.

Directed by Des McAnuff; musical direction and vocal arrangements, Linda Twine; scenery, Heidi Landesman; costumes, Patricia McGourty; lighting, Richard Riddell; sound, Otts Munderloh; musical supervision, Danny Troob; orchestrations, Steven Margoshes, Danny Troob; dance and incidental music, John Richard Lewis; choreography, Janet Watson; stage movement and fights, B.H. Barry; associate scenic design, Robert Shaw; sound effects, John Kilgore; associate producers, Arthur Katz, Emily Landau, Fred Mayerson, TM Productions, Inc.; production stage manager, Frank Hartenstein; stage manager, Steven Adler; press, Solters/Roskin/Friedman, Inc., Joshua Ellis, Keith Sherman.

Time: Sometime in the 1840s. Place: Along the Mississippi River Valley.

The adventures of Huck Finn and the runaway slave Jim on their raft on the Mississippi, in many of the details set forth in Mark Twain's novel. Previously produced in regional theater at Cambridge, Mass. and the LaJolla, Calif. Playhouse (where Des McAnuff is artistic director).

ACT I

"Do You Want to Go to Heaven?" . . . . Company
"The Boys" . . . . Tom, Gang
"Waiting for the Light to Shine" . . . . Huck
"Guv'ment" . . . . Pap
"Hand for the Hog" . . . . Tom
"I, Huckleberry, Me" . . . . Huck

"Muddy Water" .... Jim, Huck
"Crossing Over" .... Slaves, Overseer
"River in the Rain" .... Huck, Jim
"When the Sun Goes Down in the South" .... Duke, King, Huck

ACT II

"The Royal Nonesuch" .... Duke, Company
"Worlds Apart" .... Jim, Huck
"Arkansas" .... Young Fool
"How Blest We Are" .... Alice's Daughter, Company
"You Ought To Be Here With Me" .... Mary Jane, Susan, Joanna
"How Blest We Are" (Reprise) .... Company
"Leaving's Not the Only Way to Go" .... Mary Jane, Jim, Huck
"Waiting for the Light to Shine" (Reprise) .... Huck
"Free at Last" .... Jim
"River in the Rain" (Reprise) .... Huck, Jim
"Muddy Water" (Reprise) .... Company

*Aren't We All? (37). Revival of the play by Frederick Lonsdale. Produced by Douglas
Urbanski, Karl Allison, Bryan Bantry and James M. Nederlander in association with
Duncan C. Weldon, Paul Gregg, Lionel Becker and Jerome Minskoff at the Brooks
Atkinson Theater. Opened April 29, 1985.

Morton	Peter Pagan	Lord Grenham	Rex Harrison
Hon. William Tatham	Jeremy Brett	Hon. Mrs. W. Tatham	Lynn Redgrave
Lady Frinton	Claudette Colbert	Roberts	George Ede
Arthur Wells	Steven Sutherland	Angela Lynton	Brenda Forbes
Martin Steele	John Patrick Hurley	Rev. Ernest Lynton	George Rose
Kitty Lake	Leslie O'Hara	John Willocks	Ned Schmidtke

Understudies: Mr. Harrison—Peter Pagan; Misses Redgrave, O'Hara—Sybil Lines; Mr. Rose—
George Ede; Mr. Schmidtke—John Patrick Hurley; Mr. Brett—Steven Sutherland; Messrs. Pagan,
Ele, Sutherland, Hurley—David Silber. Standby: Misses Colbert, Forbes—Betty Low.

Directed by Clifford Williams; scenery, Finlay James; costumes, Judith Bland; lighting, Natasha Katz; sound, Jan Nebozenko; Miss Colbert's Scene 1 costume, Tracy Mills; associate producers, Robert Michael Geisler, John Roberdeau; production stage manager, Warren Crane; stage manager, William Weaver; press, Solters/Roskin/Friedman, Inc., Joshua Ellis, Adrian Bryan-Brown.

Act I, Scene 1: William Tatham's house in Mayfair, evening. Scene 2: Grenham Court, afternoon, two weeks later. Act II, Scene 1: The same, immediately following. Scene 2: The same, the next morning.

The first New York production of this romantic comedy took place 5/21/23, with a return engagement two seasons later. It was revived off Broadway in the 1949–50 season. This 1985 Broadway revival was previously produced in London.

*As Is (35). Transfer from off Broadway of the play by William M. Hoffman. Produced
by John Glines, Lawrence Lane, Lucille Lortel and The Shubert Organization in the Circle
Repertory Company and The Glines production at the Lyceum Theater. Opened May 1,
1985.

Hospice Worker; Business Partner;		Brother; Barney	Ken Kliban
Nurse	Claris Erickson	Clone	Mark Myers
Rich	Jonathan Hogan	Clone; Pat; Orderly	Lou Liberatore
Saul	Jonathan Hadary	Also Doctors, Pick-Ups, Bartender, Bookstore	
Chet	Steven Gregan	Patrons, PWA's, Drug Dealers.	
Lily	Lily Knight		

AREN'T WE ALL?—Rex Harrison and Claudette Colbert in the revival of the Frederick Lonsdale comedy

Standbys: Messers. Hogan, Kliban, Liberatore—Bruce McCarthy; Messrs. Hadary, Gregan, Myers —Reed Jones; Misses Erickson, Knight—Patricia Fletcher.

Directed by Marshall W. Mason; scenery, David Potts; lighting, Dennis Parichy; costumes, Michael Warren Powell; sound, Chuck London Media/Stewart Werner; associate producer, Paul A. Kaplan; production stage manager, Fred Reinglas; stage manager, Denise Yaney; press, Betty Lee Hunt, Maria Cristina Pucci.

Time: The present. Place: New York City. The play was presented without intermission.

This production of *As Is*, about the faithfulness of a homosexual lover to his partner, even though the latter has contracted AIDS, was originally produced off Broadway by Circle Repertory Company 3/10/85 for 49 performances.

A Best Play; see page 197.

*Doubles (27). By David Wiltse. Produced by Multi Production Partnership, Richard Horner, Lynne Stuart, Hinks Shimberg and Gold 'n Gay Productions at the Ritz Theater. Opened May 8, 1985.

Guy........................ John Cullum	Heather..................... Kate Collins
Lennie.................... Ron Leibman	Chuck................... Nicholas Wyman
Arnie .... Austin Pendleton	Tennis Players....... Sarah Daly, Peter Flint
George .... Tony Roberts	

Understudies: Messrs. Cullum, Wyman—Peter Flint; Messrs. Leibman, Pendleton, Roberts—David Rogers; Miss Collins—Sarah Daly.

Directed by Morton Da Costa; scenery and costumes, Robert Fletcher; lighting, Craig Miller; sound, Robert Kerzman; production stage manager, Elliott Woodruff; press, Richard P. Pheneger.

Time: The present. Place: The men's locker room of the Norwalk Racquet Club, Norwalk, Conn. The play was divided into two parts with a few months' passage of time between them.

Comedy of the ins and outs of male friendship, exposed in a weekly tennis foursome.

A Best Play; see page 220.

PLAYS WHICH CLOSED
PRIOR TO BROADWAY OPENING

Productions which were organized by New York producers for Broadway presentation but which closed during their production and tryout period are listed below.

Master Class. By David Pownall. Produced by Kennedy Center and Roger L. Stevens at the Eisenhower Theater, Washington, D.C. Opened September 9, 1984. (Closed September 16, 1984)

Marshal Zhdanov .... Dick Latessa	Shostakovich .... Michael Zaslow
Prokofiev .... Werner Klemperer	Stalin .... George Dzundza

Directed by David Trainer; scenery, David Jenkins; costumes, David Murin; lighting, Martin Aronstein; original music, John White; musical direction, Jack Lee; press, Kiki Davies.

Drama of repression of the arts in the Russia of Josef Stalin. The play was presented in two parts. A foreign play previously produced in London.

Peccadillo. By Garson Kanin. Produced by Zev Bufman and Ivan Bloch in a pre-Broadway tryout. Opened at the Bay Front Theater, St. Petersburg, Fla. February 22, 1985. (Closed at the Parker Theater, Ft. Lauderdale, Fla. March 31, 1985)

Vito De Angelis....... Christopher Plummer	Bruce .... John Mackay
Robert Epstein.............. Todd Waring	Iris Peabody............... Kelly McGillis
Rachel Garland De Angelis..... Glynis Johns	

Directed by Garson Kanin; scenery, Oliver Smith; costumes, Donald Brooks; lighting, Richard Nelson; sound, Tony Meola; associate director, Martha Wilson; production stage manager, Thomas A. Kelly; press, Judy Jacksina, Glenna Freedman.

Comedy, an egotistical orchestra conductor and his wife trying to have a ghostwriter help with their memoirs. The play was presented in two parts.

PLAYS PRODUCED
OFF BROADWAY

Some distinctions between off-Broadway and Broadway productions at one end of the scale and off-off-Broadway productions at the other were blurred in the New York theater of the 1970s and 1980s. For the purposes of this *Best Plays* listing the term "off Broadway" is used to distinguish a professional from a showcase (off-off-Broadway) production and signifies a show which opened for general audiences in a mid-Manhattan theater seating 499 or fewer and 1) employed an Equity cast, 2) planned a regular schedule of 8 performances a week in an open-ended run and 3) offered itself to public comment by critics at a designated opening performance.

Occasional exceptions of inclusion (never of exclusion) are made to take in visiting troupes, borderline cases and nonqualifying productions which readers might expect to find in this list because they appear under an off-Broadway heading in other major sources of record.

Figures in parentheses following a play's title give number of performances. These figures do not include previews or extra non-profit performances.

Plays marked with an asterisk (*) were still running on June 1, 1985. Their number of performances is figured from opening night through May 31, 1985.

Certain programs of off-Broadway companies are exceptions to our rule of counting the number of performances from the date of the press coverage. When the official opening takes place late in the run of a play's regularly-priced public or subscription performances (after previews) we count the first performance of record, not the press date, as opening night—and in each such case in the listing we note the variance and give the press date.

In a listing of a show's numbers—dances, sketches, musical scenes, etc.—the titles of songs are identified wherever possible by their appearance in quotation marks (").

Most entries of off-Broadway productions which ran fewer than 20 performances or scheduled fewer than 8 performances a week are somewhat abbreviated, as are entries on running repertory programs repeated from previous years.

HOLDOVERS FROM PREVIOUS SEASONS

Plays which were running on June 1, 1984 are listed below. More detailed information about them appears in previous *Best Plays* volumes of appropriate date. Important cast changes since opening night are recorded in a section of this volume.

344

*The Fantasticks (10,436; longest continuous run of record in the American theater). Musical suggested by the play *Les Romanesques*† by Edmond Rostand; book and lyrics by Tom Jones; music by Harvey Schmidt. Opened May 3, 1960.

*Forbidden Broadway (1,399). Cabaret revue with concept and lyrics by Gerard Alessandrini. Opened May 4, 1982. Revised (1984) version opened October 27, 1983. Revised (1985) version opened January 29, 1985.

*Little Shop of Horrors (1,189). Musical based on the film by Roger Corman; book and lyrics by Howard Ashman; music by Alan Menken. Opened July 27, 1982.

True West (762). Revival of the play by Sam Shepard. Opened October 17, 1982. (Closed August 4, 1984)

*Fool for Love (840). By Sam Shepard. Opened May 26, 1983.

The Mirror Theater. Repertory of five revivals. Paradise Lost (92). By Clifford Odets. Opened December 10, 1983. (Closed June 3, 1984) Inheritors (47). By Susan Glaspell. Opened December 11, 1983. (Closed June 2, 1984) Rain (41). By John Colton. Opened March 6, 1984. (Closed June 2, 1984) Ghosts (16). By Henrik Ibsen. Opened May 15, 1984. (Closed June 1, 1984) The Hasty Heart (40). By John Patrick. Opened May 15, 1984. (Closed July 1, 1984)

*Playwrights Horizons. Isn't It Romantic (615). Revised version of the play by Wendy Wasserstein. Opened December 15, 1983.

A . . . My Name Is Alice (353). Musical revue conceived by Joan Micklin Silver and Julianne Boyd. Opened February 24, 1984. (Closed March 11, 1984) Reopened April 8, 1984. (Closed February 17, 1985)

Orwell That Ends Well (110). Musical revue by and with The Original Chicago Second City Company; music by Fred Kaz. Opened March 4, 1984. (Closed June 3, 1984)

Roundabout Theater Company. On Approval (195). Revival of the play by Frederick Lonsdale. Opened March 27, 1984. (Closed September 16, 1984)

'night, Mother (54). Transfer from Broadway of the play by Marsha Norman. Opened April 18, 1984. (Closed June 3, 1984)

Manhattan Theater Club. The Miss Firecracker Contest (131). By Beth Henley. Opened May 1, 1984. (Closed August 25, 1984).

Nite Club Confidential (156). Musical with book by Dennis Deal; new songs by Dennis Deal. Opened May 10, 1984. (Closed September 23, 1984)

The Shadow of a Gunman (47). Revival of the play by Sean O'Casey. Opened May 22, 1984. (Closed July 1, 1984)

Circle Repertory Company. Balm in Gilead (253). Revival of the play by Lanford Wilson. Opened May 31, 1984. (Closed January 6, 1985)

---

†Rostand's title appeared in the original off-Broadway program, incorrectly, as *Les Romantiques*. The program was subsequently corrected but, as Tom Jones recently informed the Best Plays editor, "The original error still haunts us." It has also haunted 24 previous Best Plays volumes through the tenures of three editors (Louis Kronenberger, Henry Hewes and the incumbent, who regrets the error and is now relieved to assert that *Les Romanesques* is correct).

AVNER THE ECCENTRIC—Avner Eisenberg
in his solo show

PLAYS PRODUCED JUNE 1, 1984–MAY 31, 1985

Danny and the Deep Blue Sea (117). By John Patrick Shanley. Produced by Circle in the Square, Theodore Mann artistic director, Paul Libin managing director, and Robert Pesola, Ann Schindler and Stuart Bader in association with Circle Repertory Company at Circle in the Square Downtown. Opened June 6, 1984. (Closed September 16, 1984)

Roberta . . . . June Stein
Danny . . . . John Turturro

Standby: Miss Stein—Deborah Offner. Understudy: Mr. Turturro—John C. McGinley.
Directed by Barnet Kellman; scenery, David Gropman; lighting, Richard Nelson; costumes, Marcia Dixcy; production stage manager, Karen Armstrong; press, Merle Debuskey, David Roggensack.
Place: The Bronx. The play was presented in three scenes without intermission.
Subtitled, "An Apache Dance," the chance meeting and developing love story of two violence-prone people. Previously produced at Actors Theater of Louisville, Ky.

Split Second (147). By Dennis McIntyre. Produced by Philip Rose, Gus Fleming and John McDonald at Theater Four. Opened June 7, 1984. (Closed October 14, 1984)

Willis .... Bill Cwikowski Charlie .... Peter Jay Fernandez
Val Johnson................. John Danelle Alea Johnson............... Michele Shay
Parker........... Helmar Augustus Cooper Rusty Johnson........... Norman Matlock

Understudies: Messrs. Danelle, Fernandez—Count Stovall; Miss Shay—Marie Thomas; Messrs. Matlock, Cooper—Irving Barnes; Mr. Cwikowski—Robert Aberdeen.

Directed by Samuel P. Barton; scenery, Daniel Proett; lighting, Leo Gambacorta; costumes, Judy Dearing; original music, Jimmy Owens; production stage manager, Dwight R.B. Cook; press, Henry Luhrman Associates, Terry M. Lilly, Keith Sherman, Kevin P. McAnarney.

Time: The present, July 4. Place: Manhattan. The play was presented in two parts.

Crisis of conscience of a black police officer who has been goaded into killing an unarmed white prisoner.

A Best Play; see page 81.

Playwrights Horizons. 1983–84 schedule included **Elm Circle** (23). By Mick Casale. Produced by Playwrights Horizons, Andre Bishop artistic director, Paul Daniels managing director, at Playwrights Horizons Studio Theater. Opened June 13, 1984. (Closed July 1, 1984)

Janet-Ann.................... Kelly Wolf Anthony; Martin.............. Ben Seigler
Janet; Brenda.............. Cheryl Giannini Tommy; Ronnie.......... David McDonald
Tom; Frankie; Sky;
Bathroom Voice .... Edward L. O'Neill

Directed by Pamela Berlin; scenery and lighting, Bennet Averyt; costumes, Sheila McLamb; sound, Stanley Metelits; composer, Richard Weinstock; production stage manager, William Chance; stage manager, G. Franklin Heller; press, Bob Ullman.

Time: The summer of 1977. Place: U.S.A. The play was presented without intermission.

Young woman pretends she's Linda Ronstadt. Produced as a part of the Foundation of the Dramatists Guild/CBS New Plays Program.

Kennedy at Colonus (20). By Laurence Carr. Produced by Multi Production Partnership (Lynne Stuart, Hinks Shimberg, Gold 'n Gay Productions and Richard Horner) and Terry Hodge Taylor at the 47th Street Theater. Opened June 14, 1984. (Closed June 30, 1984)

CAST: Robert F. Kennedy—Christopher Curry; Actor #1 (Adam, Jack Kennedy, James Hoffa, Gen. Douglas MacArthur, Warren (Reporter), Allard Lowenstein)—Will Jeffries; Actor #2 (Ken, Joe Kennedy Jr., J. Edgar Hoover, Gov. Ross Barnett, A Bureau Man, Lyndon B. Johnson, Joseph Kennedy Sr.)—Nicholas Wyman; Actress #3 (Angie, Ethel Kennedy, Television Reporter)—Beth McDonald; Actor #4 (Television Reporter, John (FBI), Martin Luther King Jr., Mr. Smith, White House Reporter, Cesar Chavez)—Daniel Whitner.

Understudies: Messrs. Curry, Jeffries, Wyman—Elton Cormier; Miss McDonald—Mimi Bensinger; Mr. Whitner—Tommy Hicks.

Directed by Stephen Zuckerman; conceived and commissioned by Terry Hodge Taylor; scenery and costumes, Philipp Jung; lighting, Betsy Adams; sound, Robert Kerzman; associate producer, Ted Tobias; production stage manager, David Wahl; press, Henry Luhrman Associates, Kevin P. McAnarney, Terry M. Lilly, Keith Sherman, Bill Miller.

Time and Place: June 1968 in Malibu, Calif., the day of the California Primary Election, the action then moving to various times and locations between 1936 and 1968. The play was presented in two parts.

The life and times of Robert F. Kennedy.

New York Shakespeare Festival. 1983–84 schedule included **The Nest of the Wood Grouse** (46). By Victor Rozov; translated by Susan Layton. Opened June 14, 1984. (Closed July 22, 1984) **Found a Peanut** (33). By Donald Margulies. Opened June 17, 1984. (Closed July 15, 1984) **Ice Bridge** (6). By John Forster. Opened June 18, 1984. (Closed June 24,

1984). Produced by New York Shakespeare Festival, Joseph Papp producer, at the Public Theater (see note), *Ice Bridge* in the Vietnam Veterans Ensemble Theater Company, Thomas Bird artistic director, production. All plays: Associate producer, Jason Steven Cohen; press, Merle Debuskey, Richard Kornberg, Barbara Carroll, Bruce Campbell.

THE NEST OF THE WOOD GROUSE

Iskra . . . . Mary Beth Hurt	Julia . . . . Jacqueline Bertrand
Prov . . . . Ricky Paull	Valentina Dimitriyevna. . . . . . . Rebecca Schull
Zoya . . . . Julie Cohen	Ariadna Koromyslova. . . . . Phoebe Cates
Natalya Gavrilovna. . . . . Anne Jackson	Zolotarev . . . . Christian Baskous
Georgy Samsonovich	Vera Vasilyevna. . . . . . . Rosemary De Angelis
Yasyunin . . . . Dennis Boutsikaris	Foreign Visitors. . . . . Gene Lewis,
Stephen Alekseyevich Sudakov . . . Eli Wallach	Afemo Omilami
Zirelli . . . . Ernesto Gasco	

Directed by Joseph Papp; scenery, Loren Sherman; costumes, Theoni V. Aldredge; lighting, Arden Fingerhut; production stage manager, Ellen Raphael; stage manager, Barbara Abel.

Time: Early 1970s. Place: Moscow. Act I: April, early evening. Act II: May Day morning.

Domestic comedy about a contemporary Russian Foreign Ministry official's family. A foreign play previously produced (and now playing) at the Satire Theater in Moscow.

FOUND A PEANUT

Little Earl . . . . Peter MacNicol	Jeffrey Smolowitz . . . . Evan Handler
Mike. . . . . Robert Joy	Scott . . . . Greg Germann
Melody . . . . Robin Bartlett	Ernie. . . . . Jonathan Walker
Joanie . . . . Nealla Spano	Shane . . . . Kevin Geer

Directed by Claudia Weill; scenery, Thomas Lynch; costumes, Jane Greenwood; lighting, Beverly Emmons; fight direction, B.H. Barry; sound, Chuck London Media/Stewart Werner; incidental music, Allen Shawn; production stage manager, Susan Green; stage manager, Johnna Murray.

Time: Sunday, the last day of summer, 1962. Place: The back of an apartment building in Brooklyn. The play was presented without intermission.

Confrontations within a group of eight children age 5–12, played by adult actors.

ICE BRIDGE

Polar Bear . . . . Brian Delate	Snow. . . . . Anthony Chisholm
Thor . . . . James Handy	Ike. . . . . R.J. Bonds
Mick. . . . . Tom Jenkins	Voice of Teller. . . . . David Adamson
Terry. . . . . Ray Robertson	

Directed by Edward Cornell; scenery, Salvatore Tagliarino; costumes, Lee Entwisle; lighting, Marcia Madeira, Terry Wuthrich; production stage manager, Sally B. Andrew.

U.S. troops on guard with nuclear weapons in a remote Greenland outpost.

Note: In Joseph Papp's Public Theater there are many separate auditoriums. *The Nest of the Wood Grouse* played the Estelle R. Newman Theater, *Found a Peanut* played the Florence Anspacher Theater, *Ice Bridge* played The Other Stage.

Hurlyburly (45). By David Rabe. Produced by Icarus Productions and Frederick M. Zollo with Ivan Bloch and ERB Productions at the Promenade Theater. Opened June 21, 1984. (Closed July 29, 1984 and transferred to Broadway; see its entry in the Plays Produced on Broadway section of this volume)

Phil. . . . . Harvey Keitel	Donna. . . . . Cynthia Nixon
Eddie . . . . William Hurt	Darlene. . . . . Sigourney Weaver
Mickey . . . . Christopher Walken	Bonnie . . . . Judith Ivey
Artie. . . . . Jerry Stiller	

Directed by Mike Nichols; scenery, Tony Walton; costumes, Ann Roth; lighting, Jennifer Tipton; associate producer, William P. Suter; production stage manager, Peter Lawrence; press, Bill Evans, Sandra Manley.

Time: A little while ago. Place: A house in the Hollywood Hills. The play was presented in three acts.

Assortment of cocaine-era characters on the fringes of show business, self-destructing in a modern Hollywood environment. Previously produced at the Goodman Theater, Chicago.

A Best Play; see page 96.

New York Shakespeare Festival. Summer schedule of two outdoor revivals. **Henry V** (27). By William Shakespeare. Opened June 22, 1984; see note. (Closed July 22, 1984) **The Golem** (27). By H. Leivick; translated from the Yiddish by J.C. Augenlight. Opened August 3, 1984 (Closed September 2, 1984) Produced by New York Shakespeare Festival, Joseph Papp producer, with the cooperation of the City of New York, Edward I. Koch mayor, Bess Myerson commissioner of cultural affairs, Henry Stern commissioner of parks and recreation, and the New York Telephone Company at the Delacorte Theater in Central Park. Both plays: Associate producer, Jason Steven Cohen; press, Merle Debuskey, Richard Kornberg, Barbara Carroll, Bruce Campbell.

HENRY V

Chorus . . . . George N. Martin	Montjoy. . . . . Jeffrey Jones
At the English Court:	Orleans . . . . Paul Guilfoyle
Archbishop of Canterbury. . . George Guidall	Bourbon. . . . . Joseph Maruzzo
Bishop of Ely . . . . Clement Fowler	Burgundy. . . . . Jamil Zakkai
King Henry V. . . . . Kevin Kline	French Messenger. . . . . . . Christopher Bradley
Exeter . . . . Earl Hindman	Queen of France. . . . . Kristine Nielsen
Gloucester. . . . . Morgan Strickland	Katharine . . . . Mary Elizabeth Mastrantonio
Bedford . . . . David Warshofsky	Alice . . . . Vivienne Argent
Duke of York . . . . John Bauman	Ladies-in-Waiting . . . . . . Elizabeth Dennehy,
Westmoreland. . . . . Michael Wetmore	Susan Gabriel
French Ambassador . . . . Jeffrey Jones	Siege of Harfleur:
At the tavern:	Fluellen . . . . Anthony Heald
Bardolph . . . . Adam LeFevre	Gower . . . . Peter McRobbie
Nym. . . . . Larry Pine	MacMorris . . . . Joseph Costa
Pistol . . . . Dan Hedaya	Jamy . . . . Brian Jackson
Hostess Quickly . . . . Kristine Nielsen	Gov. of Harfleur. . . . . Clement Fowler
Boy . . . . Robert Macnaughton	French Messenger. . . . . Neil Bradley
At Southampton:	At Agincourt:
Scroop . . . . Christopher Grove	Michael Williams . . . . John Pankow
Cambridge. . . . . Jamil Zakkai	John Bates. . . . . Robert Schenkkan
Grey. . . . . Eriq Ki LaSalle	Alexander Court. . . . . Joseph Urla
At the French Court:	Erpingham. . . . . Clement Fowler
King of France. . . . . George Guidall	Salisbury . . . . David Wayne Nelson
Dauphin . . . . Jack Stehlin	English Herald . . . . Loren Bass
Constable. . . . . Richard Backus	M. LeFer. . . . . Pierre Epstein

Soldiers, Lords, Attendants: Loren Bass, John Bauman, Christopher Bradley, Neil Bradley, Elizabeth Dennehy, Susan Gabriel, Christopher Grove, Brian Jackson, Eriq Ki LaSalle, David Wayne Nelson.

Musicians: John Bottomley, Garry Cheddy, Edward Smith bagpipes; Ron Stinson, Bill Rohdin trumpet; Bill Uttley percussion.

Understudies, the English: Mr. Guidall—Clement Fowler; Messrs. LeFevre, Pine—Michael Wetmore; Messrs. Schenkkan, Urla—David Warshofsky; Messrs. Warshofsky, Strickland, Bauman —Christopher Bradley; Mr. Macnaughton—Neil Bradley; Messrs. Zakkai, Jackson, Costa—David Wayne Nelson; Mr. Martin—Jamil Zakkai; Mr. Hindman—Eriq Ki LaSalle; Mr. Heald—Peter

McRobbie; Messrs. McRobbie, Bass, Nelson, Wetmore—John Bauman; Messrs. LaSalle, Grove—Loren Bass; Mr. Kline—Jack Stehlin; Mr. Hedaya—Larry Pine; Mr. Pankow—Joseph Urla.

Understudies, the French: Mr. Jones (Ambassador)—Joseph Maruzzo; Mr. Maruzzo—John Bauman; Messrs. Backus, Stehlin—Christopher Grove; Messrs. Fowler, Christopher Bradley, Neil Bradley—Loren Bass; Mr. Guidall—Clement Fowler; Messrs. Jones (Montjoy), Guilfoyle—Brian Jackson; Mr. Epstein—Neil Bradley; Misses Argent, Mastrantonio—Susan Gabriel; Miss Nielsen—Elizabeth Dennehy.

Directed by Wilford Leach; scenery, Bob Shaw; costumes, Lindsay W. Davis; lighting, Paul Gallo; fight direction, B.H. Barry; music, Allen Shawn; production stage manager, Ginny Martino; stage manager, James Harker.

Part I, England. Scene 1: The Royal Palace, London. Scene 2: A street outside the Boar's Head Tavern. Scene 3: The port of Southampton; Scene 4: Before the tavern, London. Part I, France. Scene 5 (Rouen): The palace of the French king. Scene 6 (Harfleur Oct. 6–8): The battlements of the port city. Scene 7: Near the mines dug by Henry's army beneath Harfleur's walls. Scene 8: At the gates of Harfleur. Scene 9 (Rouen, Oct. 13): A room in the Royal Palace. Scene 10 (On the way to Calais, Oct. 17): The camp of Henry's depleted army on its move to the English stronghold of Calais. Scene 11 (The eve of the Battle of Agincourt, Oct. 24–25): The French camp, near midnight to 2 A.M.

Part II. (The eve of the Battle of Agincourt, Oct. 24–25) Scene 1: The English camp, 3 A.M. and after. Scene 2: The French camp, sunrise. Scene 3: The English camp, sunrise. Scene 4: (The Battle of Agincourt, Oct. 25, 1415): The field of Agincourt. Scene 5: The English camp some days after the battle. Scene 6 (Rouen): The French palace. Epilogue.

The last major New York revival of *Henry V* was by New York Shakespeare Festival in Central Park 6/24/76 for 28 performances.

THE GOLEM

Rebbi	F. Murray Abraham	Red One	Mark Margolis
Spirit of the Golem	Mario Arrambide	Blind One	Moultrie Patten
Tadeus	Joseph Wiseman	One-Eyed	Larry Block
Isaac	Daniel Marcus	Lame One	Clark Middleton
Jacob	Clay Dickinson	One With the Stump	Rick Petrucelli
The Golem	Randy Quaid	Hunchback	Joel Plotkin
Rebbi's Wife	Bette Henritze	Old Beggar	Ron Weyand
Deborah	Melody Combs	Young Beggar	
Reb Bosevy	George Hamlin	(Messiah)	Christopher McCann
Tanchum	Jamil Zakkai	Monk	John P. Connolly
Beggars:		Man With the Cross	Judson Camp
Sick One	William Preston	Shames	Carl Don

Ensemble: Loren Bass, Wendy Brennan, Umit Celebi, Ryan Cutrona, Sam Garcia, David Gregory, Richard Krohn, James Lieb, Jordan Lund, Parlan McGraw, Conrad McMillan, Joe Parisi, Lenard Petit, David Taylor, Brita Youngblood.

Vocalists: Ephraim Biran, Richard Frisch, Avery Tracht.

Understudies: Mr. Abraham—Mark Margolis; Mr. Arrambide—James Lieb; Mr. Wiseman—George Hamlin; Mr. Marcus—Loren Bass; Messrs. Dickinson, Plotkin—Umit Celebi; Mr. Quaid—Mario Arrambide; Miss Henritze—Wendy Brennan; Miss Combs—Brita Youngblood; Messrs. Hamlin, Weyand—Moultrie Patten; Mr. Zakkai—John P. Connolly; Messrs. Preston, Patten—Judson Camp; Mr. Margolis—Joe Parisi; Messrs. Middleton, Petrucelli—Clay Dickinson; Mr. Block—Clark Middleton; Mr. McCann—David Gregory; Mr. Connolly—Conrad McMillan; Mr. Camp—Lenard Petit; Mr. Don—Joel Plotkin.

Directed by Richard Foreman; scenery, Richard Foreman, Nancy Winters; costumes, Natasha Landau; lighting, Pat Collins; music and sound, Stanley Silverman; production stage manager, Bonnie Panson; stage manager, Morton Milder.

Time: The past. Place: Prague. Scene 1: Clay. Scene 2: Walls. Scene 3: Through the darkness. Scene 4: Beggars. Scene 5: The castaways. Scene 6: Revelations. Scene 7: Underground. Scene 8: The last errand. The play was presented in two parts.

Melodrama of the supernatural, with the Golem a symbol of violence tragically invoked by a Jewish

HAROLD CLURMAN THEATER—*Left,* Glenn Close in Simone Benmussa's *Childhood; right,* Alice Drummond, James Greene, Peter Evans and Alvin Epstein in the silver anniversary revival of Samuel Beckett's *Endgame*

leader for the protection of his people. The only previous New York stagings of record were by the Habimah troupe in Hebrew the season of 1947–48 and off off Broadway by Jean Cocteau Repertory 2/11/82.

Note: Press date for *Henry V.* was 7/5/84, for *The Golem* was 8/16/84.

*The Harold Clurman Theater. Schedule of six programs. **Endgame** (123). Revival of the play by Samuel Beckett. Opened June 28, 1984. (Closed October 21, 1984) **All Strange Away** (17). By Samuel Beckett. Opened September 23, 1984. Closed October 7, 1984) **A Kurt Weill Cabaret** (130). Revival of the musical revue with music by Kurt Weill, lyrics by various authors (see credits in the list of musical numbers). Opened December 20, 1985. (Closed April 21, 1985) **An Evening With Ekkehard Schall** (11). One-man performance in the German language by Ekkehard Schall of two programs of words by Bertolt Brecht: *From Laughing at the World to Living in the World*, opened February 25, 1985; and *Questions, Laments, Answers*, opened February 27, 1985. (Repertory closed March 16, 1985) **Rommel's Garden** (23). By Harvey Gabor. Opened May 15, 1985. (Closed June 2, 1985) ***For No Good Reason** by Nathalie Sarraute, translated by Kate Mortley and **Childhood** adapted by Simone Benmussa from the book by Nathalie Sarraute, translated by Barbara Wright (3). Opened May 29, 1985. Produced by The Harold Clurman Theater, Jack Garfein artistic director; *Endgame* and *A Kurt Weill Cabaret* coproduced by Byron Lasky, *All Strange Away* co-produced by Kilian C. Ganly, at the Samuel Beckett Theater; *An Evening With Ekkehard Schall* co-produced by Lucille

Lortel at the Lucille Lortel Theater; *For No Good Reason* and *Childhood* produced at the Samuel Beckett Theater.

ENDGAME

Hamm .... Alvin Epstein   Nagg...................... James Greene
Clov .... Peter Evans   Nell.................... Alice Drummond

Directed by Alvin Epstein; scenery and costumes, Avigdor Arikha; lighting, Jennifer Tipton; stage manager, Jody Boese press, Jeffrey Richards Associates, C. George Willard.

The play was presented without intermission. The last major New York revival of *Endgame* was by Manhattan Theater Club 1/1/80 for 46 performances.

Joe Grifasi replaced Peter Evans and King Donovan replaced James Greene 9/84.

ALL STRANGE AWAY

Directed by Gerald Thomas; scenery and costumes, Daniela Thomas; lighting, Howard Thies; press, Jeffrey Richards Associates, C. George Willard. With Robert Langdon-Lloyd.

Beckett's 1976 prose piece—about the last man on earth sitting on the inside of a mirrored glass cube and bargaining for more life—adapted as a one-actor play, presented without intermission. A foreign play previously produced off off Broadway 1/2/84 at LaMama ETC.

A KURT WEILL CABARET

CAST: Martha Schlamme, Alvin Epstein, Steven Blier (piano).

Lighting, Kevin Rigdon; piano arrangements and adaptations, Steven Blier; produced by special arrangement with Arthur Shafman International, Ltd.; production stage manager, Glen Hauser; press, Henry Luhrman Associates, Terry M. Lilly, Helene Greene, David Mayhew.

Revue of Kurt Weill Broadway and Berlin songs now in its 15th year of performance coast to coast, including the Broadway production 11/5/79 for 72 performances.

Harry Huff replaced Steven Blier 1/1/85.

MUSICAL NUMBERS, ACT I: "Moritat (The Ballad of Mack the Knife)" (German lyrics by Bertolt Brecht, English version by Marc Blitzstein) from *The Threepenny Opera*—Alvin Epstein; "Barbara-Song" (English version by Marc Blitzstein) from *Threepenny*—Martha Schlamme; "Alabama-Song" (lyrics by Bertolt Brecht) from *The Rise and Fall of the City of Mahagonny*—Epstein, Schlamme; "Herr Jakob Schmidt" (lyrics by Bertolt Brecht) from *Mahagonny*—Epstein, Schlamme; "Ich Habe Gelernt" (lyrics by Bertolt Brecht) from *Mahagonny*—Epstein, Schlamme; "Ballad of Sexual Slavery" (English version by George Tabori) from *Threepenny*—Epstein; "There Was a Time" (English version by Marc Blitzstein) from *Threepenny*—Epstein, Schlamme.

Also "Pirate Jenny" (English version by Marc Blitzstein) from *Threepenny*—Schlamme; "Kanonensong" (English version by Marc Blitzstein) from *Threepenny*—Epstein; "Soldatenweib" (lyrics by Bertolt Brecht, his last collaboration with Kurt Weill)—Schlamme; "Eating" (English version by Arnold Weinstein) from *Mahagonny*—Epstein, Schlamme; "That's Him" (lyrics by Ogden Nash) from *One Touch of Venus*—Epstein, Schlamme; "The Life That We Lead" (English version by Will Holt) from *Mahagonny*—Epstein, Schlamme.

ACT II: "The Saga of Jenny" (lyrics by Ira Gershwin) from *Lady in the Dark*—Epstein, Schlamme; "September Song" (lyrics by Maxwell Anderson) from *Knickerbocker Holiday*—Epstein; "Le Roi D'Aquitaine" (lyrics by Jacques DeVal) from *Marie Galante*—Epstein, Schlamme; "Moon-Faced, Starry-Eyed" (lyrics by Langston Hughes) from *Street Scene*—Epstein, Schlamme; "It Never Was You" (lyrics by Maxwell Anderson) from *Knickerbocker*—Schlamme; "Tschaikowsky" (lyrics by Ira Gershwin) from *Lady in the Dark*—Epstein; "Bilbao Song" (lyrics by Bertolt Brecht) from *Happy End*—Schlamme; "Sailor's Tango" (English version by Will Holt) from *Happy End*—Epstein; "Surabaya Johnny" (lyrics by Bertolt Brecht) from *Happy End*—Schlamme; "Survival Song" (lyrics by Marc Blitzstein) from *Threepenny*—Epstein, Schlamme; Finale.

AN EVENING WITH EKKEHARD SCHALL

Piano, Karl-Heinz Nehring; associate producer, Naomi Koncius; press, Henry Luhrman Associates, Terry M. Lilly, David Mayhew, Andrew P. Shearer. With Ekkehard Schall.

Collection of Bertolt Brecht material adapted from productions at the Berliner Ensemble and performed by Brecht's son-in-law, one of that East German theater's leading actors, in the German language in his American debut.

PROGRAM ONE (*From Laughing at the World to Living in the World*): Ballad of the adventures (1917, music by Bertolt Brecht); Mounted on the fairground's magic horses (1920); Choral of the great Baal (1918, music by Bertolt Brecht); She says she is the truest girl alive (1925, music by Hans Dieter Hosalla); Victoria's song (circa 1955, music by Rudolf Wagner-Regeny); And when we think it over (circa 1926); Salmon-song (circa 1929, music by Kurt Weill); Far be it from me to suggest that Rockefeller is a fool . . . (circa 1926); "Bilbao Song" (1929, music by Kurt Weill); New version of the ballad of the good life (1949, music by Kurt Weill); Ballad of the dead soldier (1918); On the infanticide Marie Farrer (1922, music by Karl-Heinz Nehring).

Also Song of a German mother (1942, music by Hanns Eisler); Europa is Hitler's fortress (1939); The song of the girl and the soldier (circa 1933, music by Paul Dessau); The children's crusade (1939); No one, or us all (1934, music by Hanns Eisler); The Manifesto (1945); Resolution of the communards (circa 1948); Père Joseph (circa 1948, music by Hanns Eisler); In praise of the revolutionary (1931, music by Hanns Eisler); Ardens sed virens (1939, music by Hanns Eisler); New ages (1943); Ballad on approving of the world (1932, music by Hanns Eisler); From *Arturo Ui* (1941, music by Hans Dieter Hosalla); March of the calves (circa 1943, music by Hanns Eisler).

Also Ballad of Marie Sanders, the "Jew whore" (1935, music by Hanns Eisler); Ballad of the mill wheel (1934, music by Hanns Eisler); Song of rivers (1954, music by Hans Dieter Hosalla); In praise of doubt (1939); Song of a loving woman III (1950); Seven roses on the bush (music by Paul Dessau); Song of the gentle breeze (1943, music by Hanns Eisler); Seventh song of the god of happiness I (1939, music by Paul Dessau); To eat of the meat with pleasure (circa 1954); The joy of giving (circa 1950); Luck (circa 1939); Solidarity-song (1931, music by Hanns Eisler); Communism is the moderate way (1934); Remembering Marie A. (1920, music by Bertolt Brecht).

PROGRAM TWO (*Questions, Laments, Answers*): The devil (1941, music by Karl-Heinz Nehring); To M (circa 1920); Kin-Jeh's second song to his sister (circa 1937, music by Karl-Heinz Nehring); The little rose, oh how should it be listed (circa 1954); Concerning the insecurity of the human condition (1928, music by Kurt Weill); What keeps mankind alive? (1928, music by Kurt Weill); Draft of a social contract (circa 1923); Of the seduced girls (1920, music by Bertolt Brecht); Nanna's song (1936, music by Hanns Eisler); On vitality (1920); "Alabama-Song" (circa 1926); As you make your bed, so you lie on it (circa 1926, music by Kurt Weill); O moon of Alabama (circa 1926, music by Kurt Weill); Ballad of Hanna Cash (1921, music by Hans Dieter Hosalla); Questions from a worker who reads (1935); The hopers (circa 1934).

Also Song of the smoke 1943, music by Paul Dessau); "Falada, Falada, there thou art hanging" (1938, music by Hanns Eisler); The true story of the pied piper of Hamelin (1938, music by Rudolf Wagner-Regeny); Song of the S.A. man (circa 1931, music by Hanns Eisler); Epitaph for Karl Liebknecht (1948); Epitaph for Rosa Luxemburg (1948); Song of the Courts (1932); Article One of the Weimar constitution (1930–31, music by Karl-Heinz Nehring); The ballad of paragraph 218 (1930, music by Hanns Eisler); Lullabies IV (1932, music by Hanns Eisler); Change the world: it needs it (1932, music by Hanns Eisler); Hymn to God (1917); Take not as your teacher (circa 1920, music by Hans Leo Habler); Carefully I go over (1931); Hollywood elegies (1942, music by Karl-Heinz Nehring); Hollywood (1942).

Also Germany, you blond pale creature (1920); Germany (1933); The anachronistic procession, or freedom and democracy (1947, music by Hanns Eisler); Germany (1952); Born later (circa 1920); While you're alive, don't say never! (1931); That is good (1940); In praise of Communism (1931); The spring (1931, music by Hanns Eisler); Song about good people (circa 1939); About the way to construct enduring works (circa 1931); For humanity is menaced by wars! (1952, music by Siegfried Matthus); Song against war (circa 1934, music by Hanns Eisler); Peace song (1951, music by Hanns Eisler); Mary, Mary sat her down (1938, music folk song).

ROMMEL'S GARDEN

Pvt. Ackenbaum . . . . Lonny Price
Sgt. Wolff . . . . Jay O. Sanders

Directed by Jack Garfein; scenery, Charles Henry McClennahan; costumes, Ruth Morley; lighting, Jackie Manassee; production stage manager, Robert I. Cohen; press, Joe Wolhander Associates, Megan Svensen.

Time: 1944. Place: North Africa. The play was presented without intermission.

A land-mined area places two American soldiers in deadly danger in World War II.

FOR NO GOOD REASON

Man 1	Stephen Keep	Neighbors	Michael Grodenchik,
Man 2	Max Wright		Marek Johnson

CHILDHOOD

Actress	Glenn Close	Vera	Marek Johnson
Mother	Andrea Weber	And the voice of Nathalie Sarraute.	
Father	Stephen Keep		

Understudies: Judith Novgrod, Michael Mrodenchik

Directed by Simone Benmussa; scenery and lighting, Simone Benmussa, Antoni Taulé; costumes, Gail Brassard; Glenn Close's costume, Sonia Rykiel; production stage manager, Raymond Chandler.

Childhood is Nathalie Sarraute's 1983 memoir of a difficult childhood; the curtain raiser, *For No Good Reason*, was written as a radio play about an effort to patch up a broken friendship. Both are foreign (French) works presented without intermission and previously produced in France and Italy.

Roundabout Theater Company. 1983–84 schedule included **Come Back, Little Sheba** (98). Revival of the play by William Inge. Produced by Roundabout Theater Company, Gene Feist artistic director, Todd Haimes managing director, at the Roundabout Stage One. Opened July 12, 1984. (Closed September 2, 1984)

Doc	Philip Bosco	Mrs. Coffman	Patricia O'Connell
Marie	Mia Dillon	Milkman	Michael Corbett
Lola	Shirley Knight	Bruce	Steven Weber
Turk	Kevin Conroy	Ed Anderson	Tom Klunis
Postman; Announcer	William Newman		

Directed by Paul Weidner; scenery, Lowell Detweiler; costumes, Jeanne Button-Eaton; lighting, Judy Rasmuson; sound, Philip Campanella; production stage manager, Mimi Apfel; press, Adrian Bryan-Brown.

Place: The Delaney home in a run-down neighborhood of a Midwestern city. Act I, Scene 1: Morning in late spring. Scene 2: The same evening, after supper. Act II, Scene 1: The following morning. Scene 2: Late afternoon the same day. Scene 3: 5:30 the next morning. Scene 4: Morning, a week later.

Come Back, Little Sheba was first produced on Broadway 2/15/50 for 1191 performances and was named a Best Play of its season. This is its first major New York revival of record.

Shades of Harlem (258). Cabaret musical created by Jeree Palmer. Produced by Toni Conforti and Jerry Saperstein in association with Brian Winthrop at the Village Gate Downstairs. Opened August 21, 1984. (Closed April 6, 1985)

CAST: Branice McKenzie, Jeree Palmer, Ty Stephens, Renaissance Ladies (Ludie Jones, Juanita Boisseau, Alice Wilkie), Renaissance Girls (Sheila Barker, Doris Bennett, Melanie Daniels, Alyson Lang), Frank Owens (Band Leader and Pianist).

Musicians: Emme Kemp conductor, pianist; Tommie McKenzie bass; Barry Saperstein drums; Angel Allende percussion.

Directed by Mical Whitaker; choreography, Ty Stephens; musical direction, arrangements and additional concepts, Frank Owens; scenery, Linda Lombardi; costumes, Sharon Alexander; lighting, Robert Strohmeier; directoral consultant, Adam Wade; executive producers, Sal Surace, George

Tassone; associate producters, Howard Effron, Robert Roth, Hank Thomas; stage manager, Pam Osman; press, Max Eisen, Maria Somma.

A re-creation of an evening at the Cotton Club in the 1920s, with music of the period augmented by several new numbers.

MUSICAL NUMBERS, ACT I: "Shades of Harlem" (music by Frank Owens, lyrics by Ty Stephens and Jeree Palmer)—Ty Stephens, Jeree Palmer, Branice McKenzie, Renaissance Girls; "Take the 'A' Train" (by Billy Strayhorn)—Stephens; "I Love Harlem" (music by Frank Owens, lyrics by Ty Stephens and Jeree Palmer)—Stephens; "Sweet Georgia Brown" (by Bernice, Casey and Pinkard)—Renaissance Ladies and Girls; "That Ole Black Magic" (music by Harold Arlen, lyrics by Johnny Mercer)—Palmer; "Right Key, Wrong Keyhole"—Palmer; "Satin Doll" (by Duke Ellington, Billy Strayhorn and Johnny Mercer)—Stephens; "I Got It Bad and That Ain't Good" (by Duke Ellington and Paul Francis Webster)—McKenzie; "Black Coffee" (by Paul Francis Webster and Sonny Burke)—Stephens; "The Jitterbug" (by Frank Owens)—Stephens, Sheila Barker; "Harlem Hop" (music by Frank Owens, lyrics by Ty Stephens and Frank Owens)—Company.

ACT II: "Harlem" (music by Jeree Palmer, lyrics by Branice McKenzie and Ty Stephens)— Stephens, Palmer, McKenzie; "At a Georgia Camp Meetin' " (by Kerry Mills)—Renaissance Girls; "It Don't Mean a Thing" (by Duke Ellington)—Juanita Boisseau; "If You Wanna Keep Your Man" (music and lyrics by Branice McKenzie)—McKenzie, Palmer; "Diga Diga Doo" (by Jimmy McHugh and Dorothy Fields)—Stephens, Renaissance Girls; "Stowaway" (music and lyrics by Ty Stephens)—Stephens, Barker; "I'm Just Simply Full of Jazz" (by Eubie Blake)—Palmer; "My Man" (music by Maurice Yvain, English lyrics by Channing Pollock, French lyrics by Albert Wille-metz and Jacques Charles)—McKenzie; "On the Sunny Side of the Street" (by Jimmy McHugh and Dorothy Fields)—Stephens, McKenzie, Palmer, Frank Owens; "Body and Soul" (music by John Green, lyrics by Edward Heyman, Robert Sour and Frank Eyton)—Stephens; "I Got Rhythm" (music by George Gershwin, lyrics by Ira Gershwin)—Renaissance Ladies and Girls; "Perdido" (music by Juan Tizol, lyrics by Ervin Drake and Hans Lengsfelder)—Ludie Jones; "God Bless the Child" (by Billie Holliday and Arthur Herzog Jr.)—Palmer; "Shades of Harlem" (Reprise)—Company.

The Chinese Magic Revue (16). Produced by Bill Miller and I.A.I. Productions at the Promenade Theater. Opened September 4, 1984. (Closed September 16, 1984)

Production supervised by Ben Sprecher; lighting, Alvin Ho; technical director, Tom Shilhanek; press, Jeffrey Richards Associates, Toby Mailman. With the troupe of The Chinese Magic Revue.

Limited engagement of world-touring Taiwanese jugglers, acrobats, magicians, martial arts experts, etc., in a revue format.

Elvis Mania (18). One-man performance by Johnny Seaton. Produced by Off on Broadway Theater at Off on Broadway Theater. Opened September 4, 1984. (Closed September 16, 1984)

Directed by Leslie Irons; technical director, Larry Smith; scenery, Paul Malec; costumes, Jeffery Wallach; stage manager, Larry Smith; press, Jeffrey Richards Associates, Bob Ganshaw.

The Band: Pedro Sera lead guitar, Jim Cavanagh bass guitar, Jeffrey Miller rhythm guitar, Tom Teasley drums, Daryl Davies piano.

Seaton as Elvis Presley in a concert-style set of Presley numbers from each of three decades. The show was presented in three parts.

MUSICAL SETS, SET I: The 1950s The Sun Records, RCA, Victor Records and the beginning of the big gold ones—the songs of the 1950s. SET II: The 1960s after the interruption of the Army —the movies and TV Specials began a new style of Elvis music—the 1960s songs. SET III: The Vegas years—the emergence of Elvis as a great showroom entertainer—these are the songs of the 1970s.

Blue Window (96). By Craig Lucas. Produced by The Gero Organization and Force Ten Productions, Inc. in the Production Company production, Norman Rene artistic director,

Abigail Franklin managing director, at Theater Guinevere. Opened September 18, 1984 (see note). Closed December 9, 1984.

Emily	Maureen Silliman	Boo	Christine Estabrook
Tom	Lawrence Joshua	Griever	Brad O'Hare
Libby	Randy Danson	Alice	Margo Skinner
Norbert	Matt Craven		

Directed by Norman Rene; scenery, Loy Arcenas; costumes, Walker Hicklin; lighting, Debra J. Kletter; production stage manager, M.A. Howard; press, Jeffrey Richards Associates, Louis Stern, Ben Morse.

Seven people en route to a dinner party.

Note: *Blue Window* was originally produced as an off-off-Broadway production 6/12/84 at this same theater and was raised to full off-Broadway status on the date noted above.

Jane Galloway replaced Christine Estabrook.

Viva Vittorio! (14). Program of dramatic sketches conceived by Vittorio Gassman. Produced by ICM Artists, Ltd. in the Center Theater Group/Mark Taper Forum production at the Promenade Theater. Opened September 19, 1984. (Closed September 30, 1984)

CAST: Vittorio Gassman, Rhonda Aldrich, Neil Bagg, Nino Prester.

Directed by Vittorio Gassman; scenery and lighting, John De Santis; music, Fiorenzo Carpi; stage manager, James T. McDermott; press, PR Partners, Marilynn LeVine, Merle Frimark.

Star's showcase of sketches including material from Franz Kafka's *Report to the Academy,* Alexandre Dumas's and Jean-Paul Sartre's *Kean,* Luigi Pirandello's *The Man With the Flower in His Mouth,* Luciano Codignola's *On the Harmfulness of Theater* and William Shakespeare's *Othello* and *Hamlet.* The play was presented in two parts. Previously produced in Europe, Los Angeles and elsewhere.

Avner the Eccentric (209). One-man performance by Avner Eisenberg. Produced by Jack Garfein and Byron Lasky at Lamb's Theater. Opened September 20, 1984. (Closed April 13, 1985)

Lighting, Kevin Rigdon; designer, Gordon A. Juel; production stage manager, Gordon A. Juel; press, Jeffrey Richards Associates, C. George Willard.

One-man program of clowning, mime, juggling, magic, etc. The show was presented in two parts.

Rap Master Ronnie (49). Revue with music by Elizabeth Swados; lyrics by Garry Trudeau; additional lyrics by Elizabeth Swados. Produced by Rosita Sarnoff at Top of the Gate. Opened October 3, 1984. (Closed November 10, 1984)

Reathel Bean	Mel Johnson Jr.
Catherine Cox	Richard Ryder
Ernestine Jackson	

Directed by Caymichael Patten; musical director and arranger, John Richard Lewis; scenery, Neil Peter Jampolis; costumes, David Woolard; lighting, Anne Militello; sound, Tom Gould; choreography, Ronni Stewart; production stage manager, Nancy Harrington; press, Shirley Herz Associates, Sam Rudy, Peter Cromarty.

President Ronald Reagan (played by Reathel Bean) and his aides and policies satirized in a topical revue, presented without intermission.

MUSICAL NUMBERS: "The Assistant Undersecretary of State for Human Rights"—Catherine Cox; "The Class of 1984"—Reathel Bean, Cox, Mel Johnson Jr., Richard Ryder; "Cheese"—Johnson; "The Empire Strikes First"—Company; "Facts"—Cox; "The Majority"—Company; "New

Years in Beirut, 1983"—Ryder; "Nine to Twelve"—Bean, Johnson, Ryder; "O, Grenada"—Ernestine Jackson, Johnson; "One More Study"—Cox, Jackson; "Rap Master Ronnie"—Company; "The Round Up"—Bean, Johnson; "Self Made Man"—Ryder, Company; "Something for Nothing" (with appreciation to Mayfair Music Hall)—Company; "Take That Smile off Your Face"—Jackson; "Thinking the Unthinkable"—Company; "You're Not Ready"—Bean, Cox.

After the Fall (67). Revival of the play by Arthur Miller. Produced by Roger Berlind and Ray Larsen at Playhouse 91. Opened October 4, 1984. (Closed December 2, 1984)

Quentin	Frank Langella	Mother	Tresa Hughes
Felice	Lisa Dunsheath	Elsie	Delphi Harrington
Maggie	Dianne Wiest	Louise	Mary-Joan Negro
Holga	Laurie Kennedy	Lou	Henderson Forsythe
Father	Salem Ludwig	Mickey	Benjamin Hendrickson
Nurse; Carrie	Rose Arrick	Man	William Cain

Standby: Mr. Langella—Paul Collins. Understudies: Miss Wiest—Lisa Dunsheath; Messrs. Ludwig, Forsythe—William Cain; Misses Kennedy, Harrington, Dunsheath, Negro—Lauren Klein; Miss Hughes—Rose Arrick; Miss Arrick—Anne Marie Kuehling.

Directed by John Tillinger; scenery, John Lee Beatty; costumes, William Ivey Long; lighting, Dennis Parichy; sound, Gary Harris; production stage manager, Trey Hunt; stage manager, David Conte; press, Solters/Roskin/Friedman, Inc., Joshua Ellis, Cindy Valk.

Place: The mind, thought and memory of Quentin. The play was presented in two parts.

After the Fall was originally produced by Repertory Theater of Lincoln Center 1/23/64 for 59 performances and was named a Best Play of its season. This is its first major New York revival.

Kuni-Leml (298). Musical with book by Nahma Sandrow; music by Raphael Crystal; lyrics by Richard Engquist. Produced by the Jewish Repertory Theater and Jarick Productions, Ltd. at the Audrey Wood Theater. Opened October 9, 1984. (Closed April 21, 1985)

Simkhe; Sasha	Steve Sterner	Kalmen	Gene Varrone
Yankl; Yasha	Adam Heller	Max	Scott Wentworth
Reb Pinkhos	Mark Zeller	Libe	Susan Friedman
Carolina	Barbara McCulloh	Kuni-Leml	Stuart Zagnit

Musicians: Raphael Crystal piano, Kurt Briggs violin, Deb Spohnheimer bass, Peter Hammer percussion.

Understudies: Misses McCulloh, Friedman—Joanne Baum; Messrs. Sterner, Wentworth, Zagnit —Adam Heller; Messrs. Zeller, Varrone, Heller—Joel Kramer; Messrs. Zeller, Varrone, Zagnit— Steve Sterner; Messrs. Zagnit, Wentworth, Sterner, Heller—Jack Savage.

Directed by Ran Avni; musical staging, Haila Strauss; musical direction, Raphael Crystal; scenery, Joel Fontaine; costumes, Karen Hummel; lighting, Dan Kinsley; orchestrations, Raphael Crystal; production stage manager, Gay Smerek; press, Shirley Herz Associates, Sam Rudy, Peter Cromarty, Pete Sanders; press associates, Mary Bryant, Gary Lawrence.

Time: During the reign of Czar Alexander II, within a space of 24 hours before and during the holiday of Purim in 1880. Place: Odessa in the Ukraine.

Based on the 1880 Yiddish Theater farce *The Fanatic, or The Two Kuni-Lemls* by Avrom Goldfadn, about a young couple's conniving to marry against her father's wishes. Previously produced this season off off Broadway by Jewish Repertory Theater and transferred to off Broadway in that production.

ACT I

"Celebrate" .... Simkhe, Yankel, Pinkhos, Carolina
"The Boy Is Perfect" .... Kalmen
"Carolina's Lament" .... Carolina

ROUNDABOUT REVIVALS—*Left,* Kaye Ballard and E.G. Marshall in *She Stoops to Conquer; right,* Ken Marshall and Kate Burton in *The Playboy of the Western World*

"The World Is Getting Better' .... Sasha, Yasha, Max
"Cuckoo" .... Max, Caroline
"The Matchmaker's Daughter".. Libe
"A Meeting of the Minds" .... Pinkhos, Carolina
Act I Finale .... Company

ACT II

"A Little Learning".. Pinkhos
"Nothing Counts But Love".. Max, Carolina
"What's My Name"... Kuni-Leml
"Purim Song".. Sasha, Yasha, Kalmen
"Do Horses Talk to Horses?".. Libe, Kuni-Leml
"Lovesongs and Lullabies" .... Libe, Carolina
"Be Fruitful and Multiply"... Simkhe, Yankel
Act II Finale.. Company

*Roundabout Theater Company. Schedule of five revivals. **She Stoops to Conquer** (32). By Oliver Goldsmith. Opened October 9, 1984; see note. (Closed November 4, 1984) **Joe Egg** (34). By Peter Nichols. Opened January 6, 1985. (Closed February 3, 1985 and transferred to Broadway; see its entry in the Plays Produced on Broadway section of this volume) **The Playboy of the Western World** (55). By John Millington Synge. Opened January 30, 1985; see note. (Closed March 17, 1985) **An Enemy of the People** (55). By

Henrik Ibsen; new English version by Frank Hauser with Anna Bamborough. Opened March 27, 1985; see note. (Closed May 12, 1985) *The Voice of the Turtle (12). By John van Druten. Opened May 22, 1985; see note. Produced by the Roundabout Theater Company, Gene Feist artistic director, Todd Haimes managing director, She Stoops to Conquer at the Triplex Theater, Joe Egg at the Haft Theater and the others at the Roundabout Theater. All plays: Press, Solters/Roskin/Friedman, Inc., Joshua Ellis, Adrian Bryan-Brown, Keith Sherman, Cindy Valk.

SHE STOOPS TO CONQUER

Mrs. Hardcastle	Kaye Ballard	Fellows at Inn;	
Mr. Hardcastle	E.G. Marshall	Servants	W. Erik Maeder, Derek Conte
Tony Lumpkin	Nathan Lane	Pimple	Maggi-Meg Reed
Kate Hardcastle	Tovah Feldshuh	Marlow	Norman Snow
Constance Neville	Cynthia Dozier	Hastings	John Bedford-Lloyd
Landlord;		Diggory	Dane Knell
Sir Charles Marlow	Gordon Chater	Roger	Matthew Mundinger

Directed by Daniel Gerroll; scenery, Robert Thayer; costumes, Eloise Lunde; lighting, Allen Lee Hughes; sound, Philip Campanella; production stage manager, Kathy J. Faul.

Time: September 1774. Place: In the English countryside at a place over 50 miles west of London. The play was presented in two parts.

The last major New York revival of She Stoops to Conquer was by Roundabout off Broadway 4/25/71 for 36 performances.

JOE EGG

Bri	Jim Dale	Pam	Joanna Gleason
Sheila	Stockard Channing	Freddie	Gary Waldhorn
Joe	Tenney Walsh	Grace	Margaret Hilton

Directed by Arvin Brown; scenery, Marjorie Bradley Kellogg; costumes, Bill Walker; lighting, Ronald Wallace; sound, Philip Campanella; production stage manager, Kathy J. Faul.

Place: The living room of Bri's and Sheila's home. Time: The late 1960s. Act I: An evening in winter. Act II: Later the same night.

Joe Egg, as it is familiarly known, was first produced on Broadway 2/1/68 for 154 performances under its original title A Day in the Death of Joe Egg and was named a Best Play of its season. This is its first major New York revival.

THE PLAYBOY OF THE WESTERN WORLD

Margaret Flaherty	Kate Burton	Susan Brady	Brenda Foley
Shawn Keogh	Jarlath Conroy	Honor Blake	Leslie E. Daniels
Michael James Flaherty	Rex Everhart	Sara Tansey	Maggi-Meg Reed
Jimmy Farrell	Danny Sewell	Old Mahon	James Greene
Philly Cullen	Stephen Daley	Villagers	W. Erik Maeder,
Christopher Mahon	Ken Marshall		David Spaulding
Widow Quin	Caroline Kava		

Directed by Joe Dowling; scenery, Michael Sharp; costumes, A. Christina Giannini; lighting, Judy Rasmuson; sound, Philip Campanella; production stage manager, Kathy J. Faul.

Time: The turn of the century. Place: A village on the coast of Mayo, Ireland. Act I: An evening in autumn. Act II: The following day. Act III: Later that day.

The Playboy of the Western World was first introduced to Broadway audiences by the visiting Irish Players in November 1911. Its most recent major New York revival of record was in an off-Broadway musical version entitled Christy 10/14/75 for 40 performances (and a Broadway-bound musical version entitled Back Country closed in tryout 9/24/78).

AN ENEMY OF THE PEOPLE

Billing	Barrett Heins	Petra Stockmann	Janet Zarish
Mrs. Stockmann	Ruby Holbrook	Morten Stockmann	Bart Acocella
Peter Stockmann	Paul Sparer	Ellif Stockmann	Sean H.M. Reynolds
Hovstad	Mark Capri	Morten Kiil	Jack Bittner
Dr. Stockmann	Roy Dotrice	Aslaksen	Gordon Chater
Capt. Horster	DeVeren Bookwalter		

Townspeople: Robert Brownstein, Jared Roy, Alex Stuhl, Brian Tomlinson.

Understudy: Messrs. Bittner, Reynolds—Luke Reiter.

Directed by Frank Hauser; scenery, Bob Mitchell; costumes, A. Christina Giannini; lighting, Dennis Parichy; sound, Guy Sherman; production stage manager, K. Siobhan Phelan.

Time: The 1880s. Place: A small Norwegian town. Act I: Dr. Stockmann's living room, evening. Act II: The same, the next morning. Act III: The editor's room of the *People's Messenger*, later the same morning. Act IV: A room in Capt. Horster's house, the next night. Act V: Dr. Stockmann's house, the next morning. The play was presented in three parts with intermissions following Acts II and IV.

The last major New York revival of *An Enemy of the People* was by Repertory Theater of Lincoln Center in the Arthur Miller adaptation 3/11/71 for 54 performances.

THE VOICE OF THE TURTLE

Sally Middleton	J. Smith-Cameron	Bill Page	Chris Sarandon
Olive Lashbrooke	Patricia Elliott		

Directed by Robert Berlinger; scenery, Michael Sharp; costumes, Bary Odom; lighting, Ronald Wallace; sound, Philip Campanella; production stage manager, Matthew Mundinger.

Time: Over a weekend in early April 1943. Place: An apartment in the East Sixties, near Third Avenue, New York City. Act I, Scene 1: Friday afternoon. Scene 2: Friday evening. Act II, Scene 1: Saturday morning. Scene 2: Late Saturday night. Act III, Scene 1: Sunday morning. Scene 2: Late Sunday afternoon.

The Voice of the Turtle was first produced on Broadway 12/8/43 for 1,557 performances and was named a Best Play of its season. Its only previous major New York revival was off Broadway in the 1961–62 season for 16 performances.

Note: Press date for *She Stoops to Conquer* was 10/17/84, for *The Playboy of the Western World* 2/20/85, for *An Enemy of the People* 4/10/85, for *The Voice of the Turtle* 6/4/85.

The Light Opera of Manhattan (LOOM). Repertory of one new operetta revival and 12 running operetta revivals. **The New Moon** (42). Book and lyrics by Oscar Hammerstein II, Frank Mandel and Lawrence Schwab; music by Sigmund Romberg. Produced by The Light Opera of Manhattan, William Mount-Burke founder, Raymond Allen and Jerry Gotham artistic directors, at the Eastside Playhouse. Opened October 10, 1984. (Closed November 18, 1984)

Julie	Joyce Bolton	Jacques	John Palmore
M. Beaunoir; Capt. DeJean	William Briggs	Besac	Monty Bonnell
Alexander	Donald Grove	Marianne	Sylvia Lanka
Capt. Georges Duval	Bob Cuccioli	Philippe	Gary Harger
Vicomte Ribaud	Raymond Allen	Clotilde	Janette Leslie Jones
Robert Misson	Bruce Daniels		

Ensemble of Ladies, Gentlemen, Sailors, Brides, Townspeople, Colonists: Donavon Armbruster, Rick Dohring, Brent Erdy, Herman Gaddy, Christopher Goeke, Elena Maggal, Baha Mahdi, Sharon Maxwell, Stephanie Reingold, Ruth Rome, Lori Schaffer, Mary Setrakian.

Todd Ellison conductor, organist; Brian Molloy assistant musical director, pianist; Ellen Greiss percussionist; Maria Zimmerman violinist.

Directed by Raymond Allen and Jerry Gotham; musical direction, Todd Ellison; choreography, Jerry Gotham; scenery, William Olson; costumes, George Vallo; lighting, Mary Edith Jamison; stage manager, Jerry Gotham; press, Jean Dalrymple, Bruce R. McKillip.

Subtitled "A musical romance of the Spanish Main," this operetta was first produced on Broadway 9/19/28 for 509 performances. It was revived at Carnegie Hall 8/18/42 for 24 performances and at New York City Center 5/17/44 for 44 performances.

ACT I

Overture
Scene 1: M. Beaunoir's drawing room
"Dainty Wisp of Thistledown" .... Ladies
"Servant of the King" .... Ensemble
"Marianne" .... Robert
"Marianne" (Reprise).. Marianne, Men
"The Girl on the Prow" .... Marianne, Ensemble
"Interrupted Trio" .... Marianne, Duval, Robert
"Marianne" (Reprise)... Robert
Scene 2: A wharf outside the Cafe Creole
Interlude
"Softly, as in a Morning Sunrise"................................. Philippe, Ensemble
"Stouthearted Men".. Robert, Philippe, Men
"Marianne" (Reprise) and "Softly, as in a Morning Sunrise" (Reprise)...... Robert, Philippe
Scene 3: M. Beaunoir's drawing room
Interlude
"Gorgeous Alexander"..................................... Julie, Clotilde, Alexander
"One Kiss" .... Marianne, Ladies
"Gentle Airs, Courtly Manners"... Ensemble
"Wanting You"... Robert, Marianne, Ensemble
"One Kiss" (Reprise)....................................... Marianne, Ensemble

ACT II

Entr'act
Scene 1: On board the New Moon
"Lover, Come Back to Me" .... Marianne, Robert
"Stouthearted Men" (Reprise)................................... Robert, Philippe, Men
Scene 2: Outside Marianne's cabin on the Isle of Pines
"Try Her Out at Dances".................................... Alexander, Julie, Ensemble
"Softly, as in a Morning Sunrise" (Reprise) .... Philippe, Men
"Lover, Come Back to Me" (Reprise) .... Marianne, Robert, Men
Scene 3: Inside Marianne's cabin
"One Kiss" (Reprise) and "Wanting You" (Reprise)................... Robert, Marianne
Scene 4: Outside Marianne's cabin, the next morning
"Stouthearted Men" (Reprise)... Company

LOOM's 1984-85 repertory included 12 running productions mounted in previous seasons and presented on the following schedule (operettas have book and lyrics by W.S. Gilbert and music by Arthur Sullivan unless otherwise noted): *H.M.S. Pinafore* (42), opened June 6, September 12 and January 30; *Ruddigore* (14), opened June 20; *The Pirates of Penzance* (40), opened July 4, September 26 and February 28; *The Merry Widow* (35), English lyrics by Alice Hammerstein Mathias, based on the book by Victor Leon and Leo Stein, music by Franz Lehar, opened July 18 and March 27; *Rose Marie* (21), book and lyrics by Otto Harbach and Oscar Hammerstein II; music by Rudolf Friml and Herbert Stothart, opened August 8; *The Red Mill* (28), book and lyrics by Henry Blossom, music by Victor Herbert, opened November 21 and January 2.

Also *Babes in Toyland* (30), book by William Mount-Burke and Alice Hammerstein Mathias, lyrics by Alice Hammerstein Mathias, music by Victor Herbert, opened December 5; *The Yeomen of the Guard* (14), opened January 16; *Iolanthe* (14), opened February 13; *The Mikado* (14), opened March 13; *Mlle. Modiste* (21), book and lyrics by Henry Blossom, music by Victor Herbert, opened April

10; *Naughty Marietta* (28), book and lyrics by Rida Johnson Young, music by Victor Herbert, opened May 1. (Repertory closed May 26, 1985)

Performers in LOOM repertory during the 1984-85 season included Raymond Allen, Anna Maria Alvarez, Ken Aronowitz, Patricia A'Hearn, Donavon Armbruster, Joanne Adamko, Margaret Astrup, Joyce Bolton, William Briggs, Monty Bonnell, Christina Britton, Dorcas Bravo, Bill Bryan, Bob Cuccioli, Shane Culkin, Molly Conole, Michael Cheffo, William Carter Corson, Dakota Culkin, Bruce Daniels, Shawn Davis, Michael DeVries, Rick Dohring, John DeVries, Donald Grove, Antonia Garza, Ina Goldberg, Herman Gaddy, Barry Gallo, Kathleen Gill,

Also Gary Harger, Karen Hartman, Susan Holmes, Janette Leslie Jones, Marcello Jara, Robin Jarrett, Ann K. Kirschner, Julie Kontos, Rene Kramer, Lisa Korne, Deborah Karpel, Sylvia Lanka, Karl Lindevaldsen, Scott Logsden, Leif Lorenz, Anthony Mellor, Georgia McEver, Bruce McKillip, Steve Mattar, Sharon Maxwell, Elena Maggal, Anne Mitchell, Cole Mobley, Lorie Mayorga, Demas Moyer, Ed Napler, Claudia O'Neill, Dan O'Driscoll, Susanna Organek, Stephen O'Brien.

Also John Palmore, Gary Pitts, Millie Petroski, Ruth Rome, Irma Rogers, Sarah P. Reynolds, Ruth Stoner, Stephen Rosario, Frank Reller, Cheryl Savitt, Mark Stagnaro, Leslie Skolnik, Rhanda Spotton, Karl Szilagi, Lori Shaffer, Samuel Silvers, Eileen Sameth, Lance Taubold, Stephen Todar, Randal Turner, Colby Thomas, Ernesto Valenzuela, Melissa Weick, Glenn White.

Circle Repertory Company. Schedule of four programs. **Love's Labor's Lost** (38). Revival of the play by William Shakespeare; music by Norman L. Berman. Opened October 11, 1984. (Closed November 11, 1984) **Bing and Walker** (32). By James Paul Farrell. Opened December 2, 1984. (Closed December 30, 1984) **Dysan** (34). By Patrick Meyers. Opened January 20, 1985. (Closed February 17, 1985) **As Is** (49). By William M. Hoffman. Opened March 10, 1985. (Closed April 21, 1985 and transferred to Broadway; see its entry in the Plays Produced on Broadway section of this volume) Produced by Circle Repertory Company, Marshall W. Mason artistic director, Richard Frankel managing director, at the Circle Theater. All plays: Associate artistic director, B. Rodney Marriott; press, Reva Cooper.

LOVE'S LABOR'S LOST

King of Navarre	Christopher Goutman	Dull	Jack Davidson
Berowne	Michael Ayr	Costard	Joseph Mydell
Longaville	Ben Lemon	Moth	Eric Schiff
Dumaine	Charles T. Harper	Princess	Trish Hawkins
Boyet	Edward Seamon	Rosaline	Charlotte Graham
Marcade; Forester	Kelly Connell	Maria	Amy Epstein
Armado	Ken Kliban	Katharine	Lisa Pelikan
Sir Nathaniel	Colin Fox	Jacquenetta	Sharon Schlarth
Holofernes	Michael Higgins		

Musicians: Norman L. Berman keyboards, Richard Cohen woodwinds, Elizabeth Panzer harp, Mary Wooten cello.

Directed by Toby Robertson; scenery, Franco Colavecchia; costumes, Laura Crow; lighting, Dennis Parichy; sound, Chuck London Media/Stewart Werner; instrumental and vocal arrangements, Norman L. Berman; dances, Jessica Sayre; production stage manager, Earl Hughes.

The last major New York revival of record of *Love's Labour's (Labor's) Lost* was by Royal Shakespeare Company off Broadway 2/13/75 for 13 performances.

BING AND WALKER

Arthur Walker	Jack Davidson	Eddie Bing	Edward Power
Ellie Walker	Stephanie Musnick	Diane Bing	Samantha Atkins

Directed by Dan Bonnell; scenery, David Potts; costumes, Deborah Shaw; lighting, Mal Sturchio; sound, Chuck London Media/Stewart Werner; original music, Kevin Bartlett; production stage manager, Denise Yaney.

Time: The present, late summer. Place: The Walker backyard in Woods Hole, Mass. Act I: Early afternoon. Act II: An hour later.

Spinster, taking care of handicapped family members, gets a chance for happiness.

DYSAN

Jake..................	Jimmie Ray Weeks	Dysan..................	Katherine Cortez
Eddie Pataco...............	Danton Stone	Merwan	Steven Gregan
Spider Veloci............	Charles T. Harper	Sherheriarji..................	Mark Myers

Directed by B. Rodney Marriott; scenery, Christopher Barreca; costumes, Fran Rosenthal; lighting, Dennis Parichy; original music, Robert Tomaro; lyrics, Patrick Meyers; sound, Chuck London Media/Stewart Werner; production stage manager, Les Cockayne.

Time: 1987, early September. Place: A beach home on the northern coast of California.

A love triangle which has existed through various previous lives in continual reincarnation.

AS IS

Hospice Worker; Business Partner;		Lily..........................	Lily Knight
Nurse....................	Claris Erickson	Clones........ Mark, Myers, Lou Liberatore	
Rich	Jonathan Hogan	Pat; Orderly................	Lou Liberatore
Saul.....................	Jonathan Hadary	Brother; Barney................	Ken Kliban
Chet	Steven Gregan		

Also Doctors, Pick-Ups, Bartender, Bookstore Patrons, PWAs, Drug Dealers.

Understudies: Miss Erickson—Michelle Summerlin; Mr. Hogan—Steven Gregan; Mr. Hadary—Mark Myers; Messrs. Gregan, Kliban—Ken Novice; Miss Knight—Patricia Fletcher; Messrs. Myers, Liberatore—Eric Nightengale.

Directed by Marshall W. Mason; scenery, David Potts; lighting, Dennis Parichy; costumes, Michael Warren Powell; sound, Chuck London Media/Stewart Werner; associate director, George Boyd; production stage manager, Fred Reinglas.

Time: The present. Place: New York City. The play was presented without intermission.

The faithfulness of a homosexual lover to his partner, even though the latter has contracted AIDS. A Best Play; see page 197.

Medea and the Doll (18). By Rudy Gray. Produced by The Barbara Barondess Theater Lab at the Samuel Beckett Theater. Opened October 12, 1984. (Closed October 28, 1984)

Directed by Randy Frazier; design, Don Jensen; production stage manager, Otis White; press, Jeffrey Richards Associates, Ben Morse. With Maria E. Ellis, Morgan Freeman.

Psychiatrist copes with a case of child abuse. The play was presented in two parts.

The Miss Firecracker Contest (113). Return engagement of the play by Beth Henley. Produced by The Gero Organization, Stephen Graham and Joan Stein in the Manhattan Theater Club production at the Westside Arts Theater. Opened October 15, 1984. (Closed January 20, 1985)

Carnelle Scott	Holly Hunter	Delmount Williams........	Mark Linn-Baker
Popeye Jackson.................	June Stein	Mac Sam	Budge Threlkeld
Elain Rutledge...............	Claire Malis	Tessy Mahoney ..	Joyce Reehling Christopher

Standbys: Misses Christopher, Malis—Donna Davis; Messrs. Linn-Baker, Threlkeld—Michael Countryman.

Directed by Stephen Tobolowsky; scenery, John Lee Beatty; costumes, Jennifer Von Mayrhauser; lighting, Dennis Parichy; sound, Stan Metelits; production stage manager, Louis D. Pietig; press, Henry Luhrman Associates, Terry M. Lilly, Helene Greece, David Mayhew.

Time: The end of June and the beginning of July. Place: Brookhaven, Miss., a small Southern town.

Previously produced off Broadway last season in this production by the Manhattan Theater Club 5/1/84-8/25/84 and was named a Best Play of 1983-84.

The Country Girl (45). Revival of the play by Clifford Odets. Produced by Keller Theater Associates, Ltd., Jerry Keller/Noel L. Silverman, at the Chelsea Playhouse. Opened October 18, 1984. (Closed November 25, 1984)

Bernie Dodd	Jeffrey DeMunn	Nancy Stoddard	Jennifer Joyce
Larry	Richard Zobel	Frank Elgin	Hal Holbrook
Phil Cook	Victor Raider-Wexler	Georgie Elgin	Christine Lahti
Paul Unger	Gus Kaikkonen	Ralph	Marc Umile

Understudies: Mr. Holbrook—Victor Raider-Wexler; Mr. DeMunn—Gus Kaikkonen; Mr. Raider-Wexler—Richard Zobel; Messrs. Kaikkonen, Zobel—Marc Umile.

Directed by Richard Thomsen; scenery, Jack Chandler; costumes, Julie Schwolow; lighting, Phil Monat; production stage manager, Ginny Martino; press, Shirley Herz Associates, Sam Rudy, Peter Cromarty, Pete Sanders.

Time: Autumn, 1950. Act I, Scene 1: New York, backstage. Scene 2: A furnished flat, the same day. Scene 3: Backstage, ten days later. Scene 4: The flat, a week later. Scene 5: Boston, a dressing room. Act II, Scene 1: Boston, a few days later. Scene 2: The next day. Scene 3: New York, a dressing room.

The last major New York revival of *The Country Girl* was on Broadway 3/15/72 for 61 performances.

Zelda (20). One-woman play by William Luce, performed by Olga Bellin; based on the writings of Mrs. F. Scott Fitzgerald. Produced by Fred Kolo at the American Place Theater. Opened October 23, 1984. (Closed November 10, 1984)

Directed by Paul Roebling; scenery and costumes, Fred Kolo; lighting, Kirk Bookman; projections, Pete Buchin; production stage manager, Franklin Keysar; press, David Powers.

Ms. Bellin as Zelda Fitzgerald in the story of her life, including excerpts from her letters and other writings. The play was presented without intermission.

Pacific Overtures (109). Revival of the musical with book by John Weidman; music and lyrics by Stephen Sondheim; additional material by Hugh Wheeler. Produced by The Shubert Organization and McCann & Nugent at the Promenade Theater. Opened October 25, 1984. (Closed January 27, 1985)

Reciter	Ernest Abuba	Thief	Tim Ewing
Lord Abe	Tony Marino	Commodore Perry	John Bantay
Shogun's Mother;		Madam; Russian Admiral	Thomas Ikeda
British Admiral	Chuck Brown	Old Man; American Admiral	John Baray
Kayama Yesaemon	Kevin Gray	Boy; Dutch Admiral;	
Tamate; British Sailor	Timm Fujii	British Sailor	Francis Jue
John Manjiro; Fisherman;		Warrior; British Sailor	Ray Contreras
French Admiral	John Caleb	Imperial Priest	Tom Matsusaka
Merchant	Ronald Yamamoto	Fencing Master's Daughter	Allan Tung

Proscenium Servants: Gerri Igarashi, Gayln Kong, Diane Lam, Christine Toy.

Orchestra: David Weiss woodwinds, Ray Poole harp, Bruce Doctor percussion, David Loud synthesizer, Eric Stern piano.

Understudy: John Aller.

Directed by Fran Soeder; musical direction, Eric Stern; choreography, Janet Watson (original choreography, Patricia Birch); scenery, James Morgan; costumes, Mark Passerell; additional costumes, Eiko Yamaguchi; orchestrations, James Stenborg; dance music, Daniel Troob; production stage manager, Peter J. Taylor; stage manager, Elizabeth Farwell; Press, Fred Nathan and Associates, Ted Killmer, Anne Abrams, Leslie Anderson, Bert Fink.

Time: Act I, July, 1853; Act II, from then on. Place: Japan.

Pacific Overtures was originally produced and directed on Broadway by Harold Prince 1/11/76 for 193 performances and was named a Best Play of its season and received the Critics Award for best musical. This production, based on the March 1984 York Theater production, is its first major New York revival.

The list of musical numbers in *Pacific Overtures* appears on page 340 of *The Best Plays of 1975-76.*

Between Rails (37). By Eric Hertz. Produced by New Writers at the South Street Theater. Opened October 26, 1984. (Closed November 25, 1984)

Willie-mae... Thelma Louise Carter

Produced and directed by Hal Scott; scenery, Mark Haack; costume, Karen Perry; lighting, Shirley Prendergast; production stage manager, Joseph DePauw; press, Max Eisen.

One-character play about a black woman housekeeper talking about her life in the North during a train journey to the South. The play was presented without intermission.

I Hear Music . . . of Frank Loesser and Friends (32). Musical with songs by Frank Loesser, George Gershwin, Richard Rodgers, Kurt Weill, Stephen Sondheim, Giacomo Puccini, Jule Styne and others. Produced by Henry Luhrman at the Ballroom Theater. Opened October 29, 1984. (Closed December 2, 1984)

Ed Joffe	Brian Slawson
Colin Romoff	Jo Sullivan
Douglas Romoff	Greg Utzig

Directed by Donald Saddler; musical direction and arrangements, Colin Romoff; gowns, Robert Mackintosh; lighting and production coordination, Gene McCann; sound, Sandor Margolin; press, Henry Luhrman Associates, Terry M. Lilly, Helene Greece, David Mayhew.

Jo Sullivan recapitulates songs of her career written by her late husband, Frank Loesser, and others, supported by five musician-actors. Previously produced in summer theater.

Manhattan Theater Club. Schedule of six programs. **In Celebration** (40). By David Storey. Opened October 30, 1984; see note. (Closed December 2, 1984) **Husbandry** (32). By Patrick Tovatt. Opened November 27, 1984; see note. (Closed December 23, 1984) **Messiah** (40). By Martin Sherman. Opened December 11, 1984; see note. (Closed January 13, 1985) **Hang on to the Good Times** (40). Musical revue conceived by Richard Maltby Jr., Gretchen Cryer and Nancy Ford; songs by Gretchen Cryer and Nancy Ford. Opened January 22, 1985; see note. (Closed February 24, 1985) **Digby** (37). By Joseph Dougherty. Opened March 8, 1985; see note. (Closed April 7, 1985) **California Dog Fight** (40). By Mark Lee. Opened April 16, 1985; see note. (Closed May 19, 1985) Produced by Manhattan Theater Club, Lynne Meadow artistic director, Barry Grove managing director, *In Celebration, Messiah, Hang on to the Good Times, Digby,* and *California Dog Fight* at City Center Theater, *Husbandry* at DownStage. All plays: Press, Virginia P. Louloudes, Howard Sherman.

IN CELEBRATION

Steven Shaw.................	Frank Grimes	Mrs. Shaw	Pauline Flanagan
Mr. Shaw.................	Robert Symonds	Andrew Shaw	Malcolm McDowell
Mrs. Burnett	Margaret Hilton	Colin Shaw..............	John C. Vennema

Directed by Lindsay Anderson; scenery, John Lee Beatty; costumes, Linda Fisher; lighting, Dennis Parichy; sound, Stan Metelits; production stage manager, Peggy Peterson; stage manager, Travis DeCastro.

Place: The living room of Mr. and Mrs. Shaw's house in the North of England. Act I, Scene 1: Late morning. Scene 2: Afternoon. Act II, Scene 1: Late evening. Scene 2: Morning.

Three sons return home for their parents' 40th anniversary, exposing past and present family frictions. A foreign play previously produced in London and in Washington, D.C., Los Angeles, Cleveland and off off Broadway 11/77 by Academy Arts Theater Company.

HUSBANDRY

Dee	Gloria Cromwell	Harry	James Rebhorn
Les	Richard Hamilton	Bev	Deborah Hedwall

Directed by Jon Jory; scenery, David Jenkins; costumes, Marcia Dixcy; lighting, F. Mitchell Dana; production stage manager, Johnna Murray; stage manager, Anne S. King.

Time: One evening in early spring. Place: An old farmhouse. The play was presented without intermission.

Today's American farmer battling financial and other difficulties. Previously produced at Actors Theater of Louisville.

MESSIAH

Rachel	Diane Venora	Reb Ellis	David Warrilow
Rebecca	Verna Bloom	Asher	Mark Blum
Tanta Rose	Karen Ludwig	Sarah	Margaret Gibson

Directed by David Leveaux; scenery, Tony Straiges; costumes, Linda Fisher; lighting, James F. Ingalls; composer, Robert Dennis; production stage manager, William Chance; stage manager, Karen Armstrong.

Time: 1665. Place: Yultishk, a small village on what was once the Ukranian border of Poland. The play was presented in two parts.

Victimized villagers believe a Messiah has come to rescue them.

HANG ON TO THE GOOD TIMES

Terri Klausner   Don Scardino
Cass Morgan   Charlaine Woodard

Musicians: Jack Bashkow reeds; Gary Pagin cello, bass; Tom Goldstein drums, percussion; Lee Grayson bass guitar; Cheryl Hardwick keyboards; Jay McGeehan guitar, banjo.

Standbys: Misses Klausner, Morgan, Woodard—Kirsti Carnahan; Mr. Scardino—Scott Robertson.

Directed by Richard Maltby Jr.; choreography, Kay Cole; musical direction, Cheryl Hardwick; scenery and projections, James Morgan; costumes, Karen Gerson; lighting, Mary Jo Dondlinger; sound, Sound Associates, Inc.; additional sound design, John Dumke, Jon Wolfson; orchestrations and arrangements, Cheryl Hardwick, Steven Margoshes; production stage manager, Peggy Peterson; stage manager, Karen L. Carpenter.

Collection of songs from Ford-Cryer concerts, records and musicals (*Shelter* and *I'm Getting My Act Together and Taking It on the Road*), 1967–1980, all music by Nancy Ford, lyrics by Gretchen Cryer except as indicated in the listing below.

MUSICAL NUMBERS, ACT I: "Big Bill Murphy" (lyrics by Gretchen Cryer and Nancy Ford)—Company; "In a Simple Way I Love You"—Don Scardino; "Strong Woman Number"—Charlaine Woodard; "You Can Never Know My Mind"—Terri Klausner; "Do Watcha Gotta Do" (music by Gretchen Cryer)—Cass Morgan, Company; "Too Many Women in My Life"—Scardino, Company; "You Can Kill Love"—Klausner, Morgan, Woodard; "She's My Girl"—Scardino, Klausner, Company; "Dear Tom"—Morgan; "Changing"—Woodard, Company; "Happy Birthday" —Company.

ACT II: "Goin' Home With My Children"—Klausner, Company; "Mary Margaret's House in the Country"—Woodard, Company; "White Trash Motel"—Scardino, Company; "Last Day at the Job" —Morgan, Company; "The News"—Company; "Rock Singer"—Company; "Put in a Package and Sold"—Klausner, Company; "Lonely Lady" (music by Gretchen Cryer)—Woodard; "Blackberry Wine" (music by Gretchen Cryer)—Morgan; "Old Friend"—Scardino; "Hang on to the Good Times"—Company.

MANHATTAN THEATER CLUB—Malcolm McDowell in David Storey's *In Celebration,* directed by Lindsay Anderson

DIGBY

Digby Merton .... Anthony Heald	Nelson Worth .... John Glover
Harry Crocker............ Keith Szarabajka	Mrs. Grace Evert .... Marilyn Redfield
Carl Evert .... Bernie McInerny	Alfred Becker .... Tony Goldwyn
Faye Greener............... Roxanne Hart	Lester Delehanty.............. John Polito

Standbys: Mr. Heald—Tony Goldwyn; Messrs. Polito, Goldwyn, Szarabajka—Steve Hofvendahl.

Directed by Ron Lagomarsino; scenery, James Leonard Joy; costumes, Rita Ryack; lighting, Curt Osterman; sound, Lawrence White; production stage manager, Johnna Murray; stage manager, Trey Hunt.

Place: In and around New York City. Act I: June. Act II: August.

Romantic comedy, boy looking for a platonic relationship meets girl who is not.

CALIFORNIA DOG FIGHT

Skip..................... Bruce MacVittie	Vern .... Darren McGavin
Pete...................... James Remar	Rawley .... Jimmie Ray Weeks
Sarah................. Mariel Hemingway	Lillian..................... Sheree North

Directed by Bill Bryden; scenery, Santo Loquasto; costumes, Rita Ryack; lighting, Andy Phillips; sound, Stan Metelits; animals, William Berloni; production stage manager, Scott LaFeber; stage manager, Susi Mara.

Time: The present. Place: The Sacramento delta. The play was presented in two parts.

Dog fighting as a parable of modern existence, with the program note that dogs used in this production "have been carefully and professionally trained to perform. . . . . . They have been, and will continue to be, treated in a most humane and caring fashion."

Note: Press date for *In Celebration* was 11/8/84, for *Husbandry* was 12/9/84, for *Messiah* was 12/23/84, for *Hang on to the Good Times* was 2/17/85, for *Digby* was 3/19/85, for *California Dog Fight* was 4/30/85.

The Pretender (23). By Harvey Parker. Produced by New-Cal Theatrical Productions Ltd. at the Chernuchin Theater. Opened October 31, 1984. (Closed November 18, 1984)

Directed by Ellyn Gersh; scenery and lighting, Jeffrey L. Robbins; costumes, Gail Cooper-Hecht; stage manager, John Kaywood; press, PR Partners, Marilynn LeVine, Merle Frimark. With Stanley Bojarski, Maureen Kilmurray, Cornelia Mills, Chazz Palminteri, Craig Paul Wroe.

Comedy, young man pretends to be gay in order to approach the girl next door.

*The Foreigner (242). By Larry Shue. Produced by John A. McQuiggan at the Astor Place Theater. Opened November 1, 1984.

"Froggy" LeSueur. . . . . Larry Shue	Catherine Simms. . . . . Patricia Kalember
Charlie Baker. . . . . Anthony Heald	Owen Musser. . . . . Christopher Curry
Betty Meeks. . . . . Kathleen Claypool	Ellard Simms. . . . . Kevin Geer
Rev. David Marshall Lee. . Robert Schenkkan	

Understudies: Messrs. Shue, Heald—Chet Leaming; Miss Kalember—Donna Bullock; Messrs. Shenkkan, Geer, Curry—Stephen Ahern.

Directed by Jerry Zaks; scenery, Karen Schulz; costumes, Rita Ryack; lighting, Paul Gallo; sound, Aural Fixation; associate producers, Douglas M. Lawson, Melanie Massey, Gina Rogak; production stage manager, George Darveris; press, Patricia Krawitz, Robert W. Larkin.

Time: The recent past. Place: Betty Meeks's fishing lodge resort, Tilghman County, Georgia. Act I, Scene 1: Evening. Scene 2: The following morning. Act II, Scene 1: Afternoon, two days later. Scene 2: That evening.

Comedy, very shy Englishman on vacation in Georgia pretends he can't speak the language. Previously produced by Milwaukee Repertory Theater.

A Best Play; see page 145.

Losing It (22). By Jon Klein. Produced by Mary Kell and Don Leslie at the Provincetown Playhouse. Opened November 8, 1984. (Closed November 25, 1984).

Arch Leighton. . . . . Larry Nicks	The Kid . . . . Jeff Alan-Lee
Cutty Morre. . . . . Richard Karn	

Directed by Andrew Cadiff; scenery and lighting, Paul Wonsek; production stage manager, Arlene Grayson; press, Becky Flora.

Comedy, two rustics cope with life over their backyard beers.

*New York Shakespeare Festival. Schedule of ten programs. **The Ballad of Soapy Smith** (25). By Michael Weller. Opened November 12, 1984. (Closed December 2, 1984) **La Boheme** (38). Revival of the opera based on the novel by Henri Murger; original libretto by Giuseppe Giacosa and Luigi Illica; English language adaptation and new lyrics by David Spencer; music by Giacomo Puccini. Opened November 29, 1984. (Closed December 30, 1984) ***Tracers** (169). Conceived by John DiFusco; written by Vincent Caristi, Richard Chaves, John DiFusco, Eric E. Emerson, Rick Gallavan, Merlin Marston and Harry Stephens with Sheldon Lettich; presented in The Vietnam Veterans Ensemble Theater Company production, Thomas Bird artistic director. Opened January 21, 1985. **Coming of Age in Soho** (65). By Albert Innaurato. Opened February 3, 1985. (Closed March 31, 1985) **Tom and Viv** (37). By Michael Hastings; presented in the Royal Court Theater production. Opened February 6, 1985. (Closed March 10, 1985)

Also **Virginia** (35). By Edna O'Brien; based on the lives and writings of Virginia and Leonard Woolf. Opened March 4, 1985. (Closed April 14, 1985) **Salonika** (56). By Louise Page; produced by arrangement with Hume Cronyn. Opened April 2, 1985. (Closed May 19, 1985) ***The Normal Heart** (45). By Larry Kramer. Opened April 21, 1985. ***The Marriage of Bette and Boo** (18). By Christopher Durang. Opened May 16, 1985. ***Rat in the Skull** (12). By Ron Hutchinson; presented in the Royal Court Theater production. Opened May 21, 1985. Produced by New York Shakespeare Festival, Joseph Papp producer, Jason Steven Cohen associate producer, at the Public Theater (see note). All plays: Press, Merle Debuskey, Richard Kornberg, Bruce Campbell, Don Summa.

THE BALLAD OF SOAPY SMITH

Paul Anthony
  MacAleer............ Christopher Cooper
George Wilder................ Jon DeVries
Jefferson Randolph
  "Soapy" Smith .... Dennis Arndt
Jedediah "Tripod" Schultz... James Hilbrandt
Maj. James Strong........ William Andrews
William Whitmore........... Brad Sullivan
Calvin Barkdull........... Larry Bryggman
Michael C. Sherpy............ Dierk Torsec
Frank Reid................... Kevin Tighe
Frenchie Villiers .... Jimmy Smits
Pearl..................... Lori Tan Chinn
Fritz .... Olek Krupa
Rev. Dickey................ Pierre Epstein
Tagish Sam .... E. Claude Richards
Kitty Chase .... Cherry Jones
Mattie Silks .... Marjorie Nelson

Burke Gallagher; U.S. District Commissioner
  Charles A. Shelbrede........ John Spencer
Charlie "The Reverend"
  Bowers.................. Nesbitt Blaisdell
William H. "Doc" Jackson .. Peter McRobbie
Syd Dixon .... Stephen Markle
Red Gibbs .... Timothy Carhart
Mrs. Whitmore .... Hortensia Colorado
Mrs. Barkdull; Prostitute;
  Mollie Fewclothes .... Marisa Zalabak
Mrs. Sherpy; Prostitute........ Brooke Myers
Mrs. Dickey.............. Annette Helde
Clancy; Man in Bed #1........ Peter Rogan
Jensen; Photographer .... James Eckhouse
Cpl. Egan............... Kevin McClarnon
Gov. John Brady........... Joseph Warren
J.D. Stewart............. John C. McGinley
Piano Player.............. Nancy Waldman

Skagway Townspeople, Miners, Alaska Militia, Skagway Militia, Vigilantes, Mattie Silks' Girls: Lori Tan Chinn, Hortensia Colorado, James Eckhouse, Pierre Epstein, Annette Helde, Olek Krupa, Laura MacDermott, Kevin McClarnon, John C. McGinley, Brooke Myers, Peter Rogan, Jimmy Smits, Dierk Torsel, Joseph Warren, Marisa Zalabak.

Directed by Robert Egan; music, Norman Durkee; songs, Michael Weller; scenery, Eugene Lee; costumes, Robert Blackman; lighting Jennifer Tipton; fight direction, B.H. Barry; production stage manager, Stephen McCorkle; stage manager, Mitchell Lemsky.

Time: Between 1897 and 1898. Place: Skagway, Alaska. The play was presented in three parts.

A con man's adventures in Alaska in the Gold Rush era. Previously produced by Seattle Repertory Theater.

LA BOHEME

Marcel .... Howard McGillin
(Rodolfo) .... David Carroll, Gary Morris
Colline .... Keith David
Schaunard .... Neal Kline
Benoit...................... Joe Pichette
(Mimi) .... Patti Cohenour,
            Linda Ronstadt, Caroline Peyton
Musette.................... Cass Morgan
Alcindoro.............. Merwin Goldsmith
At the Cafe Momus:
  Maitre D' .... John Herrera

Waiters .... Bill Carmichael,
                          Daniel Marcus
Trumpet Vendor............. James Judy
Bonnet Vendor............. Marcie Shaw
Lady With Pearls.......... Nancy Heikin
Parpignol............... Michael Willson
  Students: Margaret Benczak, Carol Dennis, Caroline Peyton, Joe Pichette.
In a hotel courtyard:
  Head Sweeper............... James Judy
  Sweepers .... John Herrera, Bill Carmichael

Night Clerk. . . . . Daniel Marcus
Hall Porters . . . . Joe Pichette,
    Michael Willson

Dairymaids: Margaret Benczak, Carol
Dennis, Nancy Heikin, Caroline Peyton, Marcie Shaw.

(Parentheses indicate roles in which the performers alternated)

Understudies: Misses Cohenour, Ronstadt, Peyton—Margaret Benczak; Mr. McGillin—Bill
Carmichael; Miss Morgan—Carol Dennis, Nancy Heikin; Messrs. Carroll, Morris—John Herr-
era; Mr. Klein—James Judy; Messrs. Pichette, Goldsmith—Daniel Marcus; Mr. David—Michael
Willson.

Musicians: Dale Kleps, James Ferraioulo, Richard Cohen reeds; Will Parker French horn; Peter
Prosser cello; John Feeney bass; Barbara Allen harp; Robby Kirshoff guitar, mandolin; Fred
Weldy, Edward Strauss keyboards; Glenn Rhian, Jason Cirker percussion.

Directed by Wilford Leach; musical supervisor and conductor, William Elliott; scenery, Bob
Shaw; costumes, Jane Greenwood; lighting, Paul Gallo; sound, Tom Morse; orchestrations, Michael
Starobin; assistant conductor, Vincent Fanuele; production stage manager, James Harker; stage
manager, Robin Herskowitz.

Place: Paris. Act I: A garret, Christmas Eve. Act II: The Latin Quarter and Cafe Momus,
Christmas Eve. Act III: A courtyard, some weeks later. Act IV: The garret again, late summer or
early fall. The play was presented in two parts with the intermission following Act II.

La Boheme, with a book based on *Scenes de la Vie de Boheme* by Henri Murger about Bohemian
life in Paris, was first presented at Teatro Regio in Turin, Italy, 2/1/96. Its first New York performance took place 12/26/00 at the Metropolitan Opera House with Nellie Melba as Mimi and Albert
Seleza as Rodolfo.

TRACERS

Professor. . . . . R.J. Bonds
Sgt. Williams . . . . J. Kenneth Campbell
Baby San . . . . Vincent Caristi
Dinky Dau. . . . . Richard Chaves

Habu. . . . . Anthony Chisholm
Doc. . . . . Josh Cruze
Little John . . . . Brian Delate
Scooter . . . . Jim Tracy

Directed by John DiFusco; scenery, John Falabella; costumes, David Navarro Velasquez; lighting,
Terry Wuthrich; dramaturgy, David Berry; production stage manager, Michael Chambers; stage
manager, Anne Marie Hobson.

Time: The Vietnam War, shortly thereafter and the present. The play was presented in two
parts.

Episodes of Vietnam warfare and postwar trauma, created by the original cast at the Odyssey
Theater, Los Angeles. Also previously produced by Steppenwolf in Chicago.

Music for *Tracers* (recorded), ACT I: "Walking on a Thin Line"—Huey Lewis and The News;
"Shut Out the Light"—Bruce Springsteen; "Fixin' to Die Rag"—Country Joe and The Fish; "Sympathy for the Devil"—Rolling Stones.

ACT II: "Light My Fire" and "The Unknown Soldier"—The Doors; "Four & Twenty Years Ago"
—Crosby, Stills, Nash & Young; "We Gotta Get Outa This Place"—The Animals; "Higher"—Sly
and the Family Stone; "Born in the U.S.A."—Bruce Springsteen; "Gimme Shelter—Rolling Stones;
"Born Never Asked"—Laurie Anderson.

Post-Epilogue: "Captains of Courage" (by Brian Delate and Hal Brister)—The Wise Guys.

A Best Play; see page 165.

COMING OF AGE IN SOHO

Beatrice . . . . John Procaccino
Patricia. . . . . Mercedes Ruehl
Danny. . . . . Evan Miranda
Dy. . . . . Scott DeFreitas

Puer . . . . Ward Saxton
Pasquale. . . . . Stephen Rowe
Trajan. . . . . Michael Dolan

Directed by Albert Innaurato; scenery, Loren Sherman; costumes, Ann Emonts; lighting, James
F. Ingalls; production stage manager, Jim Bernardi; stage manager, Evan Canary.

Time: The present, late winter, early spring. Place: A loft building in SoHo. Act I: Beatrice's loft.
Act II, Scene 1: Beatrice's loft, a week after Act I. Scene 2: Beatrice's loft, the same day.

Writer, confused in sexual identity and career objectives, finds himself with the help of two runaway boys. Previously produced in previews 11/30/84–12/6/84 by New York Shakespeare Festival, after which it recessed for revisions.

TOM AND VIV

Tom; Charles Marion		Louise.....................	Michele Copsey
Todd	Edward Herrmann	Rose	Margaret Tyzack
Viv	Julie Covington	Charles;	
Maurice	David Haig	William Leonard James.....	Richard Butler

Directed by Max Stafford-Clark; scenery and costumes, Antony McDonald, Jock Scott; lighting, Robin Myerscough-Walker; stage managers, Kate Salberg, Bethe Ward.

Time: Part 1, 1915. Part 2, 1921. Part 3, 1927. Part 4, 1932. Part 5, 1935. Part 6, 1937. Part 7, 1947. The play was presented in two acts, with the intermission following Part 3.

The troubled marriage of T.S. Eliot and Vivienne Haigh-Wood, his first wife. A foreign play previously produced in London in this Royal Court Theater production.

VIRGINIA

Virginia.....................	Kate Nelligan	Vita......................	Patricia Elliott
Virginia's Father;			
Leonard Woolf	Kenneth Welsh		

Directed by David Leveaux; scenery and costumes, Santo Loquasto; lighting, Arden Fingerhut; production stage manager, William Chance; stage manager, Karen Armstrong.

Time: 1882–1942. Place: London and the English countryside. The play was presented in two parts.

Study of the famous author Virginia Woolf and her friends, including Vita Sackville-West. A foreign play previously produced in London and Stratford, Ont.

SALONIKA

Charlotte	Jessica Tandy	Leonard	Thomas Hill
Enid	Elizabeth Wilson	Peter...................	Maxwell Caulfield
Ben.....................	David Strathairn		

Directed by John Madden; scenery, Andrew Jackness; costumes, Dunya Ramicova; lighting, Paul Gallo; production stage manager, Stephen McCorkle; stage manager, Robin Herskowitz.

Place: Greece, the beach at Salonika after a tide. The play was presented in two parts.

Octogenarian widow visits the grave of her husband, a World War I casualty in Greece, more than half a century after his death. A foreign play previously produced at the Royal Court Theater, London.

THE NORMAL HEART

Craig Donner; Grady;		Dr. Emma Brookner........	Concetta Tomei
Orderly	Michael Santoro	Bruce Niles	David Allen Brooks
Mickey Marcus	Robert Dorfman	Felix Turner.................	D.W. Moffett
Ned Weeks..................	Brad Davis	Ben Weeks...........	Phillip Richard Allen
David; Hiram Keebler; Examining Doctor;		Tommy Boatwright.......	William DeAcutis
Orderly	Lawrence Lott		

Directed by Michael Lindsay-Hogg; scenery, Eugene Lee, Keith Raywood; costumes, Bill Walker; lighting, Natasha Katz; song "We're Living in Wartime" by Michael Callen, performed by Pam Brandt, Michael Callen, Janet Cleary, Richard Dworkin; production stage manager, Kathleen Blair Costello; stage manager, Alan R. Traynor.

Time: Between July 1981 and May 1984. Place: New York City.

Gay activist and his friends become increasingly alarmed at the onset of the disease AIDS, to which society seems alarmingly indifferent.

THE MARRIAGE OF BETTE AND BOO

Bette Brennan	Joan Allen	Boo Hudlocke	Graham Beckel
Margaret Brennan	Patricia Falkenhain	Karl Hudlocke	Bill Moor
Paul Brennan	Bill McCutcheon	Soot Hudlocke	Olympia Dukakis
Joan Brennan	Mercedes Ruehl	Father Donnally; Doctor	Richard B. Shull
Emily Brennan	Kathryn Grody	Matt	Christopher Durang

Directed by Jerry Zaks; scenery, Loren Sherman; costumes, William Ivey Long; lighting, Paul Gallo; original music, Richard Peaslee; production stage manager, James Harker; stage manager, Pamela Singer.

Act I, Scene 1: The wedding. Scene 2: The honeymoon. Scene 3: Margaret gives Emily advice. Scene 4: The honeymoon, continued. Scene 5: Emily practises the cello. Scene 6: Bette and Boo visit their in-laws. Scene 7: Margaret gives Bette advice. Scene 8: Twenty years later, Boo has dinner with his son. Scene 9: The first child of Bette and Boo. Scene 10: Matt's favorite movie essay; arts and crafts with Emily. Scene 11: The second child of Bette and Boo. Scene 12: Bette and Margaret visit Emily in a rest home. Scene 13: Father Donnally gives Bette advice. Scene 14: Soot gives Bette advice. Scene 15: Matt talks about the Mayor of Casterbridge. Scene 16: The third child of Bette and Boo. Scene 17: Bette telephones Bonnie Wilson. Scene 18: Bette and Boo celebrate Thanksgiving.

Act II, Scene 19: Boo takes a pledge in front of Father Donnally. Scene 20: Bette and Boo go dancing. Scene 21: Matt's holiday essay; Bette and Boo celebrate Christmas. Scene 22: Twenty years later, Boo has dinner with his son; twenty years later, Bette has dinner with her son. Scene 23: Boo's second pledge in front of Father Donnally. Scene 24: Joan's birthday celebration. Scene 25: The funeral of Paul Brennan. Scene 26: The fourth child of Bette and Boo. Scene 27: Father Donnally gives Bette advice again. Scene 28: Father Donnally's marriage retreat. Scene 29: The divorce of Bette and Boo. Scene 30: Matt has dinner with Karl, Soot, Margaret and Paul. Scene 31: Matt gives Emily advice. Scene 32: The last child of Bette and Boo. Scene 33: Matt visits Bette; Bette and Boo reminisce.

Devastating cross-purposes and scarring battles of family life pictured in a series of black-comedy episodes narrated by Matt, the grown son of Bette and Boo. Previously produced in shorter versions at Yale School of Drama and the Williamstown, Mass. Theater.

A Best Play; see page 239.

RAT IN THE SKULL

Roche	Colum Convey	Naylor	Gerard Horan
Harris	Philip Jackson	Nelson	Brian Cox

Directed by Max Stafford-Clark; scenery and costumes, Peter Hartwell; lighting, Andy Phillips; stage managers, Bethe Ward, Judi Wheway.

Place: Paddington Green Police Station, London. The play was presented without intermission.

A suspected I.R.A. terrorist is detained and questioned by British and Ulster police officers. A foreign play previously produced in London in this production.

Note: In Joseph Papp's Public Theater there are many auditoria. *The Ballad of Soapy Smith*, *Virginia* and *The Marriage of Bette and Boo* played the Estelle R. Newman Theater, *La Boheme* and *Salonika* played the Anspacher Theater, *Tracers* played the Susan Stein Shiva Theater, *Coming of Age in Soho* and *Rat in the Skull* played Martinson Hall, *Tom and Viv* and *The Normal Heart* played LuEsther Hall.

Playwrights Horizons. Schedule of three programs. **Romance Language** (52). By Peter Parnell. Opened November 14, 1984. (Closed January 6, 1985) **Life and Limb** (30). By Keith Reddin. Opened January 24, 1985. (Closed February 17, 1985) **The Young Playwrights Festival** (21). Program of four one-act plays: *Field Day* by Leslie Kaufman (age 17), *Sonata* by Elizabeth Hirschhorn (age 15), *True to Life* by Marc Ratliff (age 18), *The Ground Zero Club* by Charlie Schulman (age 18); in the Dramatists Guild production, Peggy C. Hansen producing director. Opened April 11, 1985. (Closed April 28, 1985)

Produced by Playwrights Horizons, Andre Bishop artistic director, Paul Daniels managing director, at Playwrights Horizons. All plays: Press, Bob Ullman.

ROMANCE LANGUAGE

Walt Whitman	Al Carmines	Tommy; Mme. Nash	Marc Castle
Huckleberry Finn	Jon Matthews	Autie Reed	Ben Siegler
Dan'l; Lt. Varnum	Steve Ryan	Emily Dickinson	Valerie Mahaffey
Louisa May Alcott	Frances Conroy	Ralph Waldo Emerson;	
Kooloo; Raincloud	Hechter Ubarry	Mitch Bouyer	Philip Pleasants
Alcott; Lonesome Charlie	William Duell	Henry David Thoreau; George Armstrong	
Charlotte Cushman	Cynthia Harris	Custer	William Converse-Roberts
Emma Stebbins; Ellen Emerson;		Tom Sawyer	John Noonan
Dancehall Girl	Marcia Lewis	Bloody Knife	Carroll L. Cartwright

Townspeople, Cavalry, Cowboys, Barpeople, Indians: Larry Attile, Janey Borrus, Laurence Gleason, Glenn Karant, Greg Pake, David Warshofsky.

Directed by Sheldon Larry; scenery, Loren Sherman; costumes, Sheila McLamb; lighting, Jeff Davis; sound, Scott Lehrer; orchestrations and musical direction, Jack Eric Williams; fights, B.H. Barry; saloon movement, Marcia Milgrom Dodge; production stage manager, Morton Milder; stage manager, Carroll L. Cartwright; press, Bob Ullman.

Time: 1876. Act I, Scene 1: Bedroom in Brooklyn, night—Walt has a dream. Scene 2: On the docks, night—Louisa May Alcott disembarks; Walt and Huck dispose of a body. Scene 3: Dressing room Gaiety Theater—Emily Dickinson meets Hamlet. Scene 4: Ralph Waldo's house, Concord, Mass.—A tea party at Ralph Waldo Emerson's. Scene 5: Louisa May Alcott's house—The other side of Louisa May. Scene 6: In the wings, Rialto Theater—Emily is dïstressed. Scene 7: Walden, evening—Thoreau speaks. Scene 8: Concord River, night—Huck has a dream.

Act II, Scene 9: Opera house, Montana—A Romeo, Romeo! Scene 10: Mme. Nash's saloon, Big Horn, Mont.—We meet Mme. Nash. Scene 11: Outside the saloon, night—Custer and Minnie. Scene 12: Sioux camp—Captured! Scene 13: Mme. Nash's parlor—Autie Reed confronts Mme. Nash. Scene 14: Sioux Camp—No solutions. Scene 15: The plains, Little Big Horn—The battle. Scene 16: Heaven —Lucky to have quit the place.

A fantasy version of events and personalities in the American past.

LIFE AND LIMB

Franklin Roosevelt Clagg	Robert Joy	Doina	Robin Bartlett
Effie Clagg	Elizabeth Perkins	Sam; Erik	Benjamin Hendrickson
Tod Cartmell	Patrick Breen	Chris	J. David Rozsa
Jerry; Grandfather	Tom Toner		

Directed by Thomas Babe; scenery, John Arnone; costumes, David C. Woolard; lighting, Stephen Strawbridge; sound, Tom Gould; production stage manager, Melissa Davis; stage manager, Pam Edington.

Time: 1952–1956. The play was presented in two parts.

Shortcomings of the American lifestyle are laid bare and raw in a series of episodes concerning a returning Korean War veteran.

THE YOUNG PLAYWRIGHTS FESTIVAL

Field Day

Man #1	Stephen Ahern
Man #2	Robert Joy

Directed by Don Scardino. A pair of soldiers at war, and afraid.

Sonata

Little Boy	Jonathan Harold Gabriel
Little Girl	Wendy Rockman

Joseph Wallace	John Spencer
Lisa Amory	Stacey Glick
Judy Amory	Robin Groves
Clark Amory	John Martinuzzi
Man's Voice; Chief	Brian Smiar

Directed by Shelly Raffle; music scored and played by Jerry Sternbach. Parents grow indifferent to the prolongued absence of their child.

True to Life

Dallas . . . . Steven Flynn
Max . . . . Don Plumley
Woman. . . . . Lucinda Jenney
Jack. . . . . Brian Smiar
    Directed by Ben Levit. Time: The present, a
Sunday afternoon in October. Place: A small
town in South Dakota, Jack's Supper Club and
Bar & Grill. Young photographer in search of
life's meanings in a barroom setting.

The Ground Zero Club

Tourist . . . . Thomas Ikeda
Guard. . . . . Tom Mardirosian
Voice; Bob . . . . Bill Schoppert
Angela . . . . Elizabeth Berridge
Sal. . . . . Larry Joshua
Fiona . . . . Polly Draper
Tanya . . . . Lucinda Jenney
    Directed by John Ferraro. Time: Later to-
night. Place: The Observation Deck of the Em-
pire State Building. Nuclear war breaks out and
is witnessed from the top of New York's tallest
building.

ALL PLAYS: Scenery, Loren Sherman; costumes, Jennifer Von Mayrhauser; lighting, Stephen
Strawbridge; sound, Scott Lehrer; production coordinator, Melissa Davis; stage managers, M.A.
Howard, Kate Stewart.

These four plays by young authors (ages given at the time of submission of scripts) were selected
from hundreds of entries in the Foundation of the Dramatists Guild's fourth annual Young Playwrights Festival. In addition to the above full productions, staged reading were held on the Playwrights Horizons mainstage 4/21/85 and 4/22/85 of *Whatever Tomorrow Brings* by Nicole
Leigh Boland (age 10), *The Irishman* by Michael Bourne (age 18), *A Longing to Return Home* by
Benjamin Lo (age 14), *Satisfaction* by Nelly Reifler (age 16) and *Windhover* by Kathleen Ryan (age
18).

City Stage Company (CSC). Repertory of four revival programs. **Agamemnon** (33). By
Aeschylus (with prologue from *Iphigenia in Tauris* by Euripides); translated by Robert
Fagles. Opened November 30, 1984; see note. (Closed February 16, 1985) **Elek-
tra/Orestes** (*The Libation Bearers* and *The Eumenides*) (29). By Aeschylus (prologue
from *Iphigenia in Tauris* by Euripides and *Elektra* by Sophocles); translated by Robert
Fagles. Opened December 27, 1984; see note. (Closed February 16, 1985) **George
Dandin** (22). By Molière; adapted by Alex Szogyi. Opened February 21, 1985; see note.
(Closed April 6, 1985) **The Underpants** (21). By Carl Sternheim; translated by Eric
Bentley. Opened March 7, 1985; see note. (Closed April 6, 1985) Produced by City Stage
Company, Christopher Martin, Will Maitland Weiss and Craig D. Kinzer directors, at the
City Stage Company. All plays: Press, Bruce Cohen. Kathleen von Schmid; stage manager,
Bonnie L. Becker.

PERFORMER	"AGAMEMNON"	"THE LIBATION BEARERS"	"THE EUMENIDES"
Sheridan Crist		Orestes	Orestes
Essene R	Cassandra		Pythia
Ginger Grace	Prologue Iphigenia in Aulis	Elektra	Hermes
Keith Langsdale	Aegisthus	Aegisthus	
Nancy Linehan	Prologue Iphigenia in Tauris	Nurse; Prologue Iphi-genia in Tauris	Iphigenia
Charles H. Patterson	Watchman	Porter	Apollo
Guy Paul	Herald	Pylades	
Tom Spiller	Agamemnon; Pro-logue Agamemnon	Servant; Prologue Agamemnon	
Shelley Stolaroff		Prologue Iphigenia in Aulis	
Karen Sunde	Clytemnestra; Pro-logue Clytemnestra	Clytemnestra; Pro-logue Clytemnestra	Ghost of Clytemnestra
Amy Warner			Athena

CITY STAGE COMPANY—Karen Sunde
as Clytemnestra in the Oresteia of Aeschylus

Chorus in *Agamemnon*: Sheridan Crist, Ralph Dematthews, Laurence Gleason, Ginger Grace, Keith Langsdale, James Lieb, Nancy Linehan, Katherine Loague, Owen O'Farrell, Charles H. Patterson, Guy Paul, Tonia Payne, Essene R, Tom Spiller, Amy Warner.

Chorus in *The Libation Bearers*: Kathryn Klvana, Nancy Linehan, Katherine Loague, Essene R, Lisa Shea, Shelley Stolaroff, Amy Warner.

Chorus in *The Eumenides*: David Friedlander, Dierdre Frouge, Janet Geist, Ginger Grace, Keith Langsdale, Nancy Linehan, Katherine Loague, Guy Paul, Essene R, Tom Spiller, Ginny Stahlman, Shelley Stolaroff, Amy Warner.

PERFORMER	"GEORGE DANDIN"	"THE UNDERPANTS"
Sheridan Crist	Clifton	Frank Scarron
Essene R	Mrs. Simpleton	Gertrude Deuter
Janet Geist	Daisy	
Charles H. Patterson	Benny	Benjamin Mandelstam
Guy Paul	Mr. Simpleton; Collin	Theobald Maske
Tom Spiller	George Dandin	Stranger
Amy Warner	Angel	Luise Maske

THE ORESTEIA (*Agamemnon* and *Elektra/Orestes*): Directed and designed by Christopher Martin; music, Bob Jewett, Jack Maeby; masks, Laurence Maslon; associate costume designer, Blanche Blakeny; dramaturg, Laurence Maslon.

Agamemnon and *Elektra/Orestes* were presented in two acts.

The last major New York revival of *Agamemnon* was by New York Shakespeare Festival at Lincoln Center 5/18/77 for 38 performances. The last revival of all the plays in the Oresteia was by Minnesota Theater Company on Broadway 12/17/68 for 17 performances.

GEORGE DANDIN: Directed and designed by Laurence Maslon; costumes, Miriam Nieves; lighting, Rick Butler.

Place: Before George Dandin's house in the country. The play was presented in two acts.

The last New York revival of this 1668 Molière play was in the French language on Broadway 6/27/68 for 4 performances.

THE UNDERPANTS: Directed by Craig D. Kinzer; scenery and lighting, Rick Butler; costumes, Miriam Nieves.

Time: 1911. Place: Germany, Maske's living room. Act I: A Friday afternoon, spring. Act II: The following morning. Act III: That night. Act IV: The following day. The play was presented in two parts.

Comedy of scandal and cuckoldry in the middle class. This is the first New York production of record of this early 20th century play.

Note: Press date for *Agamemnon* was 1/13/85, for *Elektra/Orestes* 1/13/85, for *George Dandin* 3/2/85, for *The Underpants* 3/7/85.

*The Negro Ensemble Company. Schedule of four programs. **District Line** (31). By Joseph A. Walker. Opened December 2, 1984. (Closed January 6, 1985) **Henrietta** (69). By Karen Jones-Meadows. Opened January 25, 1985. (Closed March 24, 1985) **Two Can Play** (30). By Trevor Rhone. Opened April 11, 1985. (Closed May 5, 1985) ***Ceremonies in Dark Old Men** (19). Revival of the play by Lonne Elder III; produced in association with Citicorp/Citibank. Opened May 15, 1985. Produced by The Negro Ensemble Company, Douglas Turner Ward artistic director, Leon B. Denmark managing director, at Theater Four.

DISTRICT LINE

Actor 9 (Tweetie; Commodore)............. Graham Brown	Actor 7 (Crook; Bra' Jim).............. Samuel L. Jackson
Actor 6 (Doc).................. C. Dumas	Actor 4 (Rosette; Dovey)... Saundra McClain
Actor 2 (Cal)............... Frankie Faison	Actor 10 (Col. Fletcher).... John D. McNally
Actor 3 (Zilikazi; Cal's Father)............... Richard Gant	Actor 8 (Your Majesty/ Nancy)................. Peggy Schoditsch
Actor 1 (Andy; Richard Brown) .... John Harnagel	Actor 5 (Ike; Larry Brown)..... Larry Sharp

Directed by Douglas Turner Ward; scenery, Charles Henry McClennahan; costumes, Myrna Colley-Lee; lighting, William H. Grant III; sound, Bernard Hall; production stage manager, Jerry Cleveland; stage manager, Lisa Watson; press, Irene Gandy.

Time: The present, early May. Place: Washington, D.C. The play was presented in two parts.

The working day of cab drivers waiting for fares at the Maryland-Washington line.

HENRIETTA

Henrietta .... Frances Foster	Thomas..................... William Jay
Sheleeah .... Elain Graham	

Directed by Samuel P. Barton; scenery, Llewellyn Harrison; costumes, Karen Perry; lighting, Sylvester M. Weaver; music, Cornelia J. Post; production stage manager, Jerry Cleveland; press, Burnham-Callaghan Associates, Jacqueline Burnham, David Lotz.

Time: The present, fall. Place: Harlem brownstone. The play was presented in two parts.

A Harlem bag lady is befriended by a young, upwardly mobile female accountant.

TWO CAN PLAY

Gloria. . . . . Hazel J. Medina
Jim . . . . Sullivan H. Walker

Directed by Clinton Turner Davis; scenery, Llewellyn Harrison; costumes, Julie Asion; lighting, Sylvester Weaver; sound, Bernard Hall; production supervisor, Llewellyn Harrison; production stage manager, Jerry Cleveland.

Time: The late 1970s. Place: The home of Jim and Gloria Thomas, Kingston, Jamaica, West Indies. Act I, Scene 1: Late night. Scene 2: Evening three days later. Scene 3: One week later. Scene 4: Three weeks later. Scene 5: Two months later. Act II, Scene 1: Three weeks later. Scene 2: Next day. Scene 3: Later that evening. Scene 4: Noon next day.

Victory over male chauvinism in a two-character farce.

CEREMONIES IN DARK OLD MEN

Russell B. Parker . . . . . Douglas Turner Ward	Adele Eloise Parker . . . . Patty Holley
William Jenkins. . . . . Graham Brown	Blue Haven . . . . Keith David
Theopolis Parker. . . . . Ruben Hudson	Young Girl. . . . . Tracy Camilla Johns
Bobby Parker. . . . . . . Walter Allen Bennett Jr.	

Directed by Douglas Turner Ward; scenery, Charles Henry McClennahan; costumes, Judy Dearing; lighting, Shirley Prendergast; sound, Dennis Ogburn; production stage manager, Ed De-Shae.

Ceremonies in Dark Old Men was first produced by The Negro Ensemble Company off Broadway 2/4/69 for 40 performances and re-produced off Broadway that season a second time in independent production 3/28/69 for 320 performances. This is its first major New York revival.

Total Eclipse (5). Revival of the play by Christopher Hampton. Produced by Charles Paul Kopelman, Mark B. Simon and Gary P. Steuer at the Westside Arts Theater. Opened December 12, 1984. (Closed December 16, 1984)

Arthur Rimbaud . . . . Michael Cerveris	Charles Cros; Barman. . . . . Adam Storke
Mme. Maute de Fleurville . . . . . . Ann Hillary	Jean Aicard . . . . Adrian Sparks
Mathilde Verlaine . . . . Marissa Chibas	Eugenie Krantz . . . . Lynn Cohen
Paul Verlaine . . . . Peter Evans	Isabelle Rimbaud. . . . . Caitlin Clarke
M. Maute de Fleurville; Etienne Carlat;	
Judge Theodore T'Serstevens . . I.M. Hobson	

Directed by John Tillinger; scenery, Marjorie Bradley Kellogg; costumes, Bill Walker; lighting, Richard Nelson; music, Nick Bicat; projections, Lucie D. Grosvenor; sound, Gary Harris; fights staged by J. Alan Suddeth; associate producer, Mike Tolman; production stage manager, Marjorie Horne; press, Solters/Roskin/Friedman, Inc., Joshua Ellis, Cindy Valk.

Total Eclipse was first produced off Broadway by the Chelsea Theater Center of Brooklyn 2/23/74 for 32 performances. This is its first major New York revival.

Diamonds (122). Musical revue (see authors' credits in list of musical numbers and sketches). Produced by Stephen G. Martin, Harold DeFelice, Louis W. Scheeder and Kenneth John Productions, Inc. in association with Frank Basile at Circle in the Square Downtown. Opened December 16, 1984. (Closed March 31, 1985)

Loni Ackerman	(Dwayne Markee)
Susan Bigelow	(Wade Raley)
Jackee Harry	Larry Riley
Scott Holmes	Nestor Serrano
Dick Latessa	Chip Zien

(Parentheses indicate alternating performers)

Stadium Announcer—Bill McComb.

Musicians: Pam Drews piano; Keith Phillips synthesizers; Andy Zoob percussion, drums; Steve Usher guitars, banjo.

Standbys/Understudies: Men—Bill McComb, Gordon Stanley, Mark Zimmerman; Women—Valerie Perri, Zelda Pulliam.

Directed by Harold Prince; choreography, Theodore Pappas; musical direction and orchestrations, Paul Gemignani; scenery, Tony Straiges; costumes, Judith Dolan; lighting, Ken Billington; sound, Tom Morse; associate producer, Len M. Collura; assistant director, Arthur Masella; production stage manager, Beverley Randolph; stage manager, Bill McComb; press, Fred Nathan and Associates, Leslie Anderson, Anne Abrams, Ted Killmer, Bert Fink.

Musical celebration of the game of baseball, put together from the works of more than 40 authors and song writers.

SCENES AND MUSICAL NUMBERS—ACT I

"Winter in New York" .... Company
  (music by John Kander, lyrics by Fred Ebb)
Batting Order (by Sean Kelly and Arthur Masella)
  The Team .... Company
"In the Cards" (music by Alan Menken, lyrics by David Zippel)
  Kid... Dwayne Markee/Wade Raley
  Mother.. Loni Ackerman
"Favorite Sons" (music by Larry Grossman, lyrics by Ellen Fitzhugh)
  Arnold's Parents... Jackee Harry, Larry Riley
  Huey's Father.. Nestor Serrano
  Philip's Parents... Loni Ackerman, Chip Zien
Warner Wolf #1 (by Richard Camp) .... Chip Zien
"Song for a Pinch Hitter" (music by Larry Grossman, lyrics by Ellen Fitzhugh)
  Girl .... Susan Bigelow
"Vendors" (music by Cy Coleman, lyrics by Betty Comden and Adolph Green)
  Vendors: Jackee Harry, Loni Ackerman, Dick Latessa, Nestor Serrano, Susan Bigelow, Dwayne
      Markee/Wade Raley
Fanatics #1 (by Harry Stein and Lee Eisenberg)
  Pete .... Larry Riley
  Carl .... Chip Zien
  Businessman .... Scott Holmes
"What You'd Call a Dream" (music and lyrics by Craig Carnelia)
  Businessman .... Scott Holmes
Kāsi Atta Bat (by Sean Kelly)
  Koken .... Loni Ackerman, Susan Bigelow
  Narrator.. Dick Latessa
  Umpire.. Chip Zien
  Kāsi .... Nestor Serrano
  Ball....................................... Dwayne Markee/Wade Raley
Ballparks of the Gods (by John Weidman, media design by Lisa Podgur)
  Man .... Scott Holmes
"Escorte-Moi" (music and lyrics by Albert von Tilzer and Jack Norworth)
  Frenchman .... Chip Zien
The Dodger Game (by Ralph G. Allen)
  Comic... Nestor Serrano
  Straight Man.. Larry Riley
  Soubrette... Susan Bigelow
  Walter Johnson.. Scott Holmes
"He Threw Out the Ball" (music by Larry Grossman, lyrics by Ellen Fitzhugh)
  Woman .... Jackee Henry
  Chorus: Loni Ackerman, Susan Bigelow, Scott Holmes, Larry Riley, Chip Zien, Nestor Serrano

"Hundreds of Hats" (music by Jonathan Sheffer, lyrics by Howard Ashman)
    Old Man .... Dick Latessa
    Couple #1 .... Loni Ackerman, Scott Holmes
    Couple #2 .... Susan Bigelow, Nestor Serrano
    Couple #3 .... Jackee Harry, Larry Riley
    Boy... Dwayne Markee/Wade Riley
Warner Wolf #2 .... Chip Zien
"1919" (music and lyrics by Jim Wann)
    Narrator.. Larry Riley
    Kid... Dwayne Markee/Wade Riley
    Joe Jackson .... Scott Holmes
                                                                    Company

SCENES AND MUSICAL NUMBERS—ACT II

P.A. Announcement (by John Weidman)
"Let's Play Ball" .... Company
    (music and lyrics by Gerard Alessandrini)
Warner Wolf #3 .... Chip Zien
Psyched Out (by John Lahr)
    Shrink .... Dick Latessa
    Ballplayer.. Chip Zien
"Vendors"
    Vendors: Nestor Serrano, Dick Latessa, Loni Ackerman, Susan Bigelow, Jackee Harry, Scott
        Holmes, Dwayne Markee/Wade Riley
Fanatics #2
    Carl .... Chip Zien
    Pete .... Larry Riley
Five Ives (by Roy Blount Jr.)
    Man .... Scott Holmes
"The Boys of Summer" (music by Larry Grossman, lyrics by Ellen Fitzhugh)
    Girl at Bar... Susan Bigelow
Fanatics #3
    Carl .... Chip Zien
    Pete .... Larry Riley
"Song for a Hunter College Graduate" (music by Jonathan Sheffer, lyrics by Howard Ashman)
    Lady.. Loni Ackerman
Warner Wolf #4 .... Chip Zien
Who's on First (by Bud Abbott and Lou Costello)
    Man .... Chip Zien
    Kid... Dwayne Markee/Wade Riley
"Stay in Your Own Back Yard" (by John Weidman, music by Lyn Udall, lyrics by Karl Ken-
    nett, additional music by Pam Drews, media design by Lisa Podgur)
    Woman .... Jackee Henry
Chief Surgeon (by Alan Zweibel)
    Surgeon .... Larry Riley
    Nurses .... Loni Ackerman, Susan Bigelow
    Doctor .... Dick Latessa
    Aide .... Nestor Serrano
"Ka-razy" .... Company
    (music by Doug Katsaros, lyrics by David Zippel)
Famous People Quotes (by John Weidman)
Batting Order
    The Team .... Company
"Diamonds Are Forever" .... Company
    (music by John Kander, lyrics by Fred Ebb)

Ann Reinking . . . Music Moves Me (16). Musical revue with original music by Larry Grossman (see additional authors' credits in list of musical numbers). Produced by Lee Gross Associates, Inc. at the Joyce Theater. Opened December 23, 1984. (Closed January 6, 1985)

Gary Chryst	Sara Miles
Reed Jones	Ann Reinking
Michael Kubala	Christina Saffran
Rob Marshall	

Directed and choreographed by Alan Johnson; musical supervision and vocal arrangements, Larry Grossman; musical direction and dance arrangements, Ronald Melrose; scenery, Thomas Lynch; costumes, Albert Wolsky; lighting, Ken Billington; sound, Charles Bugbee III; assistant director and choreographer, Stephen Jay; orchestrations, Joseph Glanono, Michael Gibson, Harold Wheeler; special lyrics, Ellen Fitzhugh; production stage manager, Perry Cline; stage manager, Randall Whitescarver; press, Mark Goldstaub Public Relations, Kevin P. McAnarney, Daniel Kellachan, Philip Butler.

Band: Ronald Melrose conductor, keyboards; Ken Hitchcock Reeds; Jeff Kane percussion; Ray Kilday bass; John Redsecker drums; Dave Stahl trumpet; Steve Tubin keyboards.

Singing and dancing showcase for its star. The show was presented in two parts.

MUSICAL NUMBERS: "Another Mr. Right" (by Jonathan Sheffer and David Zippel); "Anything Goes" (by Cole Porter); "Ballin' the Jack" (by Chris Smith and Jim Burris); "Higher and Higher" (by Gary Jackson, Carl Smith and Raynard Miner); "Hit Me With a Hot Note" (by Duke Ellington and Don George); "I Can't Turn You Loose" (by Otis Redding); "If Love Were All" (by Noel Coward); "Isn't It Romantic" (by Richard Rodgers and Lorenz Hart); "Just Once" (by Barry Manilow and Cynthia Weil); "Moonlight Sonata" (by Ludwig van Beethoven); "Music Moves Me" (by Larry Grossman and Ellen Fitzhugh); "Nowhere to Run" (by Eddie Holland, Lamont Dozier and Brian Holland).

Also "Oh Baby, Won't You Please Come Home" (by Clarence Williams and Charles Warfield); "Rescue Me" (by Carl Smith and Raynard Miner); "Satin Doll" (by Billy Strayhorn, Duke Ellington and Johnny Mercer); "Sing, Sing, Sing" (by Louis Prima, trumpet solo from *Dancin'*, choreography by Bob Fosse); "Stompin' at the Savoy" (by Benny Goodman, Andy Razaf, Chick Webb and Edgar Sampson); "Tea for Two" (by Vincent Youmans and Irving Caesar); "Unchained Melody" (by Alex North and Hy Zaret); "Why Not? (Manhattan Carnival" (by Michael Camilo, Hilary Koski and Julie Eigenberg); "Wild Women" (by Ida Cox); "You and Me" (by Carole Bayer Sager and Peter Allen).

The Mirror Repertory Company. Repertory of three revivals. **The Madwoman of Chaillot** (59). By Jean Giraudoux; adapted by Maurice Valency. Opened January 30, 1985. **Clarence** (21). By Booth Tarkington. Opened February 13, 1985. **Vivat! Vivat Regina!** (32). By Robert Bolt. Opened March 14, 1985. Produced by The Mirror Repertory Company, Sabra Jones artistic director, at the Theater at St. Peter's Church. (Repertory closed May 19, 1985) All plays: Scenery and lighting, James Tilton; production stage manager, Lewis Rosen; stage managers, Nicholas Dunn, Kate Hancock; press, Mary Bryant, Becky Flora.

THE MADWOMAN OF CHAILLOT

Waiter	Phillip Pruneau	Ragpicker	Clement Fowler
Little Man	Charles Regan	Paulette; 1st Lady	Laura Galusha
Prospector	Tom Brennan	Deaf Mute	Clark Middleton
President	W.B. Brydon	Irma	Sabra Jones
Baron; 2d President	David Cryer	Broker; 3d President	Tad Jones
Therese; 2d Lady	Camilla Moore	Street Juggler	Nancy J. Nichols
Street Singer; 2d Press Agent	Michael DiGioia	Dr. Jadin; Sewer Man;	
Flower Girl; 3d Lady	Donna M. Sacco	1st Adolphe Bertaut	Bryan Clark

Countess Aurelia............ Geraldine Page
Policeman; 1st Press Agent .... Baxter Harris
Pierre .... Ivar Brogger
Sergeant .... Jess Osuna
Mme. Constance .... Carrie Nye
Mme. Gabrielle .... Madeleine Sherwood
Mme. Josephine............. Grayson Hall

2d Prospector................ Omar Lotayef
3d Prospector............. Thomas McAteer
3d Press Agent .... George McGuiness
2d Adolphe Bertaut ..... Gordon McConnell
3d Adolphe Bertaut .... Brandon Ellis
                                    Doemling

Alternate casting: Prospector—Baxter Harris; President, Broker, 2d President—James Pritchett; Street Singer, Deaf Mute—John David Cullum; Flower Girl—Laura Galusha; Irma—Donna M. Sacco; Sergeant, Little Man, Dr. Jadin—Nicholas Dunn; Countess Aurelia—Madeleine Sherwood; Pierre—Tad Jones; 2d and 3d Prospectors, Press Agents and Adolphe Bertauts—Alexander D. Carney; Ragpicker, Sewer Man, Baron—Charles Regan; Waiter—Gordon McConnell; Policeman, 1st Press Agent—Brandon Ellis Doemling; Therese—Gina Belafonte; Paulette—Nanette Werness.

Directed by Stephen Porter; costumes, Gail Cooper-Hecht; sound, Rob Gorton.

Act I: The cafe terrace of Chez Francis. Act II: The Countess's cellar, 21 Rue de Chaillot.

The last major New York revival of *The Madwoman of Chaillot* was by Classic Stage Company 3/2/78 for 29 performances.

F. Murray Abraham replaced Clement Fowler 5/7/85; Anne Jackson replaced Geraldine Page 5/14/85; Jane White replaced Grayson Hall.

CLARENCE

Mrs. Martyn .... Madeleine Sherwood
Mr. Wheeler.............. Phillip Pruneau
Mrs. Wheeler.............. Geraldine Page
Bobby Wheeler .... John David Cullum
Cora Wheeler.............. Laura Galusha

Violet Pinney................. Sabra Jones
Clarence..................... Ivar Brogger
Della.................... Donna M. Sacco
Dinwiddie................. Clement Fowler
Herbert Stem................. David Cryer

Alternate casting: Mrs. Wheeler—Madeleine Sherwood; Bobby—Alexander D. Carney; Cora—Gina Belafonte; Violet—Kim Beaty, Donna M. Sacco; Clarence—Tad Jones; Hubert Stem—Charles Regan; Dinwiddie—James Pritchett.

Directed by Arthur Storch; costumes, Arnold S. Levine; sound, Steve Shapiro.

Act I, Scene 1: The anteroom to Mr. Wheeler's private office, New York. Scene 2: The living room of Mr. Wheeler's home, Englewood, N.J. Act II, Scene 1: The same, that evening. Scene 2: The same, next morning.

The only previous major New York revival of *Clarence* was by Roundabout Theater Company 12/23/75 for 64 performances.

VIVAT! VIVAT REGINA!

Mary Queen of Scots .... Sabra Jones
Claud Nau................ Clement Fowler
William Cecil................ Bryan Clark
Elizabeth I................. Geraldine Page
Robert Dudley.............. Baxter Harris
John Knox.............. Richard Mathews
Bagpiper.............. William Driscoll
David Rizzio; Prisoner......... Ivar Brogger
Lord Morton .... Tom Brennan
Lord Bothwell............... W.B. Brydon
Bishop of Durham;
  Lord Mor .... James Pritchett
Cleric .... Omar Lotayef
Sir Francis Walsingham ..... Phillip Pruneau

De Quadra.................... Jess Osuna
Davison .... Michael DiGioia
Lord Darnley.................. Tad Jones
Ruthven .... Nicholas Dunn
Lindsey.................. Thomas McAteer
Doctor; Pope; Priest ..... Gordon McConnell
Tala................... John David Cullum
Ormiston .... George McGuiness
Scots Archbishop............ Charles Regan
Philip of Spain;
  Jailer .... Brandon Ellis Doemling
Brewer; Jailer.............. Clark Middleton
James Stuart .... Elijah Torn Burkhardt

Courtiers, Lairds, Clerks, Servants, etc.: Alexander D. Carney, Brandon Ellis Doemling, George McGuiness, Gordon O'Connell.

Court Ladies: Laura Galusha, Camilla Moore, Nancy J. Nichols, Donna M. Sacco.

Orchestra: Donald Howell musical director, Lee Sloan violin, Bob LePre percussion, Henry Oelkers lute.

Alternate casting: Mary—Katharine Houghton; Nau—William Cecil; Dudley—James Pritchett; Elizabeth—Jane White; Knox, Walsingham, Mor—Charles Regan; Rizzio—Michael DiGioia; Morton, Bothwell, Darnley, Ruthven—Thomas McAteer; Durham, Scots Archbishop, Philip, Pope—Omar Lotayef; Cleric, De Quadra—Gordon McConnell; Davison—John David Cullum; Lindsey, Ormiston, Prisoner—Nicholas Dunn; Doctor, Tala, Brewer—Alexander D. Carney; Jailer, Priest—Brandon Ellis Doemling; Courtiers, Clerics, Servants, etc.—George McGuiness, Alexander D. Carney, Gordon McConnell, Brandon Ellis Doemling, Walter Ryals, Warren Taylor; Court Ladies—Nanette Werness, Gina Belafonte.

Directed by John Strasberg; costumes, Gail Cooper-Hecht; sound, Rob Gorton; dance choreography, Elizabeth Kean.

Time: During the 16th century. Place: France, England and Scotland. Act I, Scene 1: France, spring 1560. Scene 2: Court of St. James, fall 1560. Scene 3: Scotland, fall 1560. Scene 4: Edinburgh, August 19–25, 1561. Scene 5: In Kirk. Scene 6: St. James, winter 1561. Scene 7: Hampton Court, winter 1561. Scene 8: Nonsuch Castle, 1564. Scene 9: Holyrood, 1564. Scene 10: Holyrood, March 6, 1565. Scene 11: Holyrood, January 1566. Scene 12: Holryood March 9, 1566.

Act II, Scene 1: Scotland, June 1566. Scene 2: Court of St. James, June 1566. Scene 3: In Kirk, June 1566. Scene 4: Holyrood, June 1566. Scene 5: Holyrood, Feb. 10, 1567 and later. Scene 6: Langside, June 15, 1567. Scene 7: Langside, May 1568. Scene 8: Tutbury Castle, May 1568. Scene 9: The Tower, 1570. Scene 10: Greenwich, 1580. Scene 11: Greenwich, 1585. Scene 12: Greenwich, 1586. Scene 13: Tutbury Castle, 1586. Scene 14: Court of St. James, 1586. Scene 15: Fothgringay and Court of St. James, 1587.

Katharine Houghton replaced Sabra Jones 5/8/85. Sabra Jones replaced Katharine Houghton 5/19/85.

*3 Guys Naked From the Waist Down (126). Musical with book and lyrics by Jerry Colker; music by Michael Rupert. Produced by James B. Freydberg, Stephen Wells and Max Weitzenhoffer in association with Richard Maltby Jr. at the Minetta Lane Theater. Opened February 5, 1985.

Ted Klausterman.............	Scott Bakula	Phil Kunin..................	Jerry Colker
Kenny Brewster...............	John Kassir		

General Understudy—Peter Samuel.

Directed by Andrew Cadiff; choreography, Don Bondi; musical direction, Henry Aronson; scenery and projections, Clarke Dunham; costumes, Tom McKinley; lighting, Ken Billington; sound, Tony Meola; orchestrations, Michael Starobin; associate producers, Ray Larsen, Karen Howard; production stage manager, Brian Kaufman; press, Jeffrey Richards Associates, Robert Ganshaw.

Musicians: Henry Aronson conductor; Paul Sullivan keyboards; Seth Glassman electric bass; Glenn Rhian drums, percussion; Phil Granger trumpet; Rick Heckman woodwinds I; Bob Keller woodwinds II; Brian Koonin electric and acoustic guitar.

Place: New York City and Southern California.

A trio of standup comics (for which "naked from the waist down" is show biz slang) tries to make it in the big time. Previously produced at PlayMakers Repertory, Chapel Hill, N.C.

ACT I

Komedy Klub East
"Promise of Greatness".. Ted
"Angry Guy/Lovely Day" .... Phil
"Promise of Greatness" (Reprise)... Ted
The Last Stand-Up
"Don't Wanna Be No Superstar I" .... Ted, Phil
"Operator" .... Kenny
"Screaming Clocks" (the Dummies Song).... Ted, Phil, Kenny (with dummies Mr. Dirtball, Spike, Steve)

The Funny Farm
   "Don't Wanna Be No Superstar II"................................ Ted, Phil, Kenny
   "The History of Stand-Up Comedy" .... Ted, Phil, Kenny
   "Dreams of Heaven" .... Kenny
Flight 737
   "Don't Wanna Be No Superstar III"............................... Ted, Phil, Kenny
   "Kamikaze Kabaret" .... Ted, Phil, Kenny

ACT II

"The American Dream" .... Ted, Phil, Kenny
"What a Ride I"... Ted, Phil, Kenny
"Hello, Fellas" theme
"Hello, Fellas" TV Special World Tour............................... Ted, Phil, Kenny
"What a Ride II"... Ted, Phil, Kenny
"A Father Now" .... Phil
"What a Ride III".. Ted, Phil, Kenny
"Three Guys Naked From the Waist Down" theme .... Ted, Phil, Kenny
"Screaming Clocks" (Reprise)...................................... Ted, Phil, Kenny
"Don't Wanna Be No Superstar" (Reprise)........................... Ted, Phil, Kenny
"Dreams of Heaven" (Reprise)... Kenny
"I Don't Believe in Heroes Anymore"...................................... Ted
"Promise of Greatness" (Final Reprise)................................... Ted

Cliffhanger (28). By James Yaffe. Produced by Norma and David Langworthy at the Lamb's Theater. Opened February 7, 1985. (Closed March 3, 1985)

Henry Lowenthal	Henderson Forsythe	Melvin McMullen............	Keith Reddin
Polly Lowenthal	Lenka Peterson	Dave DeVito	Tom Mardirosian
Edith Wilshire............	Natalia Nogulich		

Directed by David McKenna; scenery, Leo B. Meyer; costumes, Merrily Murray-Walsh; lighting, Jeff Davis; sound, Paul Garrity; production stage manager, Ellen Raphael; stage manager, J.R. MacDonald; press, Jeffrey Richards Associates, C. George Willard, Robert Ganshaw, Ben Morse.

Time: Late May, at the end of the semester. Place: The Lowenthal house in a small college town somewhere in the Rockies. Act I, Scene 1: Late one afternoon. Scene 2: Morning, three days later. Act II, Scene 1: Afternoon, the same day. Scene 2: A Few hours later.

A professor violently resists retirement, in a comedy-mystery context. Previously produced at Alliance Theater, Atlanta.

The Mugger (8). By Steven K. Sher. Produced by On the Street Productions at the Players Theater. Opened March 18, 1985. (Closed March 24, 1985)

Directed by Philip Price; scenery, Don Jensen; costumes, Mary Brecht; lighting, Beverly Emmons; press, Patricia Krawitz. With Stewart Zully, John DiCarlo, Jaime Perry, Evelyn Orbach, Walter Teper.

Unemployed worker turns to street crime as an occupation.

Crossing the Bar (4). By Michael Zettler. Produced by Jessica Levy at Playhouse 91. Opened March 21, 1985. (Closed March 24, 1985)

Directed by Jerry Zaks; scenery, Loren Sherman; costumes, Sally Lesser; lighting, Paul Gallo; production stage manager, T.L. Boston; press, Jeffrey Richards Associates, Toby Mailman. With Betsy Aidem, Dick Latessa, Frank Hamilton, George Guidall, Stan Lachow, Ed Setrakian, Jay Devlin, Brian Hartigan, Don Perkins.

Friends on the way to a tavern owner's funeral. The play was presented in three parts.

Before the Dawn (8). Adapted by Joseph Stein from the play *A Ladies' Tailor* by Aleksandr Borshchagovsky; translated by Lev Loseff and Dennis Whelan. Produced by Rick Hobard at the American Place Theater. Opened March 24, 1985. (Closed March 31, 1985)

Directed by Kenneth Frankel; scenery, Andrew Jackness; costumes, Jennifer Von Mayrhauser; lighting, Stephen Strawbridge; sound, Gary Harris; associate producer, Joan Firestone; production stage manager, Michael J. Frank; press, Milly Schoenbaum. With Peter Michael Goetz, Deborah Hedwall, Roberta Maxwell, David Leary, Elisa Loti, Jennie Dundas, Jeremy Peter Johnson, Jodi Thelen, Katherine Borowitz, Betty Miller, L.R. Hults, John Amedro, Pollard Brown.

Two families, one Jewish and one Christian, share love and friendship in Kiev in 1941, in the shadow of Babi Yar. The Russian-language version was previously produced in Moscow for 6 performances in 1980.

In Trousers (16). Musical with book, music and lyrics by William Finn. Produced by Roger Berlind, Franklin R. Levy and Gregory Harrison at the Promenade Theater. Opened March 26, 1985. (Closed April 7, 1985)

Marvin	Tony Cummings	His High School Sweetheart	Sherry Hursey
His Wife	Catherine Cox	His Teacher, Miss Goldberg	Kathy Garrick

Understudies: Misses Cox, Hursey, Carol Dilley; Miss Garrick—Mary Bond Davis.

Musicians: Sande Campbell piano, Laurie A. Frink trumpet, John Harvey drums, Robert J. Magnuson woodwinds, Ralph Olsen woodwinds, Edward S. Strauss synthesizers.

Directed by Matt Casella; musical direction, Roy Leake Jr.; scenery, Santo Loquasto; costumes, Madeline Ann Graneto; lighting, Marilyn Rennagel; orchestrations, Michael Starobin; sound, Tom Morse; production stage manager, Rebecca Klein; press, Solters/Roskin/Friedman, Inc., Joshua Ellis, Keith Sherman.

Husband of ten years finally gives in to his homosexual fantasies. The play was presented without intermission. Previously produced in other versions at Playwrights Horizons and Second Stage.

MUSICAL NUMBERS

In Trousers (The Dream)

"I Can't Sleep"	Marvin, Ladies
"Time to Wake Up"	Wife
"I Have a Family"	Marvin
"How Marvin Eats His Breakfast"	Marvin, Ladies
"Marvin's Giddy Seizures 1"	Sweetheart
"My High School Sweetheart"	Sweetheart, Company
"Set Those Sails"	Teacher, Ladies
"I Swear I Won't Ever Again"	Marvin
"High School Ladies at Five O'Clock"	Sweetheart, Ladies
"The Rape of Miss Goldberg"	Marvin, Teacher
"Love Me for What I Am"	Marvin, Wife
"I Am Wearing a Hat"	Sweetheart, Teacher
"Wedding Song"	Company
"Three Seconds"	Marvin
"How the Body Falls Apart"	Ladies
"I Feel Him Slipping Away"	Wife, Ladies
"Whizzer Going Down"	Marvin
"Marvin's Giddy Seizures 2"	Company
"I'm Breaking Down"	Wife
"Packing Up"	Marvin
"Breakfast Over Sugar"	Marvin, Wife
"How America Got Its Name"	Sweetheart, Teacher, Marvin
"Time to Wake Up" (Reprise)	Wife
"Another Sleepless Night"	Company
"Goodnight/No Hard Feelings"	Company

*Hannah Senesh (65). By David Schechter; developed in collaboration with Lori Wilner; based on diaries and poems of Hannah Senesh, with English translation by Marta Cohn and Peter Hay; originally developed by Dafna Soltes. Produced by William Ross and Perry Bruskin in association with Daniel Neiden in the Writers Theater production at the Cherry Lane Theater. Opened April 10, 1985.

Catherine; Hannah Senesh . . . . Lori Wilner   Young Man . . . . John Fistos
Voice of George Senesh . . . . . David Schechter

Understudy: Miss Wilner—Susan Gabriel.

Directed by David Schechter; music composed and arranged by Steven Lutvak; additional music by Elizabeth Swados and David Schechter; scenery, Jennifer Gallagher; costumes, David Woolard; lighting, Vivien Leone; production supervisor, Christopher Santee; production stage manager, Daniel S. Lewin; press, Max Eisen, Maria Somma, Madelon Rosen.

Play with music about a Hungarian Jewish heroine captured and executed as a freedom fighter in 1944. The play was presented without intermission.

MUSICAL NUMBERS: "The Rainbow Song" (words and music by Steven Lutvak); "Eli, Eli" (text by Hannah Senesh, music by D. Zehavi); "Blessed Is the Match" (text by Hannah Senesh, music by Steven Lutvak); "Soon" (words and music by David Schechter); "Shtil Di Nacht" (lyrics by Hirsh Gilk, composer unknown); "Zog Nit Keyn Mol" (lyrics by Hirsh Gilk, music by Dmitri Pokrass); "One, Two, Three" (text by Hannah Senesh, music by Elizabeth Swados).

The Singular Dorothy Parker (41). One-woman show performed by Jane Connell; adapted from the works of Dorothy Parker by Rory Seeber. Produced by Rick Seeber at the Actors' Playhouse. Opened April 14, 1985. (Closed May 19, 1985)

Directed by Laura Cuetara; scenery and lighting, Neil Prince; costumes, Deborah Bays; sound, Bruce Odland; associate producers, Entertainment Ventures, Thomas Hardy; production stage manager, Janice Booth; press, Burnham/Callaghan Associates, David Lotz.

Quotations from the bons mots of one of the wittiest of commentators, subtitled "Laughter and hope are a sock in the eye."

*Penn & Teller (51). Magic show with Penn Jillette and Teller. Produced by Richard Frankel and Ivy Properties, Ltd. at the Westside Arts Theater. Opened April 18, 1985.

Production supervised by Art Wolff; scenery, John Lee Beatty; lighting, Dennis Parichy; sound, Chuck London Media/Stewart Werner; ambient music by Yma Sumac; stage manager, Marc Garland; press, Solters/Roskin/Friedman, Inc., Cindy Valk.

Program of magic and comedy devised and performed by Jillette and Teller (who uses no first name). The show was presented in two parts.

PART I: Casey at the Bat, Ball Routine, Coin Routine, Knife Routine, A Card Trick, Cups & Balls ("Cups & Balls Suite" by James S. Campbell Jr.), Suspension, East Indian Needle Mystery, Quote of the Day.

PART II: "Spooky Stuff (instrumental), "Bacteria," "Domestication of Animals" (performance art), MOFO the Psychic Gorilla, How We Met, Shadows, 10 in 1.

*Lies & Legends: The Musical Stories of Harry Chapin (43). Musical revue by Harry Chapin; original concept by Joseph Stern. Produced by Ken Kragen, Lewis Friedman, Albert Nocciolino, Ken Yates, Stuart Oken and Jason Brett at the Village Gate. Opened April 24, 1985.

Joanna Glushak   Ron Orbach
John Herrera   Martin Vidnovic
Terri Klausner

Band: Karl Jurman piano, conductor; John Chappell guitar; Bonnie Thron cello; Howie Fields percussion; John Wallace bass.

Understudies: John Leslie Wolfe, Victoria Forster.

Directed by Sam Weisman; musical numbers staged by Tracy Friedman; musical direction and arrangements, Stephen Chapin, Tom Chapin; scenery and lighting, Gerry Hariton, Vicki Baral; costumes, Marsha Kowal; sound, Christopher Bond; pianist and conductor, Karl Jurman; associate producers, Richard Martini, Richard Grayson; creative consultant, Sandy C. Chapin; production stage manager, Kim Beringer; press, Jeffrey Richards Associates, Bill Shuttleworth.

A collection of "story songs" by the late Harry Chapin. Previously produced in Chicago.

MUSICAL NUMBERS, ACT I: "Circle/Story of a Life"—Company; "Corey's Coming"—John Herrera, Company; "Salt and Pepper"—Terri Klausner, Ron Orbach, Company; "Mr. Tanner"—Joanna Glushak, Martin Vidnovic, Company; "The Rock"—Orbach, Company; "Old College Avenue"—Klausner; "Taxi"—Herrera; "Get on With It"—Glushak, Herrera; "Bananas"—Vidnovic; "Shooting Star"—Klausner; "Sniper"—Vidnovic, Herrera, Company.

ACT II: "Dance Band on the Titanic"—Company; "W*O*L*D"—Vidnovic; "Dogtown"—Klausner, Company; "Mail Order Annie"—Herrera, Glushak; "Old Job Man"—Orbach, Company; "Dreams Go By"—Herrera, Glushak; "Tangle Up Puppet" (by Sandy and Harry Chapin)—Klausner; "Cat's in the Cradle" (by Sandy and Harry Chapin)—Vidnovic; "Halfway to Heaven"—Orbach; "Better Place To Be"—Klausner, Vidnovic; "You Are the Only Song/Circle"—Company.

*Orphans (29). By Lyle Kessler. Produced by Wolf Gang Productions, Dasha Epstein, Joan Cullman and The Steppenwolf Theater Company in the Steppenwolf Theater production at the Westside Arts Theater. Opened May 7, 1985.

Phillip................... Kevin Anderson   Harold .... John Mahoney
Treat...................... Terry Kinney

Understudies: Messrs. Anderson, Kinney—Christopher Fields; Mr. Mahoney—William Wise.

Directed by Gary Sinise; scenery and lighting, Kevin Rigdon; costumes, Cookie Gluck; sound, Gary Sinise; recorded music by Pat Metheny, Lyle Mays and Nina Vasconselos; sound supervising, Chuck London Media/Stewart Werner; stage manager, Douglas Bryan Bean; press, Milly Schoenbaum, Kevin Patterson.

Place: An old row house in North Philadelphia. Act I: A spring day. Act II: Two weeks later.

Kidnap victim powerfully affects the violent lives of two brothers, one a thief and one an illiterate shut-in. Previously produced in this production in Chicago.

*Mayor (20). Musical based on *Mayor* by Edward I. Koch; book by Warren Leight; music and lyrics by Charles Strouse. Produced by Martin Richards, Jerry Kravat, Mary Lea Johnson with the New York Music Company at the Top of the Gate. Opened May 13, 1985.

Mayor .... Lenny Wolpe

Douglas Bernstein   Ken Jennings
Marion J. Caffey   Ilene Kristen
Keith Curran   Kathryn McAteer
Nancy Giles

Understudy: Susan Cella.

Musicians: Michael Kosarin conductor, pianist; Gordon Twist synthesizer; John Redsecker drums; Jule Ruggiero bass; Raymond Beckenstein woodwinds.

Directed by Jeffrey B. Moss; choreography, Barbara Siman; musical direction and arrangements, Michael Kosarin; scenery and costumes, Randy Barcelo; lighting, Richard Winkler; orchestrations, Christopher Bankey; associate producer, Sam Crothers; production stage manager, Marc Schlackman; press, Henry Luhrman Associates, Terry M. Lilly, David Mayhew, Andrew P. Shearer.

MAYOR—Lenny Wolpe as Edward I. Koch and Kathryn McAteer as
Carol Bellamy in the Warren Leight-Charles Strouse musical based on
the New York City mayor's autobiography

Cabaret musical of songs and sketches based on material in New York City Mayor Koch's
autobiography. The show was presented in two parts.

MUSICAL NUMBERS AND SKETCHES: "Mayor"—Lenny Wolpe; "You Can Be a New
Yorker Too!" (Businessman—Keith Curran; Out-of-Towner—Douglas Bernstein; Bicycle Messenger
—Marion J. Caffey; Company); Board of Estimate (Mayor; Carol Bellamy—Kathryn McAteer;
Leona Helmsley—Ilene Kristen; Staten Island B.P.—Ken Jennings; Security Guard—Caffey);
"You're Not the Mayor" (Carol Bellamy, Staten Island B.P., Security Guard); "Mayor" (Reprise)
—Wolpe; The Four Seasons (Yentas—McAteer, Kristen; Man—Jennings); "March of the Yuppies"
—Douglas Bernstein, Curran, Nancy Giles, Company; The Ribbon Cutting, "Hootspa" (Mayor;
Mayor Lindsay—Curran; Mayor Beame—Jennings).
    Also Alternate Side—McAteer; "Isn't It Time for the People" (Carl—Caffey; Gloria—Kristen;
Assemblyman Lopez—Curran); "What You See Is What You Get" (Mayor; Sue Simmons—Giles;

Company); In the Park (Comic—Caffrey; Company); "Ballad"—Curran, Kristen; "I Want To Be the Mayor" (Harrison J. Goldin—Bernstein); On the Telephone—Mayor, Carol Bellamy; Subway, "The Last 'I Love New York' Song" (Woman—McAteer; Boy—Jennings; Girl—Kristen; Tough—Caffrey; Guardian Angel—Bernstein; Unkempt Man—Curran; Muslim—Giles).

Also "Ballad" (Reprise)—Mayor (lyrics by Warren Leight); Testimonial Dinner, "Good Times" (Mayor; Archbishop—Bernstein; Bess Myerson—Giles; Leona Helmsley; Harry Helmsley—Curran; Donald Trump—Jennings; Waiter—Caffrey); "We Are One" (Homeless People—Caffrey, McAteer; Harry Helmsley; Leona Helmsley); "How'm I Doin'?"—Mayor, Company. "My City"—Company.

Eden Court (15). By Murphy Guyer. Produced by M-Square Entertainment, Inc. (Mitchell Maxwell, Alan J. Schuster, Fred H. Krones, Marvin R. Meit) and The North Sea Group (Arthur W. Cohen, Luther Davis, Karl Mann) at the Promenade Theater. Opened May 14, 1985. (Closed May 26, 1985)

Directed by Barnet Kellman; scenery, David Gropman; costumes, Rita Ryack; lighting, Ian Calderon; sound, Bruce Ellman; production stage manager, Andrea Naier; press, Jeffrey Richards Associates, C. George Willard. With Ellen Barkin, Guy Boyd, Penny Marshall, Ben Masters.

Marital crisis taking place inside a mobile home. The play was presented in two parts.

*Man Enough (13). By Patty Gideon Sloan. Produced by RSM and Pequod Productions at the Apple Corps Theater. Opened May 19, 1985.

Josie Delaney	Marilyn Chris	Jack Delaney	David S. Howard
Joey Delaney	Bruce Roberts King	Sheila McCardle	Courtney Sherman
Donal Delaney	Will Jeffries	Tom McCardle	Richard Karn
Kit Delaney	Alissa Alban	Frank Quinn	Ron Woods

Directed by Steve McCurdy; scenery and lighting, Clark Middleton; costumes, Joy Alpern; production stage manager, Nereida Ortiz; stage manager, J.R. MacDonald; press, Mark Goldstaub Public Relations, Kevin P. McAnarney.

Time: The present. Place: The home of Josie and Jack Delaney, Flatbush, Brooklyn, N.Y. Act I, Scene 1: A late Friday afternoon in April. Scene 2: Very early Saturday morning. Act II, Scene 1: Early Saturday evening. Scene 2: Sunday morning.

Family ties re-tested and re-evaluated over an emotionally explosive weekend. Previously produced at the Houston, Tex. Country Playhouse and OOB at the Quaigh Theater.

*The Return of Herbert Bracewell (12). By Andrew Johns. Produced by Keller Theater Associates (Jerry Keller and Noel L. Silverman) in association with Kenny Karen at the Chelsea Playhouse. Opened May 20, 1985.

Herbert Bracewell	Milo O'Shea
Florence	Frances Sternhagen

Directed by Geraldine Fitzgerald; scenery, James Wolk; costumes, Julie Schwolow; lighting, Phil Monat; production stage manager, Dawn Eaton; press, Shirley Herz, David Roggensack.

Turn-of-the-century character actor reminisces about his past with his actress-wife. The play was presented in two parts.

The Acting Company. Repertory of three revivals. **A New Way to Pay Old Debts** (2). By Philip Massinger. Opened May 21, 1985. **As You Like It** (3). By William Shakespeare. Opened May 22, 1985. **The Skin of Our Teeth** (3). By Thornton Wilder. Opened May 24, 1985. Produced by The Acting Company, John Houseman producing artistic director, Margot Harley executive producer, Michael Kahn co-artistic director, at Marymount Manhattan Theater. (Repertory closed May 26, 1985) All plays: Lighting, Dennis Parichy; production stage manager, Giles F. Colahan; stage manager, Liza C. Stein; press, Fred Nathan and Associates, Anne Abrams, Bert Fink.

PERFORMER	"AS YOU LIKE IT"	"A NEW WAY TO PAY OLD DEBTS"	"THE SKIN OF OUR TEETH"
Laura Brutsman	Celia	Chambermaid; Froth	Sabina
Terence Caza	Duke Senior	Order	Announcer; Doctor
Libby Colahan	Audrey	Furnace	Mrs. Antrobus
Aled Davies	Forester #2; Oliver	Lovell	Broadcast Official; Mr. Tremayne; Professor
Matt deGanon	Duke Frederick; William	Allworth	Dinosaur; Chair Pusher
Albert Farrar	Adam; Forester #1; de Boys; Sir Oliver Martext	Amble; Tailor	Hector; Telegraph Boy; Refugee
Susan Finch	Rosalind	Lady Allworth	Ivy; Miss T. Muse
Julie Fishell	Shepherdess; Hisperia	Surgeon; Waiting Woman	Miss E. Muse
Philip Goodwin	Jacques	Greedy	Mr. Fitzpatrick; Refugee
David Manis	Touchstone	Sir Giles Overreach	Mr. Antrobus
Phil Meyer	Amiens	Vintner; Watchall; Willdo	Broadcast Assistant; Homer
Joel F. Miller	Charles; Corin	Tapwell	Mammoth; Mr. Bailey
Anthony Powell	Forester #3; Le Beau; Silvius	Marrell	Henry
Derek David Smith	Orlando	Wellborn	Fortune Teller; Judge Moses
Ann Valdes	Phebe	Margaret	Gladys

A NEW WAY TO PAY OLD DEBTS: Directed by Michael Kahn; scenery, John Kasarda; costumes, Judith Dolan.

The only previous New York productions of record of this play by a contemporary of Shakespeare's were by Equity Library Theater in the 1945–46 season and OOB by Classic Theater 9/24/83.

AS YOU LIKE IT: Directed by Mervyn Willis; scenery and costumes, Stephen McCabe; choreography, Primavera Boman; fight choreography, Bjorn Johnson; music, Jeffrey Taylor.

The last major New York revival of As You Like It took place on Broadway 12/3/74 for 8 performances.

THE SKIN OF OUR TEETH: Directed by Gerald Freedman; scenery, Joel Fontaine; costumes, Jeanne Button.

The last major New York revival of The Skin of Our Teeth took place on Broadway 9/9/75 for 7 performances.

PLAYS PRODUCED
OFF OFF BROADWAY

AND ADDITIONAL PRODUCTIONS

Here is a comprehensive sampling of off-off-Broadway and other experimental or peripheral 1984–85 productions in New York, compiled by Camille Croce. There is no definitive "off-off-Broadway" area or qualification. To try to define or regiment it would be untrue to its fluid, exploratory purpose. The listing below of hundreds of works produced by more than 80 OOB groups and others is as inclusive as reliable sources will allow, however, and takes in all leading Manhattan-based, new-play-producing, English-language organizations.

The more active and established producing groups are identified in **bold face type,** in alphabetical order, with artistic policies and the name of the managing director(s) given whenever these are a matter of record. Each group's 1984–85 schedule is listed with play titles in CAPITAL LETTERS. Often these are works-in-progress with changing scripts, casts and directors, sometimes without an engagement of record (but an opening or early performance date is included when available).

Many of these off-off-Broadway groups have long since outgrown a merely experimental status and are offering programs which are the equal in professionalism and quality (and in some cases the superior) of anything in the New York theater, with special contractual arrangements like the showcase code, letters of agreement (allowing for longer runs and higher admission prices than usual) and, closer to the edge of the commercial theater, a so-called "mini-contract." In the list below, all available data on opening dates, performance numbers and major production and acting credits (almost all of them Equity members) is included in the entries of these special-arrangement offerings.

A large selection of lesser-known groups and other shows that made appearances off off Broadway during the season appears under the "Miscellaneous" heading at the end of this listing.

Amas Repertory Theater. Dedicated to bringing all people regardless of race, creed, color or economic background together through the creative arts. Rosetta LeNoire, founder and artistic director.

16 performances each

ANONYMOUS (musical) book, music, lyrics and directed by Vincenzo Stornaiuolo; additional English lyrics, Jack Everly; additional music, Giancarlo De Matteis. October 25, 1984. Choreographer, Gui Andrisano; scenery, Janice Davis; lighting, William H. Grant III; costumes, Robert Locke; musical director, Jack Everly. With Bob Brooker, Steven Cates, Dirk Lombard, Michael Duran, Lisa LaCorte, Paul Loper.

NORTHERN BOULEVARD (musical) book, Kevin Brofsky; music and lyrics, Carleton Carpenter. February 14, 1985. Director, William Martin; choreographer, Dennis Dennehy; scenery, Tom Barnes; lighting, Deborah Tulchin; costumes, Judy Dearing. With Audrei-Kairen, Morgan Mackay, Alice Cannon, Kelly Sanderbeck, Luke Lynch, Miriam Miller, Art Ostrin, Kelley Paige, Curtis Le Febvre, Rosetta LeNoire.

AMERICAN PLACE—*Left,* Carrie Nye and Tammy Grimes in The Woman's Project production of *Paducah* by Sallie Bingham; *right,* Willie C. Carpenter and Tom McDermott in *Rude Times* by Stephen Wylie

MANHATTAN SERENADE (musical revue) based on the music of Louis Alter; written by Karen Cottrell and Alfred Heller; compiled and arranged by Alfred Heller; new lyrics, Stanley Adams and Karen Cottrell. April 18, 1985. Director and choreographer, Bob Rizzo; scenery, Mina Albergo; lighting, Gregg Marriner; costumes, Christina Giannini. With Mark Pennington, Connie Kunkle, Sally Yorke, Cliff Hicklen, Luke Lynch, Mona Yvette Wyatt, Carrie Wilder, Brad J. Reynolds, Janice Lorraine.

American Place Theater. In addition to the regular off-Broadway subscription season, cabaret and other special projects are presented. Wynn Handman, director, Julia Miles, associate director.

WHAT'S A NICE COUNTRY LIKE YOU STILL DOING IN A STATE LIKE THIS? (musical revue) (31). Music, Cary Hoffman; lyrics, Ira Gasman. October 21, 1984. Director and choreographer, Miriam Fond; scenery, Neil Peter Jampolis; lighting, Anne Militello; costumes, David C. Woolard, Marcy Grace Froehlich; musical director, John Spalla. With Brent Barrett, Jack Landron, Krista Neumann, Patrick Richwood, Diana Szlosberg.

RUDE TIMES (16). By Stephen Wylie. February 8, 1985. Director, Gordon Edelstein; scenery, Pat Woodbridge; lighting, John Gisondi; costumes, David C. Woolard. With Willie C. Carpenter, Tom McDermott, Mara Hobel, Peter J. Saputo, Kate Wilkinson.

JUBILEE! A BLACK THEATER FESTIVAL: M.L.K. (28). Conceived, performed and written by Al Eaton. Director, Larry Coen; scenery and costumes, Patrice Macaluso; lighting, Ernest Baxter Jr. CELEBRATION (26). Conceived and directed by Shauneille Perry. Lighting, Ernest Baxter Jr.; costumes, Judy Dearing. With Carolyn Byrd, Clebert Ford, Andre Robinson Jr., Fran Salisbury. LOVE TO ALL, LORRAINE (20). Adapted, written and performed by Elizabeth Van Dyke. Directors, Woodie King Jr. and Elizabeth Van Dyke. May 14–June 9, 1985.

The Women's Project

4 CORNERS (14). Conceived, directed and designed by Gina Wendkos; co-written by Donna Bond. February 10, 1985. lighting, Anne Militello; costumes, Donna Bond. With Margaret Harrington, Josh Hamilton, Ryan Cutrona.

PADUCAH (21). By Sallie Bingham. April 11, 1985. Director, Joan Vail Thorne; scenery, Karen Schulz; lighting, Anne Militello; costumes, Mimi Maxmen. With William Cain, Tammy Grimes, Laura Hicks, Lou Myers, Carrie Nye.

The Ark Theater Company. Exists to develop and produce new works in a wide variety of styles and forms, to stage plays of unusual interest from all nations and periods. Bruce Daniel, Donald Marcus, Lisa Milligan, directors.

CHARLEY BACON AND HIS FAMILY (20). By Arthur Giron. January 27, 1985. Director, Donald Marcus; scenery, Derek McLane; lighting, Richard Dorfman; costumes, Catherine Zuber. With Jonathan Hadary, Pat Lavelle, Leslie Geraci, James Handy, Stan Lachow.

LIFE IS A DREAM by Pedro Calderon de la Barca, translated by Edwin Honig. March 21, 1985. Directed by James Simpson; with Rocco Sisto, Warren Manzi, Kristine Nielsen, Laura Innes, Michael Cerveris, Thomas Richards, Jeremiah Sullivan, Daniel Moran.

CHOPIN IN SPACE. By Phil Bosakowski. May 12, 1985. Director, Rebecca Guy; with William Duff-Griffin, Phil Lenkowsky, William Mesnik, Nancy Mette, Paul Romero, Mary Lou Rosato, Sylvia Short, Noble Shropshire, Rick Thomas.

Circle Repertory Projects in Progress. Developmental programs for new plays. Marshall W. Mason, artistic director.

4 performances each

AS IS by William M. Hoffman. October 22, 1984. Directed by George Boyd; with Tobin Wheeler, Reed Jones, David Courier, Claris Erickson, Lou Liberatore.

RAMEAU LA BESQUE by John Michael Heuer. December 10, 1984. Directed by Daniel Irvine; with Nancy Killmer, Stephanie Gordon, Lynne Thigpen, Ruby Holbrook, Edward Seamon, Nancy Donohue, Bruce McCarty, Terrence Markovich, Richard Seff.

THE MUSICAL COMEDY MURDERS OF 1940 written and directed by John Bishop. February 4, 1985. With Lily Knight, Tanya Berezin, James Pickens Jr., Burke Pearson, Richard Seff, J. Smith-Cameron, Zane Lasky, Penelope Willis, Bill Elverman, June Stein alternating with Debra Cole, Stephanie Gordon, Paul Butler, Jack Davidson, Ken Kliban, Sharon Schlarth, Kelly Connell, Elaine Bromka, Charles T. Harper, Bobo Lewis.

AN EVENING OF SHORT PLAYS by Joe Pintauro. March 18, 1985. Directed by Steve Stettler; with Claris Erickson, Lily Knight, Terrence Markovich, Louis Zorich, Jo Henderson, Bill Elverman alternating with William Andrews, Kathleen Sisk, Clement Fowler.

TO CULEBRA written and directed by Jonathan Bolt. April 8, 1985. With Charles T. Harper, Jack Davidson, Edward Seamon, Barnard Hughes, Jonathan Hogan, B. Rodney Marriott, Natalija Nogulich, Richard Seff, Walter Williamson, Stephanie Gordon, Rob Gomes.

Ensemble Studio Theater. Nucleus of playwrights-in-residence dedicated to supporting individual theater artists and developing new works for the stage. Over 200 projects each season, initiated by E.S.T. members. Curt Dempster, artistic director.

THE BLOODLETTERS (38). By Richard Greenberg. November 27, 1984. Director, Shirley Kaplan; scenery, Edward T. Gianfrancesco; lighting, Richard Lund; costumes, Bruce Harrow. With Garrett M. Brown, William Carden, Nancy Franklin, Cheryl McFadden, Bruce MacVittie, Corey Parker, Stephen Pearlman.

THE CRATE (playlets) (46). By Shel Silverstein. February 11, 1985. Director, Art Wolff; scenery, Sally de Valenzuela; lighting, Karl E. Haas; costumes, Isis C. Mussenden. With Bill Cwikowski, John Fiedler, Heather Lupton, Deborah Reagan, Raynor Scheine, Howard Sherman, Robert Trebor, Janet Zarish.

ONCE ON A SUMMER'S DAY (31). Book and lyrics, Arthur Perlman; music, Jeffrey Lunden. January 17, 1985. Director, John Henry Davis; choreographer, Linda Tarnay; scenery, Philipp Jung; lighting, Michael Orris Watson; costumes, Donna Zakowska; musical director, Alex Rybeck. With Todd Graff, David Green, Frank Hankey, Carolyn Mignini, Kimi Morris, Polly Pen, David Purdham, Mimi Wyche.

MARATHON '85 (one-act play festival): MARIENS KAMMER by Roger Hedden, adapted from Georg Buchner's *Wozzeck*, directed by Billy Hopkins; THE FROG PRINCE by David Mamet, directed by Peter Maloney; MEN WITHOUT DATES by Jane Willis, directed by Shirley Kaplan; LIFE UNDER WATER by Richard Greenberg, directed by Don Scardino; THE ROAD TO THE GRAVEYARD by Horton Foote, directed by Curt Dempster; DESPERADOES by Keith Reddin, directed by Mary B. Robinson; AGGRESSIVE BEHAVIOR by Stuart Spencer, directed by Jane Hoffman; BETWEEN CARS by Alan Zweibel, directed by Risa Bramon; NORTH OF PROVIDENCE by Edward Allan Baker, directed by Risa Bramon; THE SEMI-FORMAL by Louisa Jerauld, directed by Billy Hopkins; PAINTING A WALL by David Lan, directed by Joe Gilford; ONE TENNIS SHOE by Shel Silverstein, directed by Art Wolff. May 12–June 17, 1985.

Equity Library Theater. Actors' Equity sponsors a series of revivals each season as showcases for the work of actor-members and an "informal" series of original, unproduced material. George Wojtasik, managing director.

TRIBUTE by Bernard Slade. September 27, 1984. Directed by William Hopkins; with Matthew Lewis, Dolores Kenan, Charles Major, Cynthia Babak, Caroline Aaron, Mark Rogers, Nancy Youngblut.

BELLS ARE RINGING (musical) book and lyrics by Betty Comden and Adolph Green, music by Jule Styne. October 25, 1984. Directed by Charles Abbott; with K.K. Preece, Mark Jacoby, Lorna Erickson, Becky Garrett, Kelly Woodruff, Donald McGrath, Herbert Mark Parker, Lawrence Raiken, George Emch, John-Charles Kelly, Glenn Davish.

THE DESK SET by William Marchant. November 29, 1984. Directed by Lise Liepmann; with Gloria Maddox, Jeremy Trexler, Christine Campbell, Celia Tackaberry, Denise Bessette, Anthony St. Martin, Brian Kosnik, George Bohler, William Isaacs.

JACQUES BREL IS ALIVE AND WELL AND LIVING IN PARIS (musical) production concept, English lyrics and additional material by Eric Blau and Mort Shuman, based on Jacques Brel's lyrics and commentary; music by Jacques Brel. January 3, 1985. Directed by Stephen Bonnell; with Louise Edeiken, Richard Hilton, Jan Horvath, J.C. Sheets.

THE COMEDY OF ERRORS by William Shakespeare. February 7, 1985. Directed by Kent Thompson; with Wesley Stevens, James Jenner, Richard Grubbs, Sam Pond, Maxine Taylor-Morris, Elizabeth Pearson, Bonnie Black, David Holbrook.

VERY WARM FOR MAY (musical) book and lyrics by Oscar Hammerstein II, music by Jerome Kern. March 7, 1985. Directed by Worth Howe; with Robert Grossman, Valerie Depena, Cheryl Swift, Glenn Mure, Kirsten Lind, Jay Schneider, Daniel David, Karen Longwell.

DEATHTRAP by Ira Levin. April 11, 1985. Directed by Robert Bridges; with Lewis Morgan, Maryanne Dempsey, John Donahoe, Judith Tillman, James Bormann.

A LITTLE NIGHT MUSIC (musical) book by Hugh Wheeler, music and lyrics by Stephen Sondheim. May 9, 1985. Directed by Susan H. Schulman; with Ross Petty, Kathryn Hays, Eddie Korbich, Judith Blazer, Avril Gentiles, Karen Wald, Patrick Quinn, Maris Clement, Sarah Combs.

Informal Series: 3 performances each

TRADING IN FUTURES by Robert Clyman. September 17, 1984. Directed by Gregg L. Stebben; with Valerie Beaman, James D'Apollonia.

CONSENTING ADULTS by Ralph Hunt. October 15, 1984. Directed by Gregg L. Stebben; with Anthony John Lizzul, Gale Galione, John David Barone.

DONUTS by James Nicola. January 21, 1985. Directed by Gregg L. Stebben; with David Pierce, David Trim.

WRITERS BLOC by Geoffrey Gordon and OF MACE AND MEN by Gregg L. Stebben. February 25, 1985. Directed by Gregg L. Stebben; with William Ellis, Leo Ferstenberg, Michael Iannucci, David Lough, Nancy Richards, Kathleen Marie Robbins, Christine Carter, Anita Montgomery, Victoria Page.

WHAT COMES AFTER OHIO by Daniel Meltzer. March 18, 1985. Directed by William Sevedge Jr.; with Arland Russell, Michael Waldron.

CABARET (musical revue). April 22, 1985. Directed by Dan Wolgemuth and Wes Mcaffee; with Deborah Arters, Kevin Maguire, Merrie Rich.

PAULA OF THE GREEN CLOUDS by Faustino Rothman. May 20, 1985. Directed by Rebecca Kreinen; with Grace Bentley, Martin Curland, Dan Gershwin, Cornelia Mills, Stephen Moser, Bee-be Smith.

Hudson Guild Theater Presents plays in their New York, American, or world premieres. David Kerry Heefner, producing director, Daniel Swee, associate director.

28 performances each

BURKIE. By Bruce Graham. October 24, 1984. Director, Lynn M. Thomson; scenery, William Barclay; lighting, Phil Monat; costumes, Ann Morrell. With Jeffrey Hayenga, Eddie Jones, Sam Coppola, Caryn West.

THE ACCRINGTON PALS. By Peter Whelan. December 5, 1984. Director, Daniel Gerroll; scenery, Robert Thayer; lighting, Phil Monat; costumes, Pamela Scofield. With Kate Burton, Amanda Carlin, Veronica Castang, Anthony Fusco, E. Keyishian, Denise Stephenson, Ian Stuart, George Taylor, Thomas Virtue, Amelia White.

OUTSIDE WACO. By Patricia Browning Griffith. January 30, 1985. Director, June Rovenger; scenery, Daniel Proett; lighting, Phil Monat; costumes, Patricia Adshead. With Elizabeth Berridge, Carlin Glynn, Susan Mansur, Edward Power, Kate Skinner.

SEPTEMBER IN THE RAIN. By John Godber. March 27, 1985. Director, David Kerry Heefner; lighting, Phil Monat; costumes, Mary L. Hayes; sound, Ed Fitzgerald. With Susan Greenhill, Steve Ryan.

SUBMARINERS. By Tom McClenaghan. May 22, 1985. Director, David Kerry Heefner; scenery, Daniel Proett; lighting, Phil Monat; costumes, Pamela Scofield. With John Bowman, Tim Choate, Adam LeFevre, Kevin O'Rourke, Ralph Williams.

INTAR. Innovative cultural center for the Hispanic American community of New York, focusing on the art of theater. Max Ferra, artistic director, Dennis Ferguson-Acosta, managing director.

35 performances each

IMPACT. By Juan Shamsul Alam. January 23, 1985. Director, George Ferencz; scenery, Jun Maeda; lighting, Blu; costumes, Sally J. Lesser. With Shawn Elliott, Cordelia Gonzalez, Tim Van Pelt.

COLD AIR. By Virgilio Pinera, translated, adapted and directed by Maria Irene Fornes. March 27, 1985. Scenery, Ricardo Morin; lighting, Anne E. Militello; costumes, Gabriel Berry. With Raul Aranas, Al Casas, Ivonne Coll, Miriam Cruz, Leo Garcia, Armando Molina, Katrina Ramos, Jennifer Valle.

SAVINGS (musical) book and lyrics, Dolores Prida; music, Leon Odenz. May 15, 1985. Director, Max Ferra; choreographer, Frank Pietri; musical director, Leon Odenz; scenery and lighting, Robert McBroom; costumes, Karen Barbano. With Ricci Reyes Adan, Christofer De Oni, D'yan Forest, Peter Jay Fernandez, Georgia Galvez, Judith Granite, Lawrence Reed, Edward M. Rodriguez, Carmen Rosario, Marilyn Schnier.

CURSE OF THE STARVING CLASS by Sam Shepard. May 16, 1985. Directed by Robin Lynn Smith; scenery, Brian Martin; costumes, Frances Nelson; lighting, Mark Stanley. With Rose Gregorio, Eddie Jones, Bill Pullman, James Gleason, Karen Tull, Dan Patrick Brody, Stephen Bradbury, Jude Ciccolella.

Staged readings

EXTREMES by Juan Shamsul Alam. September 29, 1984.
IMPACT by Juan Shamsul Alam. September 30, 1984.
MARTINEZ by Leopoldo Hernandez. October 2, 1984.
DUNGEON by Ana Maria Simo. October 4, 1984.
EL SUPER by Ivan Acosta. October 6, 1984.
SAVINGS (musical-in-process) book and lyrics by Dolores Prida, music by Leon Odenz. October 7, 1984.
ROOSTERS by Milcha Sanchez-Scott. October 9, 1984.

Interart Theater. Committed to producing innovative work by women theater artists and to introducing to New York audiences a bold range of theater that is non-traditional in form or theme. Margot Lewitin, artistic director.

NEW WOMEN DIRECTORS FESTIVAL: A PERFECT ANALYSIS GIVEN BY A PARROT by Tennessee Williams, directed by Carol Morley; THE BERRY-PICKER by James Purdy, directed by Waltrudis Mathes; TRIFLES by Susan Glaspell, directed by Anne West; JOE: A DRAMATIC IDIOCY and STOPS by Robert Auletta, directed by Gaylen Ross (24). June 5–July 1, 1984. Scenery and costumes, Doris Mezler Andelberg. With Maxine Hollbrook, John Istel, Mary Anne West, Dave Greenan, Gardner Brooksbank, Sal Brienza, Susan Haviland, Margaret Ritchie, Barbara Burge, Claudia Wilde, Susan Batson.

THROUGH THE LEAVES reopened at the New York Shakespeare Festival Public Theater October 2, 1984 and ran for 64 performances.

FEAST OR FAMINE (30). Conceived, written and designed by Sondra Segal and Roberta Sklar. April 19, 1985. Director, Roberta Sklar; environment, Seth Price, scenery and costumes, Beth Kuhn; lighting, Jackie Manassee. With Joanna Hefferan, Sondra Segal.

LaMama Experimental Theater Club (ETC). A busy workshop for experimental theater of all kinds. Ellen Stewart, founder; Wesley Jensby, artistic director.

LA MULATA. By Esteban Fernandez Sanchez. September 4, 1984. Director, T. Riccio; scenery and slides, Chris Wayne; lighting, Blu; costumes, Lohr Wilson. With Aminta De Laura, Christofer De Oni, Paul Knowles, Lolita Lorre, Frank Megna, Valois Mickens, Antone Pagan, Frances Ellen Thorpe, Denia Brache.

SHEPARDSETS. Trilogy of plays by Sam Shepard: ANGEL CITY, SUICIDE IN B FLAT and BACK BOG BEAST BAIT; conceived by the Cement Acting Company. October 25, 1984. Directed by George Ferencz. With Peter Jay Fernandez, Jim Abele, Stephen Mellor, Deidre O'Connell, Tom Costello, Raul Aranas, Sheila Dabney, Akin Babatunde, Zivia Flomenhaft.

NOSFERATU created by Ping Chong in collaboration with the cast; suggested by F.W. Murnau's film. February 13, 1985. Directed by Ping Chong; with R.W. Rabb, Dan Hurlin, L. Smith, Jeannie Hutchins, Michael Duffy, John Fleming, Barbara Chang, Dennis Giacomo, Debby Cohen.

ANNE'S WHITE GLOVE by Alice Notley. April 9, 1985. Directed by James Dickson; with Julia Brothers, Thomas Carey, Taylor Mead, Mary Sutton, Franck L. Goldberg, Maureen Mac-Dougall, Tom Burke.

Schedule also included:

THE AIR-CONDITIONED BEACH by Walter Hadler. June 1, 1984. Directed by Daffi.
YUP'IK ANTIGONE adapted and directed by Dave Hunsaker. June 26, 1984. With Perseverance Theater and the Village of Toksook Bay.
STRUCTURES written and directed by Rudolf Kocevar. June 27, 1984.

OTELLO, inspired by Verdi's opera, conceived and directed by Mario Martone; music by Peter Gordon. September 6, 1984. With Andrea Renzi, Licia Maglietta, Tomas Arana.

ENEIDE conceived and directed by Giancarlo Cauteruccio; music by Liftiba. September 26, 1984.

ALPHA by Slawomir Mrozek and WHO WAS THAT MAN by Tamara Karren. October 1, 1984. Directed by John Beary and Richard Harden.

RED HOUSE, written, staged and directed by John Jesserun; music by Steven Antonelli.

CUORI STRAPPATI, conceived, directed and performed by La Gaia Scienza. October 10, 1984.

SKINS by John Densmore and TONGUES by Sam Shepard and Joseph Chaikin. October 25, 1984. Directed by Tony Abatemarco; with John Densmore.

MAKING KASPAR by Benjamin Barber and Leah Kreutzer. November 28, 1984. Directed by Benjamin Barber.

PROMETHEUS BOUND by Aeschylus, translated by Peter Arnott. December 7, 1984. Directed by Bill Reichblum; with Shadow Theater Company.

BLUMFELD by Franz Kafka, adapted by Teatro Dramma of Caracas; music by Peter Gordon. December 21, 1984. Directed by Elia Schneider.

CHAMPAGNE by Jackie Curtis. January 3, 1985. Directed by David McGrath.

NUIT BLANCHE created and directed by Ping Chong. January 17, 1985. With Rob List, Pablo Vela, Tone Blevins, L. Smith, R.W. Babb, Michael Duffy, Ping Chong.

A HUMAN EQUATION written and directed by Kenny Fries. January 18, 1985.

PAGLIACCI by Ruggiero Leoncavallo, additional music by Jonathan Hart. January 28, 1985. Directed by Richard Armstrong; with Rossignol, Ian Magilton, Linda Wise, Jonathan Hart (Roy Hart Theater).

GOATMAN by Raymond Schanze. February 20, 1985. Directed by John Vaccaro.

KAFKA: FATHER AND SON by Mark Rozovsky, translated by Elena Prischepenko. February 28, 1985. Directed by Leonardo Shapiro.

1985. Directed by Gerald Thomas; with Frederick Neumann, George Bartenieff, Julian Beck.

BIG MOUTH by Sidney Goldfarb and Paul Zimet; music by Ellen Maddow and Harry Mann. April 26, 1985. Directed by Tina Shepard.

QUARRY (opera) conceived and directed by Meredith Monk. May 7, 1985.

THE MEMORY THEATER OF GIULIO CAMILLO written and directed by Matthew Maguire; music by Vito Ricci. May 24, 1985.

FRIDA Y DIEGO by David Willinger and Hortensia Colorado; music by Pilar Brache. May 30, 1985. Directed by David Willinger.

Little Theater at the Lambs. Committed to developing plays that encourage human dignity and values. Carolyn Rossi Copeland, executive director.

PORCH (24). By Jeffrey Sweet. October 15, 1984. Director, Nan Harris; scenery, Michael C. Smith; lighting, Marc D. Malamud; costumes, Neal Bishop. With Gary Bayer, Jill Eikenberry, Clarke Gordon, Lianne Kressin.

THE GIFTS OF THE MAGI (34) (musical) book and lyrics, Mark St. Germain, based on the O. Henry story; music, Randy Courts. December 3, 1984. Director, Christopher Catt; choreographer, Piper Pickrell; scenery, Michael C. Smith; lighting, Heather Carson; costumes, Hope Hanafin; musical director, Steve Alper. With Michael Brian, Leslie Hicks, Bert Michaels, Brick Hartney, Jeff McCarthy, Lynne Wintersteller.

EPISODE 26 (36). By Howard Korder. April 15, 1985. Director, Christopher Catt; scenery, Michael C. Smith; lighting, Heather Carson; costumes, Andrea N. Carini. With Eric Booth, Dan Delafield, Tom Flagg, Diane Heles, Marek Johnson, James W. Monitor, Jack Schmidt, A.C. Weary, Daniel Wirth.

Manhattan Punch Line. New York's only theater company devoted to comedy. Steve Kaplan, artistic director, Mitch McGuire, executive director, Patricia Baldwin, managing director.

KID PURPLE (24). By Donald Wollner. November 8, 1984. scenery, Steve Saklad; lighting, Joshua Dachs; costumes, Mimi Maxmen. With Joyce Leigh Bowden, Sam McMurray, Daryl Edwards, Melodie Somers, Lyn Greene, Ellis (Skeeter) Williams.

LITTLE THEATER AT THE LAMBS—Jill Eikenberry and Clarke
Gordon in a scene from *Porch* by Jeffrey Sweet

FESTIVAL OF ONE-ACT COMEDIES: WOMEN AND SHOES by Nina Shengold, directed by Mitch McGuire; THE ART OF SELF-DEFENSE by Trish Johnson, directed by Steven D. Albrezzi; FINGER FOOD by Nina Shengold, directed by William Hopkins; BACKBONE OF AMERICA by Mark D. Kaufmann, directed by Porter Van Zandt; FALSIES by Richard Gott, directed by Robert S. Johnson; MONGOLIAN IDIOT by Fredric Sirasky, directed by John Schwab; LIFE ON EARTH by Howard Korder, directed by Robin Saex; SLEEPING BEAUTY by Laurence Klavan, directed by Steve Kaplan (32). January 21-February 24, 1985. Scenery, Jane Clark and Christopher Stapleton; lighting, Scott Pinkney; costumes, David Loveless. With Peter Webster, Denise Bessette, Helen Harrelson, Kathrin King Segal, Gina Barnett, Caryn West, Cameron Charles Johann, Stephen Hamilton.

RETURN OF THE CREATURE FROM THE BLUE ZALOOM (24). Written, directed and performed by Paul Zaloom. February 28, 1985. Production design, Marc D. Malamud.

ALMOST IN VEGAS (24). By Janet Neipris. April 19, 1985. Director, Susan Einhorn; scenery, Harry Feiner; lighting, Marc D. Malamud; costumes, Donna Zakowska. With Susan Cash, David Little, Mitch McGuire, April Shawhan.

Manhattan Theater Club. This major, multi-stage off-Broadway producing organization participates in and/or houses developmental activities during the season, in addition to its regular schedule of productions. Lynne Meadow artistic director, Barry Grove managing director.

Schedule included

SECRETS OF THE LAVA LAMP (14). By Adriana Trigiani, adapted from characters and stories created by Camille Saviola. April 24, 1985. Direction and musical staging, Stuart Ross; musical direction, Joel Silberman; lighting, Jackie Manassee. With Camille Saviola, Tommy Hollis, Stephen Lehew, Scott Robertson.

D by Michael Stewart; original song, Jerry Herman. Directed by Dan Held; scenery, Peter Harrison; costumes, Karen Hummel; lighting, Steven Pollack. With Michael Zaslow, Jane Fleiss, Lynne Thigpen, Bobo Lewis, Jason Alexander, Sam Gray, Grace Keagy, Rosalind Harris, Max Chalawsky.

Music Theater Group/Lenox Arts Center. Working with a core of artists in the development of ideas flowing in all directions from the participants, based in Lenox, Mass. and showcasing productions in New York City, this season at St. Clement's. Lyn Austin, producer-director.

THE GARDEN OF EARTHLY DELIGHTS based on Hieronymus Bosch's painting, conceived and directed by Martha Clarke in collaboration with Robert Barnett, Felix Blaska, Robert Faust, Marie Fourcaut, Margie Gillis, Polly Styron; music by Richard Peaslee in collaboration with with Eugene Friesen, William Ruyle, Steven Silverstein. November 20, 1984. Costumes, Jane Greenwood; lighting, Paul Gallo; flying, Peter Foy. With Margie Gillis, Feliz Blaska, Robert Faust, Marie Fourcaut, Eugene Friesen, William Ruyle, Steven Silverstein, Polly Styron, Tim Wengerd, Lila York.

THE MAKING OF AMERICANS (musical) liretto by Leon Katz, based on Gertrude Stein's work; music by Al Carmines. March 5, 1985. Directed by Anne Bogart. With Joan Scheckel, Catherine Coray, Karen Evans-Kandel, Myvanwy Jenn, Henry Stram, Martin Moran, Scott L. Johnson, George McGrath.

THE COURTROOM. Conceived, written and directed by Bill Irwin. May 7, 1985. Music by Doug Skinner; scenery, Loren Sherman; costumes, Ann Emonts; lighting, Jan Kreze; puppets, Julie Taymor. With Bill Irwin, Michael Moschen, Bob Berky, Brenda Bufalino, Rory Mitchell, Michael O'Connor, Kario Salem, Doug Skinner, Kent Jackman.

New Dramatists. An organization devoted to playwrights; member writers may use the facilities for anything from private cold readings of their material to public script-in-hand readings. Thomas G. Dunn, director.

Staged readings and workshops September 1984-June 1985

KNIFE EDGE by Bryan Oliver. Directed by Rhea Gaisner.
BOMBS ON THE HALFSHELL by Stephen Levi. Directed by Peter Phillips.
NIGHTS AND DAYS by Emily Mann. Directed by Susan Gregg.
BODACIOUS FLAPDOODLE by Mac Wellman. Directed by Page Burkholder.
PANIC IN LONGUEUIL by Rene Daniel Dubois; translated and directed by Gideon Schein.
COP SHOP by Robert Lord.
HIDDEN PARTS by Lynne Alvarez.
TOMORROWLAND by Jeff Jones.
'ROUND MIDNIGHT by Laura Harrington. Directed by Alma Becker.
LUCIAN'S WOODS by David J. Hill.
BERT & MAISEY by Robert Lord.
THE ABLE BODIED SEAMAN by Alan Bowne. Directed by Susan Gregg.
FOR HER OWN GOOD by Tom Dunn. Directed by Cheryl Faraone.
THE WONDERFUL TOWER OF HUMBERT LAVOIGNET by Lynne Alvarez. Directed by Page Burkholder.
BETWEEN THE ACTS by Joel Schenkar. Directed by Rhea Gaisner.
HIS MASTER'S VOICE by Dick D. Zigun. Directed by John Pynchon Holms.
SALLY'S GONE, SHE LEFT HER NAME by Russell Davis. Directed by Tony Giordano.
ELEVEN ZULU by Sean Clark. Directed by John Pynchon Holms.
THE MEMORY THEATER OF GIULIO CAMILLO by Matthew Maguire.
PAVAN FOR THE PRINCESS OF CLEVES by Romulus Linney.
ENERGUMEN by Mac Wellman. Directed by Becky Harrison.
FRIED CHICKEN AND INVISIBILITY by OyamO. Directed by Peter Wallace.
END OF RADIO by Sherry Kramer. Directed by Page Burkholder.
CRUISING CLOSE TO CRAZY by Laura Cunningham.
WOMEN OF MANHATTAN by John Patrick Shanley.
FREE FALL by Laura Harrington. Directed by Alma Becker.
THE BOYS OF WINTER by John Pielmeier. Directed by Susan Gregg.
CHERRY SODA WATER by Stephen Levi. Directed by Scott Rubsam.
BANG by Laura Cunningham. Directed by Casey Childs.
MR. AND MRS. COFFEE by William Sibley. Directed by Scott Rubsam.
THE TATTLER by Terri Wagener. Directed by Peter Wallace.
HOLY GHOSTS by Romulus Linney.
SOUVENIRS by Sheldon Rosen. Directed by Page Burkholder.
THE MOLE by Shirley Hillard. Directed by Becky Harrison.
EL HERMANO by Romulus Linney. Directed by Gideon Y. Schein.
HARVEST SUN by John Olive. Directed by Bob Hall.
IT ISN'T CRICKET by Robert Lord. Directed by Ethan Silverman.
THE WHITE DEATH by Daniel Therriault. Directed by Alma Becker.
BEAUTIFUL BODIES by Laura Cunningham.
HOPE COMES AT NIGHT, book by Pam Winfrey; music by Brenda Hutchinson. Directed by Gideon Y. Schein.
SAND MOUNTAIN MATCHMAKING by Romulus Linney.
FRUGAL REPAST by Sheldon Rosen. Directed by Susan Gregg.
CHINA WARS by Robert Lord. Directed by Ethan Silverman.
UNION BOYS by Jim Yoshimura. Directed by John Pasquin.
AMERICAN LADIES by Tom Dunn.

New Federal Theater. The Henry Street Settlement's training and showcase unit for playwrights, mostly black and Puerto Rican. Woodie King Jr., producer.

OH! OH! OBESITY (15) (musical) Book, music and lyrics, Gerald W. Deas. June 7, 1984. Script collaboration and directed by Bette Howard; choreography, Ronn Pratt; scenery, May Callas; lighting, Zebedee Collins; costumes, Vicki Jones; musical director, John McCallum. With Sandra Reaves-Phillips, Karen Langerstrom, Reginald Veljohnson, Stuart D. Goldenberg, Mennie F. Nelson, Jacquelyn Bird, Regina Reynolds Hood, Erica Ariis Smith, Kent C. Jackman.

WALTZ OF THE STORK BOOGIE (20) (musical) Book, music, lyrics and directed by Melvin Van Peebles. July 12, 1984. Additional music and lyrics, Ted Hayes and Mark Barkan; choreographer, Louis Johnson; scenery, Kurt Lundell; lighting, William Grant III; costumes, Jeffrey N. Mazor, Quay Truitt. With Harold Nicholas and the Brewery Puppets.

WELCOME TO BLACK RIVER. By Samm-Art Williams. November 15, 1984. Director, Walter Dallas; scenery, Richard Harmon; lighting, William H. Grant III; costumes, Judy Dearing. With Michael O'Neill, Frances Foster, J.C. Quinn, Ejaye Tracey, Carl Gordon, Michael S. Guess, Tommy Hicks, Joy A. Aaron.

THROMBO. By Albert Bermel. January 10, 1985. Director, Leonardo Shapiro; scenery, Jane Clark; lighting, William Armstrong; costumes, Gene Lakin. With Kevin O'Connor, Janet Borrus, Esther Ryvlin, Count Stovall, Christobal Carambo, Angela Pietropinto, Frankie Faison, Larry Pine.

LONG TIME SINCE YESTERDAY (24). By P.J. Gibson. January 31, 1985. Director, Bette Howard; scenery, Charles Henry McClennahan; lighting, William H. Grant III; costumes, Judy Dearing. With Tisha Campbell, Ayana Phillips, Lee Chamberlin, Janet League, Thelma Louise Carter, Ellen Holly, Hattie Winston.

A BLACK WOMAN SPEAKS (one-woman show) (4). By and with Beah Richards. February 22, 1985.

AMERI/CAIN GOTHIC (24). By Paul Carter Harrison. March 16, 1985. Director, Woodie King Jr.; scenery, Richard Harmon; lighting, William H. Grant III; costumes, Judy Dearing. With Moses Gunn, Sylvia Miles.

New York Shakespeare Festival Public Theater. Schedule of workshop productions and guest residencies, in addition to its regular productions. Joseph Papp, producer.

ROMEO AND JULIET by William Shakespeare. June 5, 1984. Directed by John Clingerman; with Michael Golding, Constance Boardman, Marian Baer, Jeff Shoemaker. (Co-production with the Riverside Shakespeare Company.)

FESTIVAL LATINO EN NUEVA YORK: MAHAGONNY SONGSPIEL by Bertolt Brecht, music by Kurt Weill, directed by Caca Rosset, with Brazil's Teatro do Ornitorringo; LA COLLECION (anthology of Puerto Rican drama); LOS DOS HERMANOS written and directed by Felipe Santande, with Mexico's La Coopertiva Teatro Denuncia; THE KIDNAPPING by Mario Diament, translated by Maria Coburn, with Teatro Gala; THROW DOWN II written and directed by Marvin Felix Camilo, music by Gilbert Price, with The Family Theater; EL CASTILLO INTERIOR by Pedrito Santaliz, based on Euripides' *Medea*, with Puerto Rico's Teatro Pobre de America; PAPI by Carlos Gorostiza, directed by David Stivel, with Luis Brandoni, Marta Bianchi, Julio de Gracia, Dario Grandinetti; EL EXILIADO MATELUNA (collective production) with Chile's Teatro Aleph, directed by Oscar Castro; TELEDEUM (production of Spain's Teatro Els Joglars), directed by Albert Boadella; NO MORE BINGO AT THE WAKE by Pietro Pietri, with New Rican Village and Latin Insomniacs; MR. LAFORGUE by Eduardo Pavlowsky, directed by Norman Briski, with Argenta Manhattan; CUENTOS NUEVO MEXICANOS by Denise Chavez and Irene Oliver Lewis, directed by Miss Lewis, with Compania de Teatro de Albuquerque; EL ACCOMPANAMIENTO by Carlos Gorostiza; LA EMPRESA PERDONA UN MOMENTO DE LOCURA by Rodolfo Santana, directed by Vicente Castro, with Puerto Rican Traveling Theater. August 10–20, 1984.

MANHATTAN POETRY VIDEO PROJECT (live performances and premiere videos) with Allen Ginsberg, Anne Waldman, Bob Holman. September 14, 1984. Hosted by Lou Reed.

THROUGH THE LEAVES by Franz Xaver Kroetz reopened October 10, 1984. (Co-production with Interart Theater and Mabou Mines.)

HANDY DANDY by William Gibson. October 15, 1984. Directed by Kay Matschullat; with Geraldine Fitzgerald, E.G. Marshall.

POW (Professional Older Women) THEATER FESTIVAL: I-80 by Mary D. Watson, directed by Billie Allen; WINNING THE ANGRY AMERICAN RIVER RACE by Deniza Springer, directed by Alba Oms; OFFICE MISHEGOSS by Adam Kraar, directed by Maura Tighe; COLLAGE #1: SISTERS AND FRIENDS (excerpts from works) by Cynthia L. Cooper, Mary Hazzard, Julie Jensen, Kerry Cox, directed by Gail Leondar; STAG PARTY by Sally Dixon Wiener, directed by Novella Nelson; DRAGGING THEIR DEAD SANDWICHES BEHIND THEM by Mia Albright, directed by June Pyskacek; THE NEW MONTANA by Lucille Hauser, directed by Leslie Ayvazian; PAST DUE by Irene Oppenheim, directed by Margaret Denithorne; COLLAGE # 2: WOMEN AND MEN (excerpts from works) by Dorothy Velasco, Peggy Gold, Estelle Ritchie, Margaret Hayden Rector, Marcia Haufrecht, directed by Jane Whitehill; THE NEW WORLD MONKEY by France Burke, directed by Lenore DeKoven; ADMIT ONE by Elyse Nass, directed by Nancy Rhodes; NIGHT THOUGHTS by Corinne Jacker, directed by Judy Canon Ott; LIST OF HONOR by Mary Steelsmith, directed by Bryna Wortman; MAMA BETT by Elsa Rael, directed by Diane McIntyre; COLLAGE #3: WOMEN REFLECTING (excerpts from works) by Gillian Lindsay, Leigh Podgorski, Joel Ensana, Laurel Harrell, Maureen Martin, Pat Staten, directed by Romala Robb Allrud; MOLLY'S DAUGHTERS (musical) book, music and lyrics by Shellen Lubin, directed by Michael Diamond. March 11, 18, 25, 1985.

The Open Space Theater Experiment. Emphasis on experimental works. Lynn Michaels, Harry Baum, directors.

THE OTHER SIDE OF NEWARK (25). By Enid Rudd. February 25, 1985. Director, Nancy Gabor; lighting, Jackie Manassee; costumes, Gail Brassard; sound, Mike Cohen. With Laurinda Barrett, Ralph Bell, W.T. Martin, Richarda, Louise Stubbs.

Pan Asian Repertory Theater. Aims to present professional productions which employ Asian American theater artists, to encourage new plays which explore Asian American themes and to combine traditional elements of Far Eastern theater with Western theatrical techniques. Tisa Chang, artistic director.

CHIPSHOT (28). By Donald G. McNeil Jr. October 10, 1984. Director, Raul Aranas; scenery, Bob Phillips; lighting, Victor En Yu Tan; costumes, Eiko Yamaguchi. With Gerald Lancaster, Mel Duane Gionson, Stanford Egi, Michael Arkin, Susan Gordon-Clark, Bea Soong, Erol Tamerman.

STATE WITHOUT GRACE (28). By Linda Kalayaan Faigao. November 14, 1984. Director, Aida Limjoco; scenery, Robert Bullock; lighting, Victor En Yu Tan; costumes, Linda Taoka. With Mia Katigbak, John Quincy Lee, Adrienne Telemaque, Makalina, Jaime Sanchez, Tysan, Ching Valdes, Luna Borromeo.

MANOA VALLEY (35). By Edward Sakamoto. February 20, 1985. Director, Kati Kuroda; scenery, Bob Phillips; lighting, Richard Dorfman; costumes, Eiko Yamaguchi. With Alvin Lum, Carol A. Honda, Lori Tanaka, Stanford Egi, Lily Sakata, Jeffrey Akaka, Mel Duane Gionson, Kati Kuroda, Eric Miji, Barbara Pohlman.

EAT A BOWL OF TEA (28). By Ernest Abuba, based on Louis Chu's novel. April 17, 1985. Directors, Ernest Abuba and Tisa Chang; scenery, Alex Polner; lighting, Richard Dorfman; costumes, Eiko Yamaguchi. With Tom Matsusaka, Ron Nakahara, Michael G. Chin, Les J.N. Mau, Donald Li, Richard Lee-Sung, Elizabeth Sung, Mary Lum, Sandy Hom.

Puerto Rican Traveling Theater. Professional company presenting bilingual productions primarily of Puerto Rican and Hispanic playwrights, emphasizing subjects of relevance today. Miriam Colon Edgar, founder and producer.

21 performances each

ORINOCO. By Emilio Carballido. January 9, 1985. Director, Vicente Castro; scenery, Carl A. Baldasso; lighting, Rachel Budin; costumes, Maria Contessa. With Miriam Colon, Ivonne Coll.

THE DEAD MAN'S AGONY. By Esteban Navajas Cortes. March 14, 1985. Director, Manu Tupou; scenery, Janice Davis; lighting, Rachel Budin; costumes, Skip Gindhart. With Carlos Carrasco, Victor Gil De Lamadrid, Iraida Polanco, Carmen Rosario.

SIMPSON STREET. By Eduardo Gallardo. May 2, 1985. Director, Miriam Colon; scenery, Carl Baldasso; lighting, Rachel Budin. With Miriam Colon, Marta De La Cruz, Eva Lopez, Iraida Polanco, Laura Elena Surillo, Freddy Valle.

Quaigh Theater. Primarily a playwrights' theater, devoted to the new playwright, the established contemporary playwright and the modern (post-1920) playwright. Will Lieberson, artistic director.

SACRAMENTS. By Jo Ann Tedesco. June 23, 1984. Director, Sherwood Arthur; scenery, Bob Phillips; lighting, Harry F. Sangmeister; costumes, Maureen Hogan. With Rutanya Alda, Denise Assante, Cosmo Canale, Max Cantor, Richard Dahlia, Kricker James, Vera Lockwood, Dina Mattei, Julie Pepper, Gregory Salata, Marcia Savella, Judith Scarpone, Rosanne Sorrentino.

MAN ENOUGH. By Patty Gideon Sloan. October 27, 1984. Director, Steve McCurdy; lighting, Clark Middleton. With Bruce King, Florence Anglin, Ron Woods, Kerry Kienzle, Jack O'Reilly, Alissa Alban, Michael Dalby, Dan Brady.

AN OCCASION OF SIN. By Deborah Lundy. November 28, 1984. Director, Will Lieberson; scenery, Thomas Wood; lighting, Donalee Katz; sound, George Jacobs. With Keith Michl, Susan Monts, Mike Champagne, Howard Mungo, Pat Squire, Robert Haufrecht.

DRAMATHON '84 (one-act plays in marathon). Schedule included: THE SHAVED MONKEY by Charles Pulaski, directed by Joel Winston; REALLY ROSIE (musical) book by Maurice Sendak, music and lyrics by Carole King, directed by Jean Carillo; COURAGE by Kristine Nieland, directed by Carl Arnold; A PRETTY BLUE by Resa Alboher, Noreen Ellis, Daniel Donnelly, directed by Resa Alboher; STILL BEAT NOBLE HEARTS by Laurie James, directed by Clifton James; A GOOD TIME by Ernest Thompson, directed by Leslie Blake; SIMON OF CYRENE by Joseph Hart, directed by Richard Trousdell; THE ACTRESS AND THE I.R.S. by Dick Zybtra, directed by Bruce Biggins; DOWN THE DRAIN by Steve Shilo, directed by Stewart Schwartz; PARKCHESTER OVAL written and directed by Stephen Holt; CONVULSIONS: A NEURO COMEDY by Wendy Marie Goodman, directed by Charles Rudd; SIBLINGS by Demmy Tambakos, directed by Cynthia Stokes; CONFIGURATIONS by Kent R. Brown, directed by Fern Bachman; FOOD by Ross Maclean, directed by Ellen Nickles; TRIAL RUN by John Mighton, directed by David Pratt; HAPPY HOUR by Poty Oliveira, directed by Allen Frame; LADIES ROOM by Kassianni Bradoc, directed by Sheldon Deckelbaum; ROSALINE by Michael Hill, directed by Will Cantler; EGOMANIA written and directed by Peter La Villa; SHAKESPEARE: OUR CONTEMPORARY by Becca Mavnery and Joe Millet, directed by Linda M. Pilz; SUNSET by Ruth Pearl, directed by Michelle Schachere; THE JUDGMENT OF PARIS written and directed by Risa Victoria Greenberg; WINNING THE ANGRY AMERICAN RIVER RACE by Deniza Springer, directed by Ellen Lewis; WHO'S HOLDING THE ELEVATOR by Tony DeNonno and Donald Margulies; THIRD SINGLES by Thomas G. Dunn, directed by Liz Wright; FUN'S-A-POPPIN' written and directed by Tom Murphy; HOLDING OUT written and directed by Adam Kraar; THE LADY IN 5 by James Himelsbach, directed by G. Michael Trupiano; A DIM CAPACITY FOR WINGS by William Thompson, directed by Craig Butler; NO STONE LEFT UNTURNED written and directed by Mitchell S. Kobren; STAGE DIRECTIONS by Israel Horovitz, directed by Gary Canier; THE SNORE THERAPIST by Steve Shilo, directed by Rita Tiplitz; THE LADY WANTS NO CHILDREN by Oliver Goldstick, directed by Scoobie Patterson; A SHORT VISIT TO EL SALVADOR by James Castagna; TOTAL HONESTY written and directed by Kricker James; PORNOGRAPHY IS MORE HONEST THAN TEACHING ANY DAY written and directed by Marvin D. Resnick; A HELL OF A HEAVENLY TIME by Matthew Witten, directed by Barbara Head; SWEET, SWEET MONIQUE by George Ghirlando, directed by James Manos Jr.; THE BEAUTY SHOW, PART I developed by Karen Fox and Amielle Zemach, directed by Amielle Zemach; IT'S ALL IN THE EYES by Ray Alvin; BARBIE DON'T GOT NAPPY HAIR by Charles Dumas, directed by Meleesa Wyatt; THE LOVE VOODOO by Novalynne Ellis, directed by Renee Gahn; BORN AGAIN AMERICAN by James T. McCartin, directed by C.C. Catanese; MEDUSA IN THE SUBURBS by David Steven Rappoport, directed by Alan Langson; IT'S TIME by Richard Cory, directed by Robert Watson; THE CARD TABLE written and directed by Michael Ladenson, additional material by Susan Cinoman; 12:21 P.M. by F.J. Hartland, directed by Peter Gordon. December 29–31, 1984.

THEATER OFF PARK—Sharon Hope and
Wayne Elbert in *Hot Sauce* by Karmyn Lott

BLESSED EVENT by Manuel Seff and Forrest Wilson. April 2, 1985. Directed by Will Lieberson; with Jack Mahoney, Rende Rae Norman, Susan Monts, Lee Moore, Lezlie Dalton, Joyce Renee Korbin.

Lunchtime Series

RED CROSS by Sam Shepard. October 8, 1984. Directed by Sam Blackwell; with Betty Pelzer, Judith Yerby.

YUK YUK by Will Lieberson and THE LAST OF THE LONG DISTANCE TRAVELLERS by Lawrence Blackmore. October 22, 1984. With Karen Christina, Joyce Renee Korbin, Will Lieberson, Terence Cartwright.

A SEASON OF CHANGES and WEDDING DAY TRAGEDY by Thomas G. Dunn. November 5, 1984. Directed by Liz Wright; with Sharon Feldman, Daniel Jenkins, Nanette Reynolds, Barbara Wiechmann.

I CAN'T IMAGINE TOMORROW by Tennessee Williams. November 19, 1984. Directed by Shela Xoregos; with Norma Fire, John Boylan.

THE LADY WANTS NO CHILDREN by Oliver Goldstick. January 7, 1985. Directed by Scoobee Patterson; with Barbara Lehmann, Kricker James.

12:21 P.M. by FJ Hartland. January 21, 1985. Directed by Peter M. Gordon; with Tennyson Bardwell, Jon Wool, Maureen Quigley.

RATMAN AND WILBUR: A STATEN ISLAND ROMANCE by Jules Feiler. February 18, 1985. Directed by Charles Gemmill; with Alex Wipf, Daniel Neiden, Anne Pasquale.
CONFIGURATIONS by Kent R. Brown. March 4, 1985. Directed by Fern Bachman; with Peter Naylor, Adele Cabot, Maxine Schaffer-Fromm, Tony Calabro.
TRIAL RUN by John Mighton. March 20, 1985. Directed by David Pratt; with Edward Hyland, Marcus Olson.
MOLLY AND JAMES by Sheila Walsh. April 1, 1985. Directed by Leslie Blake; with Jackie Hahn, Jack Mahoney.
HOLDING OUT by Adam Kraar. April 15, 1985. Directed by Peter M. Gordon; with Risa Brainin, Timothy Hunter, Michael Oppenheimer.
THE CARD TABLE written and directed by Michael Ladenson, additional material by Susan Cinoman. April 30, 1985. With Robert Kerbeck, John Ewaniuk, David Castro, Jon Lawton, Phillip Safley, Susan Cinoman.
THE ALEXANDRIA MUNICIPAL READING LIBRARY by Saragail Katzman. May 20, 1985. Directed by K. Bell; with Deborah Mullin, John Horton.
KILLING AFFAIRS by Herb Robinson; PIECES OF APRIL by Sonny Hyles; WRITER'S LICENSE by Margaret Park; SUPPER IN CUT 'N' SHOOT by Margot Hasha; SARGASSO by Jennifer Billingsley; SIBLINGS by Sally Robinson (Playwrights' Theater of Louisiana) May 20–24, 1985.
THE DAY OF THE RACES by Julie Jensen. May 27, 1985. Directed by John Moon; with Estelle J. Greene, Dianne Busch.

The Ridiculous Theatrical Company. Charles Ludlam's camp-oriented group devoted to productions of his original scripts and broad adaptations of the classics. Charles Ludlam, artistic director and director of all productions.

THE MYSTERY OF IRMA VEP. By Charles Ludlam. October 2, 1984. Scenery, Charles Ludlam; costumes, Everett Quinton; lighting, Lawrence Eichler; original music, Peter Golub. With Everett Quinton, Charles Ludlam.

The Second Stage. Committed to producing plays of the last ten years believed to deserve another chance, as well as new works. Robyn Goodman, Carole Rothman, artistic directors.

SHORT EYES (45). By Miguel Pinero. November 13, 1984. Director, Kevin Conway; scenery, David Jenkins; lighting, Marc B. Weiss; costumes, V. Jane Suttell. With John Bentley, Richard Bright, Paul Calderon, Larry Fishburne, David Patrick Kelly, Reggie Montgomery, Esai Morales, Michael O'Keefe, Ving Rhames, Arnaldo Santana, Bari K. Willerford.

THE VIENNA NOTES (34). By Richard Nelson. March 13, 1985. Director, Carole Rothman; scenery, Andrew Jackness; lighting, Frances Aronson; costumes, Shay Cunliffe. With Mia Dillon, Gwyllum Evans, James Noble, Lois Smith.

JUNO'S SWANS (39). By E. Katherine Kerr. May 3, 1985. Director, Marsha Mason; scenery, Kate Edmunds; lighting, Frances Aronson; costumes, Ann Roth. With Betty Buckley, Daniel Hugh-Kelly, Mary Kay Place.

Soho Rep. Infrequently or never-before-performed plays by the world's greatest authors, with emphasis on language and theatricality. Marlene Swartz, Jerry Engelbach, artistic directors.

Schedule included:

THE WINTER'S TALE by William Shakespeare. May 24, 1985. Directed by Anthony Bowles; with James Denton, Erick Devine, Frank Dwyer, Suzanne Ford, Katherine Elizabeth Neuman, Ellen Nickles, Robert Shampain, Steve Sterner, Mary Testa, Sharon Watroba, Craig Paul Wroe, Helen Zelon.

Theater for the New City. Developmental theater and new American experimental works. George Bartenieff, Crystal Field, artistic directors.

Schedule included:

SMOKING NEWPORTS AND EATING FRENCH FRIES. By Sebastian Stuart. August 30, 1984. Scenery, Randy Benjamin; lighting, Anne Militello. With Helen Hanft, Debra Granieri, Steve Lott, Bill Nunnery, Ann Saxman, Richard Spore, Rick Stanley, Chris Tanner, Georgia F. Wise.

HAMLETMACHINE. By Heiner Muller, translated by Carl Weber. November 8, 1984. Director, Uwe Mengel; scenery, Jody Culkin; lighting, Craig Kennedy; costumes, Suzan Pitt. With Mary Shultz.

ACT AND THE ACTOR. By Daryl Chin. December 20, 1984. Directors, Daryl Chin, Larry Qualis; scenery, Fred Wilson; lighting, Robert M. Sudderth. With Wayne Arnold.

THE AGE OF INVENTION (AN AMERICAN TRILOGY). Created and directed by Theodora Skipitares. January 3, 1985. Music, Virgil Moorefield, Scott Johnson; dramaturg, Andrea Balis; scenery, Debby Lee Cohen, Renee Miller, Diana Yates, Eli Langner; lighting, Beverly Emmons, Ronald M. Katz. Narrators: Mike Engels, Edwin Decker, Bill Weinstein, Preston Foerder.

ON THE LAM (musical) book and lyrics, Georg Osterman; music, Jeffrey Marke. January 10, 1985. Director, John Albano; scenery, Bill Wolf; lighting, Howard Theis; costumes, Gabriel Berry. With Georg Osterman, David McCorkle, Robert Schelhammer, Crystal Field, Mark Marcante, Todd Charles, Margaret Miller, Joe Pichette, Marlene Hoffman, Florence Peters, George Bartenieff, Lola Pashalinski, Jeff Mont, Florence Peters, Todd Stockman.

THE CONDUCT OF LIFE. Written and directed by Maria Irene Fornes. February 21, 1985. Scenery, T. Owen Baumgartner; lighting, Anne Militello; costumes, Sally J. Lesser. With Sheila Dabney, Crystal Field, Pedro Garrido, Alba Oms, Hermann Lademann.

MY FOETUS LIVED ON AMBOY STREET. Written and directed by Ronald Tavel. April 11, 1985. Scenery, Ronald Kajiwara; lighting, Craig Kennedy; costumes, Jane Aire; mask design, Christina Csatary; music, Mark Marcante, David Tice. With Christian Baskous, Regina David, David Carlyon, Vince Monzo, Lana Forrester, Mark Diekmann, Kim Sykes, Mark Marcante, Brian King.

Theater of the Open Eye. Total theater involving actors, dancers, musicians and designers working together, each bringing his own talents into a single project. Jean Erdman, producing artistic director, Amie Brockway, associate artistic director.

SCAPIN reopened October 12, 1984 for 23 performances.

A CRICKET ON THE HEARTH by Charles Dickens, adapted and directed by Amie Brockway. December 7, 1984. With Alexander Peck, Leslie Carroll, George Millenbach, Joe Roesch, Michael DiGioia, Joanne Jarvis.

SHE ALSO DANCES (22). By Kenneth Arnold. February 8, 1985. Director, Amie Brockway; choreographer, Susan Tenney; music, Nikki Stern; production design, Adrienne J. Brockway. With James Dutcher, Susan Jacobson.

THE DREAM OF KITAMURA (21). By Philip Kan Gotanda. March 22, 1985. Director and choreographer, Jean Erdman; scenery, Adrienne J. Brockway; lighting, Victor En Yu Tan; costumes, Eiko Yamaguchi; masks, Ralph Lee. With William Ha'o, Jodi Long, Lauren Tom, James Pax, Glenn Kubota, Chris Odo, Maureen Williams.

MISS JULIE by August Strindberg, translated by Harry Carlson. May 13, 1985. Directed by Kent Paul; with Megan Gallagher, Marko Maglich, Susan Boehm.

Theater Off Park. Provides Murray Hill-Turtle Bay residents with a professional theater, showcasing the talents of new and established actors, playwrights, designers and directors. Bertha Lewis, producing director, Albert Harris, artistic director.

HOT SAUCE (16). By Karmyn Lott. June 7, 1984. Director, Toni Dorfman; scenery and lighting, Richard Harmon; costumes, Katherine Roberson. With Wayne Elbert, Sharon Hope, Marchand Odette, Katherine Price.

THE POKER SESSION by Hugh Leonard. October 16, 1984. Directed by Albert Harris; with Keith McDermott, Ruby Holbrook, Jessie K. Jones, Colm Meaney, Matthew Smith, Stephen Vinovich, Keliher Walsh.

HONEY, I'M HOME (36). By Julie Goldsmith Gilbert. January 15, 1985. Director, Albert Harris; scenery, Alan Kimmel; lighting, Victor En Yu Tan; costumes, Arnold S. Levine. With Ray Blackburn, Haviland Morris, Susan Plaskin.

Special events: 1 performance each
A PEASANT OF EL SALVADOR by Peter Gould, adapted and performed by Peter Gould and Stephen Stearns. October 6, 1984.
IN CELEBRATION: DR. MARTIN LUTHER KING JR. January 15, 1985. With Carolyn Byrd, Lara Teeter, Vicki Regan, Ayl Mack, Lynnie Godfrey, Dina Merrill, Doris Troy.

WPA Theater. Produces neglected American classics and new American plays in the realistic idiom. Kyle Renick, artistic director, Wendy Bustard, managing director, Edward T. Gianfrancesco, resident designer, Darlene Kaplan, literary advisor.

FEATHERTOP (33). Book, Bruce Peyton; music and lyrics, Skip Kennon. October 17, 1984. Director, Susan H. Schulman; choreography, Michael Lichtefeld; musical director, Sand Lawn; scenery, Edward T. Gianfrancesco; lighting, Craig Evans; costumes, David Murin. With Alexandra Korey, David Barron, Charles Bari, Stephen Bogardus, Laura Dean, Jason Graae.

THE INCREDIBLY FAMOUS WILLY RIVERS (35). By Stephen Metcalfe. December 12, 1984. Director, Stephen Zuckerman; scenery, James Fenhagen; lighting, Richard Winkler; costumes, Mimi Maxmen; music, Denny McCormick. With Jay O. Sanders, Hansford Rowe, Elizabeth Berridge, Kathy Rossiter, Lois Chiles, John Bedford-Lloyd, James McDaniel, John Bowman, Dave Florek.

THE HITCH-HIKERS (35). By Eudora Welty, adapted by Larry Ketron. February 19, 1985. Director, Dann Florek; scenery, Edward T. Gianfrancesco; lighting, Phil Monat; costumes, Don Newcomb. With John Anthony Lack, Peter Zapp, Timothy Carhart, Elizabeth McGovern, Wyman Pendleton, William Jihmi Kennedy, Edward Cannan, Frances Fisher.

OUT OF GAS ON LOVERS LEAP (28). By Mark St. Germain. April 23, 1985. Director, Elinor Renfield; scenery, Edward T. Gianfrancesco; lighting, Craig Evans; costumes, Don Newcomb. With Melissa Leo, Fisher Stevens.

York Theater Company. Each season, productions of classic and contemporary plays are mounted with professional casts, providing neighborhood residents with professional theater. Janet Hayes Walker, producing director.

THE MISER by Molière, adapted by Miles Malleson. November 11, 1984. Directed by Janet Hayes Walker; with John Newton, Anne Gartlan, John Rainer, Robin Haynes, Juliette Kurth, David Kroll, Brian Evers, Eric Schussler, Timothy Hall, Philip Garfinkel, Sally Dunn, Ralph David Westfall.

HOME by David Storey. February 14, 1985. Directed by Alex Dmitriev; with Kermit Brown, Robert Gerringer, Mary Hara, Patricia Falkenhain, Paul Perri.

THE BAKER'S WIFE (20) (musical) book, Joseph Stein, based on *La Femme du Boulanger* by Marcel Pagnol and Jean Giono; music, lyrics and direction, Stephen Schwartz. March 24, 1985. Scenery, James Morgan; lighting, Mary Jo Dondlinger; costumes, Holly Hynes. With Jack Weston, Joyce Leigh Bowden, Kevin Gray, Charles Goff, Hal Robinson, Judith Lander, Gabriel Barre, Florence Anglin, Bert Fraser, Paul O'Keefe, Pamela Clifford, Mayla McKeehan, Gail Pennington.

CHEROKEE COUNTY (16). By Alan Ball. May 21, 1985. Director, Roger T. Danforth; scenery, James Morgan; lighting, Mary Jo Dondlinger; costumes, Robert W. Swasey. With Clark

YORK THEATER—Jack Weston in *The Baker's Wife*

Brown, Lea Floden, Ashley Gardner, Bob Kratky, Carol McCann, Karen Sederholm, Ellen Whyte.

Special event:
JOAN OF ARK AT THE STAKE (dramatic oratorio) by Arthur Honegger. May 5, 1985. Directed by Janet Hayes Walker; conducted by Charles Dodsley Walker; with Glenn Close, William Hurt, Canterbury Choral Society.

Miscellaneous

In the additional listing of 1984–85 off-off-Broadway productions below, the names of the producing groups or theaters appear in CAPITAL LETTERS and the titles of the works in *italics*. This list consists largely of new or reconstituted works and excludes most revivals, especially of classics. It includes a few productions staged by groups which rented space from the more established organizations listed previously.

ACTORS COLLECTIVE. *Creeps* by David Freeman. April 25, 1985. Directed by Stuart Ross; with W. McGregor King, Don de Franco, Craig Fols, Kathryn Salter, Glenn Alterman, Cynthia Raftus, William Carrigan, Perry Jon Pirkkanen.

ACTORS CREATIVE THEATER. *Women of Armagh* by Joseph P. McDonald. December, 1984. Directed by Ernie Martin; with Marsha McGregor, Julie Mote, Jessica Grossman, Ann Settel.

ACTOR'S OUTLET. Paul Sills's *Story Theater*. January 23, 1985. Presented by Lone Wolf Productions. *Abel's Sister* by Timberlake Wertenbaker. March 28, 1985. Directed by Martin Nordal; with Richard Abernathy, Cynthia Hayden, Donald Most, Mim Solberg.

ACTORS REPERTORY THEATER. *I Don't Want To Be Zelda Anymore* by Marty Martin. June 7, 1984. Directed by Jason Buzas; with Margie Bolding.

AMERICAN ARTISTS THEATER ENSEMBLE. *Kid Champion* by Thomas Babe. August 16, 1984.

AMERICAN JEWISH THEATER. *Jesse's Land* by Ernest Joselovitz. September 19, 1984. Directed by Jeff Martin; with R. Michael Baker, Gary S. Nathanson, Sophie Schwab, Sylvia Gassell. *The Rachel Plays: I'm Hiding! I'm Hiding!* and *Running Home* by Leah K. Friedman. February 19, 1985. Directed by Susan Einhorn; with Maia Danziger, Regina Baff, Lisabeth Bartlett, Richie Allan. *My Old Friends* (musical) by Mel Mandel and Norman Sachs. May 1, 1985. Directed by Philip Rose; with Imogene Coca, Peter Walker, Maxine Sullivan, King Donovan, Norman Golden, Grace Carney, John Danelle, Norberto Kerner, Jean Taylor, Robert Weil.

AMERICAN KALEIDOSCOPE. *Chaos and Hard Times* by Brandon Cole. February 7, 1985. Directed by Richard Bell; with Michael Badalucco, Warren Keith, Josephine Nichols, Joel Rooks, John Turturro. *Sit Down and Eat Before Our Love Gets Cold* (musical) book, music and lyrics by Barbara Schottenfeld. April 19, 1985. Directed by Anthony McKay; with Bev Larson, Barbara Schottenfeld, John Wesley Shipp.

AMERICAN STANISLAVSKI THEATER. *The Stronger* by August Strindberg, *The Dumbwaiter* by Harold Pinter, *The Marriage Proposal* by Anton Chekhov. February 6, 1985. Directed by Sonia Moore.

AMERICAN THEATER OF ACTORS. *Take Me Home* by Ward Morehouse III. November 15, 1985. Directed by John Guitz; original songs, Gail Wynters; with Philip Cass, Paul Kassel, Dulce Mann, Patti Randol, William Morino, Dorin Seymour, Gail Wynters.

APPLE CORPS. *Ladies in Retirement* by Reginald Denham and Edward Percy. August 9, 1984. Directed by William MacDuff; with Mary Orr. *Outward Bound* by Sutton Vane. October 17, 1984. Directed by Harold J. Kennedy; with Skipp Lynch, Meg Huston, Steve Tschudy, Farley Granger, Lucille Patton, Peter Waldren, Imogene Coca, Henry Morgan, Harold J. Kennedy.

ARTISTIC NEW DIRECTIONS. *Relatively Speaking* by Alan Ayckbourn. August, 1984. Directed by Rick Meyer; with Kathleen Claypool, James Kirsch, Kristine Niven, Thomas Barbour.

BALLROOM THEATER. *Issue? I Don't Even Know You!* (satrical cabaret revue) created by Alumni of The Acting Company. December, 1984. Directed by Jack Heifner; with Casey Biggs, Harriet Harris, Diane Kamp, Jack Kenny, Wayne Knight, Anderson Matthews, Kristine Nielsen, Kim Staunton.

BANDWAGON. *Salute to Ruby Keeler* written and directed by Jerry Bell. October 31, 1984. With Loni Ackerman, Helen Gallagher, Jack Gilford, Larry Kert, Joe Masiell, Donald Saddler, Bobby Short, Charles Strouse, Margaret Whiting, Julie Wilson, Ann Reinking. *Bitter Sweet* (musical) libretto, music and lyrics by Noel Coward. April 1, 1985. Directed by Jack Eddleman; with Tammy Grimes, Juliette Koka, Sarah Rice, Ronald Young.

BILLIE HOLIDAY THEATER. *Golden Boy* (musical) new book adapted by Leslie Lee from Clifford Odets and William Gibson; music by Charles Strouse; lyrics by Lee Adams. June 7, 1984. Directed by Jeffrey B. Moss; choreography, Louis Johnson; with Obba Babatunde, James Randolph, Leata Gallaway, Ebony Jo-Ann. *Inacent Black and the Brothers* by A. Marcus Hemphill. November 1, 1984. Directed by Mikell Pinkney; with Louise Stubbs, Gwendolyn Rucks-Spencer. *Sea Rock Children Is Strong Children* by Paul Webster; music and lyrics by Ricardo Cadogan. April 28, 1985. Directed by Paul Webster; with The Caribbean Theater of the Performing Arts.

BROOKLYN ACADEMY OF MUSIC. *The Games* (opera/music-theater collaboration) by Meredith Monk and Ping Chong. October 9, 1984. (Opening production of the Next Wave Festival).

Einstein on the Beach (opera) design and direction by Robert Wilson; music and lyrics by Philip Glass. December 11, 1984.

CLASSIC THEATER. *The Imaginary Invalid* by Molière, adapted by Owen S. Rackleff. February 28, 1985. Directed by Maurice Edwards; with Owen S. Rackleff. *The Roundheads and the Pointheads* by Bertolt Brecht, translated by Michael Feingold. April, 1985. Directed by Jerry Roth; with Bill Maloney, Amy Brentano, Ellen Boggs, William Snovell.

COCTEAU REPERTORY. *Theater in the Time of Nero and Seneca* by Edvard Radzinsky, translated by Alma H. Law. September 7, 1984. Directed by Eve Adamson; with Craig Smith, Harris Berlinsky, Patrick Boyington, Mary Gratch, Craig Cook, Miles Mason. *Cymbeline* by William Shakespeare. November, 1984. Directed by Douglas McKeown; with Harris Berlinsky, Judy Jones, John Emmert, Craig Cook, Craig Smith, Margaret Dulaney. *The Importance of Being Earnest* by Oscar Wilde. January 18, 1985. *Goat Song* by Franz Werfel. February 9, 1985.

CUBICULO. *Lester Sims Retires Tomorrow* by William Curtis. September, 1984. Directed by Louis Erdmann; with George Murdock, Jennifer Rhodes, Karl Erdmann.

DANCE THEATER WORKSHOP'S ECONOMY TIRES THEATER. *The Pre-Star Condition* written and performed by Bill Talen. January, 1985. Directed by Scott Paulin and Robert Cole. *Theater of Panic* by and with Geoff Hoyle and Keith Terry. February 15, 1985.

DON'T TELL MAMA. *Sweet Will* (Shakespeare cabaret) by Lance Mulcahy. January 30, 1985. Directed by John Olon.

ECCENTRIC CIRCLES THEATER. *Love Games* by Elaine Denholtz. October 18, 1984. Directed by Paula Kay Pierce; with Aurelia DeFelice, Paula Ewin, Martha Greenhouse, Eric Himes, Johnnie Mae, Muriel Mason.

ECHO STAGE REPERTORY. *Abel's Sister* by Timberlake Wertenbaker, based on material by Yolande Bourcler. April, 1985. Directed by Martin Nordal; with Richard Abernathy, Cynthia Hayden, Donald Most, Mim Solberg.

HARBOR SHAKESPEARE FESTIVAL. *The Tamer Tamed* by John Fletcher. October 4, 1984. Directed by Jeffrey R. Cohen; with Jordan Clark, Jill Mackavey, Christine Reid, Andrew Barnicle, Rick Tolliver, Lisa Levine, Charles Anderson.

HAROLD CLURMAN THEATER. *Mr. Joyce Is Leaving Paris* by Tom Gallacher. September 23, 1984. Directed by Jordan Deitcher; with Neil Vipond, Rory Sullivan, Vince Carroll, Robin Howard, Brian Mallon.

IRONDALE ENSEMBLE PROJECT. *Jason and the Argonauts* adapted from the Greek myth and improvised by the company. October 4, 1984. Directed by James Louis Niesen. *The Ritual of Jason/Medea* conceived and directed by James Louis Niesen. December 7, 1984. Improvised by the company.

JAPAN SOCIETY. *Nomura Kyogen Theater*. July 10, 1984.

JEWISH REPERTORY THEATER. *Kuni-Leml* (musical) book by Nahma Sandrow, based on Avrom Goldfadn's farce, music by Raphael Crystal, lyrics by Richard Engquist. June 14, 1984. *Shlemiel the First*, Isaac Bashevis Singer's short stories, edited for the stage by Sarah Blacher Cohen. October 21, 1984. Directed by Edward M. Cohen; with Karen Ludwig, Zane Lasky. *Cold Storage* by Ronald Ribman. December 8, 1984. Directed by Len Cariou; with Joe Silver, Odalys Dominguez, Jay Thomas. *City Boy*, based on stories by Leonard Michaels, adapted and directed by Edward M. Cohen. February, 1985. With Max Cantor, DeLane Matthews, Scott G. Miller. *Crossing Delancey* by Susan Sandler. April 25, 1985. With Melanie Mayron, Jacob Harran, Sylvia Kanders, Geoffrey Pierson, Shirley Stoler.

JUDITH ANDERSON THEATER. *Cap & Bells* by Luigi Pirandello. October 18, 1984. Directed by John Ferraro; with Frank Gero, Angela Pietropinto, Frederica Meister, Jay Acovone, Tom Mardirosian, Carolyn Green, Lucrezia Norelli. *Be Happy for Me* by Jerry Sterner. May 15, 1985. Directed by John Ferraro; with David Groh, Philip Bosco, Priscilla Lopez, Russ Pennington.

LABOR THEATER. *Why I Left California* by C.R. Portz, J. Bentley Campbell, Gussie Harris, Bette Craig and cast; music and musical direction by Martin Burman. January 25, 1985. Directed by C.R. Portz; with M.W. Burman, Gussie Harris, Claudia Hommel, Michael Kluger, Guy Sherman.

MABOU MINES. *Pretty Boy* written and directed by Greg Mehrten; with David Drake, William Raymond, Terry O'Reilly, Ron Vawter, John Fistos, Hanne Blom, David Briar, Honora Fergusson, Greg Mehrten; and *Imagination Dead Imagine* by Samuel Beckett, directed by Ruth Maleczech; with Ruth Nelson, Clove Galilee. June, 1984.

MERIDIAN. *A Safe Light* by Adele Prandini. March 7, 1985. Directed by Francine L. Trevens; with Susan Chandler, Vickie Phillips, Teri Sheridan.

MUSICAL THEATER WORKS. *Tropicana* (musical) book by George Abbott, music by Robert Nassif, lyrics by Peter Napolitano, additional lyrics by Robert Nassif. May 29, 1985. Directed by George Abbott; choreography, Donald Saddler; with Roxann Cabalero, Constance Carpenter, Edmund Lyndeck, Lara Teeter.

NEIGHBORHOOD GROUP THEATER. *Little Birds Fly* by Harding Lemay. December, 1984. Directed by Kathryn Ballou; with Barbara Bradish, R. Dean Fourie, Tom Zurick, Cheryl Henderson, Warren Sweeney, David Wilbur, Jonathan Mandell, Sharon Shahinian, Barbara Vaccaro, Charles Brukardt.

NEW VIC THEATER. *A True Story* by Gene Ruffini. March 29, 1985. Directed by Jane Stanton; with Bill Tatum, Chris Koron, Ken Lambert, Wendy K. Matthews, Charles Honce.

NEW YORK GILBERT AND SULLIVAN PLAYERS. *The Gondoliers* December 28, 1984. With John Reed, Anthony Tamburello, Joanna Levy, Paul Tomasko, Richard Holmes, Carol Wolfe, Ellen Scrofani, Cheryl Fenner. *The Mikado*. March 8, 1985. *The Yeomen of the Guard*. May 9, 1985.

NEW YORK THEATER STUDIO. *The Cruelties of Mrs. Schnayd* by David Suehsdorf. February 2, 1985. Directed by John Pepper; with Frank Hankey, Charles Shaw Robinson, James Harper, Dion Anderson.

NO SMOKING PLAYHOUSE. *Modern Romance* by F. Latour. February 6, 1985. Directed by Bernard Barrow; with Jim Desmond, Alix Elias, John Fleming, Mark Hofmaier, David Hunt, Joseph Ragno, Geoffrey Wade.

NORMAN THOMAS THEATER. *The Golden Land* (musical) by Zalmen Mlotek and Moishe Rosenfeld. October 27, 1984. Directed by Howard Rossen; with Bruce Adler, Phyllis Berk, Joanne Borts, Avi Hoffman, Betty Silberman.

OFF-ON BROADWAY THEATER. *Elvis Mania*. August 16, 1984. Directed by Leslie Irons; with Johnny Seaton.

OHIO THEATER. *In the Jungle of the Cities* by Bertolt Brecht. February 2, 1985. Directed by Jacques Reynaud; with Carl Delo, Dana Julian, Peter Guttmacher, Nicholas Hunt. *The Crows* by Ethan Ayer. April, 1985. Directed by Patrick Brafford; with Sheila MacRae, Jerry Cunliffe, John A. Weaver, Michael Oberlander.

PERFORMANCE SPACE 122. *Loyaltown, U.S.A.* (performance art) by and with Peter Rose. November, 1984. *A Good American Novel* written and directed by Beth Lapides. December 2, 1984. *Hamlette*, adapted by Ethyl Eichberger from *Hamlet* by William Shakespeare. December, 1984. With Black-Eyed Susan, Stephen Tashjian, Agosto Machado, Ethyl Eichberger. *Fizzles* by Samuel Beckett. December, 1984. Directed by Liz Diamond; with Ryan Cutrona.

PERRY STREET THEATER. *Carla's Song* by Michelle Morris. June 29, 1984. Directed by John Glines; with Kym Le Mon, David Heyward, David Kerin, Jeanne Schlegel. *Enter a Free Man* by Tom Stoppard. September 20, 1984. Directed by Dean Button; with Jerome Kilty, Helen Stenborg, Deanna Deignan, W.T. Martin, Jeremiah Alexander, Jill Larson, Curt Williams, Charles M. Kray. *War on the Third Floor* by Pavel Kohout, translated and directed by Elizabeth Diamond. November 1, 1984. With Tom Carson, Mary Lou Rosato. *The Fantod* by Amlin Gray. March 16, 1985. Directed by Stephen Katz; with Norman Snow, Jeanne Cullen, Lorraine Morgan, Mark Moses, Charles Gregory, Burke Pearson, Martha Miller. *Sally's Gone, She Left Her Name* by Russell Davis. April 23, 1985. Directed by Tony Giordano; with Robert Leonard, Cynthia Nixon, David Canary, Michael Learned.

THE PRODUCTION COMPANY—Lesley Wise
(left) and Ara Fitzgerald in the latter's *Leverage*

THE PRODUCTION COMPANY. *Blue Window* by Craig Lucas. June 12, 1984. Directed by Norman Rene; with Matt Craven, Randy Danson, Christine Estabrook, Lawrence Joshua, Brad O'Hara, Maureen Silliman, Margo Skinner. *Private Scenes* by Joel Homer. January 13, 1985. Directed by Maggie L. Harrer; with Michael French, Donna Snow. *Leverage* by and with Ara Fitzgerald, directed by Carey Perloff, and *Baby Steps* by and with Deborah Fortson, directed by Steve Seidel. January 31, 1985. *Walk the Dog, Willie* by Robert Auletta. March 24, 1985. Directed by Norman Rene; with Larry Bryggman, Dan Butler, William Converse-Roberts, Amy Steel.

RIVERSIDE SHAKESPEARE COMPANY. *The History of King Lear*, adapted from Shakespeare by Nahum Tate. March 8, 1985. Directed by Stuart McDowell; with Eric Hoffmann, Richard Merrell, Frank Muller, Barbara Tirrell, Margo Gruber, Freda Kavanagh.

RIVERWEST THEATER. *Tender Offer* by George S. Rattner. September 8, 1984. Directed by Gordon Edelstein; with Lawrence Weber, Gretchen Trapp, Hugo Halbrich, Anthony Mannino. *Jack and Jill* (musical) book and lyrics by Bob Larimer, music by Hal Schaefer. March 21, 1985. Directed by Miriam Fond; with Lara Teeter, Jennifer Naimo, Raymond Thorne, Sheila Smith, Ernestine Jackson, David Pendleton, Edye Byrde, Daniel B. Wooten Jr. *Bruce Lee Is Dead and I'm Not Feeling Too Good, Either* by Matt Williams. April 23, 1985. Directed Suzanne Brinkley; with Lisa Ellex, Dan Moran, Paul Penfield, Marian Hampton, Ron Perkins.

SOUTH STREET THEATER. *Haven* by Joel Gross. March 10, 1985. Directed by Bruce Ornstein; with Ellen Barber, Lane Binkley, Stephen McHattie, Anita Keal, David Lynn Chandler. *Maneuvers* by Catherine Muschamp. April, 1985. Directed by Fielder Cook; with Stephen Joyce, Lise Hilboldt, David Purdham, Edmond Genest, Ron Randell, William Campbell.

STAGE ARTS THEATER COMPANY. *Sullivan and Gilbert* by Kenneth Ludwig. December, 1984. Directed by Larry Carpenter; with Etain O'Malley, George Ede, Jonathan Moore.

STANLEY EUGENE TANNEN'S FREE THEATER PRODUCTIONS. (Staged readings by established theater artists.) Readings by Jeremy Irons, June 28, 1984; Raul Julia, August 30, 1984; Joe Mantegna, October 30, 1984; George Hearn, December 4, 1984; Sharlene Hartman, Jessica James and Stanley Eugene Tannen, February 11, 1985.

THEATER GUINEVERE. *Private Scenes* by Joel Homer. January, 1985. Directed by Maggie L. Harrer; with Michael French, Donna Snow.

THEATER IN THE PARK. *Stop the World—I Want to Get Off* (musical) book, music and lyrics by Leslie Bricusse and Anthony Newley. November 1, 1984. Directed by Sue Lawless; with Jason Alexander, SuEllen Estey. *Along Came a Spider* by Robes Kossez. March, 1985. Directed by Sue Lawless; with Betsy von Furstenberg, Marie Wallace, Michael Hirsch, Betty Low.

T.O.M.I. *A Country for Old Men* by Anthony F. Doyle. June, 1984. Directed by Jerry Heymann; with Edward Seamon, Dan Lounsbery, George Gerdes, Joseph Daly. *Crime and Punishment* by Fyodor Dostoevsky, adapted by L.A. Sheldon, translated by Davis Magarshack. July, 1984. Directed by Virginia Castillo; with Shan Sullivan, Caroline Arnold. *Not Waving* by Catherine Hayes. March 6, 1985. Directed by John Donovan; with Frances Cuka, Alan Johnson, Patricia Barrett.

TOWN HALL. *Sweet Adeline* (musical) book and lyrics by Oscar Hammerstein II; music by Jerome Kern. May 20, 1985.

TRINITY CENTER THEATER. *The Pushcart Peddlers* and *The New Yorkers* by Murray Schisgal. September 12, 1984. Directed by Peter Maloney; with Phyllis Newman, Adolph Green, Amanda Green, Allen Swift.

WOOSTER GROUP.... *And That's How the Rent Gets Paid, Part IV (or, The Confessions of Conrad Gerhardt)* by Jeff Weiss. August, 1984. With Jeff Weiss, Ron Vawter, Kate Valk, Nancy Reilly, Dorothy Cantwell. *L.S.D. (... Just the High Points...)* composed by The Wooster Group. October, 1984. Directed by Elizabeth LeCompte; with Willem Dafoe, Jim Clayburgh, Norman Frisch, Matthew Hansell, Anna Kohler, Peyton Smith, Jim Strahs, Michael Stumm, Jeff Webster, Michael Kirby. *Swimming to Cambodia, Parts I and II* by Spalding Gray. November, 1984. *Trilogy: Seventeen, At That Time I Was Studying Carole Lombard* and *The Father* written and performed by Beatrice Roth. April, 1985. Special direction by Valeria Wasilewski. *Miss Universal Happiness* written, directed and scored by Richard Foreman. May 14, 1985. With Matthew Hansell, Kate Valk, Willem Dafoe, Ron Vawter, Peyton Smith, Elizabeth LeCompte, Nancy Reilly, Anna Kohler, Steve Buscemi, Michael Stumm, Jeff Webster. (Co-production of the Ontological-Hysteric Theater.)

CAST REPLACEMENTS AND TOURING COMPANIES

Compiled by Stanley Green

The following is a list of the more important cast replacements in productions which opened in previous years, but were still playing in New York during a substantial part of the 1984-85 season; or were still on a first-class tour in 1984-85, or opened in New York in 1984-85 and went on tour during the season (casts of first-class touring companies of previous seasons which were no longer playing in 1984-85 appear in previous *Best Plays* volumes of appropriate years).

The name of each major role is listed in *italics* beneath the title of the play in the first column. In the second column directly opposite appears the name of the actor who created the role in the original New York production (whose opening date appears in *italics* at the top of the column). Indented immediately beneath the original actor's name are the names of subsequent New York replacements, together with the date of replacement when available.

The third column gives information about first-class touring companies, including London companies (produced under the auspices of their original New York managements). When there is more than one roadshow company, #1, #2, etc., appear before the name of the performer who created the role in each company (and the city and date of each company's first performance appears in *italics* at the top of the column). Their subsequent replacements are also listed beneath their names, with dates when available.

BRIGHTON BEACH MEMOIRS

	New York 3/27/83	*#1 Ft. Lauderdale 11/26/83* *#2 Providence 2/8/85*
Eugene Jerome	Matthew Broderick Fisher Stevens 8/2/83 Matthew Broderick 2/7/84 Fisher Stevens 5/1/84 Roger Raines 8/7/84 Jon Cryer 9/18/84	#1 Jonathan Silverman #2 Patrick Dempsey
Stanley Jerome	Ziljko Ivanek J. Patrick Breen 8/2/83 Mark Nelson 12/4/84	#1 Mark Nelson #2 Brian Drillinger
Nora	Jodi Thelen Marissa Chibas Elizabeth Perkins 11/27/84 Wendy Gazelle 3/5/85	#1 Elizabeth Perkins #2 Lisa Waltz
Jack Jerome	Peter Michael Goetz David Margulies 8/20/84 Dick Latessa 4/85	#1 Charles Cioffi #2 Richard Greene

Kate Jerome	Elizabeth Franz	#1 Joan Copeland
	Marilyn Chris	#2 Kate Milgrim
	Barbara Tarbuck 8/84	
	Maggie Burke 1/29/85	
	Dorothy Holland 4/85	
Laurie	Mandy Ingber	#1 Olivia Laurel Mates
	Elizabeth Ward	#2 Skye Bassett
	Royana Black 8/84	Romy Berk
	Olivia Laurel Mates 4/85	
Blanche	Joyce Van Patten	#1 Barbara Caruso
	Kathleen Widdoes	#2 Rocky Parker
	Anita Gillette 8/84	
	Verna Bloom 4/85	

CATS

New York 10/7/82

Cassandra	René Ceballos
	Charlotte d'Amboise
Mistoffelees	Timothy Scott
	Herman W. Sebek
Old Deuteronomy	Ken Page
	Kevin Marcum
Rum Tum Tugger	Terrence V. Mann
	Jamie Rocco 10/84
	Terrence V. Mann 3/25/85

Note: Replacements during the 1984-85 season are listed above under the names of the original cast members. For previous replacements, see pages 415-416 of *The Best Plays of 1983-84*.

A CHORUS LINE

N.Y. Off Bway 4/15/75
N.Y. Bway 7/25/75

Sheila	Carole Bishop (name changed to Kelly Bishop 3/76)
	Susan Danielle 9/84
Mike	Wayne Cilento
	Don Correia 7/84
	J. Richard Hart 8/84
Larry	Clive Clerk
	Jim Litten 7/84
Maggie	Kay Cole
	Ann Heinricher 8/84
Richie	Ronald Dennis
	Eugene Fleming 9/84
	Gordon Owens 3/85
Cassie	Donna McKechnie
	Wanda Richert 6/84
	Angelique Ilo 10/84
	Wanda Richert 11/84

Greg	Michel Stuart Danny Weathers 8/84
Bobby	Thomas J. Walsh Ron Kurowski 8/84
Paul	Sammy Williams Wayne Meledandri 1/85

Note: Replacements during the 1984-85 season are listed above under the names of the original cast members. For previous replacements, see pages 437-440 of *The Best Plays of 1982-83*, and pages 416-417 of *The Best Plays of 1983-84*. For touring casts, see pages 472-473 of *The Best Plays of 1978-79*.

DEATH OF A SALESMAN

New York 3/29/84

Willy Loman	Dustin Hoffman
Linda	Kate Reid
Biff	John Malkovich Stephen Long 10/23/84

DREAMGIRLS

New York 12/20/81

Effie Melody White	Jennifer Holliday Roz Ryan 6/5/84
Lorrell Robinson	Loretta Devine Teresa Burrell 6/5/84 Loretta Devine 10/9/84
C. C. White	Obba Babatunde Lawrence Clayton 9/84
James Thunder Early	Cleavant Derricks
Curtis Taylor Jr.	Ben Harney Weyman Thompson 6/5/84 Ben Harney 8/84
Deena Jones	Sheryl Lee Ralph Linda Leilani Brown 6/5/84
Michelle Morris	Deborah Burrell Brenda Pressley 6/5/84 Teresa Burrell 10/84
Marty	Vondie Curtis-Hall

Note: Replacements during the 1984-85 season are listed above under the names of the original cast members. For previous replacements and the touring cast, see page 417 of *The Best Plays of 1983-84*.

THE FANTASTICKS

New York 5/3/60

El Gallo	Jerry Orbach Hal Robinson David Brummel 1/29/85 Dennis Parlato 5/7/85

FOOL FOR LOVE—As the Sam Shepard play entered its third year, its cast comprised George Gerdes and Katherine Cortez *(seated)* and Page Johnson and Stephen Mendillo *(standing)*

Luisa	Rita Gardner
	Karen Culiver 12/4/84
Matt	Kenneth Nelson
	Bill Perlach 2/5/85

Note: As of May 31, 1985, 31 actors had played the role of El Gallo, 27 actresses had played Luisa and 23 actors had played Matt. Replacements during the 1984-85 season are listed above under the names of the original cast members. For previous replacements, see pages 442-444 of *The Best Plays of 1982-83* and page 418 of *The Best Plays of 1983-84.*

FOOL FOR LOVE

New York 5/26/83

Eddie	Ed Harris
	Will Patton
	Bruce Willis
	Aidan Quinn 7/12/84
	David Andrews 10/84
	George Gerdes 5/85
May	Kathy Whitton Baker
	Ellen Barkin 2/14/84
	Moira McCanna Harris 3/12/84
	Frances Fisher 10/84
	Katherine Cortez
	Deborah Strang 4/85

42nd STREET

	New York 8/25/80	London 8/8/84
Julian Marsh	Jerry Orbach Steve Elmore 1/15/85 Don Chastain 4/85	James Laurenson
Dorothy Brock	Tammy Grimes Millicent Martin 12/84	Georgia Brown
Peggy Sawyer	Wanda Richert Lisa Brown 3/85	Clare Leach
Billy Lawlor	Lee Roy Reams Lee Roy Reams 1/8/85	Michael Howe
Maggie Jones	Carole Cook Jessica James 10/4/82	Margaret Courtenay
Bert Barry	Joseph Bova	Hugh Futcher

Note: Replacements during the 1984-85 season are listed above under the names of the original cast members. For previous replacements and touring casts, see pages 418-419 of *The Best Plays of 1983-84.*

GLENGARRY GLEN ROSS

	New York 3/25/84
Shelly Levine	Robert Prosky Howard Witt 7/2/84 Vincent Gardenia 10/31/84
Dave Moss	James Tolkan J.J. Johnston 12/17/84

ISN'T IT ROMANTIC

	New York 12/15/83	Los Angeles 10/28/84
Janie Blumberg	Cristine Rose Sally Faye Reit 11/7/84 Alma Cuervo 12/11/84 Robin Bartlett 4/9/85	Christine Estabrook
Harriet Cornwall	Lisa Banes Christine Healy 1/2/85	Anne Lange
Marty Sterling	Chip Zien Tom Robbins 4/17/84 Mitchell Greenberg 5/11/84 Alan Rosenberg 6/22/84 Tom Robbins 12/18/84 Jay Thomas 2/15/85	Michael Lembeck
Paul Stuart	Jerry Lanning Nicholas Hormann 8/14/84 James Rebhorn 1/2/85	Jerry Lanning
Tasha Blumberg	Betty Comden Marge Kotlisky 1/31/84	Joan Copeland

Barbara Barrie 5/11/84
Marge Kotlisky 8/7/84
Scotty Bloch 11/29/84
Joan Copeland 1/15/85
Elizabeth Perry 5/21/85

Lillian Cornwall   Jo Henderson   Jo de Winter
Peg Murray 3/6/84
Scotty Bloch 7/17/84
Pippa Scott 11/29/84
Julia Meade 4/2/85

Simon Blumberg   Stephen Pearlman   Barney Martin
Steven Gilborn 4/3/84
James Harder 2/5/85

LA CAGE AUX FOLLES

	New York 8/21/83	*#1 San Francisco 5/29/84* *#2 New Orleans 12/26/84*
Albin	George Hearn Keene Curtis 10/8/84 George Hearn 10/22/84	#1 Walter Charles #2 Keene Curtis
Georges	Gene Barry Jamie Ross 7/16/84 Keith Michell 8/13/84 Van Johnson 1/7/85	#1 Keith Michell Gene Barry 9/13/84 #2 Peter Marshall
Jean-Michel	John Weiner	#1 Joseph Breen #2 Peter Reardon
Anne	Leslie Stevens Jennifer Smith	#1 Mollie Smith #2 Juliette Kurth
Edouard Dindon	Jay Garner	#1 Robert Burr #2 Bob Carroll
Jacqueline	Elizabeth Parrish	#1 Carol Teitel #2 Le Clanché du Rand
Jacob	William Thomas Jr.	#1 Darrell Carey #2 Ronald Dennis
*Renaud**	Walter Charles Jack Davison 5/84	#1 Steve Arlen #2 Mace Barrett

*Character was named Duclos in first touring company.

MY ONE AND ONLY

	New York 5/1/83	*Washington, DC 3/8/85*
Capt. Billy Buck Chandler	Tommy Tune Ron Young 1/10/84 Tommy Tune 1/17/84 Don Correia 11/1/84 Tommy Tune 2/5/85	Tommy Tune
Edith Herbert	Twiggy Stephanie Ely 1/3/84	Sandy Duncan

Twiggy 1/10/84
Sandy Duncan 11/1/84

Mr. Magix	Charles "Honi" Coles	Charles "Honi" Coles
Mickey	Denny Dillon Georgia Engel 11/1/84	Peggy O'Connell
Prince Nicolai	Bruce McGill Don Amendola 11/1/84	Don Amendola
Rev. J.D. Montgomery	Roscoe Lee Browne Tiger Haynes 11/1/84	Tiger Haynes

NITE CLUB CONFIDENTIAL

New York 5/10/84

Kay Goodman	Fay DeWitt Eileen Fulton 8/30/84

ON YOUR TOES

	New York 3/6/83	*London 6/12/84*
Vera Baronova	Natalia Makarova	Natalia Makarova Galina Panova 10/1/84 Doreen Wells
Junior Dolan	Lara Teeter	Tim Flavin
Sergei Alexandrovitch	George S. Irving	John Bennett
Peggy Porterfield	Dina Merrill	Honor Blackman
Frankie Frayne	Christine Andreas	Siobhan McCarthy
Konstantine Morrosine	George de la Pena	Nicholas Johnson

Note: For New York cast changes and touring cast, see page 420 of *The Best Plays of 1983–84*.

THE REAL THING

	New York 1/5/84	*Ft. Lauderdale 2/12/85*
Henry	Jeremy Irons John Vickery 7/2/84 Jeremy Irons 11/5/84 Nicol Williamson 3/19/85	Brian Bedford
Annie	Glenn Close Caroline Lagerfelt 7/2/84 Laila Robins 11/5/84	Sara Botsford
Charlotte	Christine Baranski Sara Botsford 7/2/84	Marianne Owen
Billy	Peter Gallagher Todd Waring 6/25/84 Anthony Fusco 7/2/84 Peter Gallagher 9/24/84 D.W. Moffett 11/13/84	John Tenney

Max	Kenneth Welch Simon Jones 7/2/84	William McNulty
Debbie	Cynthia Nixon Yeardley Smith 12/10/84	Alice Haining

THE RINK

New York 2/9/84

Angel   Liza Minnelli
    Mary Testa 7/3/84
    Stockard Channing 7/14/84

Anna   Chita Rivera

SUNDAY IN THE PARK WITH GEORGE

New York 5/2/84

George   Mandy Patinkin
    Robert Westenberg 9/18/84
    Cris Groenendaal 1/15/85
    Robert Westenberg 1/22/85
    Harry Groener 4/23/85

Dot   Bernadette Peters
    Joanna Glushak 8/27/84
    Bernadette Peters 9/10/84
    Betsy Joslyn 2/26/85
    Maryann Plunkett 3/12/85

THE TAP DANCE KID

New York 12/21/83

Dipsey Bates   Hinton Battle

Ginnie Sheridan   Hattie Winston
    Gail Nelson 6/84

William Sheridan   Samuel E. Wright
    Ira Hawkins 2/5/85

Willie Sheridan   Alfonso Ribeiro
    Jimmy Tate 6/26/84
    Savion Glover 11/84

TORCH SONG TRILOGY

New York 6/10/82

Arnold Beckoff   Harvey Fierstein
    Donald Corren (eves.) 9/25/84
    Donald Berman (eves.)11/20/84
    Donald Corren (mats.)11/20/84
    Philip Astor (eves.)12/11/84
    Donald Berman (mats.)12/11/84
    Harvey Fierstein (eves.)1/7/85
    Philip Astor (mats.)1/7/85
    Philip Astor (eves.)5/4/85

Ed   Court Miller
                     Raymond Baker (eves.)6/4/84
                     Peter Ratray (mats.)6/4/84
                     Sam Freed 9/84
                     Ben Lemon 11/20/84
                     Court Miller 1/7/85
                     Tom Stehschulte 2/12/85

Note: Replacements during the 1984–85 season are listed above under the names of the original New York cast members. For previous replacements and touring cast, see pages 421–422 of *The Best Plays of 1983–84.*

TRUE WEST

              New York 10/17/82

Lee   John Malkovich
                     Peder Melhouse 7/2/84

Austin   Gary Sinise
                     Erik Estrada 7/2/84

Note: Replacements during the 1984–85 season are listed above under the names of the original New York cast members. For previous replacements, see page 422 of *The Best Plays of 1983–84.*

FACTS AND
FIGURES

LONG RUNS ON BROADWAY

The following shows have run 500 or more continuous performances in a single production, usually the first, not including previews or extra non-profit performances, allowing for vacation layoffs and special one-booking engagements, but not including return engagements after a show has gone on tour. In all cases the numbers were obtained directly from the shows' production offices. Where there are title similarities, the production is identified as follows: (p) straight play version, (m) musical version, (r) revival.

THROUGH MAY 31, 1985

(PLAYS MARKED WITH ASTERISK WERE STILL PLAYING JUNE 1, 1985)

Plays	Number Performances	Plays	Number Performances
*A Chorus Line	4.086	*Dreamgirls	1,439
*Oh! Calcutta! (r)	3,777	How To Succeed in Business Without Really Trying	1,417
Grease	3,388		
Fiddler on the Roof	3,242	Hellzapoppin	1,404
Life With Father	3,224	The Music Man	1,375
Tobacco Road	3,182	Funny Girl	1,348
Hello, Dolly!	2,844	Mummenschanz	1,326
My Fair Lady	2,717	Angel Street	1,295
Annie	2,377	Lightnin'	1,291
Man of La Mancha	2,328	Promises, Promises	1,281
Abie's Irish Rose	2,327	The King and I	1,246
Oklahoma!	2,212	Cactus Flower	1,234
*42nd Street	1,990	Sleuth	1,222
Pippin	1,944	Torch Song Trilogy	1,222
South Pacific	1,925	1776	1,217
The Magic Show	1,920	Equus	1,209
Deathtrap	1,793	Sugar Babies	1,208
Gemini	1,788	Guys and Dolls	1,200
Harvey	1,775	Amadeus	1,181
Dancin'	1,774	Cabaret	1,165
Hair	1,750	Mister Roberts	1,157
The Wiz	1,672	Annie Get Your Gun	1,147
Born Yesterday	1,642	The Seven Year Itch	1,141
The Best Little Whorehouse in Texas	1,639	Butterflies Are Free	1,128
		Pins and Needles	1,108
Ain't Misbehavin'	1,604	*Cats	1,106
Mary, Mary	1,572	Plaza Suite	1,097
Evita	1,567	They're Playing Our Song	1,082
Barefoot in the Park	1,530	Kiss Me, Kate	1,070
Mame (m)	1,508	Don't Bother Me, I Can't Cope	1,065
Same Time, Next Year	1,453		
Arsenic and Old Lace	1,444	The Pajama Game	1,063
The Sound of Music	1,443	Shenandoah	1,050

Plays	Number Performances	Plays	Number Performances
The Teahouse of the August Moon	1,027	The Pirates of Penzance (1980 r)	772
Damn Yankees	1,019	Woman of the Year	770
Never Too Late	1,007	Sophisticated Ladies	767
Any Wednesday	982	My One and Only	767
A Funny Thing Happened on the Way to the Forum	964	Bubbling Brown Sugar	766
		State of the Union	765
The Odd Couple	964	The First Year	760
Anna Lucasta	957	You Know I Can't Hear You When the Water's Running	755
Kiss and Tell	956	Two for the Seesaw	750
Dracula (r)	925	Joseph and the Amazing Technicolor Dreamcoat (r)	747
Bells Are Ringing	924		
The Moon Is Blue	924	*La Cage aux Folles	743
Beatlemania	920	Death of a Salesman	742
The Elephant Man	916	For Colored Girls, etc.	742
*Brighton Beach Memoirs	904	Sons o' Fun	742
Luv	901	Candide (mr)	740
Chicago	898	Gentlemen Prefer Blondes	740
Applause	896	The Man Who Came to Dinner	739
Can-Can	892	Nine	739
Carousel	890	Call Me Mister	734
Hats Off to Ice	889	West Side Story	732
Fanny	888	High Button Shoes	727
Children of a Lesser God	887	Finian's Rainbow	725
Follow the Girls	882	Claudia	722
Camelot	873	The Gold Diggers	720
I Love My Wife	872	Jesus Christ Superstar	720
The Bat	867	Carnival	719
My Sister Eileen	864	The Diary of Anne Frank	717
No, No, Nanette (r)	861	I Remember Mama	714
Song of Norway	860	Tea and Sympathy	712
Chapter Two	857	Junior Miss	710
A Streetcar Named Desire	855	Last of the Red Hot Lovers	706
Barnum	854	Company	705
Comedy in Music	849	Seventh Heaven	704
Raisin	847	Gypsy (m)	702
You Can't Take It With You	837	The Miracle Worker	700
La Plume de Ma Tante	835	That Championship Season	700
Three Men on a Horse	835	Da	697
The Subject Was Roses	832	The King and I (r)	696
Inherit the Wind	806	Cat on a Hot Tin Roof	694
No Time for Sergeants	796	Li'l Abner	693
Fiorello!	795	Peg o' My Heart	692
Where's Charley?	792	The Children's Hour	691
The Ladder	789	Purlie	688
Forty Carats	780	Dead End	687
The Prisoner of Second Avenue	780	The Lion and the Mouse	686
Oliver!	774	White Cargo	686

Plays	*Number Performances*	*Plays*	*Number Performances*
Dear Ruth	683	A Day in Hollywood/A Night in the Ukraine	588
East Is West	680	The Me Nobody Knows	586
Come Blow Your Horn	677	*The Tap Dance Kid	586
The Most Happy Fella	676	The Two Mrs. Carrolls	585
The Doughgirls	671	Kismet	583
The Impossible Years	670	Detective Story	581
Irene	670	Brigadoon	581
Boy Meets Girl	669	No Strings	580
Beyond the Fringe	667	Brother Rat	577
Who's Afraid of Virginia Woolf?	664	Pump Boys and Dinettes	573
Blithe Spirit	657	Show Boat	572
A Trip to Chinatown	657	The Show-Off	571
The Women	657	Sally	570
Bloomer Girl	654	Golden Boy (m)	568
The Fifth Season	654	One Touch of Venus	567
Rain	648	The Real Thing	566
Witness for the Prosecution	645	Happy Birthday	564
Call Me Madam	644	Look Homeward, Angel	564
Janie	642	Morning's at Seven (r)	564
The Green Pastures	640	The Glass Menagerie	561
Auntie Mame (p)	639	I Do! I Do!	560
A Man for All Seasons	637	Wonderful Town	559
The Fourposter	632	Rose Marie	557
Two Gentlemen of Verona (m)	627	Strictly Dishonorable	557
The Tenth Man	623	Sweeney Todd, the Demon Barber of Fleet Street	557
Is Zat So?	618	A Majority of One	556
Anniversary Waltz	615	The Great White Hope	556
The Happy Time (p)	614	Toys in the Attic	556
Separate Rooms	613	Sunrise at Campobello	556
Affairs of State	610	Jamaica	555
Oh! Calcutta!	610	Stop the World—I Want to Get Off	555
Star and Garter	609	Florodora	553
The Student Prince	608	Noises Off	553
Sweet Charity	608	Ziegfeld Follies (1943)	553
Bye Bye Birdie	607	Dial "M" for Murder	552
Irene (r)	604	Good News	551
Broadway	603	Peter Pan (r)	551
Adonis	603	Let's Face It	547
Street Scene (p)	601	Milk and Honey	543
Kiki	600	Within the Law	541
Flower Drum Song	600	The Music Master	540
A Little Night Music	600	Pal Joey (r)	540
Agnes of God	599	What Makes Sammy Run?	540
Don't Drink the Water	598	The Sunshine Boys	538
Wish You Were Here	598	What a Life	538
A Society Circus	596		
Absurd Person Singular	592		
Blossom Time	592		

Plays	Number Performances	Plays	Number Performances
Crimes of the Heart	535	Half a Sixpence	511
The Unsinkable Molly Brown	532	The Vagabond King	511
The Red Mill (r)	531	The New Moon	509
A Raisin in the Sun	530	The World of Suzie Wong	508
Godspell	527	The Rothschilds	507
The Solid Gold Cadillac	526	On Your Toes (r)	505
Irma La Douce	524	Sugar	505
The Boomerang	522	Shuffle Along	504
Follies	521	Up in Central Park	504
Rosalinda	521	Carmen Jones	503
The Best Man	520	The Member of the Wedding	501
Chauve-Souris	520	Panama Hattie	501
Blackbirds of 1928	518	Personal Appearance	501
The Gin Game	517	Bird in Hand	500
Sunny	517	Room Service	500
Victoria Regina	517	Sailor, Beware!	500
Fifth of July	511	Tomorrow the World	500

LONG RUNS OFF BROADWAY

Plays	Number Performances	Plays	Number Performances
*The Fantasticks	10,436	Your Own Thing	933
The Threepenny Opera	2,611	Curley McDimple	931
Godspell	2,124	Leave It to Jane (r)	928
Jacques Brel	1,847	The Mad Show	871
Vanities	1,785	*Fool for Love	840
You're a Good Man Charlie Brown	1,547	Scrambled Feet	831
The Blacks	1,408	The Effect of Gamma Rays on Man-in-the-Moon Marigolds	819
*Forbidden Broadway	1,399	A View From the Bridge (r)	780
One Mo' Time	1,372	The Boy Friend (r)	763
Let My People Come	1,327	True West	762
*Little Shop of Horrors	1,189	The Pocket Watch	725
The Hot 1 Baltimore	1,166	The Connection	722
I'm Getting My Act Together and Taking It on the Road	1,165	The Passion of Dracula	714
Little Mary Sunshine	1,143	Adaptation & Next	707
El Grande de Coca-Cola	1,114	Oh! Calcutta!	704
One Flew Over the Cuckoo's Nest (r)	1,025	Scuba Duba	692
The Boys in the Band	1,000	The Knack	685
Cloud 9	971	The Club	674
Sister Mary Ignatius Explains It All for You & The Actor's Nightmare	947	The Balcony	672
		America Hurrah	634
		*Isn't It Romantic	615
		Hogan's Goat	607
		The Trojan Women (r)	600

Plays	*Number Performances*	Plays	*Number Performances*
Krapp's Last Tape & The Zoo Story	582	Six Characters in Search of an Author (r)	529
The Dumbwaiter & The Collection	578	The Dining Room	511
		The Dirtiest Show in Town	509
Dames at Sea	575	Happy Ending & Day of	
The Crucible (r)	571	Absence	504
The Iceman Cometh (r)	565	Greater Tuna	501
The Hostage (r)	545	The Boys From Syracuse (r) ...	500

NEW YORK CRITICS AWARDS, 1935–36 to 1984–85

Listed below are the New York Drama Critics Circle Awards from 1935–36 through 1984–85 classified as follows: (1) Best American Play, (2) Best Foreign Play, (3) Best Musical, (4) Best, regardless of category (this category was established by new voting rules in 1962–63 and did not exist prior to that year).

1935–36—(1) Winterset
1936–37—(1) High Tor
1937–38—(1) Of Mice and Men, (2) Shadow and Substance
1938–39—(1) No award, (2) The White Steed
1939–40—(1) The Time of Your Life
1940–41—(1) Watch on the Rhine, (2) The Corn Is Green
1941–42—(1) No award, (2) Blithe Spirit
1942–43—(1) The Patriots
1943–44—(2) Jacobowsky and the Colonel
1944–45—(1) The Glass Menagerie
1945–46—(3) Carousel
1946–47—(1) All My Sons, (2) No Exit, (3) Brigadoon
1947–48—(1) A Streetcar Named Desire, (2) The Winslow Boy
1948–49—(1) Death of a Salesman, (2) The Madwoman of Chaillot, (3) South Pacific
1949–50—(1) The Member of the Wedding (2) The Cocktail Party, (3) The Consul
1950–51—(1) Darkness at Noon, (2) The Lady's Not for Burning, (3) Guys and Dolls
1951–52—(1) I Am a Camera, (2) Venus Observed, (3) Pal Joey (Special citation to Don Juan in Hell)
1952–53—(1) Picnic, (2) The Love of Four Colonels, (3) Wonderful Town
1953–54—(1) Teahouse of the August Moon, (2) Ondine, (3) The Golden Apple
1954–55—(1) Cat on a Hot Tin Roof, (2) Witness for the Prosecution, (3) The Saint of Bleecker Street

1955–56—(1) The Diary of Anne Frank, (2) Tiger at the Gates, (3) My Fair Lady
1956–57—(1) Long Day's Journey Into Night, (2) The Waltz of the Toreadors, (3) The Most Happy Fella
1957–58—(1) Look Homeward, Angel, (2) Look Back in Anger, (3) The Music Man
1958–59—(1) A Raisin in the Sun, (2) The Visit, (3) La Plume de Ma Tante
1959–60—(1) Toys in the Attic, (2) Five Finger Exercise, (3) Fiorello!
1960–61—(1) All the Way Home, (2) A Taste of Honey, (3) Carnival
1961–62—(1) The Night of the Iguana, (2) A Man for All Seasons, (3) How to Succeed in Business Without Really Trying
1962–63—(4) Who's Afraid of Virginia Woolf? (Special citation to Beyond the Fringe)
1963–64—(4) Luther, (3) Hello, Dolly! (Special citation to The Trojan Women)
1964–65—(4) The Subject Was Roses, (3) Fiddler on the Roof
1965–66—(4) The Persecution and Assassination of Marat as Performed by the Inmates of the Asylum of Charenton Under the Direction of the Marquis de Sade, (3) Man of La Mancha
1966–67—(4) The Homecoming, (3) Cabaret
1967–68—(4) Rosencrantz and Guildenstern Are Dead, (3) Your Own Thing

1968–69—(4) The Great White Hope, (3) 1776
1969–70—(4) Borstal Boy, (1) The Effect of Gamma Rays on Man-in-the-Moon Marigolds, (3) Company
1970–71—(4) Home, (1) The House of Blue Leaves, (3) Follies
1971–72—(4) That Championship Season, (2) The Screens, (3) Two Gentlemen of Verona (Special citations to Sticks and Bones and Old Times)
1972–73—(4) The Changing Room, (1) The Hot l Baltimore, (3) A Little Night Music
1973–74—(4) The Contractor, (1) Short Eyes, (3) Candide
1974–75—(4) Equus, (1) The Taking of Miss Janie, (3) A Chorus Line
1975–76—(4) Travesties, (1) Streamers, (3) Pacific Overtures
1976–77—(4) Otherwise Engaged, (1) American Buffalo, (3) Annie
1977–78—(4) Da, (3) Ain't Misbehavin'
1978–79—(4) The Elephant Man, (3) Sweeney Todd, the Demon Barber of Fleet Street
1979–80—(4) Talley's Folly, (2) Betrayal, (3) Evita (Special citation to Peter Brook's Le Centre International de Créations Théâtrales for its repertory)
1980–81—(4) A Lesson From Aloes, (1) Crimes of the Heart (Special citations to Lena Horne: The Lady and Her Music and the New York Shakespeare Festival production of The Pirates of Penzance)
1981–82—(4) The Life & Adventures of Nicholas Nickleby, (1) A Soldier's Play
1982–83—(4) Brighton Beach Memoirs, (2) Plenty, (3) Little Shop of Horrors (Special citation to Young Playwrights Festival)
1983–84—(4) The Real Thing, (1), Glengarry Glen Ross, (3) Sunday in the Park With George (Special citation to Samuel Beckett for the body of his work)
1984–85—(4) Ma Rainey's Black Bottom

NEW YORK DRAMA CRITICS CIRCLE VOTING, 1984–85

The New York Drama Critics Circle voted August Wilson's *Ma Rainey's Black Bottom* the best play of the season on its multiple-choice second ballot. 21 critics voted, 2 by proxy, and the results on the first ballot of single first choices were as follows: *Ma Rainey* 8, *Biloxi Blues* 5, *Hurlyburly* 3, *As Is* 2 and *The Marriage of Bette and Boo*, *The Ballad of Soapy Smith* and *Home Front* 1 each. No play having received a simple majority on this ballot, under the rules of their organization the critics proceeded to a second ballot of weighted choices, with 3 points given for a critic's first choice, 2 for second and 1 for third. On this second ballot *Ma Rainey* won with 37 points, 4 more than needed to win the award (three times the number of the 21 members voting, divided by two, plus one, i.e. 33 points at this session). The runner-up was Neil Simon's *Biloxi Blues* with 29 points, against 24 for *As Is*, 19 for *Hurlyburly*, 9 for *Bette and Boo*, 5 for *Soapy Smith* and 3 for *Home Front*.

Having named an American play best-of-bests, the critics voted not to give awards this season in the other regular categories of best foreign play and best musical.

SECOND BALLOT FOR BEST PLAY

Critic	1st Choice (3 pts.)	2d Choice (2 pts.)	3d Choice (1 pt.)
Clive Barnes *Post*	Hurlyburly	As Is	Biloxi Blues
John Beaufort *Monitor*	Ma Rainey's Black Bottom	Biloxi Blues	The Marriage of Bette and Boo
Michael Feingold *Village Voice*	As Is	Bette and Boo	Ma Rainey

Brendan Gill	Ma Rainey	Hurlyburly	As Is
New Yorker			
Sylviane Gold	The Ballad of	Hurlyburly	Ma Rainey
Wall St. Journal	Soapy Smith		
Mel Gussow	Ma Rainey	As Is	Bette and Boo
Times			
Richard Hummler	Biloxi Blues	Ma Rainey	Hurlyburly
Variety			
Howard Kissel	Biloxi Blues	As Is	Soapy Smith
Women's Wear			
Jack Kroll	Ma Rainey	Hurlyburly	As Is
Newsweek			
Michael Kuchwara	Ma Rainey	Biloxi Blues	Soapy Smith
Associated Press			
Don Nelsen	Ma Rainey	As Is	Hurlyburly
Daily News			
Julius Novick	Bette and Boo	As Is	Ma Rainey
Village Voice			
Edith Oliver	Ma Rainey	Hurlyburly	Bette and Boo
New Yorker			
William Raidy	Ma Rainey	Biloxi Blues	As Is
Newhouse Papers			
Frank Rich	Ma Rainey	Biloxi Blues	As Is
Times			
John Simon	Hurlyburly	As Is	Biloxi Blues
New York			
Marilyn Stasio	Biloxi Blues	Ma Rainey	Hurlyburly
Post			
Allan Wallach	Biloxi Blues	As Is	Ma Rainey
Newsday			
Douglas Watt	Home Front	Biloxi Blues	Hurlyburly
Daily News			
Edwin Wilson	Biloxi Blues	Ma Rainey	Hurlyburly
Wall St. Journal			
Linda Winer	As Is	Biloxi Blues	Bette and Boo
USA Today			

CHOICES OF SOME OTHER CRITICS

Critic	*Best Play*	*Best Musical*
Judith Crist	Ma Rainey's Black Bottom	Big River
WOR-TV, TV Guide		
John Gambling	Biloxi Blues	Abstain
Broadcaster, WOR-AM		
Susan S. Granger	Biloxi Blues	Big River
WMCA Radio, WICC, Connecticut		
Alvin Klein	The Normal Heart,	Grind
WNYC Radio	Whoopi Goldberg	
Jim Lowe	Biloxi Blues	Big River
WNEW Radio		
Jeffrey Lyons	Ma Rainey's Black Bottom	Grind
CBS Radio, Independent News		
Richard Scholem	Biloxi Blues, The	Forbidden Broadway
Radio Long Island	Foreigner, Orphans	
Leida Snow	Ma Rainey's Black Bottom	Grind
WINS-TV		

PULITZER PRIZE WINNERS, 1916–17 to 1984–85

1916–17—No award

1917–18—Why Marry?, by Jesse Lynch Williams

1918–19—No award

1919–20—Beyond the Horizon, by Eugene O'Neill

1920–21—Miss Lulu Bett, by Zona Gale

1921–22—Anna Christie, by Eugene O'Neill

1922–23—Icebound, by Owen Davis

1923–24—Hell-Bent fer Heaven, by Hatcher Hughes

1924–25—They Knew What They Wanted, by Sidney Howard

1925–26—Craig's Wife, by George Kelly

1926–27—In Abraham's Bosom, by Paul Green

1927–28—Strange Interlude, by Eugene O'Neill

1928–29—Street Scene, by Elmer Rice

1929–30—The Green Pastures, by Marc Connelly

1930–31—Alison's House, by Susan Glaspell

1931–32—Of Thee I Sing, by George S. Kaufman, Morrie Ryskind, Ira and George Gershwin

1932–33—Both Your Houses, by Maxwell Anderson

1933–34—Men in White, by Sidney Kingsley

1934–35—The Old Maid, by Zoë Akins

1935–36—Idiot's Delight, by Robert E. Sherwood

1936–37—You Can't Take It With You, by Moss Hart and George S. Kaufman

1937–38—Our Town, by Thornton Wilder

1938–39—Abe Lincoln in Illinois, by Robert E. Sherwood

1939–40—The Time of Your Life, by William Saroyan

1940–41—There Shall Be No Night, by Robert E. Sherwood

1941–42—No award

1942–43—The Skin of Our Teeth, by Thornton Wilder

1943–44—No award

1944–45—Harvey, by Mary Chase

1945–46—State of the Union, by Howard Lindsay and Russel Crouse

1946–47—No award

1947–48—A Streetcar Named Desire, by Tennessee Williams

1948–49—Death of a Salesman, by Arthur Miller

1949–50—South Pacific, by Richard Rodgers, Oscar Hammerstein II and Joshua Logan

1950–51—No award

1951–52—The Shrike, by Joseph Kramm

1952–53—Picnic, by William Inge

1953–54—The Teahouse of the August Moon, by John Patrick

1954–55—Cat on a Hot Tin Roof, by Tennessee Williams

1955–56—The Diary of Anne Frank, by Frances Goodrich and Albert Hackett

1956–57—Long Day's Journey Into Night, by Eugene O'Neill

1957–58—Look Homeward, Angel, by Ketti Frings

1958–59—J.B., by Archibald MacLeish

1959–60—Fiorello!, by Jerome Weidman, George Abbott, Sheldon Harnick and Jerry Bock

1960–61—All the Way Home, by Tad Mosel

1961–62—How to Succeed in Business Without Really Trying, by Abe Burrows, Willie Gilbert, Jack Weinstock and Frank Loesser

1962–63—No award

1963–64—No award

1964–65—The Subject Was Roses, by Frank D. Gilroy

1965–66—No award

1966–67—A Delicate Balance, by Edward Albee

1967–68—No award

1968–69—The Great White Hope, by Howard Sackler

1969–70—No Place To Be Somebody, by Charles Gordone

1970–71—The Effect of Gamma Rays on Man-in-the-Moon Marigolds, by Paul Zindel

1971–72—No award

1972–73—That Championship Season, by Jason Miller

1973–74—No award

1974–75—Seascape, by Edward Albee

1975–76—A Chorus Line, by Michael Bennett, James Kirkwood, Nicholas Dante, Marvin Hamlisch and Edward Kleban

1976–77—The Shadow Box, by Michael Cristofer

1977–78—The Gin Game, by D.L. Coburn

1978–79—Buried Child, by Sam Shepard

1979–80—Talley's Folly, by Lanford Wilson

1980–81—Crimes of the Heart, by Beth Henley

1981–82—A Soldier's Play, by Charles Fuller
1982–83—'night, Mother, by Marsha Norman
1983–84—Glengarry Glen Ross, by David Mamet

1984–85—Sunday in the Park With George, by James Lapine and Stephen Sondheim

THE TONY AWARDS, 1984–85

The American Theater Wing's Antoinette Perry (Tony) Awards are presented annually in recognition of distinguished artistic achievement in the Broadway theater. The awards are voted by members of the governing boards of the four theater artists organizations: Actors' Equity Association, The Dramatists Guild, The Society of Stage Directors and Choreographers and United Scenic Artists, plus the members of the first and second night press, the board of directors of the American Theater Wing and the membership of the League of American Theaters and Producers, from a list of four nominees in each category.

The nominations (Broadway shows only) are made by a committee of theater professionals who are appointed by the Tony Awards Administration Committee. As a result of action by both the Tony Administration Committee and the Nominating Committee, three of the 19 Tony categories have been eliminated this season: Outstanding Actor in a Musical, Outstanding Actress in a Musical and Outstanding Choreography. Since only three musicals were eligible for Outstanding Original Score, there are only three nominees in this category. The 1984–85 Nominating Committee consisted of Jay P. Carr, critic, the Boston Globe; Schuyler Chapin, dean of the arts, Columbia University; Richard Coe, critic emeritus, the Washington Post; George Cuttingham, president of the American Academy of Dramatic Arts; William Glover, former drama critic for the Associated Press; Dr. Mary Henderson, curator of the Theater Collection of the Museum of the City of New York; Henry Hewes of the American Theater Critics Association; Norris Houghton, author, producer, director and educator; Elliot Norton, former drama critic of the Boston Herald American; David Oppenheim, dean of New York University's Tisch School of the Arts, and George White, president of the O'Neill Theater Center.

The list of 1984–85 nominees follows, with winners in each category listed in **bold face type.**

BEST PLAY (award goes to both author and producer). As Is by William M. Hoffman, produced by John Glines/Lawrence Lane, Lucille Lortel and The Shubert Organization; **Biloxi Blues** by **Neil Simon**, produced by **Emanuel Azenberg, Center Theater Group/Ahmanson Theater Los Angeles**; Hurlyburly by David Rabe, produced by Icarus Productions, Frederick M. Zollo, Ivan Bloch and ERB Productions; Ma Rainey's Black Bottom by August Wilson, produced by Ivan Bloch, Robert Cole and Frederick M. Zollo.

BEST MUSICAL (award to producer). **Big River** produced by **Rocco Landesman, Heidi Landesman, Rick Steiner, M. Anthony Fisher** and **Dodger Productions**; Grind produced by Kenneth D. Greenblatt, John J. Pomerantz, Mary Lea Johnson, Martin Richards, James M. Nederlander, Harold Prince, Michael Frazier, Susan Madden Samson and Jonathan Farkas; Leader of the Pack produced by Elizabeth I. McCann, Nelle Nugent, Francine LaFrak, Clive Davis, John Hart Associates, Inc., Rodger Hess and Richard Kagen; Quilters produced by

THE KING OF *THE KING AND I*—Yul Brynner received a special Tony Award in his farewell appearance in the role he created in the Rodgers and Hammerstein musical

The Denver Center for the Performing Arts, The John F. Kennedy Center for the Performing Arts, The American National Theater and Academy and Brockman Seawell.

OUTSTANDING BOOK OF A MUSICAL. **Big River** by **William Hauptman**; *Grind* by Fay Kanin; *Harrigan 'n Hart* by Michael Stewart; *Quilters* by Molly Newman and Barbara Damashek.

OUTSTANDING ORIGINAL SCORE WRITTEN FOR THE THEATER. **Big River**, music and lyrics by **Roger Miller**; *Grind*, music by Larry Grossman, lyrics by Ellen Fitzhugh; *Quilters*, music and lyrics by Barbara Damashek.

OUTSTANDING ACTOR IN A PLAY. Jim Dale in *Joe Egg*, Jonathan Hogan in *As Is*, **Derek Jacobi** in *Much Ado About Nothing*, John Lithgow in *Requiem for a Heavyweight*.

OUTSTANDING ACTRESS IN A PLAY. **Stockard Channing** in *Joe Egg*, Sinead Cusack in *Much Ado About Nothing*, Rosemary

Harris in *Pack of Lies*, Glenda Jackson in *Strange Interlude*.

OUTSTANDING FEATURED ACTOR IN A PLAY. Charles S. Dutton in *Ma Rainey's Black Bottom*, William Hurt in *Hurlyburly*, **Barry Miller** in *Biloxi Blues*, Edward Petherbridge in *Strange Interlude*.

OUTSTANDING FEATURED ACTRESS IN A PLAY. Joanna Gleason in *Joe Egg*, **Judith Ivey** in *Hurlyburly*, Theresa Merritt in *Ma Rainey's Black Bottom*, Sigourney Weaver in *Hurlyburly*.

OUTSTANDING FEATURED ACTOR IN A MUSICAL. Rene Auberjonois in *Big River*, Daniel H. Jenkins in *Big River*, Kurt Knudson in *Take Me Along*, **Ron Richardson** in *Big River*.

OUTSTANDING FEATURED ACTRESS IN A MUSICAL. Evalyn Baron in *Quilters*, **Leilani Jones** in *Grind*, Mary Beth Peil in *The King and I*, Lenka Peterson in *Quilters*.

OUTSTANDING DIRECTION OF A PLAY. Keith Hack for *Strange Interlude*, Terry Hands for *Much Ado About Nothing*, Marshall W. Mason for *As Is*, **Gene Saks** for *Biloxi Blues*.

OUTSTANDING DIRECTION OF A MUSICAL. Barbara Damashek for *Quilters*, Mitch Leigh for *The King and I*, **Des McAnuff** for *Big River*, Harold Prince for *Grind*.

OUTSTANDING SCENIC DESIGN. Clarke Dunham for *Grind*, Ralph Koltai for *Much Ado About Nothing*, **Heidi Landesman** for *Big River*, Voytek with Michael Levine for *Strange Interlude*.

OUTSTANDING COSTUME DESIGN. **Florence Klotz** for *Grind*, Patricia McGourty for *Big River*, Alexander Reid for *Cyrano de Bergerac*, Alexander Reid for *Much Ado About Nothing*.

OUTSTANDING LIGHTING DESIGN. Terry Hands for *Cyrano de Bergerac*, Terry Hands for *Much Ado About Nothing*, Allen Lee Hughes for *Strange Interlude*, **Richard Riddell** for *Big River*.

OUTSTANDING REPRODUCTION OF A PLAY OR MUSICAL. *Cyrano de Bergerac* produced by James M. Nederlander, Elizabeth I. McCann, Nelle Nugent, Cynthia Wood, Dale Duffy, Allan Carr; **Joe Egg** produced by **The Shubert Organization, Emanuel Azenberg, Roger Berlind, Ivan Bloch, MTM Enterprises, Inc.**; *Much Ado About Nothing* produced by James M. Nederlander, Elizabeth I. McCann, Nelle Nugent, Cynthia Wood, Dale Duffy, Allan Carr; *Strange Interlude* produced by Robert Michael Geisler, John Roberdeau, Douglas Urbanski, James M. Nederlander, Duncan C. Weldon, Paul Gregg, Lionel Becker, Jerome Minskoff.

SPECIAL TONY AWARDS. **Steppenwolf Theater Company**, Chicago, Ill.; **New York State Council on the Arts; Yul Brynner**; Lawrence Langner Award for Lifetime Achievement in the Theater to **Edwin Lester**, founder and general manager for 40 years of the Los Angeles Civic Light Opera.

TONY AWARD WINNERS, 1947–1985

Listed below are the Antoinette Perry (Tony) Award winners in the categories of Best Play and Best Musical from the time these awards were established (1947) until the present.

1947—No play or musical award
1948—Mister Roberts; no musical award
1949—Death of a Salesman; Kiss Me, Kate
1950—The Cocktail Party; South Pacific
1951—The Rose Tattoo; Guys and Dolls
1952—The Fourposter; The King and I
1953—The Crucible; Wonderful Town
1954—The Teahouse of the August Moon; Kismet
1955—The Desperate Hours; The Pajama Game
1956—The Diary of Anne Frank; Damn Yankees
1957—Long Day's Journey Into Night; My Fair Lady
1958—Sunrise at Campobello; The Music Man
1959—J.B.; Redhead
1960—The Miracle Worker; Fiorello! and The Sound of Music (tie)
1961—Becket; Bye Bye Birdie
1962—A Man for All Seasons; How to Succeed in Business Without Really Trying

1963—Who's Afraid of Virginia Woolf?; A Funny Thing Happened on the Way to the Forum
1964—Luther; Hello, Dolly!
1965—The Subject Was Roses; Fiddler on the Roof
1966—The Persecution and Assassination of Marat as Performed by the Inmates of the Asylum of Charenton Under the Direction of the Marquis de Sade; Man of La Mancha
1967—The Homecoming; Cabaret
1968—Rosencrantz and Guildenstern Are Dead; Hallelujah, Baby!
1969—The Great White Hope; 1776
1970—Borstal Boy; Applause
1971—Sleuth; Company
1972—Sticks and Bones; Two Gentlemen of Verona
1973—That Championship Season; A Little Night Music

1974—The River Niger; Raisin
1975—Equus; The Wiz
1976—Travesties; A Chorus Line
1977—The Shadow Box; Annie
1978—Da; Ain't Misbehavin'
1979—The Elephant Man; Sweeney Todd, the Demon Barber of Fleet Street

1980—Children of a Lesser God; Evita
1981—Amadeus; 42nd Street
1982—The Life & Adventures of Nicholas Nickleby; Nine
1983—Torch Song Trilogy; Cats
1984—The Real Thing; La Cage aux Folles
1985—Biloxi Blues; Big River

THE OBIE AWARDS, 1984–85

The *Village Voice* Off-Broadway (Obie) Awards are given each year for excellence in various categories of off-Broadway (and frequently off-off-Broadway) shows, with close distinctions between these two areas ignored in Obie Award-giving. The Obies were voted by a panel of *Village Voice* critics (Eileen Blumenthal, Michael Feingold, Robert Massa, Erika Munk, Julius Novick with Ross Wetzsteon as chairman), plus Woodie King and Margot Lewitin as guest judges.

BEST NEW PLAY. **The Conduct of Life** by **Maria Irene Fornes**.

SUSTAINED ACHIEVEMENT. **Meredith Monk**

PERFORMANCE. **Dennis Boutsikaris** in *The Nest of the Wood Grouse*; **Jonathan Hadary** in *As Is*; **Anthony Heald** in *Henry V, The Foreigner* and *Digby*; **Laurie Metcalf** in *Balm in Gilead*; **John Turturro** in *Danny and the Deep Blue Sea*; **Frances Foster** and **Ron Vawter** for sustained excellence.

ENSEMBLE PERFORMANCE. **Charles Ludlam** and **Everett Quinton** in *The Mystery of Irma Vep*; **the cast** of *The Marriage of Bette and Boo*.

DIRECTION. **John Malkovich** for *Balm in Gilead*; **Barbara Vann** for *Bound to Rise*; **Jerry**

Zaks for *The Foreigner* and *The Marriage of Bette and Boo*.

DESIGN. Scenery, **Loren Sherman**; costumes, **Judy Dearing**; lighting, **Victor En Yu Tan**.

MUSIC. **Peter Gordon** for *Otello*; **Max Roach** for *Shepardsets*.

PLAYWRITING. **Christopher Durang** for *The Marriage of Bette and Boo*; **Rosalyn Drexler** for *Transients Welcome*; **William M. Hoffman** for *As Is*.

SPECIAL CITATIONS. **The Asia Society**; **Penn & Teller**; **Julie Taymor**; **Spalding Gray** for *Swimming to Cambodia*; the **Roy Hart Theater** for *Pagliacci*; **An Evening With Ekkehard Schall**.

ADDITIONAL PRIZES AND AWARDS, 1984–85

The following is a list of major prizes and awards for achievement in the theater this season. In all cases the names of winners appear in **bold face type**

7th ANNUAL KENNEDY CENTER HONORS. For distinguished achievement by individuals who have made significant contributions to American culture through the arts. **Lena Horne, Gian Carlo Menotti, Arthur Miller** and **Danny Kaye**.

GEORGE AND ELISABETH MARTON AWARD FOR PLAYWRITING. To recognize

and encourage a new American playwright selected by a committee of the Foundation of the Dramatists Guild. **Craig Lucas** for *Blue Window*.

1984 ELIZABETH HULL-KATE WARRINER AWARD. To the playwright whose work dealt with controversial subjects involving the fields of political, religious or social mores of the time, selected by the Dramatists Guild Council. **David Mamet** for *Glengarry Glen Ross*.

1985 JOSEPH MAHARAM FOUNDATION AWARDS. For distinguished theatrical design for original American productions presented in New York. Scenery: **Heidi Landesman** for *Big River*, **Charles Ludlam** for *The Mystery of Irma Vep*, **Angus Moss** for *Nosferatu*. Costumes: **Mel Carpenter** for *Nosferatu*, **Patricia McGourty** for *Big River*, **Everett Quinton** for *The Mystery of Irma Vep*. Lighting: **Blu** for *Nosferatu* and *Nuit Blanche*, **Lawrence Eichler** for *The Mystery of Irma Vep*, **Richard Riddell** for *Big River*. Other nominations—Scenery: Loren Sherman for *Romance Language*, Nancy Winters for *The Three Musketeers*. Costumes: Ann Hould-Ward for *Harrigan 'n Hart*, Robert Morgan for *The Loves of Anatol*, Freddy Wittop for *The Three Musketeers*. Lighting: Beverly Emmons for *The Games*, Allen Lee Hughes for *Quilters* and *Strange Interlude*, Dennis Parichy for *As Is* and *Down River*, Ronald Wallace for *Joe Egg* and *Requiem for a Heavyweight*.

WILLIAM INGE AWARD. For lifetime achievement in playwriting, given by Independence, Kan. Community College. **Robert Anderson**.

50th ANNUAL DRAMA LEAGUE AWARD. For distinguished performing: **Derek Jacobi** for *Much Ado About Nothing* and *Cyrano de Bergerac*. For outstanding musical achievement: **Yul Brynner**. Special award for unique contribution to the theater: **Royal Shakespeare Company** and **Terry Hands**.

CLARENCE DERWENT AWARDS. For the most promising male and female actors on the metropolitan scene during the 1984–85 season. **Joanna Gleason** in *Joe Egg* and **Bill Sadler** in *Biloxi Blues*.

OUTER CRITICS CIRCLE AWARDS. For distinguished achievement in the 1984–85 New York theater season, voted by critics of foreign and out-of-town periodicals. Play: **Biloxi Blues**. Musical: **Sunday in the Park With George**. Actor: **Jim Dale** in *Joe Egg*. Actress: **Rosemary Harris** in *Pack of Lies*. Off-Broadway Play: **The Foreigner**. Off-Broadway Musical: **Kuni-Leml**. Music: **Raphael Crystal** for *Kuni-Leml*. Lyrics: **Richard Engquist** for *Kuni-Leml*. Book: **Nahma Sandrow** for *Kuni-Leml*. Direction: **John Malkovich** for *Balm in Gilead*. Scenery: **Tony Straiges** for *Sunday in the Park With George* and *Diamonds*. Revival: Joe

Egg. Debut performance: **Barry Miller** for *Biloxi Blues*, **Whoopi Goldberg** for her one-woman show. Special Awards: **Forbidden Broadway**, **Henry Hewes**. John Gassner Playwriting Award: **Larry Shue** for *The Foreigner*.

1984 GEORGE OPPENHEIMER/NEWSDAY PLAYWRITING AWARD. To the best new American playwright whose work is produced in New York City or on Long Island. **Michael Brady** for *To Gillian on Her 37th Birthday*.

MARGO JONES AWARD. To the producer and producing organization whose continuing policy of producing new theater works has made an outstanding contribution to the encouragement of new playwrights. **Gregory Mosher** and the **Goodman Theater**.

41st ANNUAL THEATER WORLD AWARDS. For outstanding new talent in Broadway and off-Broadway productions during the 1984–85 season, selected by a committee comprising Clive Barnes, Douglas Watt and John Willis. **Kevin Anderson** and **John Mahoney** of *Orphans*, **Richard Chaves** of *Tracers*, **Patti Cohenour** of *La Boheme* and *Big River*, **Charles S. Dutton** of *Ma Rainey's Black Bottom*, **Nancy Giles** of *Mayor*, **Whoopi Goldberg**, **Leilani Jones** of *Grind*, **Laurie Metcalf** of *Balm in Gilead*, **Barry Miller** of *Biloxi Blues*, **John Turturro** of *Danny and the Deep Blue Sea*, **Amelia White** of *The Accrington Pals*.

GEORGE JEAN NATHAN AWARD. For drama criticism. **Bonnie Marranca**.

1984 COMMON WEALTH AWARD. For distinguished service in the dramatic arts. **Stephen Sondheim** and **Athol Fugard**.

ASCAP/RICHARD RODGERS AWARD. For outstanding contributions to the musical theater. **Harold Arlen** and **Arthur Schwartz**.

30th ANNUAL DRAMA DESK AWARDS. For outstanding achievement, voted by an association of New York drama reporters, editors and critics. Play: **As Is**. Director, play: **John Malkovich** for *Balm in Gilead*. Actor, play: **John Lithgow** in *Requiem for a Heavyweight*. Actress, play: **Rosemary Harris** in *Pack of Lies*. Actor, musical: **Ron Richardson** in *Big River*. Featured actor, play (tie): **Charles S. Dutton** in *Ma Rainey's Black Bottom*, **Barry Miller** in *Biloxi Blues*. Featured actress, play: **Judith Ivey** in *Hurlyburly*. Featured actor, musical: **Rene**

Auberjonois in *Big River*. Featured actress, musical: **Leilani Jones** in *Grind*. Score: **Roger Miller** for *Big River*. Lyrics: **Roger Miller** for *Big River*. Orchestrations, **Steven Margoshes** and **Danny Troob** for *Big River*. Book: **Jerry Colker** for *3 Guys Naked From the Waist Down*. Scene design: **Heidi Landesman** for *Big River*. Costume design: **Alexander Reid** for *Much Ado About Nothing*. Lighting: **Richard Riddell** for *Big River*. One-person show: **Whoopi Goldberg**. Revival: **Joe Egg**. Unique theatrical experience: **The Garden of Earthly Delights**. Sound and music design (tie): **Nigel Hess** for *Much Ado About Nothing* and *Cyrano de Bergerac* and **John DiFusco** for *Tracers*. Special awards: **Gerard Alessandrini** and **Forbidden Broadway**; cast and crew of *The Mystery of Irma Vep*; **Vietnam Veterans Ensemble Theater Company**; **Rex Harrison** and **Claudette Colbert**.

2d and 3d ANNUAL ELLIOT NORTON AWARDS. For professional excellence in the Boston Theater. **Robert Brustein** of American Repertory Theater (1984). **Peter Sellars** of the Boston Shakespeare Company (1985).

1st ANNUAL HELEN HAYES AWARDS. For achievement in professional Washington, D.C. theater. Production: **Cloud 9**. New play: **The Beautiful Lady** by Elizabeth Swados and Paul Schmidt. Director: **Gary Pearle** for *Cloud 9*. Leading actor: **Francois de la Giroday** in *Man and Superman*. Leading actress: **Halo Wines** in *Cloud 9*. Supporting actor: **Steven Dawn** in *Lydie Breeze*. Supporting actress: **Tami Tappen** in *Lydie Breeze*. Scene design: **Lewis Folden** for *Lydie Breeze*. Costume design: **Marjorie Slaiman** for *Man and Superman*. Lighting design: **Dan Wagner** for *My Sister in This House*.
Touring productions—Production: **Cyrano de Bergerac**. Leading actor: **Derek Jacobi** in *Cyrano de Bergerac*. Leading Actress: **Diana Frantantoni** in *Cats*. Supporting performer: **Estelle Getty** in *Torch Song Trilogy*.

12th ANNUAL JOSEPH JEFFERSON AWARDS. For outstanding work in Chicago theater in the 1983–84 season, nominated by a 40-member committee. Production of a play: **Glengarry Glen Ross** and *The Time of Your Life* by the Goodman Theater; *In the Belly of the Beast* and *Kabuki Medea* by Wisdom Bridge; *Tracers* by Steppenwolf. Production of a musical: **Gypsy**, *Windy City* and *A Day in Hollywood/A Night in the Ukraine* by Marriott's Lincolnshire Theater; *Grease* by Candle-

light Dinner Playhouse. Direction of a play: **Robert Falls** for *In the Belly of the Beast*, **Shozo Sato** for *Kabuki Medea*, **Gregory Mosher** for *Glengarry Glen Ross*, **Gary Sinise** for *Tracers*. Direction of a musical: **David Bell** for *Windy City*, **Dominic Missimi** for *Gypsy*, **Charles Repole** for *Hollywood/Ukraine*, **Dennis Zacek** for *Turntables*. Director of a revue: **Bernard Sahlins** and **Ed Greenberg** for *Orwell That Ends Well*. Principal actor, play: **Ron Galati** in *The Dresser*, **John Mahoney** in *The Hothouse*, **William L. Peterson** in *In the Belly of the Beast*, **David Pierce** in *Candida*, **Alan Ruck** in *Billy Bishop Goes to War*. Principal actress, play: **Rebecca Cole** in *Lunching*, **Amy Morton** in *Life and Limb*, **Rondi Reed** in *Fool for Love*, **Barbara E. Robertson** in *Kabuki Medea*, **Melva Williams** in *Raisin in the Sun*. Principal actor, musical: **Ron Holgate** and **Kurt Johns** in *Windy City*, **Gene Weygandt** in *Hollywood/Ukraine*. Principal actress, musical: **Bonnie Sue Arp** in *Turntables*, **Alene Robertson** in *Gypsy*. Principal actress, revue: **Meagan Fay** in *Orwell That Ends Well*. Supporting actor, play: **Randall Arney** in *Fool for Love*, **Del Close** in *The Time of Your Life*, **Terry Kinney** in *Tracers*, **Joe Mantegna** and **Robert Prosky** in *Glengarry Glen Ross*. Supporting actress, play: **Natalie West** in *Life and Limb*, **Jackie Taylor** in *Raisin in the Sun*, **Lisa A. Dodson** in *The Tempest*, **Laurel Cronin** in *What I Did Last Summer*, **Marji Bank** in *Ladies in Retirement*. Ensemble: *Hollywood/Ukraine*, *Glengarry Glen Ross*, *Lunching*, *Orwell That Ends Well*, **Tracers**. Cameo performance: **Peggy Roeder** in *Gypsy*. Scene design; **Thomas Lynch** for *The Time of Your Life*. Costume design; **Shozo Sato** for *Kabuki Medea*. Lighting design; **Michael S. Philippi** for *In the Belly of the Beast*. Sound effects: **Christian Peterson** for *Tracers*. Choreography: **Brian Lynch** for *Grease*. Original incidental music; **Michael Cerri** for *Kabuki Medea*. Musical direction: **Kevin Stites** for *Windy City*.

16th ANNUAL LOS ANGELES DRAMA CRITICS CIRCLE AWARDS. For distinguished achievement in Los Angeles Theater. Production: **In The Belly of the Beast**, **In Trousers**, **Tamara**. Direction: **Matt Casella** for *In Trousers*, **Richard Rose** for *Tamara*, **Robert Woodruff** for *In the Belly of the Beast*. Literary adaptation: **Adrian Hall** and **Robert Woodruff** for *In the Belly of the Beast*. Musical score: **William Finn** for *In Trousers*, **Randy Newman** for *Maybe I'm Doing It Wrong*. Concept: **John Krizanc** and **Richard Rose** for

Tamara. Lead performance: **Elizabeth Huddle** in *Second Lady*, **Andrew Robinson** in *In the Belly of the Beast*. Featured performance: **Joan Copeland** in *Brighton Beach Memoirs*, **Edith Fields** in *Like One of the Family*, **Karen Hensel** in *Top Girls*, **Kenneth Tigar** in *The Coming of Stork*. Ensemble performance: **Cast** of *Tamara*. Creation performance: **Penn Jillette** and **Teller** in *Penn & Teller*. Musical direction: **Roy Leake Jr.** for *In Trousers*. Orchestration: **Michael Starobin** for *In Trousers*. Scene design: **D. Martyn Bookwalter** for *Passion Play*, **Robert Checchi** for *Tamara*, **Bo Welsh** for *Steaming*. Costume design: **Theoni V. Aldredge** for *La Cage*

aux Folles, **Gianfranco Ferre** and **Diana Eden** for *Tamara*. Lighting design: **Martin Aronstein** for *Passion Play*, **Paulie Jenkins** for *In the Belly of the Beast*, **Russell Pyle** for *Billy Budd*. Margaret Harford Award "for valiantly promoting the cause of the playwright who has not been preindorsed by the commercial theater" to **Susan Lowenberg** and **L.A. Theater Works**. Special awards: **James A. Doolittle** "who has done so much to keep live theater alive in Los Angeles;" **Robert Fitzpatrick** and the **Olympic Arts Festival** "for bringing world theater to Los Angeles and Los Angeles theater to the world."

1984–85 PUBLICATION
OF RECENTLY-PRODUCED PLAYS

Amadeus. Peter Shaffer. Harper & Row (also paperback).
Archbishop's Ceiling, The. Arthur Miller. Dramatists Play Service (paperback).
Benefactors. Michael Frayn. Methuen (paperback).
Bite the Hand/Mooncastle. Ara Watson (paperback).
Christopher Durang Explains It All For You: Six Plays. Christopher Durang. Avon (paperback).
Close of Play/Pig in a Poke. Simon Gray (paperback).
Common Pursuit, The. Simon Gray. Methuen (paperback).
Da/A Life/Time Was. Hugh Leonard. Penguin (paperback).
Doonesbury: Libretto. G.B. Trudeau. Holt, Rinehart and Winston (paperback).
End of the World. Arthur Kopit. Hill & Wang (also paperback). Samuel French (paperback).
Fool for Love and Other Plays. Sam Shepard. Bantam (paperback).
Forty-Deuce. Alan Bowne. Sea Horse Press (paperback).
Four Plays by A.R. Gurney Jr. A.R. Gurney Jr. (paperback).
Hurlyburly. David Rabe. Grove.
Inner Voices. Eduardo de Filippo. Amber Lane (paperback).
Isn't It Romantic. Wendy Wasserstein. Dramatists Play Service (paperback).
Jealousy/There Are No Sacher Tortes in our Society! Murray Schisgal. Dramatists Play Service (paperback).
Jonestown Express. James Reston Jr. TCG.
Lady and the Clarinet, The. Michael Cristofer. Dramatists Play Service (paperback).
Lovers Dancing. Charles Dyer. Amber Lane (paperback).
Ma Rainey's Black Bottom. August Wilson. Plume/New American Library (paperback).
Maydays: Revised Edition. David Edgar. Methuen (paperback).
Miss Firecracker Contest, The. Beth Henley. Dramatists Play Service (paperback).
Pack of Lies. Hugh Whitemore. Amber Lane (paperback).
Rat in the Skull. Ron Hutchinson. Methuen (paperback).
Real Estate. Louise Page. Methuen (paperback).
Real Thing, The: Broadway Edition. Tom Stoppard. Faber and Faber. (also paperback). Also original London text by Faber and Faber.
Richard Cory. A.R. Gurney Jr. Dramatists Play Service (paperback).
Sally and Marsha. Sybille Pearson. Dramatists Play Service (paperback).
Shivaree. William Mastrosimone. Samuel French (paperback).
Street Theater. Doric Wilson. JH Press (paperback).
Tantalizing, A. William Mastrosimone. Samuel French (paperback).

Three Plays by Tina Howe. Tina Howe. Avon (paperback).
To Gillian on Her 37th Birthday. Michael Brady. Broadway Play Publishing (paperback).
Wild Honey. Michael Frayn. Methuen (paperback).

A SELECTED LIST OF OTHER PLAYS
PUBLISHED IN 1984–85

Anthology of German Expressionist Drama. Revised and Abridged Edition. Walter H. Sokel, editor. Cornell University Press (paperback).
As You Like It. A.L. Rowse, editor. The Contemporary Shakespeare Series. University Press of America (paperback).
Best Short Plays—1984, The. Ramon Delgado, editor. Chilton.
Busy Day, A. Fanny Burney. Rutgers University Press (also in paperback).
Collected Shorter Plays of Samuel Beckett, The. Samuel Beckett. Grove Press (also in paperback).
Coming to Terms: American Plays and the Vietnam War. Anthology. Theater Communications Group.
Congreve: Incognita and The Way of the World. William Congreve. University of South Carolina Press (paperback).
Doll Trilogy, The. Ray Lawler. Currency Press (paperback).
Doubles, Demons, and Dreamers. Daniel Gerould, editor. Performing Arts Journal Publications. (also in paperback).
Drama Contemporary Czechoslovakia. Marketa Goetz-Stankiewicz, editor. PAJ Publications.
Everyman and Medieval Miracle Plays. A.C. Cawley, editor. Dent.
Forum/Frogs. A Funny Thing Happened on the Way to the Forum by Burt Shevelove, Larry Gelbart and Stephen Sondheim and *The Frogs* by Burt Shevelove and Stephen Sondheim. Dodd, Mead (paperback).
Four Plays by Aristophanes. Aristophanes. Meridian/New American Library (paperback).
Four Plays for Radio. Tom Stoppard. Faber & Faber (Also in paperback).
Four Tudor Comedies. William Tydeman, editor. Penguin (paperback).
George S. Kaufman and His Collaborators. George S. Kaufman et al. Performing Arts Journal. (Also in paperback).
Home/The Changing Room/Mother's Day. David Storey. Penguin (paperback).
Joking Apart and Other Plays. Alan Ayckbourn. Penguin (paperback).
King Richard the Second. A.L. Rowse, editor. The Contemporary Shakespeare Series. University Press of America (paperback).
Knack, The/The Sport of My Mad Mother. Ann Jellicoe. Faber & Faber. (paperback).
Man from the U.S.S.R, The and Other Plays. Vladimor Nabokov. Harcourt Brace Jovanovich. Translated by Dimitri Nabokov.
Nine Night, The/Ritual by Water. Edgar White. Methuen (paperback).
Otherwise Engaged and Other Plays. Simon Gray. Methuen (paperback).
Plays by Augustin Daly. Augustin Daly. Cambridge (also in paperback).
Plays by Dion Boucicault. Peter Thomson, editor (also in paperback).
Plays by Marguerite Yourcenar. Marguerite Yourcenar. Performing Arts Journal (paperback).
Plays of David Garrick: Volumes 5 and 6., The. David Garrick. Southern Illinois University Press.
Selected Plays by Frank O'Hara. Frank O'Hara. Full Court Press (also in paperback).
Seven Plays by Sam Shepard. Sam Shepard. Bantam (paperback).
Six Plays by Soyinka. Wole Soyinka. Methuen (paperback).
Strindberg: Five Plays. August Strindberg. Signet (paperback).
Sweeney Todd: Libretto. Hugh Wheeler and Stephen Sondheim. Dodd, Mead. (paperback).
Three Plays by Pinero. Arthur Wing Pinero. Methuen (paperback).
Three Plays by Sartre: The Respectful Prostitute/Lucifer and the Lord/In Camera. Jean-Paul Sartre. Penguin (paperback).
York Mystery Plays. Richard Beadle and Pamela King, editors. Oxford University (also in paperback).

MUSICAL RECORDINGS OF NEW YORK SHOWS

Title and publishing company are listed below. Each record is an original cast album unless otherwise indicated. An asterisk (*) indicates recording is also available on cassettes. Two asterisks (**) indicate availability on compact discs.

Charlie Sent Me. Glendale.
Forbidden Broadway. DRG SBL. (*)
Gospel at Colonus, The. Warner Brothers. (*)
Grind. Polydor.
Jerry's Girls. Polydor (cassette only)
Leader of the Pack (two albums). Elektra. (*)
Sondheim, Stephen: A Collector's Sondheim. RCA (four albums). (*)
Tap Dance Kid, The. Polydor (cassette only).
3 Guys Naked From the Waist Down. Polydor. (*)
West Side Story (Conducted by Leonard Bernstein). DG/PolyGram (two albums). (*) (**)
Whoopi Goldberg. Geffen (cassette only).

NECROLOGY

MAY 1984–MAY 1985

PERFORMERS

Ackerman, Louis (63)—August 9, 1984
Addams, Dawn (54)—May 7, 1985
Adler, Luther (81)—December 8, 1984
Akamahou, Bill (67)—March 31, 1985
Aldrich, David C. (54)—April 3, 1985
Allen, Chet R. (44)—June 17, 1984
Allende, Juan (45)—April 23, 1985
Alvarez, Sofia (71)—April 30, 1985
Andre, E.J. (76)—September 6, 1984
Andrews, Edward (70)—March 8, 1985
Armstrong, Jimmy (63)—December 24, 1984
Ashley, Paul (71)—September 3, 1984
Auerbach, Leon (48)—September 14, 1984
Baccari, Freddie (57)—September 17, 1984
Barney, Jay (72)—May 19, 1985
Barr, Joanne Rio (52)—November 28, 1984
Barrie, Wayne (65)—August 8, 1984
Barrymore, Eugene (69)—June 15, 1984
Bartholomew, Frank (63)—July 8, 1984
Barton, Theodore (76)—March 12, 1985
Barton, Murray Nestor—August 25, 1984
Basehart, Richard (70)—September 17, 1984
Battye, Jeanne (mid-70s)—July 14, 1984
Bauer, Charita (62)—February 28, 1985
Beane, Reginald (63)—April 14, 1985
Beauvell, Jack (83)—September 27, 1984
Beck, Vincent (56)—July 24, 1984
Berle, Jack (80)—January 21, 1985
Blackstone, Harry III (25)—August 16, 1984
Blake, Arthur (70)—March 24, 1985
Bodill, Olive (47)—Summer 1984
Bond, Sudie (56)—November 10, 1984
Bonney, Gail (83)—December 7, 1984
Booth, Anthony (71)—January 2, 1985
Booth, Webster (82)—June 21, 1984
Bowers, Lally (67)—July 18, 1984
Brady, Scott (60)—April 16, 1985
Braggiotti, Sebastian H. (80)—July 29, 1984
Brambell, Wilfrid (72)—January 18, 1985
Bramson, Peggy Loeb (79)—April 8, 1985
Braun, Helen (Donohoe) (92)—December 1, 1984
Brazier, Harriet (mid-80s)—July 1, 1984
Breeze, Alice (67)—June 1, 1984
Brice, Carol (68)—February 15, 1985
Briggs, Charles (53)—February 6, 1985

Brodsky, Aaron (86)—August 20, 1984
Buloff, Joseph (85)—February 27, 1985
Burden, Hugh (72)—May 17, 1985
Burke, Walter (75)—August 4, 1984
Burton, Margaret (60)—November 23, 1984
Burton, Richard (58)—August 5, 1984
Cagney, Jeanne (65)—December 7, 1984
Campbell, Kay (80)—May 27, 1985
Carideo, Eddie (72)—January 17, 1985
Carter, Lynne (60)—January 11, 1985
Chaffee, George (77)—October 19, 1984
Chamberlin, Howland (73)—September 1, 1984
Chapin, Rosamond Y. (89)—July 30, 1984
Christopher, Milbourne (70)—June 17, 1984
Claire, Ina (95)—February 21, 1985
Clark, Judith Abbott—July 31, 1984
Clarke, Thomas S. (78)—January 20, 1985
Colasanto, Nicholas (61)—February 12, 1985
Collins, Leon (63)—May 1984
Connally, Audrey Elizabeth (20)—March 11, 1985
Cook, Clyde (92)—August 13, 1984
Cooper, Cornell (74)—October 18, 1984
Corena, Fernando (67)—November 26, 1984
Cornell, Gwynn (45)—October 31, 1984
Cowsill, Barbara C. (56)—January 31, 1985
Crane, Stephen (69)—February 5, 1985
Culver, Howard (66)—August 5, 1984
Cummings, Ruth Sinclair (90)—December 6, 1984
Cummins, Danny (70)—December 4, 1984
Cunningham, Davis (68)—June 19, 1984
Dale, James (99)—March 2, 1985
Dalton, Doris (82)—September 16, 1984
Daly, Frank J. (73)—July 30, 1984
Daniels, Jimmie (76)—June 29, 1984
Dawson, Curt (43)—January 13, 1985
Deacon, Richard (62)—August 8, 1984
Deckers, Jeanine (52)—April 1, 1985
Delmar, Kenny (73)—July 14, 1984
Denis, Prince (84)—June 21, 1984
D'Este, Yolanda (72)—December 18, 1984
Detchon, Eileen (69)—February 4, 1985
Diamond, Selma (64)—May 13, 1985
Dixon, Henry V. (75)—June 12, 1984
Dixon, Reg (69)—June 25, 1984
Dodge, Cindy (23)—December 10, 1984
Drake, John (69)—January 30, 1985

Duane, Roselyn Piccurelli (62)—February 4, 1985
Dugdale, Charlie (61)—May 18, 1985
Duprez, June (66)—October 30, 1984
Earle, Merle (95)—November 4, 1984
Elsen, Charles R. (39)—May 28, 1985
Engle, Darleen (48)—January 14, 1985
Evans, Viola Wells (82)—December 22, 1984
Faye, Vini—December 10, 1984
Fegers, Kathryn Lois Pinkney (72)—October 3, 1984
Fiedler, Ellen Bottomley (70)—October 25, 1984
Fifield, Georgia (84)—March 6, 1985
Finlay, Alec (78)—June 2, 1984
Finn, Roy (35)—November 20, 1984
Firstbrook, Peter Sprott (51)—February 22, 1985
Fitton, Doris (87)—April 2, 1985
Flint-Shipman, Piers (22)—June 2, 1984
Flowers, Bess (85)—July 28, 1984
Fogarty, John (90)—December 3, 1984
Fortus, Daniel (31)—May 19, 1984
Fowler, Mildred K. (70)—June 23, 1984
Fox, John (60)—November 9, 1984
Foy, Charles (86)—August 22, 1984
Franck, Raoul (64)—September 30, 1984
Furman, Max S. (73)—February 19, 1985
Gallo, Mario (61)—October 30, 1984
Gambill, Roger (42)—March 20, 1985
Garner, Peggy Ann (52)—October 16, 1984
Gaynor, Janet (77)—September 14, 1984
George, Ella Mae (100)—May 27, 1984
Gerber, Del (84)—August 29, 1984
Givot, George (81)—June 7, 1984
Glass, Ned (78)—June 15, 1984
Glover, Lillie Mae (76)—April 3, 1985
Gorcey, David (63)—October 23, 1984
Gordon, Noele (61)—April 14, 1985
Gough, Lloyd (77)—July 23, 1984
Granata, Anthony (72)—April 9, 1985
Greenway, Tom (75)—February 8, 1985
Grüss, Alexis Sr. (76)—February 3, 1985
Gunty, Morty (55)—July 15, 1984
Hale, Marsha (78)—June 15, 1984
Hall, Amelia (late 60s)—December 19, 1984
Hall, Holly (72)—December 26, 1984
Hamilton, John—December 5, 1984
Hamilton, Margaret (82)—May 16, 1985
Hamilton, Neil (85)—September 24, 1984
Hanneford, Grace N.—May 23, 1984
Hanshaw, Annette (74)—March 14, 1985
Hardy, Mary (52)—January 7, 1985
Harper, Cecilia DeMille (75)—June 23, 1984
Hargreaves, Christine H. (43)—August 12, 1984
Harris, Robert (63)—April 9, 1985

Hartford, Karen Kadler (50)—November 15, 1984
Hayden, Richard (80)—April 25, 1985
Hayward, Louis (75)—February 21, 1985
Heldfond, Roger (49)—November 17, 1984
Hendry, Ian (53)—December 24, 1984
Hexum, Jon-Erik (26)—October 18, 1984
Hill, Steve H. (50)—March 17, 1985
Hillpot, William Arthur (79)—February 25, 1985
Hirose, Naoe Kondo (79)—October 3, 1984
Hodynski, Walter (77)—December 20, 1984
Hogan, Monica (75)—September 5, 1984
Hollander, Adam (19)—September 24, 1984
Holliday, Bill (49)—November 13, 1984
Holms, Billy (56)—August 24, 1984
Howlett, Noel (82)—Fall 1984
Huffman, David (40)—February 27, 1985
Hughes, Beth Stone (100)—May 22, 1984
Hunter, Alberta (89)—October 17, 1984
Jerom, Ila (54)—December 22, 1984
Jewkes, J. Delos (89)—July 17, 1984
Johnson, Sunny (30)—June 20, 1984
Jones, Bessie (82)—September 4, 1984
Jordan, John Duffield (81)—November 11, 1984
Joy, Leatrice (91)—May 13, 1985
Julian, Elena (55)—May 14, 1985
Kaye, Syd (57)—January 11, 1985
Kazanova, Ulla (83)—March 22, 1985
Kendal, Jennifer (50)—September 6, 1984
Kennon-Wilson, James (53)—October 26, 1984
Kent, Larry (72)—May 1, 1985
Keyser, Harry Alexander (33)—March 2, 1985
Killip, James A.W. (77)—May 14, 1984
King, Mae House (94)—April 6, 1985
King, Walter Woolf (88)—October 24, 1984
Klavun, Walter (77)—April 13, 1984
Kogan, Edward (72)—May 4, 1984
Lake, Alan (43)—Fall 1984
Lally, Michael (82)—February 15, 1985
Lander, Toni (53)—May 19, 1985
Lathrop, Mack (82)—February 8, 1985
Lawford, Peter (61)—December 14, 1984
Layton, Lorena (77)—March 27, 1985
Lechner, Frederick (80)—October 17, 1984
LeClair, Lucille (62)—September 4, 1984
Leibert, Michael (44)—October 29, 1984
Lennox, Vera (80)—Spring 1985
Le Roy, Hal (71)—May 2, 1985
Lester, Tony (61)—Fall 1984
Libuse, Margot—October 21, 1984
Linville, Albert (66)—March 1, 1985
London, George (64)—March 14, 1985
Lotito, Adeline (80)—June 3, 1984
Lowery, Fred (74)—December 11, 1984
Lucas, William Lloyd (91)—February 8, 1985

Lupo, Alberto (59)—August 13, 1984
Lyon, Charles A. (82)—May 11, 1985
MacKay, Alex (47)—February 17, 1985
MacMahon, Jennie Simon (106)—December 29, 1984
MacVeigh, Earle (74)—April 13, 1985
Mapes, Ted (82)—September 9, 1984
Marke, Sid (89)—May 30, 1985
Marr, Richard—December 18, 1984
Martin, D'Urville (45)—May 28, 1984
Mason, James (75)—July 27, 1984
Masoner, Gene (41)—March 15, 1985
Massey, Edith (65)—October 24, 1984
Matheson, Murray (73)—April 25, 1985
Mathews, George (73)—November 14, 1984
Mattaliano, Mark (31)—April 7, 1985
Matthews, Billy (90)—April 4, 1985
Mattson, Wayne (32)—November 5, 1984
May, Doris (82)—May 12, 1984
Mayer, Kenneth M. (66)—January 30, 1985
McFadden, James (69)—January 31, 1985
McGee, Norman S. (83)—April 10, 1985
McGrath, Byron (74)—November 25, 1984
McGregor, John (55)—Winter 1985
McIntyre, Christine (late 60s)—July 8, 1984
McMurray, Richard (68)—December 11, 1984
Medeiros, Moroni (58)—May 26, 1984
Memmoll, George T. (46)—May 20, 1985
Mendoza, Leona B. (87)—March 29, 1985
Mercer, Jack (74)—December 7, 1984
Mews, Peter (63)—November 24, 1984
Michaelides, George (66)—February 1, 1985
Miller, Marvin (71)—February 8, 1985
Miller, Stanley (52)—January 1985
Minns, Albert David (65)—April 24, 1985
Minter, Mary Miles (82)—August 4, 1984
Monasch, Rose (92)—February 25, 1985
Monro, Matt (54)—February 7, 1985
Moran, Gladys (92)—February 15, 1985
Mottley, Eva (30)—February 14, 1985
Mount, William (45)—October 16, 1984
Murray, Charles (63)—January 29, 1985
Myles, Mary (93)—November 23, 1984
Nash, Murray M. (62)—August 25, 1984
Nelson, Nate (52)—June 2, 1984
Nemtchinova, Vera (84)—July 22, 1984
O'Brien, Edmond (69)—May 9, 1985
O'Brien, Kenneth (49)—January 19, 1985
O'Daniels, Barrie (81)—March 8, 1985
Ogier, Pascale (24)—October 26, 1984
Ollis, May (57)—January 7, 1985
O'Malley, J. Pat (80)—February 27, 1985
Osborn, Andrew (74)—March 13, 1985
Parfrey, Woodrew (61)—July 29, 1984
Paris, Frank (70)—August 14, 1984
Parker, Dennis (38)—January 28, 1985
Parker, Jeff (50)—July 6, 1984

Pearce, Lennard (69)—December 15, 1984
Pearce, Muriel E.T. (85)—October 13, 1984
Peary, Harold (76)—March 30, 1985
Peerce, Jan (80)—December 15, 1984
Pepper, Morris Julius (82)—February 4, 1985
Perry, Vincent G. (87)—February 22, 1985
Petgen, Dorothea (82)—March 23, 1985
Phillips, Esther (48)—August 7, 1984
Phillips, Margaret (61)—September 9, 1984
Pidgeon, Walter (87)—September 25, 1984
Pinder, Barbara Anne (76)—October 28, 1984
Pravda, George (66)—April 30, 1985
Preisser, June (61)—September 19, 1984
Purcell, Noel (84)—March 3, 1985
Raisch, William (79)—July 31, 1984
Randall, Sue (49)—October 16, 1984
Raskin, Judith (56)—December 21, 1984
Redgrave, Michael (77)—March 21, 1985
Redi, Nan (70)—May 17, 1985
Reiley, Orrin (38)—September 24, 1984
Renick, Ruth (91)—May 7, 1984
Reynolds, Marie Caldonia (63)—May 3, 1984
Richards, Norma Helen (73)—December 27, 1984
Richards, Shelah (81)—January 19, 1985
Rico, Don (72)—March 27, 1985
Rignault, Alexandre (84)—May 1985
Robson, Flora (82)—July 7, 1984
Roland, Jeff (78)—March 14, 1985
Rossiter, Leonard (57)—October 5, 1984
Roundtree, Imogene A. (84)—December 27, 1984
Ryan, Edmond (79)—August 4, 1984
Salee, Lena Nahua (90)—March 11, 1985
Salvio, Robert (45)—September 22, 1984
Sanderson, Julia Gardner (70)—September 12, 1984
Sands, Billy (73)—August 27, 1984
Sappington, Fay (78)—December 7, 1984
Sarony, Leslie (87)—February 12, 1985
Saville, Ruth (92)—March 31, 1985
Scheck, George (72)—July 1, 1984
Schweppe, Frederick (81)—June 7, 1984
Scooler, Zvee (85)—March 25, 1985
Scourby, Alexander (71)—February 23, 1985
Secunda, Betty (82)—July 30, 1984
Segarra, Ramon (43)—September 23, 1984
Sergievsky, Orest (73)—October 16, 1984
Sharp, Anthony (69)—July 23, 1984
Sheldon, Jorja Curtright—May 11, 1985
Sheridan, Phil (80)—August 21, 1984
Shields, John Webster (34)—October 6, 1984
Skinner, Ada (88)—June 9, 1984
Smith, Kent (78)—April 23, 1985
Smith, Rollin (85)—January 19, 1985
Stanley, Stan (62)—September 23, 1984
Stark, Cecillia (86)—March 2, 1985

Stein, Emanuel (73)—March 4, 1985
Stevens, Julie (67)—August 26, 1984
Stockwell, Harry (82)—July 19, 1984
Stretton, Ellen (71)—January 14, 1985
Stringer, Marcie—March 26, 1985
Suarez, Raul (51)—March 30, 1985
Sweet, Dolph (64)—May 8, 1985
Tait, Clarke (49)—December 6, 1984
Tannis, Robert E. (45)—June 19, 1984
Tanswell, Bertram (70)—June 15, 1984
Taylor, Glen—April 28, 1984
Taylor, Lance (69)—September 6, 1984
Terry, Tex (82)—May 18, 1985
Thomas, Tasha (34)—October 15, 1984
Thornton, Willie Mae (57)—July 25, 1984
Tiemroth, Edwin (69)—November 26, 1984
Townley, Toke (72)—September 27, 1984
Triest, William (71)—December 16, 1984
Tubb, Ernest (70)—September 6, 1984
Ungewitter, Robert J. (77)—May 2, 1984
Veazie, Carol Eberts (89)—July 19, 1984
Verdon, Joyce (57)—January 26, 1985
Vickery, Susan (26)—April 9, 1985
Wallenda, Herman (83)—January 22, 1985
Walters, Merri (45)—October 12, 1984
Ward, Aida (84)—June 23, 1984
Warren, Sammy (79)—April 29, 1985
Wayne, Carol (42)—January 13, 1985
Welsh, John (70)—April 21, 1985
Werner, Oskar (61)—October 23, 1984
West, Madge (93)—May 29, 1985
Weston, Steve (45)—May 12, 1985
Whitby, Gwynne (81)—July 11, 1984
White, Francia (74)—October 11, 1984
Whiteman, Margaret Livingston (89)—
  December 13, 1984
Whiteside, Rosamund (early 80s)—August 3,
  1984
Whiting, Napoleon (75)—October 22, 1984
Williams, Al (74)—May 3, 1985
Williams, Billy (74)—July 16, 1984
Wilno, Willi (80)—September 25, 1984
Wilson, Robert G. (60)—May 28, 1984
Winwood, Estelle (101)—June 20, 1984
Wynn, Beatrice Pollock (72)—May 30, 1985
Youens, Bernard (69)—August 27, 1984
Young, Joan (81)—October 10, 1984

PRODUCERS, DIRECTORS, CHOREOGRAPHERS

Artesona, Charles H. (36)—September 17,
  1984
Bourke, Lorcan (75)—July 31, 1984
Brisson, Frederick (71)—October 8, 1984
Bufman, Mordechai (81)—May 21, 1985

Bunt, George (41)—February 9, 1985
Burris-Meyer, Harold (82)—September 27,
  1984
Buzzell, Edward (89)—January 11, 1985
Cadman, Robert Royer (50)—December 8,
  1984
Carey, David (41)—March 10, 1985
Christensen, Lew (75)—October 9, 1984
Delmar, Harry (101)—August 29, 1984
Elliott, Michael (52)—May 30, 1984
Ellis, Ward (59)—May 4, 1985
Feld, Irvin (66)—September 6, 1984
Fernald, John (79)—April 2, 1985
Fontaine, Gyles (40)—March 25, 1985
Foreman, Carl (69)—June 26, 1984
Friedman, Charles (81)—July 18, 1984
Grammis, Adam (37)—January 24, 1985
Grimes, Jerry (39)—March 31, 1985
Hathaway, Henry (86)—February 11, 1985
Hibbs, Jesse (79)—February 4, 1985
Horner, Richard W. (45)—October 24, 1984
Hugh, R. John II (61)—December 16, 1984
Humberstone, H. Bruce (81)—October 11,
  1984
Jones, Charles (59)—February 15, 1985
Keighley, William (94)—June 24, 1984
Kinzer, William E. (62)—April 30, 1984
Losey, Joseph (75)—June 22, 1984
Marais, Pierre (48)—January 20, 1985
McCahon, Robert (70)—June 26, 1984
McLain, David (51)—December 15, 1984
Milford, Robert (84)—August 24, 1984
Millott, Tom (50)—August 20, 1984
Montagu, Ivor (80)—November 5, 1984
Mount-Burke, William (48)—July 8, 1984
O'Curran, Charles (79)—June 26, 1984
O'Shaughnessy, John (77)—May 3, 1985
Peckinpah, Sam (59)—December 28, 1984
Perryman, Alford A. (39)—January 19, 1985
Peterson, Edgar A. II (72)—April 22, 1985
Pincus, Irving (67)—May 13, 1984
Reveaux, Edward C. (74)—January 31, 1985
Rigby, Harry (59)—January 17, 1985
Russell, Caren McGee (29)—November 23,
  1984
Sagalyn, Robert (64)—January 9, 1985
Satenstein, Frank P. (59)—September 30, 1984
Silverman, Jack H. (53)—March 6, 1985
Socolowski, Susan C. (30)—October 18, 1984
Stuart, Martha (55)—February 15, 1984
Sunshine, William J. (46)—February 15, 1985
Sylvan, Douglas (72)—October 14, 1984
Thompson, Robert (50)—June 13, 1984
Truffaut, François (52)—October 21, 1984
VanDerBeek, Stan (57)—September 19, 1984
Welch, Lester (78)—March 6, 1985
White, Roi M. (72)—December 26, 1984

White, Stanley (53)—June 22, 1984
Wrather, Jack (66)—November 12, 1984
Young, Betty (58)—May 21, 1984

DESIGNERS

Critchley, Eric (43)—December 2, 1984
Davis, Charles (47)—December 3, 1984
Davis, Joe (71)—July 5, 1984
Dawkins, Richard (44)—March 19, 1985
Hopkins, George James (88)—February 11, 1985
Hugo, Jean (89)—June 21, 1984
Little, Thomas K. (98)—March 5, 1985
Loeb, Anton (76)—December 10, 1984
Pène du Bois, Raoul (72)—January 1, 1985
Ritman, William (56)—May 6, 1984
Sondheimer, Hans (82)—September 1, 1984
Stewart, Jack (43)—November 11, 1984
Stroock, Bianca—May 17, 1984

MUSICIANS

Assunto, Jacinto A. (78)—January 5, 1985
Baker, Norman A. (60)—March 30, 1985
Ballard, Stanley (79)—November 11, 1984
Baylinson, Leonard (71)—October 6, 1984
Berkman, Bernard A. (56)—March 17, 1985
Best, Clifton (70)—May 28, 1985
Blackwell, Robert (66)—March 9, 1985
Borrelli, Charlie (86)—August 26, 1984
Breau, Lenny (43)—August 12, 1984
Carneol, Jess (77)—September 6, 1984
Carvalho, Jimmy (56)—March 31, 1985
Caston, Ethan (71)—March 9, 1985
Cina, Louis T. (69)—December 17, 1984
Clare, Kenny (55)—January 11, 1985
Clarke, Kenny (71)—January 27, 1985
Copeland, Ray (57)—May 18, 1984
Dailey, Albert (46)—June 26, 1984
DeSantis, Vincent James (74)—September 15, 1984
Deveau, Elizabeth (79)—December 4, 1984
Dickenson, Vic (78)—November 16, 1984
Dixon, Reginald (80)—May 9, 1985
Elliott, Don (57)—July 5, 1984
Frazier, Josiah (81)—January 10, 1985
Gibson, Alfred M. Jr. (74)—May 10, 1984
Gilston, John (32)—April 23, 1984
Guarnieri, Johnny (67)—January 7, 1985
Halbman, Alexander (65)—August 20, 1984
Hampton, Calvin (45)—August 5, 1984
Hines, Herman L. (79)—March 28, 1985
Hookano, George (76)—February 4, 1985
Irwin, Mel (63)—June 10, 1984

Jacobi, Irene (93)—May 25, 1984
Jenkins, John (69)—August 15, 1984
Johnson, Albert (73)—October 18, 1984
Jones, Chester (71)—September 5, 1984
Jones, Dill (60)—June 22, 1984
Jones, Marshal M. (42)—August 18, 1984
Kamaunu, Frank (65)—January 16, 1985
Katz, Mickey (75)—April 30, 1985
Kelly, Wells (35)—October 29, 1984
Kenny, Thomas P. (60)—May 22, 1984
Klotz, Jeffrey H. (29)—December 7, 1984
Konanui, Fred P. (65)—March 17, 1985
Limonick, Marvin (63)—December 16, 1984
List, Eugene (66)—March 1, 1985
London, Evelyn M. (63)—February 2, 1985
Lyon, Jimmy (63)—November 28, 1984
Mank, Charles O.W. (82)—April 21, 1985
Manne, Shelly (64)—September 26, 1984
Martin, Richard (36)—October 5, 1984
McMickle, Dale (70s)—March 21, 1985
Molnar, Ferenc (89)—May 10, 1985
Moore, Philip III (45)—August 21, 1984
Olevsky, Julian (59)—May 25, 1985
O'Loughlin, Stanley (60)—December 24, 1984
Owen, Charles E. (72)—April 17, 1985
Pollikoff, Max (80)—May 13, 1984
Power, Dorothy B. (91)—February 27, 1985
Ramey, Gene (71)—December 8, 1984
Reno, Don (58)—October 17, 1984
Ridout, Godfrey (66)—November 24, 1984
Rose, Leonard (66)—November 16, 1984
Russin, Irving—August 4, 1984
Sanroma, Jesus Maria (82)—October 12, 1984
Sherman, Herman (61)—September 10, 1984
Sims, Zoot (59)—March 23, 1985
Spangler, Robert E. (77)—July 15, 1984
Teagarden, Charles E. (71)—December 10, 1984
Teal, Laurence L. (79)—July 11, 1984
Trombetta, Vincent (74)—January 29, 1985
Tunick, Barton M. (39)—September 6, 1984
Varga, Ruben (55)—July 26, 1984
Violin, Mischa (85)—September 3, 1984
Walcott, Collin (39)—November 8, 1984
Washington, Isidore (77)—August 5, 1984
Whittemore, Arthur (69)—October 23, 1984
Wise, Johnnie (101)—April 5, 1985
Wolman, Joseph (79)—February 28, 1985
Young, James (72)—September 11, 1984
Zimbalist, Efrem (94)—February 22, 1985

CONDUCTORS

Astor, Bob (72)—November 14, 1984
Balle, Chicho (60)—October 14, 1984
Bouillon, Joe (76)—Summer 1984

Breeskin, Barnett (70)—June 7, 1984
Cincione, Henry F. (76)—Spring 1985
Clifford, William (66)—August 1, 1984
Clinton, Larry (75)—May 2, 1985
Craciunoiu, Nick Craig (63)—March 29, 1985
Davenport, Pembroke (74)—January 27, 1985
Eber, James (61)—March 29, 1985
Elkins, Edward G. (87)—October 6, 1984
Ellington, Ray (69)—February 28, 1985
Farbman, Harry (80)—April 4, 1985
Frazier, James Jr. (44)—March 10, 1985
Gagnon, Napoleon E. (73)—August 5, 1984
Gerace, Anthony J. (78)—September 15, 1984
Golden, Robert E. (93)—September 30, 1984
Griffin, Benjamin L. (72)—March 14, 1985
Kahn, Emil (88)—January 25, 1985
Kaufman, Walter (77)—April 9, 1985
Lane, Eddie (75)—August 16, 1984
Leon, Max Manuel (80)—November 2, 1984
Martin, Thomas (74)—May 14, 1984
Miller, Jack (89)—March 18, 1985
Ormandy, Eugene (85)—March 12, 1985
Potts, Willard E. (73)—September 19, 1984
Riley, Mike (80)—September 2, 1984
Schick, George (75)—March 7, 1985
Stewart, Reginald (84)—July 8, 1984
Vashaw, Cecile (75)—January 1, 1985
Waring, Fred (84)—July 29, 1984
Womack, Robert (68)—December 24, 1984

PLAYWRIGHTS

Blackmore, Peter (75)—September 16, 1984
Brady, Leo (67)—November 18, 1984
Burrows, Abe (74)—May 17, 1985
Campbell, Gurney (62)—March 10, 1985
Capote, Truman (59)—August 25, 1984
Chase, James Hadley (78)—Winter 1985
Curtis, Jackie (38)—May 15, 1985
De Filippo, Eduardo (84)—October 31, 1984
Fabian, Josephine Cunningham (83)—
  December 20, 1984
Farren, Robert (75)—December 29, 1984
Griffiths, Drew (34)—June 16, 1984
Hellman, Lillian (79)—June 30, 1984
Hellman, Robert (65)—July 26, 1984
Herzig, Siegfried M. (87)—March 12, 1985
Johnston, Denis (83)—August 8, 1984
Kibbee, Roland (70)—August 5, 1984
Krasna, Norman (74)—November 1, 1984
Mabley, Edward (78)—December 16, 1984
Mayfield, Julian (56)—October 20, 1984
McLellan, Robert (77)—January 27, 1985
Millard, Gregory B. (37)—October 5, 1984
Murray, John (78)—June 17, 1984
O'Hara, Constance (79)—February 16, 1985

Priestley, J.B. (89)—August 14, 1984
Richardson, Howard (67)—December 30, 1984
Sauvajon, Marc-Gilbert (75)—May 1985
Spigelgass, Leonard (76)—February 15, 1985
Stebbins, Edith (79)—October 14, 1984
Sykes, Gerald (80)—July 15, 1984
Tebelak, John Michael (36)—April 2, 1985
Ward, Larry McCormick (59)—February 16,
  1985
Wexley, John (77)—February 4, 1985

CRITICS

Bell, Arthur (51)—June 2, 1984
Cameron, Loretta King—February 6, 1985
Dietz, David (87)—December 9, 1984
Dominique, Léon (91)—September 14, 1984
Edwards, John S. (72)—August 11, 1984
Gold, Edith (59)—December 3, 1984 .
Harris, Frank (73)—December 9, 1984
Johnson, Lloyd J.B. (84)—June 5, 1984
Keneas, Alexander (46)—August 10, 1984
Knickerbocker, Paine (73)—April 3, 1985
Lapole, Nick (77)—October 4, 1984
Lindeman, Edith (86)—December 23, 1984
Martin, John (91)—May 19, 1985
Masters, Anthony (36)—January 3, 1985
Movshon, George (62)—March 28, 1985
Myers, Arthur Sim (58)—August 21, 1984
O'Donnell, Francis Xavier (Mid-70s)—
  December 3, 1984
Parker, Jerome L. (45)—March 14, 1985
Peck, Seymour (67)—January 1, 1985
Rhinehart, Molly (Mid-70s)—December 17,
  1984
Swaebly, Frances (49)—November 16, 1984
Wertheimer, Howard M. (90)—September 9,
  1984
Zink, Susan W. (43)—October 19, 1984

COMPOSERS, LYRICISTS, SONGWRITERS

Addrisi, Donald James (45)—November 13,
  1984
Adler, Christopher (30)—November 30, 1984
Baron, Paul—March 22, 1985
Calliet, Lucien (92)—January 3, 1985
Cook, John (66)—August 12, 1984
Coots, J. Fred (87)—April 8, 1985
Curtis, Mann (73)—December 6, 1984
de Jesus, Luchi (61)—August 19, 1984
DeKoven, Seymour (81)—October 30, 1984
Dodd, Bonnie M. (70)—November 2, 1984

Emer, Michel (78)—November 23, 1984
Gately, Jimmy (53)—March 18, 1985
Goodman, Steve (36)—September 20, 1984
Hamilton, Nancy (76)—February 18, 1985
Hemminger, John (42)—September 30, 1984
Hironaka, Roger (20)—November 1, 1984
Jones, Keith (39)—Spring 1985
Kubik, Gail (69)—July 20, 1984
Mills, Irving (91)—April 21, 1985
Morgan, Robert Duke (76)—May 21, 1985
Morton, Brooks (51)—July 31, 1984
Newman, Emil (73)—August 30, 1984
Redding, Edward C. (68)—July 19, 1984
Robin, Leon (84)—December 29, 1984
Roemheld, Heinz Eric (83)—February 11, 1985
Schuster, Irwin (54)—September 19, 1984
Schwartz, Arthur (83)—September 3, 1984
Selinsky, Vladimir (74)—September 6, 1984
Sessions, Roger (88)—March 16, 1985
Smith, Paul J. (78)—January 25, 1985
Sour, Robert B. (79)—March 6, 1985
Spheeris, Jimmy (34)—July 4, 1984
Stock, Larry (87)—May 4, 1984
Sukman, Harry (72)—December 2, 1984
Thompson, Randall (85)—July 9, 1984
Truitt, Harry A. (76)—January 14, 1985
Willson, Meredith (82)—June 15, 1984
Wood, Isabella Cecilia (30)—April 23, 1985
Wright, Olgivanna Lloyd (85)—March 1, 1985

OTHERS

Adler, Gusti (95)—February 14, 1985
Max Reinhardt's secretary
Albin, Rodney K. (43)—May 30, 1984
Instrument maker
Alexander, Willard (76)—August 28, 1984
Booking agent
Allen, David (65)—May 25, 1984
Booking agent
Allsopp, Clarence Jr. (43)—June 6, 1984
Publicist
Antalek, Mickey (42)—August 29, 1984
Animal trainer
Aza, Lillian (82)—Summer 1984
Gracie Fields' representative
Banks, J. Vernon (84)—July 20, 1984
Publicist
Bergeron, Victor J. (81)—October 11, 1984
Trader Vic restaurants
Bloom, Julius (71)—July 6, 1984
Director, Carnegie Hall
Buchanan, Charles P. (86)—December 11, 1984
Manager, Savoy Ballroom

Buckley, William T. (76)—December 31, 1984
Lambs Club
Carr, Jesse (59)—January 4, 1985
Western Conference of Teamsters
Case, Bertha (70s)—December 11, 1984
Agent
Chance, Len (82)—October 19, 1984
Theater manager
Charles, Robert (37)—March 25, 1985
Stage manager
Coots, Clayton (51)—September 17, 1984
Company manager
Covey, Sylvan (74)—December 19, 1984
Attorney
Crowther, Florence (74)—August 9, 1984
Widow, Bosley Crowther
D'Amato, Paul E. (75)—June 5, 1984
Entrepreneur
Dearth, Earl (74)—May 19, 1984
Music editor
Devane, Katherine (71)—March 3, 1985
Capital Repertory Company
Devany, John M. Jr. (68)—September 14, 1984
ASCAP representative
Dineen, John J. (73)—January 18, 1985
Hampton Beach Casino
D'Oyly Carte, Bridget (77)—May 2, 1984
D'Oyly Carte Opera Company
Drury, Charles H. (93)—August 17, 1984
Musical director
Duckett, Alfred (67)—September 30, 1984
Publicist
Elkow, Rick (36)—April 8, 1985
Stage manager
Erbe, Carl (83)—June 4, 1984
Friars Club
Estes, Allan (29)—May 6, 1984
Theater Rhinoceros
Farr, Florence—September 10, 1984
Veterans Bedside Network
Feinberg, Preston (74)—March 24, 1985
Tropicana Hotel-Casino
Fender, Bob (80)—April 26, 1985
Publicist
Foster, Aida (89)—August 20, 1984
British stage school
Freschl, Marion Szekely (89)—November 23, 1984
Voice teacher
Friedland, Samuel N. (88)—April 9, 1985
Diplomat Hotel, Florida
Gamsjaeger, Rudolf (75)—January 28, 1985
Vienna State Opera
Gazsi, John (42)—October 14, 1984
Concertmaster
Geltman, Max (78)—May 16, 1984
Stage manager

Gendel, Meyer (67)—March 19, 1985
Friars Club
Glassman, Oscar (78)—September 24, 1984
Backer
Gold, Sheldon (55)—May 25, 1985
President, ICM
Gombos, Zoltan (79)—November 26, 1984
Budapest Symphony
Grant, Donald J. (45)—August 4, 1984
Publicist
Grant, Peggy (55)—October 18, 1984
Peggy Grant Agency
Greenfield, Jerome (60)—July 20, 1984
Armed Forces Radio
Griffin, Robert (30)—November 5, 1984
Carpenter
Grober, Wingy (83)—January 30, 1985
Cal-Neva Lodge
Hahn, Kenneth (34)—November 3, 1984
Nassau Repertory Theater
Haines, Howard (58)—January 2, 1985
General manager
Hamilton, Charles (82)—February 25, 1985
Attorney
Harden, John (81)—February 6, 1985
Publicist
Harper, Fletcher M. (56)—January 18, 1985
Investment banker
Hauser, Gaylord (89)—December 26, 1984
Fitness advocate
Hellman, Neil (76)—April 24, 1985
Albany Variety Club
Himes, Chester (75)—November 12, 1984
Author
Hofer, Walter (54)—November 7, 1984
Attorney
Hoguet, Constance (65)—July 23, 1984
Philharmonic Sympony
Holton, Robert W. (62)—February 3, 1985
Opera Musical Theater
Hughes, Del (75)—May 18, 1985
Stage manager
Hulbert, Maurice (88)—August 31, 1984
"Mr. Beale Street"
Jacobs, Morris (78)—February 26, 1985
General manager
Kapp, Paul (76)—May 15, 1984
Music publisher
Kelly, John B. Jr. (58)—March 2, 1985
US Olympic Committee
Kessler, Raymond W. (78)—October 27, 1984
Drama teacher
Klein, Jack H. (67)—March 29, 1985
Friars Club
Knopf, Alfred A. (91)—August 11, 1984
Publisher

Knowlton, Warren III (35)—August 1, 1984
Publicist
Krasny, Milt (78)—April 20, 1985
Concertmaster
Lastfogel, Abe (86)—August 25, 1984
William Morris Agency
Latman, Alan (54)—July 20, 1984
Copyright authority
Laurie, Laurence (52)—May 28, 1984
Publicist
Leddy, Mark (92)—June 17, 1984
Booking agent
Levine, Martin (75)—February 17, 1985
42d Street Theaters
Loew, Elias M. (86)—November 16, 1984
Latin Quarter
Luff, William (80)—July 9, 1984
Melody Top Theater
Madison, Harold M. (80)—November 1, 1984
Sound specialist
Marks, Grauman (80)—July 8, 1984
Theater photography pioneer
Marks, Herbert E. (83)—October 31, 1984
Music publisher
Marnatti, Mario C. (78)—September 16, 1984
Kiel Auditorium
Mayer, Alfred (81)—October 17, 1984
Publisher
Moore, Lola (93)—January 26, 1985
Talent agent
Motley, H. (83)—May 30, 1984
Publisher
Moyse, Marcel (95)—November 1, 1984
Marlboro School of Music
Mulligan, Andy (78)—September 3, 1984
Toledo Booker
Murdock, Gabrielle (43)—January 12, 1985
Joffrey Ballet
Nash, Clarence (80)—February 20, 1985
Donald Duck's voice
Novack, Benjamin H. (78)—April 5, 1985
Fontainebleu Hotel
Obodiac, Stan (62)—November 3, 1984
Publicist
Parnes, Sidmore (62)—July 31, 1984
Record World
Paul, Art Jr. (84)—February 16, 1985
Sound engineer
Perry, Joe (81)—February 7, 1985
Decca Records
Petrillo, James C. (92)—October 23, 1984
American Federation of Musicians
Plotkin, Mitchell (90)—August 9, 1984
Publicist
Quinn, Ruth O'Grady (77)—September 26, 1984
Booking agent

Righter, James H. (67)—June 9, 1984
   Buffalo Fine Arts Academy
Robertson, Cordelia Biddle (84)—November
   25, 1984
   Philanthropist
Robinson, Douglas (72)—May 19, 1984
   Chorus master
Rose, Harold (75)—July 8, 1984
   Talent agent
Rosenberg, Ben (72)—March 3, 1985
   General and company manager
Ross, Michael (78)—March 14, 1985
   Decca Records, Coral Records
Rubenstein, Bernard—December 2, 1984
   Talent agent
Samuels, Leslie R. (84)—July 19, 1984
   Philanthropist
Schacht, Al (91)—July 14, 1984
   "Clown Prince of Baseball"
Sheppard, Eugenia (80s)—November 11,
   1984
   Columnist

Silverberg, Ben (79)—June 30, 1984
   Concertmaster
Steiner, Ira L. (70)—February 8, 1985
   Famous Artists Agency
Strobach, Benjamin (61)—April 25, 1985
   Stage manager
Tannen, Phil (69)—June 25, 1984
   Music publisher
Taubman, Nora S. (74)—April 13, 1985
   English teacher
Taylor, Bob (51)—May 31, 1985
   Publicist
Westmore, Frank (62)—May 14, 1985
   Film makeup artist
Uchitel, Hy (68)—December 10, 1984
   Restaurateur
Wahl, Jim—October 8, 1984
   Honolulu Community Theater
Weiss, Jules (72)—April 19, 1985
   LaMama ETC
Woolley, Bernard (70)—Winter 1985
   British talent agent

THE BEST PLAYS, 1894–1984

Listed in alphabetical order below are all those works selected as Best Plays in previous volumes in the *Best Plays* series. Opposite each title is given the volume in which the play appears, its opening date and its total number of performances. Two separate opening-date and performance-number entries signify two separate engagements off Broadway and on Broadway when the original production was transferred from one area to the other, usually in an off-to-on direction. Those plays marked with an asterisk (*) were still playing on June 1, 1985 and their number of performances was figured through May 31, 1985. Adaptors and translators are indicated by (ad) and (tr), the symbols (b), (m) and (l) stand for the author of the book, music and lyrics in the cast of musicals and (c) signifies the credit for the show's conception.

NOTE: A season-by-season listing, rather than an alphabetical one, of the 500 Best Plays in the first 50 volumes, starting with the yearbook for the season of 1919–1920, appears in *The Best Plays of 1968–69*.

PLAY	VOLUME	OPENED	PERFS
ABE LINCOLN IN ILLINOIS—Robert E. Sherwood	38–39	Oct. 15, 1938	472
ABRAHAM LINCOLN—John Drinkwater	19–20	Dec. 15, 1919	193
ACCENT ON YOUTH—Samson Raphaelson	34–35	Dec. 25, 1934	229
ADAM AND EVA—Guy Bolton, George Middleton	19–20	Sept. 13, 1919	312
ADAPTATION—Elaine May; and NEXT—Terrence McNally	68–69	Feb. 10, 1969	707
AFFAIRS OF STATE—Louis Verneuil	50–51	Sept. 25, 1950	610
AFTER THE FALL—Arthur Miller	63–64	Jan. 23, 1964	208
AFTER THE RAIN—John Bowen	67–68	Oct. 9, 1967	64
AGNES OF GOD—John Pielmeier	81–82	Mar. 30, 1982	486
AH, WILDERNESS!—Eugene O'Neill	33–34	Oct. 2, 1933	289
AIN'T SUPPOSED TO DIE A NATURAL DEATH—(b, m, l) Melvin Van Peebles	71–72	Oct. 7, 1971	325
ALIEN CORN—Sidney Howard	32–33	Feb. 20, 1933	98
ALISON'S HOUSE—Susan Glaspell	30–31	Dec. 1, 1930	41
ALL MY SONS—Arthur Miller	46–47	Jan. 29, 1947	328
ALL OVER TOWN—Murray Schisgal	74–75	Dec. 12, 1974	233
ALL THE WAY HOME—Tad Mosel, based on James Agee's novel *A Death in the Family*	60–61	Nov. 30, 1960	333
ALLEGRO—(b,l) Oscar Hammerstein II, (m) Richard Rodgers	47–48	Oct. 10, 1947	315
AMADEUS—Peter Shaffer	80–81	Dec. 17, 1980	1,181
AMBUSH—Arthur Richman	21–22	Oct. 10, 1921	98
AMERICA HURRAH—Jean-Claude van Itallie	66–67	Nov. 6, 1966	634
AMERICAN BUFFALO—David Mamet	76–77	Feb. 16, 1977	135
AMERICAN WAY, THE—George S. Kaufman, Moss Hart	38–39	Jan. 21, 1939	164
AMPHITRYON 38—Jean Giraudoux, (ad) S. N. Behrman	37–38	Nov. 1, 1937	153
AND A NIGHTINGALE SANG—C.P. Taylor	83–84	Nov. 27, 1983	177
ANDERSONVILLE TRIAL, THE—Saul Levitt	59–60	Dec. 29, 1959	179
ANDORRA—Max Frisch, (ad) George Tabori	62–63	Feb. 9, 1963	9
ANGEL STREET—Patrick Hamilton	41–42	Dec. 5, 1941	1,295
ANGELS FALL—Lanford Wilson	82–83	Oct. 17, 1982	65
ANIMAL KINGDOM, THE—Philip Barry	31–32	Jan. 12, 1932	183
ANNA CHRISTIE—Eugene O'Neill	21–22	Nov. 2, 1921	177
ANNA LUCASTA—Philip Yordan	44–45	Aug. 30, 1944	957
ANNE OF THE THOUSAND DAYS—Maxwell Anderson	48–49	Dec. 8, 1948	286

PLAY	VOLUME	OPENED	PERFS
GOOD DOCTOR, THE—Neil Simon; adapted from and suggested by stories by Anton Chekhov	73–74	Nov. 27, 1973	208
GOOD GRACIOUS ANNABELLE—Clare Kummer	09–19	Oct. 31, 1916	111
GOODBYE, MY FANCY—Fay Kanin	48–49	Nov. 17, 1948	446
GOOSE HANGS HIGH, THE—Lewis Beach	23–24	Jan. 29, 1924	183
GRAND HOTEL—Vicki Baum, (ad) W. A. Drake	30–31	Nov. 13, 1930	459
GREAT DIVIDE, THE—William Vaughn Moody	99–09	Oct. 3, 1906	238
GREAT GOD BROWN, THE—Eugene O'Neill	25–26	Jan. 23, 1926	271
GREAT WHITE HOPE, THE—Howard Sackler	68–69	Oct. 3, 1968	556
GREEN BAY TREE, THE—Mordaunt Shairp	33–34	Oct. 20, 1933	166
GREEN GODDESS, THE—William Archer	20–21	Jan. 18, 1921	440
GREEN GROW THE LILACS—Lynn Riggs	30–31	Jan. 26, 1931	64
GREEN HAT, THE—Michael Arlen	25–26	Sept. 15, 1925	231
GREEN JULIA—Paul Ableman	72–73	Nov. 16, 1972	147
GREEN PASTURES, THE—Marc Connelly, based on Roark Bradford's *Ol Man Adam and His Chillun*	29–30	Feb. 26, 1930	640
GUYS AND DOLLS—(b) Jo Swerling, Abe Burrows, based on a story and characters by Damon Runyon, (l, m) Frank Loesser	50–51	Nov. 24, 1950	1,200
GYPSY—Maxwell Anderson	28–29	Jan. 14, 1929	64
HADRIAN VII—Peter Luke, based on works by Fr. Rolfe	68–69	Jan. 8, 1969	359
HAMP—John Wilson; based on an episode from a novel by J. L. Hodson	66–67	Mar. 9, 1967	101
HAPPY TIME, THE—Samuel Taylor, based on Robert Fontaine's book	49–50	Jan. 24, 1950	614
HARRIET—Florence Ryerson, Colin Clements	42–43	Mar. 3, 1943	377
HARVEY—Mary Chase	44–45	Nov. 1, 1944	1,775
HASTY HEART, THE—John Patrick	44–45	Jan. 3, 1945	207
HE WHO GETS SLAPPED—Leonid Andreyev, (ad) Gregory Zilboorg	21–22	Jan. 9, 1922	308
HEART OF MARYLAND, THE—David Belasco	94–99	Oct. 22, 1895	240
HEIRESS, THE—Ruth and Augustus Goetz, suggested by Henry James's novel *Washington Square*	47–48	Sept. 29, 1947	410
HELL-BENT FER HEAVEN—Hatcher Hughes	23–24	Jan. 4, 1924	122
HELLO, DOLLY!—(b) Michael Stewart, (m, l) Jerry Herman, based on Thornton Wilder's *The Matchmaker*	63–64	Jan. 16, 1964	2,844
HER MASTER'S VOICE—Clare Kummer	33–34	Oct. 23, 1933	224
HERE COME THE CLOWNS—Philip Barry	38–39	Dec. 7, 1938	88
HERO, THE—Gilbert Emery	21–22	Sept. 5, 1921	80
HIGH TOR—Maxwell Anderson	36–37	Jan. 9, 1937	171
HOGAN'S GOAT—William Alfred	65–66	Nov. 11, 1965	607
HOLIDAY—Philip Barry	28–29	Nov. 26, 1928	229
HOME—David Storey	70–71	Nov. 17, 1970	110
HOME—Samm-Art Williams	79–80	Dec. 14, 1979	82
	79–80	May 7, 1980	279
HOMECOMING, THE—Harold Pinter	66–67	Jan. 5, 1967	324
HOME OF THE BRAVE—Arthur Laurents	45–46	Dec. 27, 1945	69
HOPE FOR A HARVEST—Sophie Treadwell	41–42	Nov. 26, 1941	38
HOSTAGE, THE—Brendan Behan	60–61	Sept. 20, 1960	127
HOT L BALTIMORE, THE—Lanford Wilson	72–73	Mar. 22, 1973	1,166
HOUSE OF BLUE LEAVES, THE—John Guare	70–71	Feb. 10, 1971	337
HOUSE OF CONNELLY, THE—Paul Green	31–32	Sept. 28, 1931	91
HOW TO SUCCEED IN BUSINESS WITHOUT REALLY TRYING—(b) Abe Burrows, Jack Weinstock, Willie Gilbert based on Shepherd Mead's novel, (l, m) Frank Loesser	61–62	Oct. 14, 1961	1,417

PLAY	VOLUME	OPENED	PERFS
TABLE MANNERS—Alan Ayckbourn......................	75–76	Dec. 7, 1976	76
TABLE SETTINGS—James Lapine	79–80	Jan. 14, 1980	264
TAKE A GIANT STEP—Louis Peterson	53–54	Sept. 24, 1953	76
TAKING OF MISS JANIE, THE—Ed Bullins	74–75	May 4, 1975	42
TALLEY'S FOLLY—Lanford Wilson	78–79	May 1, 1979	44
	79–80	Feb. 20, 1980	277
TARNISH—Gilbert Emery	23–24	Oct. 1, 1923	248
TASTE OF HONEY, A—Shelagh Delaney	60–61	Oct. 4, 1960	376
TCHIN-TCHIN—Sidney Michaels, based on François Billetdoux's play	62–63	Oct. 25, 1962	222
TEA AND SYMPATHY—Robert Anderson	53–54	Sept. 30, 1953	712
TEAHOUSE OF THE AUGUST MOON, THE—John Patrick, based on Vern Sneider's novel..............................	53–54	Oct. 15, 1953	1,027
TENTH MAN, THE—Paddy Chayefsky....................	59–60	Nov. 5, 1959	623
THAT CHAMPIONSHIP SEASON—Jason Miller..............	71–72	May 2, 1972	144
	72–73	Sept. 14, 1972	700
THERE SHALL BE NO NIGHT—Robert E. Sherwood.........	39–40	Apr. 29, 1940	181
THEY KNEW WHAT THEY WANTED—Sidney Howard........	24–25	Nov. 24, 1924	414
THEY SHALL NOT DIE—John Wexley....................	33–34	Feb. 21, 1934	62
THOUSAND CLOWNS, A—Herb Gardner..................	61–62	Apr. 5, 1962	428
THREEPENNY OPERA—(b, l) Bertolt Brecht, (m) Kurt Weill, (tr) Ralph Manheim, John Willett	75–76	Mar. 1, 1976	307
THURBER CARNIVAL, A—James Thurber.................	59–60	Feb. 26, 1960	127
TIGER AT THE GATES—Jean Giraudoux's *La Guerre de Troie n'aura pas lieu*, (tr) Christopher Fry	55–56	Oct. 3, 1955	217
TIME OF THE CUCKOO, THE—Arthur Laurents.............	52–53	Oct. 15, 1952	263
TIME OF YOUR LIFE, THE—William Saroyan	39–40	Oct. 25, 1939	185
TIME REMEMBERED—Jean Anouilh's *Léocadia*, (ad) Patricia Moyes...	57–58	Nov. 12, 1957	248
TINY ALICE—Edward Albee...........................	64–65	Dec. 29, 1964	167
TOILET, THE—LeRoi Jones	64–65	Dec. 16, 1964	151
TOMORROW AND TOMORROW—Philip Barry...............	30–31	Jan. 13, 1931	206
TOMORROW THE WORLD—James Gow, Arnaud d'Usseau.....	42–43	Apr. 14, 1943	500
TORCH SONG TRILOGY—Harvey Fierstein *(The International Stud, Fugue in a Nursery, Widows and Children First)*	81–82	Jan. 15, 1982	117
	82–83	June 10, 1983	1,222
TOUCH OF THE POET, A—Eugene O'Neill	58–59	Oct. 2, 1958	284
TOVARICH—Jacques Deval, (tr) Robert E. Sherwood	36–37	Oct. 15, 1936	356
TOYS IN THE ATTIC—Lillian Hellman....................	59–60	Feb. 25, 1960	556
TRAGÉDIE DE CARMEN, LA—(see *La Tragédie de Carmen*)			
TRANSLATIONS—Brian Friel...........................	80–81	Apr. 7, 1981	48
TRAVESTIES—Tom Stoppard...........................	75–76	Oct. 30, 1975	155
TRELAWNY OF THE WELLS—Arthur Wing Pinero	94–99	Nov. 22, 1898	131
TRIAL OF THE CATONSVILLE NINE, THE—Daniel Berrigan, Saul Levitt..	70–71	Feb. 7, 1971	159
TRIBUTE—Bernard Slade..............................	77–78	June 1, 1978	212
TWO BLIND MICE—Samuel Spewack	48–49	Mar. 2, 1949	157
UNCHASTENED WOMAN, THE—Louis Kaufman Anspacher....	09–19	Oct. 9, 1915	193
UNCLE HARRY—Thomas Job............................	41–42	May 20, 1942	430
UNDER MILK WOOD—Dylan Thomas....................	57–58	Oct. 15, 1957	39
VALLEY FORGE—Maxwell Anderson.......................	34–35	Dec. 10, 1934	58
VENUS OBSERVED—Christopher Fry......................	51–52	Feb. 13, 1952	86
VERY SPECIAL BABY, A—Robert Alan Aurthur	56–57	Nov. 14, 1956	5
VICTORIA REGINA—Laurence Housman...................	35–36	Dec. 26, 1935	517

INDEX

Play titles appear in **bold face**. *Bold face italic* page numbers refer to those pages where complete cast and credit listings for New York productions may be found.